A History of England
Volume II

1603 To The Present

Fourth Edition

Stuart E. Prall
David Harris Willson

WADSWORTH

™

THOMSON LEARNING

Wadsworth/Thomson Learning
10 Davis Drive
Belmont, CA 94002-3098
USA

For information about our products, contact us:
Thomson Learning Academic Resource Center
1-800-423-0563
http://www.wadsworth.com

International Headquarters
Thomson Learning
International Division
290 Harbor Drive, 2ⁿᵈ Floor
Stamford, CT 06902-7477
USA

UK/Europe/Middle East/South Africa

Thomson Learning
Berkshire House
168-173 High Holborn
London WCIV 7AA

Asia
Thomson Learning
60 Albert Street, #15-01
Albert Complex
Singapore 189969

Canada
Nelson Thomson Learning
1120 Birchmount Road
Toronto, Ontario MIK 5G4
Canada
United Kingdom

ISBN 0-534-96853-8

The Adaptable Courseware Program consists of products and additions to existing Wadsworth Group products that are produced from camera-ready copy. Peer review, class testing, and accuracy are primarily the responsibility of the author(s).

A History of England

A History of England

FOURTH EDITION

Volume II
1603 to the Present

Stuart E. Prall

Queens College and the Graduate School/University Center
City University of New York

David Harris Willson

HOLT, RINEHART AND WINSTON, INC.
Fort Worth   Chicago   San Francisco   Philadelphia
Montreal   Toronto   London   Syndey   Tokyo

Preface

This new edition of *A History of England* has been restructured in content and redesigned in format and appearance. The book continues to cover the whole span of English history, from the earliest settlers to the introduction of the Poll Tax and the fall of Margaret Thatcher. It is a combination of narrative and analysis, incorporating new research. There is much new narrative on the lives of ordinary people, women and men. The scholarly debates over the causes of the English Revolution have been brought up to date. The post-World War II era has been restructured and expanded.

The new material has provided the opportunity to introduce a time-line at the end of each chapter. This integrates the key events and persons in a chronological frame, helping the reader to see how the variety of topics—political, economic, social, military, literary, and religious—all flow along together from one period to another. The additional maps, combined with the time-lines, provide the reader with the tools to see the history in its full setting of time and place. The additional illustrations will turn names into familiar faces and give a greater immediacy to the study of the past.

Although much is new, the basic story of England's history is still true to the original text written by the late David Harris Willson. It has been my purpose from the outset to build upon the strengths in the original while expanding and updating the work. Many scholars made suggestions before the work began and many read the completed manuscript with great care. I have benefited greatly from their suggestions. Among those most closely involved were R.J.Q. Adams, Josef Altholz, Thom Armstrong, Jaquelin Collins, Clive Holmes, Mark Neuman, Johann P. Sommerville, and Malcom Thorp. I am grateful to them all.

Special thanks must go to Martin Lewis of Holt, Rinehart and Winston, whose inspiration, encouragement, and friendly and cheerful disposition were invaluable. My graduate assistant Guanrong Shen was of tremendous help in organizing and preparing the illustrations, maps, and charts. Many libraries and galleries provided photos and permissions. I am particularly grateful to Marcia L. Lein of Wide World Photos for helping me find my way through their vast collection of prints.

The new two-volume "split" edition is designed for those who break the course of study somewhere in the seventeenth century. Recognizing that many different dates are used to separate one semester from another, both volumes contain all the chapters on the seventeenth century.

This new edition has been a challenge. It has also been fun.

S. E. P.

Hewlett, New York

Contents

Genealogical Tables

Maps

A History of England

16 James I:
The Prerogative Challenged

For over a century the Tudors had taught their subjects that loyalty to the Crown was the greatest of virtues and disloyalty the blackest of crimes. Yet forty years after Elizabeth's death a large proportion of the people took up arms against the king in the English Civil War. What were the causes of this astounding turn of events? The search for these causes has dominated, if not bedeviled, the work of historians in recent decades, with little more than exhaustion to show for their efforts. Historians have often assumed in an uncritical way that the fault lay entirely with the luckless Stuart sovereigns, James I (1603–1625) and his son, Charles I (1625–1649). The Stuarts, it must be admitted, were inept rulers. But it should be remembered that Elizabeth, despite the glories of her reign, left problems of the most serious kind to her successors. Her religious settlement, wise as it was, satisfied neither Roman Catholics nor Puritans. Parliament, grown more aggressive, more loquacious, and more difficult to manage, was reaching for control of policy. If that control were obtained, the Commons and not the king would be supreme. Elizabeth left public finance in an unstable condition. With all her parsimony she had done no more than make ends meet; the growing cost of government in a time of inflation was certain to be a thorny question. Public virtue had declined, while corruption in the government was on the increase. Even relations with foreign states were not as satisfactory as they appeared. It is true that Spain was a defeated power in 1603, but Catholicism was regaining strength throughout Europe. If Spain improved her international position, the outlook for England might darken. And meanwhile, as the war with Spain had dragged on, Elizabeth's relations with the Dutch and with Henry IV of France had grown cooler. It is not surprising that James I was unable to deal with these problems successfully. That he may be held responsible for civil war in 1642 is another question.

THE BRITISH SOLOMON

James's character contained so many contradictions that it is not easy to describe him in a few words. His councilors admired the ease and rapidity with which he comprehended business and made his decisions. He had a good memory and more than a touch of native shrewdness. James was a learned man, fond of study, especially in the area of theology. Hating war and violence, James hoped to keep England at peace; indeed, to bring peace to all of Europe. His desire was to rule well and to be good to the Church of England. An affectionate man, he wanted to be on terms of friendly intimacy with those about him. He could be jovial, witty, kindly, and good-natured.

After his death certain scandalous writers, hoping to please the Puritans, described him as a ridiculous person, a buffoon in purple, an impossible pedant without dignity or judgment. While such an interpretation was superficial it is true that his good qualities were rendered all but useless by grave defects in his character. He was astonishingly vain. No flattery was too gross, no praise too extreme for his taste. He held a lofty opinion of his own wisdom, delighting in being compared with Solomon. In his more exalted moments he felt a celestial proximity to Heaven, as though he and the Deity had much in common. He was lazy and self-indulgent, lacking in control of his emotions and given to bursts of temper. Although he was determined to dictate policy, the drudgery of daily attention to the details of government was repugnant to him, and he left it to his councilors.

Disliking London, he much preferred a country life, partly to escape the press of business, partly to indulge his love of hunting, partly to retire with his boon companions to some distant palace or country house where he could be jovial, intimate, careless, idle, and debauched. He lingered in the country for weeks at a time, at his "paradise of pleasure," when his presence was urgently needed in London. This bold hunter was normally quite timid, apprehensive, and constantly fearful of danger and of assassination. He wore heavy padded clothes which would resist the sudden thrust of a dagger. James was also very extravagant, and lacked Elizabeth's ability to scrutinize the whole fabric of public finance. Any money that came into his hands was regarded as a windfall to be squandered at once. He also lacked her power to command. "When he wishes to speak like a king," wrote Tillières, the French Ambassador, "he rails like a tyrant and when he wishes to yield he does so with indecency."

James's Scottish Background

James's training and experience as a Scottish king did not fit him to solve the difficulties left by Elizabeth. Placed on the Scottish throne as an infant, he was for many years a helpless pawn in the hands of the Scottish nobility. He lived in constant danger of capture by rival bands of nobles who wished to control the government, and especially by the wild young earl of Bothwell. Bothwell's constant misbehavior

James VI and I, artist unknown. (National Galleries of Scotland, Edinburgh)

had gradually reduced him to the life of an outlaw, but he had the notion that he could recoup his fortunes if only he could obtain possession of the king. At the same time a group of northern earls, Catholic in religion and pro-Spanish in politics, plotted and rebelled against him. The Scottish nobles did not regard the king as a sovereign lord but rather as a feudal suzerain against whom revolt was no great crime. They were themselves little kings in their own districts, combining the authority of feudal chieftains, landlords, magistrates, and heads of clans. They could raise the whole countryside against the government. In trying to suppress them James had little assistance from the weak middle class. He had to build his own power, as Henry VII had done in England. Scotland could only be ruled by tyranny—but tyranny was an evil heritage for a future king of England.

James also had to contend with the strident claims of the Scottish Kirk. John Knox, the leader of the Scottish Reformation, proclaimed that the laws of God should rule the state. Kings who fought against God, that is, kings who opposed the Kirk, should be brushed aside. Andrew Melville, who led the Kirk in James's reign, molded the theocracy of Knox into the famous doctrine of the two kingdoms. Melville made a distinction between the civil power of the king, to be exercised in temporal affairs, and the spiritual power of the Kirk, to have jurisdiction in matters of religion. The spiritual power, Melville contended, flowed directly from God to his Kirk; thus the ministers ruled the Kirk by divine right of the most immediate kind. The king was to have no share in ecclesiastical affairs. But although the independence of the Kirk was inviolable, the independence of the state was not. God spoke through his clergy, and to God's word the king should render obedience. As a matter of fact, the ministers interfered constantly in the temporal affairs of the state. Had they had their way, they would have dictated to James on all occasions. They denounced and bullied him brutally; in return he hated and loathed them. This was poor training for a king who would have to deal with the English Puritans.

In combating the pretensions of the ministers and the lawlessness of the nobility, James adopted a theory of government known as the divine right of kings. He did not originate it, but he became its ardent advocate, dwelling upon it constantly in his speeches and writing a concise and lucid description of it in 1598, *The Trew Law of Free Monarchies*. According to this theory, kings were placed on their thrones by God. Many passages in the Scriptures could be cited in support of this belief, especially those in the Old Testament in which the Israelites begged God to send them a king. God made kings, and only God could unmake them. It was God's decree that subjects obey their king, offer no resistance, and refrain from criticism, even in secret thought. Evil kings as well as good ones came from God; the only recourse of the people lay in prayers and sobs to Heaven.

James also employed history to reinforce his argument. King Fergus I, coming out of Ireland, had conquered Scotland (according to the version of Scottish history held in James's reign), and William I had conquered England. These rulers, James argued, had acquired rights in their kingdoms which amounted to absolute ownership. Absolute ownership brought absolute power. As the king was overlord of the whole land, "so was he master over every person that inhabiteth the same, having power over the life and death of every one of them." James drew an analogy from feudalism, giving the king as lord of the kingdom all the rights a feudal baron held over his fief. In a word, the king was above the law, above the church, above the Parliament. Such views were not likely to commend themselves to the English House of Commons.

During James's last years in Scotland he made surprising progress in translating his theory into fact. He dealt the nobility shrewd blows. He drove Bothwell into exile and forced the northern earls to take temporary refuge on the Continent. He imposed bishops upon the Kirk. With the aid of his able adviser, John Maitland of Thirlestane, he created a strong and loyal bureaucracy which could be trusted to govern the country in his interest. The Scottish Parliament was subject to his will. His methods, however, were those of a despot.

There were other ways in which his rule in Scotland was an unfortunate preparation for his rule in England. Early in life, under the guidance of bad advisers, he learned to intrigue with every foreign power from which he thought he might derive some benefit. He gave Elizabeth protestations of friendship but at the same time courted the good will of her enemies. In his desire to obtain the English succession he sent secret envoys to Catholic rulers, hoping to win their approval or at least to blunt their hostility. He gave them the impression that he was not unfriendly to Catholicism and, indeed, that his conversion was not to be despaired of. He conveyed the same impression to the pope. Thus he offered a secret hand of friendship to the Catholic world and was in touch with Elizabeth's foes. At the same time he secretly courted the English Puritans; yet he posed in public as the champion of the Church of England. Such scattered insinuations and contradictory half promises were certain to cause future trouble. Finally, his training in finance was very bad. A starveling prince, his poverty in Scotland was excruciating. He learned to try any dodge, however low, which offered hope of a little cash. He borrowed from his councilors and asked them to employ their private credit in his behalf. He was careless about money, in part because he never had any to be careful of.

THE RELIGIOUS SETTLEMENT

The Puritans

In Scotland James had been content with the simple ritual of the Presbyterian Kirk, but in England he became an ardent supporter of Elizabeth's church. He liked its ceremonies, partly no doubt for themselves, partly because they stressed the divinity of kings. He liked the upper clergy, many of whom were his personal friends. Above all, he liked a church which was under the firm control of bishops and of which he was the acknowledged head.

He sympathized with a movement which may be referred to as Anglican, though described in his day as anti-Calvinist, anti-predestination, or Arminian.[1] Refusing to consider the church as a political compromise, a convenient halfway house between Rome and Geneva, the Anglicans sought a more convincing foundation. Turning to the primitive church during the first five centuries of the Christian era before the rise of the medieval papacy, they studied early creeds and councils and the writings of the early fathers and reached the conclusion that the Church of England, as reformed in the sixteenth century, was the true descendant of primitive Christianity. They regarded the church of Rome as one which had fallen into error but which nonetheless had preserved in medieval times the primitive truths and godly ceremonies of the early church. Anglicanism was a conservative reaction against the rigidity of the Puritans. Its outlook was broader, more moderate, and more humane. Unfortunately its theoretical advantage was lessened by its practice. Closely allied with the king, it did not criticize the vice and corruption of the court. It was ready to strike at humble folk who were Puritans but was strangely complacent about the errors and wickedness of the great.

While James was on his journey from Scotland, he was presented with the

[1] Arminius was a Dutch professor of theology who rejected the doctrine of predestination.

*James I attending
a sermon at St.
Paul's Cross. 17th
century panel
painting. (Society
of Antiquaries)*

Millenary Petition, signed, it was said, by one thousand Puritan clergymen. The petitioners asked for discontinuance of the use of the sign of the cross in baptism, of the ring in marriage, of the terms "priest" and "absolution." They wished the rite of confirmation abolished, the wearing of the surplice made optional, and the length of the service and the amount of choral singing curtailed. They asked also for a more learned ministry, for an end to pluralities and nonresidence, for reform of the ecclesiastical courts, and for stricter observance of the Sabbath. The king reserved judgment, but he agreed to hold a conference between Puritans and Anglicans. In January 1604 this conference took place at Hampton Court. Surrounded by his bishops and councilors, James admitted a delegation of four leading Puritans and asked them what alterations they desired in the church. In addition to the points of the Millenary Petition, they asked that the doctrine of predestination be more fully recognized, that the clergy be permitted to administer Communion without subscribing to the full doctrine of the church concerning it, that there be a new translation of the Bible,[2] and that the Apocryphal books should not be read in church. As these

---

[2]The new translation, the King James Bible, was published in 1611.

points were made they were interrupted and scoffed at by the bishops, and James grew irritable.

It was then that Dr. Rainolds, the principal Puritan spokesman, used the unfortunate word "presbytery," which made the king believe that the Puritans were Presbyterians. He turned upon them in fury. A Scottish presbytery, he cried, "as well agreeth with a monarchy as God and the Devil. . . . Stay, I pray you, for one seven years before you demand that of me; and if you find me pursy and fat and my windpipes stuffed I will perhaps hearken unto you. For let that government be one up . . . we shall all have work enough, both our hands full. But, Dr. Rainolds, till you find I grow lazy, let that alone. . . . No bishop, no king. When I mean to live under a presbytery I will go into Scotland again, but while I am in England I will have bishops to govern the Church." As for the Puritans, "I will make them conform themselves or I will harry them out of this land." And so the abashed Puritans in their black gowns hastened from the court of Solomon.

James was much pleased with his part in the conference. In truth, he had done great harm. He had first encouraged the Puritans, called them to argue a case that was already decided against them, and then treated them with scorn and contempt. Clergymen who would not conform to the regulations of the church now were deprived of their livings or suspended from them. The Puritans claimed that some three hundred ministers were thus removed, but the church placed those deprived at fifty. Recent research has raised that number to about ninety. There was no further attack on the Puritans during the reign, though James's Declaration of Sports in 1618, permitting games and dancing after church on Sundays, was highly offensive to them. Drawing together into a hard core of opposition, they found much to criticize in James's government, and they were strongly supported by the House of Commons. A few refused to conform at all. A little congregation in the town of Scrooby in Nottinghamshire fled with their ejected ministers to Holland; from there in 1620 they sailed in the *Mayflower* to America. It was thus that the Pilgrims came to New England.

The Catholics

James was more enlightened and more tolerant in dealing with the English Roman Catholics than with the Puritans. He feared and distrusted Roman priests, especially Jesuits, but he distinguished between them and the laity for whom he had much sympathy and to whom he hoped to give a restricted toleration. He was, he said, opposed to persecution; on the other hand, he could not permit the number of Catholics to increase. He therefore asked two things of them: first, that they be loyal subjects, and second, that as a token of outward conformity and obedience they attend the services of the Church of England. In return he would allow the savage penal code of Elizabeth, with its heavy fines, to remain in abeyance. For about a year and a half the fines were not levied, and the king was on his way to toleration.

James found his policy of toleration difficult to maintain. It was strongly opposed by the Anglican bishops, his councilors, and his judges. Queen Anne, who was a

Catholic, favored her coreligionists in an irritating way. Pope Clement VII, deceived by James's hints before 1603, believed James was about to become a Catholic. There was a suspicion that Sir Walter Ralegh and his follower Lord Cobham were plotting with the ambassador from the Spanish Netherlands to place James's cousin Arabella Stuart on the throne. As a result of these irritations, James turned back to the Elizabethan code in February 1605.

The Gunpowder Plot of November 1605 was the result of James's broken promises to the Catholic world. It seems to have originated in the mind of Robert Catesby as early as 1603. Catesby was a Roman Catholic gentleman who had been active in many Catholic enterprises. By May 1604 he had confided his plan to four men, including his friend Thomas Percy, a relative of the earl of Northumberland, and Guy Fawkes, a soldier of great toughness of character brought over from the Spanish Netherlands. The plot involved placing barrels of gunpowder under the Parliament house and, at the opening of the next session of Parliament, to blow up the king, the queen, and Prince Henry, bishops, nobles, councilors, judges, knights, and burgesses—all in one thunderclap. The conspirators rented a house which had a cellar running under the Parliament building. Into this cellar Guy Fawkes carried some twenty barrels of gunpowder, placed iron bars upon them to increase the impact of the explosion, and laid over all a covering of faggots. The conspirators, however, ran out of funds and were forced to confide their secret to a number of people. One of these was Francis Tresham, who betrayed the plot. He wrote his brother-in-law, Lord Monteagle, to stay away from Parliament on the appointed day, and Monteagle took the letter to the government. It was not until late at night, on the eve of the meeting of Parliament, that Guy Fawkes was discovered keeping watch over the gunpowder.

The Gunpowder Plot made a tremendous impression on the men of the time. Parliament passed stricter laws against Catholics. Although James was thoroughly terrified he tried to salvage something of his program of toleration. He devised a new oath, the Oath of Allegiance, which could be offered to Catholics. It was thought that loyal ones would take this oath, whereas those who were disloyal would not. The oath, in fact, made this distinction rather neatly. James soon returned to a policy of remitting the penal fines for Catholics who were willing to take the oath. After 1614, as we shall see, his diplomacy drew him closer to Spain, and Spain demanded that the English Catholics be treated well. Hence in the later years of the reign they were better off than might have been expected.

THE PARLIAMENT OF 1604–1610

The great constitutional issue of the Stuart period was the clash of king and Parliament; in fact, the entire history of the seventeenth century was to revolve about this theme.[3] The quarrel began with surprising suddenness after James's accession. A ruler who paraded the divine right of kings and a Parliament intent upon

[3]The seventeenth century has been called "the Century of Revolution" by historian Christopher Hill.

increasing its control of policy were certain to come to blows. James's government brought evils the Commons were not slow to point out. Redress of grievances became their constant cry, but grievances meant more than new abuses. Under a ruler for whom the Commons felt no affection, as they had felt affection for Elizabeth, many aspects of government that had been tolerated before 1603 now seemed outmoded and insufferable. For some the time had come for reform. But reforms often involved a lessening of royal authority or royal revenues. As James saw it, the Commons were demanding a fundamental change that would shift power from the king to themselves: they were grasping at control of the executive. Naturally the king fought back, and thus the question of sovereignty became a major issue. Where did ultimate authority lie? And where should disputes be settled if neither the king nor Parliament would yield? The constitutional prinicple of the sovereignty of "king-in-parliament" worked only when the two would or could work in cooperation. If one or the other stubbornly refused, the path to follow was less clear.

James knew little about the English Parliament. He knew only the Paliament of Scotland which, for all its age, was a weak and primitive body that could easily be manipulated. In dealing with the English House of Commons James committed many blunders. He made too many speeches, sent too many messages, often couched in a scolding and didactic tone, and was much too quick to interfere in parliamentary business. This interference not only irritated the Commons but disturbed those avenues of influence still open to the Crown. James's principal minister, Robert Cecil, soon to be earl of Salisbury, had managed the parliamentary business of the Crown during Elizabeth's last years. He continued to do so in the new reign, though he worked under disadvantages. Now a member of the House of Lords, he could speak to the Commons only when committees from both houses met in conference. He could make use of the speaker as well as a group of officials and courtiers in the Commons, of whom the most able was Sir Francis Bacon. But Bacon was not a councilor; in fact, the number of councilors in the Commons was very small, and hence the Crown was not as well represented in the lower house as it had been under Elizabeth. Rather strangely, Salisbury had not attempted to influence elections in 1604; he could compensate for his error only by managing by-elections as the Parliament progressed. Above all, he was frustrated by the constant meddling of the king, who followed events in Parliament closely, day by day and even hour by hour, in order to send his principal minister detailed—and misguided and disturbing—instructions.

A quarrel arose as soon as Parliament met in 1604. Two men, Sir Francis Goodwin and Sir John Fortescue, claimed to have been elected to the same seat in the Commons. Where was this question to be settled? James announced that since the writs summoning Parliament had been issued by the Chancery, the Chancery had the right, if it suspected irregularity, to issue a writ for a new election. This had been the Tudor practice. But the Commons demanded the right to settle election disputes, and they promptly declared that Goodwin had won the seat in question. James asked them to confer with the Lords. The Commons refused, claiming the Lords had nothing to do with the question. Somewhat taken aback, the king told the Commons to confer with the judges and then report their findings to the Privy Council. Again the Commons refused.

James then sent them a peremptory message, commanding "as an absolute king that there might be a conference between the House and the judges," he and his councilors to be present. The Commons were astonished but decided to give way. "The prince's command is like a thunderbolt," said a member, "his command upon our allegiance like the roaring of a lion. To his command there is no contradiction." Fortunately the conference went well. James suggested a compromise: that the election of both Goodwin and Fortescue be voided, that neither stand again for the seat in question, and that a new election be held. The Commons agreed. James was delighted with his own graciousness and wisdom. But the Commons had won, for thereafter they settled election disputes without challenge. James had lost much and gained nothing.

The Commons then turned to grievances. They debated purveyance, the right of the monarch to live off the country as he traveled about. The difficulty was that James traveled a great deal and allowed his purveyors to exceed their rights. The Commons also objected to the court of wards, a court set up by Henry VIII that administered the estates of minors who were wards of the king. Wardship was undoubtedly the source of great abuse. The Commons further showed much sympathy for the Puritans, especially for the "silenced brethren" who had been ejected from their churches. When James wished to assume the style of king of Great Britain, the Commons refused their consent. They also declined to vote new taxes, since payments still were due from taxes voted to Elizabeth. At the end of the session the Commons drew up a famous document, the Apology of 1604. It was a bold declaration of right, a lecture to a foreign king upon the constitution of his new kingdom. An important point concerned the origin of parliamentary privilege. In the case of *Goodwin v. Fortescue* James had declared that the Commons "derived all matters of privilege from him and by his grant," but the Apology asserted that parliamentary privileges were the right and inheritance of the Commons—no less than their lands and goods—and did not spring from royal grace. Surveying the events of the session, the Commons justified their actions at every turn, and added a statement that the king could not alter laws on religion without their consent. James replied with a scolding speech, and so the session ended.

The parliamentary session of 1606–1607 was devoted largely to the question of closer union between England and Scotland. The two kingdoms, of course, now had the same ruler but otherwise were distinct and independent. It was James's noble ambition to draw them together into a perfect union. He would have one kingdom with one king, one faith, one language, one people alike in manners and allegiance. The names of England and Scotland should disappear in the name of Britain, the border should be erased and become the middle shires, the Englishman and the Scot should love one another as brothers. But James was in too much of a hurry. He forgot the long and mutual hostility of the two nations. Unfortunately he had brought with him to England a large number of Scots to whom he had been excessively generous, thus arousing the jealousy of the English courtiers. It is not surprising that his proposals were coldly received by the English House of Commons.

In 1606 James proposed four preliminary steps to union: the repeal of hostile laws, that is, laws of each country aimed at the other; mutual naturalization; a commercial treaty looking toward free trade; and improvement of justice along the border. The hostile laws were repealed without question, but the rest of the program met with intense opposition. A commercial treaty was completely refused, and the measures for border justice were reduced significantly. Debates on naturalization were long and interesting, but the Commons declined to naturalize the Scots unless English law was imposed on Scotland. The king grew angry, and the session ended with little accomplished. In the next year, 1608, James obtained from the English judges a decision that Scots born after the union of the Crowns were citizens of both kingdoms. The judges were unanimous in determining the status of the *post-nati* in Calvin's case. Even Sir Edward Coke supported this victory for the royal prerogative.

A major crisis developed in the parliamentary sessions of 1610. Debate revolved about the fundamental questions of the royal prerogative and the royal finance. The prerogative—that sovereign power inherent in the king to act on his own authority— had been brought to the fore by a number of issues. There had been a feud between the courts of the church, especially the Court of High Commission, supported by the combative archbishop of Canterbury, Richard Bancroft, and the courts of common law, supported by the famous judge, Sir Edward Coke, who loved the common law and became its champion against the church courts and against the royal theory of divine right. In defense of the common law Coke could be the most obstinate and difficult of men. On more than one occasion, when the king stormed at him, he fell upon his knees; yet even in that position he clung to his opinions.

A dispute arose about an ancient writ, the writ of prohibition, through which the common-law judges exercised considerable control over the courts of the church. This writ halted proceedings in any ecclesiastical court until the judges were satisfied that the matter in dispute fell properly within the jurisdiction of that court. In 1605 Archbishop Bancroft appealed to the king against the writ of prohibition. All judicial authority, he argued, began in the Crown and flowed in two streams, the temporal jurisdiction to the courts of common law, and the spiritual to the courts of the church. The two systems were on an equality, the writ of prohibition should be ended, and the king should decide disputes between the two jurisdictions. But Coke answered sharply that the writ of prohibition was a part of the law, and the law could be altered only by Parliament. Two years later Bancroft asserted that the king, as supreme judge, should hear and decide doubtful cases. "To which it was answered by me," wrote Coke, "that the king in his own person cannot adjudge any case, but this ought to be determined and adjudged in some court of justice. . . . "

The prerogative was connected closely with the question of finance. James had been living far beyond his means and had run deeply into debt. In 1608 he appointed Salisbury lord treasurer. Salisbury found that he could not lessen expenditure; he could inly increase the revenue, as he did substantially. Among other expedients he levied impositions, that is, customs duties over and above the normal schedule of tonnage and poundage authorized by Parliament. It was a dangerous experiment, for the Commons were certain to object. But Salisbury had a legal decision in his favor. In 1606 a merchant named Bate, who imported currants from the Levant, had refused to pay impositions and had been tried in the Court of Exchequer. The decision was that, since the prerogative included the regulation of commerce and

*Robert Cecil, Earl
of Salisbury,
attributed to J. de
Critz, 1602.
(National Portrait
Gallery, London)*

since impositions formed part of that regulation, the duties were legal though they had not been voted by Parliament.

The sessions of 1610 were stormy ones. The Commons insisted on discussing grievances. In a long and important debate on impositions the Commons asserted firmly that these levies were illegal unless they were granted by Parliament. Other aspects of the prerogative came under attack: the Court of High Commission, the use of proclamations to modify law, and the jurisdiction of the council of Wales over certain English shires. In July a petition of grievances was presented to the king. It was so long, said James, that he thought he might use it for a tapestry.

Meanwhile Salisbury, who was striving to extract money from the Commons, proposed that in addition to a grant of the customary kind, though of unusual size, the Commons should vote the king a permanent revenue. In return Salisbury offered that the king would abandon purveyance and most of his feudal rights, including wardship. This bargain known as the Great Contract was tentatively approved in July of 1610, but by autumn both sides wished to end it, to Salisbury's infinite sorrow. James dissolved his first Parliament in anger early in 1611.

THE PARLIAMENT OF 1614

James's first Parliament had lasted for seven years; his second, for two months. Impelled by his abject poverty, he very reluctantly summoned Parliament again in 1614. The debt was high, bills were unpaid, and future revenues were anticipated. The decay in public finance had turned to dead rot. When James faced the Commons he tried to be conciliatory and he offered a number of small concessions. Brushing aside these concessions rather impolitely, the Commons turned to more fundamental grievances. They began by a searching inquiry into the recent elections, for they had heard that a group of courtiers had plotted to influence elections on a large scale in return for promises of office. This rumor was false, and the Commons found little to complain of. Nonetheless, they expelled a privy councilor, Sir Thomas Parry, for corrupt electioneering practices, and questioned the right of the Attorney General, Bacon, to sit in the Commons.

It was clear that the Commons would debate grievances thoroughly before they turned to supply. When they took up the delicate matter of impositions, the debate grew heated. They asked the House of Lords for a conference on impositions, but the Lords refused. One bishop in the Lords made such a violent attack on the lower house that the Commons resolved to conduct no business until they received satisfaction. This sullen resolve annoyed the king, who warned them he would dissolve the Parliament if they did not vote supply. The Commons stood their ground; so did James. The Parliament was dissolved after a session of two months without passing a single bill. The king was furious: the Commons had rejected his proffered love, had assailed his prerogative, and had spoken irreverently of kings. Perhaps they sought his life. One member foolishly spoke as though there might be a massacre of the Scots in London. Thereafter, James was through with Parliaments. If he had had his way, there would have been no more Parliaments in England.

DEGENERATION IN GOVERNMENT

For the next seven years, from 1614 to 1621, James ruled without a Parliament. Unfortunately these were years of failure, of scandal, and of increasing difficulties both at home and abroad. The efficiency and the standards of government degenerated. During the first decade of the reign the king's chief minister had been Robert Cecil, Earl of Salisbury, who, as principal secretary, master of the court of wards, and lord treasurer, had been the pivot about which the entire administration revolved. If he was not a great man, he at least came close to greatness. His solid judgment and steady nerve, his prudence, sagacity, and self-control, and his tremendous industry kept affairs on an even keel and continued Tudor ideals of government in the first years of the Stuart period. Amid endless routine he did not lose sight of larger objectives. He was a man of wit and liveliness, a spirited writer and speaker, a cultured gentleman who could be warm and generous in friendship. But after his death in 1612, government fell into weaker hands.

The Howards

Several members of the Howard family became important. Henry Howard, Earl of Northampton, a man greatly trusted by James, was a worthless, self-seeking, and crafty courtier. His intense jealousy led him to dislike his colleagues. His Catholicism was only half-concealed, and he stood constantly for leniency to Catholics, severity to Puritans, alliance with Spain, and an end to Parliaments. He died in 1614. His nephew Thomas Howard, Earl of Suffolk, later lord treasurer, was a brave sailor and a loyal subject, but he was lax and easygoing, and had small strength of character. A distant cousin, Charles Howard, Earl of Nottingham, had commanded the English fleet against the Armada. He continued to be lord admiral in James's reign, but as he grew old he permitted the navy to fall into decay. Against the Howards there arose a party of opposition: Lord Chancellor Ellesmere, very Protestant and anti-Spanish; Archbishop Abbot; and William Herbert, Earl of Pembroke, the richest peer in England. The rivalries of these two factions dominated politics for many years.

George Villiers, Later Duke of Buckingham

A new favorite arose at court. This was George Villiers, a handsome young man who caught the fancy of the king in 1614. Villiers was to have a remarkable career. By 1617, when he was only twenty-five, he had become the master of the horse, a knight of the garter, earl of Buckingham, and a member of the Privy Council. He was private secretary and boon companion of the king, the channel through which suits and requests for patronage came to the ruler. He did not at first aspire to dominate policy. Rather, he gloried in his control of patronage, for this was the highest ambition of the courtier. Great men and small paid homage to him, the king foremost among his worshipers. It is small wonder that his head was turned, that he became vain, willful and arrogant, easily offended by opposition, and determined to have his way.

His rise to power brought many evils. He and his extortionate mother, Lady Compton, developed a system of spoliation and blackmail; they used Buckingham's influence with the king to extract money from all aspirants to office. But in his pride and egotism, Buckingham went further. Those who attained a place in the government must do more than pay for it: they must acknowledge their subservience to him. The ministers of state must be his creatures, swelling the crowd of his hangers-on and making the world aware of their dependence. Deviation from his wishes meant loss of office, and his path became strewn with men whom he first advanced and later ruined. His ascendancy increased the debauchery at court, where the king often was intoxicated at his jovial suppers.

In 1618 Buckingham was able to drive from office the Howards, who had always

Vandyke's original Drawing, from which the Print by Van Voerst was taken, in the Book of Vandyke's Heads. Given me by the Duke of Devonshire.

been hostile to him as an upstart. The year 1618 was one of great financial difficulty. The fiscal picture became so dark and the means of raising money so shameful—such as the sale of peerages—that even James knew something must be done. A movement for reform began. Joining this movement, Buckingham found in Lionel Cranfield a man willing to do the required work. Cranfield, a successful merchant and capitalist, had become a financial adviser of the government and was later to attain high office. In 1618, with Buckingham's backing, he investigated many departments—including the Treasury over which Suffolk presided—and showed many ways in which the king could save money. His investigations produced a struggle between Buckingham and the Howards. It was easy to show that Suffolk had mismanaged money and was probably corrupt. He was tried for embezzlement of funds, found guilty, and dismissed from office. Nottingham, the ancient lord admiral, was induced to resign without a trial, and his office was given to Buckingham. As other Howards fell in rapid succession Buckingham was left supreme. Although a few great personages at court owed him nothing, the majority of officials now received their places from him and were dependent on his good will. His appointments were not all bad. He tended to give office to devoted and efficient bureaucrats who would do as they were told; and he developed skill in obtaining work from these officials. But he and the king made all the important decisions.

The King and the Judges

Early in the reign, as we have seen, the king had clashed with the great lawyer, Sir Edward Coke. The points at issue had been fundamental: the rivalry of the courts of common law with the extralegal or prerogative courts; and the relation of the Crown to the common law. Several important cases between 1610 and 1616 underscored these issues and pointed to new ones: in 1610, in one such case, Coke delivered a clear and important opinion concerning royal proclamations, which had been increasing during James's reign. The king, said Coke, could not add to existing law or create new offenses by proclamation. He could issue proclamations only to admonish his subjects that certain laws existed and must be obeyed. In another, the Bonham Case, Coke made an unsuccessful effort to introduce the principle of judicial review. He held that "when an act of Parliament is against common right and reason or repugnant or impossible to be performed, the common law will control it and adjudge such act to be void." He would thus have allowed the judges to decide whether an act of Parliament was or was not to be enforced. This principle, so important in American history, was never established in England.

In *Courtney v. Glanvil* (1615) Coke made a crude attack upon the court of chancery, arguing that once a case had been decided in the common-law courts that case could not be reopened in the chancery. James, who regarded it as a court under his special protection, was highly irritated, and his anger was increased by two other cases which involved another principle—the independence to the bench. The Peacham Case (1615) concerned a soured and broken clergyman, Edmund Peacham, who secretly wrote notes for a sermon predicting the death of the king. James, intent on severity, decided to consult the judges before the trial, not an unusual procedure. The novelty was that James, fearing that Coke might prove difficult, hit on the plan of consulting the judges one by one and not as a group. Coke objected, declaring that "this auricular taking of opinions, single and apart, was new and dangerous." Finally, in the case of Commendams (1616), James asked the judges to postpone their decision until he had consulted with them. Coke persuaded them to reply that they could not delay justice at the king's command. In a great rage James called the judges before him; they fell upon their knees. The king then asked them whether in the future they would be willing to delay a case involving the interests of the Crown until they had spoken to him. All agreed, save Coke, who merely said that he would do what it was fitting for a judge to do. Later that year he was dismissed from the bench. By this drastic action James freed himself from the opposition of the judges, but he struck a heavy blow at the moral weight of their decisions. Coke's shortcomings were forgotten; he became a martyr of the commonwealth, a symbol of the widely held conviction that the liberties provided by the common law should be left as they were.

Foreign Affairs

England's international position, as well as her government, declined alarmingly during the interparliamentary period between 1614 and 1621. To understand this decline we must briefly review the first part of the reign. When James ascended the English throne in 1603 he was in a strong position relative to foreign powers. He was king of the most powerful Protestant state, strengthened by union with Scotland. His prestige was high in Scandinavia, northern Germany, and Holland. He was on good terms with certain Catholic states opposed to Spain: France, Venice, and Tuscany. To English friendship with France he could add the ancient tradition of Franco-Scottish alliance. Thus when he stepped into Elizabeth's place as a leader of Protestant and anti-Spanish Europe, he inherited her strength but added some of his own.

James's great departure from Elizabeth's policy was his belief that he could lead Protestant Europe and at the same time be a friend of Spain. In the past he had feared Spain greatly, but he now considered himself sufficiently powerful and well established to offer Spain his friendship and thus to make complete the circle of his amity. He was, as we know, a man who loved peace, whose ambition was not merely to keep England out of war, but to make peace universal throughout Europe. Friendly with all nations, allied with Protestant states, and on peaceful terms with Spanish lands: this was his noble vision of bringing peace and concord to Europe as a whole.

This vision, of course, was an empty one, and his failure in foreign policy was to prove the most shameful of his reign. The reasons are clear. His cardinal error was to believe that he could be a Protestant champion and at the same time a friend of Spain. This basic contradiction involved him in countless difficulties. His policy, moreover, was a personal policy he never explained to his people, who regarded him as more pro-Spanish than he was. They allowed him to be without funds, and Parliament was tempted to make for the first time a serious demand for a voice in shaping foreign policy. James was not merely averse to war; he regarded it with terror. He could not bear the sight of a naked sword or of men drilling for combat. The story was told that once when a soldier attempted to kiss his hand, the king suddenly drew it back, afraid it would be bitten. His fear of assassination played an important part in his diplomacy. Believing the king desired peace at any price, his enemies came to count on his inaction. Since he had no money he could neither fulfill his commitments nor make good his threats. Thus he became a defender who could defend no one, a champion who could do nothing but talk.

For the first decade of his reign he was much closer to Protestant Europe than to Spain. Although he made peace with Spain in 1604, thus ending the long war, the peace was no surrender. James promised not to assist the Dutch, but he allowed them to raise money and volunteers in England, whereas a similar concession to Spain meant nothing. He did not accept the Spanish claim of monopoly in the New World; in the end the treaty said nothing about Englishmen in the Spanish Indies (where they continued to go at their own risk). England and Scotland benefited by the peace. They could trade in Spain and in the Netherlands; Ireland could be pacified without fear of Spanish intervention; and Spain was left fighting the Dutch and in constant danger of war with France.

Nevertheless, the peace was an uneasy one. James quarreled with Spain over one issue after another, and as a consequence drew closer to Protestant and anti-Spanish Europe. When he looked for a bride for Prince Henry, he turned to anti-Spanish lands—France, Savoy, and Tuscany. In 1613 his daughter Elizabeth was married to Frederick V of the Palatinate, the leading Calvinist ruler in Germany. This marriage brought James into close contact with the Protestant princes of southern Germany, who in 1608 had formed a defensive alliance know as the Protestant Union. James in effect became a member. His position as Protestant champion was enchanced, and his relations with Spain became so strained that many Englishmen thought, and hoped, that the Elizabethan war with Spain would be renewed.

Then, about 1614, a shift occurred. James's international position weakened while that of Spain improved. The deaths of Henry IV of France in 1610, of Salisbury and Prince Henry in 1612, were each a grievous blow to England. Unfortunate quarrels separated James from the Dutch, from Savoy, and from France. The efficiency of English government declined and the breach with Parliament widened. Meanwhile Spain had grown stronger, at least in her relations with other powers. She had concluded a truce in 1609 with the Dutch; her relations with France had greatly improved; and she had in England a most astute ambassador, Sarmiento, later Count Gondomar.

As a result, James became more conciliatory; treating with Spain as with an equal or even a superior power, he drifted into a policy of appeasement. Left without funds by Parliament in 1614, he began negotiations to arrange a marriage between his second son, Prince Charles, and a Spanish infanta (princess) who would, he assumed, bring him a large dowry. Sarmiento eagerly advocated the marriage, but the Spanish government did not. Nonetheless, in 1615 the Spanish drew up articles to serve as a basis for negotiations. They stipulated that English Catholics be permitted the exercise of their religion through nonenforcement of the penal laws. The infanta must control the education of her children, who must be baptized according to the Roman Catholic use. They must be free to choose their own religion and, if they selected Catholicism, they must not be debarred thereby from the English succession. The infanta's household must be Catholic, her chapel must be large and open to the public, her priests must wear their normal habits. James's first reaction to these articles amounted to a refusal, but in the end he accepted them as a basis for negotiation. In 1617 the Spanish raised their terms. The English penal laws must be repealed altogether; until this was done the infanta was to remain in Spain and not a penny of the dowry was to be paid. The prince must come to Madrid for his bride, the implication being that his visit would result in his conversion. James knew that he could not repeal the penal laws; only Parliament could repeal them and such action by the Puritan Commons was unthinkable. Hence the negotiations were deadlocked. Yet James still hoped for a Spanish dowry, and the Spanish continued to negotiate with him, if only to separate him from old friends.

It was at this unfortunate moment in 1618 that Sir Walter Ralegh returned from his last voyage to the Spanish Indies. A prisoner in the Tower since 1603, he had been released in 1616 in order to seek a gold mine which he believed to exist on the Orinoco River in modern Venezuela. Delighted at the thought of gold, James seems to have convinced himself that Ralegh's voyage would make the Spanish more eager for the marriage treaty. Although Ralegh had solemnly pledged not to molest the Spaniards, he returned to England not only without gold but guilty of an attack upon a Spanish settlement. Under sharp pressure from Spain, James weakly sent Ralegh to the block, to the bitter indignation of the people.

The Thirty Years' War

In 1618 a great war broke out between Protestants and Catholics in Germany. It began as a revolt in the kingdom of Bohemia. The aged and childless Emperor Matthias, seeking to establish his cousin, Ferdinand of Styria, as successor to his dominions, had demanded in 1617 that the Bohemians accept Ferdinand as their future king. The Bohemian nobles, who were largely Protestant, refused. They rose in rebellion, broke into the palace at Prague, seized the emperor's agents, and flung them out of the window. The rebels, soon in possession of Bohemia, appealed to James for assistance, while the emperor appealed to Spain. But James's mind was taking a turn of its own. A suggestion had come to him from Spain that he, as a virtuous prince, should mediate between the emperor and the Bohemians. He eagerly accepted this proposal, not realizing it was a trick; for while he vainly attempted to mediate, Spain was left free to aid the emperor. Meanwhile, Matthias died and Ferdinand was elected emperor. Thereupon the Bohemians deposed him as their king and elected in his stead James's son-in-law, Frederick of the Palatinate. Frederick hesitated as well he might, then accepted, and traveled to Prague in October 1618.

These events caused a surge of anti-Catholic and anti-Spanish sentiment in England. James, under heavy pressure to drop his friendship with Spain and to assist his son-in-law, was in great confusion. He sharply criticized Frederick's rashness in accepting the Bohemian crown. James hated all war; but from a war to support revolt and usurpation he shrank as from the plague. He loathed the vexation of action. He had no army, and he could obtain one only by summoning Parliament. To send assistance to Frederick would ruin his reputation as the peacemaker of Europe and would end all hope of the Spanish match. The Spaniards would foster plots among the English Catholics, and his life would be in danger. Yet Frederick was his son-in-law, and Frederick's wife was his daughter. Should he desert his own flesh and blood? Torn and perplexed, the king sank into irresolution. To the exasperation of his people, month after month slipped by without taking action.

Meanwhile the Catholic powers made their plans. A secret agreement between Ferdinand and Philip III of Spain provided that Ferdinand should move against Prague while Philip created a diversion by attacking the Palatinate from the Spanish Netherlands. There is no doubt that Philip was most reluctant; his decision might have been different if James had shown clearly that he would defend the Palatinate. For although the Bohemian adventure was an act of aggression, a Spanish attack on the Palatinate would be equally aggressive. The Palatinate was Frederick's rightful possession.

A Catholic conquest of it would dissolve the Protestant Union and threaten every Protestant interest in southern Germany.

In August 1620 the blow fell when a Spanish army attacked the Palatinate. The emperor moved into Bohemia, defeated Frederick, and sent him fleeing northward for his very life. The Bohemian venture was over, and the Palatinate was in grave danger. It was under these circumstances that James summoned the next Parliament.

THE PARLIAMENT OF 1621

The Parliament of 1621 was the most important of James's reign. If the king obtained supplies, he could defend the Palatinate and perhaps could stem the tide of Catholic victory. Without money he was helpless. In view of these sobering considerations both the king and Commons acted for some months with marked restraint. Yet the Commons were in a grim mood. A mistaken foreign policy, they believed, was exposing their country and their religion to untold dangers. For one thing, they regarded the Spanish match with deep alarm. For another they were keenly aware that at home grave abuses had crept into the government. A perplexing economic depression rendered them even more irritable. They were determined, not only to improve foreign policy where they could, but also to launch a broad and searching investigation of domestic conditions.

Warned away from criticism of the king's foreign policy, the Commons turned to grievances at home. They made a thorough inquiry into patents and monopolies. These patents brought little money to the Crown but were highly profitable to certain courtiers, including a number of Buckingham's relatives. So alarmed was Buckingham that he posed as a reformer and allowed his relatives to be punished. The Commons also wished to investigate the so-called referees, that is, the councilors to whom patents had been referred for appraisal before they had been granted. Had the Commons brought formal charges against the referees, they would in effect have revived the medieval practice of impeachment. James managed to stop this attack upon his ministers, but hostility to the referees continued. When sudden dramatic charges of bribery were brought against Bacon, now lord chancellor, the Commons pushed the accusations and forced Bacon out of office. Meanwhile the foreign situation deteriorated and Frederick's cause was near collapse.

In the autumn session of the Parliament the Commons could be restrained no longer. They entered upon a long debate on foreign policy in which member after member pointed to Spain as the great enemy. Let the war be against Spain, not by pottering in the Palatinate, but by attacking Spain and the Spanish Indies on land and sea in true Elizabethan fashion. Let measures be taken against the Roman Catholics at home. The debate reached its crescendo in a violent speech by Sir Edward Coke, who poured forth vituperation upon Spain and Catholicism. The Commons voted one subsidy to aid the Palatinate over the winter. Then they prepared a petition asking for the enforcement of the anti-Catholic laws, for a war with Spain, and for a Protestant marriage for the prince.

Upon hearing of the petition James dashed off an angry letter to the Commons. They were, he said, debating matters far above their reach and capacity. He commanded them not to meddle with his government nor "deal with our dearest son's match with the daughter of Spain, nor touch the honor of that king." He added "that we think ourselves very free and able to punish any man's misdemeanors in Parliament as well during their sitting as after; which we mean not to spare henceforth." In reply the Commons drew up a protestation. It declared that their privileges were their undoubted birthright and inheritance, that weighty affairs of the kingdom should be debated in Parliament, and that every member had freedom of speech and freedom from arrest. James then dissolved the Parliament in bitter anger. Coming to the Council chamber, he called for the Journal of the Commons and with his own hands tore out the page citing the protestation.

JAMES'S LAST YEARS

The dissolution of Parliament marked the eclipse of James as a potent and respected ruler. A feeble old man sinking into his dotage and cut off from the sympathy of his people, he found his position hopeless in both domestic and foreign affairs. At home his finances fell once more into disorder. Prince Charles and Buckingham, impatient with his fumbling timidity, were eager to take control of policy. He lacked the power to intervene in continental affairs. He could not send assistance to Frederick in the Palatinate. He could only ask Spain to be kind. But he had to ask for a great deal: that the Spaniards withdraw their victorious forces from the Palatinate, that they persuade the emperor to do the same, and that, if the emperor refused, they make war upon their Catholic kinsman to please the Protestant king of England.

Though such cooperation seemed impossible, James thought it might be accomplished through the Spanish match; negotiations to this end continued through 1622. They reached their climax in 1623, when Charles and Buckingham, with romantic folly, determined to go to Spain in person, to conclude a marriage treaty quickly, and to "bring back that angel," the infanta, with whom Charles imagined himself to be in love. Luckily the two young men reached Spain in safety. But the Spanish, with the prince in their possession, naturally raised their terms. James must now proclaim that the penal laws were suspended, must swear that they would never be reimposed, and must obtain the consent of Parliament for his action. Until these things were done, the infanta was to remain in Spain even after her marriage. Charles foolishly agreed to these impossible terms; and James, terrified lest his dear son was a hostage, sadly swore the required oaths.

The Spanish marriage never took place, for Charles was at last awakened from his romantic dream. Anger and resentment against Spain extinguished his infatuation for the infanta, and when he and Buckingham returned to England, they demanded a complete reversal of policy. They wished to make war on Spain, to build a great European alliance against her, and to restore Frederick to the Palatinate by force. The old king was horrified. But his son and his favorite, treating him with some brutality, hurried him into policies he detested. A Parliament in 1624 was easily persuaded to demand an end to the Spanish treaties and the beginning of a war. The Commons voted a small supply, promising to give more when war was declared. English diplomats were dispatched in all directions to form an anti-Spanish front.

In this search for allies Charles and Buckingham turned to France, proposing a marriage between the prince and Henrietta Maria, sister of the French king. Unfortunately, and largely out of pride, the French demanded that the English Catholics be given terms as favorable as those in the abortive treaties with Spain. This condition was accepted. James died in March 1625, leaving his son a discontented kingdom, an empty treasury, a war with Spain, and a marriage treaty with France that could not possibly be fulfilled.

C H R O N O L O G Y

The First Stuart

1603–25	James I (and VI of Scotland)
1603	Millenary Petition
1604	Hampton Court Conference; the "Apology"
1605	Gunpowder Plot—Guy Fawkes; dispute over Writ of Prohibitions
1606	Bate Case; impositions approved
1607	Jamestown settled
1608	Scots born after accession of James to be citizens of England and Scotland—Calvin's case
1610	Salisbury's Great Contract proposed and rejected; Sir Edward Coke and Royal Proclamations
1611	Authorized Version of Bible—King James Bible
1612	Death of Salisbury
1616	Sir Edward Coke dismissed
1618	George Villiers in power; Declaration of Sports; Thirty Years' War; Lionel Cranfield, Earl of Middlesex, and financial reform
1620	Pilgrims sail on *Mayflower*

The Reign of Charles I to 1642

THE NEW KING, 1625–1649

King Charles I, born in Scotland in 1600 and brought to England in 1604, was very delicate as a child. As a young man at court he was healthy, though not robust, fond of theatricals and sports, an excellent horseman who delighted in hunting and in running at the ring. His early contacts with his father and Buckingham were not happy. He resented the glamorous favorite whom all must worship. James made matters worse by showing that he was fonder of Buckingham than of his son. Quarrels between the two young men became so numerous that the king called them before him in 1618 and commanded them on their allegiance to become more friendly. Thereafter their relations improved.

Although Charles was frequently embarrassed by his father's lack of dignity, he was at the same time overawed and silenced by James's rapid conversation, quick intelligence, and choleric temper. Charles was slow and halting in thought and speech and so it is probable that he felt himself inferior. If we assume these were his feelings and that he struggled to overcome them, his character becomes clearer. He schooled himself to be a brave and courageous person. With a natural love of propriety, he perhaps took refuge in laying emphasis upon what was decorous and orderly. His first act as king was to cleanse the court of the bawds and drunkards whom his father had tolerated. His family life was always dignified and correct. Perhaps to counteract any feeling of inferiority he developed a lofty and majestic deportment toward all with whom he dealt. He accepted fully the theory of the divine right of kings. James had stressed the divine origin of kingship; Charles dwelt upon the duty and obedience owed to a ruler by his subjects. He believed that opposition to the royal will was sin; and this became the constant theme of sermons by the Anglican clergy. It followed that if the people were wicked enough to force concessions from the king, the king need not keep his word to them but could revoke his promises when opportunity served. Charles thus acquired an unpleasant reputation for deceit and unreliability. There was a cold, unsympathetic rigidity about this man; he lived in his own world, alien to the feelings and ambitions of others. Nor could he understand the moral force of Puritanism or the aspirations of the Commons. In his mind the Church of England was the only possible church, and monarchy by divine right the only possible government. Such a king was certain to turn to dictatorial and arbitrary rule.

Charles, however, did not possess the vigorous personality necessary for an absolute sovereign. Left to himself he could not make incisive decisions or take strong action, and so he leaned on others more resolute than he. He relied at first on Buckingham, whose complete self-confidence and lavish extravagance symbolized the magnificence and glory of kingship. Later he was influenced by his wife who, reflecting the absolutism of France, urged her husband to play a kingly and decisive role. Later in the reign Charles relied on Archbishop Laud and on Thomas Wentworth, earl of Strafford, both advocates of authority, discipline, and coercion. When these props were gone, Charles was left with courage and tenacity, but little more.

THE CLASH WITH THE COMMONS

Diplomacy, War, and Parliament

When Charles ascended the throne in 1625 he did not understand that he was already in an awkward position. He was the unhappy heir of all the grievances and discontents that had arisen in the reign of his father. There were additional difficulties of his own making. Since he could not fulfill the terms of the marriage treaty with France, he was very likely to have difficulties with that country. He was committed to war with Spain; he and Buckingham, hoping to build a great anti-Spanish front, had promised large sums to King Christian of Denmark, the Dutch, and Count Mansfeld, Frederick's freebooting general. Money must also be spent on the English fleet. Unless Parliament came to Charles' assistance, he could not hope to honor these huge commitments. His one military venture had been Mansfeld's expedition in 1624, which had proved a shameful fiasco. The plan had called for Mansfeld to lead an English army directly across France to the relief of the Palatinate. To this the French objected; and after great uncertainty and change of plan, the English soldiers landed at Flushing in Holland. Unpaid, starving, stricken with fever, they had dwindled in a few months from an army of 12,000 men to some 3000 useless wretches.

Charles was also in difficulty at home. The terms of the French treaty were unknown, but it was suspected that they favored the Roman Catholics. Henrietta Maria, the pretty little French princess who was to be Charles's wife, was regarded as a missionary of her Catholic faith. Moreover, it soon became evident that Charles favored the High Anglican or Laudian school of churchmen. Laud's views were Arminian, not popish. But the reliance of the Arminians on the primitive church rather than on the Scriptures alone, their insistence on the continuity of the Church of England with the Roman Catholic Church before the Reformation, and their revival of medieval ritual appeared to presage a return to Roman Catholicism. The lofty position of the Anglican bishops in Charles's reign gave great offense. Their claim that episcopacy was divine in origin, their persecution of the Puritans in the Court of High Commission, their increasing pomp and dignity, and their employment by the king in high offices of state aroused the strong antagonism of many people. The courteirs were jealous of Buckingham's monopoly of power and of royal favor. And, finally, the economic depression of the 1620s had not yet lifted. It deepened momentarily in 1625 because of the plague which settled upon London and disturbed every phase of social and economic life.

Amid these difficulties Charles and Buckingham should have approached their first Parliament with care. But they acted with blind self-confidence, assuming that their success in 1624 would repeat itself. The Commons, summoned for May 17, 1625, were kept waiting in plague-stricken London for a month before Parliament began. The departure of Henrietta Maria from France had been delayed, and Charles did not wish to meet Parliament until she arrived. His opening speech was vague. He had been advised by Parliament to break with Spain, he said, and he now needed money to conduct the war, but he did not say how much was required or where the war was to be fought. This last point was important, for the Commons wanted a war at sea in the Elizabethan tradition, not a costly war in Germany. Charles's councilors in the House of Commons, having no instructions, were equally noncommittal. Taking advantage of this uncertainty, the opposition moved and carried a vote for a small supply of two subsidies. This action contained an element of trickery, which was unfortunate, but the government had invited some such move by its laxness in stating its case. About a week later Charles attempted a similar device. His councilors gave the Commons for the first time an account of the situation abroad and asked for a large amount of money. But members had been slipping away from London and the plague. Attendance was thin and those who remained refused to commit their fellow members to heavy taxation.

Charles then adjourned Parliament to Oxford, where the Commons reassembled in a rather sullen mood. At Oxford Charles and Buckingham committed new tactical blunders. Buckingham offended the Commons by summoning them before him and speaking to them as though he himself were king. The Commons criticized him sharply, attacked an Arminian divine, Richard Montague, and refused to increase their former grant. The Parliament then was dissolved. It had set a pattern of mismanagement by the Crown, of distrust between king and Parliament, and of refusal by the Commons to grant adequate supply.

Meanwhile the king and Buckingham had been gathering a great fleet at Plymouth for an attack on Spain. They hoped to assault Cadiz as Drake had done in 1587. But everything went wrong. The expedition contained only nine ships of the Royal Navy; the rest were merchant vessels pressed into unwilling service. Ten thousand soldiers and five thousand sailors were also pressed, but the former were largely vagabonds who could not be turned into an effective army. The expedition did not sail until October 1625, when the fair weather of the summer months had ended. After a long march without food in the heat of the Spanish sun, the soldiers discovered a quantity of wine and promptly became intoxicated. They could have been slaughtered by a determined attack. There was no alternative but to send them back to the ships and abandon the assault upon Cadiz, which had been strongly reinforced. Buckingham's great enterprise had ended in disaster.

The Parliament of 1626

It was under the shadow of this failure that Charles's second Parliament met early in 1626. The king had no choice but to summon it because of his many commitments and his lack of money. Knowing that Parliament would be difficult, he made what preparations he could. He ordered a strict enforcement of the penal laws against the Roman Catholics, thus breaking the pledges of the marriage treaty with France. He excluded certain leaders of opposition in the Commons by appointing them sheriffs.

In the Commons a new leader appeared, Sir John Eliot, a man of high ideals and patriotism, but of less ability and prudence than were possessed by the men whom Charles had excluded. Eliot's fiery oratory was apt to lead the Commons into rash and violent action.

The Commons, determined to have a strict accounting for what had happened, began to investigate the responsibility for Mansfeld's disaster and soon launched into a broad attack on Buckingham. They tried to impeach him, but they did so with more violence than skill. Eliot and Sir Dudley Digges, laying the charges of the Commons before the Lords, used language for which Charles sent them to the Tower. The impeachment failed, largely because the king withheld evidence and thus prevented the Commons from proving their case. In a tantalizing way the Commons had passed a resolution to give the king three subsidies but had not put the resolution in the form of a bill. After the attack on Buckingham failed, the resolution was allowed to lapse, and Charles received no money from this Parliament, which was shortly dissolved.

Charles's allies on the Continent were ruined because he could not send them the money he had promised. Mansfeld, ordered to assist the Dutch, was defeated; Christian of Denmark was badly beaten, largely because his troops would not fight without pay. Charles made matters worse by drifting into a war with France.

Louis was angered when Charles enforced the penal laws despite the marriage treaty. A coolness arose between Charles and Henrietta Maria, whose French attendants were disliked in London. Eventually Charles sent them back to France, thus breaking the treaty once more. Moreover, James and Buckingham had promised to lend the French eight English ships to be sent against the Huguenots at La Rochelle who were defying the French government. But the use of English ships to repress Protestants caused such a furor in England that Buckingham tried to prevent the delivery of the ships to France. Charles now posed as the protector of the Huguenots against Louis, each nation seized the merchant vessels of the other, and war soon followed. In June 1627, a large English expedition sent to the relief of La Rochelle made a landing nearby on the Île de Ré. But a French fort on the island could not be caputred, an English army was cut to pieces, and the expedition, another dismal failure, returned to England.

The Forced Loan of 1627

Meanwhile Charles, in trying to raise money, determined in 1627 to levy a forced loan. The money was to be collected as though it had been voted by Parliament and was to amount to five subsidies. But the widespread opposition was increased rather than lessened by the sermons of Arminian clergymen, who preached the religious duty of obedience. Sir Randolph Crew, chief justice of the King's Bench, was dismissed for refusing to declare that the loan was legal. So many men declined payment that pressures of various kinds were applied; a number of the gentry were imprisoned. Five of them brought matters to a head by applying for writs of habeas corpus, which enabled them to ask why they had been put in prison; their purpose was to force the courts to declare whether or not a refusal to contribute to the recent loan was a legal cause for imprisonment. The judges were placed in a difficult position, for it was obvious that a man could not be imprisoned merely because he would not lend his money. The judges therefore returned the knights to jail without giving any reason. But the nation believed that the judges endorsed the view that imprisonment for refusal to lend money was legal and that the king could keep men in jail indefinitely without showing cause. The episode was regarded as a dangerous attack upon personal liberty and on the rights of property.

Discontent was increased by two other grievances. Without means to feed or house his troops, Charles began to billet them in private homes. A householder was informed that he must give board and lodging to two or three soldiers, who might well be lawless rogues, and it was suspected that persons who had refused to lend their money were the first to have soldiers billeted on them. In order to deal with the many quarrels between the soldiers and their reluctant hosts and to maintain discipline in the rabble that Charles called his army, martial law was proclaimed in certain areas. These four points—forced loans, imprisonment without cause shown, billeting, and martial law—formed the basis for debate and action in Charles's third Parliament, which met in 1628.

The Petition of Right

The Parliament of 1628 differed from its predecessors. The Crown was desperate, for government simply could not be carried further without funds. The Commons, on their side, were in deadly earnest. Goaded by the nation's military defeat and by the Crown's attacks on personal liberty, they displayed a new hardness and determination.

Before the Parliament met, Buckingham had talked of a standing army, obviously to beat down opposition, and the government had considered highly dubious expedients for raising money. These wild plans were dropped and the Crown concentrated instead on winning support in the coming session. Key opponents were offered office and other rewards if they would side with the king, royal officials in the Commons were given better instructions, and an attempt was made to influence elections. All such interference failed completely. Men who had been imprisoned because they had refused to lend money were overwhelmingly elected.

The members of this House of Commons were men of position and wealth, able, it was said, to buy out the House of Lords thrice over. The opposition leaders were in complete control and had by now developed procedures—such as the committee of the whole house—by which they could obtain quick action in the Commons. They decided to drop the impeachment of Buckingham and to concentrate on the defense of personal liberties. They began by passing resolutions against unparliamentary taxation and against imprisonment without cause shown. When these resolutions were modified by the Lords, the Commons attempted to frame a bill that would guarantee the liberties of the subject. But it proved difficult to turn the wording of their resolutions into the wording of a bill. If a bill required the king to confirm old statutes and ancient liberties, the implication was that those liberties no longer existed. A member remarked that if "we tell our constituents we have confirmed old statutes, they will ask us when those statutes had been repealed." Hence the Commons adopted the happy idea of Sir Edward Coke that they employ the device of a Petition of Right to redress specific infractions by the king. Such petitions were used in the law courts in cases in which petitioners, claiming that the king had overridden the law, asked merely that they be given the law's protection. The form of a petition enabled the Commons to assert that the laws had been broken and to demand that the king not break them again. Charles endeavored to answer in vague terms, but in the end, in return for a substantial grant, he gave a firm assent.

The Petition of Right contained four points: no man thereafter should be compelled to make any gift, loan, benevolence, tax, or such like charge without common consent by act of Parliament; no man should be imprisoned or detained without cause shown; soldiers and sailors should not be billeted on private individuals against the will of these individuals; and commissions for martial law should not be issued in the future. The Petition of Right, regarded as one of the great documents of English liberty, had its weaknesses: it was not a statute, it contained loopholes, it had to be modified by later generations because it deprived the king of powers a government trusted by the people could be allowed to possess. Nonetheless, it set a limit to the arbitrary power of the Crown and was the first great check upon Stuart absolutism.

Those who hoped it would bring peace between king and Commons were shortly disappointed. Largely because of Eliot's impetuous and unreasonable tactics, the Commons drew up a remonstrance which complained of other grievances and attacked both Laud and Buckingham. A second remonstrance declared that the collection of tonnage and poundage without consent of Parliament was a breach of liberty. The duties of tonnage and poundage formed the normal schedule of the custom. For generations they had been granted to every king for life upon his accession. In 1625, however, they had been given for one year only, but the Commons' bill to this effect had never become law. Without the customs the king was all but penniless. Eliot's audacious move was beyond the wishes of moderate men. In reply the king prorogued Parliament, which did not meet again until early in 1629.

Charles and Buckingham learned little from their failures. Laud and other Arminian churchmen now were advanced to important posts. A new expedition was prepared for the relief of La Rochelle. Ships, ordnance, and provisions of all kinds were assembled at Portsmouth in the summer of 1628. Soldiers and sailors were rounded up in the usual way. But, as before, all plans went awry. The sailors were so mutinous for lack of pay that Charles himself went down to Portsmouth to pacify them. The movement of soldiers through the country revived the problem of billeting. Localities were assured in solemn terms that the king would pay for the support of his troops. But the presence of the soldiers was deeply resented, people would do nothing for them, and some Irish troopers were found to be pawning their arms in order to obtain money for food. Meanwhile merchants were refusing to pay customs duties not authorized by Parliament.

Everywhere murmurs arose against the hated duke of Buckingham. One John Felton, an unpaid and unpromoted lieutenant in the navy, bought a butcher's knife, made his way on foot to Portsmouth, and stabbed Buckingham to death as he stood amid his followers. The people rejoiced, and Felton was a popular hero. But Buckingham's blood separated Charles from his subjects in a new and bitter way. The fleet set sail for La Rochelle in September despite the lord admiral's death. But La Rochelle, where the hard-pressed garrison had been subsisting on a diet of boiled leather, surrendered to the French king in October, and the English fleet returned without glory.

Parliament met in a short and stormy session in 1629. The Commons turned at once to the collection of tonnage and poundage without their consent. They attacked the Arminian clergy, who were represented as undermining sound religion. Charles determined to end the debate. He sent a message to the Speaker to adjdourn the house. There followed a famous scene on 2 March 1629, when the Speaker sought to leave the chair but was held down by force while the Commons passed three resolutions: that whoever should introduce innovations in religion by bringing in popery or Arminianism should be accounted a capital enemy of the king and kingdom; that whoever should advise the levying of tonnage and poundage without consent of Parliament should be accounted the same; and that whoever should pay tonnage and poundage levied without the consent of Parliament should be held a betrayer of the liberty of the subject and a capital enemy of the king and kingdom. Meanwhile the king's messengers were hammering at the locked doors of the lower house. Once the resolutions were passed, the doors were opened and a royal message announced the adjournment of the Commons. A week later Charles dissolved Parliament and imprisoned a number of the opposition leaders. Some were soon liberated but others stayed in prison for years. Charles was through with Parliaments for eleven years.

CHARLES'S PERSONAL RULE

Charles was now able to rule England according to his own conception of government. He was not without idealism. He wished to be a conscientious and patriarchal king who, with the aid of his councilors, would protect his subjects in all walks of life from suffering wrong. He thought of himself as the guardian, not only of the people, but of the church and the ancient constitution against irreligious and seditious persons. The difficulty was that Charles reserved to himself, as king, all power to decide what the church should be, what rights should be protected, and what laws should be obeyed. The people were not to share in determining these matters: their duty was to obey. Charles thought in terms of the complete unity of church and state. To attack the one was to attack the other. Men who criticized the church could not be loyal subjects. Charles was prone, moreover, to determine in his own mind what the laws should mean and then to dismiss any judge who disagreed with him.

A number of reasons can be suggested to explain why Charles was able to rule for eleven years without summoning a Parliament. It is probable that the views of members of the House of Commons were more radical than those of the nation as a whole, for the English were a conservative people. Charles did not look like a tyrant. His decorous court, his habit of doing things in the traditional way, and his mediocre councilors—all made his government appear normal and innocuous. England was accustomed, when Parliament was not in session, to be ruled by the king, the Council, the law courts, and the justices of the peace. All these organs of government continued to function. Moreover, the period of personal rule was a time of economic prosperity. England was at peace, and the economy had recovered from the depression of the 1620s. Charles did not demand large sums of money. Had they been willing, the English could easily have paid what he asked.

Charles was able to withdraw rather easily from the wars in which he had become involved. In April 1629 he made peace with France without difficulty. The fall of La Rochelle showed that he could not defend the Huguenots; the terms offered them by Louis made it clear that Charles need not make the attempt. About the same time Christian IV of Denmark withdrew from the war in Germany. He had been defeated, but his enemies, afraid of Sweden, gave him favorable terms. His withdrawal relieved Charles of an embarrassing ally and enabled him to make peace with Spain more easily in 1630. Nonetheless, the treaty with Spain was a rather shameful conclusion to the long years of English intervention on the Continent since the beginning of the Thirty Years' War. The net result of English efforts was the loss of the Palatinate, the desertion of the Dutch, the fall of La Rochelle, and the defeat of Christian IV—a dismal record.

The great war in Germany was entering a new phase. Sweden, under her famous King Gustavus Adolphus, invaded northern Germany on the Protestant side. Allied with France, she faced the Hapsburgs of Spain and Austria. The two alliances were fairly evenly matched. Hence Charles could evade the burden of defending Protestantism on the Continent and could decide with which camp he wished to ally. He hoped to employ this advantage to regain the Palatinate by diplomacy. But his weak and vacillating policy, his bargaining with one side and then with the other as the fortunes of war swayed back and forth, rendered him despicable. No one wanted as an ally a king who had no military power and who might desert his friends at a moment's notice.

Charles I (1625–1649) dining in public, by Gerrit Houckgeest. (Her Majesty, Queen Elizabeth II)

Finance

Blessed with peace abroad and with tranquility at home, Charles seemed secure. In love with his queen, happy with his collection of art treasures, he believed himself to be the most fortunate king in Christendom. But by a long series of highhanded actions he gradually alienated his people and prepared the way for the sea of troubles which overwhelmed him in the 1640s. Charles's revenues from extraparliamentary sources during his years of personal rule were large but not large enough for his needs. To make ends meet he was forced to ignore the debt, to curtail expenses, and to find new sources of income. In 1629 the debt from the war years stood at nearly £1 million. Most of it never was repaid, the loudest creditors being soothed by favors and privileges of various kinds. Expenditure at court and in the administration was decreased. Ship money was a means by which Charles hoped to be relieved of the cost of the navy.

New income was raised by several devices, among them the distraint of knighthood. In the late thirteenth century Henry III and Edward I, finding that landowners attempted to evade the duties of knighthood, decreed that every man who held land worth £20 a year should become a knight. Raising the sum to £40 a year, Charles enforced this ancient rule and collected fines and compositions from persons who had neglected to be knighted. More than £100,000 were raised by this means within two years. The payments, however, were extracted from the landed classes, which were Charles's natural supporters. The value of the fines was not worth the irritation they aroused. Charles also revived the ancient laws and boundaries of the medieval forests. These forests, it will be remembered, had been extensive areas set aside for the royal sport of hunting. Redefining the forest boundaries, Charles imposed fines for the disregard of obsolete rules everyone had forgotten. For example, almost the entire county of Essex was found to be a forest, and forest law was enforced upon land which had been in private hands for centuries. As a matter of fact, very little money came to the Treasury by this means; although the fines could not be collected they aroused strong animosity among the upper classes. Wealthy families also were incensed by the increased revenues Charles obtained from the vexatious court of wards.

Moreover, Charles offended industrialists and merchants. He imposed a fine of £70,000 on certain London companies because they had not fulfilled their promises in the colonization of Ulster. Of this huge fine, he obtained only £12,000 after a long dispute. He irritated the people at large by granting monopolies to certain retailers of soap, bricks, coal, and salt. Monopolies had been declared illegal by the Parliament of 1624, but Charles evaded the letter of the law by giving monopolies to corporations rather than to individuals.

His most famous expedient was ship money. The Crown possessed an unchallenged right to impress ships from the port towns in times of emergency. Hence the first levy of ship money in 1634 for an expedition against pirates did not arouse resistance. In the following year, however, ship money was demanded once more, this time from the inland counties as well as from the ports. Opposition increased, but the money was collected. But a third levy, in 1636, met widespread hostility, for it was evident that ship money was becoming a permanent form of extraparliamentary taxation. John Hampden, a wealthy gentleman of Buckinghamshire, refused to pay. His case, watched intently by all England, came before the Exchequer Chamber in 1637, when the judges decided, though only by a vote of 7 to 5, that ship money was legal in time of danger and that only the king could decide when danger existed. Ship money continued to be levied, though its collection grew more difficult. But the Hampden Case dramatized the arbitrary nature of Charles's government. Disaffection was widespread against a system of rule and taxation in which Parliament had no share.

Persecution of Puritanism

An even deeper hostility was aroused by Charles's ecclesiastical policy. Favoring the Arminian or High Anglican churchmen, he promoted them to places of trust both in the church and in the state and defended them vigorously against the attacks of the

House of Commons. To the Puritans and to many moderate Anglicans, the Arminians seemed to be heading toward Rome. This impression was confirmed by the pro-Spanish policy of James and at times that of Charles, by the presence of Henrietta Maria and many Roman Catholics at Charles's court, by his failure to strike a blow on behalf of continental Protestantism, and by the fact that the anti-Catholic laws were unenforced whereas the full force of the law was used to persecute Puritans. It was this seeming partiality that caused dislike.

We can understand the situation better if we look at Archbishop Laud, who was hated with a violence difficult to grasp. He was a scholar, a patron of his Oxford college, a brave and resolute man, and a skillful administrator who improved the organization of the church. But although tolerant in theory, he was utterly intolerant in practice; he was a disciplinarian, an advocate of authority and of obedience. Harsh and uncompromising, he took an almost savage pleasure in punishing his opponents. Moreover, he was a meddlesome person, as zealous in matters of petty detail as in the enforcement of broad policy. And he was unfair. The Arminian clergy were to enjoy every facility for expressing their opinions, but the Puritans were to be silenced; Arminians were encouraged to defend their church, but the slightest criticism of it was to be suppressed. Laud's partiality was driven home because he was important in the state as well as in the church. A member of the Privy council, of the court of High Commission, and of the Star Chamber, he was also on commissions for the Treasury and for foreign affairs. He freely employed the power of the state to enforce his ecclesiastical policy. Sitting on the bench in cases involving Puritans, he was both a judge and a party to the suit. His lack of a sense of fair play, his great power, and his ostentatious manner of life aroused resentment, a resentment which spread to the bishops as a whole.

Laud's aim was to suppress all religious services except those of the Arminians, to hold the clergy to strict obedience and conformity, and to stifle criticism of his church. Laud's ceremonial was forced on congregations who were not permitted to worship elsewhere. Criticism of the church was brutally suppressed. No book or pamphlet could legally be printed or sold without a license, and Puritans who wrote secret pamphlets attacking the church were punished harshly. In 1630 Alexander Leighton was whipped, pilloried, and mutilated for printing abroad *An Appeal to Parliament; or Sion's Plea against Prelacy,* in which he challenged the doctrine that episcopacy was divine in origin. Four years later William Prynne, a rather obnoxious Puritan lawyer, was sentenced to life imprisonment, to a fine of £5,000, to disbarment, to mutilation, and to the pillory because of his *Histrio-Mastix: A Scourge of Stage Players,* an attack on the drama which was interpreted as a reflection on the queen. In 1637 Prynne was tried again for further pamphlet writing; Henry Burton, a clergyman, for his sermons; and John Bastwick, a doctor, for writings against the bishops. All three were sentenced to the pillory and to mutilation: and Prynne, having lost his ears in 1634, had the stubs scraped and was branded on the cheek with the letters "S.L." (Seditious Libeler). It is small wonder that by 1640 the Puritans were wholly estranged from the church.

The Explosion in Scotland

The year 1637 may be considered the first year of open opposition. It was the year of the Hampden Case, resisting ship money, and of the trial of Prynne, Burton, and Bastwick. It was also in 1637 that serious trouble arose in Scotland.

Charles handled his Scottish subjects in so highhanded a manner that he slowly drove them into rebellion. He began with an Act of Revocation in 1625 by which he recalled all grants of land (including church lands and tithes) made by the Crown since 1540. Such acts of revocation were not uncommon in Scotland, but Charles's act was so sweeping and covered so long a period of time that it affected almost every substantial landowner in the country. In 1627 he permitted the Scots to redeem their estates by money payments, but he had thoroughly alienated the upper classes. He forgot that James, as a matter of policy, had increased the loyalty of the Scottish nobility and gentry by grants from the possessions of the ancient church.

When Charles visited Scotland in 1633 he added new irritations. He introduced English innovations into the Scottish coronation service and permitted Laud to flaunt Arminian ritual before the eyes of the horrified Scots. When he attended the Scottish Parliament he noted the names of those who opposed his wishes. Upon his return to England he decided that changes should be made in the government and in the Kirk of Scotland. Very unwisely he excluded the lords of session, that is, the judges of Scotland's high court for civil cases, from membership in the Privy Council. The power of the Scottish bishops on the Council was thus increased, and in 1635 Charles named Archbishop Spottiswoode as chancellor of Scotland.

More dangerously he decided that the liturgy of the Kirk should be based on the English *Book of Common Prayer*. The prayer book prepared for Scotland used to be called "Laud's Liturgy," but a recent study has shown that it was largely the work of the Scottish bishops. Their modifications of the English prayer book, to make it more palatable for the Scots, were carefully supervised by the king. When it was used for the first (and last) time in St. Giles's Cathedral in Edinburgh in 1637 it provoked a famous riot. All Scotland was in an uproar. The Scots appointed a body of commissioners, often called the Tables, who formed a sort of opposition government. To consolidate public opinion, they issued a famous document known as the National Covenant. It contained a pledge to resist the recent innovations in religion and to support the authority of the Crown. These two points were obviously inconsistent, but they united Scotland for the moment, and thousands of persons eagerly subscribed to the Covenant. Scotland was in revolt. If Charles were to enforce his prayer book he would have to do so by military might.

THE BISHOPS' WARS AND THE SHORT PARLIAMENT

For a moment Charles bowed before the storm in Scotland. He promised that a General Assembly would meet in 1638 and a Scottish Parliament in 1639. As soon as the Assembly convened it summoned the Scottish bishops to appear before it; on their refusal, the Assembly abolished episcopacy. It proceeded to do away with the prayer book of 1637, with the canons by which the book was to have been enforced, and with the Five Articles of Perth which called for the use of High Anglican liturgical practices. It then re-established the presbyterian form of church government and decreed that nonpresbyterian clergymen should be expelled from their pulpits.

When Charles refused to recognize the actions of this Assembly both sides prepared for war. Without funds, Charles summoned the English nobility to serve at their own charge and called out the militia of the northern counties. But the men were untrained, their equipment was defective, and they were unpaid. A troop of the king's horse pushed into Scotland, saw the Scots army, turned without fighting, and fled south across the border. An invasion of Scotland became an impossibility. Charles concluded the Pacification of Berwick with the Scots in June 1639, by which both sides agreed to disband their forces. A new General Assembly and a Scottish Parliament were to determine the future government of Scotland.

This pacification was short-lived. The General Assembly confirmed all that its predecessor had done, the Parliament repealed laws in favor of episcopacy and increased its own powers, the Scottish army remained in existence. A second Bishops' war was inevitable. But Charles's resources were so limited that the momentous decision was taken to summon a Parliament in England. Charles's councilors argued that a Parliament would show the people that the king wished to obtain funds in the old accustomed way. If Parliament did not vote him supplies in his great emergency he would be free to use any means at his disposal to raise money for war. Councilors hoped that anti-Scottish feeling in England would bring support for the king; Wentworth, now summoned back from Ireland, thought that the Commons could be managed.

The result was the Short Parliament, which met from 13 April to 5 May 1640. Many of the popular leaders were returned. The Commons were told in an arrogant way that they should vote money at once and that the king would then listen to any grievances they might have. The answer of the Commons is to be found in a speech by John Pym, who presented in a moderate but devastating way the long list of grievances which had accumulated since 1629. Beginning with Charles's attacks on parliamentary privilege, Pym traced the innovations in religion and the assaults on the rights of property. He called for reform and when he sat down there were cries of "A good oration!" Under his leadership, the Commons began a systematic collection and examination of popular complaints. Grievances were to precede supply. The king, angry at a rumor that the leaders of the Commons were in secret communication with the Scots, dissolved the Parliament.

Charles was left with the old problem of fighting a war without money. His principal adviser at this crisis was Thomas Wentworth, now earl of Strafford, known to the people as "Black Tom the Tyrant." Strafford, one of the popular leaders in the 1620s, had been imprisoned in 1627 for refusing to lend money to the king. But after the Petition of Right he had come over to the side of the Crown and for this had been accused of apostasy. He was a masterful man whose temper was autocratic. He had no interest in free institutions and no sympathy with Puritanism. Skillful and resolute as an administrator, he believed in authority, demanded unquestioning obedience, and was prone to drive at what he desired without too nice an attention to legality. It was natural for such a man to take his place with the king. From 1628 to 1632 he was president of the Council in the North; from 1632 to 1640, lord deputy in Ireland. It was only toward the end of Charles's personal rule that this hard, bold, and determined man was summoned from Ireland to become one of the king's principal counselors. After the dissolution of the Short Parliament he advised Charles to prosecute the war against the Scots with vigor, to consider himself free from all normal rules of government, and to do anything "that power might admit." "You have an army in Ireland you may employ here to reduce this kingdom." Was "this kingdom" Scotland, or was it England?

It was easier to speak boldly than to raise an army. Loans could not be obtained either from London or from sources overseas. Charles called out the militia from the southern part of the country, but the men were not only half trained but half mutinous. Many of them deserted; others broke into disorders which often were demonstrations against the Laudian church. England's heart was not in the war, and the arbitrary methods of the government only increased the general discontent. The Scots, therefore, took the initiative. Crossing the Tweed unopposed on 20 August 1640, they occupied the two northern counties of Northumberland and Durham, upon which they levied £850 a day for their support. The Scots, however, had no intention of pushing farther south. With two counties and with the coal fields around Newcastle in their possession, they held hostages enough. On all sides in England the demand arose for a meeting of Parliament. Charles, not yet convinced, summoned instead a Great Council consisting only of peers, such as had not met in England for at least two centuries. The peers arranged a treaty with the Scots that left things as they were until a more lasting settlement could be made. Thus a meeting of Parliament became absolutely necessary. Charles summoned one for 3 November 1640. The years of "personal rule" and the policies of "Thorough" (or the strict and stern enforcement of the laws) attributed to Strafford and Laud were at an end.

THE FIRST YEARS OF THE LONG PARLIAMENT

The members of the House of Commons who assembled in November 1640 were in a determined mood. Estranged from the Crown by years of arbitrary government, they believed that the time had come for the removal of abuses and for curtailment of the royal prerogative. The king, defeated and bankrupt, was in their power. And yet it is probable that most members thought in the traditional fashion of redressing wrongs and driving out "evil counselors." They had no thought of revolution or of removing the king from office. But a group of leaders—men such as John Pym and John Hampden in the Commons and a handful or Puritan peers—wanted something more than did ordinary members. Not that these leaders thought in terms of physical revolt. What they wanted was a transference of power from the king to the House of Commons. It seemed intolerable to them that a wrong-headed king whose government was in shambles should formulate policy which he could not carry out—while members of the gentry, upon whom the execution of government rested, had no share in decision making. These leaders believed that sovereignty should pass from the king to Parliament. During the next few years a majority of members came to agree with them.

The Commons began by striking at the ministers of the king. It was resolved at once to impeach the earl of Strafford. In this the Commons were prompted as much by fear as by determination to punish evil deeds; they secured Strafford's imprisonment even before the charges against him were formulated. Laud also was imprisoned, but he was not thought dangerous; his trial and execution did not take place until 1644–1645.

Strafford's trial before the House of Lords began in March 1641 and ended three weeks later without a verdict. He was accused of treason for attempting to subvert the fundamental laws of the realm and for advising the king to substitute an arbitrary and tyrannical government, but it soon became evident that the Commons' case was weak. The basic definition of treason was an offense against the king, of which Strafford was not guilty. He was accused, in fact, of treason against the nation, a new concept in law. His words to the king, "You have an army in Ireland you may employ here to reduce this kingdom," might well have referred to Scotland, as he claimed they did; in any case they rested on the oath of only one witness. The impeachment seemed likely to fail.

When the Commons discovered that certain courtiers were plotting to bring down the army from the north in order to dissolve the Parliament, they dropped the impeachment in a panic and substituted a bill of attainder, which required no proof, but which must pass the Lords and be signed by the king. There was now a great deal of tumult. Mobs from the city, sometimes composed of well-dressed persons and sometimes of mere rabble, milled around Westminster. Danger arose that the mob might attack the palace; cries were heard demanding the life of the queen. Threatened with violence, the lords passed the bill in a very thin house, and the king, after days of agony, signed it, to his great loss both in strength and in honor. Strafford was executed next morning.

To secure their position the Commons passed the Triennial Act, which provided that no more than three years should elapse between the dissolution of one Parliament and the meeting of the next; and an act declaring that the Parliament now assembled should not be dissolved without its own consent. When Charles signed the second of these bills, he lost his last shred of power over the Commons. The most basic control of Parliament by the Crown had been its right to summon and dissolve at will; with the curtailment of this power the Crown was indeed laid low. Charles had decreed a perpetual Parliament.

A series of important acts followed. Ship money, forest laws, and distraint of knighthood were swept away. Tonnage and poundage, though granted for a short time, was declared illegal without the consent of Parliament. Another measure abolished the Star Chamber, the High Commission, the Council in the North, the power of the Privy Council to deal with the property rights of the people, and the jurisdiction of the Council of Wales in so far as it resembled that of the Star Chamber.

The courts of common law remained supreme, victorious in their long contest with the prerogative courts.

The early work of the Long Parliament, which we have been describing, was done with surprising unanimity, but when the Commons turned to religious issues their unanimity disappeared. They could agree that the penal laws against Catholics should be enforced, that the church should not be Laudian, that Parliament should exercise some control over it, but here agreement ended. As differences multiplied, a royalist party began to take shape in the Commons. It was composed of moderate Anglicans, people loyal to the Church of England and to its prayer book who desired to retain episcopacy with the excessive power of the bishops curtailed. But a majority of the Commons wished to overthrow the church, to end it root and branch, and to set up some form of Puritanism in its place. What form was that to be? Presbyterianism, although strong in London and in other parts of the country, did not as yet command much support in the Commons. The same was true of Independency, or Congregationalism, though the few members who supported it wielded considerable influence. Pym, followed by a majority of the Commons, thought in terms of a Puritan state church controlled by lay commissioners who in turn would be controlled by Parliament. This solution in effect would transfer to Parliament the ecclesiastical supremacy the Crown had exercised since the Reformation. As these Puritan groups emerged, the Anglicans drew together, not only in defense of the prayer book and a reformed episcopacy, but in defense of the king, whose powers, it was thought, should not be reduced any further.

Division between Puritans and Anglicans was increased greatly in the autumn of 1641, when news arrived of a rebellion in Ireland. With Strafford, who had ruled Ireland with a heavy hand, now gone, the Irish Catholics saw an opportunity to turn on their oppressors. They had hoped for a general insurrection, though what took place was a rising in Ulster, where there were many English and Scottish landowners. The stories that reached England were greatly exaggerated, but it is certain that some thousands of Protestants were murdered and that thousands more died of exposure and privation. The Commons, vowing to revenge such brutality, voted money at once for an efficient army. This raised a fundamental issue, for the Commons dared not entrust the new army to the king, and the king could not entrust it to the Parliament. In this crisis Pym and other Puritan leaders drew up the Grand Remonstrance, a long document of 204 clauses which reviewed past grievances over many years, set forth the remedies advocated by Parliament, and demanded that the king employ officers and ministers of state whom the Commons could trust. The Grand Remonstrance was opposed by the royalists, who now formed a compact party. The debates on the Grand Remonstrance became so heated that there was danger of a scuffle on the floor of the Commons. In the end the Remonstrance passed by the slim majority of 159 to 148.

Events now moved rapidly to the outbreak of war. Tumults and mobs at Westminster became common. The bishops, fearing attack, ceased to attend the House of Lords. Men drew their swords in the streets; the names of Cavalier and Roundhead came into use. Charles had a party in each house, but in a wild and foolish move he ordered his attorney general to prepare impeachment proceedings against five of the leading Puritans in the Commons. When that house would not surrender them, Charles took the fatal step of coming in person to the Commons in an attempt to arrest the five members. This was regarded as a monstrous breach of privilege—as it was—though no worse a violation of constitutional principles than the Commons' use of the mob to terrorize Westminster. The five members had slipped away to London. Four thousand men came up from Buckinghamshire to defend their hero Hampden. The Commons sent one of their number, Sir John Hotham, to secure the arsenal at Hull and passed an ordinance which placed their nominees in control of the militia. Charles withdrew to Hampton Court and sent the queen to France. In March 1642 he went to York, in April he was refused admission to Hull, and in August he raised his standard at Nottingham. The Civil War had begun.

THE CAUSES OF THE CIVIL WAR

The years between 1640 and 1660 have traditionally been treated as a single period—the Puritan Revolution, or more recently, the English Revolution. One result of this was to confuse the causes of the Civil War of 1642–1646 with those factors that caused the revolution of 1649–1660. More recently historians have come to make a distinction between the causes of the Civil War and the causes of the revolution which grew out of the Civil War. Whatever were the forces at work in society in general that surfaced in the late 1640s and the 1650s, they might not have surfaced when and how they did if there had been no Civil War to impel them.

The search for explanations, if not causes, of the events of the 1640s and 1650s began with the participants themselves. James Harrington, Thomas Hobbes, and Sir Edward Hyde, later earl of Clarendon, all contributed to the ongoing debate. Harrington's *Oceana* (1656) credited the rise of the gentry with being the force behind the rebellion. Hobbes's *Behemoth, or the Long Parliament* (1600) saw the emergence of a bourgeois ideology, and Clarendon's *History of the Rebellion and Civil Wars in England* (1702–4) was a pro-Royalist narrative history which concentrated on the events and people of the reign of Charles I.

In the nineteenth century scholars such as S. R. Gardiner, in his monumental *History of England,* saw a "Puritan Revolution" in which there was a struggle for political and religious liberty. Karl Marx and his followers saw a distinct phase in the history of class struggle—the overthrow of the feudal aristocracy by the bourgeoisie. The twentieth century has seen many historians, beginning with R. H. Tawney, seek to explain the period by combining the ideas of Harrington, Hobbes, and Marx. The rise of the gentry has been seen as the result of modern managerial techniques (Tawney). This rise has also been attributed to the gentry's connections with the royal court (Trevor-Roper). Lawrence Stone *(Crisis of the Aristocracy)* thought the temporary crisis faced by the titled nobility gave the illusion of such a rise. Christopher Hill's many books have depicted a form of bourgeois revolution. Perez Zagorin saw a struggle between "court" and "country." Margaret Judson *(Crisis of the Constitution)* saw a struggle for constitutional sovereignty between the Crown and

Parliament. This view was in the tradition of Wallace Notestein, who had earlier seen the House of Commons attempting to take the initiative in formulating legislation and making policy. Each of these scholars sought answers by looking beyond the reign of Charles I to that of James I, Elizabeth I, and even Henry VIII.

Many contemporary scholars cite more immediate causes for war and revolution. Some see a dissolution of what had been a well-run state (Conrad Russell), or else immediate conflicts over the rigid enforcement of Anglicanism by Charles and Laud (Tyacke), or the struggle between national and local governments and their respective leaders (Alan Everitt, Clive Holmes, and J. S. Morrill). Such debates have raged for three hundred years and are likely to continue.

Economic issues also played a part in bringing about the Civil War. During the early Stuart period the aggressive country gentleman, as well as the opportunistic merchant and industrialist, saw many ways in which economic profit could be made. What these men wanted was greater freedom, especially in dealing with labor, and a relaxation of Tudor control of economic life. The early Stuarts, however, believed that the regulation of the economy was a royal prerogative to be employed for the protection of the Crown and for the advancement of the general good. Desiring stability rather than progress, James and Charles were suspicious of private enterprise; they resisted economic change which, they feared, might cause unemployment and social unrest. They stood for the *status quo*. Moreover, they regarded themselves as patriarchal rulers who protected the poor against the wealthy. But their efforts in this direction were so feeble, their economic policies so inconsistent, contradictory, and full of exceptions imposed by poverty, that they irritated the landed and business classes without bringing noticeable relief to the poor.

Inflation kept up the price of agricultural products. The country gentleman who could engage in the national industry of feeding London or who owned property rich in minerals or timber could make a good thing of his estates. The agricultural frontier was moving westward into Wales and northward toward the border. Wishing to bring more land under cultivation, landowners enclosed their estates, drained marshes, and encroached upon the wasteland between villages. The government resisted these moves, partly because they injured the poor, partly because they offered opportunity to levy fines upon the rich. Nevertheless, wealthy men who loaned money to the king were allowed to act as they pleased.

The same tendencies may be seen in commerce and industry. In James's first Parliament a demand arose for freer trading conditions, that is, for a curtailment of the monopolies enjoyed by the London trading companies. But the Crown defended the rights of the London companies. Moreover, many merchants resented the government's weakness in opposing the Dutch and in allowing the navy to decay, so that it gave little protection to English seaborne trade. Industry had expanded steadily in the century before the Civil War. To a considerable extent this expansion was based upon a greater use of coal in heating houses and in new industrial techniques. A remarkable growth had taken place in the amount of capital invested in business enterprises. London grew steadily as an economic center; the population slowly increased. Yet capitalists found that they were commanded to do uneconomical things such as keeping their workpeople employed when trade was slack, that the

Star Chamber was used when the common law courts would not support the Crown, that the middleman was disliked, that economic regulation became complex and rigid, that the government broke its own rules, that monopolies increased, and that interference by the Crown in economic life did more harm than good.

As for the poor, they obtained little benefit either from the expansion of the economy or from the policy of the state. The population, though not large, was greater than the economy of the time could absorb. Underemployment and extremely low wages were common, with no protection against disaster, and little done to relieve the poor. The poor, it may be noted, did not support the king during the Civil War. The business classes, with some exceptions, were alienated; the landed aristocracy was divided at least in sympathy.

C H R O N O L O G Y

The Personal Rule

1625–1649	Charles I
1627	Relief of La Rochelle a failure; forced loan; Five Knights' Case
1628	Petition of Right
1629	"Personal Rule" begins
1630	Peace with France and Spain; Puritans settle Boston Bay
1637	Ship Money Case (John Hampden); trials of Prynne, Burton, and Bastwick; Scottish National Covenant
1639	First Bishops' War
1640	Second Bishops' War; Short Parliament; Long Parliament begins; Strafford impeached; Laud imprisoned
1641	Strafford convicted and executed; Triennial Act; rebellion in Ireland; Grand Remonstrance
1642	Militia Bill and Civil War

18 The Civil Wars and the Rule of the Saints

The Civil Wars were fought between the king and Parliament. A look at how the wars started and how different groups and individuals chose sides may give us a better understanding as to their causes.

The Civil Wars were fought with spirit and resolution. The fighting began in a rather amateurish way, but both sides soon acquired professional technique from veterans returning from the wars on the Continent. Friends and relatives found themselves on opposite sides. Both sides, seeking the support of noncombatants, treated them with respect. A fiercer spirit prevailed when Englishmen fought Scots or Irishmen; yet the war in England generally was conducted with honor and humanity.

HOW THE COUNTRY WAS DIVIDED

Some eighty of the nobility sided with the king, some thirty against him. The nobles felt instinctively that their greatness was bound up with that of the Crown; they feared the mob and the chaos of revolution. Some had a sense of personal gratitude to Charles. "Had I a million crowns or scores of sons," wrote Lord Goring, "the king and his cause should have them all. . . . I had all from the king, and he hath all again." Of the nobles supporting Parliament, a few were Puritan, a few hoped to be on the winning side. The gentry were divided, the majority for the king, a large minority for Parliament. They were influenced by the same considerations as were the nobles, though Puritanism was stronger among them than among the peers. Accustomed to riding, they had the makings of excellent cavalry officers, and they often brought a body of horsemen with them for the king's service. "The honest country gentleman," wrote a Royalist, "raises the troop at his own charge, then gets a Low Country lieutenant to fight his troop for him, and sends for his son from school to be cornet." The yeomen tended to side with the gentry of their areas; the peasants were indifferent. Although a few London merchants were Royalists, the business classes of the towns sided with Parliament; London, which was strongly Presbyterian, supplied the Commons with an inexhaustible source of men and money.

To some extent every locality was divided; the war began with a great number of small clashes as each side attempted to capture military stores and to control the militia. There was, however, a rough geographical division. The north and the west of the kingdom sided with the king, the south and the east with Parliament, while much of the Midlands formed a no-man's land. The king's territory was excellent recruiting ground, though his soldiers were difficult to discipline, prone to plunder, and apt to disappear if they did not receive their pay. The shires under Parliament's control were more amenable to discipline and to taxation, the London-trained bands were the best infantry in the kingdom at the beginning of the war, and Parliament secured the three principal arsenals of London, Hull, and Portsmouth.

Parliament held two great advantages; the first was sea power. The adherence of the navy permitted Parliament to control and to continue foreign trade, to collect customs, to hinder the king in importing munitions, and to maintain coastal towns behind his lines. Parliament's second advantage lay in money. By controlling the richer and more populous portions of the country, it could levy assessments on prosperous farming counties, sequester Royalists' estates, and raise loans in London. Although the pay of its soldiers was often in arrears, Parliament could always find new recruits. The king, on the other hand, depended almost entirely on the generosity of his followers; great nobles, such as the earls of Worcester and Newcastle, gave him huge sums. But the most lavish private gifts run out at last and are a poor substitute for taxation. As the king's finances became more and more desperate, recruiting fell off, and munitions were difficult to come by. The fact that royal troops lived off the countryside made the peasants hostile.

The first Civil War thus saw the king, the titled aristocracy, the Church of England, the North and the West, and a narrow majority of the gentry fighting against the House of Commons, London, other commercial centers with the merchant class, the South and the East, Puritans, and a large minority of the gentry. In many cases the choice of sides was a very personal one. Behind it all, it must be remembered, the House of Commons and the king could no longer trust each other. If there had been no Parliament in session, there would probably have been no Civil War.

THE CIVIL WAR OF 1642–1646

The king held an initial advantage, partly because the parliamentary general, the earl of Essex, was so dilatory that he allowed the king to grow strong. Charles moved west from Nottingham to Shrewsbury, seeking recruits and weapons. By

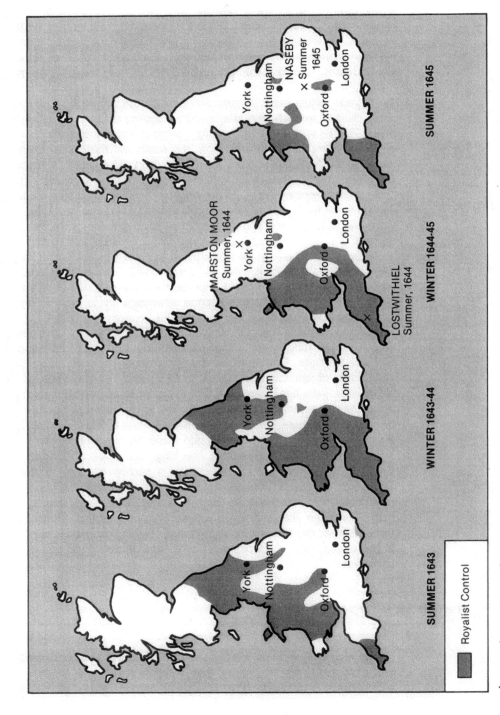

Areas under royal control.

376

October 1642 he was able to march toward London, hoping to end the war at a blow. Essex met him at Edgehill in Warwickshire in the first battle of the war. Charles's cavalry, commanded by his impetuous nephew, Prince Rupert of the Palatinate, drove Essex's horsemen from the field, but most of the parliamentary foot stood firm and the king's infantry was badly mauled. The fruits of victory fell to Charles, who entered Oxford and continued his march toward London. Although Rupert stormed Brentford a dozen miles from the city, the London-trained bands supported Essex. Charles withdrew to Oxford, which became his headquarters for the remainder of the war. He had shown more skill and daring than Essex, but he had failed to win the war in a single decisive campaign.

There was one parliamentary officer who studied these events to advantage. Oliver Cromwell, watching the battle at Edgehill, saw clearly that the parliamentary forces could never be victorious until their cavalry was equal to that of the king. He said to his cousin, John Hampden, "Your troops are most of them old decayed serving-men, tapsters, and such kind of fellows; do you think that the spirits of such base, mean fellows will ever be able to encounter gentlemen that have honor, and courage, and resolution in them? You must get men of a spirit that is likely to go as far as gentlemen will go, or you will be beaten still." Cromwell was a member of the gentry, owning estates around Huntingdon, and he obtained leave to go home to raise a troop of cavalry.

This famous troop, expanding gradually from 80 to 1100 men, was to give its spirit to the whole parliamentary army. Most of its soldiers were farmers, many owning their land and their horses. They were very religious, "having the fear of God before them and making some conscience of what they did." Cromwell was proud of his troop. "I have," he wrote, "a lovely company." Enforcing rigid discipline, he trained his men carefully. He taught them to look after and groom their horses and to keep their weapons bright and ready for use. Each trooper was armed with a pair of pistols and a sword and was protected by a light helmet called a pot and by two pieces of armor, known as back and breast, which fitted over the upper part of the body and were laced together at the sides. Cromwell trained his men to charge "at a good round trot," firing their pistols as they met the enemy and then relying upon the sharpness of their swords.

Cromwell had a natural aptitude for war. An introvert in his religious life, forever seeking flaws in his soul, he was an extrovert in battle, with a capacity for instant decision and a wonderful alertness and vitality. He was "naturally of such a vivacity, hilarity, and alacrity as another man hath when he hath drunken a cup too much." He created his own troop and selected his own officers; he saw that his men received their pay and their supplies. At first he was merely a dashing cavalry officer, but he grew with astonishing rapidity, developing into a superb general by whom all the arts and techniques of war—military, logistic, psychological—were employed with masterly success.

Following the Battle of Edgehill Parliament increased the efficiency of the war effort by dividing its territory into groups of counties known as associations. Of these the Eastern Association, consisting of East Anglia and the counties from Lincolnshire down to Hertford, was the most important. An army raised in this area was

Sir Thomas Fairfax, from Joshua Sprigg, Anglia Rediviva; England's Recovery, *London, 1647. (Department of Special Collections, Wilson Library, University of Minnesota)*

commanded by the Presbyterian earl of Manchester. Cromwell's regiment formed part of this army.

The fortunes of the king in the Civil War reached their height in 1643. In addition to the army at Oxford, there was a royal army in the north under the earl of Newcastle, who in the previous year had moved from Durham into Yorkshire, pushing back the parliamentary forces under Lord Fairfax and his son Sir Thomas. In 1643 Newcastle entered Lincolnshire and soon occupied the entire county. In the southwest a third army overran Cornwall and Devon except for the walled towns. With the capture of Bristol in July the king's hold on the west seemed secure. Thus, he occupied a central position at Oxford, with supporting forces on each flank, and there was scope for a broader strategy. Essex opened the campaign with a lunge toward Oxford, but he was checked and withdrew, allowing the queen, who had landed in the north, to enter Oxford with a large convoy of reinforcements and supplies. Encouraged by these successes, Charles planned a three-pronged assault on London by a converging movement of all his armies. But Newcastle hesitated to push south while Hull remained uncaptured in his rear; a similar dread haunted the

Royalists in the west, for they had not taken Plymouth. Charles therefore turned west to besiege the fortified city of Gloucester. Parliament was in difficulty, but it rose to the occasion, imposed new taxes, and sent Essex to Gloucester's relief. Charles abandoned the siege and met Essex at the Battle of Newbury, which was called a draw, though the king's losses were greater than those of Essex.

A crisis in the war was approaching, and both sides sought allies. The king turned to Ireland, where his Lord Deputy, Ormonde, held Dublin with a small Royalist force. Arranging a truce with the Irish Catholics, Ormonde sent troops to England, though they were not numerous enough to make any great difference. Charles was soon hoping for aid from the Irish Catholic rebels; a secret treaty was arranged which made them large concessions in return for assistance. Unfortunately a copy of the treaty was captured by Parliament, and great discredit was brought upon the king, for the use of Irish troops in England was abhorrent to all parties.

Meanwhile Parliament approached the Scots, asking for a political alliance for the resolute prosecution of the war. But the Scots wanted a religious covenant. They knew that the Presbyterian party held a strong position in the House of Commons and that Parliament was in great need of assistance. They demanded and secured the Solemn League and Covenant, a treaty containing an implied promise that Parliament would establish Presbyterianism as the state religion in both England and Ireland. This treaty had far-reaching results. It divided the Commons between the Presbyterians and another party, the Independents, to whom we will turn presently. Eventually, when the Independents came to power, the treaty brought war between England and Scotland but meanwhile it helped enormously in defeating the king.

In January 1644 a well-equipped Scottish army of twenty-one thousand men crossed the border into England. The military picture suddenly was altered. Newcastle, the king's general, turned to face the Scots and was thrown on the defensive. He was driven into York, where he was besieged by the Scots, by the Fairfaxes, and by Manchester's forces. Prince Rupert, coming to the rescue from the west, broke up the siege but made the mistake of following the parliamentary armies as they retreated and of forcing a battle at Marston Moor in July 1644. The result was a Royalist disaster. Rupert retreated with his cavalry, having lost his infantry, his guns, and his baggage. The king's hold on the north of England was crushed.

Elsewhere Charles did not fare badly. Essex was defeated in Cornwall, and a second Battle of Newbury ended in a draw, though the king should have been routed. Meanwhile the great adventurer, James Graham, marquis of Montrose, was raising the Scottish Highlands for the king, to the consternation of the Lowland Scots. Nevertheless, Charles was in a precarious position. He was almost without money or even a resolute plan.

Meanwhile Parliament reconstructed and improved its army. There had been a quarrel between Cromwell and the earl of Manchester in which, with his usual force and bluntness, Cromwell had accused the earl of inefficiency and of wishing to make peace with the king. As a result Parliament passed the Self-denying Ordinance, which forced the resignation of persons holding commands, civil or military, who were members of that Parliament. Essex, Manchester, and Waller were eliminated; Fairfax became general, Skippon, major general; the office of lieutenant general, left open for a time, was given to Cromwell. By the Self-denying Ordinance he should have been passed over, but he had a great following in the army and his services were too valuable to lose. His appointment was an indication that in a crisis the army could force its will upon the Commons. The New Model Army, as it was called, was better led and better organized; the soldiers were paid regularly by a monthly assessment levied on all the counties under Parliament's control. It was this army that speedily brought the war to a close. Charles, with no firm plan, foolishly marched into enemy territory and was crushed at Naseby in June 1645, another battle in which Cromwell played a distinguished part. Thereafter the king was a fugitive and the war subsided into sieges and small operations. In May 1646 Charles surrendered himself to the Scots.

PRESBYTERIANS AND INDEPENDENTS

To defeat the king was far easier than to construct a new government. The king could not be restored as if nothing had happened; nor could the House of Commons, which had fought a war and governed the country for five years, be set once more in its old position. King and Parliament would have to cooperate in a new government, and many wounds would have to be healed. These problems proved too difficult for solution. There were bitter quarrels—between Presbyterians and Independents, between Parliament and the army, and between England and the Scots—until chaos threatened and the Second Civil War was fought. Then the army, bitter against the king, seized control of Parliament and brought Charles to his tragic death.

When Royalist members left Parliament at the beginning of the Civil Wars, the party that remained was the Root and Branch party, determined to destroy the Anglican Church. In 1642 it summoned a meeting of clergymen, known as the Westminster Assembly, to suggest reforms. The Solemn League and Covenant gave power to the Presbyterians in the Commons, and the church gradually assumed a Presbyterian tone. A Directory took the place of the Prayer Book, the hierarchy of the Church of England was abolished, there was a new Confession of Faith as well as a new Catechism. The new church, when fully constructed, would be a Presbyterian Church, though it would be subject to Parliament and not free and sovereign as in Scotland.

A new form of ecclesiastical government—that of the Independents—was emerging in England. The Independents had begun in the reign of Elizabeth when a group of religious radicals, the Brownists or Separatists, broke from the church and set up their own congregations. The churches in New England and some English churches in Holland were of this type. They rejected any kind of ecclesiastical hierarchy, whether Anglican or Presbyterian. Each congregation, they believed, should be complete, autonomous, and sovereign in itself. Uncontrolled from above, it should select its own minister and should determine its own beliefs and ritual. The Independents laid great stress on individual interpretation of the Scriptures and believed that man could discover God's will as well as find a guide to conduct in the

Bible. "If thou wilt seek to know the mind of God in all that chain of Providence," wrote Cromwell, "seek of the Lord to teach thee what that is; and He will do it." Hence the Independents believed in new revelations, new directives, to be found in God's written word. The result was great diversity of doctrine and a great variety of sects—Congregationalists, Anabaptists, Antinomians, Fifth Monarchy Men, Seekers, Quakers,[1] and, to the far left, the Diggers, who rejected church buildings and all ritual and made religion a silent communion of the spirit between God and man. The Independents were weak in the House of Commons. They could number only fifty or sixty votes. But their leaders, such as Sir Henry Vane the Younger and Oliver St. John, were so able that they exerted an influence out of proportion to their numbers.

Presbyterians and Independents represented not only two churches but two philosophies of government. The Presbyterians proclaimed the sovereignty of Parliament. Like the members of the General Assembly in Scotland, they believed that God had given them the right to rule the state. The Independents, on the other hand, found sovereignty in the people. Democracy in the Independent churches led to democracy in politics. Just as a congregation selected its pastor, so the people should select their governors; Parliament should be kept close to the sovereign people by frequent elections. Just as the church was a voluntary association of believers held together by a covenant, so the state was an association of freemen held together by a contract. The government should not interfere in matters of the spirit. There should be liberty of conscience for every individual to believe and worship as he wished. Thus the ideas of modern political democracy were foreshadowed by the Independents.

If weak in the House of Commons, the Independents were strong in the army. All sorts of sects were to be found among the soldiers. Trusting in new revelations, they believed that God, by the victories He had given them, had marked them as the protectors of religion with a mission to control the state. The soldiers were hostile to the king. He had been their enemy, and they could not trust themselves under his power in any form of restored monarchy.

The army looked to Cromwell as its leader in politics as well as in war. He was popular with the soldiers, jovial and familiar with them, and did not stand on his dignity; and if a fiery temper underlay his joviality, this did not make him less popular. He represented their views much better in religion than he did in politics. He has been called the great Independent. Though he did not associate himself with any one sect, he sympathized with the spirit of all of them and embodied their religious ideals. As a young man of about twenty-eight he had experienced a conversion through which, after great mental and spiritual agony, he became convinced that he was one of God's elect, chosen by the Almighty to fulfill His plans on earth. It was Cromwell's primary aim to discover the will of God, and for this purpose he devoted long periods to prayer and meditation. He was a strong advocate of liberty of conscience, and he defended the sectaries in the army against the intolerance of the Presbyterians. After the Battle of Naseby he wrote to the speaker of the House of Commons:

[1]Antinomians believed Christ relieved Christians from obedience to the moral law; Anabaptists required rebaptism for true believers; Fifth Monarchy Men looked to an imminent second coming of Christ; Seekers rejected organized religion and sought truth elsewhere; Quakers also sought piety and tranquility outside a formal church structure.

Honest men served you faithfully in this action. They are trusty; I beseech you in the name of god not to discourage them. He that ventures his life for the liberty of his country, I wish he trust God for the liberty of his conscience, and you for the liberty he fights for.

In politics Cromwell did not represent the soldiers so well: his political views were those of the landowning classes. Because of his strong sense of property and his dread of chaos he labored to make the soldiers obedient to Parliament and to restrain them from using force in politics. He thus exposed himself to the suspicion of the radicals and to the charge of hypocrisy.

Parliament and the Army

Shortly after the war came to an end, the relations between Parliament and the army became extremely tense. There was no hope that Parliament, with its intolerant Presbyterian majority, would accept the Independent and democratic ideas of the soldiers. The soldiers may well have been motivated by military as much as by political considerations. The Presbyterian leaders foolishly planned to disband the army, not only without indemnity for acts committed in war but also without arrears of pay. They hoped to persuade the disbanded soldiers to enlist for service in Ireland. The degree of discontent in the army became alarming. The soldiers organized themselves politically by electing representatives called Agitators or Agents to present their views to Parliament. When the army refused to disband in the spring of 1647, the Presbyterian leaders determined to disperse it by force. The plan was to

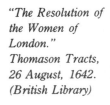

"The Resolution of the Women of London."
Thomason Tracts,
26 August, 1642.
(British Library)

bring the Scottish army into England and to employ it against the men who had won the war. At this point the army mutinied. It began by arresting the king.

Charles had been a prisoner of the Scots for eight months. He had been negotiating both with them and Parliament, but had refused Presbyterianism; in January 1647 the Scots in disgust handed him over to the English and crossed the border into their own country. In June he was seized by the English army. In August the army occupied London, and the radicals, or Levelers, drew up the Agreement of the People, to be laid before the House of Commons. This famous document demanded that the Parliament then in session be dissolved, that there be an election every two

Charles I, from Bibliotheca Regia . . . containing a collection of such of the pages of His Late Majesty . . . as have escaped the Wreck and Ruins of these times, *London, 1659. (Department of Special Collections, Wilson Library, University of Minnesota)*

years, that electoral districts be made equal, and that there be universal manhood suffrage. The king and the House of Lords were not mentioned and presumably would disappear. An assertion of natural rights followed: all Englishmen should enjoy freedom of conscience, freedom from impressment, and equality before the law. Cromwell and many officers would have been satisfied with a limited monarchy, but in the Agreement of the People the soldiers were demanding a democratic republic based on a written constitution, both novel ideas in English history. At Cromwell's urging, the Agreement was modified and presented to Parliament in the form of proposals.[2]

Events suddenly took a dramatic turn, for on the night of 11 November 1647, the king escaped from Hampton Court and made his way to the Isle of Wight off the southern coast. He had concluded a secret agreement with the Scots that he would establish Presbyterianism throughout his dominions for three years if they would restore him to his throne. There followed the Second Civil War in 1648. It consisted of scattered risings by Cavaliers, the desertion of part of the fleet, and an invasion from Scotland, but these sporadic moves were not directed by any master mind. The people as a whole were apathetic. Local risings were quelled without great difficulty, and in a lightning campaign Cromwell overwhelmed the Scots at Preston, Wigan, and Warrington in the northwest of England.

The Death of the King

After these victories the English army assumed control. Its mood was one of harsh severity against the king, whose intrigues with all parties, and especially his last treaty with the Scots, which resulted in the Second Civil War, hardened the hearts of the soldiers against him. "We came to a very clear resolution," wrote one of them, "that it was our duty, if ever the Lord brought us back again in peace, to call Charles Stuart, that man of blood, to account for the blood he had shed, and mischief he had done to the utmost against the Lord's cause and people in these poor nations." London was occupied once more in December 1648. Parliament was dealt with in a simple way. Colonel Pride, placing his musketeers at the door of the House of Commons, excluded about 140 Presbyterian members (arresting 45 of them) and admitted only the Independents, some 50 or 60 strong. This was known as the Rump (sitting) Parliament.

A court was then set up to try the king. Charles refused to recognize its jurisdiction, but it condemned him to death for treason against the nation. Charles met his fate with fortitude and courage on January 30, 1649. Steadfast in his opinions, he said on the scaffold,

> For the people I desire their liberty and freedom as much as anybody whomsoever; but I must tell you that their liberty and freedom consists in having government, in those laws by which their life and goods may be most their own. It is not their having a share in government; that is nothing pertaining to them.

[2]This document in modified form appeared again in 1649. See Charles Firth, *Oliver Cromwell and the Rule of the Puritans in England* (London: Putnam, 1901), pp. 177, 183, 236–237.

The Trial of King Charles I, 1648. (British Museum)

He then prayed for a moment, laid his comely head on the block, and signaled the executioner to strike. At one blow his head was severed from his body. A groan broke from the people—"such a groan," wrote a spectator, "as I never heard before, and desire I may never hear again."

THE COMMONWEALTH, 1649–1653

Shortly after the king's execution Parliament abolished the office of king as dangerous and unneccessary. It also abolished the House of Lords. "England," it declared, "shall henceforth be governed as a Commonwealth, or a Free State, by the supreme authority of this nation, the representatives of the people in Parliament." On another occasion the Commons affirmed that the people were, under God, the origin of all just power. But despite these democratic sentiments, the members of the House of Commons, now about ninety Independents, clung to power with the utmost tenacity. The army strongly desired an election, but no election was held. The Commonwealth was in reality a continuation of the rule of the Long Parliament under a new name. Parliament was more powerful than ever, for there was neither a king nor a House of Lords to impose restraint.

The Commons appointed a Council of State to which administrative power was entrusted; the Council, however, was to be elected annually by the Commons, and thirty-one of its forty-one members were also members of Parliament. It was no more than the Commons in administrative session. Nor could Parliament claim to represent the nation. Large areas of the country had no members in the Commons. Parliament represented only the Independents, who were a handful of sectaries, a fraction of the whole people. Parliament, moreover, did not meet occasionally as in the past. It remained in session the year round: there seemed no hope of ending it, for it could not legally be dissolved without its own consent. The Commons contained energetic and dedicated men, some of them very able, but it is not surprising that their government was highly unpopular. The army, taking its stand on the principles of the Agreement of the People, was deeply dissatisfied; it tolerated the new government only because there were enemies on every side.

At home the Commonwealth faced the hatred of Royalists and Presbyterians. These groups, and many persons outside them, could never forgive the Puritans for killing the king. The Independents had thought of Charles's death as just retribution, but it proved to be their most egregious blunder. To lay violent hands upon the king, to touch the Lord's anointed, to shed his blood as though he were a common criminal was to shock and horrify a large proportion of the people. Charles haunted the Independents from his grave. The reaction in his favor that had begun before his death was greatly intensified by the appearance of *Eikon Basilike,* a touching book about his last days of suffering. It was written by a clergyman, Dr. Gauden, who drew largely on his own imagination, but Royalists were certain that it had been written by Charles himself and that its noble thoughts were those of the king. This book kept green among Cavaliers the memory of their martyred ruler.

The popular image of the king now altered. Charles, the friend of Laud, the imposer of ship money, the shady trickster, and the man of blood disappeared; Charles the Martyr took his place. John Milton hoped to shatter this image in a learned pamphlet, *Eikonoklastes,* but no one read it. The death of the king was remembered, his weakness forgotten. For the moment the Commonwealth had little to fear from Royalists or Presbyterians. The Royalists were battered and impoverished, their estates sequestered and redeemable only by the payment of large fines. The Presbyterians, though strong among the business classes in the towns, went no further than a sullen passive resistance.

The Commonwealth was also under attack from the political radicals, known as the Levelers. Their leader, John Lilburne, a restless and unreasonable man, was an energetic pamphleteer. He denounced the Commons for refusing to grant annual elections, manhood suffrage, and complete religous liberty. He said bitter things about Cromwell, whom he regarded as a traitor to democratic principles. Cromwell believed that Lilburne was politically dangerous and ought to be suppressed. "I tell you," he said in the Council, "you have no other way to deal with these men but to break them, or they will break you." Lilburne was sent to the Tower.

Cromwell was wise enough to ignore a small and harmless group who called themselves True Levelers and were known as Diggers. Their leader, Gerrard Winstanley, was a religious mystic who applied the principle of equality not only to politics but to social and economic life. He envisaged a kind of communist utopia. Believing that the poor had been excluded from their birthright, the land of England, he wished the people to take over the land and to hold it in common. His desire was to eliminate landlords, clergymen, and lawyers. But Winstanley, a gentle rebel, began his revolution by leading a group of poor men to a village near London, where they squatted on the common, dug up the ground, and planted beans. They were shortly dispersed by the landowners of the village.

Charles's death produced a violent reaction abroad. In Russia the Czar imprisoned English merchants. In Holland the Stadtholder, William II, who had married Charles's daughter Mary, allowed Royalist privateers to refit in Dutch ports. An English ambassador at The Hague and another in Madrid were murdered by Royalists almost with impunity. France was openly hostile; Spain was a little more friendly only because she was at war with France. The Puritans were regarded on the Continent as barbarians, revolutionists, and blood-stained villains.

Surrounded by enemies, the Commonwealth perforce became a military state. It maintained an army of forty-four thousand men, of whom twelve thousand were to be sent to Ireland. This army, the finest in Europe, was commanded by officers who made it their career. The men were well paid. The famous redcoat of the British soldier was now introduced and made universal. The navy was reorganized, and some forty warships were built within three years. There was much for these forces to do. The navy hunted down royalist privateers, for some of Charles's followers, desperate in poverty, had taken to the sea and preyed upon English commerce. Small nests of Royalists were cleared from the Channel Islands, from the Scilly Isles off the coast of Cornwall, and from the Isle of Man. The North American and West Indian colonies were forced to submit to the Commonwealth. From 1652 to 1654 there was an important and fiercely fought naval war with the Dutch. Meanwhile the army had rough work to do in Ireland and Scotland.

Ireland and Scotland

Ireland was very dangerous for the Commonwealth in 1649. For some years she had been left to her own devices, but the Second Civil War and the execution of the king produced an alliance of Protestant Royalists and Irish Roman Catholics. Ireland, if left alone, would not only be independent; she would become a base for an invasion of England. Parliament therefore turned to its best general and in the summer of 1649 Cromwell landed in Dublin with a well-equipped army of some twelve thousand men. There was no Irish army that could meet him in the field; instead, the Irish relied on fortresses and walled towns to delay his progress. Cromwell at once struck north at Drogheda. When the town refused to surrender, Cromwell took it by storm and put the entire garrison of twenty-eight hundred men to the sword. Though this massacre was justified by the rules of war, it would not have happened in England and was done in a spirit of revenge. Cromwell believed that he had come to Ireland not only as a conqueror but as a judge. He termed the slaughter at Drogheda a "righteous judgment of God upon these barbarous wretches." Another massacre took place at Wexford, though, Cromwell did not order it. The terror inspired by these incidents induced other towns to capitulate; by the end of 1649 all the southern and eastern coast, with the exception of Waterford, was in English hands. Early in 1650 Cromwell struck inland into Munster and captured Kilkenny, the seat of the Roman Catholic alliance.

Cromwell left Ireland in the summer of 1650. The conquest, completed by his lieutenants, was over by 1652, when the country was utterly devastated, a third of the population had perished, and a traveler could journey for miles in some areas without seeing a living creature. The settlement of Ireland after the war was harsh. The lands of all Roman Catholics who had taken part in the rebellion were confiscated and allotted either to Englishmen who had advanced money for the campaign or to Cromwell's soldiers as arrears of pay. Some Catholics received inferior land in Connaught as compensation, but many received nothing. It is said that two-thirds of the land in Ireland changed hands, and a large part of the Irish upper classes were ordered to move into Connaught or county Clare. Ireland became a country in which the great landowners were Protestant. Cromwell's soldiers, however, who were small farmers, often married Irish women, though they were forbidden to do so. In a few generations their descendants were Catholic in religion and Irish in sympathy. The Irish peasants remained as landless laborers on the estates of the new owners. Cromwell's settlement in Ireland included a number of other points. Anti-Catholic laws were enforced, and an attempt was made to strengthen Protestant congregations. There was impartial justice in the courts, Ireland obtained thirty members in the English Parliament, and free trade was established between the two countries. But these measures benefited the English in Ireland rather than the Irish themselves. Irish hatred of England grew to white heat.

In Scotland the Presbyterians, deeply offended by the triumph of the Independents in England and by Charles's execution, at once proclaimed Charles II as their king. They sent envoys to England who demanded that he also be recognized there and that the terms of the Solemn League and Covenant be honored. In reply the English expelled the envoys and prepared for another war. This was a national war, for Scotland, like Ireland, was attempting to dictate to England how she should be governed; the struggle became one for supremacy in Britain. The Scots turned to Charles II, an exile in the Netherlands, then about twenty years old. He was told that they would place him upon the English throne on condition that he accept the Covenant and establish Presbyterianism in both England and Ireland. He resisted these terms until Cromwell's victories in Ireland ended all hope of aid from that country. Then Charles came reluctantly to Scotland. The Scots knew his acceptance of the Covenant was hypocritical, yet they insisted upon it. Charles found himself a semiprisoner of the Kirk. He was forced to deplore in public the episcopacy of his father and the Catholicism of his mother; many years later he remarked that he would rather be hanged than return to the accursed land of Scotland.

Cromwell crossed the border in July 1650. At Dunbar on September 3 he caught the Scots in an awkward position and inflicted a crushing defeat on them. Three thousand Scots fell in the battle and ten thousand were taken prisoner. The effect in Scotland was overwhelming, for the ministers had been confident of victory. Charles was able to gain some control of policy. In the next year he led an army into England, hoping for an uprising in his favor, but his army was annihilated at the Battle of Worcester. In this battle Cromwell did not merely defeat the enemy; he wiped it out. Scarcely a Scot reached home after that ordeal. Charles wandered as a fugitive for some six weeks before he found a boat to take him to France. The English conquest of Scotland followed shortly. Annexed to England, she lost her Parliament and General Assembly, though local churches were let alone. English rule in Scotland was impartial, efficient, and deeply resented.

The End of the Commonwealth

Despite these victories, there was strong sentiment in the army that the Commonwealth was a provisional government which should be superseded by something more stable and lasting. Cromwell urged the Commons to fix a date for their dissolution, but the date they determined upon was 1654, three years in the future. Meanwhile the management of constant war occupied their energies, and they had no time for much-needed reforms. A law was finally passed granting amnesty to the defeated Royalists, but it was weakened by many exceptions. There was also need for legal and social reform, for the normal relations of debtor and creditor and of landlord and tenant had been disturbed. The prisons were full of debtors; the country swarmed with beggars. Parliament appointed a commission to review the law, but few of its suggestions were adopted. A reorganization of the church was also necessary. Presbyterianism had been established in London and in a few other places, but in large portions of the country each congregation went its own way. A group of clergymen headed by John Owen, who had been Cromwell's chaplain in Ireland, presented Parliament with a comprehensive scheme for the settlement of the church. But the result was nil.

The irritation of the army with Parliament increased. When a bill was finally introduced for a new election, the commons changed it into a plan for their continuance in power, suggesting that they should remain members of all future Parliaments, and that elections should merely add to their number. Cromwell and the army officers objected and believed that the bill would be defeated. Then suddenly in April 1653, Cromwell learned that the bill was about to be passed. He came down to the Commons, berated the members soundly, and called in his musketeers. The members then filed out of the chamber and the door was locked behind them.

Like the execution of the king, the dissolution of Parliament by force proved to be a political blunder. The House of Commons had been the one last shred of legality covering the actions of government, and the only link with the old constitution. Military might was revealed as the sole source of power. Cromwell spent the rest of his life trying to give the rule of the sword some sort of constitutional form.

THE BAREBONES PARLIAMENT AND THE INSTRUMENT OF GOVERNMENT

At the dissolution of the Long Parliament, some people wished Cromwell to be king. His picture was hung up in London with the inscription:

Ascend three thrones, great captain and divine,
I' th' will of God, old Lion, they are thine.

Cromwell dismissing the Rump Parliament, 1653. Contemparary Dutch engraving. (British Museum)

But Cromwell had no wish to become either a king or a military dictator. As commander in chief he considered himself temporarily in authority but he desired to lay that authority down and divest the army of governmental power. He and the army officers determined to summon a new assembly and to place power in its hands. This assembly, however, was not elected by the old franchise. Independent churches were asked to make nominations, and from this list Cromwell and the officers selected 140 persons. They were all Puritan notables—preachers, idealists, reformers—but had no experience in government. They were strongly influenced by the Fifth Monarchy Men, who believed that Christ would soon come to rule the world and that, until his coming, "His saints should take the kingdom and possess it." This assembly was nicknamed the Little or Barebones Parliament, since one of its members was an Anabaptist preacher named Praise-God Barbon or Barebones, who seems to have contributed nothing but his name. The Parliament entered upon a reckless course of hasty and unwise reform. It abolished the court of chancery after

Oliver Cromwell, from Gregorio Leti, Historia, e memorie recondite sopra alla vita di Oliverio Cromvele, Amsterdam, 1692. (Department of Special Collections, Wilson Library, University of Minnesota)

one day's debate. It appointed a committee to codify the law, which was to be so reduced that a man could carry it in a little book in his pocket. Some members wished to abolish the law entirely and to substitute the laws of Moses. Tithes were to be abolished before any other way was found for the support of the church. Cromwell and the army officers were disgusted and alarmed, and so were the more moderate members of the Parliament. these moderates met early one morning, marched from the Parliament building to Whitehall, and returned to Cromwell the powers he had given them. The rule of the Barebone saints was over. It had lasted from July to December 1653.

Cromwell then accepted a plan advanced by certain army officers that the government should consist of a lord protector, a Council of State, and a Parliament. The plan was in the form of a written constitution, the only written constitution ever to be in effect in England. This Instrument of Government, as it was called, was written because its authors wanted something permanent, fundamental, and unchangeable. In religion they thought of a covenant between God and man, and so in politics they were led to think of a contract between man and his governors. The army officers were more conservative than they had been in 1649; the franchise was limited to property holders; Parliament was to meet only once in three years and then for only five months; it could not vote away the constitution; and there was a portion of the revenue it could not control. On the other hand, the protector had no veto; he must consult the council or Parliament or both. The councilors held office for life and could name the protector's successor. Thus the army officers built checks and balances into their constitution. The document is also interesting because in it one can see the old constitution creeping back. Finally, it guaranteed religious liberty to all Christians except to Catholics and to members of the Church of England.

THE PROTECTORATE, 1653–1659

It is ironic that Cromwell, having defeated the king in the name of Parliament, discovered as protector that he could not manage the House of Commons any more than could Charles I. Cromwell wished to rule with Parliament's consent and cooperation and not by military force; he also feared an all-powerful Parliament such as the Long Parliament, and he was determined to maintain religious toleration. He therefore took his stand on the Instrument of Government.

His Parliaments, on the other hand, were hostile to military rule and to the Instrument of Government as the work of the army. They assumed the lofty tone of the Long Parliament in claiming to be the supreme power in the state. Cromwell's first Parliament (1654–1655) began at once to amend the constitution, making elective the office of protector, bringing the council more under Parliament's control, seeking to limit religious toleration, and trying to reduce the size of the army as well as to subject it to parliamentary authority. Cromwell protested and offered compromises. He dismissed the Parliament at the earliest possible moment.

In 1655 he made a serious blunder. Amid rumors of Cavalier plots Cromwell divided the country into twelve districts and placed a major general in charge of each. This was effective as a police measure, but it brought the power of the army to every person's doorstep and intensified the hatred of military rule. The elections to Cromwell's second Parliament in 1656 went against the government. Although about a hundred members were excluded as dangerous, the Commons showed little interest in toleration and great hostility to the major generals. But they had a strong desire to return to the old constitution.

This desire took the startling form of asking Cromwell to assume the title of king. One of his Secretaries wrote:

Parliament will not be persuaded that there can be a settlement any other way. The title is not the question, but it's the office, which is known to the laws and to the people. They know their duty to a king and his to them. Whatever else there is will be wholly new, and upon the next occasion will be changed again. Besides they say the name Protector came in with the sword. . . . nor will there be a free Parliament so long as that continues, and as it savors of the sword now, so it will at last bring all things to be military.

The proposal, known as the Humble Petition and Advice, was made to Cromwell by Parliament in March 1657. He rejected it. While he saw the advantage of a settlement that would bring a sense of permanence, he knew that most of his old fellow soldiers would be deeply offended. In May the Humble Petition and Advice was presented to him again, with the word "protector" substituted for "king." This time Cromwell accepted, and he became hereditary protector, a king in all but name. There was also to be a second chamber of Parliament to which he could appoint members for life. He was also given a more ample revenue. Parliament asked for and obtained the right to control its own election disputes; the power of the Protector to exclude members was dropped. But in a second session of this Parliament a quarrel arose between the two houses. Moreover, the hard core of republicans in the Commons was violently opposed to the new arrangements. Before another Parliament met, Cromwell was dead (3 September 1658).

Cromwell's contemporaries judged him with the utmost severity. To Clarendon, the Royalist historian of the Great Rebellion, he was "a brave bad man," possessing "all the wickedness against which damnation is pronounced and for which hell fire is prepared." Clarendon, though he condemned, could not refrain from admiration, but most Royalists saw nothing to palliate the blackness of Cromwell's character. He also was assailed from the left by radicals who believed that he had betrayed the cause for which he had fought and had been led by ambition to grasp the sovereign power in the state. "In all his changes," wrote the republican Ludlow, "he designed nothing but to advance himself." These views reflect the fact that he was the leader of a party and not of the nation.

A more sympathetic estimate by his steward, John Maidston, described Cromwell the man—his fiery temper, his marvelous courage, his unselfishness and devotion to a cause, his promptness and vigor in action, his deeply religious nature, his strength and depth of character, his compassion for persons in distress. "A larger soul," wrote Maidston, "hath seldom dwelt in house of clay." Much of his work was destroyed by the Restoration; yet his great achievements stand out clearly. His superb ability as a soldier broke the absolutism of the Stuarts and changed the course of English history. He held the British Isles together and saved England from anarchy, taking hold as a strong executive in the face of chaos. Cromwell advanced the cause of religious toleration. He raised England's prestige and added to her possessions overseas, and gave her for the first time a colonial and imperial policy.[3] To this last point we must now turn our attention.

[3]See the estimate of Cromwell in the last chapter of Charles Firth, *Oliver Cromwell and the Rule of the Puritans in England.*

OVERSEAS EXPANSION

The Rise of the Dutch

English expansion overseas in the Stuart period developed naturally from the achievements of the Elizabethans. Brilliant as those achievements had been, they were for the most part experimental; when Elizabeth died in 1603 England did not possess a single colony. It was in the seventeenth century that they intensified their efforts and learned the difficult lesson that colonies must be built slowly through toil and patience and not merely through bold adventure.

Conditions of international rivalry had altered. The Elizabethans had thought of Spain as their great opponent, a belief which persisted in the reign of James I, though Spain was falling rapidly into decay. For the first three quarters of the seventeenth century it was the Dutch and not the Spanish who were England's commercial rivals. While fighting their fierce wars of independence against Spain, the Dutch had become a great maritime power. Their East India Company was far stronger and more wealthy than its English rival. During the early seventeenth century Dutch fleets swept through the Caribbean, driving the Spanish from the sea; and in 1628 Piet Hein—a Dutch Sir Francis Drake—captured the whole of the Spanish treasure fleet. By 1626 Holland had planted a settlement on the island of Manhattan; in the 1620s a Dutch West India Company established itself in northern Brazil. All over the world—in the East, the West, the Levant, Russia, the Baltic, the herring fisheries of the North Sea, and in the whaling areas of the arctic—wherever the English went to trade, to fish, or to colonize, there were the hardheaded Dutch eager to drive them out. Holland possessed a great merchant marine and hoped to monopolize the carrying trade of the world.

The English were slow to recognize the challenge of the Dutch, though there were warning voices. Sir Walter Ralegh wrote a pamphlet declaring that Holland "possessed already as many ships as eleven kingdoms, England being one of them." In 1614 Tobias Gentleman warned that the English neglected fishing: "Look but on these fellows that we call the plump Hollanders, behold their diligence in fishing and our own careless negligence." Another author contrasted the smallness of England's foreign trade with that of "our neighbors the new Sea-Herrs." These warnings fell upon deaf ears. King James, intent on the Spanish match, would do nothing; and King Charles, without resources, could do nothing if he would. It was left for the Puritans to beat back the Dutch.

English Colonies in America

Between the old war with Spain and the new ones with Holland there was an interval in which the English sought to expand overseas through the arts of peace. During the first half of the seventeenth century Englishmen swarmed to North

America and even more to the West Indies. A mass migration such as England had never seen before, it consisted of two waves. One planted Virginia, Maryland, and the English West Indies. In 1606 two companies were founded, the Plymouth and the London, to establish colonies in North America under the supervision of a royal council. The Plymouth Company accomplished nothing permanent, but the London Company in 1607 planted a colony at Jamestown in Virginia. After a period of intense suffering, the colonists found a staple crop in tobacco, much to King James's disgust, for he had conceived a strong aversion to that expensive luxury, that "precious stink." The affairs of the company became involved in English politics, and in 1624 the king dissolved the company and took Virginia under his control, making it the first Crown colony. In 1632 George Calvert, Lord Baltimore, a Roman Catholic who had been one of James's secretaries, obtained permission to establish a colony in the northern part of Chesapeake Bay. This project, carried out by his son, resulted in the founding of Maryland in 1634.

Tiny English settlements were also attempted in Guiana—an unoccupied area between the Spanish in modern Venezuela and the Portuguese in Brazil—and on the Amazon and Orinoco rivers. These settlements were failures, but they led to colonies in the West Indies. The Spanish had ignored the smaller islands, for they contained no gold, were densely wooded, and were inhabited by savage Carib tribes who had the unpleasant habit of eating Europeans.

A number of motives lay behind this wave of colonization. The first was economic, the desire for products unobtainable at home—the precious metals, naval stores, cotton, tobacco, sugar, and rare woods. There was also a social motive. England teemed with beggars, and it was thought that the country was overcrowded; hence the idea that colonies might drain off surplus population. Moreover, an English base in the New World was regarded as a great advantage in any future war with Spain. Propaganda in favor of colonization often spoke of the mission of converting the Indians, although, as a matter of fact, little was done in this direction; England did not become a missionary nation until the nineteenth century. And finally, colonial trade would help to build the merchant marine.

Another wave of expansion sprang from religious motives and produced the colonies in New England. Groups of Separatists emigrated to Holland in the early seventeenth century; in 1620 the Pilgrim Fathers crossed the Atlantic in the *Mayflower* and founded a colony at Plymouth. About ten years later a larger group of Puritan malcontents, led by men of more wealth and social standing than the Pilgrims, formed the Massachusetts Bay Company. They settled in the area of Boston and were soon the largest colony in North America, for Laud's persecution drove thousands across the Atlantic. Colonization in New England was not a normal phenomenon of overseas expansion. Rather, it was a secession of a part of the English race from the religion and government of the homeland. The Pilgrims felt a hostility toward England which for a number of years was a part of the American tradition.

The Navigation Acts of 1650 and 1651

After the Commonwealth was established in 1649 its attention was focused on the West Indies, where strange events had been taking place. About 1640, at the suggestion of Dutch traders, the English began to cultivate sugar with astonishing results. By concentrating on sugar processing, the West Indies sprang suddenly into wealth and importance. Small holdings were thrown together into large plantations, the landless were left to shift for themselves as best they could, and black slaves were imported to work the fields of sugar cane. From these changes the Dutch profited greatly. They extended credit to the planters, sold them slaves, and bought their sugar, taking it to Holland. The West Indies might be English colonies, but all the advantages were going to the Dutch. Moreover, at the end of the Civil Wars, many Royalists went to the islands. Barbados and Antigua, as well as Virginia and Maryland, recognized Charles II as king after the death of his father.

In 1650 Parliament passed an ordinance forbidding all trade with the colonies as long as they remained in rebellion. This was by way of punishment. The ordinance also contained a clause prohibiting trade by foreign vessels with any English colonies at any time, a provision thereafter enforced. A naval expedition in 1651 reduced the colonies to submission, though some clandestine trade with the Dutch continued. There followed the famous Navigation Act of 1651, which was the basis of English trade for nearly two hundred years. It declared that products from Asia, Africa, and America could be brought to England or to her colonies only in English or colonial ships of which the master and a majority of the crew were English. Products from Europe, the ordinance continued, might come to England only in English ships or in the ships of the country producing the goods. Thus foreign traders were excluded from English colonies, colonial goods must come to England in English ships, and European goods must come either in English ships or in ships of the nation in which the goods were produced. The colonists might take their products to foreign ports if they could gain access, but the bulk of their trade would be with England; the carrying trade of the Dutch was thus dealt a heavy blow. The English Parliament was legislating for the empire as a whole and was drawing the mother country and the colonies closer together.

The First Dutch War, 1652–1654

The Navigation Act of 1651, the culmination of a long period of friction, brought war between England and Holland. "The English are about to attack a mountain of gold," groaned a Dutchman; "we a mountain of iron." The mountain of gold was the vast merchant marine of Holland. During the war it sailed in convoys protected by warships, for the Dutch had to continue their trade in order to live. The mountain of iron was the English battle fleet built by the Commonwealth. Its warships were large, solid, and heavily armed; its administration was excellent; its movements were directed by the state. Three of Cromwell's soldiers—Blake, Monck, and Deane—took to the sea and gave to the navy the martial spirit of the New Model Army. The fighting was hard, close, and deadly. Both fleets sailed in line ahead formation, but the lines were often broken, and battles developed into furious melees in which new techniques developed rapidly. At first the Dutch won some advantage, but a battle in June 1653 damaged their fleet and permitted the English to blockade their coast, halting commerce and ruining hundreds of Dutch merchants. After nine pitched battles in two years, both sides were glad to make peace in 1654. The Dutch accepted the Navigation Act of 1651, agreed to salute English ships in the Channel, and paid damages for injuries inflicted upon the English East India Company. The peace, however, was a truce, and Anglo-Dutch rivalry continued.

Cromwell's Western Design

Cromwell, the first English ruler systematically to employ his power to win new colonial possessions, conceived the idea of uniting English colonies in North America with those in the West Indies, at the same time extending English possessions in both areas to form a great dominion in the West. During the Dutch war he encouraged the colonists in New England to attack the Dutch "in the Manhattoes," and, when this project was ended by peace in Europe, to attack the French in Canada. The whole area from the Penobscot River in modern Maine to the mouth of the St. Lawrence fell into English hands, though it was restored to France in 1668. When the Dutch war was over, Cromwell turned to the Spanish West Indies. He was encouraged by some of his advisers to underestimate the difficulties of the enterprise.

In 1655 Cromwell sent an expedition against the Spanish Islands, but it was not prepared with his usual care. The sailors were of good quality, but the troops consisted of men rejected by the army in England or pressed from the London slums; three thousand recruits picked up in Barbados were derelicts, "the most profane debauched persons that we ever saw." It is small wonder that an assault on Santo Domingo was a total failure. The commanders of the expedition, Admiral Penn (whose son was the founder of Pennsylvania) and General Venables, fearing the wrath of Cromwell, determined to attack Jamaica, which was weakly held by a few hundred Spanish planters. The English army, some ten thousand strong, gallantly captured this island. Cromwell was deeply chagrined, the more so because he found himself at war with Spain in Europe, but he determined to retain Jamaica, which became in time an important sugar island. His grandiose dream of a western dominion faded away, but it was the beginning of England's age-long effort to build an empire overseas.

The English East India Company

The English East India Company, as we have seen, had made an excellent beginning. Even before the friction with the Dutch had become so acute, the English had begun to turn to India. Here the Portuguese were established along the western coast, though their hold was weak. In 1612 Captain Best, after driving away a

India and the East Indies in the 17th century.

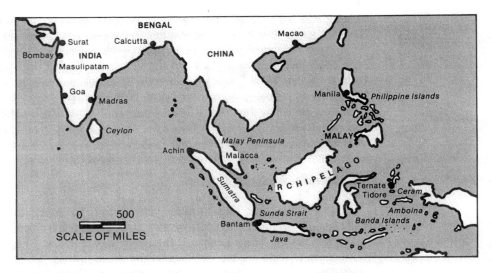

Portuguese fleet, secured from the local Mogul Governor the right to establish a factory at Surat. In 1622 the English drove the Portuguese from Ormuz at the mouth of the Persian Gulf and obtained a factory there. In 1635 a treaty was made with the Portuguese by which the English were permitted to trade in Portuguese ports. Surat remained the principal English trading area until Bombay was secured in the reign of Charles II. On the eastern coast of India the English established themselves first at Masulipatam in 1611 and later at Madras in 1639. It was not until later in the century that a firm foothold was secured in the area of Bengal. The English brought home muslins and other cotton fabrics, saltpeter, and indigo (a blue dye).

In the East the company was making headway, but difficulties arose at home. The company's system of bookkeeping was cumbersome, for each voyage was handled as a separate venture. It was accused of taking coin out of England and bringing back luxuries. Parliament was hostile because the company was a monopoly. Worst of all, it could not rely on the king, from whom it held its charter. Both James and Charles permitted interlopers to go to India, where they acted more like pirates than merchants, causing the company great harm. The company also suffered from the dislocations of the Civil Wars; for a time it ceased to trade as a corporation, though it licensed private merchants to trade as individuals. Cromwell restored the fortunes of the company and set it trading once more with a new charter in 1657.

ECONOMIC CHANGE

Historians now regard the two decades between 1640 and 1660 as highly important in the economic history of England. It was during this time that the capitalist classes—agricultural, industrial, and commercial alike—freed themselves from the

The Atlantic Ocean 1660.

The Indian Ocean 1660.

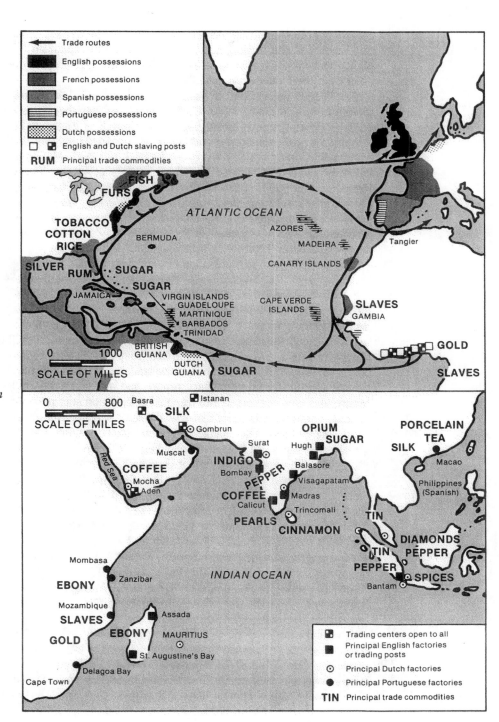

Legend:

Trade routes
English possessions
French possessions
Spanish possessions
Portuguese possessions
Dutch possessions
□ ▣ English and Dutch slaving posts
RUM Principal trade commodities

FISH
FURS
TOBACCO
COTTON
RICE
SILVER
RUM
SUGAR
SUGAR
JAMAICA
BERMUDA
VIRGIN ISLANDS
GUADELOUPE
MARTINIQUE
BARBADOS
TRINIDAD
BRITISH GUIANA
DUTCH GUIANA
SUGAR
ATLANTIC OCEAN
AZORES
MADEIRA
CANARY ISLANDS
Tangier
CAPE VERDE ISLANDS
SLAVES
GAMBIA
GOLD
SLAVES

0   1000
SCALE OF MILES

0   800
SCALE OF MILES

Basra
Istanan
SILK
Gombrun
Muscat
Surat
Hugh
Balasore
Bombay
INDIGO
PEPPER
COFFEE
Calicut
Madras
Visagapatam
Trincomali
PEARLS
CINNAMON
OPIUM
SUGAR
PORCELAIN
TEA
SILK
Macao
Philippines (Spanish)
TIN
DIAMONDS
PEPPER
TIN
PEPPER
Bantam
SPICES
COFFEE
Mocha
Aden
Red Sea
Mombasa
Zanzibar
EBONY
Mozambique
SLAVES
GOLD
EBONY
Assada
MAURITIUS
St. Augustine's Bay
Delagoa Bay
Cape Town
INDIAN OCEAN

Legend:

▣ Trading centers open to all
■ Principal English factories or trading posts
⊙ Principal Dutch factories
● Principal Portuguese factories
TIN Principal trade commodities

control over economic life formerly exercised by the Crown. "The fall of the absolute monarchy was the turning point in the evolution of capitalism." Thereafter wealthy people were at liberty to do as they pleased with their property and to manage their affairs for their own economic advantage.

A tremendous amount of land was bought and sold during this period. The government sold quantities of Crown lands—so that there was little left by 1660—and also much property belonging to the Church of England. Estates of well-to-do Royalists were sequestered and could be recovered only by the payment of heavy fines, while other estates were confiscated and sold. Moreover, many Royalists, under pressures of all kinds, sold their lands privately. These people, after the Restoration of 1660, could usually recover confiscated estates through legal action; but for lands sold privately there was no redress. Yet the majority of Royalists survived. Much land was purchased during this period by those who had made money in trade or who were connected in some way with the government. Thus the landowners after 1660 were both Cavaliers and Roundheads.

The emancipation of the landed classes may be said to have taken place in three distinct phases. In the first place, there was obvious freedom from the restrictions and burdens imposed by the government of Charles I. Indeed, the government now did everything it could to encourage agricultural productivity. Opposition to enclosing disappeared; acts were passed for the draining of the fens; improved farming methods, such as the use of clover in a better rotation of crops, were supported by the government, which also felt a new responsibility for transportation and for a postal service. In the second place, the landowning classes profited enormously from the abolition of feudal or military tenure and an end to the court of wards. Feudal tenure was now converted into freehold or common socage. So great was the desire of landowners for this relief that feudal tenure was abolished thrice over, in 1646, in 1656, and in 1660. The change has been called "possibly the most important single event in the history of English landholding." It deprived the Crown of a vital means of controlling the upper classes and it gave landowners the absolute right to do as they pleased with their estates. Knowing that their titles were secure, they were much more inclined to invest money in long-term improvements. Finally, the landed classes were able to defeat efforts by the Levelers and by other radical groups to obtain permanent rights in the land for copyholders and small tenants. Indeed, the man who bought land as an investment and the Royalist who recovered his estates after a costly struggle were apt to regard the poor with little sympathy. The temporary assertiveness of the lower classes was something to be suppressed. Hence the new developments in agriculture, although they caused productivity to leap forward, brought small benefit to the poor. There was a grave problem of rural poverty at the end of the century.

A similar story may be told of industry. The government no longer attempted to regulate prices or wages or hours and conditions of labor, or to supervise the quality of workmanship. Industrial monopolies came to an end; economic favors were no longer available to parasitic courtiers. Employers were free to conduct business enterprises along economic lines. Moreover, the common law courts, which protected the rights of the individual, were now supreme. As for the merchants, the state was willing to use diplomacy and even armed force to advance their interests in overseas expansion.

THE END OF THE PROTECTORATE

After Cromwell's death the Protectorate crumbled, and events moved quickly to the restoration of the Stuarts. Richard, Oliver's son, lacked the character and experience to remain in power. His first move was correct, for he refused a demand of the army to be allowed to select its own commander in chief. In January 1659 he summoned a Parliament which on the whole was ready to support him; but under pressure from the army he dissolved it in April. This action ended his short rule as protector. The army, left in control, recalled the Long Parliament, quarreled with it, and dismissed it. But army opinion was divided; at this point General Monck, the commander in Scotland, determined that the nation, not the army, should decide what it wished to do. Monck marched down from Scotland, outwitted the army leaders in London, recalled the Long Parliament once again, obtained a majority by adding the Presbyterian members expelled in 1648, and forced it to dissolve itself and to issue writs for a free Parliament elected under the old historic franchise. This Parliament met in April 1660 and invited Charles II to return to England. He required little urging.

C H R O N O L O G Y

Civil Wars, Commonwealth, and Protectorate

1607	Jamestown, Virginia settled
1620	Pilgrims land at Plymouth
1630	Boston Bay colony
1643	Solemn League and Covenant
1644	Battle of Marston Moor; Royalist disaster
1645	Self-Denying Ordinance; New Model Army; Battle of Naseby

(continued on next page)

Chronology, continued

1646	Charles I a prisoner
1647	Agreement of the People; Charles escapes
1648	Second Civil War; Charles recaptured; Prides's Purge
1649	Trial, conviction, and execution of Charles I; monarchy and House of Lords abolished
1649–53	Commonwealth of England, Scotland, and Ireland; Levellers in opposition; Ireland and Scotland conquered
1651	Navigation Act
1652–54	First Dutch War
1653	Long Parliament dissolved; Barebones Parliament; Instrument of Government; Cromwell lord protector
1655	Rule of major generals; conquest of Jamaica
1657	Humble Petition and Advice; East India Company rechartered
1658	Cromwell dead; Richard Cromwell lord protector
1660	Restoration of Charles II; feudal tenures abolished

19

Restoration and Revolution

THE RESTORATION

The Restoration of 1660 was a rejection of the constitutional experiments of the Puritans and a return to the ancient form of government by King, Lords, and Commons. But neither kingship nor Parliament had remained unchanged. The Crown had lost many powers. Charles II and his minister, Edward Hyde, Earl of Clarendon, wisely retained the early legislation of the Long Parliament which had been accepted by Charles I. This meant that many of the old devices for raising money and for exalting the prerogative were now gone. The king was left entirely dependent upon Parliament for money; the prerogative courts disappeared. The Crown did, however, retain control of the executive branch of government. As such, Charles II appointed his ministers, bishops, and judges, directed foreign affairs, controlled the army and navy, and supervised the daily administration and the expenditure of funds. He also summoned and dissolved Parliament. A new Triennial Act in 1664 called for a session of Parliament every three years but provided no machinery to make these sessions obligatory. Charles retained the veto and an undefined prerogative of suspending and dispensing with statutes in times of emergency.

Parliament in 1660, however, held a far stronger position than before the Civil Wars. Neither Parliament nor the king could forget that for twenty years the Commons had controlled administration, had raised armies, built a navy, fought wars, eliminated monarchy and the House of Lords, declared itself the supreme power in the state, and, above all, had brought a king to the block. Parliament after 1660 possessed an indisputable sovereignty in taxation and legislation; moreover, its competence had become all-embracing. There was no sphere in which it could not act. It assumed at once the right to arrange a settlement of the church. Parliamentary privilege was now sacred; older methods of royal influence, such as the control of the Speaker, became impossible. Charles met a storm of protest when he attempted to create a new parliamentary borough. The Commons audited his accounts and impeached his ministers. Thus Parliament entered upon the heritage of the Puritan Revolution. The great challenge of the future was to devise a means by which the Commons could control the executive without continuous crises.

Charles II

When Charles II landed at Dover in May 1660 and made his way through shouting throngs to London, the kingdom was wild with joy. Maidens strewed flowers in his path, loyal healths were drunk in endless numbers, maypoles were set up again, and Cromwell's corpse was exhumed from Westminster Abbey and hanged at Tyburn. England was England once more. The people had a king. They knew what they wanted—but they did not know what they were getting.

Charles II, born in May 1630, was a dark and ugly baby who became a dark and ugly man. He was tall and athletic and always enjoyed excellent health. His education

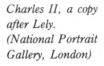

Charles II, a copy after Lely. (National Portrait Gallery, London)

was interrupted by the Civil War. As a youth he roamed about the Continent, in poverty, idleness, hopelessness, and debauchery. He grew up to be lazy and irresolute, prone to follow the course of least resistance, untrustworthy, ungrateful, and irreligious. Having few principles of any kind, he saw virtue only in dissimulation and compromise; he believed that every man and woman could be bought at a price. Because his funds were curtailed by Parliament, he used his control of foreign affairs to obtain subsidies from the king of France for which he was ready to betray the religion of his country. His sympathies were French and Roman Catholic. Confident that God would not damn a man for a little pleasure, he drank heavily, kept a harem of mistresses, and made Whitehall a licentious and wicked place. However, Charles's good qualities should not be forgotten. He made no pretense at being anything but what he was. Witty, charming, and amusing, he possessed a keen intelligence and discernment of character. He was loyal to his family and affable with his subordinates without a loss of dignity. The king had an interest in commerce, he loved the sea and the navy, he dabbled in chemistry, and was a patron of science. Though he desired a policy of religious toleration, his dark dealings with France and his sympathy with a religion hated by his people portended an explosive violence which poisoned the atmosphere at Westminster.

The Convention Parliament

While Charles was still on the Continent he had issued the Declaration of Breda, in which he promised to abide by Parliament's decision on the principal issues requiring immediate settlement. The Convention Parliament, which sat until December 1660, took action on three of these issues. An act of indemnity pardoned all those who had fought against Charles I or had taken part in the governments of the interregnum, except for some fifty persons whom the act listed by name. Of these, thirteen were executed, twelve being regicides; the thirteenth, Sir Henry Vane, was considered too dangerous to live. In an age as cruel as the seventeenth century, these thirteen lives were but a mild revenge for a Civil War and the death of a king.

Closely connected with indemnity was the question of a land settlement. Any solution was certain to cause injustice and bitterness. It was decided that Royalists whose estates had been confiscated by the Puritans should be allowed to recover their lands through the courts, but that those who had sold their estates should receive no compensation. This decision was important for the pattern of landowner-ship in the following century. It meant that many Puritans who had purchased estates during the interregnum were able to retain them after 1660. The future landowners of the kingdom were to be the descendants of Roundheads as well as of Cavaliers. The great families who had sided with Charles I were more successful in recovering their former property than were the smaller Royalists; and these great families often added to their holdings after 1660 by purchases from Royalists who were in need. There was thus a tendency for more and more land to accumulate in a few hands. The large landowners turned against James II in 1688 and often profited from the revolution in that year. Hence there emerged two classes that will become familiar in the eighteenth century: the great Whig magnate owning vast estates, and the small Tory squire, sullen, resentful, and dissatisfied.

The Convention Parliament had also to provide the king with money. The system of taxation and of government finance was antiquated, but there was no time for reform. Since money was required at once to pay off the army, Parliament quickly raised the necessary funds by levying direct assessments upon local areas. To meet ordinary expenses of government, it granted to Charles II the customs duties and an excise on beer, ale, tea, and coffee. This revenue was expected to amount to £1,200,000 a year, but unfortunately it never reached that amount. In return for this grant Charles surrendered the right to wardship and to other survivals of the age of feudalism. Feudal tenures were abolished; the great landowners now held their estates in common socage. They benefited greatly from the change, for they were relieved of heavy payments and became more independent of the Crown.

The Clarendon Code

There remained the question of a religious settlement—a most difficult question, for the country was thoroughly divided. Of England's nine thousand parish churches, some two thousand were held by Presbyterian clergymen and perhaps four hundred by Independents. There was also a large number of sectaries, comprising perhaps a tenth of the population, who went their own way, as did the Quakers, in various forms of unregulated religious life. But the Anglican clergymen, who now returned from exile or emerged from hiding, naturally expected to be restored to their former livings. So long as the Convention Parliament remained in session there was a possibility of compromise. This Parliament contained many Presbyterians who hoped that their opinions would carry weight and who were willing to accept bishops associated in some way with synods. The king was ready for toleration, and Clarendon was disposed to be moderate. A few Presbyterians were offered preferment in the church, but the moment of possible compromise quickly passed. A conference between Anglican and Presbyterian leaders broke down completely and Anglican bigotry hardened against all nonconformists. The Cavalier Parliament, elected early in 1661, contained a majority of Royalist Anglicans determined to restore the church as it had been before the Civil Wars, to drive out the Puritans, and to exclude them from political life.

Hating and fearing all forms of nonconformity, the Cavaliers passed a number of acts known collectively as the Clarendon Code, though Clarendon was only partially responsible for them. The Corporation Act of 1661 excluded from the governing bodies of the towns all persons who refused to swear to the unlawfulness of resistance to the king and who declined to receive the Communion according to the rites of the Church of England. The Act of Uniformity in 1662 issued a new Prayer Book and provided that clergymen must either accept it or resign their livings. Some twelve hundred clergymen refused, vacating their churches. Their number is an indication of the strength of nonconformity. The Conventicle Act of 1664 imposed

Edward, Earl of Clarendon, from Edward, Earl of Clarendon, The History of the Rebellion and Civil War in England, *Oxford, 1702. (Department of Special Collections, Wilson Library, University of Minnesota)*

Edward Earle of CLARENDON Lord High CHANCELLOR of England and Chancellor of the University of Oxford. An⁰ Dñi 1667.

harsh penalties on those who attended religious services in which the forms of the Anglican church were not used. The government was afraid that conspiracies might be plotted in nonconformist gatherings; the king attempted and failed to modify the Act of Uniformity by dispensing with it in individual cases. An even harsher Conventicle Act became law in 1670. In 1665 the Five Mile Act prohibited clergymen from coming within five miles of a parish from which they had been ejected. A licensing act permitted the archbishop of Canterbury and the bishop of London to control the press and the printing of books.

The Clarendon Code brought about great social changes. It divided religious life in England into two parts: the Church and nonconformity. The Church, purged of

Puritans and fanatics, was to hold the position of power: it regained its church buildings and other property, it could levy tithes, and it controlled education on all levels. Nonconformists were excluded from the universities, from many professions, from municipal government, from all offices under the Crown (by the Test Act of 1673), and from membership in the House of Commons. A social stigma became attached to nonconformity. Persons outside the Church were considered fanatic, ignorant, and "low class." Indeed, in the eighteenth century the Church was sometimes regarded as synonymous with Christianity.

These disabilities undoubtedly weakened the nonconformists greatly. People of power and ambition eventually yielded to public pressure and moved into the church; in the eighteenth century there were few persons of importance who were not Anglicans. Nonconformity, on the other hand, was now lawful. The Tudor doctrine that everyone must belong to the state church had been abandoned. Nonconformity was strong enough to remain a permanent element in English life. It had struck deep roots among the lower middle class, among shopkeepers, artisans, and small farmers. Deprived of many of the opportunities of their fellow citizens, nonconformists entered trade and business. Their industry, thrift, and sobriety brought them material success, and they eventually became merchants, bankers, and manufacturers. They were further strengthened by the rise of Methodism in the eighteenth century. As they gradually emerged from their disabilities, they formed a group apart, with a culture and a morality of their own.

THE FALL OF CLARENDON

For seven years the earl of Clarendon remained Charles's principal minister and lord chancellor. His position seemed secure, not only because of his great services during the interregnum but because his daughter Anne Hyde had become first the mistress and then the wife of James, Duke of York, the heir presumptive to the throne. But although Clarendon possessed ability and noble character, he was proud, austere, and rigid. He returned to England in 1660 to find himself old-fashioned and out of touch with the times. He was hated by the buffoons and loose women around the king, whom he irritated by lectures on morality. He was suspicious of Parliament, to which he assigned a subordinate role it resented. With many enemies, he was apt to be blamed when anything went wrong. He fell from power in 1667, largely because of mischances in foreign affairs for which he was only partially responsible.

The first was the choice of a Portuguese princess, Catherine of Braganza, as Charles's wife. Portugal offered England generous terms for a marriage alliance. The dowry was to be £800,000 in cash, along with the town of Bombay in India and the fortress of Tangier in North Africa near Gibraltar. The English were to be permitted to trade throughout her empire. The marriage was pleasing to France, for Louis XIV welcomed an alliance that weakened Spain. The Dutch, however, were furious: they wanted the Portuguese empire for themselves. The marriage alliance was accepted in London, but the results proved disappointing. The short and dumpy figure of the bride, her prominent teeth and her stolid manner contrasted sadly with the allurements of Lady Castlemaine, that voluptuous goddess who presided at Charles's court. Moreover, Catherine was childless. Bombay was a fever-ridden and profitless possession in 1661, though it became valuable later. Tangier's value as a Mediterranian base was not appreciated, and because it proved very costly Tangier was abandoned in 1683. Portugal appeared to have had the better of the bargain, for she gained a strong ally.

In 1662 Charles sold Dunkirk to the French. The cost of its garrison was heavy and it was difficult to defend from an attack by land. Dunkirk, conquered from Spain by Cromwell's redcoats, was highly prized in England; hence its sale was most unpopular. To England's great cost it was to be used later by Louis XIV as a base for privateering.

Then came a second naval war with Holland (1665–1667), which has been called the clearest case in English history of a purely commercial war. Rivalry between the two countries was again at fever pitch; even before war was declared, there had been fighting over slaving stations in West Africa, and an English squadron had seized the New Netherlands in America. This, like the first, was a war of fierce naval engagements between large and powerful fleets. It was fought for the most part in the seas between Britain and the Continent. By 1666 both sides were feeling the strain. The Dutch, having raised enormous loans, were at the end of their financial resources; England suffered two calamities which for the moment quelled her fighting spirit.

In the spring of 1665 the plague appeared in London, killing some sixty-eight thousand persons before it subsided late in 1666. Everyone fled London who could, leaving a desert of closed houses, of houses with a red cross painted on the door which meant that the plague was within, of panic and misery which paralyzed economic life. This was the final visitation of the bubonic plague, endemic in England since the fourteenth century and carried by the fleas on black rats; one explanation for its failure to return is that black rats were then driven out by brown.

To worsen matters, the Great Fire of London blazed forth in September 1666. Starting accidentally near London Bridge and driven by a high wind over parched land, the fire destroyed the greater part of the old city. The people, more intent on flight and on saving their household goods than on putting out the flames, fled through the suburbs to the countryside beyond. The fire lasted four days, destroying some thirteen thousand houses, eighty-four churches including St. Paul's, and many public buildings, none of them covered by insurance. The people stumbled back over hot ashes to begin building London anew. The new houses were usually made of brick instead of wood and plaster.

Bankrupt and without allies, England now sought peace and began negotiations. Peace was made at Breda in July 1667. The English retained New York and New Jersey; the Dutch, most of the places in dispute along the African Coast and in the East Indies. The Navigation Act was modified slightly in Holland's favor, and the English flag need be saluted only in the Channel. The war had been far from glorious.

Clarendon, as so often, received the blame. Yielding to his minister's enemies, Charles dismissed him from office. Clarendon then was impeached by the Commons, fled abroad, and spent his exile writing his famous *History of the Great Rebellion*.

THE CABAL AND THE SECRET TREATY OF DOVER

For some time after the fall of Clarendon there was no chief minister. Charles attempted a more personal rule and personal direction of foreign policy. Five of his ministers, whose initials formed the acronym "CABAL," were of more importance than the rest. One was Sir Thomas Clifford, later lord treasurer. His patron, Lord Arlington, principal secretary of state, was an experienced and industrious diplomat whose policy in general was anti-French. Both men died Roman Catholics. A third member of the CABAL, George Villiers, second duke of Buckingham, the son of the favorite of James I, was a despicable person, said to be "without principles either of religion, virtue, or friendship." He later drifted into opposition. Lord Ashley, afterward earl of Shaftesbury, was more important. A man of great courage and resourcefulness, though given to violent action, he was a strong Protestant and an opponent of arbitrary government. Like Buckingham, he was to turn against the Crown. The last of the five, Lauderdale, advised the king on Scottish affairs.

European politics in the second half of the seventeenth century centered upon two great facts: the decay of Spain and the aggressiveness of Louis XIV. Spain's sun had set in 1659 at the conclusion of a long war with France. With the death of the Spanish king Philip IV in 1665 and the accession of his sickly and half-witted son, Charles II, the Spanish empire seemed ready for dismemberment. It was still a splendid empire, including large portions of Italy and scattered footholds throughout the Mediterranean, the Spanish Netherlands, Mexico, Central and South America except Brazil, most of the larger West Indian islands, the Philippines, Morocco, and the Canary Islands. Louis XIV cast a covetous eye on these valuable territories. He had married a Spanish princess, Maria Theresa, a daughter of Philip IV; and in 1667 he put forward a claim to the Spanish Netherlands based in part on the nonpayment of his wife's dowry and in part on the law of "devolution" which governed the inheritance of property in the Netherlands. Louis attacked this area and was soon in possession of a number of fortresses within Spanish territory.

Charles's diplomacy during these years was unsettled, with many shifts and little purpose. His basic principle was friendship with France. Louis was the grand monarch of Europe, wealthy, powerful, magnificent, the symbol of absolutism and Catholicism, the model of etiquette and manners, the observed of all observers, with rich merchants, splendid diplomats, and superb armies. Charles regarded him with envy, with admiration, and with the hope of obtaining money, but his first move was to form a Triple Alliance with Holland and Sweden in 1668 to prevent Louis from absorbing the whole of the Spanish Netherlands and also, perhaps, to raise the price of English friendship. Meanwhile Louis made a secret treaty with Emperor Leopold of Austria for the division of the Spanish empire if the Spanish king died while still young, as everybody assumed he would. Hoping for greater things to come, Louis called off the war in the Netherlands in 1668; the Triple Alliance had little to do with his decision.

Louis was angry with the Dutch. They had dared to oppose his ambitions, they were France's commercial rivals, and he wanted to ensure their noninterference when the Spanish empire was divided. To isolate the Dutch, Louis sought an agreement with England. The result was the Treaty of Dover in 1670. Charles's motives in making this treaty are still debatable. Perhaps he was misled by his need for money or by his love for his sister Henrietta, who had married the brother of the French king. At any rate, the treaty was a shameful one. In it Charles declared that he was convinced of the truth of the Catholic religion and that he would announce his conversion when his affairs permitted. He had every reason to believe, the treaty stated, that his people would accept his decision, but if not, Louis agreed to provide 6000 French troops to assist in its enforcement. Meanwhile, as a token of friendship, Louis was to send Charles £166,000. (By later agreements during the next eight years Charles obtained additional subsidies. He received in all some £742,000.) The treaty also provided that England and France join in a war against the Dutch and that the English might annex certain parts of Holland, which, however, they must conquer for themselves. A public treaty contained the clauses concerning the Dutch war; the other clauses remained secret. Just before the war began in 1672, Charles issued a sweeping Declaration of Indulgence by which he suspended the penal laws against both Catholics and nonconformists.

Parliament met in an unpleasant mood in January 1673, deeply suspicious of the king. The Commons did not know the secret terms of the Treaty of Dover, but they made some shrewd guesses. "The public articles are ill enough," said a member. "What are then the private articles?" The war with Holland began abruptly with no immediate cause. The Commons were anti-Catholic and anti-French. Commercial rivalry with Holland was beginning to abate, and there was a dawning realization that France, not Holland, was the great enemy.

The Declaration of Indulgence was a bold use of the suspending power. A new apprehension was appearing—the dread of arbitrary government at home. Popery, France, and despotic power were emerging as the things to be feared. The Commons voted money for the Dutch war, but not until Charles withdrew the Declaration of Indulgence. Parliament then passed the Test Act, which prohibited anyone from holding office under the Crown, either civil or military, until he had taken the Anglican Sacrament and made a declaration against transubstantiation which no Roman Catholic would accept. All Catholic officials, including the duke of York, were driven from office.

The war did not go well. It differed from the first two wars because the Dutch, regarding France as their principal enemy, stood on the defensive at sea. One large naval battle, off the Texel in 1673, demonstrated that the English could not hope to invade Holland and that they must lift their blockade of the Dutch coast. Parliament was so insistent that Charles withdraw from the war that he did so in 1674. He had gained nothing from his crafty dealings: his Declaration of Indulgence had failed, and the Dutch war had sacrificed men and money to little purpose. Ashley and Buckingham were soon to join the opposition. Thus the year 1674 may be taken as a dividing date in the reign. Charles's attempt at personal government had broken down, leaving a legacy of fear and confusion.

DANBY, POLITICAL PARTIES, AND LOUIS XIV

The Cabal broke up after the third Dutch war. Charles's principal minister from 1674 to 1678 was the lord treasurer, Thomas Osborne, soon to be earl of Danby, a robust and vigorous man with a policy of his own. Pro-Dutch, anti-French, and anti-Catholic, he hoped, on the one hand, to draw Charles away from his unpopular policies and, on the other, to rekindle in the Commons their former loyalty to the Crown. He offered Parliament strong support of the Church of England and sound administration of public finance.

Danby paid attention to the management of the Commons. The Commons were divided, as they had been in the first part of the century, into a Court party, which normally supported the king, and a Country party, which normally opposed him. These groups now were organized into political parties, though they lacked the discipline and clear-cut division of parties today. Danby cultivated the members of the Court party, not only by offering them policies which he hoped they would like, but by judicious distribution of offices, pensions, and even payment in cash. His efforts called forth a corresponding organization of the opposition. This was the work of Shaftesbury, who drew the Country party together, established a party headquarters in London known as the Green Ribbon Club, and gradually developed an organization throughout the kingdom. He was in close contact with the political thinker John Locke, whose theories of limited monarchy were to exert great influence. Later in the reign the terms "Whig" and "Tory" came into use. The Tories, led by Danby, supported the church and the prerogatives of the Crown. The Whigs, following Shaftesbury, stood for limitation of royal power and for increased toleration for Protestants though not for Catholics.

Thus Danby organized the Court party but failed to conciliate Parliament as a whole. The Commons were tense and nervous. Their nervousness was increased by the policy of Charles and Louis as well as by a panic that resulted from a supposed Popish Plot.

After 1674 England was officially neutral in the war between Holland and France, which continued until 1678. Louis had found the war unexpectedly difficult, for the Dutch had discovered a leader in their young Stadtholder, William III, who succeeded in building a coalition of powers against France. The Commons became more and more anti-French. In 1677–1678 Charles was induced to take a step away from France by consenting to a marriage between Mary, the elder daughter of James, Duke of York, and William III. By the Treaty of Nimwegen in 1678 Louis made peace with the Dutch, who lost no territory in Europe, but, battered and broken, ceased to be a great power.

THE POPISH PLOT

The English, who by now had been living for years in an atmosphere of tension, were thrown into panic in 1678 by the false disclosures of two informers, Titus Oates and Israel Tonge. Oates was a rascal whose vices had caused him to be ejected from school, from an Anglican living, and from a Jesuit seminary. Coming forward with astonishing effrontery, he declared that he knew of a Jesuit plot to assassinate the king and to place James, his Catholic brother, on the throne. This central lie was surrounded by many lesser ones and by accusations against innocent persons. Oates had stumbled on a few facts which gave a superficial appearance of truth to his stories. It was discovered that a group of Jesuits had held a secret meeting in London and that Edward Coleman, a secretary of James's second wife, Mary of Modena, had been in dangerous correspondence with Catholics in France. Israel Tonge, the other informer, was a half-crazed clergyman, a D.D. from Oxford, who probably believed he was telling the truth.

He and Oates had first made their revelations before a London justice of the peace, Sir Edmund Berry Godfrey, who, disappearing suddenly, was found dead with a sword thrust through his back. His mysterious death was followed by a furious wave of false accusations against Catholics. Many were put to death, even though persons in authority, including the king were convinced of their innocence. For almost two years the panic continued, Oates living like a king, with no one daring to contradict his lies. The Commons listened gravely to evidence brought before them by ratcatchers, they impeached Catholic peers, and they passed a bill strengthening the terms of the Test Act. They turned on Danby, who, at Charles's command, had written one of the king's letters to Louis. Shaftesbury wildly accused the queen of treason. To save his minister from impeachment, to save his queen, and perhaps even to save the powers of the Crown, Charles dissolved the Cavalier Parliament in January 1679.

THE EXCLUSION STRUGGLE

The Catholic episode gave a new turn to English politics. Led by Shaftesbury, the Whigs embarked on a campaign to exclude the Catholic duke of York from the succession to the throne. This policy first appeared in Charles's second Parliament, elected in February of 1679, a violent Parliament in which the opposition was in full control of the Commons. It imprisoned Danby, brushed aside a compromise advanced by Charles to limit his brother's powers as king, and introduced a bill excluding James from the throne. Charles's answer was to send his brother into temporary exile and to prorogue Parliament, which he dissolved in the summer.

The question of exclusion continued to be the storm center of politics, but

Shaftesbury and other Whigs encountered difficulty in selecting a candidate to take James's place. The most obvious choice was Mary, James's elder daughter, a Protestant who had married William III. But the time had not yet come when England would accept a Dutchman as king, and Shaftesbury was anti-Dutch. He made the error of championing Charles's illegitimate son, James Scott, duke of Monmouth. Monmouth was a soldier, quite romantic in his way, but brainless, vain, and irresponsible. The Whigs were divided; some favored the succession of James with limited powers, some favored Monmouth, some Mary, and some a republic. Charles called two more Parliaments, in 1680 and 1681. The first introduced another exclusion bill which was stopped in the Lords. The second, which met in Oxford, was a wild affair to which the Whigs came armed as though to begin an insurrection. The members from London had the motto "No Popery, No Slavery" woven into their hats. This Parliament lasted for only one week and was the last to be summoned by Charles II.

Royalist Reaction

The violence of the Whigs, which appeared to be leading the nation into another civil war, caused a reaction in favor of both the king and the duke of York. Charles regained much of his early popularity. Emboldened by the support of the Tories, he ventured to arrest Shaftesbury for treason, though Shaftesbury was acquitted by a London jury. Thereupon Charles secured the appointment of Tory sheriffs who could be trusted to pack the juries of the capital. He also challenged the London charter. The charters of many other towns were examined and remodeled so as to exclude Whigs from the municipal corporations.

At first the Whigs turned from opposition to conspiracy. Some of the Whig leaders—Shaftesbury, Lord Russell, the earl of Essex, and Algernon Sidney—held secret meetings in which they talked of revolt, although their plans never reached a very advanced state. Meanwhile Monmouth was plotting in an irresponsible way with more questionable characters, and a scheme known as the Rye House Plot was devised to assassinate the king and his brother. When this was betrayed to the government, the Whig leaders, whether they were connected with it or not, knew that their cause was lost. Shaftesbury fled to the Continent, followed by Monmouth. Essex committed suicide. Russell and Sidney were convicted, not for a part in the Rye House Plot, but for their opinion that resistance to the king was lawful. Both were executed, though they were men of character and principle. Meanwhile the Tories rallied about James, displaying an extraordinary loyalty to him and proclaiming the doctrines of divine right and of nonresistance. It was their practice to fall upon their knees and drink his health as they shouted a loud "Huzzah!" They assumed that he would be a Tory king who would keep the Whigs under control, would uphold the Church of England, and would regard his Catholicism as a private affair.

In February 1685 King Charles suffered a sudden stroke and died within a few days. As the king was dying, a Catholic priest who had helped him to escape from Cromwell's forces after the Battle of Worcester was admitted to his bedchamber and received him into the Roman Church.

JAMES II, 1685–1688

King James II was fifty-one when he ascended the throne. As a young man he had served in the armies of France and Spain and was accounted a good officer. In Charles's reign he had become lord admiral, had been a successful naval administrator, and had seen action as the commander of an English fleet against the Dutch. But as king he was impossible—dull, obstinate, rigid, brusque, suspicious, blind to public opinion, and determined to have his way whatever the consequences. It is possible that he suffered a mental decline about the time he secured the throne. His soldiering left him with an inflated confidence in military power and with a callousness toward human suffering. He practiced his Catholicism openly. In less than four years he drove his people to revolution and lost his throne.

He began his reign in a strong position. The Whigs were crushed, the Tories blindly loyal. Tory town corporations could be trusted to return Tory members to the House of Commons. Thus fortified, James summoned Parliament in May 1685. It was a packed assembly, strongly Tory. The king promised "to preserve the government in Church and State as it is now by law established," and then demanded money. The Commons obligingly granted him the customs for life, so that he had an ample revenue. The Revolution, when it came, was not caused by quarrels over finance.

Meanwhile an event took place which appeared to add to his power. This was a rebellion in the southwest of England led by the duke of Monmouth. Fleeing from England in the last years of Charles's reign, Monmouth traveled to Holland where William III advised him politely to go and fight the Turks. Instead, he obtained a ship and some ammunition in Amsterdam and landed at Lyme Regis in Dorset in June 1685. Here he proclaimed himself the rightful king. The gentry did not join him, but some 6000 of the peasants, armed chiefly with scythes and other farming implements, flocked to his standard. The area was a clothmaking district in which much poverty and unemployment existed. There was not the slightest hope of success. The local militia retreated at first but soon was stiffened by regular troops, and at the night Battle of Sedgemoor Monmouth's men blundered into an impassable ditch, where they were slaughtered without mercy. This pathetic rising, the last peasants' revolt in England, was savagely punished. Some three hundred peasants were executed and some eight hundred more were sold as slaves in the West Indies. The country was shocked by the butchery of these poor simple folk. Moreover, James used the rebellion as an excuse to increase the size of the army.

In November James summoned Parliament into its second and final session. He demanded a large sum of money for the support of the army, which contained many Roman Catholic officers who had not complied with the requirements of the Test Act. The Commons, pointing to these officers, offered a considerable grant if the Test Act were enforced. But the king declined, and Parliament was prorogued after a session of about ten days. It never met again in James's reign. The king in effect had asked the Commons to repeal or modify the Test Act, and the Commons had refused to do so.

These developments startled the Tories, who had made themselves champions of

hereditary succession and nonresistance. But they were also champions of the
Church of England and of a constitution which might allow the king high prerogatives
but debarred him from despotic power. They regarded the Test Act as the bulwark
of Anglican supremacy; moreover, they loathed the thought of rule by the sword, for
they had suffered more from Cromwell's army than had any other section of the
people. If their loyalty had blinded them to reality, it had also blinded the king. James
seems to have imagined that the Anglicans were so close to Rome, and the Tories so
committed to nonresistance, that he could obtain the repeal of the Test Act and could
then place Roman Catholics in positions of authority. He should have been warned by
the parliamentary session of November 1685 that he was in error.

Nevertheless, he pressed forward. About half the army was encamped on Hounslow Heath outside London with the obvious intention of overawing the city. Roman
Catholic recruits were brought over from Ireland. A famous case in the courts
established a means of retaining Catholic officers. A collusive suit was brought
against Sir Edward Hales, who was a Roman Catholic officer in the army, but Hales
pleaded that he held a dispensation from the king to retain his place despite the Test
Act, and the judges agreed that the dispensation was legal. A Catholic commanded
the army in Ireland, another the fleet in England. The earl of Sunderland, a vigorous
but reckless man, Judge Jeffreys, the cruel judge who had dealt so harshly with the
Monmouth rebels, and a Jesuit, Father Edward Petre, zealous but unwise, became
the king's closest advisers.

In 1686 James attempted to bend the Church of England to his will by creating a
court of Ecclesiastical Commission with large powers over the clergy. This court was
illegal, for the old High Commission had been abolished in 1641 and the creation of
similar courts had been forbidden. The Ecclesiastical Commission began by suspending Henry Compton, bishop of London, from office. It then turned upon the University of Oxford, where three colleges—Christ Church, University, and Magdalen—
were placed under Roman Catholic rule; the fellows or faculty of Magdalen College
were expelled because they would not elect the king's candidate as their president.
Oxford was an Anglican and Tory stronghold; hence the king was attacking his own
supporters. Moreover, the fellows of an Oxford college, like parish priests, held
their livings as freehold property, from which they could be ejected only through due
process of law. The tyranny of the king placed the living of every clergyman in
jeopardy.

Having thus alienated the church, James sought the support of the nonconformists.
In April 1687 he boldly issued a Declaration of Indulgence which suspended all the
penal laws, leaving both Catholics and nonconformists free to worship in public and to
hold office. From dispensing with the law in a specific instance, as in the case of Sir
Edward Hales, the king now moved to the suspension by prerogative of a long list of
statutes. Had it succeeded, the king would have been free from all legal restraints.

Knowing that he could not maintain his position without the approval of Parliament,
James began a campaign to pack the Commons. The town charters again were
remodeled, Tories were expelled from town corporations, and Roman Catholics
were introduced in their places. Naming Catholics as lords lieutenants of counties, he
instructed them to ask the justices of the peace whether, if they were returned to

Parliament, they would vote for the repeal of the Test Act. The answer was so universally negative that James did not summon Parliament again.

Meanwhile, the great question remained: would the nonconformists accept the toleration offered to them by the king and ally with him against the Church of England? A few of them did, although they knew that in the long run they could expect but short shrift from a Catholic government. The Church of England promised that if ever it came to power it would grant them toleration. William III also issued a declaration supporting religious toleration for nonconformists, though not their admission to office. More and more through 1687 the dissenting bodies supported the church against the Crown. Opponents were uniting against James.

Two events in 1688 produced the Revolution. One was the trial of seven bishops. In May James had reissued the Declaration of Indulgence with the command that it be read on two successive Sundays in every parish church. Sancroft, the archbishop, and six other bishops petitioned the king to withdraw this command. They printed and distributed their petition, which was a technical breach of the law; the king prosecuted them for publishing a seditious libel against his government. The nation waited breathlessly as the seven bishops, men of high character and unquestioned loyalty, were tried by a London jury. The verdict "Not guilty" set the whole people rejoicing; the soldiers cheered on Hounslow Heath.

The second event which precipitated the Revolution was the birth of a son to James and his queen, Mary of Modena, on June 10, 1688. They had been married for fifteen years, their other children had died, and it had been assumed that they would have no more. As long as James was childless by his second wife, the throne at his death would go to one of his grown Protestant daughters, Mary or Anne. But the birth of a son altered this picture. The little prince, known in history as the Old Pretender, would take precedence over his older sisters. The fact that he would certainly be brought up in the Catholic faith opened the prospect of an endless line of Roman Catholic kings. So surprising was his birth that Catholics pronounced the event a miracle, but Protestants spread the story that the child was not of royal parentage but had been brought into the palace in a warming pan. His birth changed the course of history. A group of Whig and Tory leaders, acting together, extended an invitation to William III to invade England with a military force around which the country could rally in revolt against its present king.

THE GLORIOUS REVOLUTION

William viewed the possibility of intervention in England from the standpoint of a continental statesman. The great object of his life was opposition to Louis XIV; if he came to England he would come in order to strengthen his position against France. But developments on the Continent and in England seemed to be converging. A new war against Louis was about to begin. James, as Louis' ally, might perhaps bring England in on the French side. Resentment against James in England seemed to be about as strong as it was likely to become. By the beginning of 1688, William, who was in touch with Whig and Tory leaders, appears to have made up his mind to intervene if he could, but he acted cautiously. He refused to come, as Monmouth had done, without an invitation, and he refused to come without an army, although the presence of Dutch troops in England would certainly cause irritation.

Events played into William's hands. The Dutch naturally feared that Louis would attack them while their army was away, but the grand monarch, less interested in England than in the Rhine, sent his armies eastward against the Palatinate, opening the way for William's enterprise. Louis offered James the aid of the French fleet, but James declined this assistance; as a matter of fact, Louis had few ships to send, for his fleet was largely in the Mediterranean. Not without reason Louis believed that William's invasion would lead to a civil war which would neutralize both England and Holland while the French freely conquered parts of Germany. Hence William sailed unopposed. A fresh "Protestant" wind from the east carried him through the Channel. On 5 November, the anniversary of the Gunpowder Plot, William and his army landed safely at Torbay in Devon.

James in a panic made many concessions, but it was too late. He advanced with his army to Salisbury, returned to London, then did the one thing that was certain to overthrow his government: he ran away. Leaving London late at night, he took ship near Chatham, but was captured by some English fishermen and brought back to England. William wanted no royal martyr. The king was left unguarded and obligingly escaped once more, this time making his way to France. The English were left with little choice but to accept William as their king.

William assumed temporary control of the government and summoned a free Parliament, which met in February 1689. Whigs and Tories, sobered by a sense of crisis, met in a conciliatory spirit, though party differences soon appeared. The Whigs wanted a declaration that the throne was vacant: such a statement would break hereditary succession and give the next king a parliamentary title. The Tories, half ashamed of their opposition to James II, wished to soften the Revolution by asserting that the king had abdicated, thus absolving themselves from the sin of having deposed him. Some Tories hoped that he might be brought back with limited powers, or that William might be regent, or that Mary might be queen with William as prince consort. These suggestions were swept away by the course of events. James had no intention of returning without a French army to re-establish his former powers; William refused to be anything but king; and Mary declined to be queen unless her husband shared the royal title with her. The Commons therefore drew up a statement declaring that James, having broken the fundamental laws and having withdrawn himself out of the kingdom, had abdicated the government and that the throne was thereby vacant. William and Mary were then made joint sovereigns, with the administration vested in William.

The Revolutionary Settlement

Within the next few years Parliament passed a number of acts which, taken together, formed the revolutionary settlement. Although they sprang largely from the deposition of James II, they were remarkable for their broad conception of liberty, a theme inherent in the Puritan revolt against Charles I but made acceptable to the upper classes after 1660 by a group of political thinkers—Algernon Sidney; Henry Neville; George Savile, Marquis of Halifax; and above all, John Locke. These men rejected the egalitarian democracy of the Independents and placed political power in the hands of the property-owning classes, but insisted that all men possessed inalienable rights to personal liberty and to religious equality (though there was to be no religious toleration for Catholics).

Of these thinkers the most important was John Locke, who believed that philosophical principles must be founded on human experience. In its simplest terms, his political theory was that of a social contract between governors and governed. Rejecting all notions of divine right, hereditary succession, nonresistance, and the all-powerful state, he held that governments could be justly overthrown when they ceased to fulfill the functions for which they had been established. Locke argued further that man had certain inalienable rights, such as religious liberty and equality before the law, with which the state could not interfere. Before governments had come into existence, he argued, men were free and equal and bound only by moral law. The great end for which they had placed themselves under governments was the protection of their property. The preservation of life, liberty, and property was the solemn trust placed in the hands of the state. Governments must be limited in power to prevent them from degenerating into tyranny; this should be done by introducing checks and balances, of which the most important was the division into executive, legislative, and judicial branches which imposed restraints upon each other. Locke's reasonable, utilitarian, and liberal approach made a strong appeal to the people of his time, deeply affected government throughout the eighteenth century, and appeared in the American Constitution.

As the greatest constitutional document since Magna Carta, the Bill of Rights (1689) began by asserting that James II, abetted by evil advisers, had sought the destruction of the Protestant religion and the laws and liberties of the country. Certain actions therefore were declared illegal: the use of the suspending power without parliamentary consent; the dispensing power, first "as it hath been exercised of late," and secondly altogether; the court of Ecclesiastical Commission; the levying of money in any way other than that in which it had been granted; a standing army in time of peace without the consent of Parliament. It was further declared that elections to Parliament should be free; that free speech in Parliament should not be questioned except by Parliament itself; that Parliaments should be summoned frequently; that subjects might petition the king; that excessive bail and cruel and unusual punishments were prohibited; that jurors in treason trials should be freeholders; and finally that no Roman Catholic, nor anyone marrying a Roman Catholic, should succeed to the throne and that all future kings should subscribe to the Test Act as revised in 1678.

The Bill of Rights has been criticized because it did not deprive the king of power more completely. He remained the hereditary head of the administrative part of the government. But while this practical document sought to end abuses, it did not attempt to provide for all contingencies. Rather it asserted a number of principles which established England as a limited monarchy. It affirmed the ancient doctrine that the king was under the law, it implied the existence of a contract between the king and the nation, it asserted the sovereignty of Parliament, and it set forth the elementary legal rights of the subject. The Bill of Rights was typical of English constitutional documents in that its wording was largely limited to the specific needs of the moment. Any larger significance is always implied, not stated. In such implications the Bill of Rights has had incalculable influence at home and abroad.

The Coronation Oath (1689), prepared for the new sovereigns, was an adjunct to the Bill of Rights. This oath pledged William and Mary to rule according to "the statutes in Parliament agreed upon, and the laws and customs of the same." Former oaths had merely referred to the laws and customs of earlier kings; but now the words "the statutes in Parliament" were introduced for the first time. The new rulers also swore to uphold "the Protestant Reformed Religion established by law," as well as the Church of England and Ireland "as by law established." Although the words appear redundant, many people believed that the Church of England was too close to Roman Catholicism; Parliament included the words "Protestant" and "Reformed," words which referred to the changes brought about in the Church of England under Henry VIII and Elizabeth.

The Toleration Act (1689)[1] granted the right of public worship to Protestant nonconformists but debarred them from office in the central or local government. The Test Act and the Corporation Act remained in operation; the rest of the Clarendon Code was not enforced. The Toleration Act did not extend liberty of worship to Catholics or to Unitarians, but thereafter they were normally let alone.

A Mutiny Act of 1689, which had to be renewed annually and thus necessitated a meeting of Parliament every year, authorized the maintenance of military discipline in the army by courts-martial. Although annual sessions of Parliament had now begun, a Triennial Act in 1694 provided that Parliament should meet at least once every three years and should not be longer than three years in duration. A Trials for Treason Act (1696) stated that a person on trial for treason should be shown the accusations against him, should have advice of counsel, and should not be convicted except upon the testimony of two independent witnesses. Censorship of the press was allowed to lapse in the same year, though laws against libel remained very strict.

The House of Commons consolidated its control over finance. It assumed full responsibility for military and naval expenditures which were met—after a consideration of the estimates—by appropriations and not by grants to the king. The use of appropriations greatly assisted the government in negotiating loans, which were facilitated further by the establishment of the Bank of England in 1694. The Commons, moreover, appointed certain members as commissioners for public accounts, though the commission did not at first work closely with the Treasury. A grant known as the civil list was voted to the king to cover the expenses of civil government. It became the custom to vote this money for the reign of the sovereign.

The Act of Settlement in 1701 provided that if William or Mary's sister, Anne should die without children (Queen Mary had died in 1694), the throne should

[1]The exact title was "An Act for exempting their Majesties' Protestant Subjects, differing from the Church of England, from the Penalties of certain Laws."

descend, not to the exiled Stuarts, but to Sophia, electress dowager of Hanover, a granddaughter of King James I, or to her heirs.[2] The opportunity was taken to impose new restrictions upon the king: he must in future be a member of the Church of England; should he be a foreigner, he must not involve England in war in defense of his foreign possessions; he must not leave the British Isles without the consent of Parliament; a royal pardon could not be pleaded in bar of impeachment; judges should hold office during good behavior and could be dismissed only upon a joint address of both houses of Parliament. The final point was perhaps the most important. The judges were now independent of the Crown and were becoming the cold and impartial deities of modern times.[3]

Thus England declared herself to be a limited monarchy and a Protestant state. The ancient belief that kings governed by some divine dispensation and were supported by sacred prerogatives was dead; for all practical purposes, sovereignty resided in the nation.

SCIENCE AND THE ARTS

The age of the later Stuarts contained more than plots, intrigues, and revolutions. It was an age of great activity in overseas expansion, as will be explained briefly in the next chapter. It was also an age of intellectual and literary endeavor. Its achievements in science were remarkable. A growing interest in science earlier in the century, inspired by Francis Bacon and by the French philosopher Descartes, flowered in the reign of Charles II. The king himself, his cousin Rupert, and his favorite, the duke of Buckingham, had their private laboratories. These dilettante experiments by prominent persons constituted a danger to the spirit of pure scientific inquiry, which nevertheless made great progress. The Royal Society was founded in 1662 to promote experiments in physics and mathematics. For some time the society included talented men from various walks of life: John Aubrey, who wrote brief lives of his contemporaries; Sir Christopher Wren, the architect; John Evelyn, the botanist and numismatist; Samuel Pepys, the naval administrator and diarist; John Locke, the philosopher; and Sir William Petty, the statistician. There were also scientists: Robert Boyle, physicist and chemist, who formulated the law concerning the elasticity of gases; Isaac Barrow, a mathematician; Robert Hooke, mathematician and physicist; and Jonathan Goddard, who made telescopes. After 1684, influenced by the discoveries of Isaac Newton, the society became more purely scientific. Professor of Mathematics at Cambridge at twenty-seven, Newton was one of the great mathematicians of all time. His many discoveries concerning gravitation, calculus, optics, dynamics, and the theory of equations revealed his genius. He was president

[2]See genealogical table on page 423.
[3]Two other provisions of the act—that business normally transacted in the Privy Council should not be transacted elsewhere and that officeholders under the Crown should not be eligible for membership in the House of Commons— never became operative.

St. Paul's Cathedral (Britain on View Photographic Library, BTA/ETB)

of the society for twenty-four years. His *Principia Mathematica* (1687) became the foundation of modern science.

There was as yet no thought of a clash between science and religion. Boyle and Newton were both religious men; the first historian of the Royal Society, a clergy-man, praised its endeavors "to increase the powers of all mankind and to free them from the bondage of errors." Yet these scientists were finding paths to truth which were entirely outside theology. They were creating a mode of thought which regarded the age of miracles as past, rejected the new revelations of the Puritans, and believed that the universe was governed by natural law. One result was the decline of superstition. There was, for instance, less belief in witchcraft.

The great name in music in this age was that of Henry Purcell, a man of genius, who "wrote masterpieces in every department of music practiced in his time." Before the Civil Wars English music for the most part had been either church music or madrigals. It now broadened into many other forms. Purcell wrote operas,

HOUSE OF STUART

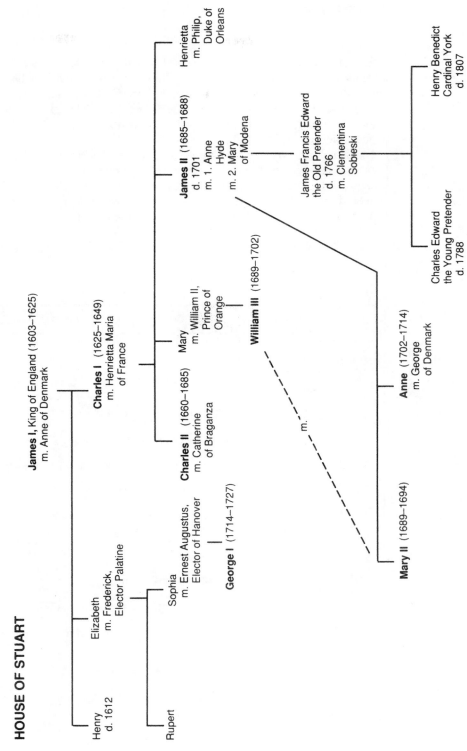

James I, King of England (1603–1625)
m. Anne of Denmark

Henry
d. 1612

Elizabeth
m. Frederick,
Elector Palatine

Rupert

Sophia
m. Ernest Augustus,
Elector of Hanover

George I (1714–1727)

Charles I (1625–1649)
m. Henrietta Maria
of France

Charles II (1660–1685)
m. Catherine
of Braganza

Mary
m. William II,
Prince of
Orange

James II (1685–1688)
d. 1701
m. 1. Anne
Hyde
m. 2. Mary
of Modena

Henrietta
m. Philip,
Duke of
Orleans

William III (1689–1702)

Anne (1702–1714)
m. George
of Denmark

Mary II (1689–1694)

m.

James Francis Edward
the Old Pretender
d. 1766
m. Clementina
Sobieski

Charles Edward
the Young Pretender
d. 1788

Henry Benedict
Cardinal York
d. 1807

423

incidental music for plays, and sonatas for strings and harpsichord. The violin was introduced into England in the reign of Charles II, when the first public concerts were given. In architecture the outstanding figure was Sir Christopher Wren, who built the modern St. Paul's Cathedral after the Great Fire. The great dome of the new cathedral, which is of the Renaissance style of architecture, still dominates the financial center of the city.

English drama had ceased for a time when the Puritans closed the London theaters, and there were only two theaters open in the early years of Charles II. The theaters of the Restoration, depending largely upon the patronage of the royal court, reflected the degenerate taste of Charles's courtiers. Plays were either heroic tragedies, melodramas of knightly love, or comedies of manners, witty but coarse and cynical. The technique of play acting was improved. Scenery now was used, and female parts were performed by actresses and not by boys, as in Shakespeare's time.

C H R O N O L O G Y

Restoration and Revolution

1660–1685	Charles II
1661–1665	Clarendon Code
1662	Act of Uniformity; Royal Society founded
1665	London struck by plague; second Dutch War begins
1666	Great Fire of London
1667	England acquires New York and New Jersey; fall of Clarendon; the CABAL
1670	Treaty of Dover
1672	Third Dutch War begins
1673	Test Act; Catholics removed from office
1674	End of CABAL; Danby in power; Shaftesbury in opposition
1678	Popish Plot and Titus Oates
1679–81	Exclusion Struggle; Whig v. Tory

(continued on next page)

Chronology, continued

1683	Rye House Plot
1685–88	James II
1685	Monmouth's Rebellion crushed
1686	James creates Court of Ecclesiastical Commission
1687	Sir Isaac Newton's *Principia Mathematica*
1688	Declaration of Indulgence; birth of son to James; trial of seven bishops; invitation to William of Orange; William lands; James flees
1689	William and Mary placed on throne; Bill of Rights and Coronation Oath; Toleration Act; Mutiny Act
1690	John Locke's *Treatises on Government*
1694	Triennial Act; Bank of England founded; death of Mary II
1696	Trial for Treason Act
1697	St. Paul's Cathedral; Sir Christopher Wren
1701	Act of Settlement

William III and Anne

WILLIAM III, 1689–1702 AND MARY II, 1689–1694

In the difficult years following the Revolution, England was fortunate in having as great a king as William III. He was not a popular ruler. His thoughts were forever on his beloved Holland, his intimates were mostly Dutchmen, and he never confided in English generals or statesmen. Small, slightly deformed, a sufferer from asthma and from a tubercular lung, he was not impressive physically. Since the smoke of London gave him a cough, he spent his time in the country as much as possible. Hence there was no court to bring him into contact with the people, as there has been under Queen Elizabeth or Charles II. He was a cold man, without social arts or graces, an exacting taskmaster, liked by the army but by few persons outside it.

William's virtues were those of the soldier–bravery in mortal danger, stoic composure in adversity, and the highest sense of duty. His life was dominated by a hatred of Louis XIV. In governing England William was somewhat highhanded, for he was an autocrat who despised the quarrels of Whigs and Tories, but he displayed both patience and magnanimity toward them. He knew that he was surrounded by treachery, that many Tories and some Whigs were in touch with James II. Yet with great forbearance, he ignored this double-dealing and employed false men if he considered them useful. He was happiest when on the battlefield. But his gifts as a soldier were far less than his powers as a diplomat and statesman. Aside from ruling England and Holland, he held together an alliance against France, fought a long war from 1689 to 1697, and prepared for a greater war which came under his successor, Queen Anne.

WAR WITH FRANCE

Ireland

William was forced at once to turn his attention to Ireland. James II had been good to the Irish Catholics, and when he called on them for help they rose in his behalf. In March 1689 James arrived in Dublin with French officers and French money. The island was soon in Catholic hands. Protestants fled to England or went into hiding or crowded into Londonderry, which withstood a siege lasting 105 days. A Catholic Parliament re-established the Roman Catholic Church and began to restore the land to its former Catholic owners. Early in 1690 some seven thousand troops arrived from France, creating a dangerous threat to England. But James's cause did not prosper. The closer he associated himself with Irish Catholicism, the less was his hope of regaining England. Moreover, his counsels were divided: he thought in terms of the English throne, but the Irish aimed at independence, and the French at a long war that would cause William a maximum amount of harm. William landed in Ireland in June 1690 with an army of thirty-six thousand men. On July 1 he fought the Battle of the Boyne, completely defeating James, who immediately fled to France. Within a year the Irish rebellion was crushed.

The Irish received condign punishment. They were hated and feared both as Catholics and as rebels, and England began a policy of ruthless repression and of impregnable Protestant ascendancy. Thereafter Catholics could neither hold office, sit in the Irish Parliament, nor vote for its members. They were barred from all learned professions save medicine, subjected to unjust and discriminatory taxation, made to suffer legal disabilities in dealings against Protestants, and excluded from almost every means of acquiring wealth, knowledge, or influence. Neither could Catholics purchase land or hold long leases. If the family owned land, it was divided at death among the sons, unless the eldest became Protestant, in which case he got it all. Catholic worship was not forbidden, but it was hedged with severe restrictions.

There was also a repressive economic code. The Irish could neither trade with the colonies, nor could colonial products come to Ireland except by way of England. Thus Ireland's shipping was all but destroyed; her many fine harbors brought her little profit. A prosperous trade in exporting cattle and sheep to England was ended, though the Irish exported cattle to other parts of Europe. They developed the manufacture of woolen cloth, but this was restricted, and in 1699 the export of woolen cloth was forbidden. Nor could raw wool be sent to England. The manufacture of linen was encouraged, but the industry was retarded by lack of capital.

The mass of the population thus was compelled to wring a precarious subsistence from the soil. It is small wonder that the Irish peasants learned to hate the law and to regard it as the enemy. But religion gave them depth and earnestness and a love of ancient custom. It taught conjugal fidelity; the Irish became a chaste people with a delicate sense of female honor. The peasant was affectionate toward family, sympathetic toward the sufferings of others, grateful for kindness, polite, tactful, and hospitable to strangers. Their character displayed contradictions. The Celtic temperament was cheerful, but sufferings produced a strain of religious and poetic melancholy. They could be patient and submissive under great provocation, yet brood over ancient wrongs while awaiting the hour of sudden revenge.

Anglo-French Colonial and Commercial Rivalry

The support given by Louis to James's enterprise in Ireland brought war between England and France. Parliament voted supplies at once to meet the French and Irish danger; war was declared against France in May 1689. The English, however, were thinking of the security of their new regime and of the defense of their country from invasion. It is conceivable that once Ireland had been subdued, England would not have joined in the European war against France. Her entry was due in no small measure to colonial and commercial rivalry.

Both Charles II and his brother gave great encouragement to commerce and colonization, courtiers and politicians followed their example, and the amount of capital available for investment increased. The result was a burst of activity in overseas expansion unequaled since the reign of Elizabeth. The older trading companies, which had suffered heavily during the Civil Wars, entered a period of prosperity. The East India Company under a new charter of 1661 did exceptionally well. On the average, the company paid dividends of twenty-five percent; at the height of its prosperity in 1683 the price of its stock had risen fivefold.

Several new companies were established. The Royal Adventurers of England Trading to Africa, chartered by Charles in 1662 with James as governor, brought slaves from West Africa to the New World. It was ruined by the second Dutch war and its stock was taken over in 1672 by a new body, the Royal African Company. James again was governor. The Hudson's Bay Company, the only one of these early companies still in existence, was begun when Prince Rupert, the Royalist general of the Civil War, became interested in the possibilities of the fur trade in the area of Hudson Bay. He obtained a charter in 1670. The company, always very conservative, operated on a modest scale and prospered in spite of French attacks.

Meanwhile the colonies in the New World were expanding. New York and New Jersey were acquired from the Dutch; the Carolinas and Pennsylvania were founded. The population of the English settlements in North America had risen by 1688 to perhaps 200,000 persons. In the British West Indies the large island of Jamaica developed slowly, and the administration of the settlements was tightened and improved.

A famous code of laws, the Acts of Trade, was devised to control colonial commerce. An act of 1660, based on the Navigation Act of 1651, provided that the trade of the English colonies, both export and import, must be conducted in English ships, and that certain enumerated articles, such as sugar, tobacco, cotton, ginger, indigo (the list grew longer in later years), must be shipped only to England or to other English colonies. From the non-English parts of Asia, Africa, and America, goods could be brought to England only in English or colonial ships directly from the place of origin. But since English vessels normally were excluded from the possessions of other powers, the practical effect of this provision was to confine the colonial trade of England to her own colonies. Colonial products other than the enumerated articles could still be taken to foreign ports. Of these products the most important were fish from the Newfoundland Banks, which were shipped to southern Europe and sold for cash, thus helping to create a favorable balance of trade. The Staple Act of 1663 provided that manufactured goods from the Continent could enter the English colonies only if the goods had been brought to England before they were shipped across the Atlantic. Finally, the Plantations Act of 1673 concerned the enumerated articles, which had long been a subject of contention. New England skippers took sugar and tobacco to continental ports in defiance of the act of 1660. To end this illegal traffic, the Plantations Act imposed new duties on exporters of enumerated articles at the port of lading unless the exporters gave security that the goods in question were bound for England.

Although the Acts of Trade have been condemned by modern historians as crude and selfish, they were not so regarded in the seventeenth century. Since the colonies had been founded by English enterprise, it was considered only just that their trade be channeled to England. The mercantile theory of the time embodied the ideal of a self-sufficing empire in which merchandise need not be purchased from foreign countries. Tropical products from the West Indies, it was thought, added directly to the wealth of England since they could not be produced at home and were often re-exported for sale on the Continent. It was argued further that the colonies were defended by the English navy and were heavily protected in the English market. The colonists made little or no objection to the exclusion of foreigners from colonial ports. What they disliked was the necessity of taking the enumerated articles to England. The Acts of Trade were not as oppressive in the seventeenth century as they became in the eighteenth. Devised by men well versed in colonial trade, they prevented the Dutch from exploiting English colonies; the English merchant marine throve under their operation. English tonnage doubled in the first decade after 1660 and continued to increase rapidly. American trade, which in 1670 amounted to one-tenth of all English foreign commerce, rose to one-seventh in 1700.

Important as it was, colonial trade was only a fraction of England's foreign business. The Merchant Adventurers and the Eastland, Muscovy, and Levant companies carried English commodities, especially woolen cloth, throughout central and northern Europe and into the Near East. The tendency at the end of the seventeenth century was to throw open these trades to a larger number of English merchants; the great trading companies became less exclusive than their structure implied. There were also unincorporated merchants who traded with Spain and Portugal. Commerce was becoming the very lifeblood of the nation. The age was one in which the techniques of manufacturing were still primitive, but in which there was no lack of capital or of business skill; the mercantile instincts of the nation turned to commerce rather than to industry. The growing community of merchants and capitalists was acquiring greater influence at Westminster than it had possessed in the past and was becoming one of the most powerful forces in the kingdom. Thus the rise of France as a colonial and commercial rival was a matter of grave concern.

In a general way the history of French expansion overseas parallels that of

England, though the French moved more slowly and founded fewer colonies. The first permanent colony was founded in 1608 at Quebec; about the same time a colony was planted at Port Royal in Acadia (Nova Scotia). The number of French colonists in Canada in 1689 was probably less than 15,000, but they ranged over an enormous area from the St. Lawrence Valley westward through the Great Lakes and down the Mississippi. The French islands in the West Indies were equal or even superior to the English ones. The French held slaving stations around St. Louis on the Senegal River in West Africa. Its early factories in India were located at Surat (1668), at Pondicherry (1674), which grew into its best town; and at Chandarnager (1690) on the Hooghly River in Bengal. These colonies were supported by the French state, by a fine navy, and by a growing mercantile marine. It is not surprising that English merchants regarded this French expansion with apprehension.

England's entry into the war against Louis in 1689 constituted a change of policy. The ancient hostility of the two countries in the later Middle Ages had subsided in the reign of Queen Elizabeth, and for almost a century, except for brief periods of hostility, England and France had been at peace. This amity was now broken. There began a century of conflict, a new Hundred Years' War, which was concluded only when Napoleon was defeated at Waterloo in 1815.

The War of the League of Augsburg, 1689–1697

The aggressions of Louis XIV against his neighbors gradually surrounded France with a ring of hostile states that formed the League of Augsburg in 1686 for their mutual protection. Just as the Revolution was taking place in England, a war broke out in 1688 when Louis attacked the Palatinate. Aligned against him were the members of the so-called Grand Alliance of England, Holland, Austria, Spain, a number of the German states, of which Brandenburg, Saxony, Hanover, and Bavaria were the most important, and later Savoy and the papacy. Sweden had joined the league in 1686 but took no part in the war. Such an alliance might appear invincible. But France had the advantage of inner lines, whereas the allied powers, scattered around the circumference, were divided by jealousies and conflicting ambitions. Decisive action depended upon what England and Holland could accomplish at sea and in the Spanish Netherlands.

The French navy, which was able at first to challenge the fleets of both England and Holland, secured temporary control of the Channel at the time of James's expedition to Ireland. But the French fleet could not control both the Channel and the Mediterranean. It was defeated by the English in 1692 at La Hogue in the Channel near Normandy; when Louis began operations against Spain and Savoy in 1694, an English squadron entered the Mediterranean, blockaded the French in Toulon, and disrupted the assault on Spain.

On the other hand, Louis had the better of the fighting in the Spanish Netherlands. He possessed every advantage of veteran troops, excellent generals, and strategic positions. He captured Mons in 1691 and Namur in 1692 and defeated William in the Battle of Steenkerke in the latter year. William again was defeated in 1693. Although

William retook Namur in 1695, Louis was winning the war on land and was dividing the allies by his diplomacy. Nevertheless, Louis was ready for peace in 1697 and so were his opponents. The Peace of Ryswick in that year provided that France restore all her conquests since 1678 except Strasbourg, allow the Dutch to garrison a line of fortresses in the Spanish Netherlands along the French frontier, and acknowledge William as King of England. The peace merely provided a breathing space before the opening of another war.

WILLIAM AND ENGLISH POLITICS

Meanwhile William was contending with political factions in England. Politics at this time are difficult to understand because although we hear of Whigs and Tories they were not like modern parties. Of the many reasons for this, perhaps the most important was the position of the king. William kept power in his own hands as far as possible. He insisted on having complete control over the army and over foreign affairs, he did not allow Parliament to meet when he was abroad, and he rarely took an English minister with him when he went to the Continent. Acting as his own prime minister, William was at liberty to control policy and to make appointments. He used all the powers of the Crown which had not been taken away and resisted any encroachment on those powers. With so strong and energetic a ruler, modern political parties which today control policy and distribute patronage were impossible.

Modern political parties were also impossible because of the aristocratic nature of society. Country gentlemen with wealth and local influence could obtain election to the House of Commons through their own efforts and were completely independent of any party organization, speaking and voting as they pleased in Parliament. There were also family groups of members. A great noble holding large estates could secure the return of his relatives, employees, and other connections; this group looked to him and not to a party for leadership. Political parties in the modern sense were also out of the question because there was no connection between a change of ministers and an election to the House of Commons. William did not appoint ministers because their party had won a majority. Indeed the reverse was true, for the king's ministers could build a Court party in Parliament. At least a hundred members were placemen who held some office in the gift of the Crown, and this patronage could be used to influence elections and to obtain votes after Parliament assembled. Members might storm at ministers but could not turn them out except by the clumsy method of impeachment.

Both parties were affected by the Revolution. The Tories lost their political philosophy. Some of them were Jacobite, but the majority accepted Locke's utilitarian view of kingship. Yet they could not pay William the respect they had accorded the Stuarts; they thought of him as the enemy of their church. The Tories represented the interests of the landowning gentry who had no inclination to pay high taxes for the support of a war on behalf of commerce. The Whigs had attacked the prerogatives of the Stuart kings but now found themselves with a ruler who used his prerogatives with vigor. Hence they were goaded into seeking further reduction in the powers of the Crown and further increases in the powers of Parliament. They stood for religious toleration, for the commercial interests of merchants and bankers, and for a vigorous prosecution of the war against a commercial rival. Finally, because both parties contained moderates and extremists their condition was confused and fluid.

Under these circumstances both the ministers of the king and the opposition to him in the Commons were apt to be coalitions of both parties; the best descriptive terms are a Country party in the Commons which criticized the government and a Court party which defended it. In the first part of the reign the Whigs had a majority in the Commons. Irritated by the king's appointment of both Whigs and Tories to the ministry, the Whigs set themselves to annoy the government. They voted money for only short periods, they made inquiries into military and naval mishaps, they set up committees to audit the accounts, they forced William to cancel grants made to his favorites, and they dealt with the affairs of the East India Company, which had previously been the province of the Crown. William naturally was irritated, but he discovered that the Tories also opposed him. They lacked enthusiasm for the war, they sought to reduce the size of the army, and some of them were in correspondence with James II.

Since the prosecution of the war was all-important to William, he brought a majority of Whigs into the government. Between 1694 and 1698 the ministry was largely Whig, although a moderate Tory, Sidney Godolphin, an official in the Treasury who was a kind of indispensable civil servant, remained in office. The leading Whigs were known as the Junto. The best work of the Whigs was the founding of the Bank of England in 1694. The subscribers to a government loan of £1,200,000 were incorporated by Parliament as a joint-stock bank with the right to issue notes and discount bills. This was a modest beginning, but the bank helped to finance the war, and since the government was not required to repay the loan so long as it paid interest, the arrangement was the origin of the national debt.

After the Peace of Ryswick in 1697, the country eagerly turned away from war. A new leader appeared in the Commons, Robert Harley, who won much popular approval but greatly angered the king by demanding a reduction in the cost of government, a smaller army than William advised, and an end to royal gifts to favorites. The Whigs were discredited by this attack and by revelations that some of them were in secret correspondence with James II. The king gradually replaced them with Tory ministers, of whom Godolphin and John Churchill, Earl of Marlborough, were the most important. Such was the situation at the end of the reign.

THE PARTITION TREATIES

The problem of the fate of the Spanish empire was growing more pressing in the last years of the century. The Spanish king, Charles II, though taking an unconscionable time in dying, would certainly do so soon. The two strongest claimants to the inheritance of Spain were Louis of France and Emperor Leopold of Austria, both of whom had married sisters of the Spanish king. A third possible heir was Leopold's grandson, Prince Joseph Ferdinand of Bavaria, who was still a child. William's great fear was that the Spanish Netherlands would fall to France, and he devoted his last years to the completion of two partition treaties with Louis by which he hoped to divide the Spanish possessions without a war and without France's obtaining the Netherlands. But neither Spain nor Austria was consulted about these treaties. The Spanish, resentful at the proposed dismemberment of their empire, believed that France could unite their possessions better than could Austria; hence Charles II, now really on his deathbed, was induced to sign a will which left the Spanish empire to Philip, Duke of Anjou, a grandson of Louis XIV, on condition that it not be divided. Louis had before him the prospect of enormous new possessions but also the sobering thought that they would have to be fought for. His decision was to accept the will.

It appeared at first that no general war would follow. Holland recognized Philip as king of Spain, and the English seemed willing to do the same, for the will provided that if Philip accepted the crown of Spain he should forfeit that of France. Louis, however, made a number of miscalculations. Hoping to prevent a war by frightening his opponents, he seized a number of strategic points in the Spanish Netherlands, in Cologne, and in Milan. These moves showed clearly that, though Philip might become the King of Spain, his policy would be dominated by France. Nor did Louis give any indication that Philip, if King of Spain, would renounce his claim to the French crown. Moreover, it became evident that French merchants would be permitted to exploit the Spanish empire: a French company was given the right to supply the Spanish colonies with African slaves. Above all, at the death of James II, Louis recognized James's son, James Edward, the Old Pretender, as king of England, a gratuitous insult which united the English against France. Tories as well as Whigs, determined to preserve the revolutionary settlement, agreed that the country must prepare for war. Preparations were under way when William died in March 1702.

QUEEN ANNE, 1702–1714

The reign of Queen Anne may seem to be dominated by the great war with France. And in a sense it was. But behind the war clouds the reign was studded with brilliant names and could boast notable achievements: Marlborough in war and diplomacy; Newton in science; Wren in architecture; Godolphin, Somers, Halifax, Harley, and Bolingbroke in politics; Pope, Swift, Defoe, Congreve, Addison, and Steele in literature—all added luster to what is often called the Augustan Age. English wealth and commerce increased while Louis' power was beaten down, the empire was enlarged, and a lasting union with Scotland was effected.

These achievements cannot be attributed to Queen Anne, a semi-invalid who suffered from gout and who had borne some sixteen children, only to see them die. A woman of very mediocre abilities, she was slow-witted, obstinate, opinionated—and rather dowdy in appearance. She disliked both the memory of William and the thought that the Hanoverians would succeed her. She was pious and devout, a strong supporter of the Church of England and of the Tory party, fond of female favorites, though devoted to her sponge of a husband, Prince George of Denmark, of whom Charles II had said, "I have tried him drunk and tried him sober, and there is nothing in him." Anne's one hobby, it has been remarked, was eating. Yet she had both courage and a sense of duty. She tried to play her part and to maintain her prerogatives. Disliking political parties, she once burst out, "Why for God's sake must I, who have no thought but for the good of my country, be made so miserable as to be brought into the power of one set of men?" Yet she could not avoid dependence on her ministers. A small inner group of advisers supplied the leadership which William had exercised personally, and thus the practice of limited monarchy was advanced during her reign.

The Marlborough-Godolphin Coalition

Anne began her reign by selecting a coalition ministry consisting of both Whigs and Tories. The most important members were the earl of Marlborough, who was captain general (that is, supreme commander of the army), and Sidney Godolphin, the lord treasurer. Marlborough, one of England's greatest generals, was a man of extraordinary gifts both as a diplomat and as a soldier. He had spent all his life at court or at war, having fought at Tangier, in Flanders, in Alsace, in Ireland, and in Flanders again before he became commander in chief. He was a splendid tactician. Armies were still small enough for a single mind to direct their movements during battle, and one must imagine Marlborough deploying troops, placing artillery, at times leading a charge in person. He taught his cavalry to charge home (as Cromwell had done), and his infantry to fire in a single volley by platoons. The grenade and the bayonet were new weapons that made close fighting more deadly. Marlborough was equally successful in planning grand strategy and in viewing campaigns as a whole. At the same time he was an excellent diplomat. Year after year he traveled from one capital to another, holding together an alliance of nations with diverse and selfish aims. His strong position at home made it possible for him to coordinate war and politics. Yet, there were serious flaws in his character. He was much too fond of money. As a young man he did not scruple to obtain advancement by becoming one of the lovers of Lady Castlemaine, the mistress of Charles II. A servant of James II, he deserted him, though only when his cause was hopeless; a servant of William, he corresponded secretly with James.

His wife Sarah, was an avaricious, violent, and overbearing woman who for many years was a favorite of Queen Anne. To place themselves on a basis of complete equality, Anne and Sarah called each other Mrs. Morley and Mrs. Freeman. This connection aided Marlborough greatly, though his wife was so partisan and vehement a Whig that she made it difficult for him to work with the Tories. Godolphin, as we have seen, was a very able administrator, sound and steady, a moderate Tory with a touch of the Jacobite. At the beginning of the reign Anne wrote to Sarah, "We four must never part till death mows us down with his impartial hand." Other members of the coalition were Somers and Halifax from the Whig Junto, Robert Harley, a moderate Tory, and a number of High Tories.

The High Tories of the coalition proved to be difficult. They raised the cry that the church was in danger, and twice attempted to pass occasional conformity bills which would have prevented nonconformists from qualifying for office by occasionally taking the Anglican sacrament. Their view of England's role in the war differed from that of Godolphin and Marlborough. Marlborough's strategy was to drive the French from the Netherlands, defeat them in a pitched battle, and so open the way for a march on Paris. But the High Tories, less interested in the war, wished England to rely on sea power and to play only an auxiliary part in the war on land. Marlborough and Godolphin broke with the High Tories, several of whom were dismissed in 1703. Robert Harley became secretary of state in 1704. Thereafter the three principal ministers, known as the Triumvirate, were Marlborough, Godolphin, and Harley. At the same time a brilliant young member of the Commons, Henry St. John, later Viscount Bolingbroke, was made Secretary at War. This moderately Tory ministry was displeasing to the extremists of both parties and would not have survived for long had not Marlborough won the victory of Blenheim in 1704.

The War of the Spanish Succession, 1702–1713

The first years of the War of the Spanish Succession did not go well. Allied with Spain, Savoy, Bavaria, and Cologne, Louis was in a strong position. He had placed French troops in a number of strategic places, and his fleet at Toulon dominated the western Mediterranean. Arrayed against him was the Grand Alliance of England, Holland, and Austria as well as Denmark, Prussia, Hanover, and lesser German states. But it was difficult, as before, for the allies to work together. Success depended largely on good relations between England and Holland, which for the most part were maintained, though the Dutch, who undoubtedly were making great sacrifices, were fearful of the pitched battles desired by Marlborough. For two years Marlborough's campaigns in the Netherlands and along the lower Rhine accomplished little, as did English operations at sea.

Successes in these years were diplomatic rather than military. In 1703 both Savoy and Portugal joined the allies. The adherence of Savoy was helpful in northern Italy and on the upper Danube against Bavaria, while the port of Lisbon supplied a naval base close to the Mediterranean. The Portuguese, however, came in only on conditions. They asked that the Emperor's son, the Archduke Charles, be declared king of Spain instead of Philip, Louis' grandson; that Charles come in person to Lisbon; and that the war continue until Spain had been won for Austria. These conditions were accepted, though they forced the allies to fight in Spain under disadvantages which in the long run proved insurmountable. There was also a commercial treaty between England and Portugal, the Methuen Treaty, by which English cloth entered Portugal and Portuguese port wine entered England at low custom rates: hence the English taste for port during the eighteenth century.

In 1704 the fortunes of the allies rose greatly. To assist the Austrians, who were pleading for help, Marlborough conceived the bold design of taking his army up the

The Netherlands 1700.

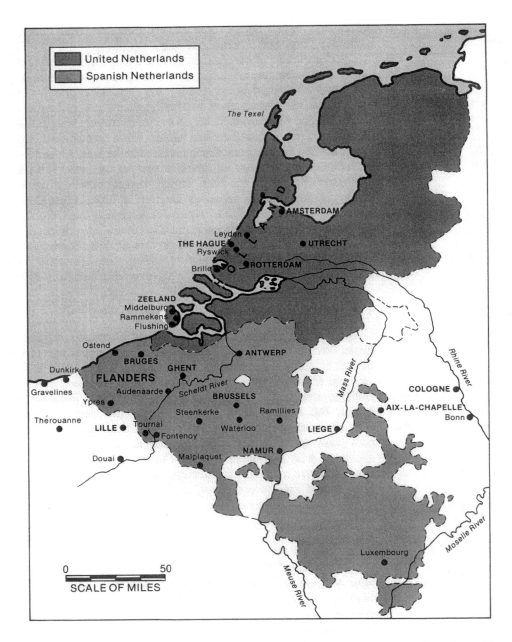

Rhine and into Bavaria to disable the Bavarians before they and the French could attack Vienna. They defeated the Bavarians at the Battle of the Schellenberg, and on August 13, 1704, met and overwhelmed a combined French and Bavarian army at Blenheim. Blenheim was a decisive battle. For the first time in two generations a large French army suffered a crushing defeat. Austria was saved, its future aggrandizement was assured, and Louis lost all hope of extending his territories beyond the Rhine. The Godolphin-Marlborough coalition was strengthened in England and remained in power for four more years. Coincidentally, Admiral Rooke captured Gibraltar and beat off a French fleet at nearby Málaga. Gibraltar remained in English hands despite counterattacks by the French and Spanish.

In the years following Blenheim the war went steadily against Louis except in Spain. Marlborough won the important victory of Ramillies in 1706, with the result that the French were cleared from the Spanish Netherlands; after another victory, Oudenaarde, in 1708, he might have pushed on to Paris but was restrained by the fears of his allies. In 1709 Louis attempted to make peace, but was offered such hard terms that he determined to continue the war. Making a supreme effort, he raised new armies and inspired France to heroic exertion. Marlborough's costly victory in the Battle of Malplaquet, also in the Netherlands, was really a strategic victory for Louis, for it stopped an advance to Paris and retrieved the reputation of French arms. In Spain, on the other hand, the allies were unsuccessful. The Spanish people did not want the Archduke Charles as their king. They wanted Philip of France, and they rallied so effectively to his cause that the allies abandoned Madrid. The Austrian cause in Spain was hopeless.

English Politics, 1705–1710

Two alterations, both gradual, took place in the relative position of parties during these years. The first came as a result of the elections in 1705 and 1708, when the Whigs increased their strength in the House of Commons. The old Whig Junto of William's reign was loud in demanding office, and since the Whigs favored the vigorous prosecution of the war, the government gradually yielded. Thus the ministry of Marlborough and Godolphin gradually was shifted from one that was moderately Tory to one containing many Whigs. The queen was most reluctant to make these changes. She thought of the Whigs as the opponents of her church and of the prerogatives of the Crown, both of which she was determined to defend. It was only with the greatest difficulty that she was persuaded to admit Whigs to office.

Following the election of 1708, however, the Marlborough-Godolphin-Whig coalition began to disintegrate. The basic cause was war-weariness among the people. The war was very costly, and although Marlborough's victories were most satisfying, they did not appear to be bringing the war to a conclusion. It was remembered that Louis had offered to make peace in 1709. The government also was weakened because Anne was at last growing tired of the domineering Sarah and was turning to a new favorite, Mrs. Abigail Masham. Mrs. Masham, a cousin of Robert Harley, was a Tory who favored a purely Tory ministry.

A famous trial in 1710 which further undermined the position of the coalition was that of Dr. Sacheverell, a Tory clergyman who attacked the Whigs in his sermons, declared that the church was in danger, and denounced the principles of the Revolution by defending divine right and passive obedience to kings. Though Sacheverell's true aim was notoriety, he did gain a great following. There was no doubt that his utterances were treasonous. The government successfully impeached him but then, knowing that severity would be unpopular, gave him a ridiculously light sentence. Sensing that the country was turning against the Whigs, Anne began to break up the ministry. She dismissed Sarah after a stormy scene, then dropped Sunderland and Godolphin, along with the Whigs of the Junto. Tories were brought in, of whom the chief was Robert Harley, lord treasurer, later the earl of Oxford, and St. John, secretary of state, later Lord Bolingbroke. Though he had won the war, Marlborough was dismissed in 1711.

The Treaty of Utrecht, 1713

The Tory ministers at once set about making peace with France. Their methods were dishonorable, for they made secret preliminary agreements with Louis safeguarding English interests before they consulted their allies. Yet the settlement was not unjust and brought England many benefits. Louis recognized Anne and the future sovereigns from Hanover as the rightful rulers of England; he banished the Old Pretender from France. The fortifications of Dunkirk, a center for French privateers, were destroyed under the supervision of English troops. England obtained important colonial concessions. The area of Hudson Bay, Acadia (Nova Scotia), and the island of Newfoundland were ceded to her by France, as was also the French portion of St. Kitts in the West Indies. From Spain England secured Gibraltar, the island of Minorca in the Mediterranean, a monopoly of supplying Spanish America with black slaves, and the right to send one ship each year to the fairs at Vera Cruz or at Cartagena.

The settlement on the Continent recognized Philip as king of Spain but provided that he renounce his claims to the French throne and that the crowns of France and Spain never be united.

The Treaty of Utrecht left France in an exhausted and bankrupt condition from which she recovered only slowly. Her colonial and commercial development also received a serious reversal, though they resumed their progress much more rapidly than did France as a whole. The Dutch sank into the position of a second-rate power—secure, wealthy, but unimportant. England emerged from the war with the most lively and busy colonial empire in the world and the largest navy. It is an indication of the prime importance of commerce to England that the Tory ministers who made this treaty were no less intent on colonial and commercial advantage than the Whigs would have been.

The Hanoverian Succession

Having dismissed her Whig ministers and appointed Tory ones in 1710, Anne dissolved Parliament. The result was a Tory victory, for she had gauged the temper of the electorate correctly. The Tories appeared to be firmly entrenched, with a

Tory queen, Tory ministers, and a Tory House of Commons. Yet within four years their party was fragmented and ruined, never to be revived in its early eighteenth-century form. The cause of this debacle was the entanglement of the Tories with Jacobitism. The story has sometimes been written as though they engaged in a deep and sinister plot, but in truth they were drawn into Jacobite dealings by the necessities of their position.

Their task was to make peace after the Whigs had won the war. Though their policy was correct, their methods, as we have seen, were questionable, for they safeguarded English interests by deserting their allies. As this came to light, the allies were deeply incensed—none more so than George, the elector of Hanover. For various reasons he had wished to fight France to a finish, and was furious over the Tory policy. So were the Whigs. Indeed, so vehement was Whig hostility that Anne was forced to create twelve Tory peers to pass the treaties through the House of Lords. Thus George of Hanover and the Whigs were drawn together. The Tories, fearful of the future, believed that if George became king they would be impeached for treason. Like many statesmen of both parties, they had occasionally flirted with Jacobitism in the past. Now they began to go further in their messages to the exiled Stuarts.

James II, of course, was dead. His son, James Edward, the Old Pretender, a young man in his early twenties, was not a promising candidate for the throne. He was a devout Catholic, his health was poor, and though he was always dignified and correct, there was a settled melancholy about him, as though he knew himself to be a man doomed to futility. His principal disadvantages as a possible king of England were his Catholicism and his dependence on France. Early in 1714, after a serious illness of the queen, Oxford, acting through the French Ambassador, inquired of the Pretender whether he was prepared to alter his religion if called to the English throne. When he replied in most definite terms that he was not he ended all chances of a Stuart restoration.

The Tories had made no secret of their approach to the Pretender, and a debate in Parliament, in which the Whigs charged that the Protestant succession was in danger, caused a quarrel between Oxford and Bolingbroke. Oxford, though an able administrator, had grown irresolute and dilatory and was intoxicated frequently. Bolingbroke, a vehement man who hated half measures, was no more Jacobite than Oxford, but he loathed a policy of drift and believed that the Tories should obtain a position of power so that they could bargain with George when the crisis arrived. He asked Anne to dismiss Oxford, which she did in July 1714. Then suddenly the crisis came. Anne was on her deathbed, but Oxford's successor as lord treasurer had not been appointed. The Privy Council, which met without the queen, was dominated by men who did not wish a Roman Catholic sovereign. They determined to suggest the duke of Shrewsbury as treasurer, and Anne accepted the appointment, perhaps without knowing what she was doing, for she died two days later. Shrewsbury, like his fellow councilors, was resolved to promote the Hanoverian succession. Bolingbroke was helpless, and all hope of a Stuart restoration disappeared.

Scene in a coffe-house, c. 1700. (Grouache, British School, British Museum)

The Scottish Union, 1707

The most important achievement of the Whigs in domestic affairs during the middle years of Anne's reign was the completion of a union between England and Scotland. At the time of the Restoration in 1660 the Cromwellian union had been dissolved. Scotland had reverted to its former position under the early Stuarts, becoming once more a separate country with its own Privy Council and Parliament. But its king remained the king of England. Charles II governed Scotland harshly through a secretary in London and an amenable Privy Council in Edinburgh. Episcopacy was re-established; the Lords of the Articles again dominated the Scottish Parliament.

It is not surprising, therefore, that the Revolution in 1688 appeared to the Scots as an opportunity to strike for greater freedom. They wished not only to be rid of a Catholic sovereign, but also to overthrow a despotic government, to reassert Presbyterianism, and to obtain a free Parliament. Hence a Scottish Convention Parliament summoned by William used stronger language than was used in England, declaring that James II had "forfeited" the Scottish throne, which was thereupon offered to William and Mary. But this offer was accompanied by an urgent request for parliamentary liberty and by a complaint that episcopacy was an intolerable grievance. Before William could respond, a revolt took place in the Highlands. It was soon dispersed.

William decided, however, that he could keep his throne in Scotland only by making concessions. He permitted the re-establishment of Presbyterianism and allowed the Lords of the Articles to be abolished, so that the Scottish Parliament was at liberty to conduct business as it chose. There was danger in this concession: the Parliaments in the two kingdoms could now go separate ways, for there was nothing uniting them except the royal veto.

Despite William's concessions, Scotland never was reconciled to his rule, and bitterness against England was increased greatly by a commercial failure in 1699. The Scots, debarred as aliens from trade with the English plantations (though they engaged in a good deal of smuggling), founded in 1695 a Scottish company to trade with Asia, Africa, and America. It was hoped at first that some capital could be secured from England, but the English Parliament opposed the plan, and in the end capital came only from Scots. Persons of every rank subscribed to the venture. The plan to trade in Asia and Africa was abandoned because of English opposition, and the company decided to plant a colony on the Isthmus of Panama. Ignoring local conditions and strangely discounting the certain hostility of Spain, the company sent out three ships with colonists and with goods (including periwigs) to be sold to the Indians. But the climate in Panama was unhealthy, the Spanish attacked the colony, and William, allied with Spain against France, would send no help. The venture ended in failure, with hundreds of Scots losing their savings in this hapless enterprise.

Smarting under this debacle, for which they blamed the English, the Scots were incensed further by the English Act of Settlement in 1701, which arranged for the Hanoverian succession without prior consultation with Scotland, and by the English declaration of war against France in 1702. In 1703 the Scottish Parliament passed an act which forbade the king to involve Scotland in war without its consent. Parliament also passed the famous Act of Security—a kind of declaration of independence—providing that unless Scotland received broad securities, she would not accept the same ruler as England after the death of Queen Anne. Fearing that Scotland might ally with France, English statesmen resolved on a closer union between the two parts of Britain. Commissioners were appointed to prepare a union with Scotland, and the threat was made that if this union were not completed quickly Scottish trade to England would be sharply curtailed.

The Scots were in a cruel dilemma. An alliance with France while England and France were at war would be disastrous. A restoration of the Catholic Stuarts would spell the ruin of the Kirk. Moreover, the only remedy for Scotland's economic plight lay in trade with England and her colonies. Scotland, in a word, faced disaster unless she accepted union. And therefore, despite its anger, the Scottish Parliament appointed commissioners to meet with those of England. A union of the two countries was accepted in 1707. The Scots gave up their Parliament. Thereafter they were to send forty-five members to the English House of Commons and sixteen representative peers to the English House of Lords.

In return the Scots received freedom of trade with England and with the English colonies. They retained Presbyterianism as their national church; they also retained their law, their local government, and their banking system. Customs duties and taxation in the two countries were amalgamated. Since Scotland would now be

HOUSE OF HANOVER

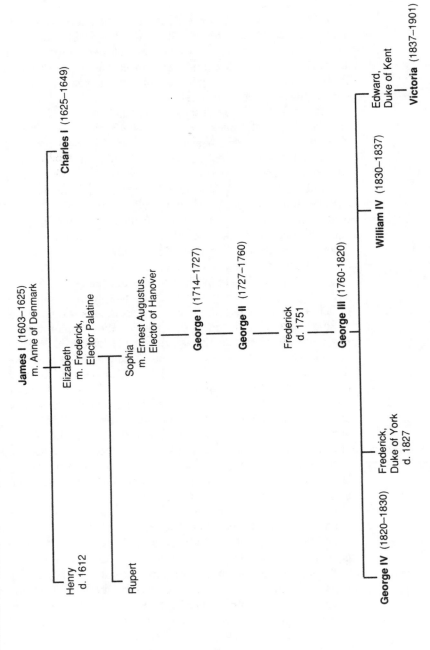

partially responsible for the combined national debt, she was given a considerable sum of money, about £398,000, known as the Equivalent. This made the union a little more acceptable; much of the Equivalent was used to compensate investors in the disastrous attempt to plant a colony in Panama.

The union gave economic opportunity to Scotland and relieved England from the danger of a Franco-Scottish alliance. In the long run it brought lasting benefits to both countries, but for at least half a century it was bitterly resented in Scotland.

C H R O N O L O G Y

Last of the Stuarts

1689–94	William and Mary; William III rules alone until 1702
1689–97	War of the League of Augsburg
1690	Battle of the Boyne; Ireland crushed
1694	Bank of England; beginning of national debt
1702–14	Queen Anne
1702–13	War of the Spanish Succession
1704	Battle of Blenheim; Marlborough and Godolphin in power; Gibraltar captured
1707	Act of Union with Scotland
1710	Trial of Dr. Sacheverell
1711	Marlborough dismissed; Harley (Oxford) and St. John (Bolingbroke) in power; House of Lords "packed"
1713	Treaty of Utrecht

21

Walpole

THE EIGHTEENTH CENTURY

The contrast between the seventeenth and eighteenth centuries was very marked. The religious fervor and political violence of the seventeenth century were regarded with abhorrence by the century that followed; the ideals of the eighteenth century were restraint, moderation, stability, correctness, balance, and proportion. Although a strong sense of personal religion by no means disappeared, as evidenced by the rise of Methodism, a good deal of indifference and skepticism existed among the upper classes. Divine worship in the Church of England was cold and formal and conducted without intensity. Political life grew more urbane and moderate, party hatreds subsided, the prevailing tone was one of compromise and expediency. Rejecting the florid and involved style of seventeenth-century writing, literary taste demanded correctness, polish, and purity of diction. Englishmen in the eighteenth century had a strong desire for social stability, for an ordered and tranquil society in which each class knew its duties and remained in its place. The tone of politics was aristocratic; it was assumed that political power should rest in the hands of the wealthy and influential. The ruling class was very small, consisting of nobles and their connections, landed gentry, rich merchants who controlled the larger trading companies and the Bank of England, and a small number of wealthy lawyers and ministers of state.

The eighteenth century was an age of art and elegance, when good taste and aesthetic feeling were fairly widespread among the upper classes. The search for excellence may be seen in the polished verses of Alexander Pope, in the artistic chinaware of Wedgwood and Spode and the furniture of Chippendale and Sheraton, and in the brilliance and poised self-confidence of fashionable society.

Yet ideals were often lost in practice. There was little moderation in the drinking and gambling which debauched society. Elegance of manners could be accompanied by coarseness and vulgarity of thought and expression. In contrast to the lavish expenditure of the aristocracy, the lower classes often were sunk in squalor, ignorance, and brutality. The constitution was idealized as a beautifully balanced threefold structure of executive, legislative, and judiciary bodies, each with its allotted functions. Yet in truth the constitution often worked poorly in the eighteenth century, and politics was littered with nepotism, corruption, and a chaos of ancient offices that had lost their meaning.

Eighteenth-century society was secular, practical, and materialistic. Weary of religious and political controversy, men turned their thoughts to ways in which they could increase their wealth. Nobles and gentry invested time and money in improving their estates. Young men on the grand tour studied continental methods of farming and introduced new flowers, crops, and vegetables at home, sometimes with an eye to the exotic, often with the thought of agricultural improvement. Great interest arose in mechanical inventions, for an improved technology in industry was greatly needed; such advancements eventually gave rise to an industrial revolution. Although commerce, colonies, and sea power continued to be fostered, industry was taking its place beside them. However, this new materialism had its dark side. The lower classes were exploited and ignored, wealth and influence were worshipped shamelessly, and there was much display and ostentation. Wars of commercial aggression were fought against other countries. Yet material wealth increased enormously and with it the general well-being of the nation.

England continued to be essentially rural. Of a population of some 5,500,000 in England and Wales in 1700, the great majority lived in tiny hamlets and small country towns. London, with a population of about 675,000, was the one great city; after London there came a tremendous drop to Bristol and Norwich, with some 50,000 each. Other areas—Manchester, Liverpool, Leeds, Sheffield, Birmingham, Coventry—were no longer sprawling villages but unsightly, unhealthy industrial towns, without sanitation of any kind, and with high death rates, especially among children. These towns increased in population only because of a steady migration from the countryside. The total population of the kingdom rose to about seven million in 1760 and to about nine million in 1801.

THE HANOVERIAN KINGS

Although the characteristics of eighteenth-century England may be seen emerging in the reign of Queen Anne, the accession of the Hanoverians marks a break in English history. George I (1714–1727) and George II (1727–1760) were thoroughly German, foreigners in the land which had made them kings. They had little sympathy with English ways or with English parliamentary institutions. Their domestic lives were grim and unattractive, and their courts were shunned by fashionable society. Their greatest asset lay in the fact that they stood for the Protestant succession against the exiled Stuarts. Hence the utilitarian view of kingship, the belief that England had a king because a king was useful, was greatly strenghened.

The Revolution in 1688–1689, despite its liberal character, left considerable powers in the hands of the king. He was hereditary head of the executive branch of a parliamentary state. Neither a figurehead nor an abstract idea, he was the supreme magistrate whose duty it was to see that the government was carried on. For this purpose he was at liberty to select his ministers. He was thus the fountain of power. His control of patronage extended far beyond his principal ministers to a host of minor places in the administration and in the royal household. The Georges snubbed and kept at a distance those politicians whom they disliked. George II was able for many years to exclude the elder Pitt from the Cabinet and on one occasion in 1746 he attempted the experiment of appointing ministers disliked by the House of Commons. But Pitt eventually was admitted to power; the experiment of 1746 ended in a few days. The Georges learned the necessity of appointing ministers who could win the confidence of Parliament, for government was impossible unless ministers and Commons acted in essential harmony. The Georges possessed the wisdom and good judgment to accept this situation and to take things in England as they found them. They made no attempt to be absolute. Though they were irascible and narrow and of only mediocre ability, and though they could and did make themselves disagreeable, they were essentially honest and sensible men, loyal to those ministers in whom they placed their confidence.

The Georges could exert some influence through the civil list, the money granted by Parliament to the Crown for the purposes of civil government.[1] The civil list included pensions and the salaries of ambassadors and of many ministers. Once granted, it was the king's for life. In two other phases of government the Georges believed they could rightfully exercise some influence. One was the army. Clinging to the tradition that the king was supreme over the armed forces, George I and George II watched the details of military administration. In the realm of foreign affairs, the Georges were deeply interested in the politics of Germany, they wished to defend and benefit Hanover, and they felt with some justice that they understood the issues involved. These issues were of growing importance because of the rise of Russia and Prussia as European powers.

GEORGE I

George I did not bother to come to England for seven weeks after the death of Queen Anne, and never took the trouble to learn English. He brought with him a large German entourage, German advisers, and three German mistresses, one of them so stout as to be nicknamed the elephant by the London mob, another so thin as to be called the hop pole. After the virtuous court of Queen Anne, George's amours

---

[1]The civil list was sharply separated from the military and naval estimates.

seemed gross and indecent. The English found him cold, awkward, silent, and aloof, preferring German to English associates, and Hanover to England. He was fifty-four years old, set in the stiff mold of a German soldier, a crude, unpleasant, grim little man, a disciplinarian toward his subordinates and a tyrant in his family circle. Yet he possessed sufficient common sense to know that England was not Hanover; and although he chafed at what he considered the absurdities of the British constitution and roundly cursed the House of Commons, he made no attempt to be absolute in England. But he was not popular with his new subjects.

It was a foregone conclusion that he would regard the Whigs as his friends and the Tories as his enemies, for the Whigs had supported the Hanoverian succession whereas the Tories had considered recalling the Stuarts at Anne's death. Even before his arrival in England, George ordered that Henry St. John, Viscount Bolingbroke, a Tory secretary of state, be dismissed from office and that his papers be retained for investigation. The duke of Ormonde, the Tory captain general, also was dismissed.

The new ministers were almost entirely Whigs. Three were of special importance. General James Stanhope, later Earl Stanhope, was a soldier and diplomat, an energetic resolute, and enterprising man. His diplomacy was, on the whole, highly successful, though some of his colleagues thought it too aggressive and too likely to lead to war. He was secretary of state for the Southern Department.[2] The other secretary was Lord Townshend, a solid Whig, whose temperament, active and warmhearted though bordering on rashness, was somewhat akin to Stanhope's. Townshend was the brother-in-law of Robert Walpole, the ablest and most promising of the new ministers. Walpole at first held the lesser but highly lucrative post of paymaster of the forces; in 1715 he became the first lord of the Treasury and chancellor of the Exchequer. The great office of lord treasurer was suppressed, never, as it turned out, to be revived, and the Treasury was placed in commission, the first commissioner being called the first lord. Walpole displayed great skill in public finance. He consolidated the national debt at a uniform and lower rate of interest, and he established a sinking fund to which certain taxes were allotted and which, it was hoped, could some day be used to pay off the national debt.

When an election in 1715 returned a Whig majority in the House of Commons, the government turned to the congenial task of dismissing all Tories from local as well as from central offices. Impeachment proceedings were begun against the former Tory ministers, including Bolingbroke, Ormonde, and Robert Harley, Earl of Oxford, who had been lord treasurer. Bolingbroke and Ormonde foolishly fled to France and joined the Old Pretender, giving the Whigs an opportunity to brand all Tories as Jacobites and traitors.

---

[2]The medieval secretary had been the private secretary of the king. It was Thomas Cromwell in the reign of Henry VIII who raised the secretaryship to a great office of state with general supervision over both foreign and domestic policy. A second secretary was added in 1540. In the later Tudor period one secretary was normally much more important than the other, but James I placed the two secretaries on a more equal basis. One was a Protestant who dealt with the countries of northern Europe; the other a man with Catholic sympathies who was concerned with southern Europe. This division was formalized in the reign of Charles II into a secretary for the Northern Department and another for the Southern Department. In addition to continental affairs, the first dealt with Ireland; the other, with the colonies.

The Fifteen

Bolingbroke and Ormonde united with the Old Pretender and his little court of exiles, hopeful that an uprising in Britain would shortly drive George from the throne. It was known that George was unpopular, that the recent purge of Tories had caused bitterness, and that there was some economic dislocation due to the transition from war to peace. Jacobite riots had become so frequent in London and in the marches of Wales that Parliament had passed a riot act by which individuals who gathered in an assembly of twelve persons to the disturbance of the peace and who refused to disperse at the command of a magistrate were guilty of felony. Misjudging these events, the Pretender and his advisers convinced themselves that England was ready for revolt. But the Pretender, now a young man of twenty-seven, had no gift for leadership. Dignified but rather melancholy, he acted as though he knew he would justify his later sobriquet of "Old Mr. Misfortune." Refusing to take advice, he showed himself incompetent and narrow. With the arrival of Bolingbroke came a flash of intelligence in the counsels of the exiled court. Bolingbroke advised that the principal rising must take place in England, that James must seek the support of the common people, and that the principles of the Revolution, now thoroughly established in English thought, must be accepted. Such advice was beyond the Pretender's imagination. He turned rather to Ormonde, who suggested a rising in Scotland and an adherence to the Stuart tradition of divine right.

From the beginning their plans miscarried. The English government, with an excellent intelligence service in France, was well informed, and its preparations were vigorous and adequate. The sudden death of Louis XIV deprived the Pretender of essential aid. Moreover, the risings were not coordinated. On two occasions Ormonde set sail from France to make a landing in southwestern England but found no support and returned to the Continent with nothing accomplished. A small group of Jacobites rose near Newcastle, wandered into Scotland, and returned to England, where they were crushed easily in Lancashire. Only in Scotland was revolt dangerous. In September 1715 a Scottish noble, the Earl of Mar—"Bobbing John," as he was called because he changed sides so often—raised the Pretender's standard at Perth. With an army of 10,000 Highlanders he advanced against a small government force under the duke of Argyll, who managed to avoid defeat at the Battle of Sheriffmuir. Mar thereupon retired to Perth, where he remained inactive and where the Pretender, landing in Scotland in December, found him. The revolt was now hopeless, for by then Argyll was strongly reinforced. Mar and the Pretender fled to France; the Highlanders, dispersing as best they could, were hunted down by government troops. The rising was over.

The failure of the Fifteen, as it was called from the year in which it took place, was a shattering blow to the Pretender and to the Tories in England. An English treaty with France forced the Pretender to leave French territory. He traveled first to Avignon and then to Italy, where he was much farther from England and so much less a threat. The Whigs continued their purge of Tories, whom they could now call traitors with some justification. Mixed ministries of Whigs and Tories were out of the question, and the Tory party of this period was ruined. The government, not wishing to face an election in such troubled times, passed the Septennial Act in 1716, which extended the life of the existing Parliament and subsequent ones from three to seven years. This act remained in force for the next two centuries.

A Rift among the Whigs

Although the future belonged to the Whigs, the leadership of the party was uncertain, and a rift appeared in which Stanhope and the earl of Sunderland[3] on the one hand were opposed to Townshend and Walpole on the other. This division was caused in part by personal animosities. The quarrel was also over policy, both foreign and domestic. Stanhope's management of foreign affairs was brilliant but bold and even rash. He succeeded admirably in wooing Holland and Austria into renewed alliance with England. These countries had been alienated in 1713 when the English, in negotiating the Treaty of Utrecht with France, had shamefully ignored their interests. Stanhope was also successful in improving relations with France.

All this was excellent. Stanhope, however, had to deal with serious problems in Scandinavia and also in Italy, where Philip of Spain was causing trouble. The Treaty of Utrecht had taken Naples and Sicily from Spain, giving the first to Austria and the second to Savoy. Philip regarded these losses as intolerable. After a short war between Spain and England, Spain yielded in 1720.

Meanwhile the Baltic was disturbed by a long war between Sweden under Charles XII and all the other Baltic powers including Russia. This war was harmful to English commerce in the Baltic, threatened to cut off her supplies of naval stores, and involved the interests of Hanover. Stanhope sent British fleets to the Baltic, often running the risk of war. His policy was to restore peace between Sweden and her enemies and to repress the rising power of Russia. In the first of these objectives he was successful, in the second he failed. On the whole his diplomacy was excellent, but it was too aggressive for Townshend and Walpole, who disliked all dangerous adventures as well as Stanhope's policies at home.

To strengthen the position of the Whigs, Stanhope was willing to allow Protestant nonconformists to hold office; and he was also willing to make concessions to Roman Catholics. Townshend and Walpole supported him in repealing two minor acts passed by the Tories against nonconformists in the last days of Queen Anne's reign, but they would go no further. In 1717 Townshend was dismissed and Walpole resigned. They strongly opposed a bill concerning the peerage which Stanhope introduced in 1719 and which was aimed at maintaining the Whig majority in the House of Lords. It proposed that the Crown be forbidden to create more than six new peerages, except for princes of the royal blood and for the replacement of noble houses which had become extinct. Had the Crown lost the right to create new nobles and hence the power to alter the composition of the House of Lords, that house would have become a closed and impregnable corporation able to impose its will on the nation. Walpole fought the measure with skill and success. Stanhope was forced to withdraw the bill

---

[3]A Whig politician who had married Marlborough's daughter.

and to admit defeat by bringing Townshend and Walpole back into the Cabinet in 1720.[4]

This division among ministers, though it might appear to weaken the Whigs, in fact strengthened them greatly. There were now Whigs in opposition as well as in the government, and if one group of Whig politicians fell from power, another group was ready and eager to take its place. Though the Whigs might quarrel among themselves, all of them supported the Hanoverian dynasty; and hope of the Tories that they might return to power, tainted as they were by the suspicion of treason, was even further removed. Indeed, a situation slowly developed during the first half of the century in which the Tory party so disintegrated that everyone who hoped for office called himself a Whig. The advantage of the division among the Whigs quickly made itself apparent.

The South Sea Bubble

Stanhope, Sunderland, and other ministers were suddenly engulfed in 1720 in the scandal of the South Sea Bubble. The national debt, which stood at some £51 million, was thought to be excessive and dangerous, and the government was intent on its reduction. Early in 1720 the South Sea Company, founded in 1711 to trade with Spanish America, came forward with a proposal to administer the debt by incorporating it into the company's finances. The company offered to pay off £7 million at once and to accept from the government a reduced rate of interest for the remainder. The company, on its side, hoped for more business and for more capital. It proposed to call in the government certificates or bonds held by the investing public and to issue instead new shares of company stock. The Cabinet found the plan attractive and accepted it, but the result was a wave of speculation in the shares of the South Sea Company. Shares that had been selling for £150 soon sold at £1000. All sorts of unlikely projects suddenly made their appearance. There were schemes to salvage wrecks off the Irish coast, to import Spanish asses, to make salt water fresh, to invent a wheel of perpetual motion. One rascal sold shares for "an undertaking of great profit in due time to be revealed" and promptly absconded with the proceeds.

In September 1720 came the inevitable crash, the investors lost large sums, and a great outcry arose against the government. The dominant faction of the Whigs suffered severely. Stanhope, though not responsible for the scandal, was placed under heavy strain, suffered a stroke, and died. When another minister committed suicide, Sunderland pushed Walpole forward to save the situation, doubtless in the hope that Walpole would fail. But he succeeded. He had not been in office when the South Sea scheme was begun, and he could not be accused of malpractice. He now persuaded the East India Company and the Bank of England to take over £18 million of South Sea Company stock. This helped to restore public credit and saved for the stockholders a fraction of their original investment. Walpole was hailed as the man of

[4]The word "Cabinet," in general use at this time, meant the small, inner group of the king's principal ministers. It did not refer to the modern Cabinet system of government, which had not yet come into existence.

the hour. In April 1721 he became first lord of the Treasury and chancellor of the Exchequer. He remained in supreme control of the government for the next twenty-one years, England's first prime minister in fact if not in name.

SIR ROBERT WALPOLE

Walople's career illustrates the great length of time that many modern English statesmen have spent in public life, for although in 1721 he was but forty-five years old, he had already served in Parliament for twenty-one years and was to remain in office for twenty-one years more. He sprang from a line of Norfolk country gentlemen. The third son in a family of nineteen children, he was at first destined for the church and studied at Eton and King's College, Cambridge. But upon the death of his two elder brothers he returned home to learn to manage the estate and to take part

Sir Robert Walpole, by Jean Baptiste Van Loo. (National Portrait Gallery, London)

in the affairs of the county. He became thoroughly acquainted with the class of hardheaded and masterful country gentlemen whom he was to meet in the House of Commons. He drank heavily, as did many politicians of the age, and filled his conversation with bawdy jests because, as he said, women formed a topic in which all could join. Although he rebuilt his country seat at Houghton in lavish style and filled it with statues and paintings, he had little interest in art or literature. A domineering man who loved power, Walpole ran the government as though it were a business with but one head, and rid himself systematically of rivals to his supremacy. Yet he had remarkable fights and was remarkably successful. With great energy, industry, and capacity for work, he possessed a clear head, a quick and solid judgment, and a keen insight into human character. Because he threw the whole force of his personality into the business at hand, he could usually enforce his will. The work of government was still on a small scale, so that he knew its details and could encompass in his own mind the whole fabric of the administration. He was intimately acquainted with his subordinates and gave them a warmhearted loyalty, though he was ruthless in dealing with adversaries. Walpole proved to be a great financial minister and a great addition to the House of Commons.

For some years after 1721 he was favored by fortune in his rise to supreme power. The way was cleared by the death of Stanhope in 1721 and that of Sunderland in 1722; and when the brilliant but arrogant Lord Carteret assumed Sunderland's role as a rival leader of the Whigs, Walpole skillfully maneuvered him into temporary obscurity by giving his place as secretary of state to the duke of Newcastle. In these early years Walpole was able to devote himself to domestic issues, of which he was master, and did not have to venture into the realm of foreign affairs, which were managed by Townshend. His fear of Jacobite plots appeared to be justified by a small rising in Scotland in 1719 and by a larger conspiracy in England in 1722. Thereafter there was small danger from the Jacobites, though Walpole kept the issue alive as an excellent slogan at election time. When George II came to the throne in 1727 it was thought that Walpole's day was done, for George had quarreled with his father and his father's minister. The new king tried the experiment of dropping Walpole, only to find that he was indispensable; Walpole quickly was recalled. Moreover, he found an unexpected ally in Queen Caroline, George's remarkably clever wife. During the 1720s Walpole and Townshend were supreme, and Walpole accomplished his best work.

Fiscal Policy

It was in financial and economic policy that Walpole excelled. He believed that the best protection against Jacobitism was a prosperous and contented people, and he set about making England loyal to the Hanoverians by making it rich. In public finance he at once began to save interest by repaying short-term government borrowings, not at stated intervals, but as money came into the Exchequer. He continued his former policy of assigning certain taxes to a sinking fund which he used to pay off portions of the national debt. By 1727 he had discharged £8.5 million of a debt of some £54 million and had reduced the interest on the balance to a uniform four percent. Had payments continued at this rate the entire debt might have been liquidated in a comparatively short time. But Walpole was determined to reduce the tax on land, a tax which fell heavily upon the country squires, who formed a majority of the House of Commons. Many squires were discontented Tories whose good will Walpole was anxious to win. In his first budget he lowered the land tax from 3s. to 2s. on each pound of assessed value. At one point he reduced the tax further to 1s., though this figure could not be maintained, and in time of war the tax rose to 4s. But he kept it as low as possible by an occasional raid on the sinking fund to meet sudden and unexpected emergencies. He had been criticized for using the sinking fund in this way. But the national debt was not large in proportion to the wealth of the nation, and Walpole was probably wise to conciliate the landed classes rather than to repay a larger portion of the debt.

He was aware that taxation should be used, not merely to produce revenue, but to stimulate commerce and industry. Aside from the tax on land and from an unpopular tax on every house (with mounting assessments according to the number of windows), the principal taxes were excises, levied internally on necessities, such as malt, candles, leather, soap, and salt; and the customs duties on imported and exported articles. The excises were more certain of collection and produced a greater yield, but they savored of oppression because the excise men descended on retailers and even entered private houses to ensure that the excises were paid. The customs, on the other hand, were a hodgepodge of illogical and complicated duties. They were out of date, for the book of rates had not been revised since 1660; they left evaluation to the guesswork of officials; and some articles, such as pepper, were subject to a number of different levies. The result was an enormous amount of smuggling, especially in such luxuries as tea, wine, and brandy.

To correct these evils Walpole issued a new and simplified book of rates. He lowered or abolished the import duties on various raw materials used in English industry, such as dyes, undressed flax, raw silk, salt for curing fish, old rags and rope for making paper, and beaver skins for hats. Duties were abolished on exported agricultural produce and on many manufactured articles, and bounties were offered for the exportation of grain, silk, sailcloths, spirits, and refined sugar. Walpole also sought to maintain high quality in goods manufactured for export. By more dubious legislation he held down the wages of artisans, since low wages were considered necessary for a successful export trade. To combat smuggling he increased the penalties for evading customs regulations and enlarged the number and authority of cutoms officials. His measures against smuggling, however, were not effective.

It is not to be thought that Walpole was in any way a free trader. He believed in high protective duties and in the Acts of Trade. English industries were heavily protected against Irish and American competition. The Molasses Act of 1733 was passed to force the American colonists to buy molasses in the British West Indies and not in the French or Dutch islands. Although Walpole was a mercantilist, he was an enlightened one who saw that the regulation of economic life must be directed by practical common sense.

In 1723 Walpole introduced a plan of bonded warehouses. Certain imported articles—tea, coffee, chocolate, and coconuts—were not to be subject to immediate duty upon being landed in England, but were to be placed in government warehouses. If these articles were then re-exported, they might be taken from the warehouses without payment of any duty at all. The arrangement greatly aided merchants who had formerly paid duties on all imported articles and then, in case of re-export, had recovered the duties from the government. If the goods were taken from the warehouses for retail sale in England they were subject to an excise. The plan worked so well that Walpole was able to reduce the excise tax on these articles and at the same time increase the sums paid to the government. In 1733, therefore, he proposed to handle tobacco in the same way, and wines were to follow.

A fierce opposition arose. The hated excise men, it was said, were to be increased in number and authority and would soon curtail the ancient liberties of the nation. The patronage at the disposal of the government would be extended, thus increasing the jobbery in public life. Here was a means to unite all of Walpole's opponents, although there were points to be made on both sides. The plan was economically wise, but the dislike of excises was rooted in the people's distrust of numerous minor government agents. As opposition grew, Walpole's majority in the Commons dwindled, and when London threatened violent measures, he yielded. He withdrew his bill from the Commons but proceeded to purge the administration of all officeholders who had not supported him. It was only at the end of the century that the younger Pitt revived the plan, with highly beneficial results.

Walpole's Decline

The failure of Walpole's excise plan in 1733 was something of a turning point in his fortunes. Afterwards he began to lose ground, for he hesitated to take any action that might arouse opposition, and fiscal reform came to an end. The death of Queen Caroline in 1737 was a severe loss which increased his difficulty in managing the king. As Walpole grew older the opposition, which was composed of many elements, took new heart. There was still a large body of Tories in the Commons. Their opposition was at its height during Walpole's regime; their number at the time of his fall from power has been estimated at 136. Old Jacobites like Bolingbroke, though they had abandoned the cause of the Pretender, carried on a constant campaign against Walpole. Moreover, a number of Whig politicians who had been dismissed by Walpole were now his personal enemies.

Meanwhile, a new figure was rising in the Commons—William Pitt, who was to be one of the great statesmen of the century. Closely allied with the merchants in London, he voiced their conviction that Walpole was too timid and nonaggressive in foreign affairs. The commerce and sea power of France, he declared, were growing so formidable that they threatened those of England; moreover, France and Spain were drawing together and France would soon dominate the trade of Spanish America. The remedy, said Pitt, was a war of aggression before it was too late. There was a brutal quality about Pitt's aggressiveness, but he opened vistas of expansion for England's colonial trade and inspired a sense of British destiny overseas. Walpole sneered at him as the "Boy Patriot" but nonetheless feared him.

To an opposition which demanded an expanding foreign trade for Britain, Walpole's policy seemed tame and not without danger. Both Russia and Prussia were emerging as powers on the Continent; yet England had won the friendship of neither. The alliance with Austria, Holland, and France, forged after Utrecht in 1713, was now breaking down. English relations with Spain continued to deteriorate.

There were many causes of friction between England and Austria. To the alarm of English merchants, an East India company, known as the Ostend Company, had been formed in the Austrian Netherlands to trade with India and China. Two years later a war broke out between Austria and France, the War of the Polish Succession, in which Walpole offended Austria by keeping England neutral. France emerged from the war with increased prestige and improved relations with Spain. After Utrecht, Philip of Spain still hoped that he might some day be King of France. This had placed him in opposition to the French government. But Louis XV had married early and had a son; Philip's chances of inheriting the French throne were now so small that he gave up his old ambition, altered his policy, and drew closer to France. The two nations agreed to cooperate in the Family Compact of 1733, which was renewed ten years later. There arose a justifiable fear among commercial classes in England that France might be the heir of Spain in Latin America.

The War of Jenkin's Ear, 1739

In 1739 the opposition in Parliament clamored for a war against Spain. Friction between the two countries had been increasing for a long time. Spain never ceased to resent the concessions—especially the surrender of Gibraltar and Minorca—made to England by the Treaty of Utrecht in 1713. Further difficulty arose over English trade in Spanish America. In the first place the treaty gave England the right to supply the Spanish colonists with black slaves. Each year one ship carrying English goods could be sent to the fairs at Vera Cruz or at Cartagena. The English also were permitted to buy land in Spanish America where Africans could be penned and brought back to health after their voyage, before they were sold. Additionally, English ships in need of repair might call at Spanish American ports. The British employed these rights to cover a large amount of smuggling. The annual English ship at the fairs was replenished at night from other vessels; the slave pens and the visits of British ships were used to carry on a large illicit trade.

The Spanish, on their side, established a system of coast guards who intercepted and searched British ships, took them to Spanish ports where the cargoes were confiscated on flimsy pretexts, or took off the goods at sea and set the ships adrift. The coast guards maltreated English sailors. A notorious case was that of Captain Jenkins in 1731, who later testified before a committee of the Commons that he had been bound to his own mast and had had one of his ears torn off. The legend runs that when Jenkins testified he carried a box which, he alleged, contained his ear. In 1739 Walpole faced a Cabinet crisis in which some of his colleagues sided with the opposition. He reluctantly agreed to war.

The fighting in Spanish America did not amount to much. Admiral Vernon, after whom Mount Vernon in Virginia was named, burned the town of Puerto Bello, but as he was about to descend upon Cartagena his men were struck by fever and he was forced to withdraw. Admiral Anson, ordered to attack the Spanish in the Pacific, completed a remarkable voyage. In the years of peace since 1713 English naval and military strength had been allowed to decay. Anson, to his astonishment, was allotted five hundred men from Chelsea Hospital, an old soldiers' home. Those with the strength to run away promptly did so, leaving Anson with invalids and men in their sixties and seventies. Nonetheless he completed his mission and sailed around the world, returning with one man and one ship for every five with which he had embarked. The war merged into a larger conflict on the Continent to which we will turn in the next chapter.

Walpole remained in office until 1742, but his influence was greatly diminished. His world had been one in which England remained at peace and increased the wealth of the upper classes, who benefited from security and low taxation and from maintaining the status quo. A new and more turbulent era was at hand, when the country, hoping for an expansion of trade and possessing the power to seize it, was eager for aggressive wars against her commercial rivals. In 1742 Walpole was defeated in the Commons and resigned.

WALPOLE AND THE STRUCTURE OF POLITICS

An inquiry into the structure of politics during Walpole's administration helps to explain his long success and his ultimate failure in the Commons. The simplest explanation of his defeat in 1742 is that the opposition in Parliament became too strong for him. He was opposed by the Tories and by many discontented Whigs whose numbers increased as he excluded from power all those who threatened his supremacy. Hence, when the war with Spain went badly, when there were tensions within the Cabinet, when some of the lesser officeholders deliberately abstained from voting in his support, and when his opponents won over many independent members, he could no longer carry on the king's business in so hostile a House of Commons. He did not resign because of any constitutional scruple that a minister defeated in Parliament must at once leave office. He had already lost a number of divisions. He resigned because it became evident that no Cabinet of which he was the head could secure the general approbation of Parliament. Thus his resignation demonstrates the fact that in the eighteenth century a minister could not survive, even though he enjoyed the confidence of the king, unless he was also acceptable to the Commons. The Commons were not telling the king whom he should employ as his minister; they were telling him whom he could not employ.

But this explanation is rather negative, and Walpole's resignation may be given a broader interpretation. The Revolution in 1688 had left the problem of how the king, who headed the administration, and the Commons, who controlled taxation and legislation, were to function together without friction. The ultimate solution was to be the Cabinet system of government. But this system is dependent upon well-organized political parties, and parties of this kind did not exist in the eighteenth century. It was necessary to find some other means to ensure the smooth cooperation of king and Commons.

It is often supposed that this cooperation was achieved through influence, that is, through the use of royal patronage to build a following in the Commons strong enough to give the king's ministers a majority. It is certainly true that patronage existed and that Walpole made use of it. Creations and promotions in the peerage, the appointment and advancement of bishops, and the bestowal of office and of pensions from the civil list were made with an eye toward obtaining support in Parliament. Men who were friendly to the administration and who controlled seats in the Commons, which they were ready to place at the disposal of ministers, were carefully chosen. The Treasury used perquisites in the dockyards and in the excise and customs service, as well as livings in the church and secret service money to influence elections in small boroughs. In this way a Court and Treasury party was constructed upon which the Cabinet could depend for support in Parliament.

Upon careful analysis, however, it becomes evident that this system was not nearly so corrupt or so effective as is often supposed. Patronage is only a part of the picture and is inadequate as an explanation of Walpole's long tenure of power. The Cabinet could not hope to influence everybody, for there was not enough patronage to go around. Of 558 members of the Commons, scarcely one-fourth held places of profit under the Crown, and the great majority were independent of any control by the government. Some of these independent members accepted small bits of patronage for themselves or for their constituencies. They might ask for a concession for a relative or for a person from their locality, or might even receive financial assistance in fighting an election. But these small favors did not bind them to constant support of the government. Patronage of a minor kind was considered a natural recompense for the time and money expended by a member in seeking election and in serving in the Commons, where he received no wages. A sharp distinction should be made between the members of the Court and Treasury party whose incomes were supplemented by the Crown and the vast number of independent members who accepted small and temporary favors.

Thus the fundamental fact emerges that most of the members of the Commons were independent. They were men of wealth and of property. Candidates in the counties usually were selected by leading families before they presented themselves to the voters. Compromises were arranged between families, so that contested elections, which were very costly, were relatively few. When they did take place, they revolved around local rivalries and local issues of which Parliament was frequently the arbiter. Country gentlemen sought election to advance the interests of their families or to heighten their local prestige. Their roots were in the country, not in London. They resided in the capital for about half the year and enjoyed its political life, but they were not part of that life and were not necessarily politicians. Indeed, they often left London before the session was over. They responded to family loyalties, to personal ties and friendships, and to local issues. The prestige of Parliament was high; it attracted talented and wealthy men. Moreover, it is absurd to think that the country gentlemen of England, having subordinated the Crown in the Revolution in 1688, would barter away their freedom of action for petty cash.

In addition to the Court and Treasury party and to the much greater number of independent members, there was a group of men who may be called politicians, who made politics their profession. They were divided between those who were in the government and those who were out. The "ins," merging with the Court and Treasury party, often held very good posts. They were the "men of business," the civil servants, active administrators who did much of the detailed work of government. They were often skilled debaters who defended the Cabinet in the Commons and sought the support of independent members. They defended the government, not from venal motives, but because they were a part of it. The government had to have them, for they represented the administrative talent and debating strength necessary for any successful administration. Seats had to be found for them in the Commons, and the Cabinet had to give seats under its control to persons already pledged to support the administration; this fact in itself restricted the wide distribution of patronage. The "outs", on the other hand, were in opposition. They hoped, by exploiting the weaknesses of the Cabinet and by winning the adherence of independent members, to force their own admission to office. Thus there existed two groups of politicians who were trying to influence independent members. But it would be quite wrong to think of this situation as representing the functioning of a two-party system.

Walpole's supporters consisted of three general classes. The first was a group of about fifty politicians or civil servants who represented the core of the Cabinet's administrative and debating talent and who seldom voted against the government. The second consisted of about one hundred other members of the Court and Treasury party. They were judicial officers, members of the royal household, army and navy officers, holders of minor posts and sinecures, and government contractors. They were loyal to Walpole while he dominated the government but became undependable as his power declined; they wanted to retain their places and had to consider who might be Walpole's successor. Family groups did not play as great a part during Walpole's regime as they came to play later in the century. There were only two of any consequence and they were small. Walpole controlled five seats, in which he placed friends and relatives. Through his family connections the duke of Newcastle controlled nine seats and managed a few boroughs dominated by the Treasury. In all he could influence about fifteen seats. He did not manage elections on a national scale until he became first lord of the Treasury in 1754. In addition, Walpole was supported by well over one hundred independent members—country gentlemen, merchants, and professional men, such as lawyers, who owed nothing to the government but were inclined to give it support.

All these groups were more independent than might be imagined. The third group was the most independent, though some of its members doubtless hoped for favors from the administration. Of the politicians and members of the Court and Treasury party, some were so well placed that they could afford to vote against the Cabinet if they disagreed with it sharply. They were entrenched in Treasury boroughs or held posts or sinecures for life. It is a mistake to think that Walpole could buy support as he pleased. The patronage of the Cabinet should be regarded as jobbery to keep a limited number of people in good humor, to support what might be termed the civil service, even at times to provide a kind of charity; it was not an attempt at universal corruption.

No organized opposition existed. It has been suggested that its absence was due to the feeling that formal opposition smacked of disloyalty and that therefore it gathered around Frederick, the Prince of Wales, who opposed his father. But in fact people went into opposition despite its ill repute; and Frederick had little to offer either as a leader or as a distributor of patronage. Two other reasons appear more plausible. In the first place, members were too independent to be controlled; it was impossible for the leaders of the opposition to exert party discipline. Secondly, the Tories kept to themselves and did not cooperate with those Whigs who were in opposition.

The Tories were in a strange position. The Hanoverian dynasty was now fully accepted and they no longer had any thought of supporting the Pretender. They had no cause to defend the church, for its position was firmly established. In fact, there was no great issue to divide a very stable society. The Tories had outlived their reason for existence and yet they refused to die out. They were a party of tradition. Almost all of them came from Tory stock and were Tories because their ancestors had been Tories. They were instinctively suspicious of the Whig government; they opposed patronage, largely because they never received any; they disliked the Septennial Act; they opposed standing armies and continental wars; they wanted the land tax reduced; and they strongly desired influence over local government. As their numbers declined some of them became Whigs. They could do this by merely ceasing to be Tories and by giving the government a general support. The term "Whig" was coming to mean little or nothing. The Whiggism of 1688 was now old-fashioned; the principles of the Revolution were fully accepted. Everyone who hoped for office was a Whig; indeed, everyone in general was a Whig unless he was distinctly a Tory.

The Office of Prime Minister

Something more than influence was needed to secure harmony between king and Commons. It was here that Walpole showed his greatness and built a unique place for himself in politics. He saw that when the king headed the administration and when the Commons controlled the purse and the making of statutes, a minister must have the confidence of both sources of power. Walpole's achievement was to gain this double confidence. He made himself indispensable to both and for many years was the link between them.

He usually is portrayed as a great Parliament man, as he certainly was. An excellent speaker, direct and forceful, whose practical arguments appealed to the squires in the Commons, he sensed their moods and prejudices, he knew their limitations as well as their good qualities, and he could judge what could and could not be done in Parliament. He paid members the compliment of giving them clear and complete explanations regarding his policies; he taught them that their function was not merely to criticize but to cooperate with ministers in conducting the king's government. They must think of themselves as a responsible senate, debating with gravity the problems of the state. He looked upon the Commons, not the lords, as the proper sphere of activity of the king's principal minister. His ascendancy depended upon clear judgment, forceful exposition, and the magnetism of a masterful personality.

But he was also a great king's man. He was the trusted minister of the king in the House of Commons as well as the trusted minister of the Commons in the king's Closet. It was this combination of function which gave him his pre-eminence and made him the first prime minister of England. For much of his time in office he was the only member of the Cabinet who was also a member of the Commons, where he defended the whole administration, of which, as we have seen, he had a firsthand knowledge. Thus he rose far above his colleagues, who were mostly peers, becoming much more than the head of a single department. His achievement was the creation of the office of prime minister, bringing king and Commons together.

But when he yielded to the demand for war with Spain, of which he disapproved, he forfeited his dominant position as prime minister. He could no longer form an effective link between the king and the Commons when both strongly supported a war he did not want. The basis of his former power was destroyed. The Commons turned against him, though George II did not. Accepting the fact that a minister must have the approbation of the Commons, he resigned, though only after a struggle, when he knew that that approbation had ended.

The office of prime minister was not understood at the time and was allowed to fall into temporary abeyance after Walpole's resignation. It reappeared in 1748 when Henry Pelham achieved a position essentially the same as that which Walpole had occupied.

C H R O N O L O G Y

Walpole and the Hanoverians

1714–1727	George I; Hanoverian Succession
1715	The Fifteen; Old Pretender crushed
1716	Septennial Act
1720	South Sea Bubble
1721	Sir Robert Walpole first lord of the Treasury and chancellor of the Exchequer (first prime minister)
1727–1760	George II
1733	Walpole's excise scheme collapsed
1737	Death of Queen Caroline
1739	War of Jenkins's Ear
1742	Walpole defeated and resigned

22 The Pelhams, Pitt, and the Seven Years' War

THE RISE OF THE PELHAMS

The office of prime minister, which Walpole had created, was not understood by the politicians of the time. Indeed, the concept of a "sole" or "overgrown" minister was thoroughly disliked and was indignantly repudiated by those in power. This hostility arose because a minister who possessed the confidence of both the king and the House of Commons was apt to remain in office for a long time. Having the patronage of the Crown at his disposal, he confined it to his followers and permanently excluded a large section of the people in public life. Nevertheless, a prime minister was coming to be a necessity. Hence Walpole's fall was followed by a period of political strife and confusion until early in 1746, when Henry Pelham achieved a position similar to that which Walpole had held. Stability then returned to political life.

The new administration formed in 1742 consisted of Walpole's followers with the addition of some new Whigs brought in from the opposition. George II wished to make as few changes as possible. His aim, in which he succeeded very well, was to give office to just enough of the opposition to secure a majority without disturbing the loyalty of the old corps of Whigs who had supported Walpole. Of these 200 or so Whigs about half were politicians, civil servants, placemen, or pensioners, plus those who sat either for Treasury boroughs or for places which they owed to patrons who were friends of the government. The other half were independent members who had normally supported Walpole. The two groups were accustomed to act together, but would have to be strengthened by additional support in the Commons. Like the king, they wished as few changes in the administration as possible.

Of the old ministers the king retained the duke of Newcastle, his brother Henry Pelham, Lord Chancellor Hardwicke, the earl of Harrington, and the duke of Devonshire. Overtures were made to Lord Carteret and to William Pulteney, Whigs whom Walpole had edged out of power. These men entered the administration. Carteret as secretary of state, an office in which he shared responsibility for foreign affairs with Newcastle, stepped into a position of great power. But Pulteney lost his influence in the Commons by accepting a peerage. The opposition, which had expected great things at Walpole's fall, was disappointed with these arrangements and was angry at Carteret and Pulteney.

Since Pulteney was now in the Lords, the Cabinet required a spokesman in the Commons. The duty fell on Henry Pelham, who became indispensable as the one commoner in the Cabinet and as the minister for the House of Commons. He was made first lord of the Treasury in 1743. A rather timid man, diffident about his own powers, he was not a person from whom heroic measures were to be hoped for; yet he was respected in Parliament for his integrity, moderation, and reasonableness. He possessed common sense, sound judgment, knowledge of business, and long parliamentary experience. The old corps of Whigs accepted him as Walpole's successor. Thus he was able to regain the confidence Walpole had lost and to act as intermediary between Cabinet and Commons.

Henry Pelham, however, did not have the confidence of the king, who much preferred Lord Carteret. Carteret, a brilliant man, an able diplomat, and a fine linguist, pleased the king by his knowledge of German politics and of the German language, as well as by his willingness to support the interests of Hanover. Unfortunately he did not make a good minister. Egotistical and overconfident, he believed that if he had the favor of the king he had everything. He treated his colleagues with contempt and arrogance, insulting them gratuitously. After some initial success, he made commitments on the Continent in 1743 which his colleagues, who had not been properly informed, refused to sanction. The result was a rupture between him and the Pelhams. Supported by most of the Cabinet, the Pelhams informed the king in November 1744 that they would resign unless Carteret, now the earl of Granville, was dismissed. With great reluctance George asked Granville to resign.

Since Granville had not been defeated in the House of Commons, his dismissal has sometimes been portrayed as the result of an intrigue by the Pelham brothers. But Granville would certainly have been defeated in the next session of Parliament. Hence the situation of 1742 was being repeated. No one could tell the king whom to employ as his minister, but if the affairs of the kingdom were mismanaged, as the Commons believed they were, the king could be told whom not to employ. The Pelhams were merely anticipating events. They were taking the precaution of removing Granville before his defeat in the Commons ruined their position as well as his.

The Pelhams then reconstructed the ministry with the aim of forming a kind of coalition government, known as the Broad-bottom administration, to which many groups were admitted. The support of the old Whigs was retained by treating them well, but some of the followers of Granville and Bath were removed to make way for new appointments from the opposition. Some of Pitt's friends were admitted to office, though the king refused Pitt himself, for Pitt had been instrumental in the fall of Granville and had opposed English support for Hanover. Yet others equally disdainful to the king were brought in; in fact, one Tory was given office.

George accepted these changes with great reluctance. He continued to show great confidence in Granville and Bath, especially in Granville, who remained a dominant figure in the government. On the other hand, the king treated the Pelhams with studied hostility. They considered resignation, for their position was most unpleasant and the king's lack of confidence was affecting their influence in the Commons. But for some time they remained in office because of a war on the Continent and a rising in Scotland in 1745. Late in that year a crisis arose over foreign policy and over the wish of the Pelhams to bring Pitt into the Cabinet as secretary at war. George violently opposed them and began arrangements to dismiss the Pelhams and to form a new administration under Granville and Bath. Thereupon, early in 1746, the Pelhams and some forty-five other members of the administration resigned. For a few days the king persisted but then gave up, and indicated that he wished the Pelhams to return. Naturally they returned on their own terms. The king's hostility to them was to end and he was to withdraw his confidence from Granville and Bath. Pitt was to be brought into the ministry, although out of deference to the king, he was to have the office of paymaster of the forces, not that of secretary at war. From this time forward, Henry Pelham, as the undisputed head of the Cabinet, enjoying the confidence of both the king and the Commons, was England's second prime minister.

The events in politics between 1744 and 1746 look more like the working of the modern Cabinet system than they actually were. The historian Sir Lewis Namier calls the whole series of crises an accident arising from what would be considered today an essentially unconstitutional situation. The Pelhams did not come to the king with a strong majority in the Commons and demand changes in the name of that majority. Rather it was the king who was the head of the state and who, through royal patronage, gave to the Pelhams their position of strength in the Commons. It is obvious that both in the government and in Parliament there was much less loyalty to the Pelhams than there was hostility to Granville and Bath. The king's power to select his ministers was challenged only in a negtive way. He was told whom he should not employ.

THE WAR OF THE AUSTRIAN SUCCESSION, 1740–1748

It was unfortunate that these crises came at a time when England was at war on the Continent. The colonial war against Spain begun in 1739 had merged into a larger conflict known as the War of the Austrian Succession. A confusing war, more significant for the Continent than for England, it is important largely because it shaped the future alignment of European powers. When Emperor Charles VI of Austria died in 1740 he left his dominions to his daughter Maria Theresa. For many years he had sought guarantees from other countries that his daughter would be

Europe in the first half of the 18th century.

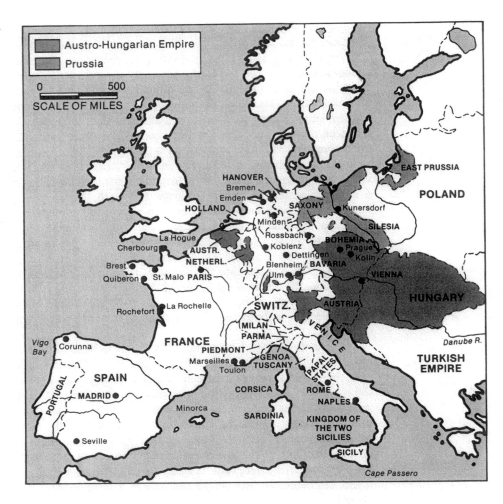

allowed to succeed him peacefully, a policy known as the Pragmatic Sanction. But Charles's death precipitated a general assault on Austria and her new ruler.

Maria Theresa called for assistance from Holland, Russia, Savoy, and England, all of whom had accepted the Pragmatic Sanction. But in the early part of the war, only Britain responded. Regarding Maria Theresa with much sympathy, the English were bound by a treaty of 1731 to come to her assistance. They were already at war with Spain, the close ally of France; they feared a French attack on the Austrian Netherlands; and George II, as elector of Hanover, was angered by Frederick's aggression in Silesia. Rather unwillingly, Walpole supplied Maria Theresa with a subsidy of £300,000 in 1741 and also agreed to pay for Danish and Hessian troops in her service. But when the French sent an army into Germany, George became alarmed. He declared the neutrality of Hanover and offered to cast his vote for Charles Albert of Bavaria as emperor, who was duly elected in 1742. Meanwhile Walpole had persuaded Maria Theresa to cede Silesia to Frederick, thus eliminating for the moment her most dangerous foe.

When Carteret became secretary of state in 1742 he threw himself energetically into European affairs. Maria Theresa was now in great danger. Carteret obtained new subsidies for Maria Theresa, persuaded George to end the neutrality of Hanover, took Hanoverian and Hessian troops into English pay, secured Frederick's second withdrawal from the war, and employed the navy against the Spanish in Italy. Moreover, he dispatched an army to the Austrian Netherlands. A rather motley host, it contained English, Hanoverian, Hessian, and later Dutch and Austrian troops. In 1743 this army, commanded by George II in person, was set in motion against the French, whom it defeated in the Battle of Dettingen. Dettingen marked the height of Carteret's influence. He now attempted to detach the enemies of Maria Theresa one by one, to unite German princes in an anti-French alliance, and to keep the slippery Charles Emmanuel of Savoy on the side of Austria. But Carteret achieved only temporary success. He was so lavish with promises of English subsidies that his colleagues refused to sanction his commitments. Moreover, he offended Frederick, who disliked English interference in German affairs. Carteret was soon dismissed from office.

The war went badly for England during the years 1744 and 1745. An English fleet in the Mediterranean failed to stop a French and Spanish squadron bound for northern Italy. In the Netherlands the English army was defeated at Fontenoy by Marshal Saxe, France's best general. By the end of 1745 most of the British forces had been withdrawn from the Continent to meet a sudden rising in Scotland on behalf of the Young Pretender.

The Forty-Five

For a moment early in 1744 the French entertained the idea of invading England. Since the Old Pretender was now a broken and gloomy man of fifty-seven, the French summoned to Paris his son, Charles Edward, the Young Pretender, known in Scottish history as Bonnie Prince Charlie. Then in his middle twenties, Charles was tall, handsome, athletic, vivacious, ambitious, spirited, and adventurous. But he was rash to the point of folly, supremely confident of his own opinions, and childishly hostile toward those who disagreed with him. When stormy weather scattered their transports at Dunkirk the French abandoned any thought of invasion and turned to a campaign in the Netherlands. Left to his own devices, Charles Edward conceived the mad notion of going to Scotland without French aid. With borrowed money he obtained two ships and boldly set forth to conquer an empire.

On 23 July 1745, he landed in the Hebrides and was soon on the mainland. The youthful glamour of his personality won him the backing of a number of the Highland chiefs. Charles Edward was idolized by his men, for he was ready to endure the hardships of the common soldier. As he marched on foot at the head of his little column, clad in the bravery of a royal Highland chief, he cast a spell on his followers, infusing them with his confidence and love of high adventure. He had but 3000 men when he reached Perth. Thanks to the blunders of his adversary, General Cope, he was able to take the city of Edinburgh, though not the castle, and to defeat the English at the Battle of Prestonpans. He then invaded England, but found that Lowland Scotland had not risen, nor did northern England. Charles Edward marched south as far as Derby, causing great alarm. But at Derby his officers, knowing that overwhelming English armies were not far distant, refused to follow him further. There was nothing to do but retreat, which he did in great dejection. Having lost his former hold on Edinburgh, Charles Edward pushed north to Inverness. At nearby Culloden, in April 1746, he was completely defeated, and five months later after many adventures he escaped to France. Thereafter he degenerated in character, drank heavily, and died in Rome in 1788. The rebellion was followed by severe punishment, with many executions and large portions of the Highlands laid waste. An attempt was made to extinguish the ancient customs of the Highland clans. Land tenure by military service and the jurisdiction of the chieftains as magistrates were abolished, the people were disarmed, and the Highland garb of kilt and tartan was forbidden.

The Peace of Aix-la-Chapelle, 1748

The war on the Continent, which continued until 1748, went badly for the English in the Netherlands but much better for Maria Theresa in central Europe. In 1746 the French Marshal Saxe occupied the whole of the Austrian Netherlands; in the next year he invaded Holland, defeating an English and allied army of more than 100,000 men in the Battle of Lauffeld. These reverses were partially offset by a success in North America. A force of New Englanders, assisted by the royal navy, captured the French fortress of Louisbourg on Cape Breton Island in 1745. In the following year, however, the French took the English town of Madras in India.

In 1747 the English navy, which grew stronger as the war progressed, intercepted two large French convoys on their way to the French colonies. These English victories at sea made the French eager for peace. Their national finances were close to collapse and their colonial trade and Newfoundland fisheries at a standstill. England also was tired of the war. Her trade had increased, but the financial strain of fighting in the Netherlands and of subsidizing allies in various parts of Europe had become burdensome. Peace was concluded at Aix-la-Chapelle in 1748.

By this Treaty England restored to France the Canadian fortress of Louisbourg in exchange for Madras in India. France relinquished her conquests in Holland and in the Austrian Netherlands, recognized the Hanoverian dynasty, and repudiated the exiled Stuarts. But the two countries made no settlement concerning their many colonial disputes in the West Indies, North America, and India. Nor did the treaty mention the Spanish coast guards whose rough treatment of smugglers had been a major cause of the war with Spain. England's monopoly of the slave trade in Spanish America and her right to send one trading ship each year to the Caribbean were renewed for four years only (and then relinquished by another treaty). Thus colonial rivalries were left unsettled.

The significance of the war is obscure because it was fought over dynastic issues, with a transient opposition and vague objectives. France was very shortsighted. She followed tradition in fighting Austria, whereas her interest lay in preparing for the colonial struggle that was certain to come with England. Even in Great Britain the true issues were not clearly understood. Carteret recognized France as the great enemy, but he attempted to defeat her on land, ignoring colonial rivalries. He also failed to see that the rise of Prussia introduced a new element in international affairs and that Maria Theresa regarded Prussia, not France, as her primary foe. Thus the war emphasized the growing importance of Prussia, the deep animosity between Prussia and Austria, and the rivalry of England and France. The Anglo-French struggle for commerce and colonies was still to be decided.

POLITICS, 1748–1754

During the years between the Peace of Aix-la-Chapelle and the death of Pelham in 1754, English politics were surprisingly tranquil. Pelham's position was secure. The king praised his care and parsimony in handling public money, and lamented his death with sincere sorrow. Pelham met with little opposition in Parliament. William Pitt, who might have been dangerous, devoted his time to the reform of his office of paymaster of the forces and gave Pelham a general support. Opposition was weakened by the death in 1751 of Frederick, Prince of Wales, around whom discontented members had rallied. Patronage, of course, played its part in maintaining a majority, but there was less need for it than in the past. The gradual disintegration of parties continued. The number of Tories was diminishing; nearly everyone by now was a Whig.

Pelham was succeeded as first lord of the Treasury by his brother Thomas, Duke of Newcastle, a man of strange eccentricities which made him appear ridiculous both to his contemporaries and to later historians. He was consumed by neurotic fears and jealousies, often imagining that he was about to be impeached, and would impose upon his friends for their support and advice in such imagined difficulties. He loved to distribute the patronage of the Crown, to dole out the financial advantages the government could offer, to manage elections, and to maintain the government's influence in Treasury boroughs. A man who wasted his time on trifles, Newcastle looked decidedly foolish. But it is probable, as a contemporary said, that "public opinion put him below his level." He possessed a wide knowledge of foreign affairs, a fund of intelligence and common sense, much warm human kindness and sincere good will, and a desire to serve his country without mean or sordid motives. Yet he must be counted as a mediocre statesman, beyond his depth in the colonial war with France that began during his ministry.

Since he was a peer, the problem arose of finding a minister for the House of Commons. Newcastle wanted someone who would not dominate the Cabinet and yet bring it additional strength in Parliament. The outstanding man in the Commons, William Pitt, was disliked by the king and had no great following; hence Newcastle selected a compromise, Sir Thomas Robinson, who proved to be incompetent. Newcastle was not a prime minister in the manner of Walpole and Henry Pelham. Little remained of that position when Newcastle left office: he had reduced it to his own dimensions.

THE CLASH OF EMPIRES

The British Empire about 1750

One should think of all the lands bordering on the North Atlantic as belonging to one great trading area. Winds and currents carried trade in a great circle. From Europe south to West Africa the prevailing winds in the autumn came from the north, while the easterly trade winds north of the equator carried vessels with ease from Africa to the Caribbean. From there a current swept north along the eastern coast of Florida. Farther north, from New England and Canada, the prevailing winds were from the west and brought the trader back to Europe.

Trade followed this circle in a general way, though there were endless variations. Cheap manufactured goods were taken to Africa to lure the Arab slave drivers, luxuries went to the wealthy West Indian planters, less costly manufactures to the colonists along the Atlantic seaboard. Slaves were brought from Africa to the Caribbean and to the southern colonies, whence sugar was carried to refineries in Europe or New England to be made into rum; from North America came tobacco, rice, cotton, lumber, and naval stores, with furs from Hudson Bay and fish from the Newfoundland Banks. Fish were taken to southern Europe or to the West Indies to feed the slaves; salt was picked up in Portugal, Venezuela, and St. Kitts. It was for control of this great area of trade that England, France, and Spain contended in the wars of the eighteenth century.

Although there were small English colonies on Newfoundland and in Nova Scotia by the middle of the eighteenth century, the great growth in the empire was taking place to the south in the English colonies along the Atlantic seaboard. Twelve of these colonies had been planted in the seventeenth century. The thirteenth was Georgia, founded in 1733 through the efforts of General James Oglethorpe, a philanthropist who hoped to make Georgia a haven for debtors who had been imprisoned in England. The American colonies had advanced from primitive and rather squalid settlements to large and flourishing communities of solid wealth and considerable culture. By 1760 their population reached the figure of almost 2 million at a time when the population of England and Wales was scarcely more than 7 million.

In the Caribbean the most valuable English possessions were Jamaica, St. Kitts, and Barbados, but there were many lesser English islands. The population of the English islands in 1750 amounted to some 320,000, of whom 230,000 were black slaves. In West Africa the English were established on the Gambia River and held a number of forts and depots on the Gold Coast, where they obtained most of their slaves. There was also solid progress in India.

The French Empire in 1750

The history of French colonial expansion at this time is one of defeat and difficulty during the wars of Louis XIV but of rapid, even striking, recovery after 1720, so that by the middle of the eighteenth century the French possessed a highly valuable empire.

The French had an energetic governor in Canada, the Comte de Frontenac, who served from 1672 to 1682 and again from 1688 to his death in 1698. He kept the western frontier of New England and New York in a state of alarm and harassed the English in Newfoundland and in the area of Hudson Bay. During the war from 1701 to 1713, however, the French were unable to send much aid to their colonies. By the Treaty of Utrecht they ceded the fringes of New France: Newfoundland, Nova Scotia, and the Hudson Bay Territory. Louis' wars also harmed the French East India Company. Its servants continued to make progress in India, but at home their affairs fell into confusion.

Between 1717 and 1720 French expansion was dominated by the schemes of John Law, a Scottish financier who proposed to combine all the French trading companies into one complex organization which would also administer the national debt and work in close association with the government. His plan, which bore some resemblance to the South Sea Bubble in England, ended in a similar crash.

French colonies and French trade overseas expanded rapidly between 1720 and 1750. The population of Canada increased from about twenty thousand in 1713 to about fifty-four thousand in 1744. It was a population of high military efficiency. The French obviously intended not only to defend Canada but to regain the territories they had lost by the Treaty of Utrecht. In 1720 the French began to build the fortress of Louisbourg which, as we have seen, was captured by the New England colonists in 1745 but returned to France in 1748. Fortified posts along the Mississippi River were constructed in order to connect Canada with New Orleans.

The French West Indian islands were making remarkable progress. French Santo Domingo, Martinique, and Guadeloupe produced much more sugar than the English islands and had largely captured the European market. The merchant marine of France increased sixfold between 1715 and 1735—from three hundred to eighteen hundred vessels. It was this rapid recovery and progress during the years of peace that alarmed William Pitt and the merchants of London.

The Coming of War

In the years following the Peace of Aix-la-Chapelle colonial rivalry between France and England moved from the stage of commercial competition to that of armed conflict. Difficulties between the two companies in India became more acute, there were disputes in the West Indies; when the French strengthened Louisbourg the English in turn fortified the town of Halifax in Nova Scotia. Nova Scotia was the source of many quarrels. Since its boundaries had never been exactly determined, each side made large claims against the other. In 1755 the government in London took the drastic step of collecting the French colonists of Nova Scotia and shipping them to various points along the Atlantic seaboard to the south.

During the years 1753 and 1754 the French pushed into the Ohio Valley. Meanwhile in the English colonies a number of companies had been formed to settle the Ohio region and to trade with the Indians. In 1754 Governor Dinwiddie of Virginia sent young Colonel Washington to expel the French from the vicinity of Fort Duquesne, but Washington was driven back by a superior force. His expedition, which resulted in some bloodshed, may be said to have begun the war for North America.

Although England and France were still at peace in Europe, both countries dispatched small armies to America in 1755. The English were commanded by General Braddock, who was instructed to raise additional troops in the colonies, to capture Fort Duquesne, and to move against the French forts along the southern shores of the Great Lakes. Obtaining a few colonial troops, he marched through the wilderness to Fort Duquesne, where his expedition was destroyed by an ambush of French and Indians. At about the same time a body of New Englanders was repulsed near Lake George. Meanwhile a French army set sail for Canada. The English Admiral Boscawen, sent to intercept it at sea, captured two French frigates and thus committed an act of war. The other French ships reached Quebec in safety. For the moment Canada was impregnable.

The year 1756 was also a time of disaster. The western frontier of the American colonies was swept by Indian raids. The French captured Oswego on the southern shore of Lake Ontario. In England there was fear of a French invasion. This threat soon faded, but the French sent an expedition from Toulon against the British naval base on the island of Minorca. Admiral Byng, the British commander, dispatched with an inadequate fleet to defend the island, fought an indecisive action, and then, believing that Minorca could not be held, sailed away and left it to its fate. An outcry arose against him in England, to which Newcastle weakly submitted. Byng was tried by court-martial and shot on the deck of his flagship.

Meanwhile, Newcastle, in attempting to build a European coalition against France, discovered that the Dutch would not be drawn into new entanglements and that Maria Theresa, though eager for revenge on Prussia, had no interest in fighting France. Newcastle's proposed coalition dwindled into a series of agreements with German states and with Russia, all backed by English subsidies. The arrangement with Russia produced an unexpected result. It so alarmed Frederick of Prussia that early in 1756 he concluded a treaty with England by which each country guaranteed the dominions of the other and promised to resist the entry of foreign armies into Germany. This treaty in turn induced the French to make an alliance with Austria, much to the satisfaction of Maria Theresa and her minister Kaunitz. Thus the alliances of the War of the Austrian Succession were reversed: England was now allied with Prussia; France with Austria. But the two great enmities of Europe—Austria against Prussia and England against France—remained as before.

The American colonies during the Seven Years' War and the American Revolution.

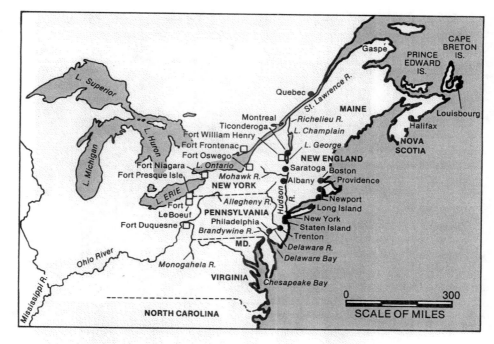

Ministerial Changes

Newcastle's fumbling policy naturally brought sharp criticism in the House of Commons, especially from Pitt and Henry Fox. As early as December 1754 Newcastle silenced Fox by bringing him into the Cabinet and by giving him the office of secretary a year later. But Pitt became more outspoken and was joined by other leaders. He refused to enter Newcastle's Cabinet when a place was offered to him. Thereupon Fox resigned; Newcastle, admitting defeat, also resigned. A long period of confused negotiations followed, until finally in June 1757 Newcastle and Pitt formed a new ministry in which Newcastle as first lord of the Treasury managed the patronage of the government while Pitt as secretary obtained the power to manage the war effort as he desired. Pitt was now a national figure. In addition to the Court party of civil servants, placemen, and pensioners under Newcastle's control, Pitt secured the wide and spontaneous support of many independent members of the Commons, much as Winston Churchill was given almost universal backing in 1940.

Pitt's Character

Pitt's genius lay in his energy, his commanding personality, his gift for leadership, and his confidence in himself and in his country. He did not belong to the aristocracy but rose from a family of aggressive merchants. For years he had demanded an

attack upon the empires of France and Spain, but he was more interested in trade than in the acquisition of territory. To him Canada meant furs, fish, and naval stores; the West Indies, sugar; Africa, gum and slaves; India, cotton fabrics, indigo, and saltpeter. He worked in close harmony with the merchants of London, to whom he offered hopes of expanding commerce and increased wealth.

Pitt acquired a commanding position in the House of Commons. Tall, majestic, and dramatic, he had a fine voice and used effective gestures in speaking; he had great oratorical power. He spoke without notes in a rapid, easy, and conversational style; yet his speeches abounded in poetic conceptions and light touches of fancy and imagination. He gave a moral grandeur to the theme of empire, as though Britian's destiny spoke through him. One of his principal weapons was a blasting invective which frightened members into silence. He did not bother to build a party; his power extended beyond the Commons to the nation as a whole. His weaknesses, however, were glaring. There was much that was bombastic about him; he was petulant, intractable, and difficult in relationships; he exasperated colleagues with his haughty manners; and he had illusions of grandeur. Often ill, both physically and mentally, his fierce aggressiveness sprang in part from his sufferings.

The Progress of the War, 1756–1763

Pitt from the first took the people into his confidence. Telling them of difficulties and of failures as well as successes, and explaining clearly the sacrifices he expected them to make, he was able to call forth their patriotic cooperation. One of his early steps was to send away the Hessian and Hanoverian troops whom Newcastle had brought to England during the invasion scare of 1756. By strengthening the militia he gave the nation a means of self-defense and at the same time made it possible to send more of the regular army overseas. He recruited Highland regiments, though the Highlands had been in revolt in 1745. The American colonists were encouraged to raise troops and were made to believe that their interests would be safeguarded. Knowing that Americans resented the arrogance of British officers, Pitt reduced friction by placing colonial officers on an equality with regulars of the same rank. He constantly sought talent among the younger men in the armed forces, often advancing them over older officers who had proved incompetent. In planning colonial campaigns, which he did with great care, he obtained detailed information concerning geography and other local conditions. But once he had placed this information before his officers, he gave them freedom to manage operations as they judged best.

Pitt's strategy was to keep the French preoccupied in Europe while he destroyed their empire and captured their trade. For his purpose he supported Frederick the Great with generous subsidies. In the past he had denounced commitments and subsidies on the Continent because they had seemed to benefit Hanover rather than England. But the situation had now altered. England already was bound by treaty to come to Frederick's assistance; and Frederick, opposed not only by France but also by Austria and Russia, might well be overwhelmed, leaving the French at liberty to concentrate on the war with England. Pitt therefore organized an army of Hanoverians and Hessians, commanded by the duke of Cumberland, the king's son, to defend Hanover and to protect Frederick's western flank against the French. He also sent commando raids against the French coast. Some of them were costly failures, which brought sharp criticism at home, but they immobilized large bodies of French troops, disturbed the plans of the French command, and made it dissipate its forces.

Pitt had a firm grasp of the strategic importance of sea power. If the French fleets could be destroyed at sea or blockaded at Brest and Toulon, the link between France and her colonies would be severed and French forces overseas would wither for lack of supplies from home. Thus an English blockade of Brest and Toulon became an essential feature of the war. It achieved much more than keeping the French inactive. A blockaded fleet suffers a sharp decline in morale and efficiency, whereas the blockading squadron remains in a state of preparedness and keenness for battle. Pitt also employed the navy skillfully to cooperate with land forces in Canada and India and to meet the French in purely naval engagements.

For some time after taking office in June 1757 he had few successes. Late in 1757 the tide began to turn. Frederick defeated the French at Rossbach and the Austrians at Leuthen. Pitt reconstructed the Hanoverian army, stiffened it with British troops, and found a new commander in Prince Ferdinand of Brunswick. Successes continued in 1758. When two French fleets with reinforcements and supplies for the war in America were turned back, English strength in the colonies became much greater than that of France. Amherst and Wolfe, two of the younger officers selected by Pitt, finally captured the fortress of Louisbourg, thus opening the St. Lawrence to British penetration. It was Pitt's plan that, while the French were occupied at Louisbourg, an attack should be made on Quebec by a force moving up the Hudson and down the Richelieu rivers; but this army, led by the dilatory Abercromby, was stopped with considerable loss at Fort Ticonderoga on Lake Champlain. On the other hand, Colonel Bradstreet captured Forts Frontenac and Oswego, thus separating the St. Lawrence Valley from the Great Lakes; an expedition across Pennsylvania against Fort Duquesne ended in anticlimax, for the French, believing that they needed all their strength for the defense of Canada, had abandoned Duquesne and the whole of the Ohio Valley. In the same year a British force expelled the French from Emden in Germany; three raids did much damage on the French coast.

The next year, 1759, brought fresh triumphs. In Germany Frederick was hard-pressed and badly defeated at the Battle of Kunersdorf, but Prince Ferdinand's victory at Minden pushed back the French and probably saved Frederick from destruction. Meanwhile, an English expedition captured the French West Indian island of Guadeloupe. Pitt was now intent on the conquest of Canada, to be accomplished by a two-pronged attack. Amherst, who was to strike north by way of Lake Champlain and the Richelieu River, failed in his purpose, but Wolfe, instructed to ascend the St. Lawrence and to capture Quebec, was successful. Ably supported by Saunders, who brought a fleet up the St. Lawrence in spite of great dangers, Wolfe landed on the Île d'Orléans in the river below Quebec. For more than two months he feigned attacks from various points along the river, then finally discovered an ill-guarded path up the steep bank to the Heights of Abraham above. Both he and Montcalm, the French commander, fell in the engagement that followed, but the French were defeated; part of their army surrendered and the remainder withdrew to Montreal. Montreal, and with it the last French army in North America, surrendered in 1760.

Meanwhile, in 1759, France once more threatened England with invasion. But the French fleet at Toulon, escaping from that port in an attempt to reach Brest, was defeated at Lagos Bay off the coast of Portugal; in September the fleet at Brest, which came out to carry French troops to England, was crippled at Quiberon Bay by Admiral Hawke. The danger of invasion passed, and the French seemed beaten everywhere.

In March 1761 the French indicated their desire to treat for peace. The Cabinet agreed to negotiate, though at the same time Pitt continued hostilities, for he had plans to capture the rest of the French West Indies and he wished to be in a position to obtain concessions for Frederick of Prussia. The Cabinet rejected a number of French proposals, which tended to stiffen as time went on. Pitt then discovered that

France and Spain had concluded a secret treaty by which the latter agreed to enter the war. Convinced that England would soon be fighting Spain, he favored an immediate attack on her, but the Cabinet was against him. Newcastle, alarmed at the mounting cost of the war, did not wish to see it extended. England, he felt, had already captured many colonies and could not afford to fight for more. Lord Bute, whom the young King George III had brought into the Cabinet, was of much the same opinion. In October 1761, Pitt would no longer endure contradiction; he resigned in disagreement with his colleagues over policy.

As he had predicted, Spain entered the war in 1762, but speedily showed herself so devoid of strength that instead of helping France she lost her own possessions—Havana in Cuba and Manila in the Philippines.

Negotiations for peace were continued by Lord Bute. A curious mood had developed in England. If France were treated too harshly, it was thought, she would soon seek a war of revenge in which she would be supported by the rest of Europe. It might be wiser to return to her some portion of her former possessions. Such a policy left Pitt cold.

The Peace of Paris, 1763

The Peace of Paris was highly advantageous to England. Great Britain retained her conquests of Canada and Cape Breton Island; St. Vincent, Tobago, Dominica, and Grenada in the West Indies; and Senegal in West Africa. Minorca passed again into English hands. On the other hand, England restored to France the West Indian islands of Guadeloupe, Martinique, Marie Galante, and St. Lucia; the post of Gorée in Africa; and fishing rights in Newfoundland with two small islands, St. Pierre and Miquelon, on which the fish could be dried. In India the French were given back their towns, but these were not to be fortified; they could be occupied by British forces whenever the British so desired. Hence the French hope of hegemony in India was gone. England restored to Spain both Havana and Manila, but received all of Florida and a recognition of the right to cut logwood in Honduras. France then completed her departure from North America by ceding Louisiana to Spain in compensation for Spanish losses. In making peace England almost entirely ignored Frederick's interests.

These treaties marked the culmination of Britain's first colonial empire and the old mercantile system. Spain, Holland, France, and England had struggled to control the trade of the North Atlantic, and now England had emerged victorious. Yet Britain's fear of dangers for the future was well founded. Within twenty years she was to see her empire shattered and Europe combined against her.

The Seven Years' War in India

The Seven Years' War determined two points of supreme importance in India. The first was the obvious one that France was defeated and that the dominant European power in India was to be England. In addition, the English emerged from the war not

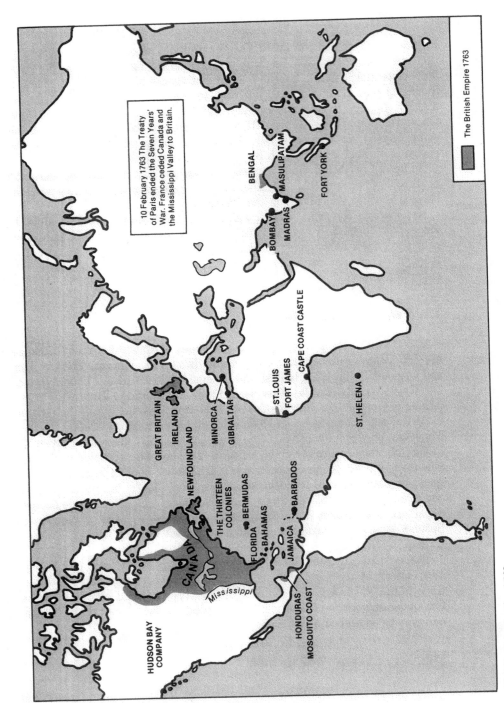

The following labels appear on the map:

HUDSON BAY COMPANY

CANADA

Mississippi

THE THIRTEEN COLONIES

NEWFOUNDLAND

GREAT BRITAIN

IRELAND

MINORCA

GIBRALTAR

BERMUDAS

FLORIDA

BAHAMAS

JAMAICA

BARBADOS

HONDURAS

MOSQUITO COAST

ST. HELENA

ST. LOUIS

FORT JAMES

CAPE COAST CASTLE

BOMBAY

MADRAS

MASULIPATAM

BENGAL

FORT YORK

10 February 1763 The Treaty of Paris ended the Seven Years' War. France ceded Canada and the Mississippi Valley to Britain.

The British Empire 1763

The British Empire 1763.

merely as merchants trading at various points along the coast but as the masters and governors of large and valuable Indian territories. This second development quickly altered the position of the East India Company in England and the role of its servants in the East.

In England the East India Company was a sound, respectable, and wealthy corporation, the largest trading organization in the kingdom, and of great importance as a part of the London money market. Its directors were men of influence in the city and were often members of the House of Commons. In close touch with the government, they were normally its allies in London politics. They possessed a certain amount of patronage both in England and in India. Of much greater importance was the fact that the Cabinet looked to the company, as it looked to the

India in the 18th century.

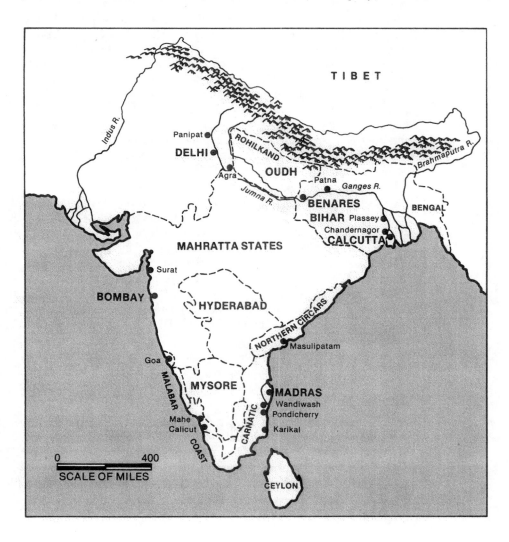

South Sea Company and to the Bank of England, for assistance in raising loans. When the government wished to borrow, it summoned representatives of the large public companies and other monied people of the city to a meeting at which amounts and terms were arranged. After a meeting of this kind in 1759–1760, when the large sum of £8,000,000 was to be borrowed, the government noted: "Mr. Burrell for the Bank of England £466,000, Mr. Bristow for the South Sea Company £330,000, Mr. Godfrey for the East India Company £200,000."[1] Thus the company was one of the corporations on which national credit depended. It issued its own instruments, known as India bonds. By 1732 the sale of its imports amounted to some £2,000,000 a year. The company, which rested on private enterprise, had as its directors sound and experienced administrators who were guided by long tradition and were well versed in foreign trade.

Meanwhile a fundamental change had taken place in the political structure of India. Since the middle of the sixteenth century the Mogul Empire, centering in the cities of Delhi and Agra, had given political stability to northern India and had imposed varying degrees of subjection on the southern principalities. For about a century and a half the Mogul Empire continued to be strong and vigorous. But Emperor Aurangzeb (1658–1707), the last of the great Moguls, brought disaster on his dominions. He has been compared with Louis XIV. His elaborate court was a heavy drain on his revenues. A bigoted Moslem, he reversed the more tolerant policy of earlier emperors and persecuted his Hindu subjects. Moreover, he was a warlike prince, who spent his strength in conquering southern India and in extending his frontier to the northwest.

Aurangzeb's campaigns brought him weakness rather than power, for in the later years of his reign he was faced with constant revolts. Weakened by extravagance, persecution, and war, the Mogul Empire rapidly deteriorated after Aurangzeb's death, when provincial governors became independent princes and robber chiefs, and military adventurers carved out dominions. An invader from Persia sacked Delhi in 1737; another from Afghanistan seized the Punjab and defeated the Marathas at Panipat in 1761. Thus India was reduced to political chaos.

This situation in India tempted the French to play a greater part in native politics. During the War of the Spanish Succession early in the century the two companies in India had arranged an unofficial truce and did not molest each other. But in the 1740s the French adopted a more warlike policy, which was largely the work of Francois Dupleix, governor first of Chandarnagar in Bengal (1730–1741) and then of Pondicherry (1741–1754). Ambitious and daring, though rather overconfident, he captured the English town of Madras in 1746. It was restored to the English by the Treaty of Aix-la-Chapelle.

The war had shown Dupleix the possibility of attracting the native princes and of forming alliances with them which could be directed against the English. His prestige among the chiefs was high, for they recognized that European troops, with their arms and discipline, were far superior to the unwieldy and poorly trained armies of India. Dupleix began to lend his troops to his allies and adherents among the native

---

[1]Quoted in Lucy S. Sutherland, *The East India Company in Eighteenth-Century Politics* (Oxford: Clarendon Press, 1952), p. 26.

rulers. The English followed a similar policy, giving military support to chieftains who were fighting the allies of the French. Thus, although England and France were at peace in Europe, their two companies were at war in India, not as principals but as allies of rival native princes. There arose a long series of intrigues and skirmishes, known as the War of the Carnatic. The English gradually gained the upper hand. In 1754 the French company recalled Dupleix, his plans collapsed, and the English candidates were successful.

When the Seven Years' War broke out in Europe hostilities began once more in India. The French sent out the Comte de Lally, a soldier of Irish extraction, who arrived in India in 1758. He at once laid siege to Madras, but he had to withdraw in 1759 at the arrival of a British fleet. In 1760 he was defeated at the Battle of Wandiwash and was besieged in Pondicherry, which surrendered in the year following. This ended the Seven Years' War in India.

It was in Bengal that the English first became master of large Indian territories; this came about because they clashed with the native ruler. Bengal, the wealthiest portion of India, was conquered with surprising ease. Its people were peaceful merchants, artisans, and peasants; the province was easily accessible from the sea through the many mouths of the Ganges. Moreover, it was divided against itself. Its rulers for many years had been foreigners, nominally officials of the Mogul Empire but in fact independent princes. The Nabob, Ali Vardi Khan, who ruled from 1741 to 1756, was an Afghan, a shrewd and able man who governed justly though severely. His rule was resented by the Hindu merchants, who looked upon him as a tyrant and a Muslim foreigner. Hence the events then about to take place in Bengal were in part a revolution of the Hindus against a foreign dynasty.

Ali Vardi Khan died in 1756 and was succeeded by Siraj-ud-daula, a weak, vicious, and headstrong young man who quarreled with the English at once. They had been forbidden to fortify Calcutta but, fearing the French, had disobeyed and strengthened the town. The English had also abused their trading privileges. Suddenly in the summer of 1756 Siraj-ud-daula marched on them with an army of fifty thousand men. The English, apparently taken by surprise, were overwhelmed in a few days. Calcutta and some upcountry agencies fell into the Nabob's hands, and for the moment the English were driven from Bengal.[2]

In Madras it was decided to send an army to Bengal, though there were fears of a French attack in the south. The command was given to Robert Clive, who sailed from Madras with about 2500 men. In January 1757 he recaptured Calcutta, fought an inconclusive action with the Nabob, and obtained a treaty restoring their former privileges to the English. Because he was in a difficult position he joined a conspiracy of discontented nobles to overthrow Siraj-ud-daula by a palace revolution and to set up the Nabob's relative Mir Jafar. Having made his bargain with Mir Jafar, Clive quarreled openly with Siraj-ud-daula, advanced against him with a small army of three thousand men, and on 23 June 1757, defeated him at the Battle of Plassey. It was a rout rather than a battle. Siraj-ud-daula's huge army fled in disorder, he himself was hunted down and slain, and Mir Jafar, who had held aloof until he saw which side

[2]The incident of the Black Hole of Calcutta occurred at this time when a number of English prisoners, placed in a small guard room, suffocated during a hot tropical night.

would be victorious, was hailed as the new Nabob. Mir Jafar was a mere puppet of the English, who were the true masters of the province. This achievement was the direct result of Clive's boldness, energy, and skill.

It cannot be denied, however, that Clive's rapacity menaced the permanence of his work. His agreement with Mir Jafar, made in the name of the East India Company, provided for gifts to himself and to other English officers. Clive mentioned these gifts in the report he sent to England, but he gave no figures. His share alone amounted to £234,000; other Englishmen received from £50,000 to £80,000 each. Many years later, when Clive was questioned by the House of Commons, he answered that he could only wonder at his own moderation. Within the next few years a number of native rulers followed each other in Bengal, and every transfer of power was accompanied by large presents of money to British officials. Clive engendered a spirit of plunder that was not eradicated for a number of years.

C H R O N O L O G Y

Pelhams, Pitt, and French Wars

1740–48	War of the Austrian Succession
1745–46	The Forty-Five; Young Pretender defeated at Culloden
1746	Henry Pelham in power
1748	Peace of Aix-la-Chapelle
1754	Pelham dead; Newcastle prime minister
1756	Diplomatic Revolution; Seven Years' War begins
1757	Pitt-Newcastle coalition; Robert Clive victorious at Battle of Plassey
1759–60	English capture Quebec and Montreal
1762	Pitt and Newcastle resign
1763	Peace of Paris; England victorious in Canada and India

Society in the Eighteenth Century

SOCIAL CLASSES IN THE COUNTRY

The Nobles

Society in the eighteenth century was dominated by the nobles. They formed a small, privileged, and wealthy caste which tended to harden as the century advanced. Custom demanded that nobles and wealthy country gentlemen seek marriages for their daughters that would afford them the highest possible rank and social position; this close intermarriage among aristocrats built up enormous estates in the hands of a few families. Estates were held together by the creation of strict entails. Thus the English peers formed a tightly knit group of about 160 persons; their number increased in the reign of George III but was well below 200 at the end of the century. The nobility, though very difficult to enter and keenly aware of its unique position, was saved from complete rigidity by two factors: the younger sons of peers remained commoners who were willing to enter the professions or even engage in trade, though this became less frequent as the century advanced; and nobles were willing to marry the daughters of wealthy businessmen. A city heiress could find her way into the aristocracy more easily than could her brother. Two of the granddaughters of Sir Josiah Child, a great merchant and banker, became duchesses.

Some of the nobles were enormously wealthy. The duke of Newcastle owned estates in twelve counties and is said to have enjoyed a rent-roll approaching £40,000 a year. The duke of Bedford owned most of Bedfordshire as well as land in London. In almost every county there were one or two noble families with large and valuable estates. Land was not the only source of a nobleman's wealth. In an age of rapid economic growth, a rich man who could secure good advice found many opportunities for profitable investment. The duke of Chandos invested large sums in building projects; in clay, coal, copper, and alum mines; in land speculations in America; in the manufacture of glass, soap, and spirit; and in diamonds and silver. He illustrates another source of income, for he had become a wealthy man by holding the lucrative post of paymaster of the forces. It was said in 1726 that one-quarter of the nobility occupied some office at court or in the government. In addition to his income from land, a noble might derive wealth from office and from business enterprises.

These rural millionaires lived on a lavish scale. They built large country mansions, filled them with fine pictures, furniture, statuary, and beautifully bound books, and surrounded them with elaborate gardens. A few of these country palaces, such as Blenheim Palace and Castle Howard, both designed by Sir John Vanbrugh, were massive and grandiose.

A reaction set in against this pretentiousness; most country houses though imposing in design and classical in inspiration, often of the Palladian school of Italian Renaissance architecture, were smaller, quieter, and in better taste. The rooms in these houses were beautifully proportioned and handsomely decorated with oval and elliptical designs on the ceilings, lovely mantelpieces and sideboards, and small columns and fanlights in the doorways. The owner of a great house was much concerned about his grounds. Early in the century gardens were formal, with straight walks and with flower beds arranged in symmetrical patterns. Later it became the fashion to give gardens a look of natural and unkempt wildness. The result, however, was frequently an increased artificiality. Contrived waterfalls and planned wildernesses were far from what nature would have produced. Gothic ruins, built to lend an atmosphere of antiquity, were merely grotesque. The landscape gardener Lancelot Brown was fond of these novelties and was so extravagant in his ideas that some men ruined themselves in making over their grounds. When Brown was called upon for advice he would begin by saying, "I see great capability for improvement here." Hence his nickname "Capability Brown."

The country palace of a noble was more than a means of satisfying his desire for ostentatious display. The administrative center for his estates and for investments, it was a symbol of his power and influence. An eighteenth-century nobleman was honored not only because he was wealthy but because he was a leader of the landed interest, which was the greatest interest in the country. Wealth in land gave greater prestige than wealth in any other form. A noble was the great man of his locality who drove about the country in a coach and four, distributed local patronage, arranged local elections, and played a large part in local government. His influence extended to national politics, for which he was trained from childhood. He was a member of the House of Lords and sometimes a member of the Cabinet. Around him gathered a group of relatives, secretaries, lawyers, and hangers-on. Having placed some of these men in the Commons, he could bargain with the government to give them offices and sinecures in return for their support. The nobility also dominated high society; their London houses were centers of fashionable life. The artists of the age painted their portraits, the architects built their houses, the writers wrote to please them. "Perhaps no set of men and women since the world began enjoyed so many different sides of life, with so much zest, as the English upper class of this period. The literary, the sporting, the fashionable, and the political 'sets' were one and the same."

The Gentry

The country gentry, or the squires, varied greatly in wealth, culture, and influence. A few were rich enough to imitate the elegance and extravagance of the nobility. A few could afford to come to London for the season, send their sons on the grand tour, or arrange rich marriages for their daughters. But for the most part, the gentry who tried to maintain such standards were apt to end in ruin. It was the burden of debt that dragged men down: many ancient families first mortgaged and then sold their estates. The gentry were in a dilemma. If they tried to ape the nobles, they lived beyond their means; if they went their own way, ignoring the peerage, they themselves were apt to be ignored while other men turned to the nobles as more promising patrons. This accounts for the sullen Tory politics of the smaller gentry, as opposed to the Whiggism of the great lords.

If, on the other hand, a country gentleman was willing to live modestly, he could enjoy rustic comfort and even abundance. Such was the case of a certain Squire Hastings, a younger brother of the earl of Huntingdon. The squire's house stood in a

The anteroom in Syon House near London. A room of great magnificence designed by Robert Adam. (Copyright Country Life)

Interior of a house at Blanford, Dorset, mid-18th century. (Copyright Country Life)

large timbered park which supplied him with firewood and venison. Fishponds and rabbit warrens on the estate also provided the squire with food. His manor house contained a great hall in which hounds and spaniels dozed before the fire or nosed among the marrowbones that littered the floor. Cats slept in the armchairs. The squire dined in the hall among his dogs and cats; he would throw the dogs pieces of meat but kept a little stick beside his plate with which he would beat them down if they became too eager. The walls of the hall were hung with the skins of foxes and polecats, the deep window ledges contained bows and arrows, on one table might be seen a bowl of oysters, on another the Bible and Foxe's *Book of Martyrs*. Scattered about in various receptacles were tobacco pipes, pheasants' eggs, and dice and cards. The hall led into a chapel which was no longer used, but the pulpit, being out of reach of the dogs, was filled with cold venison, beef, and apple pie.

Squires of this homespun variety enjoyed a few luxuries, such as tea, or wine, or oysters, but otherwise their table was much the same as that of a prosperous tenant farmer. Such squires possessed coats of arms and could pride themselves on their gentle blood; they maintained sporting establishments of dogs and horses. But their journeys beyond their own counties were rare; and their normal associates were the well-to-do yeomen and tenant farmers and the local merchants and lawyers who were their neighbors. And yet, in an age of unquestioned class distinctions, the squire regarded himself as belonging to an entirely different social order from those associates with whom he did business.

The squire was apt to be a shrewd, successful, and hardheaded manager of his estates; acquisitive, masterful, with a gift for leadership; intent on his account books and on the careers of his sons and the marriages of his daughters; or involved in local government as a justice of the peace. His position as a justice gave him power, independence, and self-confidence. A single justice or two or three acting together in petty sessions could deal summarily with a large number of minor offenses and administrative matters. At quarter sessions he and other justices heard important cases. The justices sometimes supervised local manufactures; they bound boys as apprentices, they supervised the entire operation of the poor law; they levied rates for the repair of bridges and roads, they controlled the constables and licensed fairs and alehouses. Supervision of their activities by the central government was almost nil. They were the government of the county and desired no assistance from higher authorities.

The dominance of a squire over a village in which he owned much of the land was even more marked. The village lived very much to itself. The local tradesmen and artisans regarded the squire as their best customer; the tenant farmers knew they could not offend him. It was he and his wife who brought back new ideas and new fashions from London. If agricultural improvements were to be made it was the squire who led the way. Indeed, these improvements often made the laborer more dependent on him than ever as the principal employer in the village.

The squire was not without education or interest in intellectual things. The manor house often contained a library. The squire read history and law. He was interested in architecture, liked music, and perhaps knew a little about painting. He was normally content to educate his sons in the local grammar school, though some boys were sent to Eton, or Winchester, or the fashionable school at Harrow. The sons of the gentry were less likely to attend the universities than had been those in the seventeenth century. They went into politics, into the law, into the church, into the army, and often into trade. There was little education for the squire's daughters unless they were taught by tutors brought in for the sons of the family. Most girls learned from their mothers to manage the domestic side of the manor house. Marriage was still a matter of business to be arranged by the parents of young people.[1]

The Lower Classes

Below the nobility and the gentry the rural population may be divided roughly into yeomen who owned their land; tenant farmers, a few with large holdings but most of them with small; copyholders who held perpetual leases on a few strips in the open fields; and cottagers, or landless laborers, dependent on casual employment and on trivial rights in the common land of the village. These classes did not fare alike, but speaking generally they did not prosper. A great amount of poverty and distress existed among the rural poor. The yeomen, who had flourished during the Tudor and Stuart periods and who constituted a substantial and independent middle class, were

[1]See the first chapter in J. H. Plumb, *Sir Robert Walpole, The Making of a Statesman* (London: Cresset, 1960).

still prosperous at the beginning of the eighteenth century, but their fortunes declined in time. Although this was a time of great advance in scientific agriculture, the new techniques could be exploited only by the rich who farmed on a large scale and had the capital to improve their lands. The yeoman could not afford these improvements. The price of wheat and of other agricultural products was low in the early part of the century; yet the yeoman must pay his laborers and make up his taxes. He knew, however, that he could sell his holding at a good figure, for the big farmer always wanted land and the city merchant was eager to acquire a country estate. Thus the yeoman was tempted to sell. If he did so, he might perhaps become a land agent or manager on a large estate, or he might obtain a new farm as a tenant. But he was more likely to sink in the scale of rural life.

The tenant farmer, if he rented a farm of some size, and if he had an improving landlord, might benefit from the new techniques of agriculture, but most tenants and copyholders held only small farms. Where a few men paid a rent of £70 or £80 a year, many paid only £10 or even £5. These small farmers, trying to wrest a living from a section of the open fields, were poor and insecure. A contemporary wrote that they were really not as well off as their own laborers. It was a fortunate tenant who could afford a piece of fresh meat once a week; he must be content with bacon or hanged beef, "enough to try the stomach of an ostrich." He must sell his little pigs or small chickens, his eggs, his apples or his pears in order to find the money for his rent. "All the best of his butter and cheese he must sell, and feed himself and children and servants with skimmed cheese and skimmed milk and whey curds."

The small farmer was not as well off as the small shopkeeper or artisan in the town. But he was well above the large class of landless laborers who lived in a state of misery and degradation. These cottagers, as Sir Francis Bacon had written a century before, were "but house beggars." The cottage was a shack, built on the village waste or common, to which no land was attached. The cottager might own a few pigs or geese, he might be allowed to gather faggots from the village woodland, he might work casually for a neighboring farmer, but he was never far from destitution. He had a bad name for poaching, and he was almost certain to end his days as a pauper. If men of this type drifted to the towns to work in factories they might feel a loss of liberty but their lot was no worse than before. In fact, it was probably improved. The lives of the urban workers will be discussed later.

The end of the century was a bad time for all the lesser people in the countryside. The movement toward enclosure disrupted their lives, and the Napoleonic wars inflated prices, bringing misery and starvation to the agricultural poor. We will deal with this subject in a later chapter.

THE GROWTH OF LONDON

Most English cities still gave the impression of overgrown country towns; but London, as in the reign of Elizabeth, was unique. Its life was thoroughly urban and distinct from the rest of the kingdom. Even in the clothing of its people it differed

Covent Garden in the 18th century, from Gentlemen's Magazine, *April 1749.* *(Gentlemen's* Magazine, *April 1749, New York Public Library)*

from other places, so that the rustic visitor, gazing in wonder at its crowded thoroughfares, its street lamps, its fashionable shops and handsome buildings, could easily be spotted—and often as easily fleeced. The greatest port in the country, London acquired a large proportion of the kingdom's trade; it was the center of political life; of fashion and society, of arts and letters, and of drama and music. Its population of about 675,000 in 1700 did not grow greatly until the second half of the century, but in 1801, the date of the first census, population had reached almost 900,000 and ten years later was over one million.

In the eighteenth century London spread far beyond its ancient bounds.[2] The area of Southwark across the river was filling up rapidly, especially after Westminster Bridge was completed in 1750. But the most remarkable growth was toward the west. In earlier times wealthy men had occupied houses within the walls or along the Strand between the city and Westminster, but now the fashionable world was moving westward to escape the "fumes, steams, and stinks" of old London, the prevailing winds being from the west. Lincoln's Inn Fields, Bloomsbury Square, and Soho Square were fashionable in the reign of Queen Anne; under George I the eastern end of Piccadilly was built up, houses extended along the southern side of the Oxford Road; New Bond Street and Hanover Square were completed; and Cavendish Square was under construction. But open fields still existed in Mayfair east of Hyde Park and south of Westminster and Buckingham House. By the end of the century

[2]The growth of London in the eighteenth century may be studied by examining two maps at the back of G. M. Trevelyan, *English Social History,* pp. 592–595. The first of these maps shows London under George I, the second, during the Napoleonic wars.

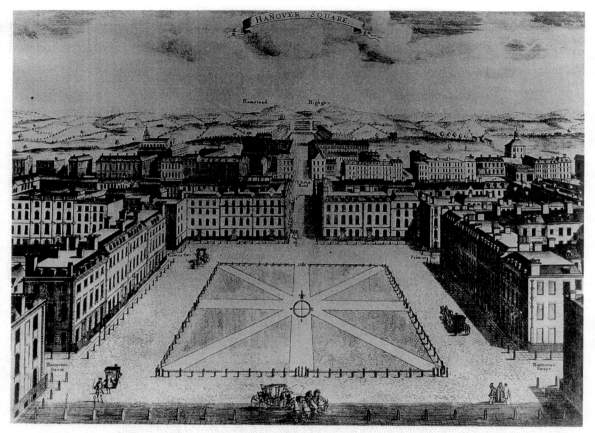

Hanover Square, early 18th century. Note the open country in the background. (Historical Pictures Service, Chicago)

Mayfair was filled with houses and many new squares—Manchester, Portman, Grosvenor, and Berkeley—had been built. These squares consisted of handsome houses, three or four stories high, built in a solid row around an open square or oval. Most of them were erected as speculative ventures. Once a fashionable square was built, it was shortly surrounded by small streets and alleys until housing covered an extensive area.

THE WORLD OF FASHION

The London season began in October and lasted until May. Fashionable life no longer centered in the royal court. Whitehall Palace, which had burned down in 1698, was not rebuilt; King William III and Queen Anne lived very quietly; the domestic life of the first two Georges was forbidding; George III, setting his face against the vices of the day, found amusement in simple domestic festivities which did not attract society. Fashionable life moved to the houses of the nobility, to public places of amusement, to clubs and gambling houses, and to the theater and opera.

The Mall above St. James's Park was a fashionable promenade where ladies and gentlemen sauntered up and down or were carried in sedan chairs, while a few rode grandly in a coach drawn by six horses. Ranelagh and Vauxhall Gardens were famous resorts. The first, in Chelsea, consisted of gardens and a large pavilion or rotunda, where visitors could walk or dine at side tables to the music of an orchestra. Vauxhall, across the river south of Lambeth, was more elaborate. Extensive gardens were laid out with walks and with replica of Greek temples and statuary, trees were festooned with colored lights, suppers were served in shaded alcoves, a central promenade called the Grove contained a pavilion or concert hall.

Later in the century the aristocracy was drawn away to other places of amusement. In the 1760s a certain Madame Cornelys, a foreign singer, presided over subscription balls, concerts, and masquerades at her "Society" in Soho Square. At clubs such as White's and Boodle's, there was nightly play for high stakes. Men sat at the card tables for twenty-four hours at a stretch. Thousands of pounds changed

The Mall, 1751, from a contemporary engraving by H. Roberts. St. James Palace is seen on the left and the west towers of Westminster Abbey on the extreme right. (Historical Pictures Service, Chicago)

The Inside View of the Rotunda in Renelagh Gardens   Vüe de la Compagnie à Déjeuner dans la Rotonde au
with the Company at Breakfast.   Milieux des Jardins de Renelagh.

The interior of the Rotunda at Ranelagh Gardens. (British Museum)

hands at a single sitting, estates were won and lost, and foolish young men encumbered their lands with debt. Ladies played as recklessly as men, though not at clubs but in their own drawing rooms. The passion for gambling was seen also in wagers of all kinds, often on the most trivial matters and on those governed wholly by chance.

There was a great deal of drinking. The Methuen Treaty with Portugal in 1703 allowed port wine to be brought into England at a low duty, and port superseded French claret as the drink of the upper classes. Port, a heady wine, was consumed in great quantities. Many of the statesmen of the eighteenth century—even such an austere person as the younger Pitt—were heavy drinkers. George III once said to Lord Chancellor Northington, "My lord, they tell me that you love a glass of wine." "Those who have informed your Majesty have done me great injustice," the lord chancellor replied. "They should have said a bottle." Some drivers of hackney coaches roamed about the West End of London late at night to pick up drunken gentlemen. If these gentlemen could supply their addresses, they were taken home. If not, they were deposited at certain inns till morning, when the drivers reappeared and took them to their houses. The oaths and vulgarities of intoxicated persons, their

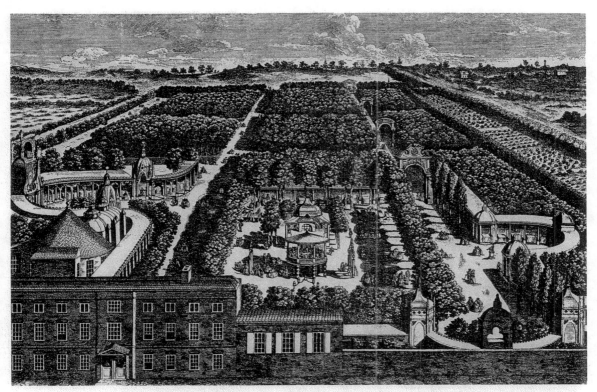

Plan of Vauxhall Gardens about 1751, from a contemporary drawing by Samuel Wale. (Historical Pictures Service, Chicago)

quarrels and disorderly conduct, and the frenzied excitement of the gaming table made society coarse and brutal despite its courtly manners. Drinking affected the health of the upper classes, enlarging their girths and shortening their lives. Suffering from gout and other disorders associated with drinking, they became old and decrepit before reaching middle age.

One cure for gout, it was thought, was to visit a spa or mineral spring and drink the waters or bathe in them. Inland spas were very popular in the eighteenth century. Charles II had patronized Epsom and Tunbridge Wells; these and similar places were visited both by high society and by the middle classes. Bath was the most interesting. It owed its fame to Richard Nash, a charming adventurer with genuine social gifts. A professional gambler, he first came to Bath in 1705 to fleece the populace at cards. When he saw the possibility of making Bath a pleasure city he persuaded the town council to build a new pump room, an assembly room, and a theater; he engaged a good orchestra, raised money to improve the road from London, and forced landlords to lower their prices and chairmen to improve their manners.

As master of ceremonies, Nash imposed a code of dress, manners, and etiquette.

A daily program was devised for visitors. The early hours of the day were spent at the baths, which were often unsanitary, accessed through unpleasant passages, and contained hot and steamy dressing rooms. Ladies and gentlemen, dressed in elaborate bathing costumes, walked about solemnly in the baths, the water coming to their waists. Ladies were provided with little floating trays on which to carry their cosmetics. After bathing they drank the waters in the pump room to the accompaniment of music. Then came breakfast, then the morning service in Bath Abbey, then riding or driving until dinner at three in the afternoon. After dinner the guests promenaded in their fine clothes till teatime and in the evening played cards, attended the theater, or danced in the assembly room. Nash did much to improve the manners of the middle classes and even those of the aristocracy.

The vogue for sea bathing also accounted for the popularity of Weymouth, Scarborough, and Harrogate. The novelist Fanny Burney tells how she bathed at Brighton in late November at six o'clock in the morning "by the pale blink of the moon" and found the water quite cold. "We then returned home and dressed by candle light."

ARTS AND LETTERS

Until the end of the eighteenth century there were few writers and artists and almost all of these were in London; they knew each other well from associations in coffeehouses and taverns. It was a great age for clubs, which were formed by men with common interests or professions who agreed to dine together each week or fortnight at a certain tavern or coffeehouse. A club might have a guiding spirit, perhaps a literary figure, whose praise or condemnation of new books reached far beyond the club's membership and might make or unmake reputations. Joseph Addison, the writer of charming essays, was a kind of literary dictator for the first two decades of the century. Surrounded by his friends at Button's Coffee House in Russell Street, he loved to talk about literature, from Virgil to the latest book in the London bookstalls. At his death in 1719 the role of literary oracle passed to Alexander Pope. He was unexcelled in the type of verse he employed— the heroic couplet—and brought it to a high state of perfection. But he spoke to the mind rather than to the heart, and a gradual revolt took place against his formal and unsentimental writing, a revolt which paved the way for the romantic movement at the end of the century. Horace Walpole, famous for his letters and memoirs, bought a small estate called Strawberry Hill. He converted the house into a strange combination of cottage and Gothic castle and filled it with pictures, statues, miniatures, and all sorts of curios, chiefly of Italian origin. Here he entertained his friends with spicy anecdotes of the great world of London. He was a connoisseur and scandalmonger, not a great writer, but he has described most vividly the eighteenth-century social scene.

The literary world of the middle of the century was dominated by the bulky figure of Dr. Samuel Johnson, who came to London from Lichfield in 1737 to earn a precarious living by his pen. The appearance of his *Dictionary* in 1755 established his

Dr. Samuel Johnson, by Sir Joshua Reynolds. (National Portrait Gallery, London)

reputation, and he gradually won a dominant position in English letters. His influence was exercised in part through the Literary Club founded in 1763 or 1764. This club included at one time or another an astonishing number of well-known men: Dr. Johnson, his biographer James Boswell, the painter Sir Joshua Reynolds, the orator Edmund Burke, the economist Adam Smith, the liberal statesman Charles James Fox, the playwright Richard Brinsley Sheridan, and such writers as Oliver Goldsmith, Edward Gibbon, and Sir Walter Scott. In the discussions of the Literary Club, Johnson's ponderous word was law; he was highly venerated by the reading public, and newcomers to the literary world sought his approval. He was a gifted conversationalist but as a writer he was more the critic than the creative artist. A man of many prejudices and eccentricities, he did not welcome new trends in literature. Yet his literary judgments usually were sound, and his standards of writing and conduct were high.

Perhaps the most important development in literature at the time was the rise of the novel. It owned much to that gifted writer Daniel Defoe, whose narratives were vivid, realistic, and entirely natural. The novels of Samuel Richardson, on the other hand, almost discarded adventure. They were written in the form of letters, emphasized the portrayal and analysis of character, and made love and society their central themes. Henry Fielding, whose humor was broad, reverted to Defoe's novel of incident and adventure; his novels, *Joseph Andrews, Tom Jones,* and *Amelia,* pictured life in England: the innkeepers, the justices of the peace, the clergymen, the people of fashion, the footmen, and the ladies' maids. Fielding, who was cheerful and optimistic, hated shams and selfishness; he was a social reformer. Tobias Smollett, once a ship's surgeon, wrote stories of the sea. He could depict character with great skill, but he was coarse and his satire was savage. A fantastic clergyman, Laurence Sterne, wrote novels, as he said, "on the design of shocking people and amusing myself." Fanny Burney was the attractive and sprightly daughter of a famous music teacher, Charles Burney. Her first and best novel, *Evelina,* portrayed the thoughts and feelings of a young girl as she first entered London society. Miss Burney accepted a position as second keeper of the robes to Queen Charlotte, the wife of George III.

To judge from the novels of the time, men in the eighteenth century liked their women to be stupid. Heroines were frail and insipid; they fainted easily and were preyed upon by the opposite sex. Yet there were many brilliant women in the eighteenth century. Lady Mary Wortley Montagu was a famous writer of letters. The daughter of a duke, she eloped on the night before her marriage rather than accept the person whom her father had selected. Another lady of the same name, Mrs. Elizabeth Montagu, created a *salon* in emulation of the *salons* of Paris. Her conversational powers, her essay on Shakespeare, and her lavish hospitality enabled her to attract to her assemblies politicians, writers, and artists—no small accomplishment in a city of masculine clubs and coffeehouses. Such ladies who combined a high position in society with an interest in letters were known as the Bluestockings.

Portrait painting had a long tradition in England, but the artists had been largely foreign. Now there arose a school of English portrait painters. Sir Joshua Reynolds settled in London in 1752, was at once successful, and remained for almost forty years a kind of national celebrity. A master of color, he was able to give each portrait a character of its own, and thus avoid the pitfall of creating a type. His name is connected with the establishment in 1768 of the Royal Academy, where paintings were exhibited for sale. Yet the very success of the academy made portrait painting somewhat stereotyped and the art was soon on its way to vulgarization. Thomas Gainsborough was both a portrait and a landscape painter. A man of real genius, he did not have Reynolds' social ambitions and was quite happy in the obscurity of his early life in Ipswich. From there he went to Bath and finally to London in 1774. The third member of this trio was George Romney, who painted portraits of much freshness and charm.

Every age in art contains its rebels. Early in the century, William Hogarth, famous as an engraver though also a fine painter, revolted from the Italian influence on English art and struck a purely native note. In a well-known series of engravings he depicted with great realism, humor, and detail the seamy side of English life and the evils of hard living. William Blake was an entirely different kind of artist, a mystic, a poet, and a painter who introduced a strange, ethereal otherworldliness into his paintings. He detested Reynolds and the comfortable, materialistic, and compromising approach to art which Reynolds represented.

The London stage was at a low ebb during the first half of the century. Plays were coarse and indecent, with illicit love their invariable theme; ladies, if they came to the theater at all, came wearing masks until the practice was forbidden in 1704. Audiences were vulgar and rowdy. An apron stage extended from the principal stage into the pit, thus bringing the performers close to the audience; some patrons, by paying an extra charge, were allowed to sit on the stage itself. These evils were reformed only slowly. Protests against the immorality of the stage grew so strong that dramatists attempted to make their plays seem moral by introducing banal lines in praise of virtue. Inevitably such plays were likely to be dull. Some managers turned from the drama to variety shows in which elaborate scenery, dancing, costumes, gods, goddesses, shepherdesses, and milkmaids at least made a pretty picture. The best feature of this development was the use of pantomime by the manager John Rich.

During the second half of the century the theater improved. Oliver Goldsmith and Richard Sheridan wrote excellent comedies which brought liveliness and wit to the stage without being indelicate. The greatest actor of the age was David Garrick, who took London by storm in 1741 with his performance of *Richard III*. He helped to bring about a revival of Shakespeare, though the plays often were mutilated. Even Garrick made unfortunate changes to please the supposed taste of his audiences. As an actor he was natural and realistic, skilled in conveying emotion through facial expression. He was also a person of refinement and intellect. Mrs. Siddons (Sarah Kemble) was an excellent tragedienne, famous as Lady Macbeth and as Queen Catherine in *Henry VIII*. Peg Woffington was popular not only for her versatile acting but for her somewhat boisterous good humor. She and Mrs. Siddons, both handsome women, were favorites of the portrait painters.

Two types of opera were to be found in eighteenth-century England. One was light opera, of which John Gay's *Beggar's Opera,* first produced in 1728, with its songs, comedy, and political allusions, proved to be the most successful. The second type was Italian opera, of rather poor quality and written largely to give the singers an opportunity to display their talents. In 1710 G. F. Handel arrived in England. Although a German he was well versed in Italian music and wrote as well as produced many Italian operas, which, however, were not much better than the others. Later he turned to the writing of oratorios, for which he became famous. Although his reputation was—and is—very great, as a foreigner he may have hindered the development of a native school of composers.

LONDON: THE EAST END

A handful of merchants, bankers, and capitalists in the city were extremely rich and lived on a scale as lavish as that of the nobility. "Some merchants are certainly far wealthier than many sovereign princes of Germany and Italy," wrote a foreign observer; "they live in great state, their houses are richly furnished, their tables spread with delicacies." Sir John Barnard, William Beckford, and Sir Francis Baring, the founder of a famous banking house, were men of this kind, national figures who were consulted by the government in matters of commerce and finance. Below them were hundreds of lesser merchants of varying degrees of prosperity who formed an upper middle class in the economic scale. They normally lived near their shops or countinghouses, though some were moving into the new parts of London. Others, as in former times, lived over their places of business, with the first floor devoted to trade or manufacturing, the second to the living quarters of the family, and the garret and cellar to servants and apprentices.

Below these groups were the working people, the mass of the London population. Distinctions and gradations among classes were sharply drawn, and one must differentiate between the artisan and the unskilled laborer, between the master and his apprentices, between the man who occupied a house and the mere lodger. An amusing contemporary list of trades descended from the "genteel" through the "dirty genteel," "the genteelish," the "ordinary," the "mean," to the "mean, nasty and stinking." Most manufacturing was done under the domestic system; boys and young men were apprenticed, though there was a great difference between the apprentice of a great London company, who might be the son of a gentleman and who looked forward to a partnership in a prosperous business, and the orphan apprenticed by the parish to a chimney sweep.

The principal distinction was between the artisan who had served an apprenticeship and the unskilled laborer whose physical strength was all he had to offer. Many artisans produced beautiful and intricate articles. Of this class were the makers of fine furniture, of watches, clocks, and nautical instruments; locksmiths and workers in metal; the painter of signs (to hang over shops); and interior decorators of all kinds. Artisans working at home produced goods on order from a master of the trade. Some artisans had shops and sold directly to the public, thus merging with the class of storekeepers. But many shopkeepers (chandlers, sellers of milk, vegetables, tripe, and gin) operated on so small a scale, perhaps in a cellar, that they must be classed as unskilled workers. The artisan, if he possessed industry and thrift, could live well above the subsistence level, though a depression in trade could easily reduce him to want.

The numbers of unskilled workers were enormous; porters, chairmen, coal heavers, dock workers, drivers of carts and drivers of cattle, watermen, scavengers, butchers and slaughterers, sailors, fishermen, and hundreds of domestic servants of all kinds. Some trades, such as weaving and silk throwing, required skill but were so badly organized that they offered little pay and only irregular employment. Lower still were hawkers selling milk, fish, vegetables, matches, and so on, who merged with the class of beggars. And below them all was a large and seething underclass without hope, who terrified those with whom they were in contact. It was easy for the poor to slip into this class, for they were never much above the subsistence level, and a slight depression could reduce them to want. Late in the century the public was shocked at the discovery of a number of women who had crept into an abandoned house and had there starved to death.

The London poor lived under dreadful conditions of overcrowding in old tumble-down tenements which had either seen better days or had been built in a cheap and shoddy way. In the sixteenth and seventeenth centuries the government had prohibited the building of new houses in the hope of keeping down the population. The results had been unfortunate. People could not build new houses; hence they patched up crumbling old ones, adding rooms in garrets and cellars and in projections fastened to the house by iron bars. Tenements sometimes collapsed through sheer dilapidation. In the eighteenth century new houses—or more often shacks—were built very cheaply in courts and alleys or on bits of wasteland until areas were covered completely with a labyrinth of dwellings to which access could be obtained only through dark and noisome passages or even through other houses. When the building was on land leased only for a short term of years, the builder, by a nice calculation, aimed at constructing houses that would be worthless about the time the lease expired.

In many of these tenements an entire family occupied a single room, which often contained nothing but a bed, a fireplace, and a few broken cooking utensils. Such rooms lacked running water and all sanitary arrangements. Filth was thrown out of the window or into a vault or cesspool at the back of the house, or allowed to accumulate in piles in open courts and alleys. In the early part of the century sewers were open ditches through which water moved sluggishly toward the Thames. The very poorest families lived in garrets under leaking roofs or in wet cellars where ventilation was impossible and even the light was dim. In such rooms many a man not only kept his family but carried on his trade, bringing the dirt and confusion of manufacture into what served him for a home. The poorest buildings were lodging-houses in which space, perhaps a part of a bed, was let for one night at a time.

Temptations of Low London Life

The poor in London were surrounded by temptations and dangers, of which the greatest was heavy drinking. Social life centered in the tavern or alehouse. A workingman, living with his family in one room, had no place to go in the evening or during weekends except to the nearest tavern. Many things combined to tempt him to drink. There was the yearning for excitement after long hours at monotonous labor. The week's wages sometimes were paid in a tavern on a Saturday night, and the money was withheld until a late hour so that drinking could go on in anticipation. Taverns were employment agencies, headquarters for benefit societies and for clubs of workingmen, places where young men met young women in what were known as cock and hen clubs to drink and sing songs.

Conditions were worse between 1720 and 1750 when the poor learned to drink gin instead of beer or ale. The abundance and cheapness of grain in the early eighteenth century led to the distilling of spirits, which increased twentyfold between 1688 and 1750. Gin shops multiplied in the poorer parts of London, for gin could be sold without a license, and every little chandler offered it for sale. A few large distillers manufactured the raw gin, but lesser people mixed it with fruit juices and distilled it again. The beverage thus produced was fiery, adulterated, poisonous, and highly intoxicating. It was primarily a drink for the poor: it was cheap, it warmed the body, and it quickly brought forgetfulness of want and misery. But it also brought a decline in the birth rate and an increase in the death rate, and contributed to the degeneration of the poor and the alarming increase in the number of criminals. Gradually the government awoke to the harm that gin was doing; an act of 1751 prohibited distillers from selling it retail, required all retailers to have a license, and sharply increased the tax on spirits. Thereafter gin drinking gradually declined.

Other hazards endangered the poor in London: no protection against unemployment existed, trades were badly organized, and the system of apprenticeship produced many evils. When the parents of a boy apprenticed him to the master of a trade, they paid the master a fee for which he agreed to teach his trade to the apprentice and to feed and clothe him for seven years. During the first part of an apprentice's time he was of little use to the master; but in the last years both were keenly aware of the valuable work done without any pay. Such a relationship could easily degenerate into neglect, brutality, and exploitation by the master and dishonesty and hatred on the part of the apprentice.

The debtors' prison was a constant menace. A man could be arrested for a small debt; once in prison he was unable to earn money either to satisfy his creditors or to support his family. Another evil arose from the tax laws concerning marriage. Some taverns and tenements around the Fleet and other prisons began a base traffic in performing the marriage ceremony for all who applied. Inside the shop or tavern a clergyman who had fallen into evil ways was ready to marry any couple for a small fee. This abuse was ended by Lord Hardwick's Marriage Act of 1753, which provided that marriages were illegal unless they were performed in a parish church of the Church of England after the banns had been properly asked on three successive Sundays. Though a grievance to nonconformists, the act was highly beneficial.

During the first half of the century a great amount of crime existed in London. Purses, hats, and wigs were snatched from people in the streets; robberies were accompanied by violence in which the victims were beaten or even killed. A turn for the better took place in 1749, when Henry Fielding, the lawyer and novelist, was appointed principal magistrate for Westminster and established a police station in Bow Street. He and his remarkable brother, Sir John Fielding, who was blind from birth, began an improved police force known as the Bow Street Runners. London was a difficult place in which to catch criminals. The mazes of little lanes and alleys and the many doors and subdivisions in old houses gave the criminal a good chance to escape. Parliament made one offense after another punishable by death until the law was so cruel that juries would not convict for petty crimes which carried the death penalty. The law was capricious in its operation, sometimes too lenient and sometimes harshly enforced. One of the pastimes of the mob was to watch public executions at Tyburn (where those who met death with swaggering nonchalance were applauded by the rabble).

These evil conditions began to be reformed about the middle of the century. In 1829, a Londoner could write: "The people are better dressed, better fed, cleanlier, better educated, in every class respectively, much more frugal, and much happier. Money which would have been spent at the tavern, the brothel, the tea garden, the skittle-ground, the bull-bait, and in numerous other low-lived and degrading pursuits, is now expended in comfort and conveniences, or saved for some useful purpose." A good many causes combined to produce this improvement. About the middle of the century, as we have seen, Fleet marriages became illegal, the traffic in gin came under some control, and the Fielding brothers introduced an improved police force, though a thorough reform of the London police did not come until the 1820s. More fundamental causes of improved conditions were the agrarian and industrial revolutions that took place in the eighteenth century and that made more food and better clothing available to the lower classes.

Moreover, London never became a factory city of the type that was growing in the north. It grew less industrial as the century advanced. Some industries migrated in search of cheaper fuel and cheaper labor; instead of being a manufacturing center, London grew as a commercial and financial center. The port of London developed tremendously, as did banking and the stock exchange. The number of schools, and hospitals, and charitable institutions multiplied. As a result, the tremendous number of unskilled laborers gradually declined, their place taken by a growing population of clerks, officials, caretakers, contractors, stockbrokers, merchants, administrators, doctors, and schoolmasters.

A gradual improvement occurred in the government of the city. Early in the century, dishonest justices of the peace had regarded the offenses and quarrels of the poor as so many opportunities to collect small fees. But the justice of the peace was becoming a police magistrate at a fixed salary. Keenly aware of the evils around him, he was sometimes a social reformer. Henry Fielding tried to inform the public of the condition of the London poor. His brother, Sir John, called attention to the number of deserted boys and girls from whom the criminals were recruited. Working with the philanthropist Jonas Hanway, he established in 1756 the Marine Society to send boys to sea, not as stray waifs but on a respectable basis. Two years later he helped to found an orphanage for deserted girls.

Some of the worst conditions were partially corrected when parish officials became more active in covering open drains and sewers, in lighting and paving the streets, and in providing more running water. It is probable that the London poor also benefited, at least to some extent, from the advance of medicine in the eighteenth century. The number of hospitals, dispensaries, and clinics and the number of physicians and surgeons increased. Two Scottish doctors, John and William Hunter, placed surgery on more scientific foundations; Sir John Pringle improved the hygiene of the army; William Smellie revolutionized the art of midwifery. Partly owing to his work, a number of lying-in hospitals were opened in London during the second half of the century; charities were developed to assist women in their homes during childbirth.

The segregation of patients with infectious diseases into separate wards and hospitals was only beginning in the eighteenth century, so that a patient might go to a hospital for one ailment and soon contract another. The training of nurses was still primitive. Although surgery might be skillful, it was surgery without anesthetics; hence a patient might die of shock; and because surgery was performed without antiseptic precautions, the patient might die from infection. The mortality rate in some of the lying-in hospitals was very high. And some practices, such as bleeding, could do great harm. Nevertheless, it is probably safe to assume that the lower classes in London received better medical attention in 1800 than they had received half a century earlier.

Certainly the lower classes profited from an increase in philanthropic work. Early in the century Captain Thomas Coram, a retired sailor, was horrified at the way in which unwanted babies were left in the streets to die. For seventeen years he labored to establish Foundling Hospital, which opened in 1745. A number of wealthy and prominent persons, including Handel and Hogarth, became interested in this project. George II presented the hospital with his portrait. The hospital admitted infants and small children and cared for them until they could be apprenticed to a trade. In the twentieth century the hospital was moved into the country; its former site is now a playground for children, appropriately named Coram's Fields. So many born in London poorhouses died there that a plan was devised to send them to be nursed in the country, where they lived and throve. Many men did philanthropic work: the Fielding brothers, Jonas Hanway, Thomas Coram, James Oglethorpe, and John Howard—the last two were especially interested in prison reform. Greater humanitarianism and greater wisdom in dispensing charity were paving the way for the reforms of the nineteenth century.

THE CHURCH AND METHODISM

During the eighteenth century the rural population attended the parish churches much as it had done in the past, and religious feelings were strong among the nonconformist bodies. But a good deal of skepticism existed among the upper classes, while thousands of the slum dwellers in the cities did not go to church at all.

A number of factors combined to weaken the spiritual leadership of the church in the first half of the eighteenth century. Like society as a whole, the church recoiled from the fanaticism of the century before. Regarding religious zeal with distaste, it taught restraint, sobriety, and common sense. It stressed the rational and reasonable aspects of Christianity, did not dwell on dogma, and played down miracles and the sacerdotal quality of the priesthood. The essence of its teaching was a cold, unemotional morality which left the heart untouched. Sermons were read like literary essays, logical and polished, but rather languid and quite devoid of inspiration.

The church had lost much of its thunder. Its two great themes before 1688 had been the wickedness of the nonconformists and the divinity of kings, dead issues in the eighteenth century. The Revolution had placed the church, as it had placed the Tory party, in an awkward dilemma. A few of the clergy had refused to swear allegiance to William and Mary and had forfeited their places in the church, but most churchmen had accepted positions under the new government. This was inevitable; yet it was a reproach to the church and clergymen were a bit ashamed of the part they were playing. William attempted to counteract this frame of mind by appointing Low-Church and liberal bishops who were sympathetic toward the new position of the monarchy. But the rank and file of the clergy remained sullenly Jacobite and Tory. It was not until the middle of the century that the church was thoroughly reconciled to the Hanoverian dynasty.

The growth of science weakened the church. The Christian had believed that God constantly intervened in the daily life of man, but this conception faded as science showed how the universe was controlled by natural laws. The church made no effort to combat scientific discoveries, for science was thought to prove that God governed the universe on rational and understandable principles. Yet in truth the progress of scientific thought tended to undermine the mystery of orthodox religion, diminish the authority of the church, and enthrone reason in its stead. Religion of a cold and rational kind led easily to deism and Unitarianism. The deist acknowledged the existence of God on the testimony of reason but rejected all revealed religion. He believed in God because he recognized that the universe must have had some creator or prime cause, but once the world had come into being, God receded into remoteness and uncertainty. The Unitarians, affirming the unipersonality of the Godhead, denied the divinity of Christ. In the eighteenth century many English Presbyterians became Unitarians.

The structure of the Church of England did not make matters easier. The higher clergy were drawn from the aristocratic classes. Bishops usually were selected from the heads of colleges in the universities, from royal chaplains, from tutors to great nobles, or from popular preachers in fashionable London churches. Worldly men with large incomes and with high positions in society, they lived in palaces and moved about the country in state. Having been appointed by the government they knew that they were expected to attend the House of Lords regularly and to vote with those who had selected them. The wonder is that eighteenth-century bishops were as learned, as conscientious, and as mindful of the church's welfare as they were.

The lower clergy, recruited from clerical families or from the middle classes, were almost always university men with some learning and culture. A few stayed in the universities all their lives. Most college fellowships required that their incumbents be in holy orders, but these men were scholars first and clerics only in a secondary way, and though they performed religious duties they did so in a somewhat perfunctory fashion. A second group of clergymen were chaplains in noble houses. They have been called the failures of the university world. They usually were easygoing men who liked hunting and country life. But since they had to retain the good will of their employer, they could not reprove his shortcomings with firmness. Their position must have been galling to persons of independence.

The parish clergy, far more numerous than the scholars or the private chaplains, obtained their churches through advowsons belonging to their colleges or to lay patrons. Having secured a living with a good income, a country parson in the eighteenth century could enjoy a pleasant and leisurely life. As improvements in agriculture increased the value of clerical livings, members of the gentry began to think it worthwhile to bestow churches on their younger sons or on their sons-in-law. The clergyman in such a parish would be a social equal of the squire and would keep the life of the parish on a plane of order and aristocratic dignity. The eighteenth-century parish priest usually attended to his spiritual duties and was kindly, sensible, and charitable in his relations with his parishioners, but he had no great spiritual earnestness and was not consumed with holy zeal.

Perhaps the greatest omission of the church in the eighteenth century was its disregard of the industrial poor. It was to these neglected souls that Methodism brought its message. John Wesley, one of the greatest men of the age, was born in 1703. His father, Samuel Wesley, was an Anglican clergyman, poetic, emotional, vivid, but a futile man in practical affairs. His mother, Susannah, was a woman of deep personal religion and of inflexible will, determined to implant her convictions in her children and to make them like herself. She taught them industry and prayer, and once a week they carefully examined the state of their souls. John Wesley inherited his mother's powerful intellect, imperious will, unflagging energy, and hard determination. For all his greatness he was a rigid, domineering man, hostile to intellectual and artistic things, and so uncompromising that he did not believe in play, even for children. Yet he also had his father's yearning for life and for love. It was to his marvelous organizing ability that the success of his movement was due. His brother Charles, the author of many famous hymns, was gentler and more poetic. The Wesleys were joined by George Whitefield, the popular preacher and revivalist.

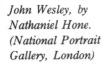

John Wesley, by Nathaniel Hone. (National Portrait Gallery, London)

In his youth John Wesley was a stern High-churchman. While at Oxford he formed a Holy Club of theological students who practiced such severe asceticism that one member died. Wesley went as a missionary to Georgia, where he failed in his attempt to impose High-Church observances on the rough colonists. Moreover, he fell in love and behaved very badly when the lady married someone else. Eventually he was hounded from the colony. On his return to England he was deeply influenced by a group of German Moravians whose personal religion and calm assurance impressed him. Then, in 1738, he experienced a conversion. "I felt my heart strangely warmed," he wrote. "I felt that I did trust in Christ, Christ alone for salvation; and an assurance was given me that He had taken *my* sins, even *mine*, and saved me from the law of sin and death."

It is important to understand what Wesley meant by conversion. Man, he believed, was in a state of sin and infamy, and in order to escape man must pass through a conversion in which he realized that Christ by his death upon the Cross had expiated human sins and had made salvation possible. This revelation brought a sense of pardon for past sin, a conviction that sin could be overcome, an assurance of salvation, and a lofty feeling of constant and eternal peace. Wesley determined to carry this message to the world. In the next fifty years he traveled some 224,000 miles and preached some 40,000 sermons, an average of 15 a week. At first he spoke in Anglican churches but soon was excluded from them. He and Whitefield preached with intense fervor and earnestness and with such paroxysms of devotion and remorse that congregations were often convulsed by sobs. Whitefield, it was said, could cause his hearers to burst into tears by the way in which he pronounced the word "Mesopotamia." It is small wonder that the Wesleys were soon shut out from the parish churches by the horrified clergy. In 1739 Wesley began the field preaching that took him to the industrial areas of the towns and to savage mining villages. He kindled a living piety among many who heard him.

Wesley created such a tightly-knit organization with his iron will that his enemies called him Pope John. The largest local unit was the society, which was subdivided carefully into small classes and bands. These smaller groups of perhaps a dozen persons met for weekly prayer, exhortation, and mutual confession. Representatives from the societies gathered in an annual conference to receive the commands of their leader. Methodism taught an active, selfless, Christian life characterized by thrift, toil, abstinence, and discipline. It was a purely religious movement, for Wesley, a rigid Tory, permitted no political overtones to creep into his society. In fact, one of the strengths of Methodism was its abhorrence of political radicalism of every kind. Although rather hostile to the upper classes, it ignored them and went its own way. Methodism not only brought an emotional release to its members but gave many of them an opportunity for social leadership. Wesley always regarded himself as a member of the Anglican Church, and it was only toward the end of his life in 1784 that he began to ordain his own ministers since the Church would not ordain them.

Methodism provided a foundation for the development of working-class culture and attitudes that offered an alternative to the emerging socialism of the nineteenth century; such an alternative was not to be found on the Continent.

C H R O N O L O G Y

Society and Culture in the Eighteenth Century

1739	John Wesley begins preaching in the fields
1745	Foundling Hospital established
1749	Bow Street Runners; first urban police force
1755	Dr. Johnson's *Dictionary*
1763–64	Literary Club founded: Samuel Johnson, James Boswell, Sir Joshua Reynolds, Edmund Burke, Adam Smith, Charles James Fox, Richard Brinsley Sheridan, Oliver Goldsmith, Edward Gibbon

24 George III and the American Revolution

Whig historians, writing in the reign of Queen Victoria, set forth a distorted and erroneous picture of George III. They believed that when he came to the throne in 1760 as a young man of twenty-two, he was determined to increase the powers of the Crown, to "be a king" as his mother urged him to do, to govern and not merely to reign. With this purpose in mind, he was supposed to have moved from one tyrannical act to another until he lost the American colonies and brought England to disaster in 1783. Then, according to this view, the people prophetically demanded that the younger Pitt be placed in power to restore the fortunes of the nation.

It is true that the first twenty years of George's reign were replete with political mistakes; otherwise this summary is inaccurate.

GEORGE III, 1760–1820

George had no wish to be absolute or tyrannical. On the contrary, he regarded the English system of government as perfect. As a young man he spoke of "the beauty, excellence, and perfection of the British constitution as by law established"; he never aimed at being more than the constitution made him, the hereditary head of the executive branch of a parliamentary state. He assumed that he could select his own ministers, as did everyone else, but he recognized fully that he could not retain them unless they were supported by the House of Commons: "George III never left the safe ground of parliamentary government, and merely acted the *primus inter pares*, the first among the borough-mongering, electioneering gentlemen of England. While the Stuarts tried to browbeat the house and circumscribe the range of its actions, George III fully accepted its constitution and recognized its powers, and merely tried to work it in accordance with the customs of the time."[1]

[1] L. B. Namier, *England in the Age of the American Revolution* (London: Macmillan, 1930), p. 4.

Unhappily, George's mind was rather disturbed. He became excited under pressure and later in life was subject to fits of insanity. Both his father, Frederick, the Prince of Wales (who died in 1751), and his mother, the Princess Augusta, from Saxe-Gotha in Germany, hated George II; and George as a child learned to hate before he learned to think. George had heard his father talk, as men out of power always talked, of the corruption of those in office. Believing what he heard, he was sure that his grandfather's ministers were "ungrateful, faithless, and corrupt." When he became king he would make them smart. Thus he grew up prejudiced and narrow, lacking in sympathy and breadth of view.

As a young man he vacillated between moments of self-abasement, when he felt himself sinful and unfit for his future position, and moments of exaltation when he fancied himself in partnership with God. In the first of these moods he was apt to become melancholy. But he was a man of pluck and courage, as he showed many times in later life. Determined to overcome his weaknesses by resolution and strength of will, his constant effort placed him under heavy strain. Such effort also resulted in obstinacy, which became his defense mechanism, his method of facing the world. And when he found himself opposed by forces his obstinacy could not overcome, he was unnerved. In his moods of exaltation he aspired to purge political life of its jobbery and corruption, for he was a pious and virtuous young man who set his face against the vicious social customs of the day. He enjoyed simple pleasures. Interested in agriculture, he wrote articles on farming and was nicknamed "Farmer George." He was loyal to those ministers whom he trusted and he was honest in politics. But he was too innocent and unsophisticated, too idealistic, and too inflexible to cope with the problems of political life. "Yet of all George III's achievements, the most significant must surely remain this, that in an era when thrones were disintegrating and ancient monarchies tumbling in the dust, the British monarchy not only survived, but survived with its standing strengthened and its popularity enhanced."[2]

SHIFTING MINISTRIES

The Resignations of Pitt and Newcastle

During the first ten years of his reign George found that his problem was not to purify government but to have any government at all. The quarrels and jealousies of ambitious politicians broke up one Cabinet after another and prevented the formation of a strong stable ministry; moreover, the unfortunate side of Pitt's character—his petulance and desire to dominate—was very marked. Seven different Cabinets held office for brief periods between 1760 and 1770. Thus the young king was in constant trouble.

The administration seemed stable enough when George came to the throne. It was dominated by Pitt, at the height of his fame as a war minister, and by Newcastle,

[2]Stanley Ayling, *George the Third* (New York: Alfred A. Knopf, 1972), p. 460.

*George III as a
young man, by
Allan Ramsay.
(National Portrait
Gallery, London)*

the manager of patronage and elections and the manipulator of personal allegiance. But the Cabinet was not as united as it appeared. Pitt conducted the war on a heroic plane with little thought of expense, while Newcastle had the mundane task of finding money to meet its enormous cost. Moreover, Pitt regarded Newcastle with apparent contempt. As a patriot who wished to win the war, George made no immediate change in the Cabinet, though he regarded both Pitt and Newcastle with suspicion.

The clash of personalities was increased when, after a few months, George added Lord Bute to the Cabinet. Bute was of sufficient importance to be placed in high office quite apart from his friendship with the king. A connection of the influential duke of Argyll, Bute had sat in the House of Lords as a Scottish representative peer. After Argyll's death in 1761, he succeeded to the management of the Scottish members of both houses. This alone made him important. In addition, his wife brought him great wealth; and his daughter married Sir James Lowther, who controlled a number of English parliamentary boroughs. Thus Bute possessed the riches to maintain a great position and enjoyed an electoral interest in both countries. He had been associated in politics with Frederick, the king's father. After Frederick's death, Bute had become the friend and adviser of Frederick's widow and the tutor of the young Prince George. Few politicians in the eighteenth century held so many trump cards and few played them so poorly.

Unfortunately, within two years of George's accession, both Pitt and Newcastle resigned, not because they were dismissed by the king, but because they disagreed with their colleagues. Yet George was glad to see them go. He was now rid of both the tyrannical and corrupting ministers of his grandfather. Had he been more experienced and sophisticated he would have known that it was dangerous to lose these men, the twin pillars of the administration. George should have done his utmost to prevent these resignations. Instead, he appointed Bute as first lord of the Treasury and George Grenville, a brother-in-law but no friend of Pitt, as secretary.

Lord Bute

Newcastle's resignation was followed by the collapse of his political empire. He did not at first understand what was happening, for he assumed that the many persons who owed their places to him would continue to follow his lead. He expected them to remain in office but to show their displeasure at his dismissal and to work for his recall. Bute, however, would not permit the placemen and pensioners of the Court party to remain half-loyal to Newcastle. In October 1762 he forced them to declare themselves either for or against the preliminaries of peace that were being arranged in Paris. Later he informed them that they must either vote with the Cabinet or else lose their places. Newcastle, meanwhile, had asked his friends to resign, but most of them did not. Holding good positions under the Crown, they refused to sacrifice them at Newcastle's bidding. Bute's purge of the "Pelhamite Innocents" was not perhaps as important as it appeared, for it was the Crown, not Newcastle, that was the source of patronage.

Although Bute appeared to be successful, a series of unpleasant episodes exposed his lack of nerve and fortitude. Peace having been made with France, the country expected a reduction in taxation. But Bute, knowing this to be impossible, introduced a tax on cider. Like Walpole's scheme in 1733, the tax was an excise and was quickly opposed as tyrannical. The government, however, did not draw back, as Walpole had done, but forced the tax through Parliament. Bute naturally suffered some scurrilous abuse. He was attacked as a Scot, as the advocate of arbitrary government, as the favorite and paramour of the king's mother. He was too thin-skinned to endure such slander. Moreover, there was an awkward quarrel with Henry Fox, who wanted a peerage. Negotiations took place between George and Bute on one hand and Fox on the other. But a misunderstanding arose: the king and Bute understood that Fox, upon becoming Lord Holland, would resign his office of paymaster of the forces, while Fox believed that he was to be permitted to keep it. A compromise finally was arranged by which Fox retained the office for two years. This episode, as it was told in public, created an impression of chicanery in the politics of the court. In April 1763 Bute resigned.

George Grenville, 1763–1765

The king was left with the problem of finding someone to whom he could give his confidence and who could also perform the difficult task of managing the House of Commons. To bring back Pitt or Newcastle would be to admit that his attempt to run the government on simple and honest lines had been a failure. He could not turn to Bute or Fox. He therefore appointed George Grenville, the secretary, as the head of a new administration. At least Grenville was not one of the old gang of George II, and he posed as an authority on the procedure of the Commons, to which he expressed great devotion.

Grenville was first lord of the Treasury from 1763 to 1765. A domineering man with considerable strength of will, Grenville was methodical, businesslike, and careful about details. Unfortunately, he was also quite devoid of imagination, with little depth of character, eloquence, and finesse. He tried to strengthen his position by rules and regulations. In order to control his colleagues and to attract the support of the Commons, he sought to show them that he enjoyed the complete confidence of the monarch. No one was to consult the king without Grenville's permission. In the same spirit Grenville ruled that all the patronage of the Crown must be in his hands; he would have no rival in the loyalty of the Court party. It is small wonder that this pedantic disciplinarian lasted for only two years.

Grenville necessarily had to deal with a political firebrand, John Wilkes, who had a flair for publicity and a knack of making ministers look ridiculous. The son of a wealthy distiller, he was well educated. He married a rich wife, bought a seat in Parliament, and secured the office of colonel in the militia. But then, separating from his wife, he entered a fast set in London, and became reckless and extreme in his politics. For a time he was supported by Pitt and other leaders of the opposition because he criticized the government. In 1763, having established a newspaper, the *North Briton,* he wrote a slashing attack upon the Cabinet. By implication Wilkes also criticised the king, who had made a speech defending the peace with France.

The Cabinet decided to punish him. It issued a general warrant, that is, a warrant which contained no names, directing the arrest of all persons connected with the offensive number of the *North Briton,* on a charge of seditious libel. Wilkes fought back fiercely. Appearing in court, he claimed that general warrants were illegal, that a secretary of state was not a magistrate who could issue a warrant, and that he (Wilkes) had freedom from arrest as a member of Parliament. The judge ruled that the secretary had acted within his rights but that Wilkes was covered by parliamentary privilege. Later, in another case concerning Wilkes, he ruled that general warrants were illegal. Meanwhile Wilkes was seeking the support of the London mob and was portraying the action of the Cabinet as an attack on the liberties of the people.

As Wilkes became more violent and disreputable he was deserted by his political allies, who refused to defend him in the Commons, where angry members unwisely voted that parliamentary privilege did not protect him from arrest. At this point, being involved in new legal difficulties and having been wounded in a duel, Wilkes fled to France, to all appearances a ruined man, though he was to return later to trouble the government once more. He should not be regarded as an apostle of liberty contending against an arbitrary government. The Cabinet had not intended to be arbitrary, but the legality of general warrants was certainly questionable; in fact, the Commons later declared them illegal. Thus the Cabinet had acted in a crude and blundering way which Wilkes could easily exploit.

Rockingham, 1765–1766

The king tolerated Grenville for two years, largely because he could find no alternative as the head of government. In 1765, however, he commissioned his uncle, the duke of Cumberland, to negotiate for a new Cabinet. Cumberland thought in terms of the old alliance of Pitt and Newcastle. But negotiations with Pitt came to nothing. Pitt merely showed that the political confusion of the period was due in no small part to him. He must have everything his own way; he would enter no Cabinet in which he did not dominate. Newcastle was now an old man. His few loyal adherents were led by the Marquis of Rockingham.

Rockingham might well have hesitated to accept office, for he would have powerful opponents and many problems. Nonetheless, in July 1765, he agreed to form an administration. He was a wealthy landowner with important connections in the House of Lords. A reasonable, sensible man, though rather colorless and with no great force or talent, he hoped to end the quarrels and jealousies of public life by forming a broad-bottom administration somewhat as Pelham had done in the middle of the century. He continued to negotiate with Pitt, though to no avail. But his friendly policy toward the American colonies split his Cabinet, Pitt played upon these differences, and after about a year the Rockingham Cabinet broke up. The king was still in search of a stable administration.

The State of Parties, 1766

The problem of instability in government, which worried many members of Parliament, was discussed at an interesting meeting of politicians in January 1766. They believed that the king should play a more active role in politics, that he should be free to select his ministers without placing himself in the hands of a single group or party. The members who attended this meeting, declaring that they had always acted upon the sole principle of attachment to the Crown, were ready to support any ministry which offered hope of permanence and stability. Prominent among them was a group of minor officials who were beginning to develop into the modern civil service. They wanted continuity in administration, partly for the sake of efficiency and partly because they wished to remain in office, for they were exposed to dismissal by every ephemeral Cabinet wishing to find places for its followers. They looked to the Crown for support, which George attempted to give them; he had learned to appreciate these industrious and loyal officials who did much of the real work of government while the party leaders wrangled. These minor officials merged into a larger group of members. Some, lacking office, wanted to obtain it, but many were ready to support the Crown in an unofficial, independent, and patriotic way without hope of gain. They were called the King's Friends. Though never organized into a political party, they represented a frame of mind. They believed themselves numerous enough to form an administration, but they lacked one essential—a leader of national stature who could become the center of a Cabinet.

The parties or factions clustering around prominent persons at this time have been carefully analyzed. One such party followed Pitt, now earl of Chatham. However, it was very small. Chatham always claimed to despise parties and to be above them, and certainly he never tried to build one. After the peace with France he lost the spontaneous support which independent members had given him during the war, retaining only a handful of hero-worshipers, such as the duke of Grafton. A second faction, the Bedford party, was a family group of three or four peers connected by marriage with that great magnate, the duke of Bedford. Each of them could place a few members in the Commons where, all told, the party controlled about twenty votes. A third party followed George Grenville. This was not a family group but rather a number of followers whom Grenville had attracted while he was in office and who remained loyal to him afterward. He could sometimes muster as many as twenty-five votes in the Commons. The Marquis of Rockingham, like Bedford, was the leader of a number of peers who were connected with each other by blood, marriage, or personal friendship.[3] Each was followed by a handful of members in the lower house, although these members had little in common save that their patrons worked together.

It is clear that no one noble controlled more than a few votes in the Commons. The great magnates, after all, were far from dominant. There remained a large segment of independent country gentlemen, normally inclined to follow the government, but quite at liberty to take an independent line whenever they chose.

Chatham and Grafton, 1766–1770

When Rockingham's Cabinet broke up in 1766, the king decided to ask Chatham to return as the head of a new administration. Chatham at last obtained what he wanted—power on his own terms. He was to select his Cabinet and follow his own policy. He appeared to have every advantage—the confidence of the king, the patronage of the Crown, the good will of the King's Friends, the support of many independent members, the prestige of his success as a war minister. And yet he threw them all away, so that stability in government was soon as far distant as before.

Chatham set out to destroy party groups and to select from the ruins those

---

[3]One of these peers was Newcastle. He suffered a stroke in 1767 and died in 1768.

ministers he desired. The duke of Grafton, detached somewhat earlier from the Rockingham faction, became the first lord of the Treasury; Henry Conway, secretary under Rockingham, was induced to remain; Lord Shelburne, formerly attached to Bute, accepted office as the other secretary. The Cabinet included Charles Townshend as chancellor of the Exchequer and Pratt, the judge in Wilkes's case, as Lord Chancellor. Chatham took the minor office of lord privy seal in order to obtain the leisure to direct the whole.

But Chatham met with a number of rebuffs. He did not destroy existing parties but rather detached a few individuals and left the rest more compact and hostile than before. He hoped to end Britain's isolation in Europe by renewing his old alliance with Frederick of Prussia, but Frederick declined to alter his policy at Chatham's bidding. He wooed the Americans, but they found new grievances. He lost his audience in the Commons, for he was now a peer. Neglecting to organize his Cabinet, he found that members went their separate ways.

Defeated on so many fronts, Chatham simply retired from politics. For more than two years, though holding office, he absented himself from the court and from Parliament. He suffered from some kind of mental illness, sitting for days in a darkened room, cut off from all contact with the world. It is possible, though one can only guess, that his imperious will could not tolerate a world it did not dominate. His colleagues acted without supervision, adopting policies of which he would not have approved. Charles Townshend, for instance, renewed Grenville's attempts to tax the American colonists. This policy divided the Cabinet, for Grafton and Shelburne were sympathetic toward America. But the Bedford group was anti-American. In the same year Chatham emerged from his retirement, though only to resign.

The duke of Grafton continued to head the Cabinet for two more years. He remained in office partly out of loyalty to the king and partly because he became involved in another encounter with Wilkes and did not wish to retire in the midst of it. But he was an incompetent person, more the grandee than the statesman; his Cabinet was weak and disorderly.

A general election in 1768 gave Wilkes an opportunity to return to England and to strike again at the government. He stood for election to the Commons first in London, where he was defeated, and then in Middlesex, the county adjacent to the city. A small county, Middlesex was already half urbanized as London outgrew its ancient borders; it contained a turbulent and radical industrial population that welcomed a candidate posing as the victim of oppression. Wilkes, who was returned in a disorderly election, then insisted upon being arrested on old charges, thus adding to his role as a martyr. In a scuffle outside his prison between his followers and a body of troops—who unfortunately were Scots—a man was killed. Wilkes used this episode to his political advantage, inciting the mob against the Cabinet. Although he had no program for the benefit of the poor, he was a symbol of revolt for industrial workers in some economic distress.

The Cabinet decided that Wilkes should be ejected from Parliament. It was not difficult to persuade the Commons to expel him, but he flourished on grievances, stood for re-election, and was promptly returned. Three times he was expelled, only to be quickly re-elected. The Commons then declared him ineligible for membership and gave the contested seat to his opponent. This blunder made the king and the Cabinet appear tyrannical. To many people, both inside and outside Parliament, the rights of the electorate appeared to have been violated. At last Wilkes had a constitutional grievance, which he exploited to form a radical party in London. Yet to other persons, including the liberal-minded Charles James Fox, the Commons had acted entirely within their rights. It was held that the Commons must maintain their freedom, not only against the court from above, but against the rabble from below. It was the right of the Commons to settle election disputes and to discipline their own members. But Wilkes, refusing to accept their decision, had employed violence and unacceptable means to force their hand. In 1770 the duke of Grafton resigned.

LORD NORTH'S ADMINISTRATION, 1770–1782

A change came over British politics when Lord North succeeded Grafton as first lord of the Treasury in 1770. The period of ministerial instability ended, and North established a firm and settled administration which lasted for twelve years. It bore many resemblances to the government of Henry Pelham.

Lord North, a son of the earl of Guilford, had received a classical education, spoke a number of modern languages, and had served an apprenticeship as a junior official in the Treasury. He became chancellor of the Exchequer in 1767 after the death of Charles Townshend. Three years later, at the age of thirty-seven, he took over Grafton's ministry. He had first been brought into office by Newcastle, but he had no close party ties and was without a personal following in the Commons. His talent lay in his ability to operate the delicate balance of political forces and to maintain a smoothly running administration.

He was shrewd but relaxed, an easygoing man of business who met problems as they arose and was not committed to a long-term program. He sought moderate and general policies which would be approved by the majority of members. He had the advantage of being in the Commons, where his easy and natural manner, his disarming humor, his good sense, good temper, and affability helped to calm the storms of political life. Honest, reliable, and steady, if not very exciting, he won the approbation of both king and Commons as a minister worthy of trust.

So far as possible North avoided controversial issues. He refused to clash with Wilkes, who was allowed to take his seat in the Commons after the election of 1774. The problems of discontent in America and improvement in the government of British India were both approached in a moderate and conciliatory way. The Rockingham group, which was the principal party of opposition, could find no popular issue on which to fight him. And he won general applause by his skill and care in handling financial business.

Like Pelham he was not greedy for personal power but sought to broaden his administration by seeking talented debaters and admitting former opponents to office. The Bedford faction, which had joined the government in 1768, was retained as a political ally. The Grenville party, which did not survive its leader's death in

1770, was brought back to the support of the government. The duke of Grafton was offered and accepted office. In this way North constructed a broad coalition of various groups and opinions. The stability of his administration was especially acceptable to the civil servants and to others in the group known as the King's Friends.

North's position appeared unshakable by 1774. After that time, however, he became involved in difficulties with the American colonists and proved less successful as a wartime than a peacetime minister.

THE REVOLT OF THE AMERICAN COLONIES

Causes of the Revolt

While British politicians quarreled and refused to cooperate during the first decade of George's reign, discontent of a serious nature arose among the American colonists. Having grown into prosperous and stable communities with a sense of constitutional and economic freedom, the colonies refused to be taxed by a Parliament in which they were not represented. Their refusal led to lawlessness and defiance; in fact, they developed a frame of mind in which any act of the British government was regarded with suspicion. They began to question and then to repudiate Parliament's right to legislate for them as well as to tax them, and ultimately they rejected the king himself.

The English, on their side, had no wish to dominate the political life of America, toward which they felt a somewhat contemptuous indifference. Their principal aim was to regulate commerce, for they were still traders, not imperialists. It was taken for granted in England that Parliament was supreme; hence the American challenge to Parliament's authority was resented. The Americans, it was felt, must be put in their place. This in turn led to unwise and provocative attempts at punishment which, far from cowing the colonists, increased their truculence. Exasperation mounted on both sides of the Atlantic until fighting erupted in 1775. The British had no wish to be tyrannical, but they lacked sufficient knowledge of conditions and opinions in America, they acted in anger, and they assumed a moral superiority, as though they knew how to manage America better than the Americans did themselves. The British also suffered from a lack of continuous and consistent policy: they were paying the price for the instability of politics at home.

There was a strong tradition of liberty in America. Freedom had been won because Parliament had subdued the king and had established the principle that the king could not take an Englishman's property without his consent expressed through a representative body. The colonists exulted in this victory, which they compared with the victory of their elected assemblies over the royal governors. Consequently, they thought, in America as in England citizens should levy their own taxes, make their own laws, and run their own affairs.

This tradition of liberty was strengthened in several ways. Except for the regulation of trade, the English government had allowed the colonies great autonomy.

An American might live his entire life without seeing an imperial official. Indeed, there were very few such officials in America except for the governors and for those entrusted with the enforcement of the Navigation Laws. The governors, of course, were appointed in England (except for the popularly elected governors of Connecticut and Rhode Island), but every colony possessed an assembly which controlled finance. The assembly, representing local and popular interests, and the governor, representing imperial and royal interests, were often at odds. It was the governor who usually gave way, for his salary came from the assembly and he was not certain of the support of the home authorities in any quarrel with the colonists. Serving for a short term, he tended to take the line of least resistance, to ease his relations with the colonists by concessions, and to allow basic differences to drift. The assemblies pushed their fiscal advantage against the governors in an aggressive and self-righteous way, much as Parliament in the seventeenth century had pushed its advantage against the poverty-stricken Stuarts.

The home authorities did not appear to be disturbed by these developments. The administration of the colonies was part of the executive jurisdiction of the king, who left it in the hands of the secretary of state for the Southern Department. The secretary relied heavily upon a Board of Trade and Plantations created in 1696 which considered colonial business and advised him what to do. The secretary then made his decision, which was passed on to the royal governors. But the colonists normally did what they pleased and were accustomed to a very loose control. What control there was came from the king and his ministers. The colonists failed to realize that a command from the king was really a command from Parliament also.

A sense of liberty was increased by the fact that most Americans lived on the soil. It is now believed that most of them owned the land they cultivated. Such ownership gave them economic independence, for by industry they could make it yield a fair return and could thus be free from control by other men. Moreover, it gave them political independence, for ownership of land conferred the right to vote. Property was not merely a possession to be cherished and increased: it was the foundation of life and liberty. The concepts of property and liberty were thus intertwined. But a person had no security for his property if it could be taken from him without his consent.

Historians of a generation ago laid great stress upon the Acts of Trade as a cause of the American Revolution. These acts required that many colonial raw products, if they were exported, could be taken only to England or to other English colonies, and that imported manufactured articles from Europe must come from England, having been either produced there or brought to England from the Continent. All colonial trade, export and import, was confined to English and colonial shipping; high duties were placed on certain imports of non-British origin; and the colonists were forbidden to engage in many forms of manufacture.

At the present time, however, the Acts of Trade are not considered a primary cause of the Revolution, for two reasons. In the first place, the acts permitted trade to flow in its natural channels. Trade would have followed much the same course had there been no acts at all. Great Britain was the natural market for America's raw products and the natural source of her manufactured imports. Secondly, the acts were not strictly enforced, at least not in New England. The Molasses Act of 1733, for example, was one that might have imposed hardship. The New Englanders had built a large industry upon molasses. It was brought from the West Indies and made into rum, which was sold throughout the colonies or taken to Africa to exchange for slaves. So extensive had this industry become that the British West Indies could not supply molasses in sufficient quantities, and New England skippers bought it in the French and Dutch islands. To protect the British planters, the Molasses Act imposed a prohibitive duty of 6*d*. per gallon upon molasses imported into the colonies from non-British sources. Had the act been enforced, an important segment of colonial trade and industry would have been crippled. But a standard bribe of 1*d*. to 1½*d*. per gallon was arranged between New England traders and the venal customs officials in America, and the trade continued as before.

A New Imperial Policy

After the close of the Seven Years' War in 1763 the British government felt compelled to pay greater attention to colonial problems. The vast territories acquired from the French in Canada and in the area west of the Appalachian Mountains would have to be pacified and defended. It was thought that for this purpose an army of ten thousand men was necessary at a cost of some £350,000 a year. Moreover, the lax enforcement of the Acts of Trade had been underlined during the war when, to the exasperation of the British, Americans had continued to trade with the French West Indies.

It was George Grenville who first moved to meet these problems during his administration between 1763 and 1765. He began by placing the trans-Appalachian West under direct imperial control. The plan was to keep this territory roughly as it was. A line was drawn along the mountains, and "for the present" the colonists were not to expand beyond it. Grenville, who feared that a sudden rush across the mountains would cause Indian wars, wished to make treaties with the Indians, to foster the fur trade, and to divert American migration to Nova Scotia and Florida. In due time he would release the western lands for settlement in an orderly and gradual way. But the so-called Proclamation Line ignored a number of factors. Colonial settlements already existed west of the mountains. Several of the colonies claimed that their western boundaries extended to the Mississippi. During the recent war volunteers had been recruited in America by the promise of western lands, and land companies had been formed to exploit the West. To many groups in the colonies the Proclamation Line was a great disappointment.

Grenville also began the policy of taxing the American colonists. The Acts of Trade were now to be made to produce revenue. American skippers must prepare elaborate papers for every voyage. The navy was to hunt down smugglers, who were to be tried by Admiralty courts and not by colonial juries. In 1764 Grenville passed the Sugar Act, which superseded the Molasses Act and cut the duty from 6*d*. to 3*d*. per gallon, but he warned that the new duty would be collected. In 1765 he passed the Stamp Act. Stamped paper, on which a tax had been paid, must be used for all legal documents, deeds, bonds, ships' papers, as well as for almanacs, newspapers, and advertisements.

To British statesmen these taxes seemed fair and just. The Seven Years' War had brought great benefit to the colonies, freeing them from the threat of the French in Canada and opening lands to the West (though these lands might be withheld for the moment); but the war had doubled the British national debt and had been followed by an economic depression in Britain. It was felt that though the colonies could never pay for the cost of defeating the French, they should at least meet the bill for the ten thousand troops sent to guard the lands west of the mountains. Most of the cost of defending the colonies, including all the charges of the navy, would still be born by the British taxpayer.

The colonists, on the other hand, viewed these taxes quite differently. They had learned the importance of the taxing power from their struggles with the colonial governors; they regarded a tax to which they had not consented as an attack upon their property. They raised the fundamental question whether Parliament could levy taxes on them and claimed that it could not. Parliament in England, they held, was a representative body which protected the British citizen from arbitrary taxation. But since the colonists were not represented, Parliament gave them no protection. On the contrary, when it asked them to pay ungranted taxes over which they had no control, it became a threat. The colonists made no distinction between indirect taxes levied through customs duties and direct taxes, such as that imposed by the Stamp Act.

In England, at the instance of Grenville, one of his subordinates, Thomas Whateley, wrote a pamphlet[4] to answer the Americans. Many Englishmen, the pamphlet argued, did not vote and yet enjoyed virtual representation because their interests were the same as the interests of Englishmen who possessed the franchise. The colonists, then, were as fully represented as those Englishmen who could not vote. Moreover, members of the Commons represented the whole empire and not merely their own constituencies. These arguments fell flat in the colonies, as they deserved to do, and were demolished in an answer[5] by Daniel Dulany, a lawyer in Maryland. A nonvoting Englishman, said Dulany, might have the same interests as the Englishman who voted, but an American did not. American interests, far from being identical with those of England, were frequently the complete opposite. Members of the Commons might in theory represent the empire, but in fact their interests normally were confined to their own localities. Nor would the presence in Parliament of a few American representatives be any solution, for such members would have no influence on Parliament's decisions.

Meanwhile the Stamp Act could not be enforced. Rioters burned the stamps and intimidated the distributers of the stamped paper, radicals formed societies known as "Sons of Liberty," merchants refused to import British manufactures, resolutions were passed denouncing taxation by Parliament, a Stamp Act Congress met in New York to which nine colonies sent representatives. This assembly, after acknowl-

---

[4]*The Regulations Lately Made concerning the Colonies and the Taxes Imposed upon them, considered* (London, 1765).
[5]*Considerations on the Propriety of imposing Taxes in the British Colonies, for the Purpose of raising a Revenue, by Act of Parliament* (Annapolis, Md., 1765).

edging the king as supreme head, made a distinction between Parliament's right to legislate for America, which was accepted, and Parliament's right to tax, which was denied.

These events came as a shock to England. Many members of Parliament believed that concessions should not be made to rioters and that weakness in Britain would spell the end of all control over the colonies. But Rockingham, who succeeded Grenville as head of the Cabinet in 1765, had opposed the Stamp Act and was under pressure from English merchants injured by the disruption of American trade. He therefore repealed the Stamp Act in March 1766. But he found the Commons reluctant to make concessions; hence the repeal was accompanied by a Declaratory Act which asserted the right of Parliament to make statutes binding the colonies "in all cases whatsoever." Unfortunately Rockingham allowed members to receive the impression that the colonists objected only to direct taxation and not to indirect taxes through customs duties, although no such distinction existed in America. Rockingham recognized that the Sugar Act was a burden on the economy of New England, and so the duty on non-British molasses imported into the colonies was reduced to 1d. per gallon.

William Pitt, now earl of Chatham, whose administration began in July 1766, was even more friendly toward the colonists than was Rockingham. But when he attempted to persuade them to tax themselves in order to supply food and shelter for the soldiers stationed in America, his request was resisted. After his physical collapse American affairs fell into the hands of Charles Townshend, the chancellor of the Exchequer, a clever but shallow man. Grasping in a sharp legalistic way at the supposed distinction between direct and indirect taxes, he devised a plan to impose new customs duties on glass, lead, paper, paints, and tea imported from Britain into the colonies. He also established a board of customs commissioners in Boston to manage the customs service along the whole American coast. The proceeds from the customs would be used first to support the army in America and then to pay the salaries of British officials in the colonies, thus freeing them from dependence on the assemblies.

The Townshend duties proved disastrous. Their yield, which was estimated at only £40,000, was quite inadequate for the ends Townshend suggested. His talk of paying officials from the proceeds of the customs aroused suspicion in America; his new duties made possible a sinister interpretation of what the Declaratory Act really meant. Agitation and disorder began again in the colonies, with nonimportation agreements and vigorous denials of Parliament's right to tax. One part of Townshend's legislation, which suspended the assembly in New York for its refusal to billet soldiers, was regarded in America as an attack on all the colonial assemblies. Moreover, the customs commissioners established in Boston proved to be corrupt men who used their powers to enrich themselves at the expense of American traders. The Sugar Act, as passed in 1764, gave the commissioners authority to seize the ships and goods of violators, a power they used to the full. Soon cordially hated in Boston, they called on the authorities in England to send troops for their support.

Persuaded that Boston was in the hands of smugglers and rowdies, Lord Hillsborough, who held the newly created post of secretary for America, sent troops in September 1768. Their presence aroused hostility not only in Boston but in the other colonies. Here was proof that Parliament's power to legislate was fully as dangerous as its power to tax. Nonetheless, an uneasy calm existed in Boston for many months. In March 1770, however, in a collision between the soldiers and the mob five Bostonians were killed.

This explosion had a sobering effect on both sides. Many Americans thought that Boston had gone too far and that mobbing was becoming dangerous. At almost the same time Lord North became head of the Cabinet at home. In a move toward conciliation, he repealed all the Townshend duties except that on tea and informed the colonies that no further taxes would be imposed on them for the purpose of raising revenue. There followed a period of almost three years in which relations between England and America improved. Nonimportation agreements ceased to operate. Some of the old good will between the two countries returned. The colonies were prosperous, constitutional issues receded, and it was hoped in England that North's conciliation had solved the American question.

But beginning in 1772 new causes of friction arose which quickly brought matters to a head. One such cause was the rapacity of the customs commissioners in Boston, who continued to confiscate colonial shipping. Benjamin Franklin obtained possession in England of a number of letters by British officials in America who urged the home government to take strong measures against the colonists. The publication of these letters aroused strong resentment. The colonists were therefore in a state of alarm and excitement when in May 1773 Lord North passed a Tea Act which permitted the East India Company to carry tea directly to America, where it would be distributed to retailers, thus bypassing the wholesale merchants in both countries. North's purpose was to assist the East India Company, but the wholesale merchants in America denounced the act as a subtle scheme to raise new revenues in America. The people took alarm. In most ports the captains bringing the tea were persuaded to take it away without unloading it; but at the infamous "Boston Tea Party" the colonists dumped it into the harbor.

Lord North's answer was to pass the Coercive Acts to punish Boston. The port was closed, the Governor's council was to be appointed by the king, town meetings were forbidden except for the election of officials, trials might be transferred to England at the Governor's discretion, troops were again stationed in the town, and General Gage, their commander, became governor of Massachusetts. Coincidentally, Parliament passed the Quebec Act, which established a new government in Canada and extended the province of Quebec southward to the Ohio River. This act was misinterpreted in America as another indication of British hostility. The First Continental Congress, which met in Philadelphia in September 1774, declared that the colonies had the right to legislate for themselves in their provincial assemblies, subject only to the veto of the British Crown. This claim placed the assemblies upon an equality with Parliament, for it meant that the king should govern the colonies through the assemblies just as he governed England through the Parliament. Yet the resolution adopted by the Congress contained a somewhat contradictory statement that Parliament should continue to regulate the commerce of the empire as a whole.

*The solid
enjoyment of bottle
and friend, 1776.
(SNARK/Art
Resource)*

The SOLID ENJOYMENT of BOTTLE and FRIEND.

The assembly of the First Continental Congress appeared to the British as nothing short of treason. Other acts were passed restricting the commerce of New England. Meanwhile the colonists in Massachusetts had collected arms and ammunition at Concord. An attempt of the British to seize these arms led to the skirmish at Lexington in April 1775 and to the attack on the British troops as they returned from Concord to Boston. The Second Continental Congress, meeting in May 1775, found itself conducting a war and selected Washington as commander in chief. Before he reached Boston, the Battle of Bunker Hill had taken place in June. Although the Congress was preparing for war, it sent a petition to George III urging him to withstand the efforts of Parliament to deprive the Americans of their liberty. But no one in England was more eager than the king to uphold the sovereignty of Parliament over the colonies. As the Americans hesitated, they were influenced strongly by a pamphlet, *Common Sense,* written by Thomas Paine, a radical Englishman who happened to be in Philadelphia. The logical conclusion of the colonists' course, said Paine, was independence. Any trust in the king was a delusion, for George was worse than his ministers.

In May 1776 the Congress adopted a resolution advising each colonial assembly to assume the powers of government in its own locality. In June a resolution declaring independence was moved in the Congress. It was adopted on 2 July. Two days later a more famous declaration of independence, the work of Thomas Jefferson, was also formally adopted.

The War with the Colonies

As the colonists moved from discontent to open war, British opinion hardened against them. The opposition in Parliament led by Rockingham, still friendly to the Americans, appeared factious and unpatriotic. Independent members, rallying behind the throne and its ministers, gave North a large majority in the Commons and greatly strengthened his political position, but a good deal of discord existed in the Cabinet. Lord George Sackville Germain, who became the American secretary in November 1775, was anxious to advance the war with vigor and to end it by a series of quick decisive blows. He criticized North for hoping that a reconciliation might still be effected. Barrington, the secretary of war, was gloomy, contending that British land forces were insufficient to subdue America. He advocated instead a naval war. But Lord Sandwich, the head of the Admiralty, feared an attack from France and did not want to send many ships to America.

North, who did not control the Cabinet properly, tried to soothe differences of opinion by compromise rather than by leadership. His reputation rested upon his economies in finance and upon his wish, like Walpole's, to avoid controversial issues. Yet he was committed to a policy of teaching the Americans a lesson. He allowed several policies to be pursued at once, tried to keep down costs, and soon showed that he was a poor war minister. From the first the Cabinet lacked a strong, long-range planner, as Pitt had been in the Seven Years' War.

The military problem in America was really very difficult although the colonists rarely possessed an army that could face the British in the field. The British could capture almost any point they wished but they could not occupy the whole country. Once they left an area behind, their control over it was likely to disappear. When they ventured inland they were harassed and ambushed by irregulars who gathered quickly from farms and small towns. These irregulars knew how to use firearms, and though they were undependable in pitched battles, they could turn a British victory parade into a hasty retreat. In a word, this was a people's war. The American armies could count on local support. The loyalists, from whom the British hoped so much, made a poor showing. The British had to bring their supplies all the way from England; moreover, their commanders were often dilatory and failed to make the most of their opportunities. Such a war might well have ended in stalemate had not foreign aid given the Americans an opportunity to win.

In the early days of the war the American cause looked bleak. General William Howe, who had succeeded General Gage as commander in Boston, was forced to evacuate that city and to withdraw to Halifax in Nova Scotia. But in July 1776, just as the Americans were declaring their independence, he landed unopposed on Staten Island with a considerable force. He was shortly joined by his brother, Admiral Lord Howe, who brought a fleet and reinforcements from England. The army on Staten Island soon numbered more than thirty thousand men, and at the Battle of Long Island in August 1776 Washington was badly beaten. General Howe thereupon occupied New York and pushed Washington in a southwesterly direction across New Jersey to the Delaware. For the time this seemed sufficient, and Howe went into winter quarters. But on the night of 25 December 1776, Washington recrossed the Delaware and made a surprise attack on the British at Trenton, capturing about one thousand Hessians and British cavalry. This victory, though not of great military importance, revived the hopes of the colonists and showed that their cause need not collapse.

The British made a more determined effort in 1777. France and Spain were sending aid to the colonists, British finances already were strained, and it was felt that the war must be ended quickly. In 1775 the Americans had invaded Canada. Although this invasion was both a military and a political failure, it had alarmed the British, who had sent an army of some size to Quebec. In planning the campaign for 1777, General John Burgoyne, working with Lord George Germain, devised a plan to bring this army down from Montreal by way of the Richelieu River and Lake Champlain to the Hudson and so to Albany, where it could be met by General Howe coming up from New York. The British forces would thus be united and New England would be severed from the rest of the colonies. In retrospect this has usually been considered sound strategy, though it failed in execution. But, as a matter of fact, the plan was ill-conceived. Since New York was already in English hands, and since communications between New England and the rest of the colonies were largely by sea, even if successful, the plan would not have been very effective. Nonetheless, Burgoyne was on Lake Champlain in June with seven thousand men; in July he took Ticonderoga.

At this point, however, General Howe moved the bulk of his forces to Philadelphia. His reasons for doing so are not entirely clear. He had long been considering an attack on Philadelphia, and had obtained Lord George Germain's consent to this change of plan. Howe believed that Burgoyne was doing well. It has been argued that he did not want to go to Albany too soon and so give Washington freedom of action along the seaboard. Whatever Howe's motive, the result was disastrous. After a difficult voyage along the Jersey coast, he entered Chesapeake Bay, defeated Washington at Brandywine Creek, and entered Philadelphia. But once in the city he could not go north to meet Burgoyne, who was in serious difficulty. With his communications very extended, Burgoyne found himself in a hilly and roadless wilderness some forty miles north of Albany, hemmed in and harassed by large numbers of American troops and irregulars. General Clinton in New York was unable to send adequate reinforcements. In October 1777, at Saratoga, Burgoyne surrendered his army, now shrunk to five thousand men.

This defeat altered the entire character of the war. Ever since 1763 the French had been hoping for a war of revenge. They had strengthened their navy and had sought a close alliance with Spain. Their plan was to secure their position in the Mediterranean and to obtain compensation for the loss of Canada by acquiring new possessions in the Caribbean. But the American revolt opened new prospects. Even before the colonists asked for assistance, the French Foreign Minister, Vergennes, had persuaded Louis XVI to grant them one million livres (roughly one million pounds of silver) for the purchase of arms. Vergennes persuaded Spain to do the same, and other credits followed.

The French would not commit themselves to military and naval assistance until they were sure that the American war would be a long and difficult struggle for Britain. Saratoga convinced them that this would be so. In February 1778 they concluded two treaties with Benjamin Franklin, whom the colonists had sent to Paris. One was a treaty of amity which recognized the United States and dealt largely with commerce. The other was a treaty of military alliance in case a war should follow between France and England, as it did in June of the same year. The French agreed not to make peace until the independence of the United States was secured. They disclaimed any ambition to acquire territory in North America, though French conquests in the West Indies were to be recognized by the United States. These highly advantageous treaties gave the colonists a firm foundation for success.

In 1779 Spain entered the war against England. She did not conclude an alliance with the Americans, however, for their independence would be a bad example for the Spanish colonies in the New World. The Spanish objective was to regain the possessions Spain had lost to Britain since the beginning of the century. The English also faced the hostility of neutral nations whose ships were stopped by the British navy and searched for contraband of war. When Holland refused to tolerate this practice, England declared war on her in 1780. The same grievance brought Russia and the Scandinavian powers together in a League of Armed Neutrality. With an inefficient and unwarlike government, England faced a hostile world. She also had to meet serious difficulties in India and Ireland.

Recognizing his own inadequacy, Lord North begged to be allowed to resign. But he remained in office at the earnest solicitation of the king, who could find no one to replace him. No other member of the Cabinet would do. Nor did the opposition offer better prospects. The Rockingham group advocated the independence of America, which was anathema to the king. Chatham and his follower, Lord Shelburne, who were also in opposition, were ready to conciliate the colonists though not to capitulate to them.

The war effort in America necessarily slackened. Sir Henry Clinton, who succeeded General Howe as commander, was given new instructions. If he could not bring Washington to a decisive battle, he was to confine himself to raids against the coastal towns and to the destruction of American shipping. He was to send part of his army to the West Indies to cooperate with the navy in an attack on the French island of St. Lucia. Meanwhile he should evacuate Philadelphia and return to New York, which was exposed to an assault by sea. Shortly after his arrival a strong French fleet under the Count d'Estaing approached New York. But thanks to the energy and daring of Admiral Howe, D'Estaing moved on to Newport, Rhode Island, where he disappointed the colonists by not attacking the town, then to Boston to refit, and finally to the West Indies.

In 1779 Clinton continued a policy of raids along the coast, especially in the South, where he was so successful that the Cabinet allowed him to open an offensive on land. Late in 1778 a British force captured Savannah in Georgia and quickly brought the entire colony under royal control. A more important triumph followed. Clinton attacked the city of Charleston in South Carolina, which surrendered in May 1780 with some seven thousand American troops. He then returned to New York, for D'Estaing was again in American waters.

The general left in charge of southern operations was Lord Cornwallis. At first he was very successful. In August 1780 he defeated the Americans severely at Camden, South Carolina. But as he moved through the interior he felt the pressure of a hostile population. Constantly harassed by an able American commander, General Nathanael Greene, Cornwallis marched north rather quickly into Virginia and established himself at Yorktown, expecting reinforcements from Clinton in New York.

Disaster now came quickly upon Cornwallis. A powerful French fleet under command of the Count de Grasse won temporary control of the sea off the coast of Virginia and blockaded Cornwallis at Yorktown. Washington, after feigning an attack on New York, marched south, strengthened by a French army under the Count de Rochambeau. Cornwallis was besieged by sea and land, many of his men were ill, the French and American guns swept his camp. His surrender in October 1781 virtually ended the war in America.

The War in Europe

England continued the war against France and Spain for another year, winning an important naval action in the West Indies which helped her greatly in the negotiations for peace, but in general the war was disastrous for her. Constantly on the defensive, without an ally in the world, and governed by a minister who recognized his own imcompetence in war, she was fortunate to fend off the attacks of the Bourbon powers as well as she did. The combined navies of France and Spain were superior in fighting strength to that of England. Hence the British could not always control the Channel.

Meanwhile large French and British naval units were operating in the West Indies. When De Grasse returned to the West Indies in 1781 after the surrender of Cornwallis, the English islands appeared to be gravely menaced. But in the following year Admiral George Rodney, the most enterprising admiral of the war, inflicted a severe defeat on De Grasse which ended the French threat in the Caribbean.

The Spanish displayed unusual vigor. They were strong enough to besiege both Gibraltar and Minorca and at the same time send an army to West Florida. The French were active in India, intriguing with native princes against the English; for a time a French squadron operated in Indian waters. The British navy, faced with so many foes and fighting in so many theaters, was under enormous strain. Toward the end of the war Lord North could raise money in Britain only at ruinous rates of interest. His majority in the Commons having melted away, he resigned in the spring of 1782.

The Peace of Paris, 1783

The ministers who followed North and who made the peace of 1783 were members of a coalition of the Rockingham and Shelburne groups who had recently been in opposition. Shelburne was secretary for Home and Colonial Affairs, while the secretary for Foreign Affairs was Charles James Fox. Peace with America fell within Shelburne's jurisdiction; peace with France within that of Fox. Unfortunately, the two men disliked each other and did not work together. A difference arose over policy in making peace with America. Fox wished to recognize the independence of the United States at the beginning of negotiations, thus taking America out of the war and making possible a firmer tone with France. Questions of American boundaries and trade could be dealt with later. Shelburne, on the other hand, wished to postpone the granting of independence until independence was defined clearly. He still hoped that the Americans would be satisfied with freedom to manage their domestic affairs and could be persuaded to cooperate with Britain in commerce and foreign policy. He wanted the two countries to be partners in the trade of the Atlantic, and he hoped that the king and his ministers might still be allowed to control the foreign policy of both. He was willing to grant to the United States the lands between the Appalachian Mountains and the Mississippi.

American negotiators in Paris were shrewd enough to take advantage of these differences. When France and Spain opposed the extension of American territory west of the mountains, the Americans made what amounted to a separate peace with England despite the treaty of alliance with France. By the terms of the peace (September 1783) the United States became independent. Her territory, with a northern frontier not very different from what it is today, was extended westward to the Mississippi, and south to the thirty-first parallel, leaving Florida in the hands of Spain. The treaty recognized that debts owed by Americans to Englishmen were valid debts. The Americans received no commercial privileges in Britain, but they secured the right to fish off the Newfoundland Banks and gave no guarantee that the loyalists would escape persecution.

The settlement between England and France was largely based upon a mutual restoration of conquests in the West Indies. The French regained their fishing rights off Newfoundland and received both Senegal and Gorée in West Africa. Spain kept her conquests of Minorca and Florida.

RADICALS AND CONSERVATIVES

Under the impact of the American war, politics in Britain took a new turn. The radicalism associated with John Wilkes in the 1760s was renewed, though not by Wilkes himself, and a demand arose for reform in political life and for drastic changes in the constitution. These proposals were disliked by the independent country gentlemen in the Commons, whose instincts were basically conservative. Suspicious of radical reformers, independent members resisted change, preferring to support Lord North as a minister who represented long-established methods of government. Thus a revived radicalism was opposed by a new conservative impulse.

At the beginning of the war Lord North enjoyed a large majority in the Commons, but by 1778, as disasters mounted, his political strength had greatly diminished. His very manner betrayed indecision and lack of energy. As a result of his weakness, the opposition in the Commons began to take new hope. This opposition consisted largely of the followers of Rockingham and those of Lord Shelburne, Chatham's political heir. Both groups were sympathetic toward America and both contained men who were to be important: Charles James Fox, Rockingham's close friend, Edmund Burke, who was Rockingham's private secretary, and, somewhat later, William Pitt the Younger, Chatham's son, who entered political life as a follower of Shelburne.

The weakness of the opposition lay in the fact that its criticism of the Cabinet during a war appeared unpatriotic. But the leaders claimed they were justified in opposing a war which was badly managed and that England would not have suffered such disasters if they had been in power. They also asserted that they were kept from office by the excessive influence of the Crown, which employed its patronage to build Lord North's majority. Too strong an executive, they argued, had corrupted the self-righting forces of the constitution and kept them out of power.

In 1779 two movements for reform began outside Parliament, both quite separate from the politics of parliamentary life. Their fundamental cause was the general disappointment and chagrin at the failures of the American war. The blame had to be placed somewhere, and it was easy to place it upon the parliamentary system of the day. One part of this reforming movement arose among the old associates of Wilkes in the county of Middlesex. The people, it was argued, should have greater power to influence events in Parliament. There should be more organization among voters and a larger number of constituencies—such as Middlesex and the city of Westminster— in which a large and articulate electorate gave force and vigor to parliamentary elections. A second movement for reform began in the north. A meeting in Yorkshire expressed the view held by many persons that the counties—where an electorate of some size chose country gentlemen as knights of the shire—were the soundest and purest part of the constitution. Country gentlemen of means and standing in their localities would shun corrupting influences and would take an independent line in politics. Again reformers stressed the excessive power of the Crown. They wanted more independent members who, it was assumed, would not tolerate bungling ministers like North. The Yorkshire leaders sent petitions to the House of Commons. Their program was a demand for rigorous economy (which North was practicing already), for the addition of one hundred new county members to the total membership of the Commons, and for annual elections.

The members of the opposition pressed forward to take part in these movements and if possible to lead them. William Pitt, Charles James Fox, John Wilkes, and a number of the nobility all were interested. In the Commons Edmund Burke introduced several bills calling for radical reform. He wished to abolish sinecures, to investigate and prune the civil list, and to end the Board of Trade. Other members of the opposition called on the government to publish the list of pensioners. This rather petulant demand for reform reached its climax in a motion by John Dunning "that the influence of the Crown has increased, is increasing, and ought to be diminished," which was adopted by the Commons in April 1780. The truth of this famous resolution was highly doubtful. George III had not kept Lord North in power against the will of the nation. For a long time North's policies had had general support. It was only when his government ran into difficulties that the country, less loyal than the king, turned upon him as a scapegoat for the failure of the war. He himself had created a false impression by his frequent assertions that he would like to resign.

Dunning was able to carry two other motions: that the Cabinet should disclose the amount of money given to members from the civil list, and that subordinate members of the king's household should be debarred from Parliament. But a bill to disfranchise revenue officers was defeated; and a radical proposal that Parliament should continue until a better balanced constitution had been obtained was soundly defeated.

A reaction set in against the reformers and in favor of North. If North resigned, his place would be taken by an opposition that was showing itself to be wild, oppressive, and factious. The violence of Charles James Fox, for example, was already making men doubt the soundness of his judgment, however much they liked him personally, And it presently became evident that independent country gentlemen much preferred the broadly based and relaxed administration of North, who represented moderation and tradition, to the intense fury and unpredictable policy of the radical reformers. This feeling was strengthened immensely by the Lord George Gordon riots in June 1780. Beginning in a foolish demonstration against an act that allowed Roman Catholics to enlist in the army without taking old-fashioned oaths against their religion, the rioting in London got completely out of hand and raged for a week before order was restored. This famous riot was a sharp reminder of the danger of exciting the mob over political issues. Horrified country gentlemen turned against reformers who made themselves responsible in any way for agitation among the people. The strength of North was revealed to be far deeper than mere support of the Crown. He remained in power until his majority disappeared as a result of Yorktown.

Thus Parliament was divided between the radical reforming zeal of Fox and Rockingham and the conservative instincts of independent country gentlemen.

C H R O N O L O G Y

George III and Revolution

1760–1820	George III
1763	John Wilkes and the *North Briton;* Proclamation Line
1764	Sugar Act replaces Molasses Act

(continued on next page)

Chronology, continued

1765	Stamp Act and Stamp Act Congress
1766	Stamp Act repealed; Declaratory Act; The King's Friends
1766–70	Pitt (Chatham) returns to power
1767	Townshend Acts
1768	Wilkes again in opposition; British troops in Boston
1770	Lord North prime minister; Boston Massacre; Townshend Duties repealed
1773	Tea Act passed; Boston Tea Party
1774	Wilkes in Parliament; Coercive Acts; Quebec Act; First Continental Congress
1775	Lexington and Concord; Second Continental Congress: Battle of Bunker Hill
1776	Declaration of Independence; Tom Paine's *Common Sense*
1777	Battle of Saratoga; British defeated
1778	France allied with Americans
1780	John Dunning's resolution; Gordon Riots
1781	Battle of Yorktown
1782	Lord North resigned
1783	Peace of Paris; American Independence recognized

25

The Industrial Revolution

The economic changes that took place in the eighteenth century laid the foundations of our modern industrial world. The invention of heavy machines propelled by water power or by steam, in place of light ones turned by the human arm, and the advance of technology on every side began to undermine the domestic system of manufacturing and to substitute the industrial plant or factory as we know it today. This development, as it gathered momentum, vastly increased the volume of production, altered the working conditions of the laboring classes, created a new type of industrial capitalist, and deeply affected the daily life of the entire population.

This sharp fundamental change is commonly called the Industrial Revolution, however, that term has fallen into some disrepute among historians. The writers of the late nineteenth century, who first talked about the Industrial Revolution, frequently came to erroneous conclusions. They imagined that the revolution began quite abruptly about 1760 with a group of great inventors who suddenly appeared from nowhere, that factories came in with a rush, and that by 1820 the domestic system had all but disappeared. These writers idealized the domestic system, dwelling upon the happy state of the domestic worker who combined a little agriculture with manufacturing in the contented atmosphere of the home.

These notions have now been modified. It is realized, in the first place, that technological progress did not begin in 1760 but had been gradually evolving for centuries. There was, of course, a tremendous increase in the number of inventions between 1770 and 1800, but they had their roots in the past. "The developments which took place in the reign of George III must therefore be regarded as the quickening of an age-long evolutionary process, rather than as a violent break with the past and a fresh beginning." Secondly, it is understood now that industry as a whole changed very slowly. To be sure, some industries, such as the making of cotton thread, advanced rapidly. But cotton was not typical, and other industries lagged far behind it. The manufacture of woolen goods, for example, remained largely in the hands of domestic workers after most of the cotton industry had passed into factories. Some processes in an industry might become mechanized whereas others might not; and the invention of a machine was no guarantee that it would pass at once into general use. It is believed that even in 1830 no single industry was completely mechanized and more than half of the industrial workers were still outside the factories.

Thirdly, despite the obvious evils of the factories and the factory towns, it is now held that on the whole the workpeople derived more benefit than misfortune from the changes that were taking place. Here, of course, we are partly in the realm of the intangible. A peasant family coming to the city doubtless longed for the peace and quiet of the countryside. But they were probably better fed, better clothed, and received better medical attention. The workers hated the discipline of the factories, and this gave the factories a bad reputation. But at least some of the evils for which the factories have been blamed were also to be found in the domestic system, which had its own shortcomings. Finally, industrial change cannot be studied in a vacuum. It must be connected with an increase in population, with improvements in agriculture, with better methods of transport, as well as with inventions and the factory system.

INDUSTRY IN THE FIRST HALF OF THE CENTURY

Industry under the domestic system was found in the cities but also was scattered through many rural areas and small towns. There were independent domestic artisans in the country who were self-employed, who carried on manufacture in their houses, who owned their tools, bought their raw materials, perhaps employed a few helpers in a shed, and sold their products at the local market. But most of the domestic workers were employees of some wealthy merchant manufacturer. This was particularly true in the large textile and metal industries. The master clothier, employing a network of agents and middlemen, sent out his wool over a wide area to be manufactured into cloth. The iron and brass made into cutlery, nails, swords, buckles, spurs, and bits for horses by the domestic workers in the metal trades were given out by capitalists who owned the foundries, forges, and slitting mills. Not only was the domestic system highly capitalized, with large funds in the hands of the wealthy few; there was also a great deal of specialization and division of labor among workmen who performed one process only. Both developments had gone about as far as they could profitably go. The great need was for a more advanced technology.

The domestic system should not be idealized. The notion of the happy domestic worker at his loom, surrounded by his wife and children carding and spinning—all contented and busy, with a vegetable garden and perhaps a cow on his little plot of land—is a fallacious notion. It is based in part on a famous description by Defoe of the woolen industry near Halifax in Yorkshire. Defoe found the district populous with many villages "and at every considerable house a manufactury." The hills supplied coal and pure running water. Each master clothier kept a horse or two to take his cloth to market. His workers lived in "an infinite number of cottages," in which women and

Domestic industry. The women are spinning; the man is at a frame for knitting stockings. From the Universal Magazine, *August 1750. (Historical Pictures Service, Chicago)*

children were carding and spinning. There were no beggars. The master clothier's house was surrounded by a plot of ground on which he kept a cow, but the cottagers had no land. This pleasant picture perhaps owed something to Defoe's love of honest work and productive activity; it applied only to a restriced area and was not, strictly speaking, a description of the domestic system at all. It was rather a picture of a small factory, for the men came to work at the house of the master.

The normal domestic worker was in quite a different position. He brought into his home the dirt and confusion of manufacturing as well as the nervous strain of sweated industry. He did not combine agriculture with manufacuring, for the weaver was a weaver, the farmer a farmer. The chasm between the domestic worker and the wealthy clothier was as wide as that between the factory worker and factory owner in later times. The clothier was tempted to squeeze his workmen and to pay them in truck, that is, in provisions, often of poor quality, instead of in cash. He could easily shift the burden of a depression onto the shoulders of his employees. He merely stopped giving out work; he could do so with much smaller loss than that suffered by a factory owner who shut down his factory. In Nottingham and Leicester the clothier owned the stocking-frames used by the hosiery workers who paid him rent whether he supplied them with work or not. There was great irregularity of employment. Periods of demand were followed by periods of depression; some industries were so dependent on the weather that exports and imports could be delayed for weeks by contrary winds.

The domestic worker lost time between the completion of one assignment of work and the beginning of the next. He must often carry his finished goods to the employer, perhaps trudging for an entire day in each direction. Such irregularities bred bad habits. The domestic worker was tempted to produce shoddy goods. Since he could determine his own hours, he also was tempted to spend the first days of the week at the alehouse, celebrating Saint Monday and even Saint Tuesday, and then to rush through the week's work in three or four days of very long hours. Sedentary workers, like weavers, felt the deadly monotony of repeating the same mechanical processes for hours on end; even the most reliable sought occasional solace in drink. Hence employers came to believe that higher wages would merely result in greater debauchery. And to what could the domestic worker look forward in his old age except the poor house?

The cities which grew most rapidly in the eighteenth century were those in which new industries were established or in which old ones employed new techniques. London was unique, displaying conflicting tendencies. It contained a vast amount of domestic manufacture—trades connected with navigation, luxury trades to cater to the world of fashion, new trades growing from the grain and cattle brought to feed the metropolis (flour mills, breweries, the manufacture of soap, glue, and candles, and the processing of leather). Yet London did not grow as a factory city but as a commercial and distributing center. Goods came from every quarter of the kingdom to be finished, to be exported, and to be distributed throughout the country. London's future could be seen in the development in the early eighteenth century of the fashionable shop, in which as much money went into elegant decorations and furnishings as into the stock itself. As a manufacturing city London lost ground in the eighteenth century. Bristol, England's second city in 1700, grew as a port and as a center for the manufacture of iron and other metals, but it declined in textiles and by 1800 was surpassed by Liverpool in commerce. Norwich, the third city in 1700, sank rapidly into a provincial town. At the time of the census of 1801 "the eight greatest towns of Britain were London with 864,000, Manchester 84,000, Edinburgh 82,500, Glasgow 77,300, Liverpool 77,000, Birmingham 73,000, Bristol 68,000 and Leeds 53,000." Not far behind were Sheffield, making knives, swords, and razors; Nottingham and Leicester, hosiery; and Newcastle-upon-Tyne, articles connected with mining and navigation.

A number of important inventions were made in the first half of the century. The steam pump of Savery and Newcomen, constructed in 1712, was used to lift water from coal mines. This unwieldy and largely imperfect contrivance was very wasteful of fuel, it acted on the principle that condensing steam created a vacuum which sucked water from the coal pits. This engine helped to solve the problem created by water that seeped into the mines as they grew deeper. Another invention saved the iron industry. In the past the foundries where iron ore was smelted had used wood in the form of charcoal as a fuel, but in the eighteenth century the forests of Britain were all but gone and the lack of charcoal seemed destined to kill the iron industry. The solution was found by the two Abraham Darbys, father and son, of Coalbrook-

The Savery and Newcomen engine, early 18th century. (Historical Pictures Service, Chicago)

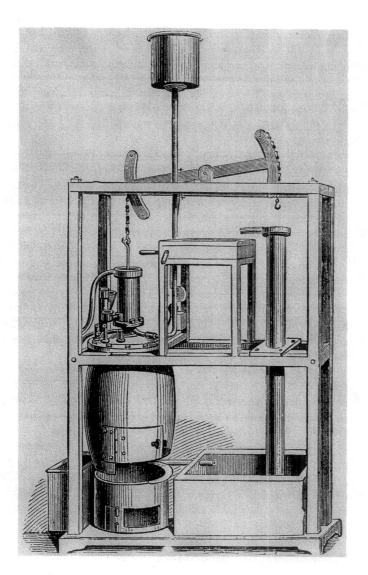

dale in Shropshire, who discovered a means of smelting by coal in the form of coke. This method was used by the elder Darby in about 1709 and later was improved by his son. But for years they kept it a trade secret; it did not pass into general use until about 1750. After that date, the iron industry recovered lost ground and expanded enormously.

A third invention was John Kay's flying shuttle, patented in 1733. This ingenious device could be attached to a hand loom and enabled one man to weave a broader piece of cloth than before. Formerly, if a broad piece of cloth was being made, two workers were needed to throw the shuttle back and forth. But the use of Kay's flying shuttle did not spread rapidly; the great need at the time was for a faster method of spinning thread. Another important contrivance of the early eighteenth century was the use of the overshot water wheel in place of one that was undershot. By this substitution a small flow of water could be made to produce as much power as a larger flow had formerly done. At Coalbrookdale one of Newcomen's engines was used to throw back water from below the mill run so that it continually passed over the water wheel.

As industry grew there was a tendency toward larger units of production in which many workers were gathered in a single building or factory. The state fostered this tendency both by example and by government contracts. In the early years of the century the naval dockyards and arsenals at Chatham formed the largest single unit of production in the kingdom. Government contracts for cannon, shoes, uniforms, and blankets were naturally given to firms with sufficient facilities and with sufficient control of labor to ensure high quality and rapid production. On a much smaller scale, the parish workhouses in which paupers were assembled to perform simple industrial tasks may have served as examples to later owners of factories. The rise of industrial towns increased the tendency toward larger units. When a new industry settled in a town the workers had to be trained and supervised; hence the work was done in buildings provided by the firm. This was also true of silversmiths and manufacturers of costly imported wool, for these materials were too valuable to be scattered among workers in their homes.

The greatest pressure toward larger units, however, was the need for power, which at first was water power. Power was responsible for the first large factory built in England, the famous silk mill of John and Thomas Lombe at Derby. In 1716 John Lombe had gone to Italy and had obtained, by less than scrupulous means, the secret of an Italian process of making silk thread by machinery. Between 1717 and 1721 the Lombe brothers built a large factory four hundred feet long and five stories high, with twenty-six thousand wheels, in which they employed over three hundred women and children. When John Lombe died shortly after, it was rumored that he had been poisoned by a vengeful Italian, but Thomas continued the works and made a fortune. There was thus a full-fledged factory in England by 1721.

CAUSES OF THE QUICKENING OF INDUSTRY

Population

Of the many factors that converged to quicken industry one was an increase in population. The causes of the increase are not entirely clear, but it seemed to be primarily due to a larger number of early marriages in rural areas. As the old pattern of village life was disrupted in the eighteenth century, restrictions on marriage imposed by custom or by parental authority were weakened, and young people tended to marry earlier. Thus the span of childbearing years for a married woman was increased, with a cumulative effect over a number of generations. The growth of population provided a larger market for the sale of manufactures and swelled the labor force. In the eighteenth century the employment of children in industry was not regarded as an evil but as a boon to the poor and a benefit to society. Children of five and six years of age worked in factories. The labor force was augmented further by a more systematic employment of paupers and by a steady stream of Irish immigration.

An increase also took place in the numbers of the lower middle classes from which many of the new industrial leaders arose. They were men of ability and of some education, with habits of thrift and hard work, drive, and a tough determination to make their way in the world. Many of them were nonconformists. Discussions in the Methodist chapel or in the Quaker meetinghouse sharpened their wits, and in the schools and academies founded by dissenting bodies they learned languages, bookkeeping, and elementary science. The expansion of industry brought them opportunity.

Agriculture

A movement toward improved methods of agriculture begun in the later seventeenth century and continued into the eighteenth was largely the work of well-to-do country gentlemen who could afford to experiment and who combined the pleasure of creating model farms with the practical aim of obtaining increased profits. One of the first was Jethro Tull, who owned estates in Oxfordshire and Berkshire. Although something of a crank and often wrong in his opinions, he had a keen eye for improvements in agriculture. He invented an important device known as a drill, a little horse-drawn contrivance by which it was possible to plant seeds in rows instead of scattering them broadcast over the ground. He advocated the cultivation or pulverization of the soil between rows of crops; for this purpose he invented a horse-drawn hoe. By using these methods he grew wheat on one field for thirteen consecutive years without the addition of fertilizer. His experiments continued through the first decades of the century, though it was only in the last ten years of his life (1731–1741) that he published accounts of his advancements.

Another name famous in agriculture was that of Lord Townshend, a landowner in Norfolk. When Turnip Townshend, as he was called, was driven from office in 1730 by his brother-in-law Sir Robert Walpole, he abandoned politics and experimented on his estates with grasses and root crops. He publicized a rotation of crops—wheat, turnips, barley or oats, and clover or rye—by which he eliminated the wasteful practice of leaving one field fallow every year. Turnips and clover could be fed to sheep and cattle during the winter, thus making unnecessary the slaughter of the weaker animals that was customary in the autumn.

Experiments in stock breeding also took place. By intense inbreeding, Robert Bakewell, a Leicestershire farmer, greatly increased the weight of his sheep and cattle. He also developed a breed of strong black horses, much used by the army. He treated his animals with tender care, keeping his rams as clean as race horses.

By the end of the century an astonishing transformation in English livestock had taken place. Sheep ceased to be the small, stunted animals of the past—looking like a cross between a dog and a goat[1]—and became valuable for meat as well as for wool. Cattle grew sleek and fat; the roast beef of old England was the pride of Englishmen, though few could afford to eat it. The weights of sheep and oxen more than doubled between 1710 and 1795, while that of calves increased threefold. Bakewell was visited by celebrities whom he entertained so lavishly in his farm kitchen that eventually he went bankrupt.

A number of improvers revolutionized the agriculture of East Anglia. Of these the best known was Thomas Coke of Holkham, later the earl of Leicester, who enriched the light soil of his estates in Norfolk by marling. Marl was a fertilizer, a clay containing carbonate of lime. Although its value had been known in the Middle Ages, the practice was lost, then resumed in the eighteenth century. Giving his tenants long leases, Coke required them to employ the latest methods of agriculture. The success of these experiments created a wave of enthusiasm for agricultural improvement and it became fashionable for gentlemen to improve their lands. There were farmers' societies, cattle shows, and medals for superior crops. In 1793 the government established a Board of Agriculture, of which the secretary was Arthur Young, perhaps the greatest of all English writers on agriculture. His accounts of his tours through Britain and on the Continent, written with singular enthusiasm and charm, combined sprightly anecdotes with sober descriptions of agricultural improvements. He published a journal, the *Annals of Agriculture,* to which George III contributed under the name of Ralph Robinson, his shepherd at Windsor.

Improvements were impossible unless the old open fields were enclosed and broken into smaller units, each surrounded by its fence or hedgerow. We have often heard of enclosing in English history. It was done to some extent in the medieval period and it became important under the Tudors as fields were converted into sheep runs, but it is surprising that so much of England remained unenclosed in the early eighteenth century. After 1750 the movement picked up speed and continued at a faster tempo until, by about 1830, the countryside had acquired its present appearance and an unenclosed field was a relic of a bygone age.

The reasons for this rapid increase in enclosing are fairly clear. The growth of population was both a cause and a result of improved agriculture. Better roads enabled farmers to take their produce to market, and the great coaching days at the end of the century meant an increase in the number of horses which had to be fed. Moreover, wars brought large government orders of foodstuffs for armies and navies. Thus pressure on the land to produce more food grew ever stronger so that by 1773 or thereabouts England ceased to export grain in any quantity. An increasing population brought about enclosures, and enclosures made possible the growth of population. That enclosures produced more food than the open fields is certain, but unfortunately their utilization benefited the large landowners at the expense of the small ones and imposed new hardships on the poor.

---

[1]The phrase is that of J. H. Plumb, *England in the Eighteenth Century* (Baltimore: Penguin Books, 1964), p. 83. See his table of weights of animals on p. 82.

Agriculture 1700–1800.

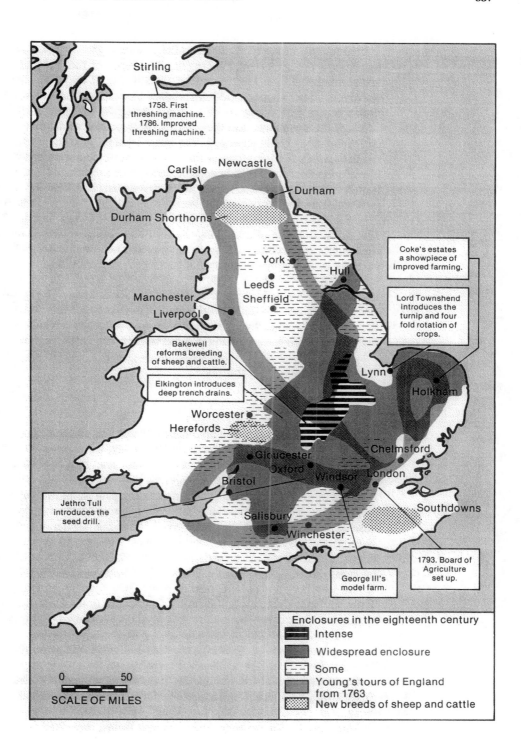

Stirling

1758. First
threshing machine.
1786. Improved
threshing machine.

Newcastle

Carlisle

Durham

Durham Shorthorns

Coke's estates
a showpiece of
improved farming.

York

Hull

Leeds

Sheffield

Lord Townshend
introduces the
turnip and four
fold rotation of
crops.

Manchester

Liverpool

Bakewell
reforms breeding
of sheep and cattle.

Elkington introduces
deep trench drains.

Lynn

Holkham

Worcester

Herefords

Chelmsford

Gloucester

Oxford

Windsor

London

Bristol

Jethro Tull
introduces the
seed drill.

Southdowns

Salisbury

Winchester

George III's
model farm.

1793. Board of
Agriculture
set up.

Enclosures in the eighteenth century

Intense

Widespread enclosure

Some

Young's tours of England
from 1763

New breeds of sheep and cattle

0   50

SCALE OF MILES

In order to enclose the lands of a village in the eighteenth century it was necessary to obtain a private act of Parliament. A number of the wealthier landowners of a village might petition Parliament for such an act. If they obtained it, the land was surveyed, then reapportioned in compact blocks, each owner receiving an amount proportionate to the size of his former holding. In this process the open fields, the pasture, the commons, and the waste all disappeared as distinct entities, and a new pattern of small fields emerged. The large owners, who profited greatly, possessed the capital to pay their share of the costs of the act, to drain and level their fields by filling in the depressions between the strips, and to plant hedges. But the small-scale farmer often suffered: perhaps he received an allotment of land too small for profitable farming, or perhaps he lacked the captial for the necessary improvements. If he sold his land he might rent a farm from a larger owner, but he was more likely to sink to the position of a landless laborer. The cottagers also suffered, for they lost their rights in the commons and in the waste. These rights had so little value that the cottager could not be given land but received a sum of money, which was soon spent. Moreover, he lost the possibility of improving his status, for he could no longer hope to obtain a piece of land and thus rise in the social scale. The gulf between the rich and the poor grew wider, and though the population of the villages did not decline, the number of small farms did. Wages rose with the advance of agriculture, but prices rose even faster. An agricultural laborer could attain a modest prosperity only if his wife and children found some employment. Toward the end of the century disaster fell upon the rural poor.

Transportation

The increasing tempo of industrial production was connected closely with improvement in transport. Good roads came only slowly; throughout the eighteenth century England depended to a large extent on the sea. It was said in 1774 that some eighteen hundred ships were engaged in the coal trade alone, and that about nine hundred more carried other commodities. Shipping along the western coast was not so great, but it was considerable, amounting perhaps to four hundred or five hundred vessels. Cargoes for the most part consisted of the heavier and bulkier goods—coal, slate, stone, clay, and grain—which could be transported by land only at prohibitive prices. These goods were carried long distances by sea rather than very short spans by land. But this coastwise traffic had disadvantages. Sailing ships were dependent on the weather and could be held up for days and weeks on end by contrary winds. They stayed in port during the dead of winter. In time of war they were exposed to capture or destruction by enemy action, and their crews might be pressed into the navy. Goods paid considerable duties as they reentered the country; moreover, thievery from ships at anchor in the Thames was a major problem. Manufacturers and farmers looked first to inland waterways and then to improvement in the roads.

The possibility of improving the rivers was limited. Of English streams, the Severn was best suited to navigation, for it could be traversed without the use of locks and floodgates. Barges traveled from Bristol to Gloucester, Worcester, Kidderminster, Shrewsbury, and even into Wales, and could ascend a number of the river's tributaries. The Thames was navigable as far as Oxford. Smaller streams presented many difficulties, some of them manmade, for mills and fishweirs formed obstructions to river traffic. Nonetheless, considerable work was done in the late seventeenth and early eighteenth centuries to improve the rivers. By 1725 more than a thousand miles of river were open for navigation.

An age of canal building began about 1760. The Sankey Navigation, started in 1755, was constructed to carry coal from a nearby mine to Liverpool. A more famous canal was built between 1759 and 1761 by the duke of Bridgewater, with the aid of the engineer James Brindley, to bring coal to Manchester from the ducal mines at Worsley. The canal was only eleven miles in length, but it presented some difficult problems of engineering and caught the imagination of the public. At Worsley a portion of the canal ran underground to the very site of the mine; at Barton an aqueduct carried the canal over the Irwell River, so that barges above and below passed each other at right angles. This intersection illustrated the way in which a canal substituted capital for labor. Half a dozen of the duke's barges coupled together moved easily along the canal, drawn by a horse or by two men, while below eight or ten strong men pulled and hauled to move a small boat up the Irwell River. The moment the canal was opened the price of coal in Manchester was cut in half.

Many other canals were built in the years that followed. At first they were constructed to bring a raw material such as coal to an industrial area or to connect that area with the sea. Ultimately engineers conceived the bolder plan of linking the major ports of the kingdom by a network of canals. For technical reasons it was some time before London became part of the system. By 1830 over four thousand miles of canals in England and some five hundred miles in Scotland and Wales were in operation. After that date the building of railways caused the abandonment of canal construction. The building of a canal required both engineering and organizing skill. Large amounts of stone and other materials must be collected at out-of-the-way places; great numbers of laborers, many of them Irish, must be assembled, housed, and controlled.

Tudor legislation had made each parish responsible for the maintenance of the

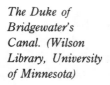

The Duke of Bridgewater's Canal. (Wilson Library, University of Minnesota)

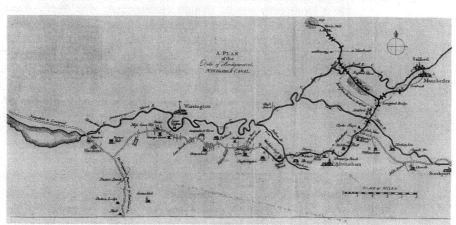

roads within its boundaries. Parishioners were summoned each year to work for a few days on the roads without compensation. But under this arrangement the roads were neglected and tended to degenerate. It is probable that in the eighteenth century most country roads, which were nothing but dirt lanes, sufficed for the limited needs of the locality; but the main highways, especially those leading to London, now subjected to heavy traffic, were cut by the narrow wheels of carriages and churned into a sea of mud by herds of cattle driven to the London market. These roads were impassable for wagons during the winter months, when goods could be carried only by pack horses. The Great North Road from London to Edinburgh fell into such a state of disrepair that men and horses were known to have drowned in its great holes. Parliament attempted improvement without much success, regulating the loads to be carried by large wagons, the number of horses to each, and the width of the wagon wheels. A broad wheel was thought to do less damage to the road (though more to the vehicle) than a narrow one. Tolls were arranged so that wagons with broad wheels, sometimes sixteen inches wide, were given preferential treatment.

It soon became evident that less attention should be paid to the traffic and more to the surface of the roads. The task of improving the highways was entrusted more and more to corporate bodies, known as turnpike trusts, which were authorized to charge tolls on sections of road in return for keeping them in repair. These companies employed engineers who introduced new techniques in building roads. John Metcalf, the blind engineer of Knaresborough, constructed roads by digging out the soft dirt, placing heather on the ground, covering the heather with stone, and the stone with gravel. At the end of the century Macadam and Telford were building good highways by topping them with small crushed stones which the traffic ground together into a hard surface. These roads were slightly convex so that water ran off to the sides.

With the development of hard-surfaced roads, stagecoaches traveled at a faster pace. Express coaches carrying mail and passengers, who had to be persons of some fortitude, were introduced in 1784. By changing horses frequently, the coach from Liverpool to Manchester raced along the road at fourteen miles per hour. Such speed for a lumbering coach, though picturesque, was highly dangerous: coaches could easily overturn. Travelers who could afford the cost hired chaises and post horses. For fear of highwaymen coaches often carried a redcoated guard armed with a blunderbuss. In 1775, when a coach was waylaid in Epping Forest, the guard shot three of the highwaymen before he himself was slain. By the end of the century coaches were running on advertised schedules between the more important towns of the country. These great coaching days continued until the coming of the railways.

Inventions

By the middle of the eighteenth century the impulse to invent was widespread, and an ever-increasing number of discoveries, inventions, and improvements enabled industry to exploit new sources of energy, to reduce the cost of labor, to conserve materials, to liberate capital, and to produce in greater volume.

The spinning of cotton thread was the fastest-growing industry of the 1770s and

1780s. Fine cotton fabrics had been imported for centuries from Italy and later from India, but they were very costly. Early in the seventeenth century a small cotton industry had developed in Lancashire, where cotton from the Levant and linen yarn from Ireland had been woven into a cloth known as fustian. In 1738 Lewis Paul patented a machine to produce cotton thread by passing the raw cotton through rollers; ten years later he invented a carding machine to brush the cotton into long stringy fibers before it was spun. These devices, however, were not successful; the most important invention, Kay's flying shuttle,[2] was an improvement in weaving, whereas the great need was for new techniques in spinning. Weavers could use more thread than the spinners could produce; hence the shortage of yarn was chronic.

The problem was solved by three inventions. In the 1760s a poor weaver, James Hargreaves, who lived near Blackburn in Lancashire, invented the spinning jenny, a multiple spinning wheel, turned on its side, with spindles in place of wheels. It could spin eight threads at a time, and soon it was improved and enlarged to spin one hundred threads. A simple machine that could be set up in a cottage and driven by hand, it was patented in 1770. A year earlier the wealthy entrepreneur Richard Arkwright had invented the water frame. Beginning life as a barber, he had traveled from village to village collecting human hair to be made into wigs. It is probable that his water frame owed something to Lewis Paul, for it was a machine which produced cotton thread by passing the raw cotton between a series of rollers. As the thread emerged from the last set of rollers it was given a twist to make it tough and strong. The water frame was a heavy machine which required artificial power and could not be placed in a cottage. Hence Arkwright built factories. His first machines were powered by horses, who walked round and round in a circle, but he soon turned to water power. He displayed great ability, not only as an inventor, but also as a man of business who could promote his enterprises, organize his factories, and use his employees to the best advantage. Eventually he was conducting under one roof all the processes required to make raw cotton into finished cotton thread. More than anyone else he made the spinning of cotton thread a factory industry.

In 1779 Samuel Crompton, a Lancashire spinner, invented a machine, known as the mule, which combined features of the jenny and the water frame. By 1800 this beautiful and fairly intricate machine could spin four hundred threads of the finest yarn. The industry forged ahead because its problems could be solved by relatively simple machines, its supply of raw material from America was unlimited, and it enjoyed a highly flexible market. The weaving of cotton cloth still continued to be done by domestic workers. In 1785 Edmund Cartwright, a clergyman, invented a mechanical loom run by water power, but it was not a success; it was not until the 1820s that a power loom brought the weaving of cotton fabrics into factories, condemning the hand weavers to a bitter and hopeless struggle for existence.

The mechanization of spinning and weaving woolen goods was much slower, for wool was a fragile material which required gentle handling. The spinning of woolen yarn was not a factory industry until the early nineteenth century; the weaving of high-grade woolen cloth remained a domestic industry until the 1870 and 1880s.

[2]See page 533.

The iron industry expanded rapidly in the second half of the eighteenth century. It was aided, as we have seen, by the discovery of the Abraham Darbys that coke could be used in smelting in place of charcoal, a discovery which became generally known about the middle of the century. Iron thus produced was pig or cast iron. The ironmasters greatly increased the variety of cast-iron products and created a wide market for them. But cast iron contained carbon and other impurities which made it brittle and apt to break under stress or heavy blows. Malleable or wrought iron, which would bend rather than break and which could be hammered into various shapes, was obtained by removing these impurities.

These improvements made possible the production of good wrought iron at comparatively cheap rates, so that England was soon manufacturing the cheapest iron bars in Europe. In 1825 the cost at Cardiff was £10 a ton, whereas in France the cost was £26; by 1830 almost three-fourths of the British product was wrought iron. The uses to which iron could be put was expanded enormously. An imaginative ironmaster, John Wilkinson, believed that iron could be used for every purpose for which wood or stone was commonly employed. "He produced railroads for mines (1767), built the first iron bridge in the world over the Severn (1779), built an iron chapel for the Wesleyans, saw the first iron boat afloat (1787), and finally was buried suitably in an iron coffin (1805)." The industry was most efficient when concentrated in a few great plants, such as the Carron works in Scotland and the Dowlais works in Wales, where all the processes of manufacture were performed together under one management. They were located in areas producing both coal and iron; some firms owned and operated their own mines. Thus the industry was highly capitalized.

A coal wagon on rails, from The London Magazine *1764. (Historical Pictures Service, Chicago)*

*Industry
1715–1815.*

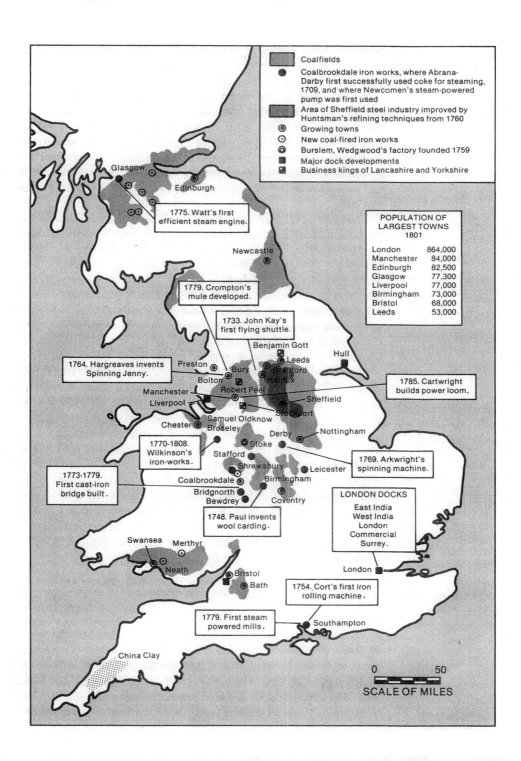

Coalfields

Coalbrookdale iron works, where Abrana-Darby first successfully used coke for steaming, 1709, and where Newcomen's steam-powered pump was first used

Area of Sheffield steel industry improved by Huntsman's refining techniques from 1760

Growing towns

New coal-fired iron works

Burslem, Wedgwood's factory founded 1759

Major dock developments

Business kings of Lancashire and Yorkshire

POPULATION OF
LARGEST TOWNS
1801

London	864,000
Manchester	84,000
Edinburgh	82,500
Glasgow	77,300
Liverpool	77,000
Birmingham	73,000
Bristol	68,000
Leeds	53,000

Glasgow
Edinburgh

1775. Watt's first efficient steam engine.

Newcastle

1779. Crompton's mule developed.

1733. John Kay's first flying shuttle.

Benjamin Gott

Hull

1764. Hargreaves invents Spinning Jenny.

Preston
Leeds
Bradford
Halifax
Bolton
Bury
Robert Peel
Manchester
Liverpool
Sheffield

1785. Cartwright builds power loom.

Samuel Oldknow
Chester
Broseley
Stockport
Derby
Nottingham

1770-1808. Wilkinson's iron-works.

Stoke
Stafford
Shrewsbury
Leicester

1769. Arkwright's spinning machine.

1773-1779. First cast-iron bridge built.

Coalbrookdale
Birmingham
Bridgnorth
Bewdrey
Coventry

LONDON DOCKS
East India
West India
London
Commercial
Surrey.

1748. Paul invents wool carding.

Swansea
Merthyr
Neath

Bristol
Bath

London

1754. Cort's first iron rolling machine.

1779. First steam powered mills.

Southampton

China Clay

0   50
SCALE OF MILES

Yet the metal trades in which iron was made into a great variety of small objects continued to be carried on by domestic workers until well into the nineteenth century.

The demand for coal steadily increased, though not as rapidly as might be supposed, because of the frequent use of water power. Perhaps four times as much coal was mined in 1800 as had been mined a century earlier. As the miners worked farther and farther away from the bottom of the mine shaft, iron rails were installed underground on which carts, drawn by horses or human beings, carried the coal to the bottom of the shaft, where it was raised to the surface by new hoisting machinery. There was great need for an industry to manufacture machines according to exact specifications. Such an industry did not appear until the nineteenth century, but a step toward it was made in 1794 when Henry Maudsley invented a side rest for the lathe.

The making of china, porcelain, and other potteries became an important industry in the eighteenth century. Royal Potter Josiah Wedgwood displayed great skill in every department of this manufacture. He not only developed a high quality of chinaware but created artistic shapes and designs. An enterprising and aggressive businessman who extended the market for his wares throughout Europe and America, he became one of the great industrialists of the century. Another manufacturer of chinaware was Josiah Spode, whose willowware design, a modification of a Chinese pattern, is still used extensively today. Pottery works also produced less expensive china which the lower classes could afford to buy. Much easier to clean than pewter, chinaware was a factor in improving the health of the nation.

The development of the steam engine, of prime importance in the Industrial Revolution, is connected with the name of James Watt, an inventor of genius. He was at first a maker of scientific instruments at the University of Glasgow, where he prepared apparatus for experiments in astronomy and physics. In 1763 he began a study of the principles of the Savery and Newcomen engine. Over a period of many years, handicapped because he could not obtain parts cut to exact specifications, he gradually constructed a vastly improved engine and adapted it for use in industry. His engine, a true steam engine in that steam was fed into each end of a closed cylinder and pushed the piston up and down, was patented in 1769. Between 1782 and 1784 Watt perfected a device by which his engine could turn a wheel. The invention of an engine using coal and turning the wheels of a factory made industry independent of water and opened an new phase of the Industrial Revolution. About three hundred of Watt's engines were in use by the year 1800.

FIRST RESULTS OF THE INDUSTRIAL REVOLUTION

Of the more immediate effects of these changes the most striking was the enormously increased volume of production at greatly reduced costs. The imports of raw cotton into England rose from 4 million pounds in 1761 to 56 million in 1800 and to 100 million in 1815. The cost of production of cotton thread declined between 1779 and 1812 in the ratio of 100 to 7; between 1779 and 1882 in the ration of 100 to 2. In 1796 there were 21 million yards of cotton cloth manufactured; in 1830 the figure had risen to 347 million. A machine tended by a young girl who mended broken threads could weave as much cotton cloth as could ten weavers working by hand. The same astonishing acceleration may be seen in the iron industry. In 1740 England produced 17,000 tons of pig iron; in 1796, 125,000 tons; in 1806, 256,000 tons. There was a corresponding increase in British shipping. The tonnage of ships that cleared from British ports rose from 289,000 in 1709 to 2,130,000 in 1800. At the height of the struggle with Napoleon, between 1800 and 1810, the English constructed thirty acres of new iron docks in London, making it by far the greatest port in the world.

The inventions of the age made a deep impression on the people. As they saw the new canals and factories, the speeding coaches, and the new machines, as they breathlessly watched the first daredevil ascend in a balloon (from a spot, as was noted, near Bedlam), they were filled with wonder and astonishment. The newspapers of the time were constantly using such words as "amazing," "unprecedented," and "astounding." The agricultural writer Arthur Young, in attempting to prove that population was rising (which some people doubted), wrote as follows: "View the navigation, the roads, harbors, and all other public works. Take notice of the spirit with which manufactures are carried on. . . . Move your eyes which side you will, you behold nothing but great riches and yet greater resources. It is vain to talk of tables of births and lists of houses and windows, as proofs of our loss of people; the flourishing state of our agriculture, our manufactures and commerce, with our general wealth prove the contrary." Here was born that belief in progress which in the nineteenth century became almost a religion. Such wonder at the achievement of machines and such faith in the idea of progress may seem naïve, but to people living in the year 1800, mechanical gadgets appeared the symbols of a brave new world.

There was at the same time a change in economic thought. The mercantile views which, as we know, had dominated the thinking of the early modern period laid emphasis on trade rather than on production, assumed that a nation increased its commerce by seizing the commerce of some other power, and set up a favorable balance of trade as the great goal of the nation. Gold and silver were believed to constitute wealth. To attain these objectives it was the duty of government to regulate minutely the economic life of the nation, not with the individual merchant in mind but for the corporate economic good of the commonwealth. These theories were demolished by a famous book, Adam Smith's *Wealth of Nations*, published in 1776. It was a declaration of independence no less than the one in America. It held that wealth did not consist of the precious metals but of consumable goods—of buildings, canals, machines, and industrial plants; of the useful articles being produced. Adam Smith laid emphasis on production rather than on commerce. The way to increase production, he believed, was to allow the individual manufacturer the greatest possible freedom, for his self-interest would lead him to produce the goods that society wanted. The state should not interfere, but should permit the private enterprise of the manufacturer to come into gradual alignment with the needs of society. Artificial barriers to trade should be removed. This was the doctrine of *laissez faire* (to let alone) which led England eventually to adopt free trade. For some time the effect of this thinking was merely negative. The government stopped making new regulations but did not repeal old ones. Later, in the 1820s, regulatory laws began to be removed from the statute book.

The first scientific census, carried through by John Rickman in 1801, showed that the population of England and Wales had risen to about nine million, whereas it had stood at about 5.5 million in 1700. Also because of the census, an important shift of population, dimly perceptible throughout the century, was now made clear. Population was leaving the south and east of the country and was moving to the north and west, to Lancashire and to the West Riding of Yorkshire, to Newcastle, to Birmingham and Coventry, to cities in the Severn Valley, and to South Wales—in a word, to the coal fields and the manufacturing towns. This shift of population was slow, quiet, subtle, almost unobservable, a kind of caterpillar crawl, by which the people living near a town moved into it and the places they left vacant gradually were filled by other people living farther away. The south and east of England, except for the area of London, lost its old preeminence in the national life and subsided into a quiet land of large estates. The future of England lay in the industrial north. From time out of mind the southern counties had returned more than their share of members to the House of Commons, and the movement of population to the north made ever sharper and more glaring the inequities of the electoral system.

The growth of industry produced a type of capitalist who was a newcomer to the English scene. He was likely to have risen from humble origins. It was said that as a middle-aged man Richard Arkwright devoted an hour a day to the improvement of his English and his penmanship. The new capitalist was a businessman, tough and

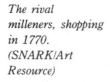

The rival milleners, shopping in 1770. (SNARK/Art Resource)

rugged in temperament, with drive and determination, who had clawed his way up the ladder of success from poverty to riches. He had many admirable qualities, but he was not a gentleman. The aristocracy looked upon him with hostility. He found himself excluded from the social circle of the country gentry and from that preserve of English gentlemen, the life of politics. Occasionally a millionaire like the elder Sir Robert Peel, a magnate of the cotton industry, could secure, at least for his children, a place in society and politics, but most of the industrialists could not. Many of the smaller factories were in the country, the squalid cottages of the workers clustering about the manufactury. The owner was in close proximity to the local gentry. The result was a mutual dislike and bitterness which in time produced its political repercussions.

The new wealth was distributed badly, and the poor got little of it. Their condition was rendered much worse at the end of the century by the long war with France which began in 1793 and continued, with one short intermission, until 1815. War brought inflation and high prices for food; wages, though they rose, did not keep pace with this increase. The fortunes of war and the opening and closing of markets on the Continent made business conditions unstable and employment uncertain. Factory hours were unbearably long. The slums of the industrial towns showed little improvement. It is not surprising that there were frequent riots, sometimes for food and sometimes against the burden of poverty and overwork thrust upon workers. Yet the factory worker was better off than the landless agricultural laborer who was dependent upon low wages and who could not afford to buy the food he himself had helped to raise. Rural slums could be nearly as horrid as urban ones.

The lower classes, in both town and country, suffered from the bad administration of the Poor Law. The Elizabethan Poor Law of 1601 was still in force, though it often was modified in practice. The parish remained the unit of poor relief: it must support its own poor in the parish workhouse, and many were the dodges of local officials to shift the burden of the poor, whenever possible, to some other parish. Employers living in one parish favored laborers living in another so that if work became slack the support of the unemployed would fall upon the parish where the laborers resided. The diseased and the infirm, even persons at the point of death, were hustled out of a parish when some excuse could be made for their support by another. The workhouse was often a place of filth and misery into which were crowded together the young and the old, the diseased and the healthy, the vagabond and the honest laborer. All were supported—or, rather, kept from starvation—by rates levied on their grudging fellow parishioners. As the condition of the poor grew worse, the justices of the peace of Berkshire, meeting at Speenhamland in 1795, adopted the policy of outdoor relief, that is, the practice of taking money from the poor rates to supplement the wages of laborers who were not living in the workhouse. This local measure designed to meet a local emergency soon spread to other parts of the country and the results were disastrous: wages sank below the level of subsistence, for employers need not pay a living wage when the parish would made up the difference; the independent laborer who wished to support himself could not compete with laborers subsidized by the poor rates; the poor rates rose alarmingly and threw an intolerable burden on the middle class. Thus the century ended darkly for the poor, especially for those in rural areas.

Generations of historians have argued about the effects of the Industrial Revolution. Some, when comparing the conditions between 1750 and 1850, point to the obvious improvement of life for vastly greater numbers of people. Others have stressed the demoralizing conditions in which so many urban dwellers struggled to survive. The latter, however, have generally not compared the plight of the poor with their plight in earlier and later periods. Relatively speaking, life in the long run did indeed improve, and the number of those enjoying the better life increased tremendously.

C H R O N O L O G Y

Industrial Revolution

1701	Jethro Tull invents the seed drill
1709	Darby smelting techniques begin
1712	Savery and Newcomen steam pump
1717–21	John and Thomas Lombe build first factory at Derby
1732	Lord Townshend's turnips; Robert Bakewell and selective breeding of cattle
1733	John Kay's flying shuttle
1750	Enclosure movement begins
1759–61	Duke of Bridgewater's canal
1769	Richard Arkwright's water frame; Josiah Wedgwood appointed Royal Potter; James Watt patents steam engine
1770	James Hargreaves patents spinning jenny
1776	Adam Smith's *Wealth of Nations*
1779	Samuel Crompton's mule; first iron bridge (over Severn) built by John Wilkinson
1784	Express coach service begins
1785	Edmund Cartwright invents power-loom
1793	Board of Agriculture and Arthur Young
1795	Speenhamland system of "outdoor" poor relief
1801	First population census

26 The Younger Pitt and the Great War with France

The peace with America in 1783 was followed first by a short period of political crisis and then by a decade of reconstruction and recovery under the premiership of William Pitt the Younger, a statesman of remarkable ability and dedication. Pitt steadily improved the efficiency of government in a quiet and unobtrusive way. It was well for England that he did his work so effectively. In 1789 came the shock of the French Revolution, which greatly alarmed the English upper classes. In 1793 England and France went to war. From then until the final defeat of Napoleon in 1815 the energies of the nation were absorbed by the struggle with France, and domestic reform of any kind became nearly impossible.

POLITICAL INSTABILITY, 1782–1784

The fall of Lord North's administration in March 1782 was followed by two years of political instability. A demand for peace with America compelled the king to find a minister who had not been closely associated with the war; he was forced to turn to the opposition. The new ministry was a coalition of the group led by Rockingham, which included Charles James Fox and Edmund Burke, and the group led by Shelburne, the political heir of Chatham. Rockingham became the first lord of the Treasury; Shelburne and Fox, secretaries; and Burke, paymaster of the forces.

The new Cabinet did not promise to last long. The Rockingham group did not like Shelburne, a man of ability, knowledge, and breadth of view. Even his opponents admired his clearness of thought and his ruthless sense of purpose, but he was considered too close to the king, too secretive in his methods, and too masterful in action. Fox began to talk as though Shelburne represented a royal faction within the new ministry and declared that he planned to give the influence of the Crown a stout

549

blow. As a matter of fact, the Crown's influence was at a low ebb. George had wished to continue the war because he believed that France was on the verge of collapse, he feared that an American victory would spell the end of the empire, and he felt that radical and dangerous forces were abroad which ought to be suppressed. He now saw all his policies reversed. He regarded Fox as his enemy, partly because of Fox's offensive speeches and partly because Fox was a friend of the Prince of Wales, whom he was leading into gambling and debauchery.

Both groups in the Cabinet desired reform, but their approach and their objectives differed. Shelburne wished to reform the Commons by increasing the number of independent country members. He also suggested reforms of administrative methods. He began an inquiry into abuses in raising loans during the American war, he advocated the payment of officials by salaries and not by fees, and he proposed clearer divisions between the work of administrative departments. At the same time he hoped to raise the standing of the Crown and to preserve its position in politics.

Burke and Fox, on the other hand, obsessed with the idea of the king's excessive power, aimed directly at reducing the possibility of royal influence over the Commons. They passed an act which disfranchised the revenue officers of the Crown as persons open to direct pressure from the government. Another act disqualified men who held government contracts from sitting in the Commons. Burke also obtained a measure which compelled the paymaster of the forces to separate his private funds from those belonging to the state and to keep the latter in an official account at the Bank of England. He further devised an act concerning the civil list which was to be so arranged that ministers' salaries were to be paid only after other items charged to the civil list had been provided for. The purpose was to make ministers economical, but they soon disregarded the act as a dead letter.

The Rockingham-Shelburne coalition ended in the summer of 1782, when Fox resigned after a quarrel with Shelburne over the peace negotiations in Paris. Rockingham died in July. His followers hoped that the king would appoint the duke of Portland as head of a Cabinet dominated by Fox, but the king offered the first place to Shelburne, who accepted.

It was estimated that at this time three main groups existed in the Commons. Shelburne, who commanded about 140 votes, was followed by those who thought of him as a disciple of Chatham, as the true reformer of the day, and as the head of the government who could bestow political favors. Fox headed a party of about 90 members. The leader of the Rockingham group, he had added followers of his own who felt the charm of his personality and thought that he would soon be in power. The third group was North's, numbering some 120 members. It consisted of men who had attached themselves to North during his long period of office and who now felt some awkwardness in breaking away, though desertions were taking place as his position weakened. Beyond these factions, more than 100 members maintained complete independence.

Although no one group could control the Commons, Shelburne made the attempt. Disliking party government, he did not negotiate with party leaders. He hoped that as his administration became stable it would attract individuals from other groups and would gain the support of independent country gentlemen. But his career was ended by the peace settlement negotiated in Paris. The country accepted the peace but repudiated the man who made it; Shelburne fell in February 1783.

An alliance of two of the three groups in the Commons was now essential. The one which emerged was a coalition of Fox and North, a coalition which held office only from April to December 1783 and which has often been portrayed as unnatural and almost wicked. It was certainly an alliance of convenience, but it was not as strange as it appeared. Although the two men had opposed each other during the American war, that war was over and differences of opinion could be forgotten. Both North and Fox believed that they were better off with each other than either of them would have been with Shelburne. It was true that North was conservative whereas Fox stood for radical reform. But Fox, thinking perhaps that reform had gone far enough for the present, agreed not to push it further in the immediate future. Thus the alliance could be justified in a number of ways, although it made a painful impression in the country: Fox appeared to be abandoning his principles in order to obtain power. The king was so deeply incensed that for over a month he did not summon his new ministers to take office.

The short life of the coalition revolved around Fox's India bill, which was an attempt to take control of Indian affairs away from the East India Company without placing that control in the hands of the king. Seven commissioners, assisted by nine others expert in commerce, were to govern British India. Unfortunately, the commissioners named in the bill were all members of the parties of Fox and North. The country came to the conclusion that Fox was seeking to place the patronage of India in the hands of his friends. For this reason the bill alienated public opinion.

To the king, who was ready to believe the worst, the bill appeared a monstrous abuse of power. Duty compelled him, he thought, to stop the bill if possible and to remove ministers who advocated such legislation. He was within his constitutional rights to make the attempt, though if the country did not support him, the result might be disastrous. He discovered that North was being deserted by some of his followers. The possibility arose that the twenty-four year old William Pitt, who was free from any connection with the American war, might be able to attract these deserters and thus form a stable administration. In December 1783, therefore, George took the unusual step of using his personal influence to bring about the defeat of the bill in the House of Lords. He then dismissed Fox and North and appointed Pitt as first lord of the Treasury. The king was taking the chance that in the long run the Commons would approve this action. And in the long run they did.

Pitt came forward as the opponent of faction and of party government. He hoped to succeed where Shelburne had failed in building a nonparty administration upon a broad basis of general support. It was Fox who embodied party, but he had made party government appear unscrupulous and clannish. Pitt hoped to become what the Commons and the country wanted—an able, sensible, incorruptible, and patriotic leader who symbolized national unity and offered calm and practical administration, as opposed to the heated imaginations of Burke and Fox. Pitt stood for a reconciliation of king and Commons; he was both a friend of the king and a minister pledged to reform.

Pitt's lifelong opponent in politics was Charles James Fox, a man of ability and

William Pitt the Younger, by John Hoppner. (National Portrait Gallery, London)

charm. Warmhearted and generous, with humor, vitality, and attractive manners, he possessed far more personal magnetism than did the austere Pitt. A true liberal, he espoused the causes of the American colonists, Ireland, and the French revolutionists; he was a strong opponent of the slave trade. Fox was an excellent debater, very skillful in reply, able to grasp the significance of each argument in debate, develop it logically, and present it to the Commons with remarkable clarity. His excellent memory supplied him with apt quotations. He was thus a formidable figure in the Commons.

PITT'S RISE TO POWER

Pitt's first months as prime minister were difficult ones. He did not have a majority in the Commons, and the way in which he had come to power by a kind of palace intrigue embittered Fox and his followers. But Fox made the mistake of being too violent, using his majority to hold up supplies and to postpone the normal passage of the Mutiny Act. He persuaded the Commons to send a representation to the king asking him to dismiss his present ministers. The fact that he also denounced the possibility of a general election showed that Fox feared its consequence. Such vindictive measures told against him, for he appeared to be denying the king's right to dissolve Parliament and to select his ministers.

Pitt, on the other hand, played his cards with coolness and judgment. He carefully cultivated the business community in London and the friendship of reformers like Wilberforce. He brought in an excellent India bill, which was defeated by only eight votes. He showed that he was making a serious attempt at sound government, and many people believed that he represented the last possibility of decent administration. Thus, when the election was held in April 1784, Pitt won a surprising victory and Fox went down to ignominious defeat. It is true that Pitt had the support of government patronage, which was used freely in his behalf. He also received financial backing from a number of wealthy men, such as those in the East India Company, who had been terrified by Fox's proposed solution of the Indian problem. Some of Fox's followers, seeing little hope of election, decided not to stand for Parliament.

Charles James Fox, by Karl Anton Hickel. (National Portrait Gallery, London)

Public opinion, aroused in an unusual way, supported Pitt. One hundred and sixty of Fox's followers either did not stand or were defeated. George's calculation in dismissing Fox and North was justified by the result.

PITT AS A PEACE MINISTER

Administration and Finance

Pitt's greatest achievement, upon which his reputation justly rests, was his thorough investigation and steady reform of administration and finance. He did not concentrate on the civil list, as Fox and Burke had done, but looked at the work of every clerk in the employment of the state and at every item of receipt and expenditure. It was this constant scrutiny of details that slowly improved the machinery of government. It is truer to think of Pitt as a patient reformer of the details of government all his life than to call him a reformer in his youth and a reactionary in middle age. He worked quietly and slowly, avoiding strife and publicity so far as possible. Thus he preferred to end sinecures, not by a sweep of the pen, as Burke would have done, but by waiting until the holder of a sinecure died and then refusing to appoint a successor. On the whole this was cheaper than to abolish the sinecure and compensate the incumbent. In substituting salaries for fees he was also slow, and for much the same reason. But civil servants discovered that the volume of their work steadily increased. Much more application was now expected of them, so that the government received value for its money.

Pitt improved financial arrangements in the customs service by having all customs duties paid into one consolidated fund instead of into a number of funds as in the past. He thus eliminated many offices and also simplified bookkeeping. The civil list, formerly the preserve of the Crown, was now reviewed by Parliament, and a beginning was made in appropriations for separate items, leaving to the king only such money as was required for his private necessities. In raising loans for the government Pitt obtained better terms by asking that competitive bids be offered in sealed letters.

It was necessary to obtain new sources of revenue. Pitt's early budgets imposed taxes on luxuries in a rather haphazard way. Thus a tax on windows in houses, which he made an important part of the tax structure, proved to be less a levy on the rich than a discouragement to the building of windows in lower class housing and in factories, where windows were badly needed. Pitt's taxes, however, became more scientific as time when on. Finding that high duties on tea, wines, and tobacco increased smuggling, he reduced the duties, extended the excise to these articles (as Walpole had vainly attempted to do), and struck fiercely at the smugglers. A disciple of Adam Smith, Pitt sought to remove impediments to the growth of industry and to promote freer trade. In 1785 he attempted to establish free trade with Ireland, though the opposition of business interests in England forced him to drop the measure. He succeeded in concluding a commercial treaty with France by which both countries lowered their tariffs. English cloth entered France more cheaply than before, and French wines came into England at lowered prices. To reduce the national debt, which stood at £238 million in 1783 and consumed half the government's income in interest charges, Pitt revived the sinking fund set up by Walpole.

In ten years Pitt raised the government's revenue by a third and paid off £11 million of the debt. He was able to balance the budget, though only by reduction of military and naval expenditure. His financial success depended on the maintenance of peace and ended under the strain of the war with France. Nonetheless, a rapid revival of the English economy took place between 1783 and 1793. The resilience and buoyancy of the new industrialism came as a gratifying surprise.

India

Shortly after the election in 1784 Pitt reintroduced his bill on India, which became law in the same year.

The history of the East India Company was highly complicated during this period. This trading corporation enjoyed a monopoly of commerce between England and India, but in Bengal it was also gradually assuming the powers of government. This trend raised serious problems because the commercial interests of the company might easily conflict with its duty in governing a large native population. At home the company not only conducted eastern trade but was also a financial and banking house to which the government turned when it wished to borrow money. The company itself raised funds by issuing bonds. It possessed a good deal of patronage, which was highly valuable because even a minor clerkship in the East offered a young Englishman an opportunity to become wealthy. Moreover, the directors of the company were important men in London who could influence city politics and help return members to Parliament. In fact, they were courted by the government. This history of the company was further complicated by the existence of feuds and factions within the group of directors.

Some of the company's servants were coming home with enormous fortunes. These "nabobs," as they were called, with their Orientalized manners and vulgar display of wealth, became familiar figures in the English social scene. The opportunity for illegal gains in Bengal was fostered by Clive's dual system of government, through which the company drew revenue not only from trade but also from the native treasury, though responsibility for law and order was left in the feeble hands of the native ruler. During a parliamentary investigation Clive committed suicide.

In 1772, Warren Hastings became the governor of Bengal. A great administrator with a firm grasp of the essentials of Indian government, he combined boldness in decision with grim determination to fight to the finish against his many foes. He was not a reformer. During his first two years in office he laid the foundations for a greatly improved system of finance and administration. Following orders from home, he abolished Clive's dual system and assumed full control of the government of Bengal. The taxes were collected by native officials supervised by Englishmen drawn from the senior ranks of the service. They also tried civil cases, though criminal cases were left in the hands of native judges using Hindu and Muslim law. Two courts of appeal, one civil, the other criminal, also were established. Here was the beginning of an administrative system which fused English and native elements and which could be understood by the Indians.

Partly because of French intrigue and partly because of the blunders of the English in Madras and Bombay, Hastings was drawn into war with an alliance of the three most powerful native states in India—the Marathas, Mysore, and Hyderabad. He could hope for little aid from home but he fought the war with great energy and determination. By his able diplomacy he split the alliance and was able to make peace with his enemies one by one.

During this struggle Hastings engaged in several questionable practices. He levied an enormous fine on Chait Singh, the Raja of Benares, an ally of the company, and pressed for payment until Chait Singh rose in wild revolt and had to be dethroned. When the Nabob of Oudh claimed that he could not make certain payments to the English because he was owed money by his great-aunts, the Begums, or princesses, of Oudh, Hastings sent soldiers to seize the treasure of the elderly Begums. These episodes formed the counts against Hastings when he was later impeached in England.

The Indian problem was still to be solved when Pitt came to power. Pitt's bill separated the government of Bengal, which was to be controlled by the Cabinet, from the management of commerce and from patronage, both of which were left to the company. Officials sent to India continued to be named by the company, though the cabinet influenced major appointments. But when these officials reached the East, they received their instructions in civil and military matters from the government at home. A board of control was established in London; its president was a member of the Cabinet; it was he who governed British India so far as it could be governed from London. By a supplementary act in 1786 the powers of the Governor General were increased. His council was reduced from four members to three, he could override its decisions if he took full responsibility, and his control over Bombay and Madras was made complete.

Hastings came home in 1785. Led by Fox and Burke, who acted in a kind of partisan frenzy, the opposition in the Commons insisted that Hastings be impeached. The impeachment dragged on for seven years; and Hastings, though acquitted at last, was ruined by the expenses of the trial. It was a poor return for saving India.

The next governor general, sent out in 1786, was Lord Cornwallis. Despite his defeat at Yorktown, he continued to enjoy the confidence of his countrymen. He went to India with great power and prestige. He was not a servant of the company, but an officer of the Crown, a noble lord, the friend of Pitt and Dundas. Answerable only to the board of control, he could defy the company. Under his wise administration, the honesty and efficiency of English officials in India steadily improved.

Other Attempts at Reform

Although the Commons accepted Pitt's financial reforms and his bill on India, they did not hesitate to defeat some of his other proposals. In 1785 he introduced a bill to eliminate thirty-six pocket boroughs (with generous compensation to borough owners), to transfer the seats to London and to large counties, and to extend the franchise by giving the vote to copyholders whose lands were worth forty shillings a year. The measure was defeated by a large majority. Accepting this verdict, Pitt made no further move to alter the electoral system. Indeed, he conferred peerages on owners of pocket boroughs, so that his friend Wilberforce lamented that he governed through influence rather than through principle.

Pitt also wished to abolish the slave trade. This traffic, which had been accepted as a matter of course until the middle of the century, was now under attack by the Quakers, by the Methodists, and by an evangelical movement within the church. In 1772 Judge Mansfield ruled that a slave became free if he set foot in Britain. An Abolitionist Society was founded in 1787. Pitt brought the question before the Commons in 1788 and on subsequent occasions, but the opposition of vested interests was so strong that the matter dragged on until it was lost in the conservatism resulting from the French Revolution.

Foreign Affairs

During the ten years of peace between 1783 and 1793 Pitt conducted the foreign affairs of England with considerable success. His aims, apart from temporary crises, were to end the isolation in which Britain found herself after the American war, to frustrate the designs of France on Belgium and Holland, and to resist the advance of Russia into eastern Europe.

A serious crisis developed in Holland, where conflict arose between the Stadtholder and an aristocratic party which desired to overthrow him. France allied with the Dutch insurgents; England and Prussia supported the Stadtholder. In 1787, using a somewhat thin excuse, Prussia sent troops into Holland and firmly established the Stadtholder in power, a course which England approved. Faced with bankruptcy at home, France made no move to intervene. This was a diplomatic victory for Pitt. In the year following he was able to construct alliances of England with both Prussia and Holland, thus ending British isolation.

In another episode in a quite different part of the world, French financial decay again played its part. English fishermen had established a settlement on Vancouver Island on the Pacific coast of North America. But the Spanish, claiming a monopoly of the entire Pacific shore, seized an English ship in Nootka Sound off Vancouver. Pitt protested while Spain prepared for war. Then finding that no help would be forthcoming from France, Spain gave way and the crisis passed.

Pitt was less successful in opposing Russia. In a war between Russia and Sweden, England, acting with Holland and Prussia, assisted the Swedes by forcing Denmark to remain at peace. But in 1791, when Pitt wished to fight the Russians, who were about to seize certain Turkish territories in the vicinity of Oczakov on the Black Sea, he was unable to obtain support in England for a war in defense of Turkey. He was forced to accept this extension of Russian possessions.

THE FRENCH REVOLUTION

Meanwhile events were taking place in France which were to reshape the political and social structure of Europe and to have a profound effect upon England. We are apt to think of Britain in the eighteenth century as aristocratic and oligarchical; yet England was democratic in comparison with France. In France, without the principle of primogeniture, there were some 110,000 nobles who enjoyed a disproportionate amount of wealth and privilege at the expense of the rest of the nation. They owned almost half the land, monopolized the higher offices in the church and in the government, and were enriched further by frequent gifts from the king. They paid practically no taxes.

Below the nobility were the bourgeoisie, a middle class of lawyers, doctors, and bureaucrats, of merchants, manufacturers, and heads of guilds. The most modern and progressive part of the nation, they were irritated by the privileges of the nobility and by the rigid class distinctions dividing society. Yet, speaking very broadly, the middle class was not dissatisfied; it could normally obtain what it wanted.

At the bottom of French society were the peasants, who formed the mass of the population. They were for the most part freemen and were probably better off than the peasants in other parts of the Continent, but their lot was hard enough. They lived in poverty; yet they paid most of the taxes. They owed labor and produce to the seigneur, tithes to the church, and oppressive payments to the state.

These conditions might have been born had the government been efficient and successful. It was not. The king claimed to rule by divine right and to be the embodiment of the state, but he was merely the captive of an evil system of government which brought extravagance at court and confusion in every department of administration. Although the kingdom was bankrupt, vested interests defied attempts at reform. The conviction arose that the existing state of affairs was unnecessary and absurd. The American Revolution had supplied a stirring example of what a determined people could do.

We can do no more than outline the course of the Revolution. Once the Estates General was assembled in 1789, the third estate declared itself a National Assembly and assumed control. It was protected by the Paris mob. The early work of the Assembly was of fundamental importance: the abolition of feudalism, serfdom, and all feudal dues; the abrogation of special privilege; the declaration that all classes should be taxed on a basis of equality; and the ending of tithes. The National Assembly declared that men were born free and equal, with rights to "liberty, property, security, and resistance to oppression." Religious toleration, freedom of the press, and free speech were guaranteed, as was the right of every citizen to have a voice in the selection of officials.

The Assembly decreed a constitution in 1791 which was idealistic and impractical. It made the king responsible for good government but denied him the power to achieve it. As a result he was constantly at odds with the Assembly. Meanwhile the country was faced with invasion and other dangers, and a break occurred between the bourgeoisie, who had controlled the Revolution so far, and the lower classes, who felt they were being excluded from its benefits. In August 1792 the mob in Paris rose in revolt, and the more radical elements seized power. France was declared a republic, the king and queen were executed, and nobles and bourgeoisie alike were sent to the guillotine. This Reign of Terror lasted about a year in 1793 and 1794. Then, following the fall of Robespierre in 1794, more moderate groups among the revolutionaries regained control and set up a government known as the Directory in 1795. But it was weak and corrupt and in 1799 was overthrown by its most brilliant general, Napoleon Bonaparte, who made himself the head of the state as First Consul and became the emperor of the French in 1804.

ENGLAND AND THE FRENCH REVOLUTION

The first events of the Revolution were well received in England. When Fox heard of the fall of the Bastille, he exclaimed, "How much the greatest event that has happened in the world and how much the best." English reformers rejoiced to see a progressive spirit in France. Political societies, formed to celebrate the centenary of 1688, remained in existence to acclaim the French. Poets found it "bliss to be alive." Even conservative Englishmen were glad to see constitutional monarchy replacing absolutism, and if France chose to weaken herself by internal strife, so much the better.

But as the Revolution grew more violent and radical, as the lower classes obtained control, as monarchy ended in bloody butchery, as the intervention of Austria and Prussia was repulsed, English opinion altered and the English upper classes first became disgusted, then alarmed, then panic stricken. Seeing the awesome power of the mob, they were convinced that the principles of the French Revolution, if applied in England, would bring about their destruction. It was Burke who first sounded a note of terror in his *Reflections on the Revolution in France,* published in October 1790. With his belief in the sanctity of ancient institutions and his veneration for the aristocracy, he regarded the Revolution as a catastrophe. Unless it was crushed it would spread to other countries, ruin the civilization of Europe, and could lead to an orgy in which cutthroats persuaded the mob to guillotine kings, despoil churches, and confiscate the property of the well-to-do. Burke made a profound impression, giving a strong conservative bias to English society and politics. He was answered by Tom Paine's book, *The Rights of Man,* which only increased the terror of the upper classes. Paine, though of Quaker origin, was a firebrand in politics. In America he had urged the colonists to revolt. Now in England he declared that government was derived from the people, that the monarchy and the House of Lords should be abolished, and that a democratically elected House of Commons should take control. His book was revolutionary propaganda.

A number of radical societies sprang up in England. The leadership did not come from Fox or from the poorest class of industrial workers, but from lower middle-class persons, such as John Telwall, a tailor and attorney's clerk, and Thomas Hardy, a shoemaker, backed by "artisans, shopkeepers, dissenting ministers, and schoolmasters." The societies talked the jargon of the Revolution, corresponded with clubs and societies in France, rejoiced in French victories, and passed resolutions assuring the French that English arms would never be used against them. The London Corresponding Society, founded by Thomas Hardy in 1792, aimed at a national organization based on local committees. It held a convention in Edinburgh in 1793 which challenged authority by acting as though it would substitute itself for Parliament. After England and France went to war in 1793, the radicals talked as though they sympathized with the enemy; the high price of food led to riots in the industrial towns; a stone was thrown at the glass carriage in which George III was riding to open Parliament; and Ireland was close to rebellion.

Yet there was really no danger of revolution in England. The clubs, for the most part, were frothy and clamorous rather than violent. Even the Corresponding Society, basing its radicalism on John Locke, did not talk of revolution but of manhood suffrage, annual Parliaments, less expensive government, and a simplified legal system. Nonetheless, the country gentlemen in the Commons may perhaps be forgiven if they became alarmed. Following Burke, they reverenced ancient institutions, but then went further in forming their own philosophy. Fiercely on the defensive, they were determined to preserve the position of the upper classes. Maintenance of the *status quo* was all important; fear of radical upheaval became hysterical. Pitt assumed a new significance: he was valued above all as the resolute opponent of French ideas.

The difference of opinion between Burke, who continued to denounce the French Revolution, and Fox, who continued to praise it, led eventually to a split in the opposition. The two men quarreled openly in the Commons in 1791. His quarrel with Fox ended Burke's political career.

A long series of repressive measures followed. A proclamation in 1793 against seditious writings warned that a conspiracy was under way against the state. An Aliens Act placed foreigners under strict surveillance; habeas corpus was suspended; a Treasonable Practices Act extended treason to the writing or speaking of words inciting to treason; and a Seditious Meetings Act prohibited gatherings of more than fifty persons without prior notice to a local magistrate, who might stop the meeting at any time. The press was controlled; clubs and societies were forbidden; trials and convictions were savage. But when Hardy and others were tried for treason in 1794, with death as the penalty demanded by the state, they were acquitted, and Pitt received a warning that repression must not be carried too far. Gradually the fire went out of the clubs, partly because of Pitt's measures, partly because of disillusion over the course of events in France. An agitation among the lower classes in 1798 was not revolutionary; it was industrial, inspired by hard times and high prices. It was answered by the Combination Acts (1799–1800), which prohibited any combination or union of workingmen for any purpose whatever. This legislation sprang from fear of the new industrial proletariat and formed a prelude to the class struggles of the nineteenth century.

PITT AS A WAR MINISTER

The French War, 1793–1797

In February 1793 France declared war on England, Holland, and Spain. In the summer of 1792 Austria and Prussia had invaded France, intent on crushing the Revolution. But the French had checked the invaders at Valmy in September and had forced them to retreat. The ardor of the French made them aggressive and they pushed into the Rhineland and into Savoy. Promising assistance to any people who sought to overthrow their rulers, the French invaded the Austrian Netherlands, won the Battle of Jemappes, threatened Holland, and declared that the Scheldt River, closed to commerce by international agreements, should now be opened. To open the Scheldt, which connected Antwerp with the North Sea, was to overthrow the commercial balance of the area. It was a fixed principle of English policy to prevent France from dominating the Austrian Netherlands and Holland. Hence Pitt reluctantly accepted the challenge of war in 1793.

Although Pitt was to guide the war for many years, he was not a good war minister. England's strategic objective in 1793 should have been a direct thrust at the heart of France, but Pitt entered the war with very limited aims. He believed that there were certain areas of Europe—the Austrian Netherlands, the Mediterranean, and the Baltic—which were vital to British interests, and these must be defended. But he did not plan to fight on the Continent as a principal. The fighting there should be left to Britain's allies, to whom Pitt was ready to give handsome subsidies. England's true interests, he believed, lay outside Europe: his aim was to capture French trade and French colonies, especially in the West Indies.

This, in a general way, had been Chatham's policy, but times had changed. Pitt fought a France with a new spirit, a nation in arms, with patriotic troops and ruthless commanders, soon to be reinforced by the genius of Napoleon Bonaparte. He in turn was allied with the reactionary and hesitant powers of Austria, Prussia, and Russia, all more intent on the partition of Poland than on the war with France.

Pitt's blunders are obvious. He expanded the army in an unfortunate way which allowed some men to buy exemptions from service and took others into the militia when they should have gone into the regular army. For many years there was no commander in chief; and Dundas, who became secretary for war, was no better strategist than Pitt. Pitt placed too much confidence in English gold. He constantly underrated the strength of France and overrated the power of his allies. He could not understand how France without money or prestige, could withstand the nations allied against her. These nations—Austria, Prussia, Sardinia, Spain, Naples, and Portugal, with an empty promise of help from Russia—Pitt formed into the First Coalition. The word "coalition" implies a closer alliance than really existed. The one point on which the allies were united was their common desire to secure British funds. Above all, Pitt made the error of scattering his energies in many small expeditions, none of them strong enough to achieve its objectives.

As a result there were years of dismal failure, although Britain met with some success at sea and in the West Indies. On 1 June 1794, Admiral Howe mauled a French fleet some four hundred miles off the coast of Brittany and Pitt carried forward his plan of capturing the French and Dutch colonies. His principal effort was against the French West Indies. A number of islands were taken, but the cost in human life was high. By 1796 the British had lost forty thousand dead; as many more were made unfit for military service. For Pitt and Dundas to pour half the army into the West Indies to fight rebellious blacks and to die of yellow fever was, to say the least, a grave error in judgment.

After two years of war the French army had not been defeated and the French navy had not been destroyed; even their seaborne trade, though greatly diminished, had not disappeared. Worse was to follow.

Between 1795 and 1797 the First Coalition broke up. Prussia, having spent Pitt's money in Poland, made peace with France and lapsed into neutrality. Spain and the small Italian state of Tuscany abandoned the struggle in 1795. The French were thus free to concentrate against Austria. Led by their brilliant young general, Napoleon Bonaparte, they defeated one Austrian army after another and imposed the Peace of Campo Formio in 1797. Austria ceded the Netherlands, accepted the Rhine as France's eastern frontier, and agreed to abandon Italy except for Venice. The first half of 1797 was a difficult time for England, now alone in the war against France. Taxation was extremely heavy, food was scarce, and prices were cruelly high. So much gold had been sent to Austria in a vain attempt to keep her in the war that a financial crisis developed in London. Ireland was restive. A mutiny in the fleets off Portsmouth and off the mouth of the Thames was due to bad conditions, meager pay, and the poor quality of some seamen. A demand for peace arose in England; talks were held with the French at Lille, but they came to nothing.

Revival of British Sea Power

The mutiny in the fleets was only a passing episode. The last quarter of the eighteenth century was notable for a marked revival of British sea power. A generation of famous admirals—Rodney, Howe, Keppel, and Hood—steadily improved the fighting quality of the navy and gave it a new spirit. Horatio Nelson was to become the most famous. Nelson's fighting genius and his chieftain's experience and professional competence formed an excellent combination. British sea power revived only just in time, for late in 1796 the French tried to invade Ireland. But their fleet was scattered by a month of storms and they failed to accomplish their goal. Although the French had acquired the navies of both Spain and Holland, these fleets had been destroyed by the end of 1797. Early in that year Admiral Jervis won a decisive victory over the Spanish fleet off Cape St. Vincent near Cadiz, a battle in which a bold maneuver by Nelson added to the impact of the British assault. In October Admiral

Duncan destroyed a large portion of the Dutch fleet off the coast of Holland. These victories ended for the time any threat of French invasion.

The navy played a great part in the fighting in 1798, the year in which Napoleon conceived his plan for an expedition to Egypt as a step toward French control of the Mediterranean and toward the ultimate conquest of India. After capturing Malta, Napoleon was soon established in Egypt. The British sent Nelson after him. Nelson was the supreme embodiment of fighting spirit at sea, as Napoleon was on land. But there was much more to the "Nelson touch" than desperate courage and joy in combat. He had the power of instant decision and he was a master of naval tactics, which he planned and discussed with his captains, his "band of brothers," until each captain knew what was expected of him in almost any circumstance. Nelson's patriotism, his devotion to duty, and his confidence of victory made him a spiritual force. His object was not the defeat but the annihilation of the enemy. Entering the Mediterranean, he at first had some difficulty in locating Napoleon's squadron. At sundown on 1 August 1798, he found it in an exposed anchorage in Aboukir Bay at the Rosetta Mouth of the Nile. He attacked instantly, the forward ships of his line coming in on both sides of the enemy's van, so that the concentration of numbers was 8 to 5. The French, caught unawares, received a crippling bombardment. Of thirteen French warships only two escaped destruction or capture in one of the most overwhelming defeats in naval history. Control of the Mediterranean was won at a blow; Napoleon was left a hopeless adventurer cut off from France.

This victory enabled Pitt to form the Second Coalition of Great Britain, Austria, Russia, and a number of smaller powers. At first it met with success. But they soon melted away, and the Second Coalition dissolved in 1799 and 1800 for much the same reasons that had ruined the first. Nelson displayed personal weakness by falling under the captivating influence of Lady Hamilton, who was living in Naples. Pitt sent no troops to Italy, but dispatched an expedition against Holland which was a failure. In August 1799, Napoleon, deserting his army in Egypt, slipped back to France. Within a year he defeated Austria, forcing upon her a peace which left him master of western Europe. Russia had withdrawn from the coalition, and England was once more alone.

Sea power, however, enabled England to defeat the French in Egypt and to capture Malta. When it appeared that the Danish fleet would fall into French hands, an English squadron was sent to the Baltic. Its admiral was the rather cautious Sir Hyde Parker, but Nelson was second in command, and at the Battle of Copenhagen in 1801 he destroyed much of the Danish fleet. From this engagement emerges the most famous of Nelson stories. At a critical moment Parker signaled to discontinue action, but Nelson, putting his telescope to his blind eye (lost in fighting in Corsica), disregarded the signal. The war was becoming one in which France appeared invincible on land and England invincible at sea.

The Union with Ireland, 1800

In March 1801 England was stunned by the news that Pitt had resigned. He resigned over disputes involving Ireland, and we must turn for a moment to Irish affairs. Until the middle of the eighteenth century Ireland had lain prostrate under the religious and economic code imposed upon her after 1688. Then conditions began slowly to improve, bitterness between Catholics and Protestants diminished, and many of the penal laws were laxly enforced. Ireland achieved a modest prosperity. A society of some wealth, culture, and learning arose in Dublin. The Irish House of Commons began to agitate against the restrictions by which it was bound.

Despite these stirrings, the institutions of the country were firmly in the hands of the Protestant minority and were controlled from England. The upper clergy and the senior officials in Ireland were appointed by the Cabinet in London as part of its normal patronage; scarcely an Irishman was to be found in the higher ranks. The Irish establishment in both church and state was far more elaborate and costly than the country required. Even by English standards the Irish Parliament was narrow and corrupt: no Catholic could vote in an election or be a member, Presbyterians were excluded in practice because various tests debarred them from the town corporations which controlled the majority of elections, and Poynings' law, restricting the Irish Parliament, was still in force. By an act of 1719 the English Parliament possessed the right to make laws that were binding in Ireland.

The American and French revolutions gave Ireland an opportunity to strike for freer government and freer trade. As troops were withdrawn from Ireland to be sent to America and as the danger of French invasion mounted, both Protestant and Catholic Irishmen enrolled in a national militia known as the United Volunteers which eventually had eighty thousand members. At the same time a group of reformers appeared in the Irish Parliament, led by Henry Grattan and Henry Flood, who used the threat of Irish revolt to obtain concessions from Britain. In the years between 1778 and 1783 England yielded a number of important points: Roman Catholics were permitted to inherit property and to hold long leases; the Acts of Trade were modified; Irishmen were allowed to trade with the British colonies; and the Irish Parliament was given its independence. Poynings' law, enacted under Henry VII, and the Act of 1719 were repealed; the Irish Parliament could legislate as it wished, though the English Crown retained a veto; and the English Parliament ceased to pass laws concerning Ireland. The Irish, however, had not obtained self-government. Their Parliament was elected on so narrow a franchise that it could be controlled through patronage and the manipulation of pocket boroughs. It possessed no power over the executive officials in Dublin Castle, who were appointed in England. Religious disabilities and a wretched agrarian system continued.

The French Revolution brought wilder hopes and passions. Irish radicals, looking to France for aid, dreamed of complete independence—the goal of the Society of United Irishmen, founded in 1791 by Wolfe Tone, though its nominal purpose was to press for parliamentary reform. The society at first included both Catholics and Protestants, but animosities arose between the two religious groups. Catholics clamored for admission to Parliament but, though they obtained the vote in 1793, they still were excluded from membership. Fear of French radicalism and French invasion rallied the Protestants to the support of the government, but many Catholics were ready to cooperate with France. Secret societies were formed along religious lines—Protestant "Peep-o'-Day Boys" against Catholic "Defenders." The government caught the spirit of panic which prevailed in England. It permitted Protestant magistrates and militiamen to suppress the Catholics; the irregular troops, in the name of law and order, committed outrages—torturing, flogging, and shooting in cold blood. The result, a Catholic revolt in 1798, was never formidable and was easily suppressed.

Watching these developments, Pitt became convinced that in such dangerous times the Irish Parliament could not be allowed freedom of action. As was true of England and Scotland before the union of 1707, independent Parliaments in England and Ireland could and did take conflicting action on very important issues. Pitt came to believe that there must be a legislative union by which the Irish Parliament would cease to exist and Irish members would be added to the Parliament in London. He planned to couple union with far-reaching reforms. In particular he wished to grant Catholic emancipation, that is, the admission of Catholics to the English House of Commons; he also wished to modify the tithes paid by Irish peasants to the Anglican Church, to provide salaries for the Irish Catholic priesthood, and to establish free trade between the two countries.

Unfortunately he passed the union without the reforms. By the distribution of bribes and pensions, by promotions in the Irish peerage, and by promises that Catholic relief would follow, the Irish Parliament was induced to vote itself out of existence in 1800. One hundred Irish members were added to the British House of Commons; four Irish bishops, sitting according to a scheme of rotation, and twenty-eight lay peers, elected by all the Irish nobles from their own number, were to sit in the British House of Lords. The seats in the Commons were not reserved for Irishmen. On the other hand, since the twenty-eight Irish peers in the Lords were elected for life, other Irish nobles might seek election to the British House of Commons. But when Pitt turned to Catholic emancipation, he met the implacable opposition of the king. George was again on the verge of insanity, and since the very mention of Catholic emancipation disturbed him greatly, Pitt felt that he could not press the issue. He therefore resigned. It is strange that he had not come to an understanding with George earlier, for the king's views were well known. Union without emancipation embittered the Irish Catholics, who felt that they had been deceived.

THE PEACE OF AMIENS, 1802

Pitt was succeeded as prime minister by his friend Henry Addington, who had been speaker of the House of Commons for many years. An extremely conservative and cautious man, Addington possessed common sense and reliability but no great talent. He represented the war weariness of many Englishmen. Although he regarded the war with France as just, he was ready to end it in a draw because of its great expense. In opposing any kind of domestic reform as dangerous experimentation, he seems to have personified the mood of the moment. With only a small following of his own in the Commons, he received that general support which many members had grown accustomed to give to the government of the day. He had very few friends among the leading politicians. But with the support of the king, Pitt, and a majority in the Commons, his administration seemed likely to last for some time.

Addington stood for peace and retrenchment. He opened negotiations for peace with France. Napoleon, on his side, welcomed a breathing space but drove a hard bargain. Except for Ceylon (captured from the Dutch) and Trinidad (captured from Spain), England restored all the colonies taken from France and her dependencies, whereas Napoleon promised little more than to evacuate Egypt and to withdraw from southern Italy. This one-sided peace was possible only because the English assumed that Napoleon, in the Treaty of Lunéville with Austria in 1801, had guaranteed the independence of Switzerland, Holland, and northern Italy. Addington then began to cut down the size of the army and navy and to concentrate on financial reform. At first the peace was popular in England. It soon became clear, however, that Napoleon had no thought of enduring peace. He continued in his aggressive policies: armed peace was to carry on the work of war. Hostilities with England began again in May 1803 after a cessation of fourteen months.

Addington thought in terms of a defensive war, but his military preparations for even this limited objective were so bungled and his prospects as a war minister appeared so dim that opposition mounted in the Commons and he resigned in May 1804. Pitt then returned to office. He wished to form a Cabinet of complete national unity in preparation for a great struggle, but quarrels and squabbles had developed among politicians. Thus Pitt was compelled to form a narrow ministry from his own followers and from those of Addington, though the two groups disliked each other. It was not a strong Cabinet.

THE WAR, 1803–1815

Napoleon at the Height of His Power

"Make us master of the Channel for three days," Napoleon had once said in his grand way, "and we are masters of the world." Addington's concentration of defense gave Napoleon the opportunity to bring his army to the Channel ports of France. Fortunately the French plans were mismanaged. Napoleon hoped at first to rely on surprise and to take his army across the Channel on a dark night in small boats armed only to resist light attack. Then he concluded that a French fleet must have temporary control of the Channel. In 1805 there were French squadrons at the naval bases of Brest, Rochefort, and Toulon, and Spanish ships at Cadiz and El Ferrol. They were blockaded by English units, but the English could not watch all of them all the time. The French units at Rochefort and Toulon evaded the blockade and sailed for the West Indies. This was intended at first merely as a diversion, but Napoleon conceived the idea that if his fleets could rendezvous in the West Indies, they might return to Europe together, pick up the Spanish units, and hold the Channel long enough for a French army to cross to England. The plan miscarried, partly because fleets could not be moved on an exact timetable, partly because the Toulon fleet, which Nelson followed to the West Indies, failed to effect its junction with the main French fleet, but chiefly because Austria reentered the war against France in August 1805.

Pitt's countermove against the threat of invasion had been to construct a Third Coalition of Britain, Russia, and Austria. Its existence was brief. Abandoning the plan of invasion, Napoleon quickly turned his armies eastward. On 20 October 1805, he defeated the Austrian vanguard at Ulm. On 2 December he crushed the combined Austrian and Russian armies at Austerlitz, perhaps the greatest of his victories. When Pitt heard the news, his face assumed what was called the "Austerlitz look," his frail health gave way, and in January 1806 he died.

England, too, won a great victory. On 21 October 1805, the day after the Battle of Ulm, the French Admiral Villeneuve sailed from Cadiz with a French and Spanish fleet in a dash for the Mediterranean. Off Cape Trafalgar he was met by Nelson. The French and Spanish line extended in a great half-moon. Dividing the bulk of his fleet into two attacking columns, Nelson dared to approach the enemy almost at right angles. His forward ships were badly mauled, but he broke the enemy line and inflicted an overwhelming defeat in which eighteen ships were captured or destroyed. Nelson was killed in this action. The effects of Trafalgar were far reaching. Napoleon's naval power was ended for the time being, though it was later to revive; a French invasion of England became impossible. Each side looked for new ways to attack the other. To the English, Trafalgar suggested the possibility of a land front which could be sustained from the sea.

On land Napoleon continued his victories. King Frederick William III, the foolish ruler of Prussia, after leaning toward alliance with Napoleon, suddenly declared war against him in 1806. At the Battle of Jena in October Prussia was totally defeated. Her military power collapsed, Napoleon entered Berlin in triumph, and Prussia was shorn of large portions of her dominions. In the following year, after defeating Russia at the Battle of Friedland, Napoleon made an alliance at Tilsit with the impressionable young Czar, Alexander I. Napoleon's power had reached its height. His supremacy in Europe appeared impregnable. French ideas in government, in law, and in education, as well as in war, were accepted and admired throughout the Continent.

English Politics, 1806–1815

Pitt's Cabinet broke up after his death in 1806. The king accepted a coalition drawn from the opposition. It was known as the Ministry of All the Talents because it included Fox, Lord Grenville, and Addington (now Lord Sidmouth). In reality the new Cabinet was narrowly Foxite. Fox proved to be a good man in office, both as a leader and as a colleague, though he accomplished little against Napoleon either in war or in diplomacy. Having opposed Pitt's coalitions with continental powers, Fox tried again to make peace only to discover that an honorable peace with Napoleon was impossible. He might have held office for a long time, but he died in 1806. The one important domestic measure of the ministry was the abolition of the slave trade throughout the empire. On another liberal issue, a proposal to admit Roman Catholics to high office in the armed forces, the Cabinet encountered the opposition both of the king and of many members of the Commons. Thereupon the coalition Cabinet broke up.

It is possible, in speaking of the Ministry of All the Talents, to use the terms "Whig" and "Tory" without confusion. Fox's heirs were Whigs. Pitt, who had never ceased to call himself a Whig, was now dead; and George Canning, one of his disciples now coming into prominence, adopted the word "Tory" to denote his conservative principles.

Yet in 1807 the groups in the Commons again were broken and divided. A Tory Cabinet was patched up under the duke of Portland (1807–1809), an elderly and rather slow-witted man. Its interest lies largely in his younger colleagues, who were to give the country Tory government for many years to come. One was Lord Eldon, an ultraconservative lawyer who opposed change of any kind. Another lawyer, Spencer Perceval, who succeeded Portland as prime minister in 1809, was also very conservative, especially on the Catholic question, but he possessed a good mind and great courage.

This Cabinet also contained Lord Castlereagh, the eldest son of the Irish marquis of Londonderry. A brilliant diplomat and man of action, Castlereagh was calm and unruffled in demeanor, with a simple massive dignity, though with no great skill in debate. Cautious and sound, with solidity of character and judgment, he acquired an extensive experience in foreign affairs. More than any other man, he held the foes of Napoleon together until victory was won and a settlement of Europe achieved. Portland's Cabinet included George Canning, the son of an Irishman of good family but of straitened circumstances. Canning's mother was an actress, a woman of great beauty. Young Canning was well educated by an uncle, entered politics, and became a follower of Pitt. An able administrator, a shrewd and daring diplomat, a brilliant speaker, he was, unfortunately, egotistical, difficult, and ambitious, with a sharp tongue that earned him enemies. Disliking Castlereagh, he intrigued against him. The two men fought a duel in 1809 and both resigned from the Cabinet. Castlereagh returned as foreign secretary in 1812, a position he retained for a decade. Canning was out for a longer period, holding only minor office until 1822, when he succeeded his rival as foreign secretary. Another member of this Cabinet was Lord Liverpool, who was to be prime minister for an extraordinary length of time, from 1812 to 1827. His principal talent was his ability to keep difficult colleagues working together as a team. These men pushed the war with new vigor and with more strategic insight than had prevailed in the days of Pitt.

The Decline of Napoleon

After 1808 the nature of the war began to change. Although Napoleon was older and naturally more inclined to take his ease, he retained more authority than any one man, however brilliant, could hope to employ properly. The character of his army also altered. When he had first led it to victory, it had been inspired by patriotism and by the ideals of the Revolution. But these ideas were fading: the army was now selfish and materialistic—a host of mercenaries who followed a plundering tyrant for their own advantage. Napoleon quartered his troops outside France, forcing other nations to support them. Because of this heavy burden France began to be considered, not as a liberator, but as a despot which squeezed the lifeblood from its victims. Resentment fostered a sense of nationality among the exploited peoples. The ideals of liberty, equality, and fraternity, taking root in Germany, Spain, and elsewhere, worked against Napoleon and not for him. Because of England's resistance, his rule meant constant war: he brought neither peace, nor prosperity, nor permanence.

Napoleon's Continental System angered Europe and prepared the way for his downfall. Knowing that he could not defeat England by invasion, he attempted to ruin her economy by excluding her goods from Europe. By a series of decrees between 1806 and 1810 he commanded that every country under his control or in alliance with him refuse to admit British manufactures or raw materials from British colonies. The English answered by a number of Orders in Council which declared Europe to be in a state of blockade, cut off from trade with the rest of the world. England suffered from the Continental System, especially between 1810 and 1812, and became involved in quarrels with neutral countries who wished to trade with the Continent. These difficulties were the principal cause of a short war with the United States (1812–1814). The Americans had suffered more from the British enforcement of the Orders in Council than from the French Continental System. The ensuing war was of great importance to the Americans but was of little concern to the British, then or later. It became evident that the Continent suffered more from the blockade than England did from lack of markets. Italy and Holland saw their commerce throttled; Germany and Russia could obtain neither manufactured articles nor tropical products. Moreover, if the Continental System were to be effective, it must be universal.

In 1808 the English sent an army to the Continent once more. In the preceding year Napoleon had attacked Portugal in order to tighten the Continental System. In 1808, having an army in Spain, he deposed the Spanish ruling house, though he was in alliance with it, and installed his brother Joseph as king of that country. The result was a Spanish uprising. For the first tme Napoleon found himself at war with a continental people fired by the spirit of nationalism. Although the Spanish could not face his armies in the field, they were excellent guerrillas and their constant attacks and ambushes forced him to keep large garrisons in Spain. In July 1808 Sir Arthur Wellesley, later the duke of Wellington, was sent with a small army to drive the French from Portugal. This he succeeded in doing but he was then superseded by other English generals. One of them, Sir John Moore, after a daring raid into Spain, was forced to retreat over desolate country in winter weather and evacuate his shattered army at Corunna. The English were discouraged. Nonetheless, the government persevered, and Wellesley (now Lord Wellington) returned to Portugal in 1809. Thereafter there was always a British front in Spain and Portugal. Sometimes Wellington could move into Spain, at other times he merely held his position in Portugal. Eventually he defeated the French at Salamanca (1812) and at Vitoria (1813), fought his way through the Pyrenees, and invaded southern France late in 1813.

Napoleon then had to either fight Russia or give up his one great weapon against Great Britain. His invasion of Russia and his retreat from Moscow during the winter

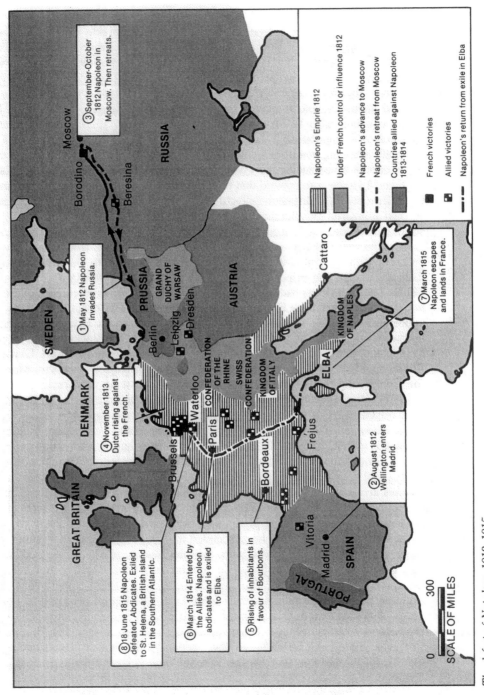

The defeat of Napoleon 1812–1815.

The map legend:

Napoleon's Emprie 1812

Under French control or influence 1812

Napoleon's advance to Moscow

Napoleon's retreat from Moscow

Countries allied against Napoleon 1813-1814

French victories

Allied victories

Napoleon's return from exile in Elba

① May 1812 Napoleon invades Russia.

② August 1812 Wellington enters Madrid.

③ September-October 1812 Napoleon in Moscow. Then retreats.

④ November 1813 Dutch rising against the French.

⑤ Rising of inhabitants in favour of Bourbons.

⑥ March 1814 Entered by the Allies. Napoleon abdicates and is exiled to Elba.

⑦ March 1815 Napoleon escapes and lands in France.

⑧ 18 June 1815 Napoleon defeated. Abdicates. Exiled to St. Helena, a British island in the Southern Atlantic.

GREAT BRITAIN

SWEDEN

DENMARK

RUSSIA

Moscow

Borodino

Beresina

PRUSSIA

Berlin

GRAND DUCHY OF WARSAW

Leipzig

Dresden

AUSTRIA

CONFEDERATION OF THE RHINE

SWISS CONFEDERATION

KINGDOM OF ITALY

Waterloo

Brussels

Paris

Bordeaux

Fréjus

Vitoria

Madrid

SPAIN

PORTUGAL

ELBA

KINGDOM OF NAPLES

Cattaro

SCALE OF MILES

0   300

570

of 1812 were disastrous. All Europe turned against him. In the three-day Battle of Leipzig he was driven from Germany. His empire beyond France quickly collapsed. In April 1814 Napoleon abdicated as Emperor and was sent to the island of Elba, off the west coast of Italy. In May the allies signed the Treaty of Paris with Louis XVIII, of the Bourbon line of kings, now restored in France. But many questions remained to be settled by a congress of powers which met in Vienna in September. While the victors were negotiating and quarreling in Vienna, Napoleon suddenly reappeared in France on 1 March 1815, and was soon at the head of a large army. His return united the allies against him. At the Battle of Waterloo in Belgium in June 1815 he was thoroughly defeated by Wellington and by the Prussians under General Blücher. He then was exiled to the island of St. Helena, far away in the South Atlantic Ocean, where he died in 1821.

THE SETTLEMENT OF EUROPE

Castlereagh and Wellington, who represented England at the Congress of Vienna, believed that Europe would be more peaceful and stable if France were treated well. The Treaty of Paris had restored her frontiers as of 1792 and had returned the bulk of her colonies, but this settlement was made more severe at Vienna. France now received her frontiers of 1790, was forced to pay a large indemnity, to support an army of occupation until the money was paid, and to return the works of art which Napoleon had looted from the capitals of Europe. Yet even this was generous treatment.

In order to restrain France from aggression in the future, Castlereagh sought to strengthen the states along her borders. Belgium was placed under the king of Holland, Prussia was given lands along the Rhine, the kingdom of Sardinia was enlarged, and Austria dominated the rest of northern Italy. In central Europe Castlereagh hoped to strengthen Prussia and Austria as a counterpoise to Russia in the east and France in the west. Russia received the lion's share—Finland in the north, most of Poland in the center, and Bessarabia from Turkey in the south.

England's gains were colonial. During the war she had swept up not only the French possessions overseas but also the whole of the Dutch empire in the Malay Archipelago. These colonies now were returned except for Ceylon, ceded by Holland in 1802, and the French West Indian islands of Tobago and St. Lucia. In the Caribbean area England also acquired Trinidad from Spain and a portion of Dutch Guiana from Holland. In the east she kept French Mauritius and the Seychelle Islands. She also retained the Cape of Good Hope, for which she paid Holland a compensation of £2 million, to be used in building fortifications against France. In European waters England obtained Heligoland in the North Sea, Malta in the Mediterranean, and the Ionian Islands in the Aegean.

These possessions made England the greatest imperial power in the world and gave her a firm hold on the principal sea lanes of the world's commerce. Her supremacy at sea was undisputed until the end of the nineteenth century.

C H R O N O L O G Y

Younger Pitt and World War

1783	Pitt the Younger prime minister
1784	Pitt's India Bill enacted
1785	Warren Hastings impeached
1789	French Revolution began
1790	Burke's *Reflections on the Revolution in France;* Paine's *The Rights of Man*
1791	United Irishmen founded by Wolfe Tone
1792	London Corresponding Society founded
1793	France declared war on Britain; First Coalition; Alien and Sedition Acts
1798	Nelson won Battle of the Nile; Second Coalition
1799–1800	Combination Acts
1801	Nelson won Battle of Copenhagen; Henry Addington prime minister; union of Great Britain and Ireland
1802	Peace of Amiens
1803	War resumed
1804	Pitt returned as prime minister
1805	Battles of Austerlitz and Trafalgar
1806	Pitt dead; Ministry of All the Talents; Fox dead; Napoleon began Continental System; Britain issued Orders in Council
1812	Wellington victorious at Vitoria; War of 1812; Napoleon reached Moscow
1814	Napoleon defeated; sent to Elba
1815	Napoleon returned to power; Battle of Waterloo; Congress of Vienna

Transition from War to Peace

ENGLAND IN 1815

Englishmen hailed the peace of 1815 with great joy, and with good reason. Of all the nations of Europe they alone had never bowed to Napoleon; rather, they had continued the struggle against him after their allies had collapsed. Their navy had prevented invasion, had broken the sea power of the French, and had made possible the expansion of trade and empire. Their armies had played a great part in defeating Napoleon as had their statesmen in making the peace. The English constitution had weathered the stress of a generation of war. Manufacturers, merchants, and landlords, on the whole, had prospered. Industrial development had made steady progress. As Englishmen considered all this, they drew a sharp distinction between themselves and the peoples on the Continent, whom they regarded with condescension and with a sense of moral superiority.

This was the bright side of the picture; there was also a darker side. For many reasons, as we shall see, the transition from war to peace was to be extremely difficult, for other and more fundamental problems existed. England was entering a new age. The old world of the eighteenth century had been shattered by the growth of population, the rise of the northern industrial towns, the American and French revolutions, and the Napoleonic wars. The new world of the early nineteenth century was a harsh world, with sharp distinctions between classes as well as bitter class antagonisms. At the top of society were the nobility and gentry, in the heyday of their power and influence, with their monopoly of political life, their landed estates, their church, their pocket boroughs, and their privileged universities. The middle classes included a larger and larger variety of many kinds of people, from rich merchants and bankers to small shopkeepers. But though they were growing in wealth and numbers, they were largely excluded from political power. Below them

573

Beau Brummell and his tailor. (Granger Collection)

were the depressed agricultural laborers, the seething mass of industrial workers in the towns, and many special groups, such as miners, sailors, and domestic servants.

The poor were often in desperate straits. Scientific agriculture and high prices for agricultural products had enriched the landowners and tenant farmers but had often inflicted hardship on the rural laborer, who found himself deprived of ancient rights and almost wholly dependent on his wages. A bad harvest, a stretch of unemployment, or a rise in the cost of living could easily reduce him and his family to the verge of starvation. The increase of mills and factories had brought a steady stream of laborers into the towns. These grimy workpeople, living a squalid life in slums and factories, were uneducated, brutal, even savage, totally unorganized and totally unprotected against exploitation and sudden unemployment. Unless the English harvest was abundant, they paid high prices for food, for there had been little opportunity to import grain during the French wars. A bad system of poor relief increased the number of paupers, demoralized the lower classes, and imposed a heavy financial burden on the nation.

England thus was faced with new and difficult problems. Most of her institutions, devised in an earlier and simpler age, were inadequate for the complex problems of the nineteenth century: the poor law was Elizabethan; so was the church which, with its many abuses, its badly distributed revenues, and its neglect of the urban poor, had not been overhauled since the Tudor period; the Acts of Trade, a product of the seventeenth century, were still in force; the universities and the Inns of Court were just awakening from their eighteenth-century slumbers; the law was in great need of reform; there was an exaggerated respect for the rights of property and of vested interest. England might boast of her constitution, but in truth she was inefficiently governed by a small landed aristocracy whose standard of conduct, both in public service and in private morals, was not high. Although the power of the Crown in politics had diminished, it could still influence the composition and actions of the government. The Cabinet system had advanced, yet Cabinet coherence and discipline were still in their infancy, and most ministers thought of themselves as the servants of the king. Above all, Parliament was unreformed: the franchise in the counties was governed by a law of 1430, new boroughs had not been added since 1688, and the industrial north was grossly underrepresented. Old Sarum, which was uninhabited, continued to send members to the Commons; Birmingham and Manchester, which were nearing populations of 100,000 each early in the century and doubled in size during the next thirty years, sent none. Reform in a broad sense could hardly be achieved until the House of Commons was reformed.

The French Revolution and the Napoleonic wars came at a most unfortunate time for England. There had been hope of reform after the American war. But the French Revolution frightened the upper classes, ended all possibility of immediate change, and poisoned the relations of rich and poor. Proposals for mild and needed reform were branded as dangerous and radical. Men do not stop to repair their houses, said a member of Parliament, while a hurricane is raging.

There was a deep and unreasoning fear of the mob. A phrase such as the "swinish multitude," heard in the Commons in the early nineteenth century, would not have been used before the Revolution. Any demonstration of discontent on the part of the poor inspired terror as though it was the prelude to insurrection, and men believed that at any time they might be compelled to take up arms against the violence of the lower classes. The word "democracy" was a nasty word, recalling the guillotine and the French Reign of Terror. The years since 1789 had been years of profound economic and social change, but the government, intent on the war, had done nothing to guide the forces of industrial development and rapid urbanization. Employers had managed their factories as they pleased; the new towns had grown up raw and hideous. With reform deferred, with antiquated institutions, with a vast national debt, with inflationary prices and depreciated currency, with suffering among the poor and apprehension among the rich, and with a difficult transition from war to peace, it is no wonder that the years after 1815 were years of stress and conflict.

HARD TIMES, RADICALISM, AND REPRESSION

Agriculture had enjoyed a boom during the war. Landlords who had received good rents and tenant farmers who had enjoyed good incomes were tempted to speculate by growing grain on marginal land which could be farmed profitably only when the price of grain was high. Conditions suddenly altered at the end of the war: grain could be imported from abroad, the government ceased to buy for the armed forces, and there was a bumper crop in 1813. The price of grain sank rapidly. Bankrupt farmers laid off their laborers until rural unemployment became a tragedy rendered more acute as demobilized soldiers returned to their villages. The poor rates became so onerous that they dragged down the small yeoman farmers.

Meanwhile, the landowning members of Parliament attempted to raise the price of wheat by legislation. The Corn Law of 1815 prohibited the importation of foreign wheat until the price in England had risen to 80s. per quarter (eight bushels). The act was a failure, for it did not hold the price at 80s., nor did it save the landowning classes from a long period of agricultural depression; it did, however, arouse the bitter hostility of the poor, who blamed it for the high price of bread. This hostility was shared by the factory owners, who believed that cheaper wheat would mean lower wages. As a matter of fact, however, the price was determined far more by the abundance of the English harvest than by the availability of foreign wheat, and the effect of the Corn Law was exaggerated on both sides. Certainly the Corn Law did not stabilize the price of wheat, which fluctuated violently and fell in 1822 as low as 38s. 10d. The law was so inadequate that in 1828 the government experimented with a sliding scale. Foreign wheat could be imported duty-free when the price was 74s. or above in England; there was a duty of 1s. when the price was 73s.; thereafter the duty rose sharply as the English price declined. This measure, however, led to speculation and was not satisfactory. The price of wheat and the distress of the laborer continued to rise and fall with good or bad harvests. Bad harvests between 1828 and 1831 reduced the rural poor in the south to such abject misery that the starving laborers sought vengeance by burning the hayricks of wealthy landlords. Agriculture remained generally depressed for many years. In fact, it was not until the middle 1830s that conditions improved and a more even prosperity returned to the countryside.

Like agriculture, industry had prospered during the war, but it had been even more speculative. One manufacturer might make enormous profits whereas another, his market suddenly closed by the fortunes of war, might be ruined. The management of a factory posed new problems to which businessmen were as yet unaccustomed. They could not borrow money easily, and once their private capital had been exhausted they could only shut down and discharge their workpeople. They made mistakes in calculating future demand, especially in 1815. Assuming that Europe was eager to buy their goods, they laid in large supplies, only to discover that the Continent was too impoverished to purchase English manufactures. Furthermore, war orders from the government at home came abruptly to an end.

In these unhappy years trade was badly depressed, wages were cut, factories were closed, and the poor suffered greatly through unemployment. Angry mobs destroyed the machines they thought were robbing them of employment and sacked bakers' and butchers' shops in their search for food. Rioting and arson occurred in Norfolk and Suffolk. In 1817 a band of poor weavers in Manchester, desperate at their pitiful wages, determined to march on London. They set out, each carrying a blanket for protection at night, from which their journey was called the March of the Blanketeers, but they soon were dispersed by force.

Although the cause of these disturbances was simply the misery of the poor, popular radicalism was increased by popular orators, of whom "Orator" Hunt and

Cartoon of soldiers attacking a gathering at St. Peter's Field in Manchester in 1819, by Phiz. (The Mansell Collection)

William Cobbett were the most famous. Hunt, though a good public speaker, was violent and thoroughly disreputable. Cobbett was more interesting and more personable. The son of a small farmer and innkeeper, he looked back to the village life of his youth with nostalgia and hated the new industrialism with all his heart. Completely ignorant of economics, he turned easily to abuse and rash statements that excited the passions of the mob. He was not a revolutionary but a kind of John Bull incarnate, and his racy writings were the vigorous protests of the hearty countryman against the evils of the time. He taught the people to agitate for the reform of Parliament. Other reforms were impossible, he argued, until the electoral system had been widened. It was Parliament which caused bad government and economic distress. But if, by its reform, the poor could obtain a voice in the House of Commons, then somehow enlightened legislation could restore the old England that was being destroyed by machines. Cobbett began a radical journal, the *Political Register,* reduced its price from a shilling to twopence, and for a time sold thousands of copies a week. Societies were formed, mass meetings were held, and petitions in favor of reform were sent to the House of Commons. This campaign for a democratic suffrage, however, was a working-class movement from which the middle classes held aloof.

The government offered nothing but repression. Tory ministers, with their fear of the mob, believed that a conspiracy existed to overthrow the government and to despoil the rich. In 1817 the Cabinet suspended habeas corpus, passed harsher measures against seditious meetings, and urged local magistrates to enroll special constables and to make prompt arrests. The number of government spies and informers was increased. Public meetings came to an end. Agitation among the lower classes subsided, partly because of a good harvest in 1817, but rose again in 1819, when another cruel depression in trade brought lowered wages and much unemployment. The bitterness and discontent of the poor reached alarming proportions and monstrous protest meetings were held in many cities. One meeting in St. Peter's Field in Manchester ended in tragedy. A throng of 50,000 to 60,000 persons, many marching in ranks carrying banners with such slogans as "Annual Parliaments" and "Universal Suffrage," met in orderly fashion to hear a speech by "Orator" Hunt. The magistrates permitted the crowd to assemble; then, losing their nerve, they attempted to arrest Hunt as soon as he appeared. A body of mounted yeomanry was sent to make the arrest. Jostled and pushed about by the crowd, the yeomanry drew their sabers but had to be rescued by a troop of soldiers. In the following panic many persons were trodden under foot, some were sabered, eleven were killed, and some four hundred were injured. The government congratulated the magistrates on their conduct, but to the poor the events in St. Peter's Field, renamed Peterloo in mocking comparison with the Battle of Waterloo, became a symbol of harsh tyranny that was long remembered.

The Cabinet then passed six acts to suppress disorder. Three of them, which hastened trials for offenders, prohibited drilling, and authorized search for hidden arms, were reasonable, but the others were very reactionary: they restricted public assemblies, authorized seizure of seditious literature, and increased duties on pamphlets and newspapers. The hostility between rich and poor was growing dangerous.

Two events in 1820 provided the lower classes with an opportunity to express their feelings. One, a wild plot known as the Cato Street Conspiracy, aimed at nothing less than the assassination of the entire Cabinet. It was discovered and crushed, but the lower classes were plainly disappointed that the plot had not succeeded. In the same year a scandal in the royal family permitted the people to display their dislike of and comtempt for their rulers. King George III had finally passed away and was succeeded by his disreputable son, George IV (1820–1830). The matrimonial affairs of the new ruler were somewhat unconventional. As a young man in 1785 he had married a Roman Catholic, Mrs. Fitzherbert, a marriage that might have cost him the throne because the king of England could not marry a Catholic. He was saved by another law which provided that the Prince of Wales could not marry legally without his father's consent. Ten years later he married a German princess, Caroline of Brunswick-Wolfenbüttel. He did not like his wife and he treated her with brutality. Some years later Caroline left England and spent her time in Italy, where her conduct was rather indiscreet. When George IV became king he asked the Cabinet to obtain a divorce for him by special act of Parliament. Meanwhile Caroline returned to England and demanded her rights as queen. The lower classes took up her cause with enthusiasm, pulled her carriage through the streets when she appeared in public, and demonstrated wildly in her favor. The bill for divorce passed the House of Lords, but its prospects in the Commons were so doubtful that it was withdrawn. The queen died shortly thereafter. This episode, sordid as it was, provided a safety valve for the emotions of the poor and eased the tension between classes. An improvement in trade after 1820 also helped to relieve the crisis.

The Tories who held office in the terrible years following Waterloo should not be regarded as cruel or evil men. Liverpool, the tactful prime minister; Eldon, the ultraconservative lord chancelor; Wellington, with his great prestige and high sense of duty; Sidmouth, the timid home secretary; Castlereagh, the brilliant diplomat— these were men of intelligence and common sense, but they were also narrow and unimaginative, without much hope of improving things. Determined to preserve the position of the upper classes, they feared that any change might be for the worse. And it must be remembered that most of the Whigs supported the repressive measures of the Tories and that even though the Cabinet had attempted to give relief to the poor the administrative machinery at its disposal was quite inadequate.

THE BEGINNING OF A MORE LIBERAL ERA

The suicide of Castlereagh in 1822 was followed by a reconstruction of the Cabinet. Liverpool remained as prime minister; George Canning became foreign secretary and leader of the Tories in the House of Commons; Sir Robert Peel became home secretary; and William Huskisson, president of the Board of Trade. The ultraconservatism of the war generation was softened into a more moderate kind of Tory policy. Canning, Peel, and Huskisson were Tories, but they were not reactionaries; they were conservative but open-minded men. Some of the older type of Tories remained in the Cabinet, however, and this division was to split the party after Liverpool's resignation in 1827. But for a time, from 1822 to 1827, he presided over a strong and able Cabinet.

Canning's Foreign Policy

Canning followed the principles of foreign policy laid down by Castlereagh, but he employed bolder methods and he explained his actions to the British public, which Castlereagh had never done. Hence the change after 1822 appeared more fundamental than it actually was. Both Castlereagh and Canning had to deal with the autocratic states of Austria, Russia, and Prussia, with whom England had formed a Quadruple Alliance, first to defeat Napoleon and later to preserve the peace settlement of 1815. Castlereagh hoped for close cooperation among the great powers, and it was at his suggestion that they agreed to hold periodic conferences to discuss the problems of Europe. But from the first there arose a difference between England and her allies. Austria, Russia, and Prussia were eager to suppress revolutionary movements. Alexander of Russia, in particular, desired the allies to guarantee not only the

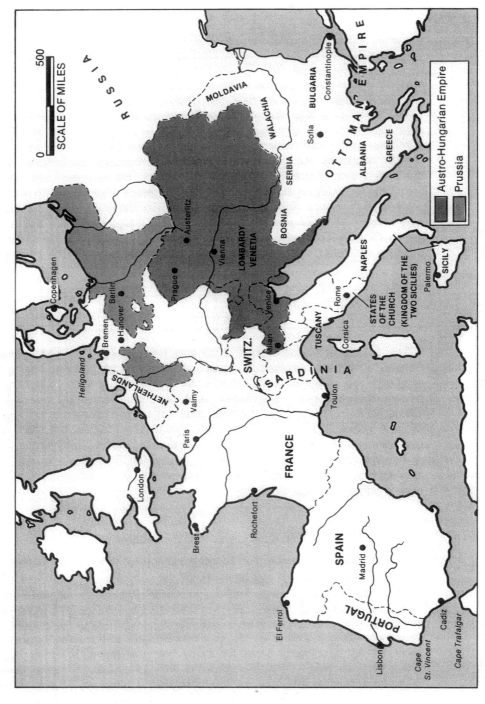

RUSSIA

MOLDAVIA

WALACHIA

BULGARIA

Constantinople

O T T O M A N   E M P I R E

Sofia

SERBIA

BOSNIA

ALBANIA

GREECE

Austerlitz

Vienna

LOMBARDY
VENETIA

Copenhagen

Berlin

Prague

Venice

Bremen

Hanover

Milan

SWITZ.

NAPLES

Rome

STATES
OF THE
CHURCH

(KINGDOM OF THE
TWO SICILIES)

Palermo

SICILY

Heligoland

NETHERLANDS

TUSCANY

Corsica

S A R D I N I A

Valmy

Toulon

Paris

FRANCE

London

Rochefort

Brest

SPAIN

Madrid

El Ferrol

PORTUGAL

Lisbon

Cadiz

Cape
St. Vincent

Cape Trafalgar

Austro-Hungarian Empire

Prussia

500

SCALE OF MILES

0

Europe in 1815.

frontiers but also the existing governments of Europe. To this Castlereagh objected. He was willing to put down any Bonapartist rising in France, but he refused to commit England to a general policy of suppressing revolts or of guaranteeing borders. The test came in 1820, when there were revolts in Spain, Naples, and Portugal against the despotic governments set up in 1815. When the eastern autocracies wished to intervene, Castlereagh refused to meddle in the domestic concerns of small independent states. Thus Castlereagh broke with the Quadruple Alliance before his death, but he regretted the necessity of doing so.

Canning, on the other hand, welcomed the break, emphasized it in every way he could, and sought to destroy the alliance of the autocratic powers. But it was at this time that revolt was spreading among the Spanish colonies in Latin America, and it was obvious that British trade in that area was increasing as Spanish power declined. Canning therefore let it be known that the European system of repression was not to be extended to the Spanish colonies and that the British fleet would prevent intervention in America. He sought to interest the United States in a similar policy. In 1823 President Monroe issued his famous doctrine that from now on the New World was not to be considered a sphere for further European colonization. This was somewhat more than Canning had bargained for, especially as Monroe's brave words were rather empty without the backing of the British fleet. Yet the result was that the Spanish colonies secured their independence, and Canning could boast that if the Bourbons ruled over Spain once more it was a Spain without the Indies. British policy stood forth as liberal in contrast to the tyranny on the Continent.

Canning also had to deal with the Near East, where a smoldering revolt of the Greeks against their Turkish rulers burst into open rebellion in 1821. This revolt was regarded quite differently by the various powers. Austria and Prussia saw nothing more than another rebellion which should be suppressed as soon as possible. But Russia, with her great desire for Turkish territory, was likely to intervene on the side of the Greeks. British policy was opposed to Russian expansion at the expense of Turkey, for the British feared, as they feared all through the nineteenth century, that Russia aimed at Constantinople and at a position in the Near East which might open a path for Russian expansion toward India. Meanwhile a wave of sympathy for the cause of Greek independence swept over France and England. Educated men were familiar with the glories of Greek antiquity and did not realize that conditions in modern Greece could hardly be compared with those in the Age of Pericles. The death of the poet Byron, who championed the cause of the Greeks and who died in Greece in 1824, profoundly affected public opinion. The war was going against the Greeks; moreover, the Turkish Sultan obtained aid from his nominal vassal, Mehemet Ali of Egypt.

Canning handled this complicated situation with skill. By playing on the differences of Austria and Russia, he split the alliance of the autocrats beyond repair. He had two choices of policy in Greece. He might, as England did both before and after him, support the Turks against Russia; or he might restrain Russia by cooperating with her in the Near East. He chose the second of these policies. In 1827 he secured an agreement with France and Russia to force a settlement on the Turks on the basis of Greek self-government under Turkish suzerainty. A combined British, French, and

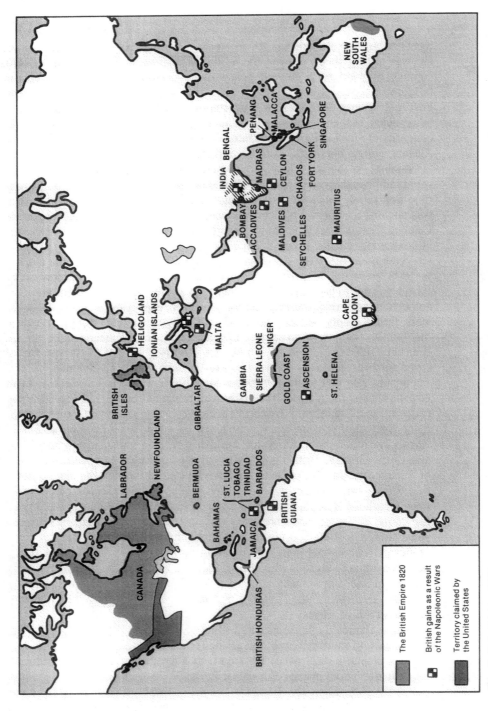

NEW SOUTH WALES

PENANG
MALACCA
SINGAPORE

INDIA BENGAL
MADRAS
CEYLON
FORT YORK

BOMBAY
LACCADIVES
MALDIVES
CHAGOS
SEYCHELLES
MAURITIUS

HELIGOLAND
IONIAN ISLANDS
MALTA

CAPE COLONY

BRITISH ISLES

GIBRALTAR

GAMBIA
SIERRA LEONE
NIGER
GOLD COAST
ASCENSION
ST. HELENA

LABRADOR
NEWFOUNDLAND

BERMUDA

ST. LUCIA
TOBAGO
TRINIDAD
BARBADOS

BAHAMAS

JAMAICA

BRITISH GUIANA

CANADA

BRITISH HONDURAS

The British Empire 1820

British gains as a result
of the Napoleonic Wars

Territory claimed by
the United States

The British Empire 1820.

Russian fleet sent to Greece blockaded Turkish and Egyptian squadrons in Navarino Bay. When the Turks and Egyptians sailed out of the harbor their ships were blown to bits. A few months before this event Canning died and in 1828 the duke of Wellington became prime minister. Disliking cooperation with Russia, the duke drew back from Canning's policy. After a short war between Russia and Turkey, Russia received most of the credit for the peace in 1829 which gave the Greeks their independence.

Peel at the Home Office

Sir Robert Peel, who became home secretary in 1822, was to be one of the leading Tory statesmen for the next quarter of a century. He did not spring from the aristocracy. His father, the first Sir Robert, had made a huge fortune in the cotton industry and was determined that his son should have a great career in politics. In fact, the younger Peel was trained for parliamentary life. He was educated at Harrow and at Christ Church, Oxford; his father then found him a seat in the Commons, gave him a fine house in London, and provided him with an ample income. Peel soon made his mark in the Commons; within a few years he was secretary for Ireland. Although he was brought up in Tory principles, he was a man open to conviction, ready to examine facts, and honest enough to alter his opinions in the light of what he saw. Thoughtful and cautious, with a high sense of dedication, he possessed great ability in handling public business. His manner was cold and reserved. The Irish statesman O'Connell, who disliked him, said that Peel's smile resembled the silver plate on the top of a coffin.

As home secretary he cleared out the gang of government spies and informers who had done so much to exasperate the lower classes. He also made important reforms in the criminal law, which contained many barbarities, for Parliament in the eighteenth century had imposed the death penalty upon one offense after another until people could be hanged for any one of some two hundred petty crimes. The death penalty, for example, could be inflicted for stealing a fish from a fish stand, for taking forty shillings or more from a dwelling, or for appearing on the road with a blackened face, a disguise used by highwaymen. These savage punishments did not deter the criminal. The police were so inadequate that there was always a good chance of escape, and juries frequently refused to convict when a minor offense might bring the death penalty. Yet punishment could fall with terrible severity on unlucky persons.[1] For some years rather fruitless efforts had been made to modify the criminal code. Within a few years Peel cut in half the number of offenses punishable by death. Peel also was interested in prison reform. Here again there had been a long agitation, led in the eighteenth century by John Howard and in the early nineteenth by Elizabeth Fry, a Quaker who worked for more humane treatment of female prisoners. Peel began the inspection of prisons and provided salaries for jailers in place of fees, but his work was limited and did not affect debtors' prisons, which continued until the middle of the century.

[1]The need for reform of the criminal law was dramatized in 1818 when, in the celebrated case of *Ashford v. Thornton,* a man on trial for murder suddenly demanded the medieval right of trial by battle against his accuser. Parliament abolished trial by battle in 1819.

Peel recognized that crime would decline only when detection and punishment became more certain, but he also knew that surer detection could be obtained only through a better police force. No adequate police force existed. The fumbling old constables in most county towns were hopeless. In London the Bow Street Runners and the Thames police were more efficient, but the magistrates in various parishes did not cooperate properly; there was much room for improvement. The upper classes feared disorderly crowds partly because there was no means of control, except to call in soldiers and begin to shoot. Peel established a new metropolitan police force which was soon extended to all of London. Its headquarters was in Scotland Yard and it was responsible to the Home Office. The men were drawn from retired noncommissioned officers in the army, wore top hats and blue, belted coats, and were armed with clubs but not with firearms. The "bobbies" or "peelers" were regarded at first with some derision but soon won general respect. They learned to establish contact with disorder very quickly, to prevent the formation of dangerous mobs, and to make the apprehension of criminals far more certain. They also developed such a tradition of politeness that until recently the modern British bobby, combining firmness with good manners, had become a model for the world. The London police was gradually copied throughout the country. Peel established mounted patrols to deal with highwaymen and took action against innkeepers who protected criminals. The picturesque but barbarous figure of the highwayman disappeared from English life.

Huskisson and the Board of Trade

William Huskisson, president of the Board of Trade, reformed the customs duties. A man of humble origin, he possessed great ability and was in closer touch with the new world of business than his predecessors had been. As a disciple of Adam Smith he agreed with merchants and manufacturers that the way to promote foreign trade was to remove restrictions on the free enterprise of the commercial classes. He found, however, a host of government regulations of many kinds, some dating back to the old colonial system, and others passed more recently as war measures.

Huskisson could not hope to introduce complete free trade, for a large proportion of the government's revenue was derived from customs and excises, and his aim was to substitute protective for prohibitive duties. He lowered import duties on silk, wool, and rum, on cotton, linen, and woolen goods, and on glass, paper, porcelain, coffee, copper, zinc, lead, and iron. A general duty on imported manufactured articles was lowered from about fifty to about twenty percent. The Navigation Acts, which had already been modified in 1822 to allow freer trade with South America and to permit British colonial products to be sent directly to the Continent, were relaxed further in 1823 by ending the extra duties levied on goods imported into England in foreign ships. Thus Huskisson lowered duties, allowed freer colonial trade, and modified the Navigation Laws.

TORY DIVISION

Canning, Peel, and Huskisson, who had dominated the Cabinet since 1822, had not been able to pass their enlightened measures without opposition from the ultraconservative members of the Tory party led by Wellington and Eldon. It had only been Liverpool's tact and skill in handling difficult colleagues that had kept the party together; when he resigned in February 1827, after a paralytic stroke, the rift among the Tories became an open one. Neither Canning nor Wellington would serve under each other. Canning became the new prime minister, forming a coalition of his followers with a few Whigs who accepted minor positions in the Cabinet. This coalition was important because it showed a tendency, obvious by 1830, for the liberal elements in both parties to draw together. Wellington, Eldon, and Peel refused to join Canning's Cabinet. Canning's term in office was brief and troubled, and in August 1827 he died. For a few months his friend, Viscount Goderich, known as Goodie Goderich, stumbled along as prime minister and then tendered his resignation amid a flood of tears.

The king turned to the duke of Wellington. Wellington's Cabinet was composed at first of High Tories and Canning's followers, but dissensions between the two groups continued, and Wellington complained that he spent his time in "assuaging what gentlemen called their feelings." In May 1828 he found an opportunity to dismiss the Canningites and seized it with soldierly brusqueness. For almost three years, until late in 1830, the country was ruled by the High Tories alone. It did not enjoy the experience, and it became increasingly impatient with what one Whig called "the stupid old Tory party." On almost every issue Wellington failed to satisfy the nation: his policy in the Near East after the Battle of Navarino was considered weak and pro-Turkish, his sliding scale of duties on imported wheat was unsatisfactory, his attitude toward parliamentary reform became clear when he refused to give to Manchester two seats from a small borough disfranchised for corruption. Wellington possessed sound judgment and solidity of character but he lacked the skill and finesse of the successful politician.

Nevertheless, much against his will, Wellington passed one reform of first-rate importance: the Catholic Emancipation Act, which permitted the admission of Roman Catholics to membership in Parliament. The measure was significant, not only because it advanced religious toleration, but because it involved Ireland.

Ireland in the 1820s

The Irish question was to appear in many forms during the nineteenth century. Essentially, however, there were three principal Irish grievances. One was religious. The Church of England was the established church in Ireland, though it served only a small minority of the population. Although it was more than amply endowed, the Roman Catholic peasants were required to pay tithes for its support. The harsh penal code imposed on Irish Catholics in an earlier age was now largely relaxed, they could hold land on equal terms with Protestants, they could vote for members of the English House of Commons, but they could not hold civil or judicial office, nor could they sit in the English Parliament.

The second grievance was political. The Irish had lost their Parliament in 1800, and they longed to have it reinstated. Home Rule, as it came to be called, meant the restoration of the Parliament in Dublin. The Irish believed that the first step toward such a restoration was the admission of Irish Roman Catholics to membership in the English Commons; hence the importance of Catholic emancipation.

The third great grievance was agrarian. As in the eighteenth century, many landlords were absentees, renting their estates on long leases to middlemen who sublet them to the peasants in small parcels. The peasants often subdivided and sublet the land even further, until an estate might be teeming with people, all dependent on the potato to keep them from starvation. The population was growing rapidly, the land was used unscientifically, and the quality of the potatoes was declining. From June to September, when the crop of the preceding year had been eaten and the new crop had not yet been harvested, many a poor peasant family was without means of subsistence; wife and children went on the road to beg while the husband sought casual employment, often in Britain. Neither landlords nor peasants felt any incentive to improve their methods of agriculture. A peasant who attempted more scientific farming might find that he had merely raised the rent by his pains. A landlord who wished to improve his estate could do so only by clearing out some of the peasants and combining small parcels of land into larger fields. This process meant evictions and more suffering for the poor, who cordially hated the improving landlord. Yet the number of evictions was high. The landlord was permitted by law to seize the crops and cattle of a peasant in arrears with his rent; a peasant who thus lost his means of livelihood was almost certain to be evicted in the long run.

Believing that the law was loaded against him the peasant sought to protect himself and to enforce a wild justice by terrorism and crime. Secret societies took vengeance on evicting landlords, on their agents, and on peasants who took up holdings from which other peasants had been expelled. But landlords were usually out of reach and their agents were protected by the police; consequently, vengeance often fell on persons who were not responsible for an injustice. Agrarian crime brought terrible evils to Ireland. It challenged the government in a way that could not be ignored, alienated English opinion, prevented the investment of capital and the improvement of agriculture, and poisoned the relations of landlord and tenant. It spread to the towns and retarded industry. Ireland required nothing less than an agricultural revolution which would have been very costly, would have temporarily increased the sufferings of the poor, and would have interfered with the rights of private property. Yet the English cannot be excused for their neglect of Irish wrongs, for the union of the Parliaments carried with it the responsibility of legislating wisely for Ireland.

Wellington and Catholic Emancipation

Catholic emancipation could be granted more easily than most Irish demands because it did not affect property and because it was favored by most Whigs and by some Tories. Yet it would not have been won so soon but for a curious series of circumstances. In 1828 Wellington had accepted a Whig proposal to repeal the Test and Corporation Acts which, since the reign of Charles II, had debarred dissenters from holding national or municipal office. The measure was merely the removal of a formal grievance, for annual indemnity acts had long permitted dissenters to ignore these laws. But political equality for dissenters renewed the question of Catholic emancipation.

In the 1820s an Irish patriot, Daniel O'Connell, conducted a great campaign for Catholic emancipation. He was a gifted speaker, a shrewd lawyer, and an able organizer, but he was not a revolutionary. He dared to attack agrarian crime, and he proposed to use force but not violence. In 1823 he formed the Catholic Association, which collected a "Catholic rent" of a penny a month, from the peasants and organized their voting power under the leadership of their priests. Until then the Catholic voter had normally supported his landlord's candidate. O'Connell ended this practice. In 1828 he stood for election to Parliament from county Clare; headed by the priests, the peasants marched to the polls; O'Connell was returned, though as a Catholic he could not take his seat. He was prepared to employ similar tactics all over Ireland. Wellington and Peel became convinced that they must either grant Catholic emancipation or else face an Irish civil war. They decided to yield and passed a bill, over the protests of their own followers, permitting Roman Catholics to sit in Parliament, to hold any office in Great Britain except those of regent or lord chancellor, and any in Ireland except lord chancellor and lord lieutenant. A Roman Catholic could not act as high commissioner to the General Assembly of the Church of Scotland.

But Wellington and Peel yielded with poor grace. They did not conceal their detestation of what they were doing, they insulted O'Connell by forcing him to be elected over again, and they disfranchised the forty-shilling Irish freeholders and substituted a voting qualification of ownership of land worth £10 a year. This, it was hoped, would prevent O'Connell from controlling the Irish vote, and provision was taken to suppress associations such as O'Connell had employed. Hence the English gained little credit in Ireland. Rather, they taught the lesson that force could bring concessions when right and justice could not. The High Tories were furious with Wellington for granting emancipation. Protestant ascendancy in Ireland had long been a Tory battle cry, and the Tories now were divided not only between Canningites and High Tories, but between High Tories who sought vengeance against Wellington and those who stood by him. He was defeated in 1830 and the Whigs came into office.

FORCES MAKING FOR CHANGE

The policies of Canning, Peel, and Huskisson in the period from 1822 to 1828 had shown that moderate and cautious reform was possible without upheaval or danger of revolution, and many sections of the middle classes, growing in prosperity and in their standards of living, saw the desirability of further reform. They were dissatisfied with the old aristocratic world of special privilege and monopoly of political power by the nobility and gentry. The return of more rigid and conservative government under the duke of Wellington (1828–1830) produced irritation and disappointment.

Jeremy Bentham

An important force making for change during these years was the influence of the gentle lawyer-philosopher Jeremy Bentham, whose excellent health, long life, and private fortune gave him the opportunity to develop his ideas. As early as 1776 he had published his *Fragment on Government,* which challenged the complacent view of the eighteenth century that British society, government, and law had attained as great perfection as could be hoped for. Bentham declared that all law and government were continual experiments in promoting the general welfare—"the greatest good for the greatest number"—and could never be regarded as final. Every institution, he held, must be subjected to constant investigation and reform and tested by the question, "What is the use of it?" He supplied a formula which was often followed in the nineteenth century: thorough inquiry by a government commission, corrective legislation by Parliament, careful administration of this legislation by the ministers of state, and official inspection and report.

There was a good deal of pedantry about Bentham, whose view of human nature was much too simple and mechanical. Yet he and his followers, known as philosophical radicals or utilitarians, because they applied the test of utility, did a great service. Bentham's spirit, with its emphasis on reason and utility, underlay much of the movement for reform in the nineteenth century. Indeed, his influence was so great that there is danger in making it appear even greater than it was. Many reforms came into existence, not because of any movement or any philosophy, but because officials detected weaknesses in the laws and traditions by which they governed and quietly made improvements.

Bentham was the great foe of special privilege. He saw that antagonisms were certain to exist between those who ruled the state and those who were governed, and he sought a reconciliation by an extension of the franchise. His *Reform Catechism,* published in 1817, advocated the suffrage for all householders. He fully accepted the doctrine of laissez faire as set forth by Adam Smith. He believed that when men promoted their own profit (without doing harm to others) they promoted the general good, and that the state should stand aside in economic matters. There was, however, a contradiction in Bentham's philosophy, a contradiction which ran through much of the political thinking of the nineteenth century. If the state was to investigate, reform, and inspect, it must by necessity invade the sphere of social and economic life and interfere with the rights of private property. If, on the other hand, it followed a policy of laissez faire, no such reform was possible. It became increasingly obvious as the century advanced that laissez faire was too negative, that women and children working in factories required protection, that social and economic evils could be removed only by the action of the government, and that interference and control by the state were necessary for progress.

The Evangelical Movement

Alongside the utilitarians, who appealed to reason and were often freethinkers in religion, must be placed the growing evangelical movement. The movement had begun in the eighteenth century and had created the strong and tightly knit organization of the Methodists. In the early nineteenth century various groups of Methodists broke away from the parent body, but nonetheless that body continued to grow and to do a great work among the poor. Methodism in its various branches became the largest religious organization in the country except for the Church of England. Other denominations, such as the Congregationalists and the Baptists, experienced a revival, and the number of nonconformists constantly increased. The influence of these groups on social change was at first rather negative but they made clear their conviction that the methods and morals of the eighteenth century could no longer be regarded as satisfactory; that standards of conduct must be raised; and that new classes, which had counted for little in the past, must now be allowed to express themselves.

Methodism had evoked a corresponding movement in the Church of England. The philanthropist William Wilberforce and the writer and schoolteacher Hannah More had brought intelligence, wit, and social standing to the aid of religion. They had labored for a disciplined and industrious working class within the Church of England. Their movement, however, had been conceived in the spirit of the eighteenth century when privilege and social distinctions had been taken for granted. The poor were expected to lead godly, righteous, and sober lives but could not expect improvement in their social or economic lot.

The evangelicals in the church fought with success against the grosser forms of vice, against brutal amusements such as bullbaiting, against dueling, and against slavery in the British Empire. For many years they conducted a great campaign against slavery, a campaign in which the nonconformists joined and which showed how moral indignation could be organized politically. The supreme victory of Wilberforce was the abolition of slavery within the empire in 1833. In that very year he died, but something of his spirit was carried on by Lord Ashley, later the earl of Shaftesbury.

Shaftesbury was an aristocrat who devoted his life to good works: factory legislation, public health, reform of the lunacy laws, improvement in the lot of the agricultural laborer, the protection of the poor little urchins who sometimes were suffocated or burned to death as they cleaned the chimneys of great houses. He taught his fellow peers that they must feel responsibility for the welfare of the poor. But in his mind reform must be the work of the upper classes and he was suspicious of democracy and cold toward any movement of self-help among working people.

The evangelicals and the Benthamite utilitarians did not always see eye to eye. The humanity of the religious bodies, for example, condemned child labor in factories, but utilitarian businessmen wanted labor to be as cheap as possible. Industrialists, however, were also advocates of change. They had to apply reason to the management of their affairs, they were faced with new problems and they sought new solutions without regard for traditional beliefs. To them tradition meant the old restrictions of the guilds and the regulations imposed by government. They were rationalists, quite ready to break with the past. Concerned only with measuring, counting, and observing, they thought in terms of the present and the future, not of the past.

The Artisan Reformers

Among men of business Robert Owen was unique. He was a manufacturer who combined great executive ability with a deep desire to improve the lot of the working classes. "His mind and character never lost the mark of an upbringing among poor people and among people aspiring earnestly towards an ideal outlook on everyday things." He was naïve and often absurd; yet he taught the great lesson that the new industrialism should not merely be admired or shuddered at but should be controlled by corrective legislation, by cooperation in place of competition, and by a moral approach to social and economic problems. One of the founders of British socialism, he believed that people's characters are formed by hereditary and environmental forces, and hence they can be molded by the conditions surrounding them. At the cotton mills at New Lanark in Scotland, of which he became manager and part owner while he was still in his twenties, he conducted a great social experiment. These mills, when he had taken charge of them, were a shocking example of the evils of the factory at its worst. Within a few years he created a model industrial community, with good housing, good pay, and reasonable hours, with care for the education, recreation, and social security of his workpeople, and with the first nursery school in Britain. The resulting high morale among his employees enabled him to make his factory pay a handsome return. He proved that under enlightened management the evils of the factory and the slum could be avoided without impairing efficiency or lessening profits. He made philanthropy profitable.

Owen failed to interest his fellow industrialists in copying his ideas, and when he came to London in 1815 and naïvely laid his plans for the welfare of the workers before the Cabinet, ministers were polite but unconvinced. For some years Owen collaborated with the elder Sir Robert Peel in advocating a bill for the protection of children in factories, but the bill as passed in 1819 was easily evaded and did little good. Having failed with the factory owners and with the government, Owen turned in his later years to self-help among the laboring classes—to trade unions, workmen's cooperatives, and utopian schemes for self-governing and cooperative communities such as that at New Harmony, Indiana. He had little interest in the reform of Parliament. Nonetheless, he made a profound impression on the social thinking of the time and set in motion ideas which persisted throughout the century. The success of the mills at New Lanark—philanthropy joined with handsome profits—could not be explained away.

Francis Place, "the radical tailor of Charing Cross," was a workingman who had risen through thrift and business skill to a modest affluence and who sponsored the cause of the laboring classes. "For nearly fifty years he was one of the mainsprings of the democratic movement." He was not an idealist like Owen, but a shrewd and practical man with a rather high opinion of himself and a profound contempt both for other labor leaders and for the "gabbling Whigs" in Parliament. A born manipulator, he employed the art of lobbying to induce Parliament in 1824 to repeal the Combination Acts of 1799 and 1800 which formed part of the repressive code enacted in the decade after the French Revolution. These acts prohibited trade unions among laborers but placed no check on associations of employers. Workers were thus denied the small advantages that might be theirs under the doctrine of laissez faire, although it was common decency to permit them the same rights of combination that were allowed the mill owners.

After a series of strikes, with some violence and intimidation, the Tories called loudly for restoration of the Combination Acts. But Place obtained a new act in 1825 which permitted trade unions to bargain about wages and hours of labor, though with strict provisions against intimidation. Thus the prohibition of trade unions came to an end; their growth was rapid during the next decade. Owen and other leaders conceived of vast combinations of workers which would transform all industry into one great cooperative enterprise. The Grand Consolidated Trades Union expanded under Owen's control into an organization of more than half a million workers. Unfortunately, it rested on faulty foundations and collapsed in 1834 when mill owners refused to employ union members and the government conducted cruel prosecutions. Thereafter, trade unions began a slower and less ambitious but more solid and conservative period of growth.

Romanticism

A movement of a very different kind also swelled the desire for change. This was the romantic movement in literature, which often is said to have begun with the publication in 1789 of William Blake's *Songs of Innocence* and to have ended with the death of Sir Walter Scott in 1832. The romantic writers, revolting from the formal and unsentimental verses of the eighteenth century, relied upon emotion, instinct, and imagination. They wished to escape from what was familiar into a world of their own imagining, into that "serene and blessed mood," as Wordsworth called it, in which the poet, free from earthly contamination, believed he saw into the reality of things.

They sought escape from reality in writing about things that were far away, about the marvelous, the abnormal, and the supernatural, about haunted castles, pleasure palaces, subterranean rivers, demon lovers, and magic casements opening on the foam of perilous seas in fairyland forlorn. Seeking a return to a state of nature, these writers were interested in the life of the savage, the peasant, and the child. There was also an interest in the Middle Ages, as something that was vague, remote, and mysterious. The romanticists were lovers of liberty and haters of oppression in any form.

William Blake, both artist and poet, lived in a world of his own imagination in which vague but mighty forces strove for mastery. His symbolism is confusing but vivid: evil forces of disunity, regimentation, and oppression are opposed by freedom, passion, and love, which is identified with imagination, poetry, and art.

God Creating
Adam, *engraving*
by William Blake.
(Tate Gallery,
London)

William Wordsworth, the nature poet, rose steadily in poetic power until in the decade from 1797 to 1807 he was writing lofty and majestic verse. Thereafter his powers declined, though he lived until 1850. At first a young radical, admiring the French Revolution, he became disillusioned with events in France and adopted a philosophy of patriotism and a love of English institutions which turned him into a conservative. In 1798 he and Samuel Taylor Coleridge published their famous *Lyrical Ballads.* Wordsworth explains that he sought material for this volume in humble and rustic life and employed the language of ordinary people, coloring homely episodes with imagination and seeking insight into the laws of human behavior. A self-centered man, he probed into his own development in an autobiographical poem, *The Prelude.* He recalled the profound impressions made upon him in childhood by the beauties of nature and how these impressions, which had once opened his youthful mind to visions of reality, faded away in middle age. Here perhaps is the secret of his decline.

His intimate friend Coleridge, with whom he published the *Lyrical Ballads,* was a man of great mental powers marred by a disordered private life. Both philosopher and bard, he wrote a handful of great poems but devoted most of his life to philosophical speculation. His role in the *Lyrical Ballads* was to deal with "persons or characters supernatural or at least romantic." The result was *The Rime of the Ancient*

Mariner. Other poems—*Christabel* and *Kubla Khan*—were also highly romantic in character.

The most popular of these writers was Sir Walter Scott. He was fascinated by the romance, rapid action, and martial tone of Scottish history, by Scottish ballads and folklore, and by the superstitions, character, and dialect of the Scottish peasant. Scott knew the history of the clans and of noble families; he had an eye for scenery. All these elements were woven together with great skill and imagination in his narrative poems and historical novels. Scott excelled in vivid descriptions of striking scenes and episodes and in fine character sketches; he virtually created the historical novel; and he made a profound impression upon the culture of his age.

A new generation of romantic poets, more rebellious than the old, arose in the early nineteenth century. By far the most famous in his day was George Gordon, Lord Byron, a dissipated young peer who traveled in southern Europe and in the Levant and wrote romantic descriptions of strange lands and tales of amorous adventure in mysterious oriental settings. His *Childe Harold's Pilgrimage* (1812) made him famous. Besieged by women, he began a period of notorious living, which became so scandalous that in 1816 he left England forever. After wanderings chiefly in Italy, he espoused the cause of Greek independence and died in Greece in 1824. His masterpiece was *Don Juan,* the story of a young rake who wandered in many lands and found amours in each one. The poem is a satire upon the oppressions and hypocrisy of society; it is hostile to war and to the normal conventions of morality. In style Byron vacillates between classical tradition and the newer types of verse. He had moments of grandeur, but today he is rated more highly as a satirist than as a poet.

The conventional and well-to-do background of Percy Bysshe Shelley contrasts strangely with his poetic genius, his radical politics, and his determination to devote his life to a struggle against injustice and oppression. In a similar way his noble ideals contrast with his pathetic incompetence in practical affairs. Thus at the age of eighteen he eloped with a young lady of sixteen whose father had "persecuted her in a most horrible way by endeavoring to compel her to go to school." Shelley's restless wanderings, his financial difficulties, and his unconventional relations with women brought disaster upon himself and those he loved until he was close to insanity. His poetry is not easy to understand. One of the most erudite of poets, he gave his poems a thoughtful and philosophic content as well as great artistic beauty. Undoubtedly his most significant work was the poetic drama *Prometheus Unbound,* composed during his stay in Italy. His current wife Mary Wollstonecraft Godwin Shelley had already published her soon-to-be-famous *Frankenstein.*

John Keats was the apostle of beauty, as Shelley was of freedom. Rising from humble origins and taken out of school at the age of fifteen, Keats had at least the encouragement of friends who introduced him to other literary people in London. At the age of eighteen he determined to devote himself to writing poetry and applied himself to that art with the greatest earnestness. The rapidity of his development was astonishing. His first long poem, *Endymion,* was flamboyant and undisciplined, but he recognized these faults and set about correcting them. At the age of twenty-six he died of tuberculosis. Perhaps his greatest gift was his skill in using words to evoke a rich and well-formed image of the mood or object he was describing.

Jane Austen is now regarded as one of the great writers of the Romantic era. Although she was little recognized by contemporaries, perhaps because she was a woman, the Prince Regent admired her. We learn much about the life of the gentle classes from her novels, especially about the relationships between parents and children and those between the sexes. While her writings satirized the styles of the age, they did not challenge its structure as did the writings of Mary Shelley's mother, Mary Wollstonecraft, in her *Vindication of the Rights of Woman.*

Thus during the 1820s forces of widely different kinds and widely different origins combined to break down the old, irrational dislike of change. New classes were developing that refused to accept the standards of the eighteenth century, expecting instead more humanity, more justice, more rationality in government and law, and a greater role for women. The old regime, with its privileged aristocracy, corruption, complacency, and heartlessness must come to an end and make way for a world in which all had some share in their government. These ideas were fostered by the romantic movements in literature, by the growth of evangelical religion, and by a new faith in progress. It was no longer held that material improvement was rendered doubtful by the growth of population, or that the sufferings of the poor were unavoidable.

In contrast to literature, the greatest painter of the period was John Constable, whose work glorified the natural, not the supernatural. He admired the classical landscapists of the past and anticipated the impressionists of the future. His *Hay Wain* in 1824 took England by storm.

C H R O N O L O G Y

War Followed by Peace

1798	*Lyrical Ballads* by Samuel Taylor Coleridge
1802	*Cobbett's Political Register* began
1811	Jane Austen's *Sense and Sensibility,* first of her novels
1813	Robert Owen reorganized his mills at New Lanark
1814	Sir Walter Scott began Waverley novels
1815	Corn Law enacted
1817	March of the Blanketeers dispersed; *Habeas Corpus* suspended; Jeremy Bentham's *Reform Catechism*

(continued on next page)

Chronology, continued

1818	John Keats's *Endymion;* Mary Wollstonecraft Shelley's *Frankenstein*
1819	Peterloo Massacre; Six Acts passed
1820	Cato Street conspiracy; death of George III
1820–30	George IV
1823	Monroe Doctrine supported by Canning
1824	Repeal of Combination Acts; Francis Place; beginning of trade unions
1828	Test Act repealed
1829	Catholic Emancipation; Peel established Metropolitan Police (Bobbies)
1830	Wellington out; Whigs in power
1833	Abolition of slavery in the British Empire; William Wilberforce and the Evangelical Movement

28 Reform and Discontent, 1830–1846

The period from 1830 to 1846 was a time of active reform. And yet, despite these reforms, the period was one of discontent and bitterness. Discontent was due primarily to economic misery, especially in the cruel years of deep depression and unemployment between 1837 and 1843. The lower classes were discontented, as were many middle-class radicals. They were convinced, moreover, that they were unjustly and needlessly deprived of their share of the nation's wealth. There were two movements of protest. One was Chartism, an interesting though futile attempt of the poor to help themselves; the other was a prolonged and highly emotional agitation by the middle classes against the Corn Laws. Thus during these years the tensions of class hostility, economic distress, and political radicalism continued to plague the nation.

THE WHIGS IN OFFICE

A general election in the summer of 1830, following the unlamented death of George IV, gave to the Whigs thirty additional seats in the House of Commons. Wellington continued as prime minister, but after a rash statement in which he opposed parliamentary reform of any kind he fell in November and the Whigs took office. The return to power by the Whigs meant a major shift in politics, for they had not held office since the brief Ministry of All the Talents in 1806 and 1807.

The new prime minister, Earl Grey, an elderly and rather austere nobleman and an aristocrat of aristocrats, had all the prejudices of the eighteenth century against any form of democracy. He had not the slightest thought of disturbing the political supremacy of the ruling class, but the Whigs had a tradition of constitutional reform. As a young man in the Commons, Grey had advocated reform of the electoral system, and now as an older man in the Lords he was ready to return to his early policy. His Cabinet consisted almost wholly of peers. Its aristocratic nature was really an asset, for if noblemen such as these were willing to reform the House of Commons, then reform could not be very dangerous. By including some of the Canningites, Grey had combined the liberal wings of both the old parties. His Cabinet also contained a few radicals, such as Henry Brougham and Lord Durham, Grey's liberal son-in-law.

Grey assumed office at a moment of dismay and danger. A financial crash in 1825–1826 had caused a return of economic depression. Wages were reduced and there was widespread unemployment, especially among agricultural laborers. Radical societies, including both middle- and lower-class elements, sprang up in various cities. Grey feared some sort of political upheaval led by portions of the middle class. A revolution of this kind had occurred in France during the summer of 1830, when almost without bloodshed the reactionary Charles X had been driven from the throne, the Citizen King, Louis Philippe, had taken his place, and the supremacy of the middle classes had been established. If such a victory could be won so easily in France, might it not occur in Britain? The parliamentary Reform Bill of 1832 was in a sense an aristocratic appeasement of the middle classes and especially of the numerous shopkeepers. By admitting these classes to the franchise, the nobility and gentry erected a bulwark against the turbulent demands of the classes further down.

The Reform Bill of 1832

The Reform Bill, as first introduced in 1831, swept away about fifty of the smallest boroughs, took one member from some thirty more, all without compensation to the borough owners, and distributed the seats thus released to new industrial towns and populous county areas. But the extension of the franchise was very small. Grey believed that to pass such a final measure was the conservative thing to do, for he thought it would silence demand for further reform. The bill was introduced in the Commons by Lord John Russell, a younger son of the duke of Bedford. As he read in his high, thin voice the list of boroughs to be disfranchised, the Tories burst into shouts of derisive laughter. But when the bill was given a second reading three weeks later, members were aware that it had tremendous support throughout the country. The second reading passed by a vote of 302 to 301.

With so small a majority, Grey knew that the bill could not pass through its later stages, and he persuaded the new king, William IV, a timid, conservative, and slightly ridiculous old sailor, to dissolve Parliament and to hold an election. Such a direct appeal to the people on a single issue, especially one in which the interests of the upper classes were involved, was in itself a novel event. The Whigs were returned with a comfortable majority. Even in the days of an unreformed House of Commons, the nation was able to express its opinion in moments of crisis. The Tories in the Commons, after the election, could do no more than delay the bill during the summer of 1831. On the first of October it was sent to the Lords. A week later, after an all-night session, the Lords threw it out, as well-informed people fully expected they would.

Parliamentary
representation
before 1832.

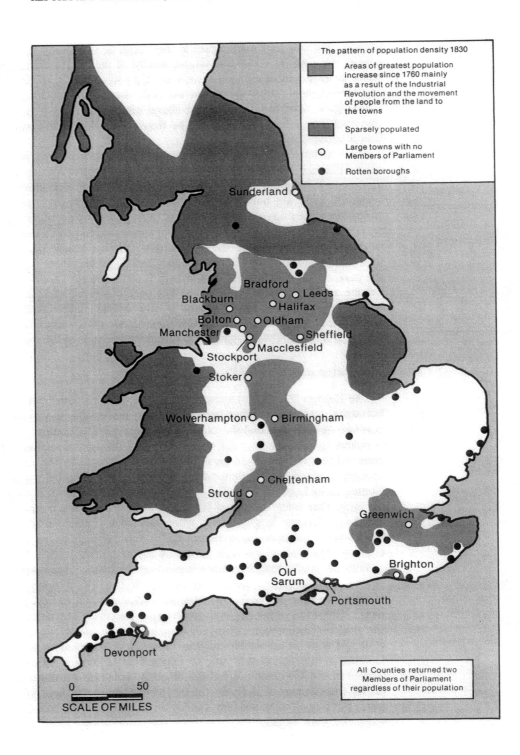

The pattern of population density 1830

Areas of greatest population increase since 1760 mainly as a result of the Industrial Revolution and the movement of people from the land to the towns

Sparsely populated

○ Large towns with no Members of Parliament

● Rotten boroughs

Sunderland

Bradford
Blackburn   Leeds
Bolton   Halifax
Manchester Oldham
        Sheffield
    Macclesfield
Stockport
Stoker

Wolverhampton Birmingham

Cheltenham
Stroud

Greenwich

Brighton
Old
Sarum
Portsmouth

Devonport

0   50
SCALE OF MILES

All Counties returned two
Members of Parliament
regardless of their population

Parliamentary reform 1832.

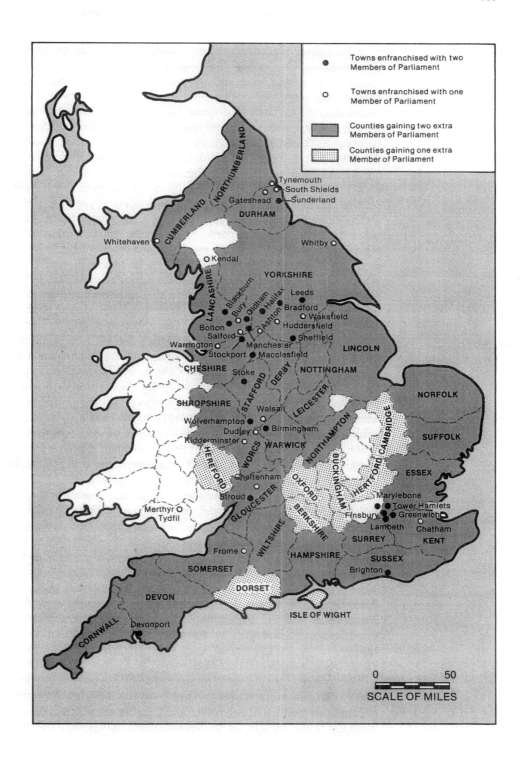

Towns enfranchised with two Members of Parliament

Towns enfranchised with one Member of Parliament

Counties gaining two extra Members of Parliament

Counties gaining one extra Member of Parliament

SCALE OF MILES

In the eighteenth century, when a defeat in the Lords was as serious as a defeat in the Commons, Grey would doubtless have resigned. But he decided to stay in office because the people were furious with the House of Lords. There was a riot in Bristol, and groups of workingmen were drilling in various places as though they intended to revolt. Grey prorogued Parliament for two months and then reintroduced the bill in December. It passed quickly through the Commons, but the problem of securing its passage through the Lords remained. One method of meeting this difficulty, though a very drastic one, would be the creation of new peers in sufficient quantity to form a majority for the bill in the upper house. The only precedent for such an action had occurred in the reign of Queen Anne, when twelve peers had been created. But sixty new peers might be needed to pass the Reform Bill, and Grey shrank from such a violent remedy. As it happened, there was a group of lords, nicknamed the Waverers, who opposed the bill but dreaded the opprobrium of rejecting it outright. They conceived the idea of allowing it to pass its second reading in order to satisfy the people and then to modify it quietly in committee. The Waverers attempted this strategy in the spring of 1832, but Grey would not permit his bill to be mutilated. He went to the king and demanded the creation of a sufficient number of peers to pass the bill. When the king refused, Grey resigned.

A strange situation thus arose. The nation was greatly excited, the Commons were determined to support Grey and pass the bill, but the Lords stood in the way. In May 1832 the king turned to Wellington, asking him to form a Tory Cabinet and to pass a reform bill less drastic than Grey's. But Wellington discovered he could not form a Cabinet. Leading Tories, including Peel, refused to join him. They argued that, having fought the Reform Bill tooth and claw, they could not honestly support a substitute for it. The king was forced to recall Grey's Cabinet, but Grey would not return without a promise that new peers would be created if that became a necessity. When the Tory nobles discovered that Grey possessed this power, they stalked out of the House of Lords in dignified procession, and thus, by absenting themselves, permitted the bill to pass. It became law in June 1832.

The Reform Bill did not alter the total number of seats in the House of Commons. It disfranchised 56 boroughs and took one member from 30 others. Of 143 seats thus released, 65 were given to large towns and cities, 65 were given to newly created rural constituencies in populous counties, and 13 were added to the representation of Ireland and Scotland. In rural areas the forty-shilling freeholders retained the vote, but the franchise was extended to copyholders and to long leaseholders whose lands were worth £10 a year, as well as to short leaseholders and to tenants at will with lands worth £50 a year. In the boroughs the old jungle of voting qualifications was swept away, and one universal rule gave the vote to persons who occupied property either as a residence or as a place of business rated at £10 a year. There was to be a register of voters, the money spent on an election would be controlled, and the polls would remain open for two days only.

The changes brought about by the Reform Bill were not as great as its terms might imply. The number of pocket boroughs was reduced, but they continued to exist; it is thought that they could still return about eighty members. The new £50 voters in the counties were certain to be conservative; moreover, the members allotted to industrial towns were balanced rather neatly by new county constituencies in which the landed aristocracy continued to influence elections. Influence in various forms was perhaps even greater after 1832 than before. Both rural and urban voters, in the absence of a secret ballot, were subjected to the scrutiny of their superiors. The process was still quite disorderly: "Election day was still a carnival which usually ended in a fight." The franchise was not extended greatly. The electorate in England and Wales was increased only from 435,000 to 657,000, while that in all of Britain and Ireland rose only from 478,000 to 814,000. The gentry and nobility, who continued to dominate the political life of the nation, were in a stronger position than before, for they had abandoned the absurdities of the old system without losing ultimate control.

The way in which the bill was passed through Parliament strengthened the Cabinet system of government and illustrated its principles. Supported by the House of Commons, the Cabinet had forced its will on the king and the House of Lords. Wellington, without that support, had been unable to form a ministry. Although both parties were conservative by modern standards, the passage of the Reform Bill opened the way for other liberal measures.

The Abolition of Slavery in 1833

The great victory of the evangelicals was the abolition of slavery in 1833. The slave trade had been illegal since 1807, but so long as slavery was permitted in the British colonies there was always a market for blacks smuggled across the Atlantic; the slave trade, though greatly reduced in volume, continued to exist, often under worse conditions than in the eighteenth century. Severe penalties against slavers made them brutal toward the blacks; captains of slaving vessels in fear of capture were known to have thrown their blacks overboard. In 1823 Wilberforce founded an Anti-Slavery Society and began an extensive and well-organized campaign. In 1833 the government passed a measure abolishing slavery in the British empire. The act provided for a period of semiservitude under the guise of apprenticeship, but this arrangement proved unsatisfactory, and by 1838 the slaves had been freed without reservation. A sum of £20,000,000, about half the commercial value of the slaves, was voted as compensation to their former owners.

In only two parts of the empire was slavery deeply entrenched. One was the West Indies. The few British planters, who were usually very wealthy, were violently opposed to emancipation, but as their influence at Westminster had declined they could only submit in helpless rage. Slavery also existed in South Africa, where the Dutch farmers, known as Boers, living in Cape Colony, lost not only their slaves but part of their compensation, for the money was payable only in London. West Indian planters had London agents who collected the money for them, but a simple Boer farmer at the Cape had to sell his claim at a discount. The Boers, however, were not helpless. Hostile to British rule for many reasons, they began in 1837 a mass migration, the Great Trek, into the interior, where eventually they established two semi-independent republics.

The Factory Act of 1833

In 1833 an important act was passed for the protection of children working in textile factories. As in the campaign to abolish slavery, the drive behind this act was largely humanitarian. When it became known that younger children were working for fourteen or sixteen hours a day, the public demanded reform irrespective of party. The movement was led by evangelical Tories who delighted in exposing the mill owners, largely Whigs and Benthamite radicals. As manufacturers, the owners thought in terms of profits, wanted long working hours, and normally opposed factory legislation. The question of child labor became connected with a demand by workingmen for a ten-hour day. In many factories the work of children was integrated closely with the work of adults, so that if children obtained a ten-hour day adults might hope for it also.

There had been a movement since 1800 for the regulation of child labor, but legislation had not been effective. In 1830 a new agitation was begun by Richard Oastler and Michael Sadler, two evangelical Tories. Sadler, a member of Parliament, secured the appointment of a select committee of investigation. Its report aroused the public and convinced Lord Ashley, later the earl of Shaftesbury, that legislation was essential. In 1832 he introduced a bill which provided a working day of ten hours for young persons under eighteen. His bill in effect would have established a ten-hour day for all workers. The factory owners, taking alarm, obtained a new inquiry; and on the basis of its findings the Cabinet introduced a bill to take the place of Lord Ashley's. The government bill prohibited the employment of children under nine in textile mills, provided that children under thirteen should work no more than nine hours a day and young persons under eighteen no more than twelve, but permitted children to come to the factories in relays so that the mills could operate for fourteen or sixteen hours daily. Adult workers, who had hoped for a ten-hour day, were bitterly disappointed. However, one of its principal features was the introduction of government inspectors. This was an important innovation, for the trained inspector, as he gained skill in judging the condition of factories, was later to play a great part in the control of industrial enterprises.

An act of 1842 prohibited the employment of women and girls and of boys younger than ten underground in coal mines. In 1844 the working day of all children under thirteen was restricted so six and a half hours, and the working day of all women and girls to twelve. An act of 1847 provided a ten-hour day for women and children. This act, however, was modified in 1850 so that factories could remain open for twelve hours a day with an hour and a half for meals. Workers again were disappointed, but at least a normal day of ten and a half hours with a half holiday on Saturday had been established. Shorter hours did not decrease production, as employers had feared, for increased efficiency more than made up for a shorter working day.

The Poor Law of 1834

The Poor Law Amendment of 1834 was not passed to assist the poor but to relieve the middle classes of the burden of the poor rates; both the act and its operation bore the mark of Benthamite utility in a harsh and unpleasant form. There was certainly great need of change. The Elizabethan system, which was administered by the parish vestry and which gave relief only to persons living in the parish workhouse, had broken down in the late eighteenth century. After 1795 relief was given to persons outside the workhouse by supplementing wages from the poor rates. The results were disastrous. Wages declined, the independent poor could not compete with the subsidized laborer, pauperism increased, and the poor rate rose from some £600,000 in 1750 to some £8,000,000 in 1818. The new poor law of 1834 applied a drastic remedy. Its aim was to end outdoor relief for the able-bodied poor and to make the workhouse so unattractive that the poor would resort to it only as a last expedient. In order to spread the burden of the rates more evenly, parishes were combined into larger units, known as unions, and administered by locally elected officials. A central commission with great authority supervised the entire system.

The outstanding member of the commission was Edwin Chadwick, a disciple of Jeremy Bentham. Although he was an able and energetic man, he administered the poor law in an unsympathetic way, allowing an element of harshness to dominate poor relief, as though paupers were necessarily idle and vicious and ought to be chastised. But it was impossible to make the workhouse so unattractive that it frightened away the idler and at the same time make it comfortable and consoling for the aged and infirm. The new bastilles, as the poor called them, became very bleak indeed. Husbands were separated from wives, and children from parents; silence was imposed at meals; paupers were buried at the lowest possible cost without the normal decencies. The poor law, as Disraeli later said, outraged the manners of the people. In 1847 the commission was replaced by a central poor law board with less autocratic powers; thereafter the poor were treated with greater humanity.

Chadwick had hoped that the new law would reduce the poor rates and would at the same time induce employers to raise wages. The rates declined, but wages did not increase. Indeed, during the years of depression after 1837, they tended to go down and did not recover until the more prosperous era of the 1850s.

The new poor law established an administrative pattern which was to become familiar: administration in detail by locally elected bodies, local responsibility for finance, but close supervision by the central government. Inevitably the bureaucratic machinery of government was increased and the functions of the state were extended.

The English Municipal Corporations Act, 1835

The English Municipal Corporations Act of 1835 was a direct response to the demand of the middle classes for a drastic reform of local government in the towns. There were nearly 250 incorporated towns in England and Wales, each governed by a corporation consisting of a mayor, aldermen, and common councilors. Over the centuries most of these corporations had become close, exclusive, and self-perpetuating bodies, from which dissenters were excluded by the Corporation Act of 1661. The old town corporations need not be painted too darkly. During the eighteenth century they had governed the towns well enough according to the standards of the time, but hostility mounted against them in the early nineteenth century as the number of dissenters increased and as industrial growth brought wealth into new hands. Their doom was assured when the Corporation Act was repealed in 1828 and when the Reform Bill of 1832 ended their power to manipulate parliamentary elections.

The act of 1835 made sweeping changes. The old corporations were abolished. The government of some 70 of the smallest towns was merged with that of the shire. About 178 towns received new town councils to be elected by all householders who had resided in the town for three years and who paid the local rates. The new councilors served for three-year terms, chose one of their own number as mayor for a term of one year, and selected certain councilors as aldermen for terms of six years. The new corporations expanded their functions rapidly, introduced social services, and became employers on a large scale, but they could not float loans without the consent of the central government, which also audited their books once a year. They had no control over the law courts or over the appointment of judges, nor could they regulate the liquor traffic or license public houses. The Municipal Corporations Act effected a revolution in local government much more complete than did the Reform Bill of 1832 in the structure of Parliament.

Education

In 1833 the Whigs began a modest grant of £20,000 a year for the support of elementary education. The money was shared by two religious societies which sponsored schools for the lower classes: the British and Foreign School Society, which was nonconformist, and the National Society for Promoting the Education of the Poor in the Principles of the Church of England. Their schools were not very good. It was believed at the time that children could be educated in large numbers, several hundred in a room, by the use of child monitors, clever boys or girls who, having learned a short lesson from the master, repeated it over and over to the other children until they learned it by rote. This method could impart very simple ideas, but many of the children never learned to read or write, and the experiment gradually was abandoned. A great step forward was taken in 1839, when the distribution of funds was entrusted to a committee of which Sir James Kay-Shuttleworth was the leading spirit. A man of ability and drive, he established the first training college for teachers. In 1846 a system was begun which consolidated the principles of training colleges, of a teaching certificate, and of additional pay for trained teachers. This was the foundation of the teaching profession. By the middle of the century England had a system of public education, though it was grossly inadequate: half of the children of the poor never went to school at all.

LORD MELBOURNE, 1834–1841

After 1835 the reforming zeal of the Whigs began to slacken. Although they remained in office until 1841 (with two brief Tory intervals), their last years were lethargic and aimless. For this lack of purpose there were three principal causes:

An election in 1841. (Giraudon/Art Resource)

the character of the prime minister, the problem of Ireland, and weakness in financial management.

Upon Grey's retirement in 1834, the king called upon Lord Melbourne, a conservative Whig, to become prime minister. Melbourne was an aristocrat of affability, but he was idle, disillusioned, and contemptuous of vulgarity in any form. He had no great desire for office, he disliked radicals, and he regarded the Benthamites as fools. He also had little sympathy for the poor. Indeed, he had no program of any kind save to manage affairs with as little trouble as possible. His greatest service was his influence on Queen Victoria during the first three years of her reign. When William IV died in 1837, his brother, the duke of Cumberland, became king of Hanover and his niece Victoria became queen of England. She was only eighteen, the daughter of George III's fourth son, Edward, Duke of Kent, who had been dead for many years. Victoria had been brought up in seclusion by her mother, the German princess Victoria of Saxe-Coburg, and her education differed little from that of any young woman of the upper classes. She was attractive and virtuous, a little headstrong, with high notions of the powers of the Crown, but with a most sincere desire to do her duty. It was Melbourne's happy function to employ his charm and tact in teaching her those constitutional principles upon which a British sovereign must base her actions. She liked Melbourne personally and profited greatly from his instruction.

During the first years of her reign the fact that she was surrounded by Whigs resulted in a minor constitutional crisis in 1839. In that year Melbourne resigned, and Peel, asked to form a Cabinet, felt that there should be more Tory influences surrounding the queen. He asked her to remove some of the Whig ladies of her bedchamber and to replace them with Tory ladies. When Victoria refused, Peel abandoned his attempt to construct a ministry, and Melbourne returned for two more meandering years. In 1840 Victoria married her cousin, Prince Albert of Saxe-Coburg-Gotha. A serious young man, he was interested in science, in inventions, in economics, and in the practical problems of government. He exercised a steadying influence on Victoria. Their household was a model of hard work, devotion to duty, and domestic virtue. Victoria created in the public mind a new conception of monarchy. This was of great importance, for the sons of George III had brought kingship into such disrepute that it might not have survived another such generation.

Ireland

In 1832 the Cabinet introduced some reforms in the finances of the Anglican Church in Ireland, suppressed ten of twenty-two Irish bishoprics, and taxed those that remained for the maintenance of ecclesiastical buildings. But when in 1834 Russell suggested that the revenues of the Anglican Church in Ireland were greater than necessary, he broke up the Cabinet. Peel and the Tories came in for a few weeks; then Melbourne returned with a reconstructed ministry.

Melbourne did his best to conciliate O'Connell. The English poor law was extended to Ireland and Irish municipal corporations were reformed. In 1838 tithes were turned into a tax payable by landowners; the money still came from the peasants but it was collected as part of their rent. More important, the undersecretary in Dublin, Thomas Drummond, governed with a new and admirable impartiality. He divided patronage between Protestants and Catholics, recruited Catholic policemen, permitted Catholics to serve on juries, and astonished owners by reminding them that property had responsibilities as well as rights. For some years Ireland was quiet, but in 1841 O'Connell began a great agitation for repeal of the parliamentary union. The English, of course, were adamant in refusal, and O'Connell was shortly faced with the dilemma of either dropping his campaign or sanctioning insurrection. He dropped his agitation and thus lost face with his followers. A new group of leaders, very violent and nationalistic, began a movement they termed "Young Ireland." Insurrection would surely have followed, but soon the entire picture in Ireland was altered by the potato blight.

Finance and Depression

A third difficulty of the Whigs concerned finance. Since taking office in 1830 they had never produced a first-class financial minister. Annual deficits followed one another in dreary succession. Not only were the Whigs incompetent in finance; they failed to recognize that the tax system rested on an unsound foundation, being far too dependent on customs and excises which burdened trade and industry. In periods of economic depression, when the yield from customs and excises was small, the revenues of the state declined in a dangerous way. The first five years of Whig rule had been fairly prosperous, but late in 1836 there were signs that a period of depression was approaching. Conditions grew worse until, by 1840, prosperity had disappeared, many manufacturers had been ruined, and the working classes had sunk into a miserable plight. Wages in the factory towns declined to about a third of their former figure, scarcely one man in ten could find employment, a fourth of the houses were empty, with thousands of families living in the workhouse or subsisting on relief administered at the rate of one shilling a head each week.

As the depression deepened, there was naturally much thought concerning the advantages and disadvantages of the Industrial Revolution. Two contrasting points of view were evident. Businessmen stressed the achievements of industry. In their opinion it had brought wealth and opportunity, not only to themselves but to the people as a whole. The depression was merely a pause in industrial growth; if industry could be liberated from the shackles of tariffs, and especially from the Corn Laws, which benefited the landowner at the expense of everyone else, then progress would be resumed and new achievements beneficial to all would follow. The Tory landlord and the workingman regarded the matter quite differently. The Industrial Revolution, they believed, had brought ruin to many independent workers, had exploited women and children, and had unleashed forces which appeared to be reckless, uncontrollable, and destructive of security. Depression, it was held, could not be blamed on the Corn Laws. The fault lay with the manufacturers, who had been guilty of overproduction and speculation until the world was glutted with their goods and no one could make a profit.

THE GROWTH OF POPULATION

Much of the misery of the poor had its roots in a deeper cause: the increase of population which began in the eighteenth century and continued throughout the nineteenth at a growing rate. In 1801 the population of England and Wales stood at a little under nine million; in 1851 it was almost eighteen million; in 1871, nearly twenty-three million; in 1881, almost twenty-six million. The causes of this tremendous increase are still somewhat obscure. It is no longer believed that it was caused by a decrease in the death rate or by improved medical care, for the growth of population was rapid in an area such as Connaught in Ireland, where medical services were at a minimum. Historians now think that it sprang primarily from altered conditions in rural life which made for earlier marriages and thus increased the span of a woman's childbearing years. Early marriages increased the birth rate, and, as they continued through successive generations, they produced an explosion of population. This was a rural phenomenon, for the cities continued to be unhealthy places and grew largely by immigration. Many people were on the move in England and Scotland in the early nineteenth century—people from crowded rural areas in

England, from the Scottish Highlands, and especially from Ireland. After the Irish potato famine in 1845–1847 the number of Irish in Britain became very large.

These wanderers drifted to the towns, for there was no place else to go. But the cities were not prepared to receive such numbers of immigrants. Although we hear of town improvements in the eighteenth century, they were largely in the main streets and not in the slums and alleys. The towns never caught up with the influx of newcomers to which they were subjected. Despite efforts at improvement, most towns in the first half of the nineteenth century reproduced the evils that had existed in London a century earlier. The poor first crowded into old decaying houses which had seen better days. The squalid suburbs arose outside the old center. Speculators ran up flimsy buildings in long continuous rows, each unit attached to others, side to side and back to back, completely hemmed in except in front, without proper light or ventilation and often without water or means of sewage disposal. Dwellings of a similar kind were built in inner courts and in the centers of city blocks until an area was completely choked with housing. Refuse of all kinds, including human excrement, was piled in courts and alleys until it was carted away. Although a practicable water closet had been patented in 1778, sewage flushed away by water was merely deposited in nearby rivers, pools, or open ditches.

It was very difficult to remedy these conditions, for they had become unmanageable before engineers learned how to collect the great quantities of water needed by a modern city, how to pump it to residential areas, or how to build proper sewers. The danger of disease was great, as was apparent in the outbreaks of cholera during the 1830s. The cause of these conditions was not the Industrial Revolution; rather, it was the increase of population and the growth of cities.

CHARTISM

Chartism, a passionate and resentful protest of the poor against the harsh conditions under which they lived, took the form of a working-class demand for the franchise and for a radical reform of Parliament. The movement began in 1836, when William Lovett, a small shopkeeper, an embittered but cautious man, founded the London Working Men's Association composed of upper-class artisans who were intelligent and fairly well paid. The purpose of the association was to draw the working classes together, to inform the public of the conditions in which laborers lived, and to agitate for the political and social rights of all classes. In 1838 Lovett, aided by Francis Place, drew up a program for the reform of Parliament, a program which came to be called the People's Charter. It contained six points: universal manhood suffrage, equal electoral districts, the secret ballot, removal of property qualifications for membership in the House of Commons, payment of members, and annually elected Parliaments.

Unfortunately the movement soon fell into the hands of demagogues. The Charter was issued at a time when the poor were in great distress, when they were discouraged by their failure to obtain the vote in 1832 and by the collapse of Robert

A slum in London, wood engraving after Gustave Doré. (The Granger Collection)

Owen's plan for a gigantic trade union, and when a bitter campaign was in progress in northern England against the new poor law. Workers in the north, inclined to physical force, were not likely to be satisfied with Lovett's dignified agitation for the reform of Parliament. They adopted the Charter as a kind of battle cry and found a more congenial leader in Feargus O'Connor, an Irish radical who talked wildly about force without understanding the implications of what he was saying. A large man with a tremendous voice, O'Connor was a powerful public speaker, but his character was low and he was described even by a friend of the people as a "foolish, malignant, and cowardly demagogue." He ruined the Chartist movement. He began a newspaper in Leeds, the *Northern Star*, which fanned discontent and incidentally brought him a good deal of money.

It was now proposed that a petition, signed by millions of people, should be presented to Parliament urging the adoption of the six points of the Charter and that the Chartist leaders should hold a convention in London while the petition was being presented to the House of Commons. About fifty delegates met in London in February 1839. They were earnest but naïve men, vastly impressed with the responsibility entrusted to them. Some of them wrote the letters "M.C." (Member of Convention) after their names, in imitation of the "M.P." used by members of Parliament. Chartist leaders had to consider what the next step would be if Parliament rejected their petition, as it was most likely to do. They were not prepared for insurrection, but they thought that a threat of one might be helpful. They asserted, therefore, that the people had the right to arm, they talked of a refusal to pay rent and taxes, and they considered a general strike. Their petition, presented to Parliament in May, was neglected because of a Cabinet crisis, but was rejected in July.

Meanwhile the country was becoming alarmed. Troops were sent to various points in northern England, though there was no fighting. The convention moved from London to Birmingham, where its coming was the occasion of some ugly riots. After Parliament rejected the petition, the Chartists set a date for a general strike. But they knew that many of their followers had no employer to strike against and that those workpeople who had employment were not likely to leave it. Hence the convention lost its courage, canceled the strike, and dissolved in confused defeat. Talk of an insurrection dwindled away, though there was a small uprising in Monmouthshire which was crushed instantly.

This was the first and most interesting phase of Chartism. Thereafter it degenerated, falling completely under the sway of O'Connor, who merely led the people astray. In May 1842 a new petition with more than three million signatures was presented to Parliament, only to be promptly rejected. Disappointment combined with hard times to produce a number of dangerous strikes. Chartism became connected in the public mind with violence, the strikes failed, some of the Chartist leaders were arrested, and the movement subsided once more.

The final defeat of Chartism occurred in 1848, a year of revolution in Europe. Expectation of change was in the air, and O'Connor, untaught by failure, was ready to play the demagogue again. A monstrous petition, said to contain five million signatures, was prepared to be brought to Parliament by a vast throng assembling at Kennington Common in London. O'Connor appeared at the assembly. The government brought up troops and special constables and informed O'Connor that the crowd would not be permitted to cross the Thames to the Parliament buildings. At this moment of crisis O'Connor weakly told the crowd to disperse; in place of an overwhelming demonstration of popular strength the petition was carried to Parliament in three hansom cabs. The ignominy of this fiasco was increased when the petition was found to contain many bogus signatures such as Flatnose, No Cheese, and Jack Frost; moreover, the signatures of the duke of Wellington and of Queen Victoria, which appeared on the list, were not likely to be genuine. Thus the last effort of the Chartists faded away amidst the relief and the ridicule of the upper classes. Yet Chartism must not be dismissed as mere folly. It was a sincere and vigorous effort of the lower classes to help themselves, and the energy it generated passed into other movements. It helped to build the self-respect of laborers and called the attention of the nation to the plight of the poor. John Stuart Mill justly named it the victory of the vanquished.

PEEL'S ADMINISTRATION, 1841–1846

Sir Robert Peel became prime minister in 1841 after an overwhelming Tory victory at the polls. A contemporary called Peel "the best man of business who was ever prime minister." With his great abilities, his tremendous capacity for work, and his high sense of dedication, he brought new order, efficiency, and conscientiousness into government. Perhaps more than any other man in the nineteenth century he raised the standard of public life. He introduced his own budgets, drew up minutes for the Cabinet on all important questions, prepared himself for every debate, and answered in his own hand an enormous number of letters from people of all kinds. His conservatism was not merely that of the landed aristocracy or of the wealthy manufacturers; he wished to support every substantial interest in the country and to draw the middle classes to the new Toryism. At the same time, he felt genuine sympathy for the poor.

PEEL'S BUDGETS

Peel's greatest work was in finance. The whole structure of taxation was in need of reform, not merely to balance the budget but to stimulate the lagging tempo of industry and commerce. Four-fifths of the government's revenue came from customs and excises and thus placed a heavy burden on industry and foreign trade. Peel discovered that although there were duties on more than a thousand articles, the bulk of the revenue came from very few. If the customs were considered primarily as a source of income, they could be lowered on many articles without great loss. British industry, in fact, was so far ahead of the industry of other countries that it did not require protection; moreover, freer trade would facilitate the entry of British manufactures into foreign markets.

Peel therefore began a series of famous budgets which, greatly reducing customs duties, took England far on the road toward free trade. The budget of 1842 lowered duties on 769 articles, establishing a rate of about five percent on imported raw materials, of about 12 percent on semimanufactured articles, and of about twenty percent on fully manufactured goods. Although Peel believed that in the long run the income of the government would not suffer, he foresaw a temporary decline. To meet this immediate loss of revenue and to balance the budget, he persuaded Parliament to accept for three years an income tax of 7d. in the pound. By this measure the burden of taxation, which had fallen with unfair severity on the business classes, was distributed more equally over the nation as a whole. The success of the measure was phenomenal. Industry and commerce revived and expanded, employment increased, and prosperity slowly returned. Lowered duties did not bring serious foreign competition. In the budgets of 1845 and 1846 Peel went further, abolished altogether the customs on 430 articles, lowered the duties on imported raw materials, and allowed most manufactured articles to enter the country with an ad valorem duty of about ten percent. During his term of office he remitted taxation at the rate of about £2.5 million a year and yet produced a surplus. He repaid £14 million of the national debt, and by establishing confidence in the credit of the government he reduced the interest on the debt that remained, at an annual saving of £1.5 million. But he found that the income tax could not be dropped; it became fundamental for government finance.

The Anti–Corn Law League

In this general reduction of tariffs there was one great exception. Peel had not touched the Corn Laws save to readjust Wellington's sliding scale. To a large part of the landed aristocracy, and even more to their tenant farmers, the Corn Laws were the very foundation of agricultural prosperity. Yet Peel was gradually converted to free trade in wheat, and in 1845 he broke with his party over this issue.

A campaign had arisen for the repeal of the Corn Laws. It was begun in the autumn of 1838 by a group of Manchester businessmen who, early in the next year, formed the Anti–Corn Law League. The league found support among large sections of the

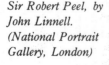

Sir Robert Peel, by John Linnell. (National Portrait Gallery, London)

middle classes. It was an attack upon privilege, and it offered a rallying point for all those who disliked the aristocracy. Like the agitation against slavery, it was nationwide. Highly emotional in its approach, the league also appealed to religion—and it was well organized. The league had a clear and simple objective. It made a direct appeal to manufacturers, who regarded the Corn Laws as a tax on the whole community for the enrichment of the landowners; and it also appealed to laborers, who hoped for cheaper bread. The struggle was not merely one between town and country. The aristocracy was supported and even urged forward by the tenant farmers, but agricultural laborers opposed the landlords. A favorite device of the league was to produce a rural laborer who would say at a public meeting, "I be protected and I be starving."

The league possessed two remarkable leaders. One was Richard Cobden, a manufacturer in Manchester, highly critical of the aristocracy, which he branded as aggressive and warlike. He had a fine, reflective mind and a wonderful gift for lucid and forceful exposition of economic questions. The other, John Bright, was a manufacturer of Quaker background and developed into one of the great orators of the age. He could be bitter and vindictive in speaking, but he added liveliness and popular appeal to the arguments of Cobden. The campaign of the league was waged on a tremendous scale. It conducted mass meetings, sent out lecturers, and distributed millions of closely argued tracts which found arguments to appeal to every class except the offending landlords, who cordially hated the league because it held up the aristocracy to the people as a group of knaves and plunderers.

The Irish Potato Famine, 1845–1846

In 1845 Peel became a convert to free trade in wheat. But if he repealed the Corn Laws he could be accused of betraying the interest of the party that had put him in power. Hence he planned to take the issue to the country in a general election, when he would offer aid to agriculture to cushion the shock of change. He also believed that he would be supported by the growing Toryism of the middle classes. But his attention was diverted by the Irish famine of 1845–1846. In both these years the Irish potato crop failed completely; some 4 million persons dependent on potatoes for food faced starvation. Cholera and various fevers fastened on the stricken population, and during these tragic years perhaps a million people died in Ireland. Peel responded. By 1847 some 700,000 Irishmen were employed on public works; food was distributed to some 2 million more. The Corn Laws did not mean much in Ireland, for the Irish could not afford to buy foreign wheat, but Peel felt that nothing should be done to keep wheat out of Ireland. He saw a lesson for England in the Irish experience: the English peasant must not be forced into dependence on the potato because of the high price of bread.

In December 1845 Peel announced to his Cabinet that the Corn Laws must be repealed. Most of his ministers resisted, the Cabinet broke up, and Peel resigned. Lord John Russell, asked to form a Whig ministry, should have done so, for he had recently declared himself a convert to free trade in wheat. But the Whig aristocrats were landlords no less than the Tories. Russell foresaw a split in his party and an unpleasant struggle in the House of Lords. His efforts to form a Cabinet were halfhearted and he soon abandoned the attempt. Peel was recalled. In June 1846, with the support of a section of the Tories, most of the Whigs, the radicals, and the Irish, he repealed the Corn Laws. Wellington, faithful to a colleague, pushed the measure through the House of Lords. In the case of the Corn Laws, as in the case of Catholic emancipation, Peel and Wellington looked upon themselves as servants of the state who must follow the right or necessary course of action regardless of party or public opinion; but in 1846, in contrast to 1829, the agitation of the league had brought public opinion—though not Tory party opinion—to favor their course of action.

The duty on wheat and other grains was lowered drastically over a period of three years until, in 1849, these grains could enter the country at the nominal rate of one shilling a quarter.

The Results of Repeal

The impact of repeal was greater on politics than on the economic life of the nation. Repeal of the Corn Laws divided the Tory party and ended Peel's career as a great leader. Many Tories had grown restless as Peel had moved toward free trade. Believing that they had been betrayed they turned against him in bitter anger. They found a spokesman in Benjamin Disraeli who had been passed over for office in 1841 and had been critical of Peel ever since. Peel, on his side, believed that his party had deserted him. He was always aware to some extent that he was the son of a manufacturer and not an aristocrat. He now denounced the men whom he had been leading. He would not, he said, by the mere tool of a party. "To adopt the opinions of men who have not access to your knowledge, and could not profit from it if they had, who spend their time in eating and drinking, hunting and shooting, gambling, horse racing, and so forth, would be an odious servitude to which I never will submit." The split in the Tory party was irreparable. Those Tories who remained faithful to Peel, of whom Gladstone was the greatest, held aloof from both parties for a time but eventually united with the Whigs. Most Cabinets for the next twenty years were Whig Cabinets.

On the other hand, the effect of repeal on the economy was surprisingly small. In good years England could still supply most, though not all, of the wheat she required, English farming methods were as advanced as any in the world, and the vast wheat fields of the American West had not yet been opened by railways and cheap ocean transportation. English agriculture continued to prosper; indeed, it enjoyed a golden age. The price of wheat held up very well, averaging about fifty-two shillings a quarter, though it would probably have gone higher if the Corn Laws had been retained. It was only in the 1870s that English farming, unable to compete with grain from America, fell from its high position. The repeal of the Corn Laws has sometimes been portrayed as the final victory of the middle classes. But this was not so. Hostility to the landowning aristocracy, as evidenced by Cobden and Bright, was still insufficient to dislodge the old ruling class from its predominant position in politics. That predominance continued for thirty years after the repeal of the Corn Laws.

The potato famine added new bitterness to Anglo-Irish relations. Lord John Russell, who followed Peel as Prime Minister in 1846, did not administer Irish relief skillfully. Nor was the governmental machinery equipped to meet such an emergency. Suffering in Ireland was intense. The population dropped in a few years from 8 million to some 6.5 million. Thousands of Irishmen left their native land to emigrate to various parts of the empire; even more thousands went to the United States, taking with them a hatred of England intensified by their miseries. This hatred was to make the problem of Ireland much more difficult.

THE COLONIES

Meanwhile important developments were occurring in the British colonies overseas. The highly complicated history of the empire in the nineteenth century is more readily understood if one thinks in terms of three distinct types of expansion. The first was a continuation of the mercantile empire of the seventeenth and eighteenth centuries whose purpose was trade. This mercantile expansion consisted of a series of units, each of which served some trading purpose. These included plantations, commercial centers, and naval bases or strategic points from which trade could be controlled and protected. A second kind of expansion was the military conquest and administration of areas in Asia and Africa containing large native populations. An obvious example was British India. A third type of empire, which will be discussed in detail, consisted of colonies of permanent white settlers, chiefly of British stock. These colonies had the potential to grow in wealth and population until they formed new nations; they arose during the first half of the nineteenth century in Canada, South Africa, Australia, and New Zealand. Like the North American settlements before them, these colonies posed problems quite different from those of trade and conquest.

These latter colonies did not arouse much interest in England at the beginning of the nineteenth century. They contained few British settlers. In 1815 Canada was strongly French; South Africa was Dutch and black; the West Indies contained a small class of white planters and many thousands of black slaves; there were even fewer Englishmen in India; Australia was a penal colony. To utilitarians and businessmen in Britain the cost of these colonies seemed greater than their worth. There was also criticism of the Colonial Office, a rather stuffy department with much jobbery and little imagination. Remembering the American Revolution, the Colonial Office was suspicious of white settlements and much preferred a mercantile empire devoted to trade.

Nonetheless, interest in the colonies gradually increased. In South Africa this interest was largely humanitarian. British missionaries, shocked at the way in which the Boers treated the blacks, worked with evangelicals in England to bring about the abolition of slavery.

Colonization in Australia began very badly. In 1787 Captain Arthur Phillip was sent out with an expedition of some 1100 persons, of whom about 750 were convicts. Early in the following year he founded a penal colony, not at Botany Bay, but at a nearby harbor, which he named Sydney. He annexed the eastern half of Australia, to which the name New South Wales was given. The first free settlers were soldiers who, having served their time with the garrison, later took up land. Although free settlers from Britain came out very slowly, new colonies were gradually formed: Van Diemen's Land (later Tasmania) in 1823, Western Australia in 1829, South Australia in 1834, and Victoria in 1850. A colony was founded in New Zealand in 1839. The white population of Australia increased enormously when gold was discovered in Victoria in 1851, so that by 1860 there were 350,000 people in New South Wales and 538,000 in Victoria.

Systematic Colonization

Greater attention in England was directed toward the colonies in the 1830s by a group of men who wished to introduce new methods of colonization. Their leader was Edward Gibbon Wakefield. An original thinker of remarkable ability, Wakefield might have had a great career in politics but for a private scandal. In 1830 he founded the National Colonization Society of which Charles Buller, Sir William Molesworth, and the radical earl of Durham, Grey's son-in-law, were later members.

Believing that emigration would bring relief to economic misery at home, Wakefield set forth a plan for what he termed "systematic colonization." He saw that throughout the empire there were vast stretches of unoccupied land but a scarcity of capital and labor for their development. His proposal was that the government should not give these lands away but should sell them at reasonable prices. Land would thus pass into the hands of persons with a little capital, and the money obtained by the government could be used to assist the emigration of poorer classes who would serve as laborers until they were able to purchase land of their own. If a supply of labor was thus obtained, men with capital would be more willing to emigrate. The entire process should be supervised by the government in a systematic way. Land should be surveyed and evaluated before it was sold; emigrants should be received at colonial ports and, to discourage them from lingering in the port towns until their money was gone, should be dispatched at once to areas where employment was available. Wakefield's views were theoretical and never were applied in their entirety.

The Durham Report

It was in Canada that colonial self-government first became a reality. The settled parts of the country in the early nineteenth century consisted largely of three areas. The first was the province of Lower Canada (Quebec) along the banks of the St. Lawrence, the home of the French population. The second was Upper Canada (Ontario), a huge western province, in which the early settlements were made in the region between Montreal and the modern city of Detroit. This area, divided from Lower Canada in 1791, had begun to grow when some ten thousand American loyalists had migrated north after the Revolution. The third region, the Maritime Provinces, consisted of Nova Scotia, New Brunswick, Prince Edward Island, and Newfoundland. The government as it existed in 1837 consisted of a governor general for all the Canadian colonies (except Newfoundland where there was a naval governor), and of a lieutenant governor, an appointed council, and a popularly elected assembly in Lower Canada, in Upper Canada, and in each of the Maritime Provinces except Newfoundland. The assemblies had little control of policy, for the lieutenant governors were given revenues the assemblies could not touch. There were many causes of friction: French hostility toward the growing British minority in Lower Canada, discord among the provinces, and quarrels in each province between its governor and its assembly.

In 1837 small insurrections took place in both Upper and Lower Canada. It was then that the prime minister, Lord Melbourne, sent out Lord Durham to investigate and to propose a solution. Wakefield and Charles Buller accompanied Durham to Canada in 1838, and with their assistance Durham collected the material on which he based his famous *Report on the Affairs of British North America*. Its conclusions were twofold. It proposed, in the first place, that Upper and Lower Canada be thrown together into one province so that a united nation could develop and a British majority could be obtained in a united assembly. But it also proposed that Canada be given responsible government, that is, that the Governor should act only as the king acted in England and that the members of his council should retain office only so long as they were supported by a majority in the Assembly. The power of the assembly should be confined to domestic affairs. The first part of Durham's *Report* concerning the union of the two provinces was adopted at once by the British Parliament. The second part was delayed until 1847, when Lord Elgin, a liberal governor general and a son-in-law of Lord Durham, began to put its principles into practice. From then on, Canada enjoyed self-government. Once granted in Canada, it was quickly extended to other colonies in South Africa, Australia, and New Zealand.

Self-government led to a desire for federation. By the British North America Act of 1867 most of the Canadian provinces united to form the Dominion of Canada, subordinate to Britain in imperial matters but self-governing in domestic affairs. Federation came to New Zealand in 1852, and responsible government in 1856. But the union of the Australian colonies was achieved only in 1900, and in South Africa only in 1910.

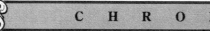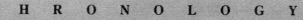

CHRONOLOGY

Whigs and Reform

1830–37	William IV
1830	Lord Grey and Whigs in power
1832	Reform Bill passed
1833	Slavery abolished; Factory Act
1834	Poor Law Amendment and Edwin Chadwick; Lord Melbourne prime minister
1835	Municipal Corporations Act
1836	London Working Men's Association begun by William Lovett
1837–1901	Queen Victoria
1838	The People's Charter, Feargus O'Connor; Anti–Corn Law League, Cobden and Bright
1839	First training college for teachers; Sir James Kay-Shuttleworth; Durham Report
1841	Peel prime minister
1845–47	Irish potato famine
1846	Corn Laws repealed
1848	Chartism defeated
1867	British North America Act; dominion status for Canada

29

The Mid-Victorians

The years between 1846, when the Corn Laws were repealed, and 1868, when Gladstone formed his first ministry, constitute a distinct period in the history of nineteenth-century Britain. At the beginning of this era a radical such as John Bright believed that the work of fundamental reform would go forward rapidly, that the lower classes would soon obtain the franchise, and that the aristocracy would lose its hold on political life. But these expectations were not fulfilled. In spite of a series of lesser reforms between 1850 and 1854, it is nonetheless true to say that in the middle of the century there came a pause, a time of ineffectiveness in Parliament and of diminished desire for drastic change. The nobility and gentry continued to dominate the political life of the nation.

The most obvious reason for this lull was the remarkable prosperity of the time. Thriving on free trade and untroubled by foreign competition, Britain entered into the full enjoyment of industrial leadership. Not only was she the workshop of the world, she represented a new kind of industrial civilization which other nations envied and sought to emulate. British prosperity was more widely distributed than in the past; agriculture did well despite the repeal of the Corn Laws; and large sections of the working classes enjoyed higher wages and better food. The healthy state of the economy was reflected in a lessening of class tensions, a pride in the achievements of industry, and a confidence in future progress. In politics this was a time of instability, with no large party majorities in the Commons. Cabinets rose and fell in rapid succession without much alteration in policy.

INDUSTRIAL ACHIEVEMENT

Prosperity was based on solid industrial advance. The cotton industry, which continued to expand, was supplying cotton cloth not only to the home market and to the Continent but to many other parts of the world. In 1815 Britain had imported eighty-two million pounds of raw cotton; in 1860 that amount had increased to one billion. Changes in the woolen industry came more slowly, but the spinning of wool by machinery had advanced rapidly in the first quarter of the century, so that by 1850 most wool was spun and woven in factories, though there was some weaving of fine fabrics by hand. Raw wool was imported from Australia, New Zealand, and the Cape.

Advance in the heavy engineering and metal trades was even more spectacular. The annual production of iron rose tenfold during the first half of the century, the iron industry receiving a tremendous impulse from the building of railways and later of iron ships. The manufacture of iron machinery became a great new industry. Instead of buying wooden machines or iron ones constructed painfully by hand, a manufacturer could now buy iron machines cut to exact specifications and thus increase the durability of his equipment as well as the quality of his product. After restrictions on the exportation of British machinery were removed in 1843, the value of exported machines rose fivefold in the next twenty years. The production of coal more than tripled during the first half of the century, and by 1870 Britain was mining more than 110 million tons a year. The steam printing press was invented in 1814; the sewing machine was invented in France in 1830 and strengthened in the 1850s to pierce leather and thus make shoes; and the telegraph came about in the 1830s—these advancements opened a host of new industries. The use of petroleum as a lubricant (first developed in Pennsylvania in 1859) was a great improvement over the animal and vegetable fats employed in the past.

The Railways

The early history of railways is the story of bringing rails and the steam engine together. Wooden rails, over which carts were drawn by horses, had been used underground in coal mines since the sixteenth century. By 1800 these rails were made of iron, the flange that kept the wheels in place had been transferred from the rail to the inner side of the wheel, and tracks had been laid above ground to transport coal for short distances from the pit-head, normally to navigable water. Tracks on the surface naturally suggested longer lines. It was proposed in 1799 to build a railway from London to Portsmouth to carry goods; a portion of the line was opened in 1804. The first steam engines, of course, were stationary. Then about 1782 James Watt invented an engine that could turn a wheel; and attempts were soon made to construct a self-propelling engine.

The Stockton and Darlington Railway, opened in 1825 in a mining area south of Durham, was built by promoters who rented the tracks to anyone wishing to run his own vehicles over the line. Trucks for coal and lighter carriages for passengers were both to be drawn by horses, but when the line was half built, the promoters decided to use locomotives. A famous inventor, George Stephenson, constructed a steam engine weighing seven tons which could haul a ninety-ton train at a speed of four to eight miles an hour. Stephenson's engine, its smokestack red hot from its exertions, was the wonder of the countryside. Stationary engines on the tops of hills pulled trains up steep inclines by cables.

A coal mine, 1814. Part of the mine appears on a hill in the background. A steam engine, built by Mr. Blenkinsop, draws a train of coalwagons to nearby Leeds. From Edward Hailstone, The Costume of Yorkshire, London, 1885. *(Historical Pictures Service, Chicago)*

The Liverpool and Manchester Railway, which was opened in 1830, was the first modern railway. Stephenson had been conducting experiments which demonstrated the drastic way in which a grade reduces the pulling power of a locomotive. He persuaded the company to abandon stationary engines on the top of hills and to accept the basic principle that tracks must be laid on the level. The company held a competition for the best engine, and Stephenson's locomotive, the *Rocket*, proving far superior to other entrants (two of which would not start), was adopted by the line. The *Rocket* could travel easily at a speed of thirty miles per hour; in one breathless test it covered a distance of four miles in four and a half minutes. Other railways were rapidly constructed in many parts of the country. Such progress was not made without difficulties and mistakes. There were technical problems: boilers burst, trains ran off the tracks, and strong resistance to the railways came from the owners of canals and stagecoach lines, from farmers who feared for their local markets, from gentlemen who saw their hunting disturbed, and from educators at Eton and Oxford. Rapid construction led to speculation, extravagance, and jobbery. But by the middle of the century Britain was supplied with an excellent network of railways.

*Railways
1825–1914.*

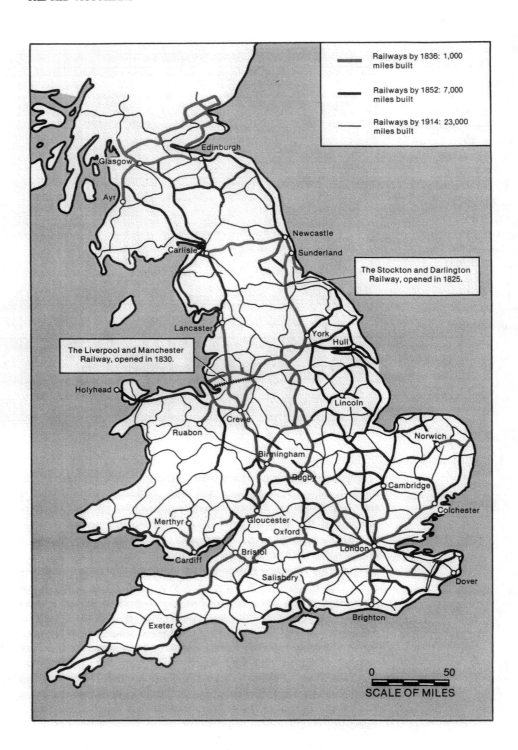

Railways by 1836: 1,000 miles built

Railways by 1852: 7,000 miles built

Railways by 1914: 23,000 miles built

The Stockton and Darlington Railway, opened in 1825.

The Liverpool and Manchester Railway, opened in 1830.

Glasgow
Edinburgh
Ayr
Newcastle
Carlisle
Sunderland
Lancaster
York
Hull
Holyhead
Lincoln
Crewe
Ruabon
Norwich
Birmingham
Rugby
Cambridge
Colchester
Merthyr
Gloucester
Oxford
London
Cardiff
Bristol
Salisbury
Dover
Brighton
Exeter

0   50
SCALE OF MILES

The railways exerted a tremendous influence on English life. Quickening all aspects of the economy, they caused a great increase in the production of coal and iron, they became large employers of labor, and they immensely influenced industry. Cheaper and faster transportation increased all production, reduced prices, and attracted foreign buyers. English firms built railways in many parts of the world. Agriculture was scarcely less affected than industry, for perishable goods could be carried long distances, cattle could be brought to market, and fertilizers and farm machinery could be more widely distributed. Railways required large capital funds and offered a new form of investment, thus affecting the structure of credit and finance.

Their social effects were no less important. They broke down the isolation of rural areas, enabled city and country folk to visit back and forth, and opened the age of the commuter. The number of passengers was far greater than had been anticipated. An act of 1844, compelling railways to run one train a day on every line at the fare of a penny a mile, made travel possible for the poor. The railways forced inveterate people into an acceptance of change and encouraged others to think of the future. Brushing prejudice and vested interests aside, they brought obvious advantage to society as a whole. Railways were also heralded as a triumph of private enterprise. The state never built a railway, though it reserved the right to purchase them.

London: A Pilgrimage, *1872 wood engraving after Gustave Doré. (Granger Collection)*

Commerce

The tonnage of British shipping remained fairly constant between 1815 and 1840 but nearly doubled in the next twenty years. In the same way the value of British exports, after rising very little between 1815 and 1834, increased rapidly thereafter, from a value of £42 million in 1834 to £199 million in 1870. The total value of imports was much greater: £152 million in 1854 and £303 million in 1870. The difference was made up by earnings in carrying freight by sea and by income from investments abroad. In the middle of the century businessmen obtained better facilities for organizing corporations and for obtaining credit. An act of 1844 made incorporation easier; legislation between 1855 and 1862, limiting the liability of stockholders to the value of their investment, encouraged the public to buy stocks. Before 1850 businessmen had suffered from lack of facilities for borrowing from banks, from unsound banking practices, and from inefficiency in the administration of the Bank of England. Conditions in these matters improved greatly after 1850.

THE IDEA OF PROGRESS

The achievements of industry and the increase of wealth bred a spirit of satisfaction with the present and fervent faith in the idea of progress. Mid-Victorians believed in the worthiness of themselves and their world. They had problems, but problems could be solved: the tone of the age was buoyant and optimistic. Great opportunities appeared to lie ahead for those who were earnest and industrious. It is also true that the age was materialistic, that great emphasis was placed on the production of wealth, that the aesthetic side of life was neglected.

The pride of the Victorians had finer qualities than vulgar exultation in new riches. Industrial achievement represented a victory over the brute forces of nature, a victory of intelligence over outworn modes of thought. There was pride in the capacity to strive and to achieve; the smoke hovering over a factory town was sometimes compared with the smoke of a great battle. Material progress was leading to a more civilized life. Cheap cotton cloth increased cleanliness; street lighting reduced crime; safe drinking water and cheaper tea and coffee decreased drunkenness. The speeches of business leaders expressed the hope that expanding commerce would bring peace and unity to all the world. There was belief in the perfectibility of human beings, in "the creation of certain nobler races, now very dimly imagined." The Great Exhibition of 1851, the first world's fair, caught the imagination of the people and symbolized national pride in the industrial wonders created during the last half-century.

RELIGION

Religion played an enormous part in mid-Victorian England. Some sections of the lower classes were so neglected and so sunk in ignorance as to be outside the life of the churches. Indeed, only about twenty percent of the people attended regularly.

Some skepticism resulted from the advance of science, but most members of the more prosperous classes were Bible-reading, Sabbath-keeping, sincere, and devout Christians. The flocking of earnest men and women to the churches every Sunday, the zeal for missions both at home and abroad, the popularity of hymns and religious verses no matter how dismal, the number of newly built churches, the attack on drunkenness, a more energetic and appealing type of preaching, an increased use of ritual and music by nonconformists, and greater beauty in the services of the Church of England—all offered proof of a deep and widespread interest in religion. Many working-class citizens were untouched by this, however.

Religion was evangelical. Whether one attended Wesleyan or other nonconformist chapels or the services of the Established Church, one was taught a personal religion which emphasized conscience and moral conduct. The soul must recognize its sinfulness, must seek salvation through Christ, and could thus emerge from a state of wickedness to one of goodness and virtue. Conscience must be an omnipresent guide, sitting in constant judgment over every thought and action. The mid-Victorians were taught a literal interpretation of the Scriptures, an anthropomorphic God, a belief in the Last Judgment, in the joys of Heaven, and in the pangs of Hell.

Some historians have seen in eighteenth-century Methodism the origin of the nineteenth-century revival of religion. But the revival had a broader base. There had been an evangelical movement within the Church of England during the eighteenth century, and some of the older nonconformist sects had become more active. The French Revolution had produced in England by reaction a deep conservatism both in politics and in religious faith, and the victory over Napoleon had added a certain moral vanity and ethical assurance. Thus the evangelical movement, drawing strength from various sources, advanced on a broad front in the nineteenth century until it became almost universal.

The movement hardened into a social code which, with its etiquette, its taboos, and its prudery, divided society sharply into those who were godly and those who were not. Unless a person was respectable, unless one's doings would bear investigation, unless one was careful, vigilant, and earnest—unless, in a word, one lived according to the evangelical code—that person was looked at askance by his neighbors. Hence the supermorality of the age. In speech and in writing there was an anxious avoidance of anything indelicate and a most guarded reticence toward all matters relating to sex. It was improper to refer to the human body, or to the nasty conditions in the slums, or to that much-maligned plant, the potato (which was commonly called "the root"). The sheltered education of girls made them guardians of the code; and the yards of cotton cloth in which women of the middle classes encased themselves testified both to their inordinate modesty and to their sedentary lives. The social code stressed cleanliness and neatness—a German professor scoffed that the English mistook soap for civilization. There was also an assurance of ethical rectitude, a sense that England, a nation of the elect, was justified in the eyes of the Almighty. The code was probably more rigid in the lower middle classes than elsewhere, which was possibly an indication that new classes were trying to establish themselves and must therefore stress their respectability. The code was also the result of the emergence of society from the brutality of the eighteenth century to a more decent and civilized standard of conduct.

The Growth of Nonconformity

Nonconformity grew enormously during the half century after 1800. Although there was some splintering among the Methodists—we hear of the Primitive Methodists, the Calvinistic Methodists, the Methodists of the New Connection—the parent organization steadily increased its membership and appealed strongly to the working classes. Baptists, Congregationalists, Unitarians, and Quakers also grew in strength and numbers. They tended to attract more middle-class people than did the Methodists, although they made efforts to appeal to the poor. And there were humbler religious bodies of various kinds among the lower classes. A religious census in 1851 disclosed the fact that of all the people who attended a place of worship upon a certain Sunday about fifty-two percent went to services of the Church of England and about forty-eight percent to some sort of dissenting chapel or to a Catholic church.

The census also revealed that a great many of the poor, especially the unskilled factory workers, did not go to any church. Of a population of 17 million in England and

Wales, at least 5 million were outside any religious body. Some of these people had no place of worship near them. Others disliked the way in which the poor were crowded into the free seats at the back or at the sides of the church, or they resented being told that their poverty was the result of idleness and vice, or they had no Sunday clothes. But many others were absent because religion had no meaning for them. Although both the Church of England and the dissenting groups made strenuous efforts to Christianize the mass of unchurched that still remained in Britain, these efforts were only moderately successful.

The Church of England

The Church of England had been subjected to sharp attack in the 1830s because it contained abuses, because the bishops voted against the Reform Bill, and because religious thought at Oxford appeared to be moving toward Catholicism. One cause of criticism was the enormous gap between the incomes of the upper and the lower clergy. A few of the bishops enjoyed princely revenues. The see of Canterbury was worth £30,000 a year, and a few other bishoprics, of which Durham was the richest, brought their incumbents annual incomes of £15,000 to £20,000. On the other hand, there were cases of abject poverty among the lower clergy.

Absenteeism and pluralities were still serious abuses. In 1827, of 10,500 beneficed clergymen, 4500 were absentees from one of their livings. It should be remembered that there were no pensions for clergymen, so that a priest who was aged or ill could do little but ask permission to be nonresident. The constitution of the church was cumbersome; bishops often could not discipline their clergy except through action in the ecclesiastical courts. The renting of pews to well-to-do parishioners, so that the poor were crowded into a few free seats, was another unfortunate practice. Many industrial parishes were so thickly populated that clergymen could not hope to administer properly to the people entrusted to them.

During the thirty years between 1830 and 1860 these matters were largely corrected. It was Sir Robert Peel, more than any other man, who saved the Church of England. In 1835 he established the Ecclesiastical Commission to investigate clerical incomes; the salaries of the highly paid clergy were reduced drastically and the number of canons allowed each cathedral was controlled. Peel also facilitated the subdivision of large parishes. Other legislation, passed by the Whigs, forbade clergymen to hold more than two livings simultaneously, created the bishoprics of Ripon and Manchester, and commuted tithes to small money payments. The ecclesiastical courts were reformed. Later, in the 1850s, new central courts of probate and divorce took these areas of jurisdiction away from the courts of the church, leaving them little to do. A charity commission administered nonecclesiastical trusts, that is, money left for educational and charitable purposes but often consumed in sinecures. There was also a great amount of church building; the number of clergymen was increased; and a new spirit of reform, of dedication, and of spiritual earnestness transformed the church with thoroughness and rapidity.

The Oxford Movement

These ecclesiastical reforms were disliked by certain churchmen. In 1833 a group of scholars and clergymen at Oriel College, Oxford, of whom John Henry Newman, John Keble, Edward Pusey, and Hurrell Froude were leaders, formed an Association of Friends of the Church and began to publish pamphlets known as *Tracts for the Times*. This was the origin of the Oxford movement. The writers of these tracts were young men, sincerely religious, but rather given to cleverness and to a subtle type of argument which sometimes appeared sophistic. They were really ignorant of the world to which they addressed their teachings; hence they were impractical and academic. Repelled by the materialism and by the liberalism of the age, they feared that the church was in danger and that those who sought its reform were in reality seeking its destruction. The Tractarians assailed the government for redistributing the revenues of the church and further opposed the admission of nonconformists to Oxford and Cambridge. Although they found themselves on the side of reaction, they did have noble aims. They sought to foster a spiritual conception of the church as a divinely constituted society, above the state's control. They laid stress on ritual, on the church's historic role, and on the doctrine of the apostolic succession which carried the church back without a break to Christ and the apostles.

The thinking of the Tractarians inclined them to Roman Catholicism. In 1841 Newman published Tract No. XC, which argued that the Thirty-nine Articles of Faith of the Church of England contained nothing contrary to the teachings of Rome. W. G. Ward, another Tractarian, declared that the articles could be given a Catholic interpretation and that in subscribing to them he had renounced no Roman doctrine. In 1845 Newman and Ward became members of the Roman Catholic church. These and other spectacular conversions broke the Oxford movement. A wave of anti-Catholicism swept the country. When in 1850 the papacy established Roman bishops in England, the prime minister, Lord John Russell, was applauded for rather foolishly denouncing "papal aggression." The Oxford movement, however, awakened in the clergy a deeper sense of the spiritual significance of the church and of their dedication to a sacred calling, and it made them less inclined to mingle in the work and pleasure of the world. The movement affected the Anglican service, which gradually was made more refined and more beautiful, with greater simplicity and greater reverence.

Later in the century other disputes arose within the Church of England that may be traced to the Oxford movement. A good many of the Anglican clergy, known as Anglo-Catholics, moved toward more elaborate ritual and toward a higher conception of the priesthood. They were opposed, however, by evangelical groups within the church, both lay and clerical, who wished to keep the service simple and distinctly Protestant. So bitter did these disputes become that in 1874 Disraeli passed a Public Worship Act to regulate Anglo-Catholic practices. These divisions also produced the Broad Church Movement, sponsored by liberal churchmen who wished the church to accept the teachings of science and of biblical criticism but also to stress the broad and unifying essentials of faith on which all Anglicans could agree.

Skepticism

Few of the mid-Victorians were disturbed by religious doubt. Yet there were forces at work which challenged religious orthodoxy and fundamentalist belief. The church was not troubled by the advances in astronomy, for as the universe was shown to be ever more vast, the location of Heaven could be projected into space. But geology was another matter. It apparently showed that the earth had not been created in the manner described in Genesis. Biblical scholarship, moreover, was proving that the Scriptures had not been written in the way the churches taught. Most difficult of all was the theory of evolution, set forth in Darwin's *On the Origin of Species by means of Natural Selection* (1859), which undermined the orthodox conception of human creation. In a word, the religion of the evangelicals could not be reconciled with the teachings of science. People who thought about these conflicting ideas were perplexed and anxious. Some became skeptics who doubted the truth of the Christian religion, or agnostics who held that the nature of God as a first cause was beyond human knowledge and understanding. One reason for the popularity of Tennyson's *In Memoriam* was its recognition of religious doubt and its comforting assurance that somehow all might yet be well.

The physical sciences, with their objective investigations, their organized attack on one problem after another, and their revelation of unalterable laws, led people to apply similar methods to social studies. H. T. Buckle, in his *History of Civilization in England,* tried unsuccessfully to explain human history in terms of climate and terrain. Walter Bagehot began to apply scientific concepts to politics, and Herbert Spencer, to sociology. Historical research, influenced by the German seminar method, became more objective and scientific; similar tendencies appeared in the study of language, as in the great project of the *Oxford English Dictionary.*

LITERATURE

The great variety and fullness of life in mid-Victorian England offered essayists, novelists, and poets ample themes on which to write. John Stuart Mill's essay *On Liberty* carried the conception of personal freedom about as far as it could be carried in an ordered society; Samuel Smiles's *Self-Help* set forth in a striking if naïve way the doctrine that hard work and devotion to duty were the keys to material success. Charles Darwin's *Origin of Species* was followed in 1860 by *Essays and Reviews,* in which seven distinguished persons courageously accepted the discoveries of science and of biblical scholarship. The year 1859 saw the publication of Tennyson's *Idylls of the King* and Dickens's *A Tale of Two Cities,* works that followed literary and Christian tradition; but two novels, George Eliot's *Adam Bede* and George Meredith's *The Ordeal of Richard Feverel* treated moral issues in an objective, almost pagan, way. Edward Fitzgerald's *Rubáiyát of Omar Khayyám,* in its spirit of resignation and its desire for ease and pleasure, struck a most un-Victorian note.

Despite the individualism of mid-Victorian writers, one can observe certain general characteristics. The mood of social indignation, evident in the period from 1830 to 1850, continued into the middle of the century, but some of the best novels now dealt with the comfortable life of the upper classes. Concern with religious topics persisted; authors appeared as diverse as Thomas Henry Huxley, the champion of science, and Cardinal Newman, who regarded a dogmatic and traditional faith as the only bulwark against irreligion. Although many writers abandoned Christianity, they retained the moral assumptions of an evangelical society. Thomas Carlyle, for example, having rejected Christianity, constructed a new personal faith in which the attributes of Scottish Calvinism played no small part. Indeed, writers were compelled to conform to the conventions of the time if they wished to retain an audience. While some authors followed Macaulay in glorifying material progress, others were convinced that economic success was exacting too high a toll in human misery. Mid-Victorian writers were more concerned with form and craftsmanship than the Romantics had been. A characteristic unpleasant to modern readers was the role of prophet or sage assumed by some popular authors. But the Victorians, earnestly seeking guidance, expected this from authors. Finally, we must admire the vitality and creative force of Victorian writers.

Authors of nonfictional prose were among the finest thinkers of the age. Thomas Carlyle, historian, biographer, and social critic, was the son of Scottish peasants, from whom he derived a belief in frugality, work, and discipline. A blasting social critic, he felt some sympathy with the Chartists and hinted at the inevitability of revolt. His great message was a call to action. "Stop moping," he seemed to be saying, "there is work for all of us to do." Contemptuous of middle-class bungling, he became disillusioned with democracy and turned to the dubious notion of the strong man or hero who would cure social ills by autocratic action. Another prose writer, Matthew Arnold, son of the schoolmaster Dr. Thomas Arnold, was a refined and sensitive critic who wrote with wit and urbanity. He was at first a poet; but his melancholy verse seemed the broodings of an intellectual disturbed by the ferment around him. He abandoned poetry for prose in a determined effort to be more resolute and active. Turning to literary criticism, he held that literature was a potent force in shaping a civilized society; hence the writer should be highly serious, a thinker who offered guidance to the world. As social critic Arnold attacked the materialism of the age, its worship of wealth, its crudity in business life, and its bad taste in aesthetic values. These faults he attributed to ignorance. He called the aristocrats Barbarians who liked honors, sports, and pleasure; the business classes, Philistines who occupied themselves with fanaticism, moneymaking, and tea meetings; the lower classes, the Populace, of which, he wrote, "the sterner self liked bawling, hustling, and smashing; the lighter self, beer."

Bad taste in art, in architecture, and in domestic furnishings was attacked by John Ruskin, a critic and historian of art, who turned social economist and reformer. A brilliant but erratic man, he wrote with great eloquence and moral intensity. He believed that religious faith and morality formed the basis of aesthetic feeling; that the attributes of God were to be found in things of beauty; that bad art revealed a decadent society and good art resulted from good social conditions. In the 1860s

Ruskin began to express radical opinions upon economics, the condition of the poor, and utopian schemes of reform. Although his views were often eccentric, his attacks upon the cruelty of laissez faire and the social apathy of the well-to-do displayed a nobility of character and a deep sense of social wrong.

Of writers in the field of politics, John Stuart Mill was probably the greatest. An advanced liberal, he held that "genius can only breathe freely in an atmosphere of freedom" and that "the individual is not accountable to society for his actions, in so far as these concern the interests of no person but himself." Mill argued that self-government was more important than efficient government, that the franchise should be extended, that all special privilege should be abolished, that women should have equal rights with men, and that the state should intervene in economic life to protect and to control, even to the point of interference with the rights of property.

A number of famous novelists were writing in the mid-Victorian period. Perhaps the most gifted was Charles Dickens, whose bubbling humor, buoyancy in telling a story, and skill in creating characters placed him in the first rank of novelists. Yet the plots of many of his novels were trite; his pathos approached vulgarity. But he

Charles Dickens. (A.P. Wide World Photos, Inc.)

understood the London poor as few writers have ever done. Exposing the evils of society, he taught the moral that poverty was not the result of depravity but of virulent social conditions. He portrayed the patience and good nature of the poor. He had no program of reform, however, beyond a larger humanitarianism. Two other novelists, William Makepeace Thackeray and Anthony Trollope, described the life of the upper classes. Thackeray was a disillusioned man who satirized romantic sentiment and gave his characters reality partly by emphasizing the unpleasant side of human nature. His realism, however, was urbane and was lightened by ironic comedy. His greatest novel, *Vanity Fair,* was a picture of contemporary life, though the story was laid in the early part of the century. Trollope wrote pleasant though unexciting novels of clerical life in the country and of politics in London. There is no better way to become acquainted with the Church of England in the middle of the century than to read his novels of the clergy in the imaginary cathedral city of Barchester. Mary Evans, writing under the pen name of George Eliot, was an agnostic who defied convention in her private life. Yet in her novels she was preoccupied with problems of conscience as it gained in strength or degenerated into weakness.

The most popular of mid-Victorian poets was Alfred Tennyson. His early poems, written in a mood of romantic melancholy, contained no depth of thought but offered promise that the author would become a great master of words. This promise was amply fulfilled. A "lord of language," Tennyson developed a wonderful sense of stately cadence and full-voiced vowel sounds. His mind was somber and ponderous. When he gave himself time for reflection, his ideas were worthwhile. His long elegy, *In Memoriam,* written over a span of seventeen years, dealt gravely with problems of religion and faith and of man's relationship with God and nature. But when he wrote on impulse, he became sentimental and trivial. He wished to deal with contemporary themes; he was fascinated by science and by engineering; and he took pride in England's material progress. But there was always an element of doubt, a fear that an advancing society might end in retrogression. He was essentially a poet of somber introspection, of romantic melancholy, of musical lyrics, a lover of nature who could create scenery appropriate to the mood he wished to portray.

Unlike Tennyson, Robert Browning was a self-confident poet who wrote with great vitality and did not hesitate to break with literary tradition. He was interested in strange and occult tales, in myths of ancient times, in human psychology, especially in the workings of the criminal mind, and in Italian history and social life. His poetry was sometimes obscure. He tended to think that matters clear to him would be clear to his readers, and he often masked his thoughts and opinions in one way or another. This reticence led him to employ the dramatic monologue, a form of poetry in which a speaker in the verse discourses at length, gradually revealing his ideas and indirectly those of the poet. An optimistic man, Browning handled the religious problems of his age with more buoyancy than depth. He implied that the obvious defects of this world would be remedied by the perfection of the world to come, a hope that brought comfort to his more naïve readers. At the same time there was a realism about Browning that is quite modern; he employed colloquial phrases, discordant sounds, and jaw-breaking diction to obtain the effects he desired. Romantic and impulsive, he eloped with the poetess Elizabeth Barrett in order to save her from the domestic tyranny of her father.

Three other important poets should be mentioned: Dante Gabriel Rossetti, both poet and artist, whose polished verses remind one of Tennyson; William Morris, interested at first in poetry and the arts but later in the rise of socialism; and Algernon Charles Swinburne, whose wonderfully musical poetry challenged the moral and intellectual assumptions of the mid-Victorians.

In mid-century a significant change occurred in the place accorded to women writers. Previously, Jane Austen had to maintain anonymity; the Brontë sisters made various uses of the names Ellis, Currer, and Acton Bell, and Mary Evans employed the name George Eliot. Now the frequent use of the pseudonym and the recourse to anonymity had ended. Elizabeth Barrett Browning boldly used her own name and successors followed her example. Literature thus became a branch of the arts where women could both excel and be accepted as women.

SOCIAL CLASSES

The structure of society continued to be aristocratic. A handful of nobles and gentry owned most of the land; the middle classes were proportionately smaller than they are today; the laboring poor made up the vast bulk of the population. Of this

*Child labor.
(SNARK/Art
Resource)*

working population, the largest single group of laborers (1,790,000) comprised those connected with agriculture, still the greatest of English industries; the second largest contained the domestic servants (1,039,000). These figures should be compared with 527,000 cotton workers, 284,000 wool workers, 103,000 workers in linen and flax, 133,000 in silk.[1] Thus large numbers of the laboring class were still on the soil or in domestic service; and many thousands of workers—miners, men in the building trades, merchant seamen, blacksmiths, shoemakers, tailors and dressmakers, and those engaged in unspecified labor—although affected indirectly by industrial developments, did not work in factories but used skills which were preindustrial in nature.

The lot of the agricultural laborers was grim. Unless they lived in an area where industry competed with agriculture for his services, their wages were low, housing was bad, and hours of labor were excessive. In the towns the condition of factory workers varied greatly. Abject poverty, ignorance, want, drunkenness, and brutality existed at the bottom of the scale. But there was now an upper crust of skilled or semiskilled workers who received much higher wages than in the past. They formed a class of decent and respectable laboring people who lived in modest comfort, with enough money for a little pleasure and with enough leisure to enjoy it. Parks, free

[1]Figures taken from G. Kitson Clark, *The Making of Victorian England,* pp. 113–114. Based on the census of 1851.

The only photo of Charlotte Brontë. (A.P. Wide World Photos, Inc.)

concerts, museums, football matches, and cheap excursions on the railways as well as libraries and institutes for those of a serious turn of mind—these made life more interesting for the respectable poor. Perhaps a third of working-class women worked outside the home, increasingly in the textile industry. The factory acts had limited their opportunities while protecting them from extremely dangerous working conditions. Household service had been and would continue to be a major outlet for working-class women.

It is not easy to define the middle classes. They contained some businessmen of great wealth who for one reason or another, perhaps because they clung to nonconformity, were not considered more than middle class. On the other hand, there were people with very little money who asserted their superiority over peers. The ranks of the lower middle class consisted of all kinds of clerks, bookkeepers, and commercial travelers, of an enormous number of small retailers who operated little shops, of saloonkeepers, and of such people as foremen in factories and in the building trades. The middle classes were striving professionals, devoted to industry and commerce, but often narrow and grasping. In religion they were evangelical, stressing the business virtues of sobriety, industry, and thrift; they were apt to think that the same qualities which brought economic success would also pave the way to Heaven. They had much more money than in the past. They lived in solid comfort, as the growth of suburbs made evident, but in shockingly bad taste. The invention of metal springs began the age of upholstered chairs and sofas, bulbous in form and elephantine in size. Cheap building materials, cheap foreign wood, ugly architecture and furniture, and endless knickknacks made in factories, killed the art of local craftsmen and produced a dreary vulgarity in domestic arrangements.

But just as prosperity created an upper crust of laborers, so it also produced an upper middle class of successful business and professional men, a class with wealth, leisure, education, and frequent connections with the aristocracy. New luxuries, new means of enjoyment, and new opportunities for thought and culture gave poise and urbanity to this upper middle class and enticed it from the meanness and rigidity of middle-class life. The secret of this advance was the reform of the universities and of what the English call the public schools. The mastership of Dr. Thomas Arnold at Rugby from 1828 to 1842 opened a new era for these schools, making them more scholarly and more devoted to the building of character. Arnold developed the ideal of the Christian gentleman dedicated to public service. The development of a tax-funded school system in the second half of the century created opportunities for women as well as men to obtain an education and to earn a teaching position. Meanwhile, Oxford and Cambridge, under pressure of parliamentary inquiry and legislation, reformed abuses, removed sinecures, broadened curriculums, and opened their doors to the upper middle class.

The position of the aristocracy was surprisingly strong. Nobles and gentry, numbering together perhaps three thousand persons, were the great landowners of the country. About a quarter of the land in 1871 was in the hands of twelve hundred individuals; some years later there were twenty-eight nobles each of whom possessed estates of more than one hundred thousand acres. Many large estates, which were normally managed well, produced revenue not only from agriculture but also from other sources, such as coal mines or urban property, or from the development of a seaside resort or a port town. Their owners were apt to be sober and practical men who were also putting money into commercial and industrial enterprises. They were by far the wealthiest class in the nation.

Greatly overrepresented in Parliament, the aristocracy continued to dominate politics. Their influence in borough elections was diminishing, but their hold on the countryside was strong; they could exert many pressures on the "deferential" rural electorate. The aristocracy stood at the top of the social scale. Great deference was paid to birth. The pleasures of country life and the possession of landed property fascinated the upper middle classes. The world of the aristocracy, its manners softened and its morals improved, was still an enchanted realm the wealthy business-man admired, imitated, and secretly longed to enter. And yet the rule of the aristocracy, with its inheritance of special privilege, could not continue indefinitely to satisfy the new England of industry and commerce.

LIBERALISM AND POLITICS

Mid-Victorians were liberal in a broad sense. The Tories never had a majority in the Commons during this period, and the Whigs reflected the liberal tone of the country. Even the Whig aristocrats had a liberal tincture, though their liberalism was somewhat tepid. Liberalism meant a belief in reform and progress, a respect for the dignity and worth of the individual, a vague desire to give the lower classes an opportunity for self-improvement, a pride in England's free institutions, a hostility toward autocracies, a sympathy with national aspirations, and a hatred of slavery in any part of the world. There were advanced liberal thinkers, as we know, and also sharp critics of the contemporary scene.

These liberal impulses failed to produce a major movement of reform. However, that solicitude for the welfare of the lower classes had not disappeared. Between 1850 and 1854 a series of acts provided for the safety of miners and merchant seamen; for the regulation in London of burial grounds, lodging houses, and the nuisance of smoke; for an increased number of juvenile reformatories; and for supervision of lighthouses and pilot authorities. On the other hand, moves to widen the franchise came to nothing. This failure was partly due to the fact that intelligent and educated people both in and out of politics, though they might agree with Mill in theory, hesitated to extend the franchise to the lower classes. What they knew of American democracy did not attract them, and they were repelled by the uncultured and sentimental language of nonconformist leaders and businessmen who asked for reform. The constitution, as it stood, was fairly liberal; it provided for government by discussion, though admittedly the role of the aristocracy in politics was far too great.

Nor did the nature of politics in the middle of the century lend itself to the passage of drastic reform. Politics were unstable and confused; Cabinets, without dependable majorities in the Commons, were overthrown on trivial issues. One reason for this instability was the lack of discipline in the Commons. In the eighteenth century members had been controlled by patronage and by the authority of the Crown; later in the nineteenth century they were controlled by party organization. But in the 1850s they did much as they pleased. Without proper discipline, they debated issues in a purposeless way which did not lead to action.

Both Whigs and Tories, moreover, were divided and poorly organized. For some time after 1832 there had been two coherent parties, but the Tory party had been broken by its internal quarrel over the Corn Laws. The free-trade followers of Peel—known as the Peelites—had split from the protectionist Tories who had turned Peel out of office. After the election of 1847 the Peelites numbered about a hundred members and were strong in talent. But they were only a group in the

Commons; they refused to work with other Tories and yet would not join the Whigs. The protectionist Tories were better organized but never had a majority. The Whigs as a group were so poorly constructed that they could hardly be called a political party. They were divided between a small radical wing, composed chiefly of businessmen, and a much larger segment of more conservative Whigs. Some of the Irish members, moreover, were inclined to draw together and to vote as an independent bloc. Hence, the impossibility of forming a strong majority in the Commons.

Political Leaders

The man of the future among the Peelites was W. E. Gladstone. Trained by Peel in public finance, he made a superb chancellor of the Exchequer. His budgets completed Peel's work in making England a free-trade country. He moved slowly but steadily from a conservative to a liberal point of view. Already a man of eminence and a giant in debate, he continued to grow in stature, though his greatness belongs to a later period.

The protectionist Tories were headed by the earl of Derby, with Benjamin Disraeli as leader in the Commons. Derby had been important in politics since 1830. He had served as a cabinet minister under Earl Grey and under Sir Robert Peel, but, essentially conservative in spirit, he had resigned from the first of these Cabinets over Irish policy and from the second over the repeal of the Corn Laws. A skillful debater and parliamentarian, the holder of a great position in fashionable society, he was a man of ability, influence, and solid judgment. He had serious defects, however, as a party leader. It was only slowly that Disraeli established his leadership of the Tories in the Commons. A Jew by background though an Anglican by conviction, Disraeli did not come from the social class of the men he was leading.

Lord John Russell was prime minister from 1846 to 1852 and again in 1865–1866. A younger son of the duke of Bedford, he was the old aristocratic type of Whig. Self-confident, didactic, and egotistic, he permitted personal feelings of pique and vanity to override party loyalty. But he was liberal in policy, a good debater, and a man of courage.

The most prominent statesman of the age was Lord Palmerston. First obtaining office at the age of twenty-three, he served as a lord of the Admiralty, as secretary of war, as foreign secretary, as home secretary, and finally as prime minister from 1855 to 1858 and again from 1859 until his death in 1865. In a span of almost sixty years he was seldom out of office. This remarkable achievement is an indication that below his buoyant and lighthearted manner there was a foundation of hard work and application to the business at hand. His special interest was foreign affairs. He had a knack of explaining his policy to the people and of appealing directly to them for support. In the middle years of the century he was tremendously popular. "His gaiety, his love of horses, his easy-going courage, good temper, and fine bearing, stood in his favor with a high-spirited and overconfident nation."

He followed a liberal foreign policy, looking with favor on the constitutional states of Europe and with disfavor on the despotisms. He saw no reason to conceal his opinions. "England is one of the greatest powers of the world," he wrote to Victoria, "and her right to have and to express opinions on matters . . . bearing on her interests is unquestionable; and she is equally entitled to give upon such matters any advice which she may think useful." Unfortunately Palmerston offered his advice with a bluntness and truculence that were deeply resented abroad. "Generally when Lord Palmerston talks of diplomacy," wrote a contemporary, "he also talks of ships of war." As he grew older he became more rash and bouncy. The people enjoyed his blusterings, but his colleagues did not. Often acting without consulting them, he attempted to make the Foreign Office independent of Cabinet control.

In 1850 occurred the Don Pacifico case. Don Pacifico was a Portuguese money-lender of dubious honesty who claimed to be a British citizen because he had been born in Gibraltar. His house in Athens having been burned by a mob, he made extravagant claims against the Greek government and appealed to Palmerston for help. Palmerston at once sent a gunboat to blockade the coast of Greece. This episode involved a quarrel with France and exposed Palmerston to attack by the opponents of his policy. He defended himself in an able speech ending with the words: "As the Roman, in days of old, held himself free from indignity, when he could say 'Civis Romanus sum,' so also a British subject, in whatever land he may be, shall feel confident that the watchful eye and the strong arm of England will protect him against injustice and wrong." The speech was a popular triumph and made him more than ever the idol of the masses.

Palmerston's methods infuriated Victoria, who regarded foreign affairs as a sphere in which the sovereign might still participate, and she was far more sympathetic toward German and Austrian autocrats than was Palmerston. After the Don Pacifico episode, she urged Russell, then prime minister, to dismiss Palmerston or to shift him from the Foreign Office. She sent Palmerston a memorandum demanding that in submitting dispatches to her he should make his policies perfectly clear so that she would know to what she was giving her consent, and that once she had approved dispatches they should not be altered. Palmerston agreed but went on much as before. In 1851 he expressed to the French Ambassador his personal approval of Louis Napoleon's *coup d'état* in Paris. This angered Russell so much that Palmerston was dismissed. He blithely opposed Russell in the Commons and brought about his defeat in the following year. Thus, he had his "tit for tat with John Russell." After a brief interlude of Tory under Derby and Disraeli, a coalition of Whigs and Peelites was formed by Lord Aberdeen. Palmerston returned to office as home secretary. It was this Cabinet which drifted into the Crimean War.

The Crimean War, 1854–1856

The Crimean War, in which England and France allied with the Turks against Russia, was caused by the decay of Turkey, the aggressiveness of Russia, and the fumbling policies of England and France. Time and again in the nineteenth century the Turkish Empire, its government careless, untrustworthy, and corrupt, appeared to be on the verge of collapse. The Christian peoples over whom it ruled in the

Balkans were restless, eager to follow the example of the Greeks who had won their freedom in the 1820s. In the first half of the century Turkey had been menaced also by its overmighty vassal, Mehemet Ali, the Viceroy of Egypt. Above all there was Russia, Turkey's ancient foe, longing for greater influence in the Near East. Suspicion of Russia was strong in England. To prevent Russian encroachment in the Near East was a cardinal principle of British diplomacy, for Britain was a Mediterranean power whose interests would be threatened by Russian advance. Russia was building a navy and had erected a naval base at Sebastopol in the Crimea. Moreover, the Russians were pushing into central Asia east of the Caspian Sea. This expansion, if continued, would bring them to the northwest frontier of India.

In France Louis Napoleon was desirous of gaining the support of the Catholic party. He attempted to do so in 1852 by reminding the Turks of an old Franco-Turkish treaty of 1740. This treaty provided that the holy places in Palestine (shrines connected with the life of Christ) were to be under the jurisdiction of the Roman Catholic Church. But in recent years these holy places had been partially controlled by the Greek Orthodox Church, to which Russia adhered.

Russia saw an opportunity to gain advantage over Turkey. Early in 1853 the Czar sent a special envoy, Prince Menshikov, to Constantinople. Menshikov, not a tactful man, demanded not only that the holy places remain under the jurisdiction of the Greek Orthodox Church but that Turkey recognize a Russian protectorate over the Greek Christians in the Balkans. The Turks yielded to Russia's demand concerning the holy places but refused the protectorate. There was great indecision in the British Cabinet. Russell thought that the Russians should be resisted; Palmerston was loud for "a bold, firm course." Aberdeen, the prime minister, was horrified at the thought of war. Not a strong man, he hesitated, but took steps which brought war closer. In June 1853 he sent a British fleet to Besíka Bay to defend Constantinople if the need arose. The Russians then invaded the Danubian Principalities, the Turks declared war, and British and French warships entered the Black Sea. A demand was made that Russia keep her fleet at Sebastopol. When Russia refused, war began.

An English expeditionary force set sail in February 1854 commanded by Lord Raglan, a keen soldier but a man of only ordinary ability. The troops were sent first to Varna on the Black Sea coast of Bulgaria. The Russians, however, retreated from the Danubian Principalities, the coast at Varna was malarial, and the allies decided to attack the naval base of Sebastopol on the Crimean peninsula. The allied army, which did not reach the Crimea until September, consisted of some twenty-six thousand British, thirty thousand French, and five thousand Turkish troops. It is thought that if the allies had stormed Sebastopol at once they might have taken it, but the French commander, St. Arnaud, insisted that the armies move to a plateau south of the fortress and organize a formal siege. This course was followed. Lord Raglan unwisely selected as his base an inlet known as Balaclava, from which only one dirt road ascended a steep hill to the plateau. He neglected to put a hard surface on the road. The British troops, camped on the plateau, were exposed to Russian attack and bore the brunt of two battles, Balaclava and Inkerman, in which the Russians were repulsed. The Battle of Balaclava is famous for the charge of the Light Brigade.

Because of a poorly worded order by Raglan, which was misunderstood, 600 British cavalrymen charged up a long valley commanded by Russian guns. The guns were overrun, but few of the Light Brigade survived.

An early blizzard wrecked supply ships in the harbor and rendered the road up the hillside impassable for wagons. The troops on the plateau, though close to the shore, could not be properly supplied. Exposure and disease, combined with lack of food, inadequate clothing, and insufficient medical supplies, all but wiped out the little British army during the winter of 1854–1855. Such miseries had often been the lot of the common soldiers of all nations, but in the Crimean War, for the first time, newspaper correspondents sent home accounts of conditions at the front. The vivid dispatches of William Russell of the *Times* horrified a public unacquainted with war. Accustomed to efficiency in government, the British were indignant at the way in which the war was being mismanaged. A Cabinet crisis caused the resignation of Aberdeen; and Palmerston, to the disgust of many, stepped—or, rather, bounded—into the place of prime minister.

Conditions gradually improved at the front during the spring of 1855. Florence Nightingale organized a good base hospital staffed with well-trained nurses. Palmerston gave the war effort new vigor. In September the fortress of Sebastopol was finally taken. Peace was signed early in 1856 whereby Russia was forbidden to have warships on the Black Sea or to construct naval installations on its banks; a commission of the states along the Danube was given power to control its navigation; Russia renounced her claim to protect the Christian subjects of the sultan; the independence of Turkey was guaranteed by the powers of Europe; and the Turks promised to reform their government in the Balkans. This treaty stopped the advance of Russia in the Near East for about twenty years, but it did little more.

THE INDIAN MUTINY

Alarming news reached England from India in the summer of 1857. The native troops, or sepoys, in the Bengal army had mutinied; the position of the British in all of northern India appeared to be threatened. Judged from a military point of view, the Mutiny was not as dangerous as it seemed. It was confined, as things turned out, to the Ganges Valley. Its back was broken within four months, and British power was fully restored in seven. Yet the Mutiny had deep and lasting effects on India and on Anglo-Indian relations.

British possessions in India had expanded rapidly during the first half of the nineteenth century. Pitt's India Act had forbidden any further extension of British territory, but the attempt to govern British India in isolation from the rest of the country soon broke down. The British possessions were scattered and without natural frontiers. The existence of powerful and lawless native princes, the plunderings of robber bands, the intrigues of the French, the oppressive government of many native rulers—all rendered British intervention inevitable.

The first surge forward was made by Lord Wellesley (governor general from 1798

India in 1857.

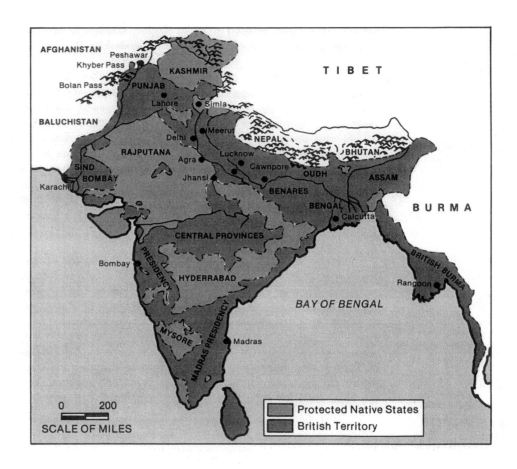

to 1805), an elder brother of the duke of Wellington. An imperious man, Wellesley was angered at the failure of native rulers to honor their treaty obligations and at their cruelty to their people; moreover, he was highly suspicious of French intrigue. By wars, annexations, and treaties he pushed the British frontier far up the Ganges Valley and brought most of southern India under British control. He made treaties, known as subsidiary treaties, with many native princes by which they placed themselves under British protection: the British guaranteed the territories of the native prince against aggression, and the prince continued to rule the domestic affairs of his state, but his foreign relations were controlled by the British. Troops of the East India Company were stationed in his territories and gave him protection but they were also a reminder that he would be wise to observe carefully the terms of his subsidiary treaty. Wellesley acquired territories so rapidly that he was recalled by the frightened authorities at home. But the expansion of British India continued. In 1849 the British annexed the Punjab.

A series of wars and annexations inevitably aroused resentment among the

Indians. Under Lord Dalhousie, governor general from 1848 to 1856, grievances tended to multiply. Some were political. Like Wellesley, Dalhousie was irritated by the inefficiency and despotism of native rulers and sought opportunities to bring native states under British administration. He employed a device known as "the doctrine of lapse" by which, under certain circumstances, a native state lapsed to the British if its ruler died without an heir. It was the custom for native rulers to adopt a son if they did not have one, but Dalhousie held that an adopted heir could not inherit a state without the consent of the paramount power. The princes, believing that they were to be gradually liquidated, were deeply alarmed.

Moreover, there was another difficulty. Whenever an annexation occurred, with its transfer of administration to British officials, the peasants benefited but the upper classes were likely to suffer. They lost their position as administrators under a native prince, and their opportunities to take part in the government of their country diminished. As a result many Indians of the upper classes were resentful and looked upon the English as their enemies.

Religious and social grievances also existed. There was resentment, especially among the Brahmin priests, at the abolition of suttee, a custom by which a Hindu widow flung herself on the funeral pyre of her husband and perished in the flames. The British also prohibited the murder of unwanted infant girls. New laws permitted the remarriage of Hindu widows and protected Hindu converts to Christianity. Indians also disliked the Western inventions which Dalhousie brought into the country. He built the first railway and set up the first telegraph system. In a word, he moved forward too rapidly for the deep conservatism of the Indians, bringing even the most ignorant and apathetic Hindu into close contact with the spirit of the West. The Mutiny was a military rising, but it came at a moment when there was much civilian discontent.

The sepoys had their own grievances. Their religion forbade them to cross the sea. This taboo had caused such inconvenience in sending troops to Burma that Dalhousie issued an order that all future recruits must agree to serve wherever they were sent. The Bengal army contained many Brahmins who were highly sensitive to all matters relating to caste and who suspected that Dalhousie's order was an attack on their caste position. Finally, by a grave error in the factory at Woolwich, cartridges for the new Enfield rifles were greased with animal fat. The cow was sacred to the Hindu and the pig was unclean to the Muslim; hence, when the sepoys bit off the cap on a cartridge, as the easiest way to be rid of it, both Hindus and Muslims were defiled. The sepoys knew that the British position in India was momentarily weak. Some European troops were still in the Crimea, and those that remained in India were scattered; moreover, sepoys in the Ganges Valley outnumbered Europeans five to one.

The Mutiny began at Merut on 10 May 1857, when three native regiments rose, killed their British officers, marched to Delhi, the ancient capital of Muslim India, and massacred the Europeans in that city. A handful of British blew up the magazine, killing themselves and a thousand mutineers. The Mutiny slowly spread down the Ganges Valley. This desperate situation called forth heroism on the part of the British forces. An army of some thirty-five hundred men under Sir Henry Barnard, coming down from Simla, defeated thirty thousand rebels and took up a position on a ridge outside Delhi. Meanwhile there was heavy fighting in Oudh. The mutineers captured Cawnpore after a siege of three weeks and massacred their European prisoners. Cawnpore was retaken in July by Sir Henry Havelock. Lucknow was beseiged but did not surrender. In September Havelock was able to fight his way into the city, but the rebels closed behind him, and Lucknow had to be relieved a second time. Meanwhile another British army under John Nicholson, coming from the Punjab by forced marches of twenty-seven miles a day over a period of three weeks, joined the British outside Delhi and took the city by storm in September. With Delhi again in British hands and with the taking of Cawnpore and the strengthening of Lucknow, the tide turned against the mutineers. Strong forces and excellent commanders arrived from England; the last months of the Mutiny consisted of mopping-up operations on a large scale. The rebels degenerated into groups of brigands.

The Mutiny failed because of the devotion of the British on the spot, because the mutineers never developed great leaders, because they never escaped the ancient hostility of Hindu against Muslim, and because the Mutiny was localized. It did not touch the Punjab, Afghanistan, or the bulk of southern India. Many native princes, fearing the anarchy that would follow a British defeat, remained loyal.

The Mutiny brought many changes. An act of 1858 dissolved the East India Company and placed the rule of India entirely in the hands of the government. The change was largely formal, for the company had long since lost its political power. The Board of Control now was abolished, and a Secretary of State for India governed that country from London. In India the governor general became a viceroy. Over the years, however, he tended to lose power to the secretary of state, who could telegraph his instructions to India. The Indian army was reformed, the proportion of European troops was increased, and all artillery units were composed of Europeans. The British renounced the doctrine of lapse and thenceforth fostered the native states with great care. India entered on a period of peace and rapid material progress, but bitterness remained: the memory of atrocities committed by both sides during the Mutiny could not be erased. Hindus turned away from Western ideas and looked to their own civilization and to their own religion as protections against absorption by the West. The gulf between the English and the Indian races tended to widen. British officials in India could visit England more easily than in the past, there were more English women in India, and the British, who lived their own lives instead of adopting native customs, were more aloof and less sympathetic than before.

CHINESE WARS

Two short wars with China were fought during this period. The East India Company had traded at Canton since 1684 and had learned that combination of long-suffering and bribery necessary in dealing with Chinese officials. But in 1833 England ended the company's monopoly and opened the trade at Canton to all British merchants. Without the experience of the company's agents, these merchants were soon in trouble. Moreover, a new difficulty arose. In 1839, when the Chinese

Emperor determined to end the importation of opium from India by the British, a high official from Peking seized all the opium in Canton and quarreled with the British over the trial of English nationals in Chinese courts. This led to a short war in which Canton was bombarded. By the Treaty of Nanking in 1842 the Chinese opened Canton, Shanghai, and three other ports to foreign trade, ceded the island of Hong Kong to England, and paid an indemnity to the British merchants at Canton.

Difficulties continued. The Chinese, refusing to admit the equality of foreigners, attempted to curtail the concessions they had made; the British merchants wanted freer access to a rich market. A second war took place between 1856 and 1860 in which British expeditions bombarded Chinese forts near Canton, captured other forts on the Pei-ho River, and burned the Emperor's summer palace at Peking. The Chinese yielded in the Treaty of Peking in 1860, when they opened Tientsin and other ports. They also agreed to the presence of foreign diplomats at Peking and accepted the opium trade on an open and legal basis. There was a strong feeling in England that Palmerston's actions were too highhanded, but he held an election in 1857 and won a majority. In the next year he fell from power, though he returned as prime minister in 1859 and continued in that office until his death in 1865.

PALMERSTON'S LAST MINISTRY

Palmerston was now an old man who perforce shared power with Russell as foreign secretary and with Gladstone as chancellor of the Exchequer. The period is important for three phases of foreign policy. The first concerned the unification of Italy which culminated in 1859–1860. British policy was constantly on the side of Italian liberty and unification. English policy was of great assistance to the Italians and displayed a rare combination of liberalism, detailed knowledge of events in Italy, and enlightened self-interest.

English relations with the United States during the American Civil War, on the other hand, were badly handled. Ministers knew next to nothing about conditions in America. They were strongly opposed to slavery, and Lincoln's first inaugural address was taken to mean that the North accepted slavery in principle. The English sympathized with the right of the South to form a new nation, and it was believed that an independent South would be to England's commercial advantage. Neutrality was proclaimed as soon as the war began, but it was, as Russell admitted, a neutrality hostile to the North. This caused great bitterness in the northern United States.

Two incidents increased ill will. One concerned two southerners, Mason and Slidell, sent abroad by Jefferson Davis to plead the cause of the South. They boarded a British ship, the *Trent*, at Havana. But an overzealous northern captain, intercepted the ship. Acting without orders he forced the southerners off the *Trent* and brought them to the United States. The English were furious. A sharp note demanded an apology and the return of Mason and Slidell. For a short time feeling ran high on both sides of the Atlantic. But Lincoln, with his hands full at home, saw the insanity of a war with Britain. Hence he yielded. The other incident concerned the *Alabama,* a commerce raider built for the South in England. English law forbade

British firms to supply equipment to ships of a power at war when England was neutral. But because of Russell's carelessness and official red tape, the *Alabama* left Liverpool on a trial run and did not return. She did a great deal of damage to northern shipping before she was destroyed. This also angered the North, and Russell was careful to see that the incident was not repeated.

A final crisis in foreign relations concerned a short war between Prussia and Denmark over the two duchies of Schleswig and Holstein. There was great sympathy in England for the Danes. Edward, the Prince of Wales, had recently married the Princess Alexandra of Denmark, who was very popular in England. Palmerston indulged in some of his usual saber rattling. If an attempt was made upon the independence of Denmark, he said, those who made the attempt would find that the Danes did not stand alone. But Bismarck continued his plans against Denmark, the English people had no intention of fighting over this issue, and Palmerston suffered the humiliation of seeing his threats ignored.

C H R O N O L O G Y

Mid-Victorians

1830	Liverpool and Manchester Railway opened
1833	Oxford Movement began
1842	Opium War; Britain took Hong Kong
1845	John Henry Newman converted to Roman Catholic Church
1847–48	Thackeray's *Vanity Fair*
1850	Elizabeth Barrett Browning's *Sonnets from the Portuguese*
1852	Russell replaced by Aberdeen as prime minister
1854–56	Crimean War
1854	Battle of Balaclava; Tennyson's "Charge of the Light Brigade"
1855	Palmerston prime minster; Florence Nightingale
1856	Peace of Paris
1857	Sepoy Mutiny
1858	East India Company was dissolved
1859	Darwin's *Origin of Species by Means of Natural Selection*; Tennyson's *Idylls of the King*; Dickens's *A Tale of Two Cities*; Fitzgerald's *Rubáiyát of Omar Khayyám*; George Eliot's *Adam Bede*; J. S. Mill's *On Liberty*; Samuel Smiles' *Self-Help*; a truly remarkable year

30 Gladstone and the Liberal Party, 1865–1886

The mid-Victorian interlude described in the last chapter, when politics were confused and reform was of secondary importance, ended about 1867. After that date political life became more stable and effective. By 1867 the Peelites had merged with the Whigs, and Gladstone, the greatest Peelite, had moved to the position of an advanced Liberal. At the same time, new forces were emerging in the middle and lower classes which added greatly to the strength of the Liberal party, making it truly Liberal rather than Whig. This party won the election in 1868, in 1880, and again in 1885, and formed the dominant fact of political life for twenty years. But in 1886 the Liberals were shattered by Gladstone's Irish policy, the Conservatives gathered strength, and the era of Liberal power came to an end.

The period from 1865 to 1886 had other distinctive features. It was a time of radical reforms which stressed the removal of special privilege and the importance of social questions, such as education. Two parliamentary reform bills brought manhood suffrage and began the era of true political democracy. A new interest in imperialism was to reach its crescendo in the 1890s, but it began in the 1870s encouraged by Disraeli, disliked by Gladstone. Ireland became increasingly difficult, until the Irish problem convulsed and dominated politics. Finally, the two great giants, Gladstone and Disraeli, gave to parliamentary life a fascination unparalleled in English history. Debates in the Commons were reported at length in the newspapers and were followed with zest throughout the country by rich and poor alike.

GLADSTONE AND DISRAELI

Neither Gladstone nor Disraeli rose from the aristocracy. Gladstone's family, of Scottish origin, had settled in Liverpool and had amassed a fortune in shipping and in the slave trade. Gladstone, who had been educated at Eton and at Christ Church,

W. E. Gladstone,
by George
Frederick Watts.
(National Portrait
Gallery, London)

Oxford, was a very learned man, with a deep interest in theology. A devout member of the Church of England, he had at one time considered becoming a clergyman. He entered Parliament in 1833 as a Conservative. In 1841 Peel had made him vice-president of the Board of Trade. His training in finance was of the utmost benefit to him, and he became one of the greatest of financial ministers. As we have seen, he broke with the Conservatives in 1846, was a Peelite in the 1850s, and emerged in 1865 as a Liberal, "unmuzzled," as he told his new constituents in south Lancashire. He combined a respect for antiquity with a passion for improvement.

He took politics very seriously, almost with a sense of religious mission, approaching political problems with great moral earnestness. This led him at times to give the impression of a very good man stuggling against wicked-minded opponents, but his appeal to morality fitted the temper of the age and pleased the nonconformists. He was rarely ill, could work fourteen hours a day, and could crowd more business into an hour than most men could do in twice that time. For all-round parliamentary ability he has never been surpassed. He acquired great skill in drafting legislation and in guiding it though the Commons. His impressive appearance, fine voice, tremendous vitality, and wonderful power over words made him a superb speaker, a human

Benjamin Disraeli, by Sir John Millais. (National Portrait Gallery, London)

tornado in debate whom few men could challenge with success. Although he remained in politics too long and developed weaknesses in his old age, in his prime he was a great leader. The statute book is studded with his reforming legislation.

Disraeli was born in London in 1804. His father, Isaac Disraeli, was a wealthy Jew whose family had migrated from Spain to Vienna and then to London in the eighteenth century. The younger Disraeli was educated privately, read widely in his father's library, traveled abroad, and wrote a number of novels. He entered Parliament as a Conservative in 1837. In the struggle over the Corn Laws he made himself the spokesman of the protectionist Tories and did much to destroy Peel's position in the Commons. Disraeli then moved toward the leadership of the Conservatives, but it was an uphill fight. A Jew[1], a romantic novelist whose rococo effusions showed

[1]Benjamin's father Isaac had left Judaism without becoming a Christian, and had Benjamin and his brother baptized in their youth. Benjamin was thus eligible for membership in the House of Commons. Yet, he never denied his origins. On the contrary, he took great pride in his ancestry.

more than a touch of vulgarity, an upstart whose brilliance often was regarded as impudence, was not a likely leader of the country gentlemen of England. Yet Disraeli, in his own phrase, "climbed to the top of the greasy pole." He did so through ability, audacity, and strength of will. He was a brilliant speaker. There was an imaginative quality in his speeches, a sparkle of wit and humor, a gift for epigram, sarcasm, and irony. But he had more than sparkle. A deadly fighter, he could hit hard and wound deeply. He possessed great courage and a cool, imperturbable solidity. In facing Gladstone he never lost his nerve and always maintained a fighting front.

He had a human quality, a capacity for affection, a gift for managing people which Gladstone lacked. The difference may be seen in their relations with Victoria. Gladstone treated her with great respect and forbearance, but coldly and formally, as though, it was said, she were a public department. She never liked him. Disraeli, on the other hand, gradually overcame her early suspicion; in the end she regarded him as an intimate friend. He had cultivated her carefully and late in life he developed a fantastic attachment to her, thinking of her as a second Gloriana and to his intimates referring to her as "the Fairy."

He is remembered for his ideas rather than for his legislation. He believed in the Church of England, in the monarchy, and in imperialism. He believed in the nobility. Then, passing over the middle classes, he had faith in the British laborer. He stood also for a spirited foreign policy, perhaps because Gladstone could be accused of weakness in this area. But he was not Gladstone's equal. To Disraeli politics was a competitive game, not the means to constructive statesmanship. His measures were largely expedients, or the result of momentary inspiration, or the work of his subordinates.

The Reform Bill of 1867

For the first few years after the death of Palmerston in 1865 neither Gladstone nor Disraeli held the office of Prime Minister. Lord John (now Earl) Russell succeeded Palmerston; Gladstone remained as chancellor of the Exchequer. Gladstone introduced a reform bill in 1866, a moderate measure which in the boroughs would have lowered the voting qualification for householders from £10 to £7 and in the counties would have created a new class of voters whose premises were worth an annual rent of £14.

There was at first little interest in the bill; then suddenly the issue of parliamentary reform caught fire. The change was due in part to the tactics of a group of conservative Whigs. Led by Robert Lowe, these Whigs attacked the bill on the ground that the lower classes were too ignorant and too vicious to be trusted with the franchise. Lowe and his followers voted with the Conservatives, defeated the bill, and caused Russell to resign. Another Derby-Disraeli Cabinet took office (1866–1868). It did not have a majority because Lowe and his followers returned to the Whig side of the Commons. The country was demanding a reform of Parliament. Lowe's tactics had caused a wave of resentment among the workers; the lower middle classes, some of whom were still without the franchise, pressed for reform.

In the great surge of liberal sentiment that swept the country there was a slight touch of violence. When the government closed the gates of Hyde Park in order to prevent a demonstration in favor of reform, a crowd pressed gently against the railings, broke them down, entered the park, and held its demonstration. This episode helped Disraeli decide to introduce a bill of his own. He was afraid not to do so, and his belief in the laborer prompted him to act.

Disraeli supported reform for a variety of reasons. One, surely, was his belief that if reform of the franchise was inevitable, it is better to do it yourself than to have it done by your opponents. The rapid passage of the bill was a personal triumph for Disraeli and he soon replaced the ailing Derby as prime minister in his own right. This important bill, which on the surface appeared to be quite radical, gave the vote to all householders in parliamentary boroughs, thus enfranchising large numbers of workingmen; created in the counties a new class of voters whose premises were worth £12 per annum; and took forty-five seats from small boroughs. In general, it enfranchised the urban factory worker but the agricultural laborer was still without the vote.

The bill, however, was not as radical as it appeared. Many boroughs now had a greatly enlarged electorate but continued to send two members to Parliament as before; thus their power in the House of Commons was not increased. Of the small boroughs, 87 survived and still returned 105 members. The new £12 qualification in the rural areas continued the exclusion of the agricultural workers. Hence the changes wrought by the bill were not decisive. Although after 1867 the number of businessmen returned by urban constituencies rapidly increased, the ascendancy of the nobility and the gentry in the counties was not fatally impaired. The bill was important in two respects: by doubling the electorate, it was an acceptance of the principle of democracy; and it created new political activity in the boroughs and greatly stimulated the organization of both parties.

THE LIBERAL PARTY

A change came over politics in the years following the Reform Bill of 1867. This change was due less to the bill itself than to the development of the Liberal party. The general increase in wealth in the middle years of the century had created new forces and new classes in the manufacturing towns. These new forces were welded into a unit by the dynamic personality of Gladstone. To the old aristocratic Whigs new elements were now added: (1) wealthy industrialists, such as Joseph Chamberlain, the mayor of Birmingham, men who wished to be prominent in politics and were ready to take a radical line; (2) the lower middle classes of clerks and shopkeepers; and (3) an upper crust of skilled artisans and craftsmen. Gladstone, who could work with the Whigs, held the key to the situation. But he had become an advanced Liberal, and he had developed a style of speaking which appealed to people outside the educated classes. The sympathy of these audiences affected his thinking and made him more radical.

At the same time the Liberals developed a strong party organization which helped greatly in producing victories at the polls. Local associations were formed of party members, so that for a time it was possible for workers to have some share in these associations by attending the meetings in their wards. In 1877 Joseph Chamberlain founded a National Federation of these local groups. The National Federation seemed democratic enough, but in truth it placed control of the party in the hands of wealthy manufacturers. It imposed increasing discipline upon Liberal members of Parliament, and it returned to the Commons a new type of member who was likely to be a businessman, a radical, and a nonconformist. The number of members in the Parliament of 1868 who were willing to disestablish the Church of England was surprisingly large.

GLADSTONE'S FIRST ADMINISTRATION, 1868–1874

The Liberals won an overwhelming victory in the election of 1868, and Gladstone formed his first and greatest ministry. He had a unique opportunity; he was at the height of his mental and physical powers, he had a large majority, and he had been given a popular mandate to press on with the work of reform. It is significant that one of his first measures was the disestablishment of the English church in Ireland. Other reforms came in rapid succession.

One of the most important concerned elementary education. Now that the poor can vote, said a member of the Commons, "we must educate our masters." It was indeed high time to improve the education of the lower classes. In 1833 Parliament had begun to make annual grants for this purpose. These grants had increased to well over half a million pounds a year, but the government's support still went to schools sponsored either by the Church of England or by nonconformist bodies, and almost half the children of school age did not go to school at all. Gladstone found that he could not avoid religious controversy. Both nonconformists and the Church of England insisted upon religious instruction, but the nonconformists wanted a system of secular schools in which there would be no denominational teaching. Such schools, they hoped, would gradually replace the schools of the Church of England. The church defended the denominational principle.

Gladstone and his minister, William E. Forster, approached the problem from the standpoint of education and not of politics. Their Education Act of 1870 retained all existing schools with good records and increased the subsidies of the government. This benefited the Church of England because its schools were more numerous than those of the nonconformists. New schools were set up in areas in which the old ones were inadequate. The new schools were known as board schools because they were controlled by locally elected boards of education. They were financed by government grants, local rates, and small student fees, though the boards could excuse the payment of fees by children of the very poor. Religious teaching in the board schools was to be nondenominational and was to be given during the first or last hour of the day so that parents could remove their children if they so desired. Gladstone's act placed a school within the reach of every English child. In 1880 attendance was made compulsory and in 1891 all student fees were dropped. But Gladstone was to discover at the next election how deeply he had offended his nonconformist followers.

In 1870 Gladstone improved the civil service by basing appointments on competitive examinations. From the beginning of central civil administration ministers had used patronage in the civil service as a means of keeping their followers in good humor. Persons influential in government circles could obtain places for their friends and relatives, with the inevitable result that there was much laziness and inefficiency in the offices at Whitehall. In 1853 a commission of inquiry had recommended competitive examinations. Examinations began in 1855, but heads of departments were not required to make appointments on the basis of these examinations until Gladstone's act of 1870. Competitive examinations soon proved their worth; thus another blow was struck at the special privileges of the old ruling classes.

The same may be said of a series of reforms in the British army. The Franco-Prussian War of 1870 was a rude shock to England, for it revealed the great inferiority of the British army to Prussia's. Fortunately, Gladstone's secretary for war, Edward Cardwell, was a man of unusual ability. His first reforms were to abolish flogging in the army in time of peace, to withdraw troops from the self-governing colonies, and to secure a royal order making the commander-in-chief, the duke of Cambridge, a cousin of the queen, subordinate to the secretary for war.

The measure for which Cardwell is best known was the abolition of promotion in the army by purchase. Prior to this reform a senior officer upon retirement was normally entitled to sell his commission to his successor. This practice, which was deeply rooted, was based on the assumption that officers should be drawn from the upper classes and that their rank in the army was a piece of property which could be sold. The system enabled rich men to buy positions for which they were not trained, and it obstructed, though it did not prevent, promotion by merit. The Crown could, if it wished, deny an officer the right to sell his commission, could dismiss without compensation an officer who had purchased his commission, and could commission an officer who had not the means to purchase one. But the Crown did not normally exercise these rights. A bill in 1871 abolishing purchase passed the Commons with difficulty but was shelved by the Lords. The practice then was abolished by royal warrant. This forced the Lords to pass the bill, for the bill provided compensation to officers who had purchased their commissions whereas the royal warrant did not.

Cardwell also shortened the term of enlistment from twelve years to six with the colors, and six in the reserve. He associated each regiment with a county or with a similar area in Great Britain or Ireland. A regiment was provided with a depot in the county, and, being recruited from this area, could develop local associations. Each regiment contained two battalions, one of which served abroad while the other was training at the depot. Cardwell combined efficiency with economy, which won him Gladstone's confidence.

The Hight Court of Judicature Act of 1873 (as amended in 1876 and 1880) remodeled the central law courts in London and fused the legal systems of common law and equity. In 1873, there were eight central law courts of first instance: the ancient courts of Queen's Bench, Common Pleas, and Exchequer; the Chancery; the Hight Court of Admiralty, the Court of Probate, the Court for Divorce and Matrimonial Cases, and the London Bankruptcy Court. Procedure differed from court to court, there were various methods of appeal, and there were anomalies and unreasonable practices. The Judicature Act combined these courts into one High Court with three divisions: Queen's Bench, with which Common Pleas, Exchequer, and Bankruptcy were merged; Chancery; and Divorce, Probate, and Admiralty. The rules of common law and of equity were administered concurrently in all these courts, with the rules of equity prevailing in case of conflict. A new Court of Appeal was created to hear appeals from all three divisions. It was at first intended that this appeal should be final, but the House of Lords objected, asserting its ancient role as the highest court in the land. Hence it was made possible to appeal a case from the Court of Appeal to the House of Lords. To handle such appeals four distinguished lawyers were placed in the House of Lords; they held life peerages and were known as law lords. They were also made members of the Judicial committee of the Privy Council, which heard appeals from courts overseas throughout the empire.

A number of other measures should be mentioned briefly. An act of 1872 introduced the secret ballot. Of considerable importance in England, this act was to bring startling changes in Ireland. A University Tests Act in 1871 opened fellowships and appointments at Oxford and Cambridge to persons of all religious faiths. Another act of 1871 recognized the legal status of trade unions, though it prohibited picketing in any form during industrial disputes; the Licensing Act of the year following regulated the hours during which public houses could remain open.

The Decline of Gladstone's Ministry

The pace of reform during this famous ministry was strenuous indeed. After 1870 the Cabinet's popularity declined. Gladstone had pushed forward without considering with sufficient care the way in which voters were likely to regard his legislation. He discovered that every measure offended some group or interest: his generosity to the Church of England in his Education Act had been deeply resented by nonconformists; his Irish policy and his curtailment of special privilege had irritated the aristocracy; his bill against picketing had angered the lower classes; his licensing bill cut deeper than anyone would have imagined.[2] The liquor interests turned to the Conservatives; and many pubs became centers of support for the Conservative party. The saloonkeeper emerged as a man who could sway votes as much as the political orator. The Conservatives, it is true, were a little ashamed of their new ally; but the liquor interests made such substantial contributions to the party chest that their help could not be refused. And gradually other businessmen followed the liquor trade into the Conservative camp. Even Gladstone's supporters in the Commons felt they had been driven very hard.

Another criticism of Gladstone's policy was of a completely different kind. It was

---

[2]The Licensing Act of 1872 was a modest measure, but in 1871 another bill (which did not pass) would have permitted magistrates to determine the number of public houses an area required. This proposal alarmed the liquor trade.

felt, not quite fairly, that he permitted England's prestige abroad to suffer loss. During the Franco-Prussian War in 1870 Bismarck made every effort to conciliate Russia, and at his secret suggestion Russia suddenly announced that she would no longer abide by the naval restrictions placed upon her at the end of the Crimean War. Englishmen were angered to think that Britain, with all her wealth and industrial superiority, had suddenly become so impotent in Europe. Gladstone also was accused of weakness in allowing the claims of the United States in the case of the *Alabama* to be settled by arbitration. Gladstone's action was that of a statesman. But arbitration was not popular in England, nor was the payment of an indemnity of £15 million to the United States. Gladstone lost the election of 1874, and Disraeli came to power with a good working majority.

DISRAELI'S MINISTRY, 1874–1880

In view of Disraeli's brilliance and imagination, his ministry was rather disappointing. Its meager achievement can easily be explained. Disraeli had campaigned on a platform of protecting the country from Gladstone's reforming zeal which, he claimed, menaced "every institution and every interest, every class and every calling in the country." England under Disraeli's government may have profited from a period of repose, but repose is scarcely progress. And although Disraeli was a social reformer, desirous of improving the lot of the working classes, he was also the leader of a conservative party containing wealthy men who had little to gain, and possibly much to lose, by a policy of social reform. Moreover, Disraeli's period in office was a time of economic depression. There was a serious slump in trade between 1876 and 1878. The old unbounded confidence in Britain's industrial future was somewhat shaken. At the same time there was a depression in agriculture. Cheap ocean transportation in iron ships and the extension of American railways to the western prairies made possible the importation of American wheat into England at very low prices. Disraeli had to decide whether to defend the British farmer by protective tariffs, knowing that any tampering with free trade or any increase in the cost of the poor man's loaf of bread would spell disaster for the Conservatives at the next election. Disraeli's decision, therefore, was against protection. Disraeli became prime minister at seventy, still deeply grieving the recent death of his wife and suffering severely from gout.

Social Legislation

Disraeli's desire for social reform was reflected in a number of measures. A Trade Union Act in 1875 permitted unions more freedom of action in conducting strikes. The act allowed peaceful picketing and declared that actions by a group of persons engaged in a trade dispute were not illegal if the same actions were legal when done by an individual. An Artisans' Dwelling Act passed in the same year empowered municipalities to demolish buildings in slum areas and to erect better housing for the poor. The public was protected by a Food and Drugs Act which prohibited the use of ingredients injurious to health. A Public Health Act, also in 1875 and including provisions from many earlier acts, created a code of sanitation. The Liberals scoffed at this measure as a "policy of sewage," and Disraeli enlivened a dull subject by saying, "Sanitas sanitatum, omnia sanitas"; but the act remained the basis of sanitation law for many years. In 1876, partly because of an unruly outburst in the Commons by Samuel Plimsoll, the Cabinet passed a Merchant Shipping Act which established regulations for the safety of merchant vessels. In 1878 a Factories and Workshops Act codified a large amount of earlier legislation concerning hours and conditions of labor for factory workers. This honest humdrum, as Disraeli called it, benefited the working classes in practical ways without endangering the interests or arousing the opposition of wealthy Conservatives. Disraeli's measures were steps away from laissez faire toward regulation of a mildly socialistic kind by the state. Increased rights for women were also advancing, albeit slowly, during these years. In 1878 the Factory and Workshops Act gave married women control over their wages. In 1882 the Married Women's Property Act gave them control over inherited property. Disraeli and Gladstone were more accepting of this progress than was Queen Victoria.

Imperialism

The drabness of social legislation was offset by the glamour of imperialism and a spirited foreign policy. Although the empire had expanded steadily during the first half of the century, its development had followed unspectacular lines and, as we have seen, had aroused no great interest. But in the 1870s forces were gathering which rendered the idea of empire far more attractive, and Disraeli was shrewd enough to see something of what the future would bring. It was India, that rich jewel in Britain's imperial crown, which stirred his imagination. And it was primarily of India that he was thinking when in 1875 he purchased from the Khedive of Egypt a large bloc of shares in the Suez Canal Company (seven-sixteenths of all the shares outstanding).

The canal, built by the French engineer Viscount de Lesseps, had been opened in 1869. Its importance for Britain was obvious. Four-fifths of the shipping which passed through it was British. The route through Suez was by far the shortest route from England to India, to Australia and New Zealand, to the Malay Archipelago, and to China and Japan. A sailing ship early in the century, voyaging around Africa, had taken six months to journey from England to India. Now a fast steamship, using the Suez Canal, could reach India in three weeks. Suez altered the shipping lanes of the world. Parliament was not sitting when Disraeli learned that the Khedive, who was deeply in debt, wished to sell his shares. Disraeli made the purchase on his own responsibility. This was recognized at once as an act of outstanding wisdom and leadership. Merely as an investment, the purchase price of £4 million brought an eightfold return over the next half century. And the strategic advantage of Britain was enormous.

Disraeli offers the Crown of India to Queen Victoria. (SNARK/Art Resource)

In 1876 Disraeli proclaimed Victoria Empress of India. The title of empress recalled to Indians the glories of their past under the mogul emperors. Moreover, it gave to India a new status as a country with a ruler of its own who was thus something more than the queen of a distant power; the concept of an Indian empire appealed to Indians and strengthened their loyalty to Britain. The new title, however, was criticized by the Liberals with unnecessary sharpness. This criticism angered Victoria and increased her bias against the Liberals.

The Congress of Berlin, 1878

Meanwhile, a crisis had arisen in the Near East. Pan-Slavism, the doctrine that all Slavic peoples should draw together under the aegis of Russia, was prompting her to renew her drive for influence in the Balkans at the expense of Turkey. The Turks were in a desperate strait. Their promises made at the end of the Crimean War to reform their government in the Balkans had not been fulfilled, and Europe was growing weary of Turkish abuses. The Turks also were faced with a growing sense of nationality among the Balkan peoples. The Greeks, independent since 1829, longed to annex various areas inhabited by people of Grecian stock. The Serbs and the Rumanians, though tributary to Turkey, had obtained partial self-government and naturally wanted more. The Bulgars were less developed and were ruled directly by Turkey. To the west, moreover, Austria-Hungary entertained hopes of annexing the Turkish provinces of Bosnia and Herzegovina. In the summer of 1875 a revolt broke out in these provinces and spread to Serbia and Bulgaria in the following year. In retaliation the Turks proceeded to massacre the hapless Bulgarian peasants. To Russia the condition of the Balkans appeared most inviting.

Disraeli was deeply suspicious of Russia. He remembered how Russia in 1870 had repudiated her obligation to have no ships of war on the Black Sea. He believed that if Russia became a power in the eastern Mediterranean through the dismemberment of Turkey she would pose a threat to the Suez Canal. And he was aware that the British Empire contained millions of Muslims who regarded the Sultan as the head of their religion. Hence Disraeli adopted a policy of supporting Turkey against Russia.

To Disraeli's disgust Gladstone took a different line. Deeply shocked by the massacres in Bulgaria, Gladstone began a famous campaign to incite the English against the Turks. He wrote a pamphlet, *The Bulgarian Horrors and the Question of the East*, which sold 40,000 copies within a few days. "Let the Turks," he wrote, "now carry away their abuses in the only possible manner, namely, by carrying off themselves. Their Zaptiehs and their Mudirs, their Bimbashis and their Zusbashis, their Kaimakams and their Pashas, one and all, bag and baggage, shall I hope clear out from the province they have desolated and profaned." To Disraeli, striving to stand up against the Russians, this seemed foolish and ill-timed. Gladstone knew little about the Balkans and was apparently unaware that massacre in the Balkans was no Turkish monopoly; yet he saw one vital point Disraeli missed; that the nationalism of the Balkan peoples, if strengthened by independence from Turkey, might prove a strong deterrent to Russian expansion.

A conference of the great powers, including England, met at Constantinople in December 1876 and urged the Turks to make reforms. The Turks refused. Thereupon Russia declared war on Turkey early in 1877. Advancing through friendly Rumania, the Russians at first made rapid gains. Then they were held up for months by an able Turkish general, Osman Pasha, who occupied a fortified camp at Plevna. But in December 1877 Osman capitulated; in March 1878 the Russians dictated the Treaty of San Stefano. The most important provision of this treaty created a greatly enlarged Bulgaria. Though nominally under Turkish suzerainty, Bulgaria was to become an autonomous principality with a Christian government and a national militia. The Christian government was to be organized by Russia; and if Bulgaria fell eventually into Russian hands, as Disraeli believed it would, the Russians would be on the Mediterranean. Other Balkan nations were given increased independence; though she retained Constantinople, Turkey was almost driven from Europe.

For some months a war fever had been rising in England. She had been neutral in the recent war, but she found it galling to stand by while her old friend Turkey was thus mauled by the Russian bear. A song in the London music halls added a new word, "jingo,"[2] to the English language:

We don't want to fight, but by jingo, if we do,
We've got the ships, we've got the men, we've got the money too.

Disraeli made a number of warlike moves; a British fleet was sent to Constantinople, in a dramatic gesture Indian troops were brought to Malta, Parliament voted a large war credit. Exhausted by the Turkish war, Russia yielded to these threats and agreed to a revision of the terms of the Treaty of San Stefano. The revision was made at the Congress of Berlin (13 June to 13 July 1878), a glittering assembly of the leading diplomats of Europe. The large Bulgaria set up by the Russians was now divided into three parts. The southern third was handed back to Turkey without safeguards for the welfare of the inhabitants. The central section, known as Eastern Rumelia, was also restored to Turkey, though it became a separate province with a Christian governor appointed by the Sultan. The northern portion was made an autonomous Bulgarian principality, dependent on Turkey but to be organized by Russia. Bulgaria thus was reduced in size and was excluded from the Aegean; Turkey appeared once more as a European power. Serbia and Montenegro retained the independence given them by the Treaty of San Stefano. But Austria obtained the right to occupy and adminster Bosnia and Herzegovina, though the provinces remained nominally Turkish; Disraeli secured the island of Cyprus for England. Disraeli, returning to England in the summer of 1878, declared that he brought back "Peace with honor" and was hailed by the populace.

The popularity withered away during his final year and a half in office. The depression in trade lifted somewhat after 1878, but the depression in agriculture did not. Moreover, Disraeli became involved in two small imperial wars, both costly, both unexpectedly difficult, both showing that imperialism had its dark and seamy side.

The first war was in Afghanistan, the small mountainous country just beyond the northwest frontier of India, inhabited by fierce Muslim tribesmen, and of growing strategic importance as the Russians approached it from central Asia. There were two schools of thought in India regarding Afghanistan. One was to keep out of the country and to rely on the Afghans' fanatic spirit of independence to resist any Russian advance. The second, or forward, policy was to push into the wild country between India and Afghanistan and to secure control of the Khyber, Kurram, and Bolan passes through which armies could march from central Asia into northwest India. Disraeli sent out Lord Lytton as Viceroy to pursue the second of these policies. In 1878, when the Russians sent a military mission to Afghanistan, Lytton acted. Three British armies marched into Afghanistan. The Russians fled. Lytton then arranged for a British agent to reside at Kabul, the Afghan capital, and for British control of the passes. As soon as the British armies were withdrawn, however, the tribesmen murdered the British agent, and the war began anew. This was the situation when Disraeli resigned, leaving an awkward problem for his successor.

Policy also was fumbled in South Africa. During the 1830s, as we have seen, a large number of the Boer farmers living in the area of the Cape had become so

[2]A jingo came to mean an ardent nationalist.

discontented with British rule that they had migrated into the interior. There they had established two semi-independent republics, the Transvaal and the Orange River Colony. It was the Transvaal which caused difficulty for Disraeli. Its government was extremely weak. The Boers, ranging over an enormous area, administered a crude frontier justice and often refused to pay taxes. In 1877 a British official discovered that the Boer treasury contained 12s. 6d. Moreover, the Boers were frequently at war with the fierce Bantu tribes of the interior. Under these circumstances Lord Carnarvon, Disraeli's colonial secretary, wished to annex the Transvaal, not only to strengthen its government but to pave the way for a unification of all the European colonies in South Africa. The annexation was proclaimed in April 1877, but the Boers objected violently. At about the same time a very costly war broke out with the Zulus in which some British troops in an exposed position were massacred in a sudden raid. This war was highly unpopular in England.

The Election of 1880

In the election of 1880 Gladstone exploited the unpopularity of these two wars. He regarded imperialism as both provocative and evil. In a series of flaming speeches known as the Midlothian campaign, since it took place in Scotland, Gladstone stumped the country in a way unknown in English history. Older people were shocked to see a British statesman addressing crowds from the rear platform of a railway carriage. But democracy was bringing new methods of electioneering, and the superior organization and more daring methods of the Liberals gave them an advantage at the polls. The party was more united than it had been in 1874. These factors, together with the depression in agriculture, sufficed to win the election which brought Gladstone back to power. Disraeli died in 1881.

GLADSTONE'S SECOND MINISTRY, 1880–1885

Gladstone's second ministry was less successful than his first. Although the Liberals had united against Disraeli, there was internal division in the party between its more conservative members, such as Lord Granville and Lord Hartington, and the radicals. Gladstone, though radical himself, had given most of the places in his Cabinet to the conservative wing of the party; indeed, the only effective radical to be admitted was Joseph Chamberlain. There was further division over imperialism. The Liberals as a party were anti-imperialist; yet there were Liberals, such as Chamberlain and Sir Charles Dilke, who were deeply interested in the empire and who saw no reason for allowing the absorbing possibilities of imperialism to become a political monopoly of the Conservatives. Gladstone was much more interested in Ireland. But the problem of Ireland was becoming so extremely difficult that solution appeared all but hopeless. Finally, a minor but irritating problem was posed by Charles Brad-laugh, an atheist member who asked permission to affirm his allegiance instead of taking the parliamentary oath. He should have been allowed to do so. But the Speaker, instead of ruling firmly, allowed the point to be debated. A little group of four Conservatives, nicknamed the Fourth party, of whom Lord Randolph Churchill and A.J. Balfour were members, saw an opportunity to make trouble for Gladstone by rallying Conservatives, Irish members, and nonconformist Liberals against Bradlaugh. Gladstone pleaded nobly for religious toleration but was voted down. This threw discredit upon his ministry. There was a painful scene in which Bradlaugh, a powerful man, was removed from the Commons by ten policemen.

Afghanistan and South Africa

Wishing to reverse the forward policy of Disraeli in Afghanistan and South Africa, Gladstone determined to withdraw all British forces from Afghanistan. Such a move would have been interpreted in Asia as sheer weakness of which the Russians would have taken advantage. Gladstone was saved by the British generals on the spot and by the wisdom of the new Amir, Abdur Rahman. The generals withdrew, but only after marching through Afghanistan in a way that showed their mastery. Abdur Rahman, who was shrewd enough to see the advantages of British friendship, refused to accept a British resident, for he knew that the barbaric customs of his tribesmen would make bad reading abroad, but accepted what was in effect a subsidiary treaty. By this treaty the British were to conduct his foreign affairs, protect him from Russian aggression, and pay him a subsidy. He ruled his country well until his death in 1901. Gladstone was fortunate.

During the electoral campaign of 1880 Gladstone had attacked Disraeli's annexation of the Transvaal and had given the Boers the impression that, should he come to power, the annexation would be annulled. Such was his intention, but on assuming office he was busy with many matters and allowed affairs in South Africa to drift. Suddenly, in December 1880 the Boers in the Transvaal revolted. When a small British force advanced against them they defeated it decisively at Majuba Hill in February 1881. The Transvaal was granted independence subject to British suzerainty and to British control of its foreign relations. Thus a temporary settlement was made at the cost of future trouble.

Egypt and the Sudan

Gladstone was soon carried into a much larger imperial venture which he disliked and mismanaged—the English occupation of Egypt in 1882. Britain, of course, was deeply interested in the Suez Canal, but the immediate cause of the occupation was financial. The Egyptian Khedive Ismail was an irresponsible spendthrift who had borrowed heavily in Europe and had squandered the money on the toys of Western civilization: palaces, railways, steam yachts, and, for the ladies of his harem, bicycles and player pianos. What Egypt required was reform of a fundamental kind. Its officials were notoriously corrupt and its people downtrodden to the point of serfdom. For many weeks every year the peasants labored without pay, cleaning the irrigation canals; they were ruled by the wicked sting of the kurbash, a whip of hippopotamus hide.

For Ismail the reckoning arrived at last. In 1878 the governments of England and France, prompted by the bankers who had loaned money to Ismail, demanded reforms in Egyptian finance and established a Dual Control by which European advisers were installed in Cairo. When Ismail resisted reform the Sultan in Constantinople was persuaded to depose him and to recognize his son Tewfik as Khedive. Meanwhile a dangerous nationalism was rising in Egypt. Led by an army officer, Col. Arabi Pasha, it was aimed indiscriminately at Turks, Christians, and Europeans. Gladstone was persuaded to send a British army to Egypt. He invited French cooperation, but the French declined, and England went into Egypt alone. Arabi's forces were crushed rapidly and Gladstone solemnly declared that the British troops would be withdrawn as soon as order was restored. But it became apparent that the Egyptian government had collapsed. If the British withdrew, some other power would certainly intervene, and this Britain could not permit because of the canal.

Gladstone could have annexed Egypt or declared a protectorate. Instead, he clung to the idea of a temporary occupation. The Khedive retained his throne and his Egyptian ministers, but British advisers, headed by the banker Sir Evelyn Baring, Lord Cromer, were installed throughout the Egyptian administration; their advice could not be disobeyed. This cumbersome arrangement was successful only because of Cromer's outstanding ability.

Throughout the nineteenth century the rulers of Egypt had made constant efforts to conquer the area south of Egypt known as the Sudan. It was inhabited by a people, part black, part Arab, and fanatically Islamic. In 1881, a revolt had broken out, led by Mohammed Ahmed, a Sudanese who had proclaimed himself to be the Mahdi, or Muslim messiah, and had begun a holy war against the Egyptians. Broken as she was, Egypt could not hope to quell the uprising, but Gladstone refused to be drawn into further adventures. To placate Egyptian feeling, however, he agreed to send a British expedition to evacuate the Egyptian garrisons, who would otherwise be slaughtered by the Mahdi's forces. The man selected for this mission was General Charles Gordon, a popular hero in England, a Bible-reading soldier who had fought in the Crimea, China, and the Sudan. Upon reaching Khartoum in February 1884 he should have evacuated at once, for the Mahdi was closing in between him and Egypt. Not wishing to abandon outlying garrisons, he devised a plan to set up another Sudanese as a rival to the Mahdi. This proposal was vetoed by the British Cabinet. Meanwhile the Mahdi surrounded Khartoum, and the problem became one of extricating Gordon. Gladstone and his Cabinet delayed. When at last a British expedition fought its way to Khartoum, it arrived too late. Two days earlier, on 26 January 1885, the Mahdi's forces, having stormed Khartoum, massacred every Englishman and Egyptian in the fortress. So great was the popular resentment in England that Gladstone's government never recovered from this blow. The fault had been partly Gordon's, but blame must rest far more on Gladstone and his colleagues for their unaccountable delay and negligence. For the next ten years the Sudan was left to fire and sword; the British did no more than defend the southern frontier of Egypt.

The Reform Bill of 1884–1885

Gladstone's preoccupation with the empire and with Ireland made it difficult for him to enact important reforms during his second ministry. One of the minor measures permitted the burial of nonconformists in graveyards of the Church of England; another allowed farmers to kill hares and rabbits that destroyed their crops; two acts increased the pay and added to the welfare of seamen in the merchant marine; and married women were given the right to control their own property. A Settled Land Act ended old restrictions on the transfer and sale of land. These restrictions had been imposed in order to hold large estates together; their abolition was another loss of special privilege for the aristocracy. An indication of modern times may be seen in the first Electric Lighting Act.

But such measures were a meager return for the majority given to Gladstone in 1880. He therefore pushed forward an important measure of parliamentary reform. It passed easily through the Commons but was bitterly attacked in the Lords and became law only after a series of conferences between Gladstone and Salisbury, the Conservative leader. It was divided into two parts. The first, passed in 1884, extended the franchise to all male householders in the counties as the act of 1867 had extended it to all householders in the towns. Some 2 million new voters were thus created in Britain, and about 700,000 in Ireland. The act gave Ireland a larger electorate and a greater representation in Parliament on a basis of population than any other part of the United Kingdom. Parnell, the Irish leader, who knew the power the act would give him, kept very quiet.

The second part of the act abandoned the ancient principle of representation by counties and boroughs and divided most of the country into single-member constituencies of roughly equal population. By this act England became a political democracy in the sense that every man (with a few trifling exceptions) who occupied a permanent home, either as a householder or lodger, could vote for a member of Parliament. The act was a severe blow to the political power of the aristocracy. The acts of 1832 and 1867 had protected in various ways the influence of the landed magnates over the rural electorate, but the act of 1884–1885 disregarded the interests of the landlord, destroyed the last of the pocket boroughs, and placed town and country on political equality. It also ended an electoral device of the Liberals, who had often run a Whig and a radical in a two-member constituency in the hope of capturing both seats. After 1885 the radicals tended to crowd out the old aristocratic type of Whig in the new single-member constituencies.

GLADSTONE AND IRELAND, 1868–1886

When a message was brought to Gladstone in 1868 indicating that he was about to become Prime Minister he was found engaged in his favorite exercise of cutting down trees on his estate. He leaned on his ax and exclaimed with deep earnestness: "My mission is to pacify Ireland." It is greatly to his credit that he was willing to grasp that bramble and to give to Ireland more intense and sympathetic study than any other prime minister of the nineteenth century.

For some years after the potato famine of 1845–1846 Ireland lay prostrate and subdued. But in the 1860s a new era of violence was opened by the Fenian Brotherhood, an organization of Irish-Americans founded in New York in 1858. The Fenians, Irishmen who had left Ireland after the famine, had carried with them a deadly hatred of England. Hoping to terrorize England into granting independence to Ireland, they perpetrated a series of senseless outrages. They attempted an invasion of Canada from the United States. They attacked police barracks in Ireland. In England they attempted to capture Chester Castle, which was used as an aresenal; to rescue Fenian prisoners from a police van in Manchester (killing a policeman in the process); and to free other Fenians from Clerkenwell Prison in London by blasting an outer wall with a barrel of gunpowder. The explosion, with an impartiality that might have been predicted, killed twelve persons and injured ten times that number. But the Fenians won little support in Ireland, either from the Catholic clergy or from the people.

Gladstone hoped—vainly, as it proved—that the redress of religious and economic wrongs might yet reconcile Ireland to English rule. In 1869 he introduced a bill to disestablish the English Church in Ireland. The ease with which this important measure passed through Parliament was an indication of the strong nonconformist element among Gladstone's followers and of the moderation of the House of Lords. The church in Ireland was reduced to a private corporation without connection with the state. Tithes disappeared; so did the Irish church courts and the Irish bishops in the House of Lords. The church in Ireland retained its buildings and some £14 million of its endowment of almost £20 million. The balance was devoted to public purposes in Ireland, such as education and relief work for the unemployed. Thus the religious grievance ended.

An Irish Land Act in 1870 also passed easily because Gladstone aimed to help the Irish peasant without infringing upon the rights of property. The act compelled a landlord to pay compensation to a tenant who was evicted while paying rent and to reimburse him for unexhausted improvements made at the tenant's expense. The act, however, did not forbid evictions, nor did it prevent a landlord from raising the rent; hence, it did not reach the heart of the agrarian problem and did little to conciliate Irish opinion. One feature of the act was to be important in the future. A fund was established from which Irish tenants could borrow on easy terms in order to purchase their holdings from the landlord and thus end the constant friction of their relations with him. This principle was to be adopted on a large scale later in the century.

Policy and legislation devised for England but imposed on Ireland in a mechanical way could produce unexpected results in that country. The secret ballot introduced by Gladstone in 1872 had a far greater impact on Ireland than on England. It enabled the Irish peasant to vote independently, free from the scrutiny of his landlord. In a similar way Disraeli's vital decision not to protect British agriculture by a tariff against cheap American wheat was based on conditions in England where the interests of the urban worker were thought to be paramount. But Ireland was a land of farmers. There was little Irish industry except around Belfast. Hence the agricultural depression of the 1870s and 1880s meant widespread ruin to Ireland. Rents that were based on earlier economic conditions simply could not be paid, and an Irish tenant who failed to pay his rent was evicted almost as a matter of course. By 1880, when Gladstone became prime minister for a second time, the misery in Ireland was appalling. Some ten thousand persons were evicted in that year. The peasants' answer was agrarian violence; in 1880 there were twenty-five hundred such outrages.

Meanwhile a demand was growing in Ireland for an end to the union with England and for the restoration of an Irish Parliament in Dublin. In 1870 an Irish member of the House of Commons, Isaac Butt, had founded the Irish Home Rule Association. He had coined the phrase "home rule" because the older word, "repeal," meaning the repeal of the parliamentary union, was resented in England. Butt's movement made rapid progress; in 1874, thanks to the secret ballot, fifty-nine of the Irish members in the Commons belonged to his party. He was a pleasant, likeable man who presented home rule as a reasonable and moderate proposal which deserved acceptance as a matter of justice. But he was ignored. In 1878, just before Gladstone returned to power, a new Irish leader, Charles Stewart Parnell, became the official head of the Home Rule party.

Parnell was not a typical Irish leader. He was a Protestant, a landlord, an aristocrat, a handsome and fastidious man of fashion. He was also cold, hard, and unemotional, dominating his followers by sheer will and intellectual power. He was a forceful speaker, though not a learned man. He had a deep sense of Irish wrongs, a hatred for England—inculcated, it was said, by his mother, who was the daughter of an American admiral—and a contempt for English parliamentary tradition. Butt admitted no force but argument; Parnell, no argument but force.

He developed a fighting front both in the Commons and in Ireland. In Parliament he employed obstruction to disrupt the work of the Commons and to drive the members to a consideration of Irish questions. Filibustering was quite unheard of and caused a great sensation. In Ireland Parnell came to terms with certain Fenians, though he was not a member of the group. He and Michael Davitt, a Fenian who had served seven years in prison, formed the Irish National Land League in 1879, which channeled agrarian crime into an organized reign of terror against evicting landlords and against persons who rented land from which a tenant had been evicted. Barns were burned, cattle mangled, landlords and their agents assaulted and even murdered. A man marked for vengeance might awake in the morning to find a grave dug before his doorstep. Or he might be ostracized by his neighbors, who refused to have contacts with him of any kind. The name of the first victim of this practice, Captain Boycott, added a new word to the language.

Gladstone combined coercion with conciliation. A Coercion Act in 1881 suspended habeas corpus in Ireland, empowering the government to make arrests and to hold prisoners without trial. In the same year Gladstone passed a second Irish Land Act. This act conceded a large part of what the Irish peasants claimed they were fighting for—the three Fs: fair rent, fixity of tenure, and free sale of their tenancies. The act set up a Judicial Commission in Ireland with power to determine rents. Upon application by an Irish tenant, the commission could establish what it considered a fair rent for his holding; if he paid that rent he could not be evicted for a period of fifteen years. If he left his holding at the end of that time he could sell unexhausted improvements to his successor.

The weakness of this measure lay in the fact that it conceded to crime and violence what had been refused to justice and reason. The lesson was not lost upon Parnell, who continued his campaign as before. In October 1881 he was arrested under the Coercion Act. He warned that if he was imprisoned "Captain Moonlight" would take his place; this indeed happened, for agrarian crime increased to unbearable proportions. After six months of this war of nerves, Gladstone made a bargain with Parnell in April 1882. Some 100,000 Irish tenants owed large amounts in back rent; they could not appeal to the Judicial Commission until that rent was paid. Gladstone agreed to wipe out this debt with an Arrears Act and to free Parnell if the latter would use his influence to diminish crime. As a token of good will Gladstone appointed a new secretary for Ireland, Lord Frederick Cavendish, an able, personable, and popular man who had married a niece of Mrs. Gladstone. Cavendish went to Ireland but within a few hours of his arrival he was assassinated in Phoenix Park by a murder band known as the Invincibles, who butchered their victim with long surgical knives. England and Ireland were horrified at this atrocity. Parnell himself was unnerved. Believing he was to be the next victim of the Invincibles who opposed his policy, he carried a revolver with him at all times. Yet for the next few years Ireland was quieter. Gladstone fulfilled his pledge of an Arrears Act, and Parnell for various reasons was willing to approve a temporary truce. A Crimes Act gave the government in Ireland extraordinary powers in suppressing disorder.

The Defeat of Home Rule in 1886

Discredited by Gordon's death at Khartoum, Gladstone resigned in June 1885, though he still commanded a majority in the Commons. There was an element of trickery in his resignation. A general election could not be held for some time because the new voters enfranchised by the act of 1884–1885 had not yet been registered. Hence Gladstone's Conservative successor, the marquis of Salisbury, would not command a majority in the Commons. The Conservatives, since they were in a minority, began to woo Parnell and his Irish Nationalists. The government of Ireland became more lenient. The Conservatives passed the Ashbourne Act, by which money was loaned to Irish peasants with which to buy out their landlords and thus become the owners of their little holdings. This expedient, first suggested by Gladstone's act of 1870, was now greatly extended and became a permanent policy of the Conservatives. There was also a secret interview between Lord Carnarvon, the new viceroy in Ireland, and Parnell, in which a mild measure of home rule was discussed in a tentative way.

Parnell believed that he might obtain more from the Conservatives than from the Liberals, and in the election in November 1885 he swung the Irish vote in England to the Conservative side. The result of the election increased his importance. Some of the large cities turned against Gladstone, but the newly enfranchised rural voters gave him a majority of eighty-six votes over the Conservatives. By a strange coincidence, Parnell, having swept Ireland, returned with a compact Irish party of exactly eighty-six members. He had become the arbiter of governments. If he voted with the Conservatives, he could keep them in office, though he could not give them a majority. If he joined the Liberals, the Irish Nationalists and the Liberals together would command an overwhelming lead.

Meanwhile, in the summer of 1885, a momentous change had taken place: Gladstone had become converted to home rule. His principal reason, apparently, was his conviction that problems of Ireland could never be solved so long as the two parties in England attempted to make political capital of Irish questions. He wished to take Ireland out of English politics. He would gladly have avoided the thankless task of forcing a measure of Irish home rule through the British Parliament. His own party was divided on this issue. As he saw Parnell and the Conservatives drawing together he hoped that the Conservatives would pass home rule with some Liberal support, as Peel had abolished the Corn Laws in 1846 with Liberal assistance against the protectionist Tories. Gladstone decided to keep his conversion a secret for the moment because, if he supported home rule, the Conservatives might draw away from it. Hence, all through the autumn and through the election in November, he did not commit himself.

Suddenly on 15 December his son, Herbert Gladstone, from pure but mistaken motives, revealed to the press that his father was ready to support home rule. This announcement caused a great sensation. The alliance of Parnell and the Conservatives quickly ended, and Parnell sought Gladstone's support. Gladstone found himself in a most awkward position. The Conservatives, as he had feared, were now ready to fight home rule as a Liberal measure. The Liberals were divided. The Liberal leaders were angry because Gladstone had not confided his change of opinion to them. Joseph Chamberlain, in particular, had been kept in the dark under highly irritating circumstances. Furthermore, it was speculated that Gladstone had adopted home rule just when such action might bring him back to power.

Moreover, new obstacles appeared. Ulster, the northeast province of Ireland, contained many Presbyterians of Scottish ancestry who had no wish to be ruled by a Roman Catholic Parliament in Dublin. As the prospects for home rule brightened, the Ulstermen became more bitter in their opposition; had the measure become law there might well have been an insurection in Ulster. It also became clear that the British people were more opposed to home rule than was the House of Commons. Lawlessness and crime in Ireland had created the impression that the Irish were not ready for self-government. There was fear that Ireland, in her hostility to England, would use home rule to break the union and would combine with England's foes. And finally, Parnell's tactics in the Commons and his contempt for English tradition had aroused a deep resentment among the English people. This was an aspect of the problem which Parnell had not foreseen.

In view of all these difficulties, Gladstone might well have drawn back from forming a government committed to home rule. Yet he did not hesitate when Salisbury resigned in January 1886. Gladstone was now seventy-six. Old age had a curious effect on him; he retained astonishing physical and mental powers and his speeches continued to be masterly, forceful, and persuasive; but he became less prudent, and made some serious mistakes of judgment. In April 1886, amid intense excitement, he introduced his home rule bill. It would have created an Irish Parliament and an Irish Cabinet in Dublin, but there were many reserved subjects which the Irish government could not touch: the Crown, the army and navy, foreign relations and the question of peace and war, customs and excises, post office and currency, and weights and measures. Irish taxes, moreover, were to be determined in London; some forty percent of the proceeds were to go for imperial defense and for interest on the national debt. The Irish Parliament was not to consist of houses but of two orders which were to sit together, though they might vote separately. There were to be no Irish members in the British Parliament. This provision was liked at first but later recognized as a weakness; the Irish, if taxed and restricted by an imperial Parliament in which they were not represented, would certainly continue to struggle for greater liberty.

In June the bill was defeated because a large number of dissentient Liberals voted against it. The margin of defeat, however, was not large. Under these circumstances the cabinet system gave the prime minister a choice: he could resign, or he could dissolve Parliament and hold an election on the assumption that the country supported him and would give him a majority in a new House of Commons. But the second of these alternatives was highly dangerous when the party in power was divided against itself. Nonetheless, in a frenzy of mistaken zeal, Gladstone adopted it, although there had been an election only eight months before. He thus shattered the Liberal party. The results at the polls tell the story: 316 Conservatives; 78 dissentient Liberals who came to be called Unionists and eventually merged with the Conservative party; 191 Gladstonian Liberals; and 85 Irish Nationalists. Gladstone resigned at once; Salisbury formed his second ministry. With one Liberal interlude the Conservatives governed the country for the next twenty years.

C H R O N O L O G Y

Gladstone and Disraeli

1866–68	Derby-Disraeli cabinet
1867	Second Reform Bill
1868	Gladstone prime minister
1869	Church of Ireland disestablished

(continued on next page)

Chronology, continued

1870	Education Bill passed; Civil Service examinations inaugurated; Irish Land Act; Irish Home Rule Association founded
1871	Purchase of army commissions abolished; universities opened to all faiths; trade unions legalized
1872	Secret ballot adopted; Licensing Act
1873	High Court of Judicature Act
1874	Disraeli prime minister
1875	Trade Union Act; Public Health Act; Artisans' Dwelling Act; Suez Canal shares purchased
1876	Victoria empress of India; economic depression began
1878	Factory and Workshops Act; Congress of Berlin; married women may control earnings
1879	Irish National Land League founded
1880	Gladstone victorious in "Midlothian" campaign
1881	Irish Coercion Act; second Irish Land Act—the three Fs
1882	Married women may control property; Irish secretary murdered in Phoenix Park
1884	Third Reform Bill
1885	Gordon defeated at Khartoum by the Mahdi; single-member parliamentary constituencies
1886	Gladstone supported Irish Home Rule; Gladstone defeated; Lord Salisbury prime minister

Salisbury and Imperialism

The marquis of Salisbury, who formed his second ministry in August 1886, was prime minister three times (1885–1886; 1886–1892; 1895–1902), a total of more than thirteen and a half years. He was the last noble to hold that office. A descendant of the Cecils, who had been statesmen under Elizabeth I and James I, Salisbury was a handsome, dignified, impressive man with a great black beard. His mind was of a somber, aristocratic cast, calm and imperturbable in temper, massive in wisdom and judgment, highly critical, and not given to optimism. He was a powerful debater who could expose the weaknesses of his opponents with devastating and sometimes savage force. His gift for epigram was second only to Disraeli's, and there was a sardonic quality about his wit that gave it a cutting edge. His principal interests were foreign and imperial affairs, which he handled with subtlety and admirable judgment. However, he did not plan ahead as did Bismarck; he was content to meet problems as they arose. This negative approach was even more evident in his domestic policy. He had little faith in the value of popular reforms. Indeed, he disliked change, was content to leave things much as they were, and had no constructive program. He did not control his colleagues with Disraeli's finesse, but left them alone unless they sought his advice. Always the aristocrat, he had nothing but contempt for the tricks and devices of the low politician.

Politics in 1886

Salisbury was not in a strong position in the early days of his second ministry. He was dependent on the votes of the Liberal Unionists, who had broken with Gladstone over home rule, but the Unionists did not coalesce with the Conservatives until 1895.

Salisbury also was troubled by his colleague Lord Randolph Churchill. Churchill had risen to prominence in 1880 when his skill and boldness in debate had enabled him to oppose Gladstone with success. He was much closer to Disraeli's tradition of Tory democracy than was Salisbury. Indeed, he was something of a radical. He had fought the more conservative elements of his party and had built up the party machine, much as Joseph Chamberlain had done among the Liberals. In Salisbury's second Cabinet Churchill received the brilliant appointment of chancellor of the Exchequer and leader of the House of Commons. At the age of thirty-seven he was the youngest man to hold these positions since the younger Pitt.

He began very well, but a quarrel developed in the Cabinet over his first budget. Wishing to make economies, he tried to squeeze the budgets of his colleagues. When they resisted, he wrote to Salisbury that he would resign if they were not overruled. This dangerous and highhanded device was a failure. Salisbury would not overrule other ministers, and Churchill, having published his resignation in the *Times*, had to carry it through. He assumed that he would be recalled to office, but he was not. By a willful and petulant act, which showed him to be impossible as a colleague, he had ruined his political career. Salisbury's position, however, was strengthened.

Moreover, the debacle among the Liberals became increasingly obvious. They lost Joseph Chamberlain, their second greatest figure, who took the city of Birmingham with him into the Unionist camp. They lost some of the London radicals who drifted off toward socialism. Almost the entire Whig aristocracy deserted the Liberal party and gave the Conservatives a solid permanent majority in the House of Lords. Furthermore, there was a fundamental shift of political forces about this time. In the great days of the Liberal party Gladstone had attracted a number of successful businessmen who were willing to take a radical line and welcomed an opportunity to attack the landed aristocracy. But these businessmen had now reached an economic and social position which might well be threatened by radical policies. There was a general movement of business interests from the Liberal to the Conservative side; the Conservative party had become the party of the well-to-do. The Liberals retained the alliance of the Irish Nationalists, but the Nationalists soon were weakened, and the Liberals were thus dependent on the nonconformist Celtic fringe in Wales and Scotland.

Parnellism and Crime

It was also an advantage to Salisbury that Ireland continued to be the center of politics and thus kept alive the issue of home rule. Interest centered in Parnell, the Irish nationalist. In April 1887 the *Times* published some sensational letters, supposedly written by Parnell in 1882, in which he expressed approval of the assassination of Lord Frederick Cavendish by the Irish murder band, the Invincibles. These letters were the talk of the town. The assassination had horrified England, and Parnell had denounced it in the strongest terms. If, then, he was shown to have approved it in secret, he stood revealed as thoroughly dishonest. With great passion Parnell declared that the letters were forgeries and asked for a parliamentary inquiry. After some delay the government appointed a commission of three eminent judges to conduct an investigation, which was long and thorough. Among the witnesses was a disreputable Irish journalist, Richard Pigott, who did not stand up well under cross-examination. Later he fled the country, mailed a confession to the *Times* acknowledging that he had forged the letters, and committed suicide in Spain. Completely exonerated, Parnell stood at the height of his influence.

Within a year, however, he came crashing down when named as correspondent in the divorce case of Captain W. H. O'Shea against his wife. A few people had known for a long time that a liaison existed between Parnell and Mrs. O'Shea, but the news came as a shock to the public, and the story told in court by Captain O'Shea was more damaging to Parnell than the truth would have been. For private reasons Parnell did not contest the case. He believed at first that the scandal would not disturb his position in politics; indeed, most of his Irish followers expressed confidence in him. But the stigma attached to divorce was very great, and the nonconformists in the Liberal party were deeply offended. They intimated to Gladstone that they would not tolerate his continued alliance with Parnell; the Irish must select a new leader. When Parnell refused to give way there followed a long and unseemly wrangle among the Irish members, who split into two groups, one remaining with Parnell, the other

Reading the local news. (Art Resource)

seceding from him. He fought fiercely against great odds, but the contest shattered his health and in October 1891 he died. As a parliamentary tactician he has rarely been surpassed. As a patriot fighting for the welfare of his country he must be ranked among the great. The Irish members continued to rend each other, thus greatly weakening the cause of home rule.

Meanwhile, trouble was renewed in Ireland. According to a new device known as the Plan of Campaign the tenants of each Irish estate were encouraged to organize and to decide upon a fair rent for their holdings. This sum was to be offered to the landlord; if he refused, the money was to be paid into a central fund. The result was a new wave of evictions and an increase in crime. But A. J. Balfour, the Irish secretary, secured new coercive legislation and ruled Ireland with a firm hand. At the same time he extended the Ashbourne Act, which gave tenants the opportunity to borrow money and to buy out the landlords. After three tumultuous years Ireland subsided into comparative quiet.

The Local Government Act of 1888

Although the Municipal Corporations Act of 1835 had democratized the government of the towns, rural areas had remained under the ancient jurisdiction of the justices of the peace. A Local Government Act of 1888, which was symbolic of what was happening in the countryside, transferred their administrative and some of their police functions to elected county councils.

The Decline of Aristocratic Control over the Countryside

For many centuries, as we know, the rural areas of Britain had been dominated by the nobility and gentry in both an economic and a political sense. This domination had survived the Reform Bills of 1832 and 1867, the repeal of the Corn Laws, and the disappearance of special privilege. The prints of hunting scenes from the middle of the century, with their robust squires and pretty girls in attractive riding habits, depict a rural aristocracy still firmly entrenched. But in the 1870s and 1880s the hold of the aristocracy over the countryside was undermined by the advance of democracy and by the harsh impact of economic change. Nonagricultural income would be increasingly necessary if the landed families were to maintain their positions in the countryside. The Secret Ballot Act of 1872, the Corrupt Practices Act of 1883, and the Reform Bill of 1884–1885 which ended pocket boroughs–all tended to deprive the landed classes of their old influence over the rural voter.

Of far greater importance than these reforms was the ruin of British agriculture as cheap American wheat began to flood the English market. This wheat, grown on the virgin soil of a new continent, was so low in price that British farmers simply could not compete. It was no fault of theirs that disaster fell on agriculture in Britain, where farming was highly scientific. Her farm animals were carefully bred, her rotation of crops was excellent, and her yield per acre was very great. In fact, Britain was leading the world in agriculture almost as much as in industry. Prior to about 1875

British agriculture had maintained a certain supremacy over trade and commerce. The largest single British industry, it employed the greatest number of persons and produced great wealth. But now the railways on the American prairie, the improvement in ocean transportation, and the invention of agricultural machinery for prairie farming brought catastrophic results in Britain. The price of wheat sank from 56s. 9d. per quarter in 1877 to 31s. in 1886; to 26s. 4d. in 1893; and to 19s. 8d. in 1894. Thereafter it rose slightly, though not very much. The acreage under wheat in Britain was cut in half between 1872 and 1900. Rents had to be reduced both in England and in Ireland. In 1888 they stood at about £59 million per annum; in 1901 at about £42 million. Agricultural wages declined, and there was a steady exodus of laborers from the countryside. In 1901 only about one-fifth of Britain's total population remained on the land. Britain became increasingly dependent on imported wheat. During the 1890s about sixty-five percent of the wheat she consumed came from overseas. British agriculture might have been saved by a tariff. Other European nations faced the same problem, and almost all of them protected their farmers with tariff walls.

A run of poor harvests between 1874 and 1879—of which the last was especially poor—also contributed to the difficulties of British agriculture. Despite the scarcity of homegrown wheat, prices did not rise because of the wheat that came in from abroad.

And yet the old life of the country gentleman continued, though it was no longer supported by agricultural rents. This was possible because large numbers of the aristocracy now drew their incomes from nonagricultural sources—investments, directorships, the law, political office, a lucrative marriage, perhaps with an American heiress. There was also the ancient process by which old families sold their estates and newly rich ones bought places in the country. By the end of the century the automobile made it possible to live far from the city and yet maintain close connections with it. Country life continued to flourish because wealthy people liked to live in the country, and rural society reshaped itself to cater to their wishes. A number of people whose gentility was derived from past ownership of land now lived in the city, most likely in London, where they were courted by other city dwellers who craved a gentility to which they had no pretension.

A LIBERAL INTERLUDE, 1892–1895

The election of 1892 gave the Liberals and Irish Nationalists a small majority over Conservatives and Unionists. Gladstone at once formed his fourth Cabinet, but his prospects were bleak. He was then almost eighty-three and, though still a formidable debater, he was not the power he had been in his prime. He was burdened by a long list of proposed reforms known as the Newcastle Program to which his party had committed itself. Moreover, he was faced by a hostile and overwhelming opposition in the House of Lords. Indeed, he remained in politics only because of his intense desire to settle the Irish question.

His chief concern was a second home rule bill. Like the bill of 1886, it provided for a Parliament and an executive in Dublin, but with many reserved subjects that could be handled only by the imperial Parliament in London. The new feature of the second bill was a provision for 80 Irish members at Westminster who were to take part in the work of the Commons only when Irish or imperial affairs were under discussion. This provision answered an objection to the first bill that it left the Irish unrepresented in London, but it would have played havoc with the operation of the Cabinet system of government. The bill was defended by Gladstone in a long series of eloquent arguments and was denounced with great power by Chamberlain. It passed through all its stages in the Commons but was thrown out by the Lords in a vote of 419 to 41 and thus came to an end. However, it had made far greater progress than the first bill and its chances of revival were good. Gladstone was keenly aware of the problem created by the Tory majority in the Lords: the Lords defeated the home rule bill, they mangled an important bill on local government (which set up parish councils),

Joseph Chamberlain, by Frank Hall. (National Portrait Gallery, London)

and they killed a bill for employers' liability in case of injury to workmen. They created a state of affairs which, Gladstone asserted, could not continue. In March 1894 he resigned, sixty-one years after he had first spoken in the Commons.

The Liberal government limped along for another sixteen months under the premiership of Lord Rosebery. Its position was weaker than ever. Rosebery was a personable man—young, handsome, rich, and eloquent—but he was not an adroit politician, and he never aroused the loyalty of his followers. Many of them thought that Sir William Harcourt, the chancellor of the Exchequer, should have been Gladstone's successor. The nonconformists were suspicious of Rosebery, not only because he was a Whig aristocrat and an imperialist, but because he was a great patron of the turf. Twice while he was prime minister his horses won the Derby. He had few other successes. The House of Lords was adamant in its opposition to all Liberal measures. Cabinet ministers were furious and sent up measure after measure which they knew would be defeated. They thought that "fillin up the cup" of the Lords' iniquities would turn the nation against the upper chamber. But to the people such a policy appeared weak and ineffective. Although the Lords had their way and practically drove Rosebery from office, in the long run they were digging their own grave.

The Lords did not dare touch the budget. Harcourt's important budget of 1894 increased death duties by taking all the assets of an estate, landed and otherwise, and taxing them as a unit instead of taxing the several fractions that went to various beneficiaries. This was a new form of direct taxation which later chancellors of the Exchequer were not likely to forget. Its drawbacks were that it could be increased easily and that the government was taking capital and spending it as income.

Rosebery resigned in June 1895. An election gave the Conservatives a good majority, and Salisbury formed his third Cabinet, containing five Unionists, including Chamberlain. As colonial secretary, Chamberlain was now enormously powerful; his attention shifted from Ireland and radical reform to questions concerning the empire.

THE NEW IMPERIALISM

British interest in the empire increased during the last quarter of the nineteenth century until imperial expansion became a dominant theme in British thought and policy. The desire for empire and the acquisition of colonies were not confined to England. Between 1870 and 1900 the nations of Europe divided almost the whole of Africa among themselves, acquired large sections of Asia, and annexed hundreds of islands throughout the Pacific Ocean. The British added some 5 million square miles to their empire until by 1900 it included a fifth of all the land on the face of the globe. So eager were the nations for colonies and spheres of influence that competition brought dangerous international crisis.

A fundamental reason for imperialism was economic. England's position is highly instructive. The wonderful prosperity she had enjoyed in the middle years of the century reached a climax about 1870, when British foreign trade was greater in value than the combined foreign trade of France, Germany, and Italy. England's production of pig iron—the basis of both puddled iron and steel—was larger than the production of all the rest of the world. She was mining almost half the world's coal, her shipbuilding industry reached outstanding pre-eminence, and she was selling vast quantities of textiles in Europe, America, and the East. But after 1874 came a period of industrial and commercial depression, falling prices, and increased foreign competition. During a serious depression in the years 1876–1878 about ten percent of the working population was unemployed; a second depression quickly followed between 1883 and 1886. These two slumps, coming in rapid succession, ended the buoyant optimism of the mid-Victorians. Indeed, England was never again quite the same. In absolute terms her wealth continued to increase, her population to grow, and her foreign trade to expand, but the pace was slower than in the past, much slower than the rate of increase in either Germany or in the United States. In brief, Britain was no longer the only workshop in the world. Germany, the United States, Belgium, and, to a lesser extent, France, Japan, and portions of the British Empire were becoming industrial nations. They protected their industries by tariff walls against British goods. Total exports of British iron and steel increased, but the amounts sold to countries with high tariffs declined. By 1900 Germany produced more steel than did Britain, and the United States produced twice as much. British exports of cotton goods, which declined slightly, were sold for the most part in India, China, and the Near East; they were almost excluded from Europe and the United States.

The articles of British export which showed an increase were indicative of changed conditions. One was machinery. The value of exported machinery more than doubled between 1880 and 1900. But exported machines increased the industrial potential of foreign countries and reduced their demand for British goods. Britain also built many ships for foreign customers. But as the world's greatest carrier of goods by sea, she was making other nations less dependent on her by selling them ships. Finally, the export of British coal greatly increased. It was admirably suited for use by steamships and was mined close to the sea, but coal was an irreplaceable national asset which should have been saved for the industrial needs of the future. There was still cause for optimism, however, for Great Britain was a very wealthy country with enormous resources at home and abroad.

These developments made the empire appear more attractive now as a market for British goods. The quantity of cotton cloth sent to India, for instance, was enormous; British iron and steel and countless other manufactured articles were sold in the empire all over the world. The empire was a source of raw materials—cotton, wool, oil, rubber, lumber, jute, palm oil for soap, sugar, tobacco, tea, and coffee. Improvement of transportation by sea enabled ships to carry larger cargoes at greatly reduced freight rates. The change from wooden sailing ships to iron and steel ships propelled by steam had been very slow. It was only in the 1860s that iron largely replaced wood and only in the 1880s that steel replaced iron. Many iron ships (including the composites with wooden walls over an iron frame) were propelled by sail, for the early steamers consumed such quantities of coal that little space was left for cargo. But after compound engines, introduced about 1863, cut in half the amount of coal required, the number of steamships increased rapidly. And once the change was made, it brought enormous advantages. Iron and steel ships could be many times the size of wooden ones; they were safer than wood, lighter, and less costly in repairs. Independent of the wind, steamers could run on regular schedules and could make many more voyages than sailing ships in a given time. They could penetrate easily in areas where sailing ships had trouble, such as the rivers of China or the coast of West Africa near the equator. The speed of steamers was increased greatly in 1881 by the introduction of triple-expansion engines. Three years later the Cunarder *Umbria* (not, of course, a freighter) crossed the Atlantic westward in five days and twenty-two hours.

The empire also provided opportunities for the investment of surplus capital. Many enterprises at home had reached a point at which increased investment did not produce great profit, perhaps bringing a return of only two or three percent. On the other hand, an investment in some undeveloped area might offer dividends of fifteen or twenty percent, though the risk was greater. In the last quarter of the nineteenth century between one-half and two-thirds of surplus British capital was going abroad; by 1914 the British had invested some £4 billion in enterprises overseas. If she was no longer the workshop of the world, she was the world's capitalist, its landlord, its banker, and its bond and mortgage holder. The stocks of hundreds of companies throughout the empire were bought and sold on the London Stock Exchange.

There were other motives for imperialism. The possession of colonies was the symbol of a great power. Nations with colonies took pride in them; nations without them, such as Italy, struggled to obtain them and cast envious eyes at the huge British Empire. The acquisition of colonies became a game at which a nation must not be outdone by its neighbors. Imperialism was popular with rich and poor. One can understand why manufacturers, merchants, shipowners, bankers, and diplomats favored it. Surprisingly, the English lower classes also liked it. Empire meant employment. Moreover, it offered the thrill and excitement of international conflict as well as an opportunity for chauvinistic excesses. This taste was catered to by a cheap sensational press that appeared in England toward the end of the century and by a literature of adventure and stories of the sea, spiced with depictions of brutal and vulgar living. Meanwhile, the upper classes were influenced by such mis- understood phrases from Darwinian evolution as "the survival of the fittest" and "the struggle for existence," which appeared to justify the conquest of weaker peoples by the imperialists of Europe. It is only fair to add, however, that imperialism also carried a sense of mission. Europe must assume "the white man's burden" and must take civilization to the backward peoples of the world. A part of the "civilizing" mission was the role of the missionary. The dedication and the sacrifice of great numbers of men and women ministered to the spiritual, educational, and health needs of thousands, especially in Africa. The very existence of a vast empire created its own need for defense. Indeed, an empire was needed in order to protect the empire.

The Partition of Africa

The scramble for Africa was precipitated by three events. The first was the achievement of the explorer H. M. Stanley in crossing tropical Africa. In 1874 he plunged into the wilderness on the east coast with three other white men who died

on the way. He attempted in vain to interest the British government in the Congo
Basin and then reluctantly entered the service of King Leopold of Belgium, who
eventually created the Congo Free State and became its ruler. A second development was the action of the French, who pushed inland from their settlements on the
Senegal River, crossed to the upper reaches of the Niger, consolidated this inland
empire, and began to connect it with their stations along the western coast. And in
1882 Bismarck annexed the territory known as German Southwest Africa, which up
to that time the British might have had for the taking.

    Salisbury's diplomacy obtained a great deal of African territory for England without
causing a war with other powers, but the initial effort came from a remarkable group
of men—explorers, merchants, and shipowners—who penetrated or sent agents

Africa in 1914.

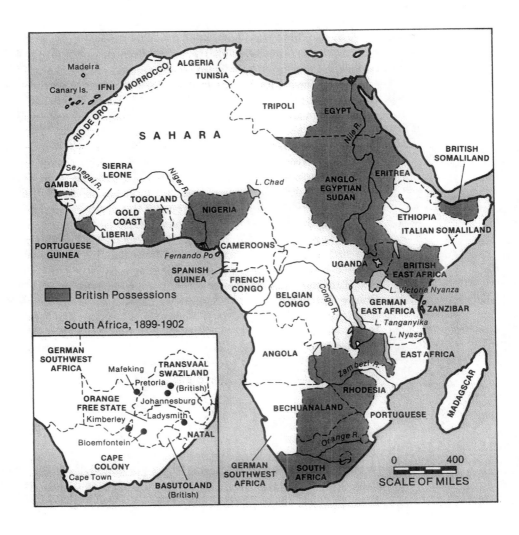

into the wilds of Africa and made treaties with native chiefs on which British diplomacy could base its claims.

In West Africa Sir George Taubman Goldie acquired modern Nigeria for Britain. In East Africa Sir William Mackinnon and Sir John Kirk became advisers of the Sultan of Zanzibar and employed Stanley to make treaties with the chiefs on the mainland. The British East Africa Company, chartered in 1888, obtained for Britain what is now Kenya and Uganda. Expansion in South Africa was the work of Cecil Rhodes. The son of an English clergyman, he went to South Africa in 1870 just as diamonds were discovered in the vicinity of Kimberley. Rhodes, who made a great fortune in diamonds and later in gold, became prime minister of Cape Colony in 1890. A year earlier he had obtained a charter for the British South Africa Company, which, pushing northward, claimed for England the territories known as Northern and Southern Rhodesia.

But local agreements with African chiefs meant nothing unless they were backed by diplomacy in London and resulted in international treaties. In 1890 three important treaties concluded with Germany, France, and Portugal delineated African boundaries and went far toward easing tension among the great powers.

A sharp clash with France in 1898–1899 was known as the Fashoda incident. It concerned the Sudan, the area south of Egypt from which the British had been driven in 1885 when Gordon had been slain at Khartoum. The Sudan was important because it controlled the Nile, the key to the control of Egypt. The British, therefore, determined upon its reconquest. In 1896 the Sudan was invaded from the north by Sir Herbert Kitchener, the commander of the British army in Egypt. He moved slowly, consolidating his conquest and building a railway as he advanced. In September 1898 he defeated a large army of dervishes at the Battle of Omdurman and entered nearby Khartoum, thus avenging the death of Gordon. Suddenly he heard that a French expedition had appeared at Fashoda five hundred miles farther up the Nile. This expedition was commanded by Captain Marchand, a gallant French officer who had made his way across Africa from the French Congo. Kitchener quickly reached Fashoda, where a dramatic meeting took place between the two commanders. Kitchener was in superior force, but any violence might have caused war with France. Kitchener therefore handed Marchand a written protest, hoisted the English and Egyptian flags, and referred the matter to London. The French could hardly have hoped to acquire the Sudan although they may have thought they could obtain a corridor from French West Africa to the Nile. But Salisbury was absolutely firm, and after several months of great tension the French gave way and Marchand was recalled. Thus the English were entrenched firmly throughout the entire Valley of the Nile.

The Boer War

Meanwhile events were approaching a crisis in South Africa. When the Cape had been acquired by the British in 1815 it had contained about twenty five thousand Boer farmers, about thirty thousand black slaves, and perhaps another twenty thousand free blacks. The Boers had never been handled properly. As we have seen, they resented British rule and hated British missionaries. After the abolition of slavery in 1833 a large number of Boers, perhaps as many as 10,000, had sought to escape from British control by moving into new territory to the north and east. A small white population thus was scattered over an enormous area. By the middle of the century there were four separate colonies in South Africa: the Orange Free State and the Transvaal, which were entirely Boer; and Cape Colony and Natal, which contained both Boers and British settlers. The Boer governments were weak, unstable, and primitive; relations among the four colonies were far from satisfactory. Disraeli annexed the Transvaal in 1877, but Gladstone reversed this action.

The normal development of the area was disturbed further by the discovery of great mineral wealth. In 1870 a Boer farmer found his children playing with a bright little stone which turned out to be a diamond worth $25,000. The mines at Kimberley soon were producing most of the world's diamonds. When, in 1886, rich deposits of gold were discovered on the Witwatersrand in the Transvaal, foreigners rushed in to exploit the gold mines. Johannesburg, the capital of the Transvaal, became a large city, but trouble was certain to arise between the foreigners, or Uitlanders, and the Boers. The newcomers, pushing and aggressive, determined to make money quickly, and intolerant of the Boers, were far from ideal settlers. Most of them, though by no means all, were British. The Boers, on the other hand, were frontiersmen whose ancestors had lived for centuries in great isolation from the rest of the world. They were independent and courageous, but stubborn, ignorant, unprogressive, religious in a narrow sense, deeply suspicious, and thoroughly exasperating.

It was the policy of Paul Kruger, the president of the Transvaal and the very incarnation of the Boer character, to make the Uitlanders pay heavily for the privilege of exploiting the mines. Some ninety percent of the taxes came from the miners. Kruger also obstructed trade between the Transvaal and the Cape. He began to buy armaments from Europe, he employed Dutch civil servants who were very anti-British, and he sought support from continental powers, especially Germany.

The Uitlanders organized and plotted insurrection. Most unfortunately, Rhodes, although he was prime minister of Cape Colony, allowed himself to be drawn into these conspiracies. A revolt was planned for 1895. Part of the plan was to collect on the western frontier of the Transvaal a force of mounted police who would make a dash for Johannesburg at the moment of the revolt, but for various reasons the uprising was postponed. Nonetheless, Dr. Jameson, the commander of the mounted police, who had not been properly warned, invaded the Transvaal with his little force on 29 December 1895. Four days later he fell into an ambush and surrendered.

The Jameson Raid completely altered the situation in South Africa. The raid was utterly unjustifiable; it ruined Rhodes, who resigned as prime minister; it caused an outburst of anti-British feeling in Germany; and it united all the Boers in South Africa against Britain. The Kaiser sent Kruger a telegram congratulating him on his success in repelling invasion. Joseph Chamberlain, who was colonial secretary, did know of Jameson's plans, and the suppression of some of his messages to Rhodes made the Boers suspicious. From that point Kruger openly prepared for war.

The war may be divided into three well-defined stages. The first (October 1899 to

February 1900) was one of Boer aggression and success. The British had only some fifteen thousand regulars in South Africa to oppose fifty thousand Boers, who were greatly superior in artillery. There were a number of British defeats, and the Boers besieged the British towns of Ladysmith, Kimberley, and Mafeking. These sieges were strategic errors: had the Boers made straight for Cape Town they might have overrun the country and been in a very strong position. Their delays gave the British time to send strong reinforcements under their best generals. The arrival of Lord Roberts and Lord Kitchener opened the second phase of the war (February to September 1900), in which the British took the offensive and defeated the Boer armies. Roberts invaded and annexed both the Orange Free State and the Transvaal. When organized resistance came to an end, the British thought they had won the war.

But the third and longest period was to come (September 1900 to May 1902). This consisted of prolonged guerrilla warfare by mobile bands of Boer commandos who harassed the British armies and inflicted serious local reverses upon them. The Boers did not wear uniforms, so that a Boer could be a dangerous sharpshooter one moment and a peaceful farmer the next; indeed, every farmhouse was a base of operations. Kitchener divided the whole country into compartments surrounded by heavy wire fences, then swept every person by compartment into concentration camps. The result was unavoidable suffering, with high mortality among the children. Peace was signed in May 1902. The British insisted on complete sovereignty, but once that point was settled they gave very generous terms. Representative government was to be established at once and self-government was to follow shortly; a free gift of £3 million to restore agriculture was supplemented by loans; the Dutch language was safeguarded, though the official language was English. The Boers never had more than 60,000 men in the field; the English sent 450,000 at a cost of £222 million. The war made apparent the great need for a British general staff and for a better military intelligence service.

THE CONTINENTAL SYSTEM OF ALLIANCES

During the Boer War England felt very much alone in a hostile world. She had no ally, no friendly nation to give her moral and diplomatic support, and it was obvious that profound changes had taken place on the Continent. The fundamental cause of these changes was the sudden rise of Germany in 1870 to a position of great military strength with which England could not hope to compete. England had a large navy but a small army, for the people would not have tolerated conscription, though it became the norm on the Continent. The consequence was that England no longer enjoyed the place of pre-eminence she had formerly occupied in the affairs of Europe. She had, for example, played an important part in the unification of Italy before the Franco-Prussian War but had exerted no influence whatever on the unification of Germany which followed that war. Moreover, a system of alliances had grown up in Europe in which England had no part. For a time this did not seem to matter.

England exulted in her "splendid isolation" which gave her freedom to determine her policy solely on the basis of her own interests. But the Boer War brought doubts and questionings.

To understand the European system of alliances one must begin with Bismarck. His policy after the Franco-Prussian War was twofold: to isolate France so that she could never wage a war of revenge, and to maintain friendly relations with both Austria and Russia. In 1872 Bismarck arranged a meeting in Berlin of Kaiser William I of Germany, Emperor Francis Joseph of Austria, and Czar Alexander II of Russia. This meeting proclaimed the friendship of the three powers and their informal alliance was called the League of the Three Emperors. In 1879 Bismarck concluded with Austria a secret defensive alliance which remained the cornerstone of German policy. It was joined in 1882 by Italy, thus becoming the Triple Alliance. But Bismarck also made treaties with Russia. In 1881 he managed to revive for a time the League of the Three Emperors. As Bismarck hoped, these treaties isolated France, but they had to be handled with great skill. Kaiser William II did not renew the convention with Russia, a coolness ensued between the two countries, Russia drifted first into isolation and then into friendship with France. France and Russia concluded a general entente in 1891 and a formal alliance in 1894.

Thus England, faced with two alliances, found it more difficult than ever to obtain friendly cooperation. Her sprawling empire made her vulnerable. Other powers were building navies, and the invention of the torpedo and the submarine created the danger that small ships could attack large ones and that a sudden knockout blow could destory British naval supremacy. Under these circumstances British statesmen, regarding isolation as no longer possible, began a search for allies.

The Search for Allies

The two powers with whom British had been clashing over imperial questions were Russia and France. At the Congress of Berlin in 1878 Disraeli had suspected Russian designs not only in the Balkans but also in the Persian Gulf, in Egypt, and in Suez. Russian expansion into central Asia led her toward Persia and the northwest frontier of India. In the 1890s Anglo-Russian rivalry shifted to China. Taking advantage of Chinese weakness after her defeat by Japan in 1894–1895, various European powers encroached on Chinese territory. The British acquired Weihaiwei in 1898, but strongly resented Russian expansion into Manchuria and the Liaotung Peninsula and the obvious Russian interest in Korea. Meanwhile the French, smarting under their defeat by Prussia, set out to find compensation in an empire. This led to friction with Britain in West Africa, in Indochina, and in the Sudan. In 1887 England concluded a secret treaty with Italy and Austria to maintain the status quo in the Mediterranean, a treaty aimed at Russia and France. An alliance with either of these powers seemed quite out of the question.

England's relations with Germany were friendly as long as Bismarck was chancellor. In the late 1880s Bismarck had played with the idea of an Anglo-German alliance, and though this had not developed, the two countries had reached a comprehensive adjustment of their African disputes in 1890. But Germany under William II became more difficult. The kaiser, desiring colonies in Africa and elsewhere, pushed his policy with vigor. He fell into an irritating habit of demanding compensation whenever any other power made acquisitions. There was a brusqueness about German diplomacy that angered the English. The kaiser's telegram to Kruger in 1896, for example, was a gratuitous insult. Shortly thereafter Germany began in earnest to build a navy.

Nonetheless the British Cabinet preferred to try for an agreement with Germany rather than for one with France and Russia. In 1898 Chamberlain obtained permission to suggest an alliance to Germany. It was to be a defensive alliance based on settlement of differences in China and elsewhere, but Germany declined the British offer. The Germans feared that an alliance with Britain might lead to war with Russia. They assumed that England would never settle her disputes with either Russia or France and that Germany could probably obtain better terms from Britain some time in the future. The possibility of an alliance was discussed once more in 1901. But the Germans, thinking again that they could afford to wait, asked that Britain make commitments to both Austria and Italy. This the British declined to do. When these negotiations, which might have altered the course of history, came to an end, Britain turned elsewhere for allies.

To the astonishment of the world, Britain concluded an alliance with Japan in 1902. It was a defensive alliance against Russia. Japan was determined to fight if Russia attempted to acquire Korea; England wanted protection for her commercial interests in China. Both feared that, if events in the Far East brought war with Russia, the French would come to Russia's assistance. The agreement provided that if either of the contracting powers, because of their interests in China or Korea, were attacked by a third power, the other party would come to its assistance. This was England's first major break from her old policy of splendid isolation.

THE END OF THE CENTURY

The death of Queen Victoria in 1901, after the longest reign in English history, and the retirement of Salisbury in 1902 underlined the fact that an era of history had ended. It is worthwhile to contrast the England of 1900 with the England of the mid-Victorians. Many of the social and moral characteristics of the middle of the century had begun to disappear around 1890. The old taboos had been relaxed, the passion for respectability had subsided, and there was far greater latitude in thought and conduct. In short, it was a freer age. There was also more diversity, more uncertainty, and more doubt and apprehension about the future.

A marked decline took place in religious belief and in the observance of the Sabbath. Evangelical religion was losing its hold on the educated classes. The number of brilliant young men at the universities who took Anglican orders greatly diminished. Many other careers were now open to them, for they no longer regarded

HOUSE OF SAXE-COBURG-GOTHA-WINDSOR

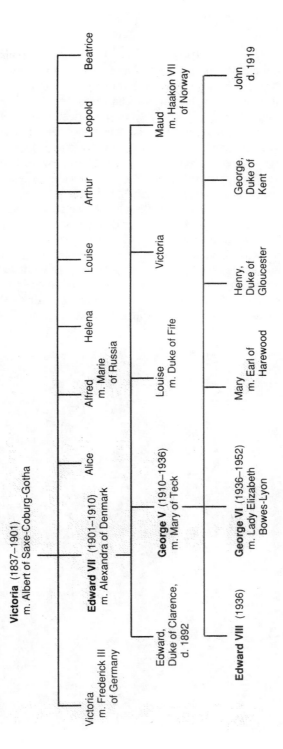

religion as the central theme of life. The difficulty of recruiting men for the ministry was also felt by the nonconformists, for able young men of the lower middle classes could now find places in the world of business or in the labor movement. Church attendance fell off greatly, especially in the cities. Family prayers and teaching in Sunday schools declined. Since Sunday was no longer a day devoted to worship, the necessity arose to provide other means of spending it profitably. Museums and art galleries were opened on Sunday afternoons, there were public concerts and cheap excursions on the railways. The weekend in the country, leaving the cities strangely deserted on Sundays, became a national institution.

There was also a revolution in the press. The newspapers of the mid-Victorians had been dignified and responsible but dull and stuffy, appealing only to intelligent readers. They were now driven out by a cheap, sensational press that put everything in the form of a story, used short sentences and short paragraphs with glaring headlines, and served up the news in chatty and spicy tidbits for uneducated minds. The new journalism did not aim to inform; it aimed to amuse, to pander to low taste, and to make money. This revolution was the work of Alfred Harmsworth, later Lord Northcliffe, who founded the *Daily Mail* in 1896. He ran competitions and offered a

Shopping in the Italian quarter of London. (SEF/Art Resource)

trifling form of insurance to increase his circulation, and was immensely successful in his endeavors. His paper was read by thousands who considered themselves far above the working class.

By the turn of the century middle-class women were beginning to attend Oxford and Cambridge and to enter the teaching profession. The franchise had been granted in municipal and county elections, and organized feminist movements were appearing. Women could now be elected to town councils and school boards and employed as factory inspectors and poor-law officers. In 1897 the National Union of Women's Suffrage Societies was formed amid mounting demands for women's suffrage.

The 1890s were years of increased comfort and general well-being in spite of trade depressions. They were also years of technological advance. Electric lights, telephones, cables, the wireless, electric trolleys and underground railways, the internal combustion engine that opened the way for automobiles and airplanes, finer and stronger steel that could be used for a thousand purposes, industrial chemistry, new drugs and better medical research, the adding machine, the cash register, and the dictaphone, faster transportation by sea, and, unfortunately, vastly improved armaments—all made this period one of unprecedented progress.

The problem of the poor remained. A large proportion of the people lived in extreme poverty and miserable slums and tenements, where they easily fell into vice and depravity. The collapse of agriculture had caused a new migration into the towns. To many thinking people the great challenge of the age was to probe the causes of poverty and to apply what remedies were possible.

THE RISE OF SOCIALISM

Socialism in Britain was in part a product of the Victorian conscience. Perhaps the most important of the new social service agencies was the Salvation Army, founded in 1878 by William Booth and his devoted wife, Catherine Mumford. It was intended to be a purely religious movement, revivalist in nature, but it was soon a center of social service. Booth's book, *In Darkest England and the Way Out* (1890), was a description of urban poverty that shocked the world. Booth was interested in the fate of the agricultural laborers who had drifted to the towns, and he advocated a program of training that would fit them for emigration. Toynbee Hall, founded in 1884, was the first of many settlement houses in East London. Many nonconformist churches preached a social gospel of aiding the poor. Two strikes caught the attention of the public. One, in 1888, was a strike of seven hundred girls employed in making lucifer matches in London. Public support enabled this defenseless group in a toilsome industry to win. Another strike that aroused much sympathy was that of the London dock workers in 1889. Miserably paid, they had only casual employment and lived in chronic poverty. They struck for a wage of 6d. an hour and for four consecutive hours of employment at a time. They obtained most of their demands. In 1889

Charles Booth, a wealthy man not related to William Booth, began to publish a series of studies of the London poor. His conclusion was that thirty percent of Londoners lived in abject poverty, often below the subsistence level. He also was interested in the problem of the aged poor.

Meanwhile there was a growth of socialist ideas. Although Karl Marx wrote his explosive book, *Das Kapital,* in England, English socialism did not adopt his doctrine of the war of classes or of the violent overthrow of capitalism. For the most part English socialism has been idealistic, utopian, and good natured. It was strongly influenced by an American book, Henry George's *Progress and Poverty* (1879), which advocated the nationalization of land. George's phrase "the unearned increment," referring to a rise in the value of land due to the progress of society and not to any effort by the owner, became widely current in England. Edward Bellamy, in *Looking Backward* (1887), and William Morris, in *News from Nowhere* (1891), sketched impossible utopias. Much more influential among the lower classes was *Merrie England* (1894) by Robert Blatchford, who also published a weekly, the *Clarion,* which caught the fancy of young people by its springly articles about cycling, music, arts and crafts, feminism, and other timely topics. High spirits, fun, happiness, courtship, and socialism were all jumbled together. Blatchford had no program, but his writings stressed the injustice of the economic system.

The Fabian Society, founded in 1884, achieved a fame out of proportion to its size because of its distinguished members George Bernard Shaw and Beatrice and Sidney Webb. The Fabians, as their name implies, suggested that socialistic change must come gradually and gently without revolutionary upheaval. They combined a strong desire to improve the lot of the individual with a deep respect for existing institutions of law and government. Rejecting the violence of Marx and the emotional approach of men like Blatchford and William Morris, the Fabians held that socialistic objectives could be attained through the normal processes of parliamentary legislation and that the state could thus be molded into an agent for the promotion of the general good. Socialism, said Webb, was merely the economic side of democracy. The Fabians sought practical legislation on both the national and the local levels. They worked, for example, for the municipal ownership of public utilities, from which they derived the nickname "gas and water socialists."

Socialism could not go far in politics without the financial support of the trade unions, but for a long time the older unions were not interested either in politics or in socialism. In 1875 they had obtained the right of collective bargaining; they had a central agency, the Trades Union Congress; they represented a small aristocracy of skilled labor; and they had placed a few workingmen in Parliament who voted with the Liberals and were known as Lib-Labs. The old trade unions had no wish to experiment. But a new unionism composed of unskilled workers appeared in the 1890s. Led by socialists, it wanted a party organization separate from that of the Liberals. One of its great personalities, Keir Hardie, who had gone to work in Glasgow at the age of seven and had become a miner at the age of ten, broke with the Liberals and formed a Scottish Labor party. In 1892 this party placed three members in the House of Commons of whom Keir Hardie was one. He came to the opening of Parliament wearing his miner's costume and preceded by a man blowing a horn. Other members in the customary morning dress must have lifted their eyebrows.

Shaw and Webb also supported a separate party for labor. In 1893 a conference of socialists of many shades of opinion and some trade-union leaders was held at Bradford and founded the Independent Labor party, an event of great significance. There was now a popular socialist party devoted to the interests of labor. Its object was the "collective ownership of all means of production, distribution, and exchange"; its method was to work through Parliament. Associated with it were many persons famous in the history of the labor movement: Hardie, Blatchford, Shaw, the Webbs, Ben Tillett, and Tom Mann, who had organized the dock workers' strike in 1889, G. N. Barnes, and later Philip Snowden and James Ramsay MacDonald.

By 1900 the Trades Union Congress, feeling less secure than of old, was also ready for parliamentary action. It summoned a congress of cooperative, socialist, trade-union, and other working-class organizations which set up a labor representation committee to secure the election of laboring men to Parliament. The secretary of that committee was Ramsay MacDonald. It did not aim to form a party; it merely hoped to establish a labor group in the Commons which would cooperate with any party whose program favored labor. In the election of 1900 it contested only fifteen seats and won only two. In the election of 1906, however, it won twenty-nine seats, and these members formed the parliamentary Labor party, which is the party that we know today.[1]

THE BALFOUR MINISTRY, 1902–1905

In 1902 Salisbury was followed as Conservative prime minister by his nephew, A. J. Balfour. The new administration lasted for a little more than three years and then ended in disaster. Proposals to abandon free trade and to adopt tariffs that would give the colonies a favorable position in the British market divided the Conservatives, united the Liberals in opposition, and brought about a Liberal victory at the polls in 1906.

The Education Act of 1902 abolished the school boards and gave control of elementary, secondary, and technical education to the county councils, except in large urban areas which were to have authority over their own elementary schools. In a complicated arrangement the county councils were also to control the schools that had been managed for almost a century by the Church of England or by nonconformist bodies. These schools were now to be supported by public funds.

---

[1]In addition to these twenty-nine members, twenty-four other Labor members were elected in 1906. Of the additional twenty-four, a few were Lib-Labs of the ordinary kind, but most of them were officials of miners' unions. Thus in 1906 the Commons contained a total of fifty-three Labor members.

The arrangement pleased the church, straining under the burden of supporting its schools, but infuriated the nonconformists, who had hoped that the church schools would disappear through lack of funds. The act continued the church schools and supported them by taxation which must be paid in part by the nonconformists.

An Irish Land Purchase Act of 1903 facilitated the Conservative policy of lending money to Irish peasants to buy out their landlords. The new act enabled Irish peasants on an estate to purchase the entire estate as a unit rather than to buy it piecemeal in small parcels. A Licensing Act of 1904 was another controversial measure. The country contained far too many saloons or public houses, and there was pressure, especially from nonconformist bodies, to reduce the number of licenses. But if a publican lost his license, not as a punishment for disorder but as a result of general policy, he had a grievance. Balfour's act gave him compensation from a levy on the whole liquor industry. But the nonconformists opposed compensation in any form. In foreign affairs there were momentous events: the conclusion of the Boer War, the alliance with Japan, an entente with France, and a crisis over Morocco in 1905.

Imperial Federation and Tariff Reform

To understand the division among the Conservatives over tariff policy we must return for a moment to one aspect of imperialism in the nineteenth century.

In the 1880s and 1890s there was a movement in England for some kind of federation between Britain and the self-governing colonies. The purpose was to bind the colonies closer to the mother country and to devise some kind of imperial council by which the empire could act as a whole. The Imperial Federation League was founded in 1884, though it never formulated its rather vague proposals. The idea of federation also was furthered by the stirring and elaborate jubilees of 1887 and 1897 commemorating the fiftieth (golden) and sixtieth (diamond) anniversaries of the queen's accession. Since the prime ministers of all the self-governing colonies were present in 1887, it was suggested that a conference be held between them and the ministers in Britain. The first in a long and important line of colonial conferences, it was addressed by Salisbury, who took as his theme the necessity of united action for self-defense. But the conference came to no conclusions. A second conference in 1894, held in Ottawa, Canada, was a rather small affair. It had been summoned to discuss oceanic cables and faster mail service. The Canadians introduced the subject of preferential tariffs.

A third colonial conference in 1897 dealt with imperial federation, naval and military cooperation, and preferential tariffs. But again the results were rather disappointing. Chamberlain, now colonial secretary, urged federation. He asked for a central imperial council which, he hoped, would develop into a federal body to determine common policy. The colonies did not respond to this suggestion.

There were also differences concerning imperial defense. The British naturally thought in terms of high strategy for the defense of the empire as a whole. But the colonial prime ministers were laymen who did not understand grand naval strategy: they wanted battleships in their own waters. They were far more interested in preferential tariffs, for such tariffs would be greatly in their favor. But the position of England was very different. Her tradition was one of free trade and in order to give preference to the colonies she would have to erect tariffs against the rest of the world. Only a fraction of her trade was colonial, and it was by no means certain that British industry as a whole would benefit from tariffs.

At a fourth colonial conference, which met in 1902, the colonies pressed again for preferential tariffs. And Canada, after giving British goods a preference and being punished by German tariffs for doing so, declared that if Canadian goods received no preference in England then Canada would act as her interests demanded. This conference convinced Chamberlain that England should grant colonial preferences. A tariff, he came to believe, not only would help the colonies but would protect British industry and could be used as a weapon against the world at large. What was needed, he said, was not free trade but fair trade. At once there was opposition in the Cabinet. Balfour should have made up his mind one way or the other. Instead, he offered compromises and said that the matter should be discussed. Few prime ministers have had such a dangerous issue raised by a friendly colleague. The Cabinet began to break up. Chamberlain resigned and made a series of speeches which moved closer to a purely protective tariff policy. The free traders in the Cabinet also resigned, and in 1905 Balfour followed their example. The election of 1906 was a Liberal landslide. Tariffs as yet made no appeal in either agricultural or industrial constituencies.

Chamberlain's campaign had a number of results. It gave a bad fright to the Germans, who profited greatly from British free trade. It also gave the Liberals an issue on which they could unite. They had been badly split over the Boer War, but they could now re-form their ranks in defense of free trade. They became more radical. When they were again in office they had to find new sources of revenue; having rejected tariffs they had to turn to new methods of raising taxes. Finally, Chamberlain had turned the thoughts of Englishmen toward colonial problems in a new way.

Before the Conservatives left office they thoroughly alienated the laboring classes. One issue was the importation of Chinese coolies to South Africa to work in the mines. The coolies were housed in compounds they were not permitted to leave, and they were not accorded the normal rights of free men. There was also a legal decision which caused great alarm in labor circles. During a strike against the Taff Vale Railway in Wales the railway had suffered some injury to its property. It sued the railway union and obtained damages. But if a union could be sued for damage done by its members during a strike, the labor movement was in great peril.

Balfour was blind to the feelings and convictions of labor. The Conservative party, leaving Tory democracy far behind, had become the party of the upper classes and was too exclusively concerned with the interests of its own members. It paid the penalty at the polls in 1906.

C H R O N O L O G Y

Salisbury and Imperialism

1878	Salvation Army founded by William Booth
1882	Triple Alliance formed (Germany, Austria, and Italy)
1884	Fabian Society founded
1887	Parnell under attack; Golden Jubilee
1888	Local Government Act; East African Company chartered; match girls strike
1889	London dock strike
1890	Cecil Rhodes prime minister of Cape Colony; Labor Representation Committee
1892	Gladstone again prime minister; Home Rule Bill defeated
1893	Independent Labor Party founded
1894	Gladstone retired; Rosebery prime minister
1895	Salisbury returned to power; Jameson Raid
1896	Kruger telegram
1897	Diamond Jubilee
1898	Fashoda Incident; Battle of Omdurman
1899–1902	Boer War
1901	Death of Queen Victoria; Edward VII king; Taff Vale Decision
1902	Anglo-Japanese alliance; Balfour prime minister; Education Act
1903	Irish Land Purchase Act
1904	Licensing Act
1905	Free trade issue arose; Balfour resigned; Campbell-Bannerman prime minister
1906	Liberal election landslide

Social Reform and War

The Liberal victory early in 1906 was one of the most sweeping on record. The Liberals won 337 seats, the Conservatives only 157; there were 83 Irish Nationalists and 53 Labor members who were certain to vote with the Liberals, giving that party a very large majority. The composition of the Commons was more varied than in the nineteenth century. Although country gentlemen were still to be found in Parliament, members were also drawn from many other classes and occupations—from the law, from business, from journalism, and from labor. This election made it clear that the urge toward social democracy ran very deep. It was not nineteenth-century Liberalism that won the victory in 1906; rather, it was the electoral power of the laboring classes demanding a higher standard of living, more equality of opportunity, and greater protection against such causes of poverty as sickness, unemployment, and old age. Many Liberals, as well as Labor members, were ready to vote for advanced legislation of this kind.

The desire of the working classes for radical social reform was not the result of acute suffering. The national economy between 1900 and 1914 was fairly prosperous, with employment at a higher level than in the 1890s. There was, it is true, a certain stagnation in industry; as a result of a lack of capital investment it did not expand, nor did it take full advantage of new techniques. Opportunities for investment abroad, in the Dominions and elsewhere, were so attractive that too much money was sent overseas while industry at home was starved for capital.

SIR HENRY CAMPBELL-BANNERMAN, 1905–1908

The new prime minister, Sir Henry Campbell-Bannerman, was quite ready to adopt a program of social reform. A shrewd and wealthy Scot, he had become leader of the Liberals in 1898, when their prospects were dim. He had shown ability, steadfastness, and devotion during long years in opposition, and he proved even more effective in office. Though not a brilliant speaker, he could succinctly express the sentiment of the Commons, as on the famous occasion when he reproved Balfour for making politics a kind of sport for gentlemen rather than a serious task for dedicated men. Like Gladstone, he moved to the left with advancing years. And in his kindly and generous old age he proved an excellent leader for a Commons containing many idealistic but inexperienced members. His Cabinet was unusually rich in talent, with three Liberal imperialists from Rosebery's ministry: Herbert Asquith, Sir Edward Grey, and R. B. Haldane. Other members of unusual ability were John Morley, James Bryce, Augustine Birrell, and David Lloyd George; younger men outside the Cabinet included Reginald McKenna, Winston Churchill, Herbert Samuel, and Walter Runciman.

The Cabinet had a clear mandate from the people to enact a program of social reform. Yet the House of Lords contained a large and permanent majority of Conservative peers. When Rosebery had been prime minister, these peers, as we have seen, had voted along strict party lines and had wrecked legislation merely because it came from a Liberal House of Commons. In the years after 1906 the Lords were not as intransigent as this. They believed that in opposing the measures of the Cabinet they were acting as wise amenders of hasty and ill-advised legislation. Yet they often voted as Conservatives ready to employ the constitutional power of the upper chamber in deciding which of the measures proposed by a Liberal government should be allowed to pass.

Social Legislation

A clash between the two houses forms an important and dramatic part of the history of this period, but social legislation, though less spectacular, was really more important. The Lords allowed a good deal of it to become law, for many reasons. Old-age pensions, for example, had been accepted in principle by both parties, and could be considered as part of a Conservative program. In other matters, even in some rather radical ones, the Lords hesitated to incur the antagonism of the working classes. And certain measures could be regarded as nonpartisan.

In 1906 they passed three pieces of social legislation. One, a measure for workmen's compensation, extended the principle that employers must compensate laborers for injuries suffered during hours of employment; some 13 million workers, including domestic servants, now were protected in this way. Another bill provided free or cheap meals for children who were sent to school in the morning without any breakfast. A more controversial measure was a Trade Disputes Act. Labor had been greatly alarmed by a legal decision in 1901 awarding damages to the Taff Vale Railway when it had sued a union for injuries suffered during a strike. A Trade Disputes Act now declared that unions could not be so sued. Indeed, it gave them a broad immunity from legal actions. So radical a measure might well have been questioned by the Lords, yet they allowed it to pass.

An important Old Age Pensions bill was sponsored by Lloyd George in 1908. Old

Bank Holiday, *painting by W. Strang. (Tate Gallery, London)*

age was an obvious cause of extreme poverty, for a worker could not normally hope to accumulate savings for old age. The pension provided by the bill was modest enough: to qualify for it a person must be seventy and must have an income of no more than 10s. a week. The pension was to be a weekly sum of 5s.; the pension of an elderly couple living together was frugally reduced to 7s. 6d. Yet even this slender sum might suffice to keep a man or woman from the stigma of the poorhouse. The Lords began to tamper with the bill, but were outmaneuvered because it was attached to the budget and so they let it through. Another measure limited the working day of miners to eight hours.

In 1909 a royal commission appointed by Balfour in 1905 to study the operation of the Poor Law published its conclusions, which included a minority report. Both majority and minority reports proposed to abolish the local guardians of the poor established by the act of 1834 and to entrust poor relief to the county councils. The minority report—the work of Sidney and Beatrice Webb—suggested that poor relief as such be ended altogether and that various welfare services be extended to provide a minimum standard of life for everyone. The Cabinet failed to act on these proposals. Winston Churchill sponsored the Labor Exchange Bill through which unemployed laborers could obtain information about jobs in various parts of the country. Churchill was also responsible for the Act for the Establishment of Trade Boards in certain industries. Under this act a board appointed to examine an industry could establish a minimum wage in that trade. These measures were passed by the House of Lords.

Bills Rejected by the House of Lords

There were other measures, however, which the Commons sent up to the Lords, only to have them rejected. The most important of these in the session of 1906 was an education bill. On this bill the Liberals had set their hearts, for they regarded Balfour's Education Act of 1902 as far too generous to the Church of England. The Cabinet clearly had a mandate to enact a new bill, but the Lords destroyed the education bill of 1906 by hostile amendments. They also threw out a plural voting bill which would have restricted every voter to one vote although he qualified in several constituencies. In 1907 four measures concerning land were either rejected or mutilated by the House of Lords.

As a result of these rejections an important debate took place in the House of Commons concerning its relations with the House of Lords. Campbell-Bannerman declared that "in order to give effect to the will of the people, it is necessary that the power of the other House to alter or reject bills passed by this House should be so restricted by law as to secure that within the limits of a single Parliament [a period of seven years] the final decision of the Commons should prevail." In the debate that followed, Lloyd George remarked that the House of Lords was not the watchdog of the constitution: it was merely Mr. Balfour's poodle. Churchill referred to the Lords as unrepresentative and irresponsible.

HERBERT ASQUITH

Early in 1908 Campbell-Bannerman died and was succeeded as prime minister by Herbert Asquith. A Yorkshireman of nonconformist stock, Asquith was a lawyer whose strength lay in the admirable precision and lucidity with which he could present complicated matters to the Commons. He never lacked for cogent arguments in defense of Liberal measures. He had a clear head for business, and he employed tact and moderation in keeping the strong-willed members of his Cabinet working together. He gave his colleagues loyal support but he was not a crusader. He was perhaps somewhat lacking in imagination, and after the war began in 1914 he did not develop into a great war leader. He had entered Parliament in 1886 as something of a radical, and served in Gladstone's Cabinet in 1892. After 1895, when his party was out of power, he had become less influential in politics. His marriage to Margot Tennant took him into high society, an enjoyable circumstance which unfortunately weakened his Liberal connections. He returned to office as Campbell-Bannerman's chancellor of the Exchequer and then succeeded him as prime minister.

In 1908 the Lords rejected an important licensing bill, a temperance measure that was well thought out and well framed. It was greatly needed, for the amount of drinking in the early twentieth century was excessive and the number of pubs enormous. The bill would have gradually reduced them by about one-third (some thirty thousand) over a period of fourteen years; compensation would have been given for licenses revoked.

The outlook for the Cabinet seemed bleak: it could not get its most desired bills through the Lords, trade was depressed in 1908, and by-elections were going against the government. In 1909 a naval scare resulted in a decision to lay down eight battleships in one year, a most costly undertaking. The old-age pensions plan was also proving expensive. Lloyd George, now chancellor of the Exchequer, would have to find £15 million in new taxation.

The Budget of 1909 and the Parliament Act of 1911

This was the background of Lloyd George's budget in 1909. The Conservatives later regarded this budget as a cunning trap set for the downfall of the House of Lords. The budget was aimed at the rich. Death duties were increased sharply, so that estates could be taxed up to twenty-five percent of their total value. The income tax also was increased, with surtaxes on incomes above £5000 and with heavier duties on incomes derived from stocks and bonds than on those derived from salaries. Heavy duties also were laid on automobiles, furs, tobacco, liquor, and other luxuries. There were two new taxes: one a twenty percent tax on the unearned increment of land whenever it change hands, the other a small tax on the capital value of undeveloped land and minerals. Conservative hostility to the budget was intense. Not only would it tax the wealthy very heavily; its enactment would eliminate all hope of tariff reform and it might well be the opening wedge for a much more radical program of socialism.

Conservative opposition to the budget was uncompromising in the Commons; the Lords pledged themselves to fight it in their own chamber. Lloyd George began a series of speeches in which he denounced the peers as rich and selfish men who cherished special privilege and sought to escape their share of taxation. The more violently the Lords replied, the more certain the public became that their motives were sinister. In the Cabinet some members wished to draw back, but Asquith supported Lloyd George. The Lords then rejected the budget. This action was clearly unconstitutional, for if any principle of the constitution had been steadily maintained since 1688 it was that the Commons had complete control of finance. Asquith at once carried a resolution in the commons that "the action of the House of Lords in refusing to pass into law the financial provisions made by this House for the service of the year is a breach of the constitution and a usurpation of the rights of the Commons."

An election was fought in January 1910 on the merits of Lloyd George's budget and on the larger question of the veto power of the House of Lords. As a result of the election the Liberals came back with 275 seats, the Consevatives with 273, the Irish with 82, and Labor with 40. The Liberal victory was greater than the figures seem to imply. As the Liberals had been losing ground it was thought that the Conservatives would win. But in fact the Conservatives lost about 100 seats they were considered likely to win, Labor and Irish members were solidly behind a reform of the House of Lords—Labor in the hope of further social legislation, the Irish in the hope of home rule. The budget was now accepted by the Lords. But the larger question of curbing the power of the upper chamber remained.

The Cabinet was preparing its campaign when it was interrupted in May 1910 by the death of King Edward VII. His successor, George V, hoped for a compromise. In the long series of conferences between committees of the two houses, nothing was accomplished. A second election held in December 1910 did not materially alter the party figures in the Commons. It then became known that Asquith had the king's permission to announce the creation of a great number of new peers unless the House of Lords gave way. Although a group of diehard Conservatives wished to force this creation, it was avoided because the more moderate peers abstained from voting and allowed the bill to pass.

The Parliament Act of 1911 contained three essential provisions. Money bills were to become law one month after passage by the Commons even if the Lords had not passed them. Should there be a question about whether a certain bill was a money bill, the issue was to be decided by the speaker of the House of Commons. Bills that were not money bills might become law without the consent of the House of Lords if the Commons passed them in three successive sessions. This provision enabled the Lords to delay a bill for two years but not to block it permanently. Thus the Lords could no longer challenge the supremacy of the Commons. Finally, the legal life of a Parliament was reduced from seven to five years.

THE MONARCHY

When Edward VII came to the throne at the death of Victoria in 1901 he was almost sixty. A brilliant man of the world had succeeded a recluse. After Albert's death in 1861 Victoria had retired for many years from almost all public activities, and though she emerged from her seclusion about 1874, her court was never lively. Edward referred to Buckingham Palace in her reign as a sepulcher. But when he became king it was a sepulcher no longer. Edward liked high society, he was fond of shows and displays, he delighted in uniforms and decorations, and he played the host in a truly regal fashion. Balls and dinner parties attracted the fashionable world to Buckingham Palace. Edward was widely traveled, was personally acquainted with most of the important people in Europe and in the empire, and possessed a knowledge of the world through contacts with all kinds of people. As a symbol of empire he was valuable to the state. Yet his influence over its affairs was much less than

*Edward VII's car.
(A.P. Wide World
Photos, Inc.)*

Victoria's. Victoria had been willing to spend her days laboriously reading dispatches. Edward occupied his time more pleasantly; there was a general impression that he was fond of good cheer, of race horses, and of pretty women. Early in life he had rebelled against the strictness with which he was being educated. He turned away from books. As a man he never read anything except the newspapers and an occasional novel. Victoria had excluded him from the business of the state. He was fifty before she allowed him to see the reports of Cabinet meetings. But if he lacked industry, he had his gifts: he could be both dignified and charming; he could handle people with great tact; he was a good linguist and possessed an excellent memory.

In 1910 Edward was succeeded by a very different kind of person. George V, resembling Victoria, was grave and serious, with a high sense of duty. Like her, he disliked society. He was very conventional and rather distrusted intellectuals. So far as possible he wished to live the life of a simple country gentleman. During World War I he displayed an impressive spirit of dedication and self-sacrifice, and he was truly beloved. He was an ideal sovereign in an age when the king must maintain the dignity of kingship but must not aspire to influence the affairs of the state.

DOMESTIC ANARCHY

The years from 1910 to 1914 were disturbing ones for moderate and sensible Englishmen. Not only was the international horizon more threatening; unrest, disunity, and violence were chronic in domestic affairs. The Liberal alliance with Labor and with the Irish Nationalists weakened. There was also much labor disquiet. Home rule for Ireland again convulsed the nation. The Conservatives continued the bitter and uncompromising tone they had adopted during the curbing of the House of Lords. Many people set forth their principles in a militant way without respect for the principles of others, for violence seemed to obtain better results than patient and orderly conduct.

Labor Unrest

The strength of the labor movement throughout the country was greater than the number of Labor members in the Commons would indicate, and the Labor party believed that it did not carry the weight in Parliament to which it was entitled. Labor also felt its defeat in the Osborne Case, a court decision declaring that unions could not impose compulsory levies on their members in order to raise funds for political purposes. The decision was a blow to some Labor members who had no income beyond the support they received from their unions. To meet this grievance the government in 1911 secured a financial resolution in the House of Commons providing a salary of £400 a year for each member. Nonetheless, the Labor party was dissatisfied. Growing cool toward the Liberals, it fostered a socialist program of its own.

There was a corresponding change in the thinking of labor leaders, who turned away from Parliament toward syndicalism, that is, toward the notion that the union and not the state was the center of democratic action. Labor leaders should influence Parliament, not by becoming members, but by direct action outside politics, by the sympathy strike, by the general strike, and even by sabotage. Similar ideas appeared in other countries, for there was labor unrest in most industrialized nations at this time. A number of strikes took place in Britain during the years from 1910 to 1912. The most important were a railway strike in 1911 and a strike of coal miners in 1912. The strike on the railways lasted only two days, but it paralyzed the nation during that period. The miners' strike continued for five weeks, affecting 850,000 miners and 1,250,000 workers in other industries. Strikes tapered off with better times in 1913–1914. But three of the most aggressive unions—those of the railway workers, the miners, and the transport workers—formed an industrial alliance in 1913. If the 2 million workers in these trades all struck at the same time they could cripple industry as well as prevent the distribution of food.

In 1911 the Cabinet secured the passage of a National Insurance Act which protected almost the entire working population in case of sickness. It was true insurance in that the worker, the employer, and the government each contributed a few pennies a week to a central fund. Benefits included medical care and small money payments, varying according to circumstances over a period no longer than twenty-six weeks. An attempt made to insure workers in certain trades against unemployment was admittedly experimental. Contributions were arranged as in sickness insurance; benefits were payable over a period of fifteen weeks, during which time it was assumed that a laborer could normally find new employment. The Conservative party was furious. The measure would never have become law if the Lords had possessed the power to stop it. The contributions made by laborers (normally 4*d.* a week) were denounced as robbery of the poor, noble ladies exhorted workingmen to resist such tyranny, and the medical profession was urged to refuse the government its cooperation.

Violence of another kind arose from the woman-suffrage movement. An agitation for woman suffrage had been conducted for some time in an orderly fashion. But in 1903 Mrs. Emmeline Pankhurst organized the Woman's Social and Political Union, which resorted to violence in order to promote its cause. Public meetings were disrupted, pictures were slashed in art galleries, fires were set, acid was poured into mail boxes, women chained themselves to the galleries of the House of Commons so that they could not be easily removed. One woman threw herself before the horses as they ran in the Derby. In prison the suffragists resorted to hunger strikes. A "Cat and Mouse" Act was passed by which prisoners could be released when ill and arrested again when they had recovered. The willingness of many women to suffer the physical and mental agony of forced feeding has remained a monument to the cause. Mary Leigh recorded the experience in a letter to her lawyer in 1909:

> The sensation is most painful—the drums of the ears seem to be bursting and there is a horrible pain in the throat and the breast. The tube is pushed down twenty inches. I have to lie on the bed, pinned down by the wardresses. . . . I resist and am overcome by weight of numbers.[1]

The public turned against the "suffragettes" and for the time the movement produced no results.

Home Rule

In 1912 the government introduced a Home Rule Bill for Ireland. This bill was certain to be controversial; it increased the bitterness of political life and inflamed the tendency toward violent action regardless of the law. It was based upon a federal concept. Ireland was to be autonomous in domestic affairs, with a Parliament and a responsible government in Dublin, but the imperial Parliament in London was to remain supreme and was to handle many matters of wider importance in Anglo-Irish government. Forty-two Irish members were to sit in the English House of Commons. Conditions in Ireland had altered greatly since Gladstone's first Home Rule Bill in 1886. The Irish land problem had been solved. Irish peasants, thanks to loans from the English government, had largely bought out their landlords and had become prosperous and self-respecting small farmers. Through a system of county and

[1]Midge Mackenzie, *Shoulder to Shoulder: A Documentary* (New York: Alfred A. Knopf, 1975), pp. 128–129.

district councils introduced in 1898 they had become accustomed to self-government in local affairs. Moreover, John Redmond, the Irish Nationalist leader, had none of Parnell's hatred of England. Unfortunately a problem arose in the area of Ulster, where the population, largely of Scottish ancestry, was Protestant and industrial in contrast to the Roman Catholic and agricultural society of southern Ireland. Ulstermen were determined not to be placed under the domination of a Catholic Parliament in Dublin. The conservatives in England, in their furious opposition to home rule, fostered a spirit of revolt in Ulster. Sir Edward Carson, an Irish member of Parliament, and Bonar Law, the official leader of the conservative party, gave full support to preparations in Ulster to resist home rule by force. As volunteer armies organized both in Ulster and in southern Ireland, the country was headed for civil war.

Asquith handled the situation badly. He might have known that Ulster could not be forced to accept home rule and he should certainly have taken vigorous steps to suppress the private armies springing up in Ireland. Instead, he permitted matters to drift and remained committed to a bill which placed all Ireland under a Parliament at

Dublin. Meanwhile Carson and Law were making speeches calculated to induce the British army to refuse to coerce the Ulstermen. Such open defiance of law and order was highly scandalous and most unsettling for the nation as a whole. When the bill became law, after the Lords had delayed it for two years, World War I had begun. The operation of the act was deferred for the duration of hostilities.

THE EMPIRE

Between 1906 and 1914 the Liberals took important steps toward the extension of self-government within the empire. They were generous to the Boers. The treaty at the end of the war in 1902 had promised the Boers representative government in the near future and responsible government at a later time. Campbell-Bannerman decided to skip the representative stage and to grant responsible government at once. This move was strongly denounced by the Conservatives. Self-government was granted to the Transvaal in 1906 and to the Orange River Colony (formerly the Orange Free State) in 1907. General Botha, who was elected prime minister of the Transvaal, with General Smuts as his principal colleague, cooperated fully with the British to make the new government a success. The Union of South Africa was formed in 1909.

The Liberals also took a tentative step toward self-government in India. A nationalist movement has arisen in India during the second half of the nineteenth century. In 1885 it had taken shape in the establishment of the Indian National Congress, a body composed largely of Hindu intellectuals educated in the Western tradition. They were moderate, they recognized the benefits of British rule, and they requested that representative institutions be introduced into India as rapidly as possible.

Anti-British feeling rose in the years between 1898 and 1905 when Lord Curzon was Viceroy. An extremely able but a rather autocratic ruler, he was eager to introduce reforms and was impatient of criticism from Hindu sources. A violent campaign in Bengal against many of his policies led to assassinations, bomb throwing, and constant disturbance of the peace.

India was governed by a secretary of state in London and by a Viceroy in India. A small executive council, whose members for the most part were the heads of large departments, assisted the Viceroy. There was also a legislative council composed of a much larger group of lesser officials. Both councils were almost exclusively British. The Indian civil service, a body of about twelve hundred British officials of very high quality, was responsible for all kinds of administration and often governed a small areas within the provinces. In addition, in some 500 native states, internal affairs were administered by native princes, but foreign relations were conducted through the British government.

In 1909 the Liberals passed the Morley-Minto reforms, John Morley being secretary for India and Lord Minto being the viceroy. The reforms included the appointment of an occasional Indian to the executive councils. The legislative councils were greatly enlarged to include many Indians who were elected by constituencies representing various classes, interests, and religions. Members of the legislative councils could criticize the proposals of the government, including financial proposals, but the executive could disregard these criticisms. Thus India received representative government of a restricted kind, with responsibility remaining in British hands. This halfway house on the road to self-government could be no more than a temporary measure.

THE APPROACH OF WAR

The Entente with France

About the turn of the century, as we have seen, Britain had abandoned her traditional isolation and had begun a search for allies. Her first approach had been to Germany, but she had been repulsed; in 1902 she had announced her alliance with Japan. In 1904 she concluded a much more important agreement with France. This was not an alliance but an entente, an understanding, an attempt to end the constant friction over colonies and empire that poisoned relations between the two countries. Disagreements were seen to fall into two categories. The first was a long series of local irritations and minor disputes which were ironed out in hard bargaining. They dealt with Newfoundland, West Africa, Siam, Madagascar, and the New Hebrides.

The second category was a matter of high policy. Ever since the English had occupied Egypt, the French had used their treaty rights in that country to obstruct British administration. England had been forced to seek the support of Germany in Egyptian affairs. Now, however, the French were interested in Morocco, where the government of the Sultan was slowly disintegrating. Possession of Morocco would connect Algeria with French West Africa and would strengthen French naval power. Thus a bargain was possible. France agreed to give England a free hand in Egypt, and the English recognized French interest in Morocco. Success in these negotiations was the result of good will on both sides of the Channel. The British foreign minister, Lord Lansdowne, was quite pro-French, and he was assisted in winning French approval by a visit of Edward VII to Paris in 1903. Although Delcassé, the French foreign minister, did not love the British, he was convinced that France could never sustain a war with Germany without more assistance than she was likely to obtain from the Russians.

Thus from the beginning the entente may have been anti-German in the minds of the French, but there is no evidence that this was so in England. It was later developments that turned the entente into an anti-German alliance of France and Britain. One of these was the steady increase in the size of the German navy. Even in the days before the entente the British had been strengthening their naval bases in Scotland and had begun to assemble naval units in home waters. British naval power in the Mediterranean had been reduced. This policy was gradually expanded until, in 1914, the British fleet was concentrated in Scottish bases facing Germany across the

North Sea, while the French fleet was concentrated in the Mediterranean. No such close cooperation had been foreseen in 1904.

A second influence drawing England and France together was the Russo-Japanese War, which weakened Russia and thereby increased the relative strength of Germany. There was also the first Moroccan crisis in 1905–1906. As French ambitions in Morocco became clearer, the Kaiser suddenly visited Tangier in March 1905, where he asserted that Morocco was an independent country in which Germany and other nations had interests. The German move was a challenge to the entente and an attempt to weaken it, but the result was quite the opposite. At an international conference at Algeciras in Spain in 1906 English diplomacy supported France, and Germany obtained nothing. The entente had been greatly strengthened.

Meanwhile Lord Lansdowne had been succeeded by Sir Edward Grey as British foreign secretary. A Liberal imperialist, Grey saw no reason to alter the policy of his predecessor.

As the Algeciras conference was about to begin, Paul Cambon, the French ambassador in London, told Grey that France greatly feared a sudden attack by Germany. Cambon asked whether England would assist France in resisting such an attack and whether she would permit military conversations between the two powers concerning possible cooperation. Without such conversations, Cambon argued, British assistance would be futile. Grey replied that he could not commit his country in advance; but after consultation with Campbell-Bannerman, Asquith, and Haldane (the secretary for war), though not with the whole Cabinet, he permitted the conversations to begin. They continued for many years. They included arrangements for rushing the British army to France within a period of a few days. The nature of the entente thus was transformed. Grey might insist that England was not bound by treaty to come to the aid of France if France was attacked by Germany. Nonetheless, the military conversations implied a moral obligation: how could England make detailed plans to assist the French and then not do so when the crisis came? There were also naval conversations leading, as we have seen, to French concentration in the Mediterranean and to British concentration in the North Sea. But if, while this arrangement continued, the German fleet should attack the northern coast of France, how could the British escape the moral duty of intervention?

In 1907 a treaty was signed with Russia. It, too, was an entente, similar to the agreement with France, for it did no more than settle imperial differences between Russia and Britain. Friction between the two countries had lessened in both the Near and the Far East, and it was only in the Middle East that serious difficulties remained. They concerned Persia, Afghanistan, and Tibet. Each of these countries was treated differently. Persia was divided into three zones: a northern one in which the Russians might seek concessions, a southern one in which the British might do the same, and a central one in which both countries might be active. The Russians recognized the special interest of Britain in Afghanistan and agreed to have no dealings with the Afghans except through British sources. Both countries agreed to stay out of Tibet. By 1909 Europe thought in terms of the Triple Entente as a counterbalance to the Triple Alliance.

Armaments and Crises

Britain continued to be preoccupied with the problem of defense. In 1906 she completed a new battleship, the *Dreadnought,* the first all-big-gun ship, which revolutionized naval design. Earlier battleships had normally carried four heavy guns with a number of medium guns and light, quick-firing ordnance. The designers of the *Dreadnought* swept aside all secondary armaments and equipped the vessel with eight of the heaviest guns then made. The *Dreadnought* rendered all other battleships obsolete. As Admiral Fisher boasted, it could sink the whole German navy. The Germans agreed. They laid down four such ships in 1908, whereas the British only laid down two. Admiral von Tirpitz planned four more in 1909, and by accumulating guns and equipment well in advance he greatly shortened the time required for construction. In the ensuing naval scare in Britain Asquith suggested that four battleships be built in 1909, with four later if the need arose. The public was not satisfied. "We want eight and we won't wait," was the theme of the music halls. The government then yielded to pressure and laid down eight dreadnoughts in one year.

Meanwhile the secretary for war, R. B. Haldane, took in hand the reorganization of the army. Knowing that English opinion would not tolerate conscription, upon which the huge armies of the Continent were based, he kept the regular army small (160,000 men) but made it very good. This army, with its transport, artillery, and medical services, could be sent to France within a few days. Haldane also created a second army, known as the Territorial Force. Composed of volunteers, it stood between the regular army on one hand and the militia on the other; by 1910 it numbered 176,000 men. A general staff was now established for the first time; a war council, which did not amount to a general staff but made an advance in that direction, also was created for the navy.

Between 1908 and 1914 a series of international crises brought Europe closer to war. The Bosnian crisis of 1908 arose from the rivalry of Austria and Russia in the Balkans. Taking advantage of difficulties in Turkey, Austria suddenly announced the annexation of the provinces of Bosnia and Herzegovina, which she had administered since 1878. The Kaiser disliked this move, but he supported Austria by suggesting that the annexation be approved in an exchange of notes among the great powers. When the Russians delayed their answer, Germany demanded a reply in peremptory terms. Russia gave way but was deeply humiliated. The Agadir crisis of 1911 concerned Morocco once more. Since 1906 the French had been continuing their penetration of that country. In 1911 they dispatched a small army to quell some rebellious tribesmen. Germany at once sent a gunboat to Agadir, a port on the Atlantic coast of Morocco. Her purpose was to secure some compensation to balance Morocco's absorption by France, but Grey thought that she planned to seize Agadir as a naval base.

In 1912 interest shifted once more to the Balkans. Serbia, Bulgaria, Greece, and Montenegro won surprising victories in a war against the Turks. In the next year, however, they fell out among themselves and waged war on each other. Relations between Austria and Serbia remained tense and hostile.

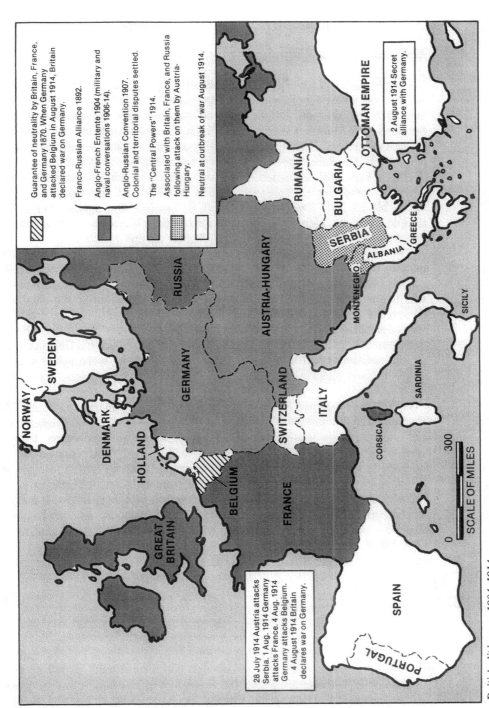

Guarantee of neutrality by Britain, France, and Germany 1870. When Germany attacked Belgium in August 1914, Britain declared war on Germany.

Franco-Russian Alliance 1892.

Anglo-French Entente 1904 (military and naval conversations 1906-14).

Anglo-Russian Convention 1907. Colonial and territorial disputes settled.

The "Central Powers" 1914.

Associated with Britain, France, and Russia following attack on them by Austria-Hungary.

Neutral at outbreak of war August 1914.

2 August 1914 Secret alliance with Germany.

28 July 1914 Austria attacks Serbia. 1 Aug. 1914 Germany attacks France. 4 Aug. 1914 Germany attacks Belgium. 4 August 1914 Britain declares war on Germany.

SCALE OF MILES

0   300

British diplomacy 1904–1914.

707

The Outbreak of War

On 28 June 1914, the Archduke Francis Ferdinand, heir to the Austro-Hungarian throne, and his wife were assassinated at Sarajevo, The capital of Bosnia. The deed was done by Bosnian nationalists who had received inspiration and guns from Serbians. The Austrian government, though it could not trace the assassination to the government of Serbia, determined to use the incident to deal with Serbia once and for all. The kaiser gave his approval for strong action. On 23 July Austria sent Serbia a very stiff ultimatum which was meant to bring about war. The Serbs, however, gave way on almost every point. Nonetheless, the Austrians declared war on Serbia 28 July. The Russians began to mobilize first against Austria and then against Germany. Hence the Germans also began to mobilize. On 1 August Germany declared war against Russia and on 3 August against France.

The rapidity of these events astonished both the British Cabinet and the British people. Grey's proposal of a conference in London of the ambassadors of the great powers was accepted by France but refused by Germany. Thereafter the question was not whether England could prevent the war but whether she should enter it. Russia and France pressed desperately for a commitment. But the British Cabinet was divided, and Grey had to reply that he could give no pledge. He obtained permission to inform Germany that Britain would not tolerate a German naval attack on the northern coast of France. France and Germany were asked whether they would respect Belgian neutrality. The French reply was satisfactory; the German reply was not.

On the afternoon of 3 August Grey presented his case in the Commons. He argued that although the military conversations with France did not bind England to come to her support, there was a moral obligation to do so. He pointed out that if France were crushed, the British Empire would be in jeopardy. He reported the Cabinet's decision to defend the northern coast of France. Then he came to Belgium. On the previous day the Germans had demanded from Belguim the right to send troops through that country; the violation of Belgium was certain to follow. It had long been British policy to prevent the occupation of Belgium by any great power. The Commons strongly supported Grey. Next day an ultimatum was sent to Germany threatening war if Belgium was invaded. The ultimatum expired at 11 P.M. on 4 August. Thereafter Britain and Germany were at war.

THE FIRST WORLD WAR, 1914–1918

The master plan of the Germans, which led them to violate Belgian neutrality, was to make a great, semicircular sweep into northern France, to roll up the French against other German armies on the Franco-German frontier, and to crush France within six weeks. Holding the Channel ports, such as Calais and Boulogne, the Germans could then fend off any English attack while they turned their full strength on Russia, bringing about her speedy collapse. The war was to be ended quickly.

This plan was frustrated at the Battle of the Marne in September 1914, when the Germans were stopped by the French and British armies. Instead of lasting a few weeks the war dragged on for fifty-two months. It destroyed the German, Austrian, and Turkish empires, it precipitated the Russian Revolution, and it brought about profound changes in England and the British Empire.

British strategy remained essentially the same as it had been in other great wars, such as those against Louis XIV and Napoleon. In each case a dominant continental power controlled the land mass of Europe. British strategy was twofold. It consisted, in the first place, of a naval blockade to halt the flow of raw materials to the enemy and to deny him access to world markets. In the second place, Britain sought allies along the periphery of the continental power, assisting them with men, money, and munitions. Thus the British began at the circumference and worked toward the center.

But the First World War differed greatly from earlier wars because of the development of weapons. Artillery was vastly more effective than in the past. Machine guns, barbed wire, and grenades gave great defensive strength to trench warfare. Zeppelins, airplanes, poison gas, and wireless added new dimensions to war; torpedoes, mines, and submarines altered the conditions of blockade and revolutionized naval combat. The British navy carried on under the new conditions. German merchantmen disappeared at once from the oceans; a few German warships in scattered parts of the world were soon run down and destroyed. The British Grand Fleet at Scapa Flow in the Orkneys, with light craft at Harwich, and the second Fleet at Sheerness in the mouth of the Thames, maintained a remote blockade of the German High Seas Fleet in its fortified harbors in northern Germany. Vast numbers of soldiers were taken across the Channel, or brought from the Dominions, or later from the United States with very little loss. Food and war materials flowed into Britain. The blockade was effective, though it caused the usual friction with neutral nations. In spite of a large shipbuilding program carried on in Britain her navy was under great strain.

Britain continued to search for allies. Belgium was perforce one from the beginning. So was Serbia, at war with the Austrians. Japan quickly pounced on German possessions in the Far East. But although every effort was made to conciliate Turkey, she threw in her lot with the Central Powers. This was of vital concern. Surrounded by enemies in Europe, Germany possessed no outlets save those of the Balkans, Turkey, and Asia Minor. Moreover, Turkey blocked communications between the western Allies and Russia as well as threatened British power in both the Near and the Middle East. After some hesitation Bulgaria also sided with the Central Powers. Rumania remained neutral until 1916, then joined the Allies, only to be quickly crushed. Italy also joined the Allies and her entrance into the war opened a new front which engaged large numbers of Austrian troops.

A British army of some 100,000 men, placed in France within a few days, was too late to help the Belgians but gave great assistance to the French. It fought delaying actions against the advancing Germans at Mons and at Le Cateau; it took part in the Battle of the Marne, which stopped the Germans and forced them back to the Aisne; it defended a forward salient at Ypres in desperate fighting to save the Channel ports

British troops in Flanders. (A.P. Wide World Photos, Inc.)

of Calais and Boulogne. Had these ports been captured by the Germans, British communications with France would have been much more difficult. As a result of these battles, the British Expeditionary Force was reduced to a small fraction of its original size. Meanwhile, however, new armies were being recruited at home. Lord Kitchener, the popular hero of many imperial campaigns and now secretary for war, called initially for 100,000 volunteers, who were quickly sent to France, along with the Territorial Force and troops from the Dominions. The Western Front was already stabilized in a line of trenches extending six hundred miles from the Channel to the Swiss frontier. This front swayed back and forth over small distances in an agony of shells, machine guns, barbed wire, and mud, with frightful casualties on both sides.

There were various schools of high strategy among the Allies. To the French, fighting on their own soil, with their iron- and coal-producing areas in enemy hands, the Western Front seemed all-important. Many British soldiers agreed with them. Admiral Fisher, on the other hand, advocated an attack on the Baltic in an attempt to break through to Russia. This plan was abandoned as too dangerous. Lloyd George believed that a landing in the Balkans would gain allies and open a way into Austria. Winston Churchill, First Lord of the Admiralty, urged a drive through the Dardanelles to Constantinople, thus knocking Turkey out of the war and gaining access to the Black Sea. When this was attempted in 1915 it began as a naval operation; but the Turks had German advisers, the forts on the Dardanelles were strongly held, the Straits were mined, and the naval attack was a failure. A month later troops were landed on the Gallipoli Peninsula. With the element of surprise lost, only exposed beach heads could be occupied. The troops were withdrawn at the end of the year. Another defeat fell on the British in Mesopotamia. After enduring many privations the British forces there surrendered to the Turks in 1916.

Meanwhile the Western Front in 1915 was the scene of heavy fighting and severe British losses. British offensives at Neuve-Chapelle and at Festubert in March and in May, another battle at Ypres, and an offensive known as the Battle of Loos in September all resulted in more and more casualties without an appreciable gain against the German lines. Sir John French was replaced by Sir Douglas Haig as supreme commander. An obvious cause of British failures was a shortage of shells and other types of arms. The number of shells required was fantastic: in one battle the British used more than were used in the whole South African war. These reverses caused a Cabinet crisis in May 1915. Asquith remained in power but formed a coalition Cabinet which included a number of Conservatives and one member of the Labor party. A Ministry of Munitions was created and placed in the vigorous hands of

British cavalry in France. (A.P. Wide World Photos, Inc.)

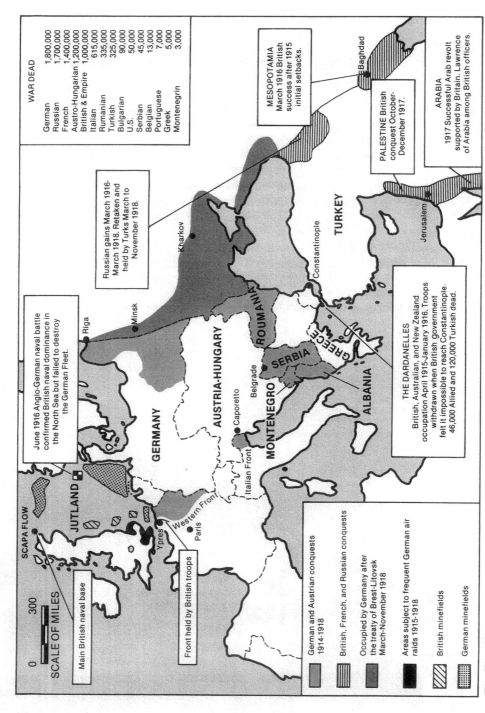

The First World War 1914–1918.

WAR DEAD

German	1,800,000
Russian	1,700,000
French	1,400,000
Austro-Hungarian	1,200,000
British & Empire	1,000,000
Italian	615,000
Rumanian	335,000
Turkish	325,000
Bulgarian	90,000
U.S.	50,000
Serbian	45,000
Belgian	13,000
Portuguese	7,000
Greek	5,000
Montenegrin	3,000

MESOPOTAMIA March 1916 British success after 1915 initial setbacks.

ARABIA 1917 Successful Arab revolt supported by Britain. Lawrence of Arabia among British officers.

PALESTINE British conquest October-December 1917.

Russian gains March 1916-March 1918. Retaken and held by Turks March to November 1918.

June 1916 Anglo-German naval battle confirmed British naval dominance in the North Sea but failed to destroy the German Fleet.

THE DARDANELLES British, Australian, and New Zealand occupation April 1915-January 1916. Troops withdrawn when British government felt it impossible to reach Constantinople. 46,000 Allied and 120,000 Turkish dead.

Baghdad

Jerusalem

TURKEY

Constantinople

Kharkov

Riga

Minsk

GERMANY

AUSTRIA-HUNGARY

ROUMANIA

SERBIA

GREECE

MONTENEGRO

ALBANIA

Belgrade

Caporetto

Italian Front

Western Front

Paris

Ypres

JUTLAND

SCAPA FLOW

SCALE OF MILES

0   300

Main British naval base

Front held by British troops

	German and Austrian conquests 1914-1918
	British, French, and Russian conquests
	Occupied by Germany after the treaty of Brest-Litovsk March-November 1918
	Areas subject to frequent German air raids 1915-1918
	British minefields
	German minefields

Lloyd George. Production of shells increased greatly, though it hardly affected the fighting in 1915.

The year 1916 brought new reverses. The Germans, deciding that Russia could be ignored, concentrated their power against the French lines at Verdun. France had already suffered 2 million casualties, and the Germans thought that she could now be crushed or at least bled white. For almost half a year the Battle of Verdun engaged the entire French army at a cost of some 350,000 casualties, but when the fighting slackened, Verdun was still in French possession. The British were naturally expected to relieve the pressure by opening an offensive on the western section of the front. This offensive, known as the Battle of the Somme, was thus a political necessity though a bad military risk because the Germans were well prepared to meet it. Still short of artillery, the British lost 60,000 men on the first day and some 410,000 before the offensive was abandoned. In return for this heavy loss of life they could show only an advance of six or seven miles along a thirty-mile front. Britain and the Western world had never experienced such catastrophic losses in war before. Nor would they in World War II. The people back home never understood what the men at the front went through. This lack of comprehension was to be an important factor in postwar readjustment.

The one naval engagement on a grand scale between the British and the German fleets was the Battle of Jutland in the North Sea in May 1916. This battle has been the subject of great controversy. There was natural disappointment that although the British fleet was superior (twenty-eight battleships and nine battle cruisers against sixteen battleships and five battle cruisers), the Germans not only escaped destruction but inflicted more damage than they received. But many answers can be given. The British losses occurred before the two main fleets were engaged; during their brief encounter the Germans were worsted and never tried again.

The net result of the battle was that the British hold on the North Sea was left intact though the Grand Fleet had to maintain its vigil and the British navy could continue its countless tasks. The Germans lost hope of defeating the British Grand Fleet.

The year 1917 brought tremendous developments and offered hope for the future, though the present was grim. In March the Revolution began in Russia, overthrowing the Czar and demoralizing the Russian armies. Their disintegration exposed the Allies to new dangers, for the Austrians were then able to send large numbers of troops to Italy. At Caporetto in October the Italians were defeated disastrously.

As Russia was leaving the war, the United States was entering it because of a change in German policy in the use of the submarine. During the first two years of the war the depredations of German submarines had not been great, nor did submarines normally sink vessels without warning. The sinking of the Cunard liner *Lusitania* in May 1915, with the loss of 100 American lives, brought a sharp protest from President Wilson, and the Germans agreed not to sink ships without warning. But at the beginning of 1917 the morale of the Germans was low. They had been fighting on many different fronts and their standard of living had suffered from the British blockade. In February 1917, therefore, the Germans decided to disregard neutral nations and to embark on unrestricted submarine warfare. It was more

The first British troops to cross the Rhine at Cologne, December 1918. (A.P. Wide World Photos, Inc.)

important, they thought, to strike fiercely at Britain than to keep the United States out of the war. Losses of British shipping rose ominously. In April these losses reached 875,000 tons, a rate that would soon have reduced England to starvation. Unrestricted submarine warfare, however, brought the United States into the war in April.

The Allies gradually learned how to fight submarines. The best protection for shipping was the convoy; the best method of detection was constant scouting by surface craft. The hydrophone was developed to pick up underwater sounds.[2] Toward the end of the war submarines were destroyed so rapidly that they averaged only about six trips each, a mortality rate which had a numbing effect on the crews. Nonetheless, submarines demanded a far greater effort on the part of the Allies in combating them than on the part of Germany in building them.

The year 1917 was a tragic one for the Allies in France. The Germans retired a short distance to new defenses, the Siegfried—or Hindenburg—line, which greatly strengthened their position. An overoptimistic offensive by the French General Nivelle ended in collapse. Nivelle was superseded by General Pétain, the commander at Verdun. Later in the year Haig launched an offensive at Passchendaele toward the coast of Flanders. This also failed.

British arms met better fortune in fightng the Turks. A new push up the Tigris and

[2]An even better sonar device, known as Asdic, was not invented until after the war was over.

Euphrates Valley captured Baghdad; and an invasion of the Holy Land from Egypt resulted in the capture of Jerusalem.

Early in 1918 the Germans opened a great offensive. Staking all on one desperate thrust, they gambled on cracking the Allies before the strength of America could be brought fully into play. The Treaty of Brest-Litovsk with the Bolsheviks not only ceded large sections of Russian territory to Germany but also liberated German troops to fight on the Western Front. The full fury of this offensive fell first on the British under Haig, who had his back to the wall but held on. In May the offensive shifted to the French, who retreated. Now was fought the second Battle of the Marne. Regarding Marshal Pétain, the French commander, as too pessimistic, Haig accepted General Foch as the supreme commander of all the forces on the Western Front. The German offensive came to a halt.

Therafter the Germans were on the verge of defeat. Bulgaria collapsed, Turkey surrendered, and Austria capitulated after a defeat of her armies in Italy. A mutiny broke out among the seamen in the German fleet. The armistice signed on 11 November brought the war to an end.

The Home Front

Criticism of the government was regarded as unpatriotic in the early days of the war. The leadership of Asquith's Cabinet—in which the war effort was directed by the prime minister, by Kitchener, and by Winston Churchill—was accepted loyally by all parties. But difficulties arose in May 1915 as a result of reverses in France. Kitchener came under criticism. His dual position as commander in chief and as secretary for war made for overcentralization. The shortage of shells and the quarrels between Churchill and Admiral Fisher over the Dardanelles campaign also caused adverse comment. The Conservatives under Bonar Law thereupon informed the prime minister that they would oppose the government unless Churchill and Haldane (who was thought to be sympathetic toward the Germans) were removed from office.

It was then that Asquith constructed the coalition Cabinet mentioned earlier. Grey and Kitchener retained their places, but Haldane was dropped and Churchill was relegated to minor office, while four Conservatives—Bonar Law, Carson, Balfour, and Lord Curzon—were brought into the Cabinet, as was also Arthur Henderson, the leader of the Labor party. Lloyd George was placed in charge of the new Ministry of Munitions to end the shortage of shells, a task in which he succeeded admirably. Hailed as the one man who could win the war, he found his prestige rising rapidly. When Kitchener was drowned at sea in June 1916, his place as secretary for war was given to Lloyd George.

But the coalition was not working smoothly. The Conservatives thought that the Liberals still held the key positions and that Liberal reluctance to interfere with the rights of private citizens hindered the war effort. The Liberals, for instance, opposed conscription. But voluntary enlistment no longer supplied the number of soldiers required; it had drained away the most idealistic young men and had sacrificed them

David Lloyd George, by W. Orpen. (National Portrait Gallery, London)

in the first years of the war. In January 1916 a Military Service Act, supported by the Conservatives as well as by Lloyd George, made all men under forty-one liable for service. An unexpected consequence to the act was the magnificent way in which British women stepped forward to perform all kinds of work formerly done by men, who now went to the front.

New criticism of the government arose in the autumn of 1916. It was directed as Asquith, who was thought to lack vigor and decisiveness. Lloyd George complained that the prime minister came to Cabinet meetings without a policy, listened to what was said, summed up the debate with admirable clarity, and then postponed decision. Some of the newspapers began to attack Asquith; Bonar Law joined the opposition. It was suggested to Asquith that he remain as prime minister but that the direction of the war be placed in the hands of a War Council headed by Lloyd George. After several days of confused intrigue Asquith resigned, convinced that Lloyd George had betrayed him. The result was a split in the Liberal party, some members following Asquith, some Lloyd George who, despite his arguments with Asquith, quickly combined the office of prime minister with the direction of the war effort.

Lloyd George created a small War Cabinet of five men—he himself (the only Liberal), Bonar Law, Milner, Curzon, and Arthur Henderson. Largely free from departmental duties, the Cabinet could devote itself almost entirely to the larger issues of the war. It was assisted by a Cabinet secretariat and by the innovation of keeping minutes of Cabinet meetings. The new prime minister was a remarkable man, combining resourcefulness, vigor, decision, and imagination with unusual administrative ability and great oratorical power. More than anyone else he was the organizer of victory. Unfortunately, he displayed a ruthlessness and a lack of loyalty to his colleagues which made him the object of distrust and suspicion.

At the beginning of the war the Cabinet encouraged the impression that business and ordinary civilian life should continue as usual. The war was to be conducted with as little interference as possible with private enterprise and personal liberty. But it became evident, as the war continued, that the state must exercise firm controls and that the war required a total mobilization of the country's resources, both human and material. The powers of the government over the economy steadily increased. A series of Defense of the Realm Acts (nicknamed DORA) gave the Cabinet power to issue general regulations for the public safety and to exercise broad controls over economic life. Lloyd George's vigorous administration of the Ministry of Munitions discarded trade-union rules, diluted skilled labor with unskilled male and female workers, limited war profits, outlawed strikes, and curtailed excessive drinking. Before the war was over the government was managing coal mines and all means of transport, determining the hours and wages of labor, and settling industrial disputes. The number of civil servants expanded into a large bureaucracy. As the submarine menace grew more dangerous, Lloyd George created new ministries of Food, of Blockade, of Pensions, and of Labor. The rationing of food was introduced early in 1918.

Women railway porters at Marylebone, 1915. (Mansell Collection)

Because goods and services were in short supply, inflation could not be avoided. It is thought that up to the end of 1917 prices rose at a rate of about 27 percent each year, though after that date further increases were slowed by controls of prices and wages and by heavy taxation. Even so, wholesale prices at the end of the war were about 140 percent above their prewar level; the pound had shrunk to about 8s. 3d. in purchasing power. The national debt rose to the astonishing figure of some £7 billion. Yet England paid the cost of the war more fully by current taxation than did most other nations. The income of the Exchequer was four times as high at the end of the war as at its beginning; large incomes were taxed at the rate of 6s. in the pound.[3]

The war was a profound emotional experience for every Briton. It began with a mood of exultation and idealism, shortly followed by bewilderment, and then by grim determination and dogged resolve. As the war continued month after month with little change in position on the Western Front there was a declining interest in following its details and a growing sense of agony at the appalling casualty lists. In many cases this agony was followed by bitterness and cynicism and by an utter loathing of that horrible thing called war. In the end there was exhaustion. Yet the British also had hope for better things; in Lloyd George's phrase, they longed for "a country fit for heroes to live in."

C H R O N O L O G Y

Social Reform and World War

1903	Women's Social and Political Union
1904	Entente Cordiale between Britain and France
1905	Balfour resigns; Campbell-Bannerman prime minister
1906	Liberal landslide; Trade Disputes Act; Workmen's Compensation Act; school meals; Algeciras Conference
1907	Anglo-Russian Treaty
1908	Old Age Pensions Bill; Asquith prime minister
1909	Labor Exchange Bill; eight Dreadnoughts ordered; "People's" Budget defeated; Morley-Minto Reforms (India); Triple Entente in place (Britain, France, and Russia)
1910	Liberals win two elections in one year; Death of Edward VIII; King George V

(continued on next page)

[3]These figures are taken from Henry Pelling, *Modern Britain 1885–1955* (Edinburgh: T. Nelson, 1960), pp. 81–82.

Chronology, continued

1911	Parliament Act; railway strike; National Insurance Act; Agadir Crisis
1912	Coal miners strike; Home Rule Bill introduced
1913	"Triple Alliance" formed (railway workers, miners, transport workers)
1914	Francis Ferdinand assassinated; World War I
1916	Verdun and the Somme; Battle of Jutland; Military Service Act; Asquith out; Lloyd George prime minister
1917	Russian Revolution; United States entered war; Jerusalem captured
1918	Second Battle of the Marne; the Armistice

33 Politics and Depression 1918–1931

The First World War was followed by a period of intense readjustment for Britain. More shattering than at first imagined, the war had disrupted Britain's foreign trade and had shaken her position as a world power. Britain had reduced her ownership of foreign investments by £300 million. Forty percent of the merchant fleet had been sunk. The war had severely weakened her economic base and she was a short-term debtor nation. It was followed by depression and unemployment and by difficulties in foreign and imperial affairs. At the end of the war the Labor party and large numbers of the working classes hoped for an advance toward socialistic goals. These hopes were disappointed. Yet by an interesting paradox, economic necessity forced Conservatives, who were in power most of the time, to do a number of things that looked toward socialism. Twice during this period the Labor party was in power. Though it was unable to accomplish much, this unique experiment in British democracy held significance for the future.

LLOYD GEORGE AND POSTWAR PROBLEMS

The Peace Treaties

Much of the government's time in 1919 was occupied by the Peace Conference at Paris, in which Lloyd George, assisted by British experts, played a major role. His mandate from the British electorate was to impose a harsh peace on the Germans, but he found himself mediating between the idealism of President Wilson, who stood for self-determination of peoples and for no annexations, and the realism of the French leader Clemenceau, who was interested primarily in the subjugation of

Germany and the exaction of heavy reparations. In return for a number of concessions, Wilson obtained support for the League of Nations—an idea which owed
much to British opinion. Germany was disarmed. Her army was limited to a force of
100,000 enlisted men; she was to have no military aircraft, no submarines, and no
battleships of more than 10,000 tons. The map of Europe was drawn anew. France
received Alsace-Lorraine and semipermanent posession of the Saar. A number of
new states appeared—Czechoslovakia, Yugoslavia, and Poland, with a corridor of
land extending to the Baltic and separating East Prussia from the rest of Germany.
Rumania, Greece, and Italy obtained additional territory; Bulgaria, Austria, and
Hungary were greatly reduced; the Turks lost their empire.

Britain's share, as usual, was colonial. Colonies were not given to her in complete
ownership, however, but as mandates under the League of Nations. The idea of a
mandate had been developed by various writers in the Labor party. Its principle was
that the League should assume responsibility for the welfare of colonial peoples, but
that the administration of colonies should be entrusted to individual powers under the
supervision of the League. By the end of the war a number of former German
colonies were in the possession of the British Dominions. The South Africans held
German Southwest Africa; the Australians, North-East New Guinea; and the New
Zealanders, Samoa. The Dominions were permitted to keep these areas as mandates
and to administer them as integral parts of their own territories. Great Britain
obtained a mandate over German East Africa (renamed Tanganyika) and over the
former Turkish possessions of Mesopotamia and Palestine.

The treaties concluded in Paris—Versailles for Germany; Saint-Germain for Austria; Trianon for Hungary; and Sevres for Turkey—left many questions unsettled,
and there followed a long series of international conferences in which Lloyd George
took a leading part. Yet in the end he failed to achieve a stable European settlement.
A major difficulty was that the Senate of the United States refused to ratify the treaty
with Germany and thus withdrew from all responsibility for the affairs of the
Continent. This action increased the desire of the British to withdraw also, but it
intensified the determination of the French to obtain some sort of security against
future German attack. France made alliances with the newly created states of
Europe as a protection against Germany.

Security was connected closely with reparations and war debts. It became evident
very quickly that the Germans would have to pay reparations in goods and not in
money. But German goods as reparations—German coal, for example—destroyed
the British market on the Continent and delayed Britain's economic recovery. Hence
Lloyd George began to urge a more lenient tone toward Germany. The French,
however, were adamant in demanding reparations. A serious rift appeared between
England and France, and the two countries ceased to cooperate in European policy.
France was interested in reparations partly because of her war debts to Britain and
to the United States. Britain could not afford to be generous. Of the £1740 million
she had loaned to her allies, £568 million loaned to czarist Russia were completely
lost, and she owed £842 million to the United States.[1] The United States insisted on

---

[1]These figures are taken from Henry Pelling, *Modern Britain 1885–1955* (Edinburgh: T. Nelson, 1960), pp. 88–89.

repayment. Under these circumstances Lloyd George struggled against increasing difficulties, his prestige diminished, and his fall from power in 1922 was imminent.

A conference on disarmament called by the United States and held in Washington, D.C., in 1921–1922 had some success. Clashes between the British and the French prevented any reduction in land forces. However, the United States proposed that all naval tonnage under construction be scrapped, that a naval holiday be established for the next ten years, and that the existing ratio between the five naval powers be kept at 5–5–3–1.75–1.75. This arrangement provided for parity between the United States and Britain, for a ratio of about sixty percent for Japan, and about thirty-five percent for Italy and France. The proposal was accepted by Britain, whose former naval supremacy thus was reduced to parity with that of the United States. The latter also persuaded Britain to abandon her alliance with Japan and to substitute for it a four-power treaty between the United States, Britain, France, and Japan to guarantee existing conditions in the Pacific.

Ireland

Soon after the end of the war Lloyd George had to face a new crisis in Ireland. An Irish Home Rule Bill, introduced by the Liberals in 1912, had become law in 1914, though its operation had been deferred until the end of hostilities. It was soon quite out of date. The Home Rule party of Parnell and John Redmond declined and was superseded by a much more radical movement known as Sinn Fein (We Ourselves), which demanded an independent Irish republic extending over the whole island. An army formed in southern Ireland was known as the Irish Volunteers. In 1916 the Sinn Feiners and the Volunteers rose against English rule in a rebellion known as the Easter Rising. This revolt was quickly suppressed. As a result, however, the movement for independence was seized by extremists when the British showed no mercy, executing the leaders, Patrick Pearse, James Connolly, Tom Clarke, and Sir Roger Casement. When Lloyd George held a general election in 1918, the Sinn Fein party swept Ireland, returning seventy-three members. These members refused to come to London. Instead, they met at Dublin (that is, twenty-six of them did; most of the others were in jail) and formed their own Parliament, the Dail Eireann. This body proclaimed the independence of Ireland and the establishment of an Irish republic. The Volunteers, organized by Michael Collins, became the Irish Republican Army. Other Irish leaders were Arthur Griffith, the founder of Sinn Fein; Cathal Brugha, a man who lived for fighting; and Eamon de Valera, the only one of the four to survive these desperate times. His survival may have been due in part to Britain's diplomatic ties with the United States—de Valera's mother was an American.

Soon a state of war existed between the Irish Republican Army and the Royal Irish Constabulary, a government police force hastily strengthened by new recruits who wore khaki uniforms and black helmets and who were nicknamed the Black and Tans. They lacked the discipline of trained police. Both sides soon were committing barbarities—assassinations, ambushes, tortures, and kidnappings—which shocked the world. A turn for the better came in 1921, when King George V in a speech at

Belfast pleaded for an end of hostilites and for a negotiated settlement. In a prolonged series of conferences between Lloyd George and the Irish leaders, Lloyd George offered southern Ireland the status of a dominion (the Irish Free State) whose only link with England would be an oath of allegiance to the Crown. This arrangement was accepted by Collins and Griffith. De Valera, on the other hand, demanded a republic, denounced allegiance to the Crown, and approved only of some vague external connection with the empire. A new civil war broke out between the two wings of the Sinn Fein party. Having recognized the Irish Free State in 1922, England left the Irish to fight among themselves. In the following year De Valera decided to resist no longer, though he did not abandon his ideas. In 1949 southern Ireland became a republic. Ulster remained a part of the United Kingdom of Great Britain and Northern Ireland.

The Election of 1918

Meanwhile, in December 1918, a few weeks after the ending of the war, Lloyd George held an election. Wishing to remain in office, he proposed a continuation of the coalition which had brought the war to a successful close. The Labor party, however, withdrew from the coalition, and Lloyd George was unable to make peace with the official Liberal party under Asquith. He therefore sought the support of the Conservatives and of those Liberals who had continued to follow him. His colleagues in the War Cabinet were Conservatives; he had no party machinery of his own. As a result, some 400 Conservative candidates stood for election, but only about 140 Lloyd George Liberals. All coalition candidates were given a written endorsement signed both by Lloyd George and by Bonar Law, the leader of the Conservative party. Asquith contemptuously called this endorsement a "coupon" or ration ticket, and the election became known as the "coupon" election. Lloyd George offered an attractive program of reconstruction, but the election was fought in an emotional atmosphere in which revenge on Germany was the dominant note. The result was a sweeping victory for the coalition. It was returned with 484 seats in the Commons, of which 338 were held by Conservatives and 136 by Lloyd George Liberals. Labor won 59 seats, the Asquith Liberals only 26. The 73 Irish members, as we have seen, refused to come to London.

There were many important aspects of this election. One was the shattering of the Liberal party. It had been weakened before the war by the violence connnected with Ulster and with other issues, and the split between Lloyd George and Asquith in 1916 weakened it further. In 1918 the continuation of that split was fatal. The Liberals came back with less than half their former strength, and that half was itself divided. Moreover, the rise of the Labor party deprived them of radical support. As their position as a middle party became less and less tenable, they gradually sank to a position of insignificance. Although Labor increased its strength only from forty-two to fifty-nine members, its gain in popular votes was far greater than these figures suggest. The Conservatives, of course, came back in great numbers. They were to be the dominant party for the next twenty years. Their victory placed Lloyd George in a precarious position, for they could dispense with him at any time and form a Conservative government with a majority in the Commons. His actions afterwards often reflected this uncertain state.

The election, however, had a deeper meaning: it emphasized a new alignment in political life. In the nineteenth and early twentieth centuries Liberals and Conservatives had been largely drawn from the same social classes. They looked alike and fundamentally they thought alike. But now at the end of the war there was a marked distinction between Conservative and Labor members. It was the difference between the right and the left, based on economics and on class distinctions. The Conservatives in the new House of Commons contained many successful businessmen, directors of corporations, and leaders in commerce and finance. The remark that they were "hard-faced men who looked as if they had done well out of the war" was unjust but contained an element of truth. They thought in terms of capitalism and private enterprise, of the maintenance of the gold standard, of tariffs for the protection of British industry. Proud of the empire, distrusting the masses and distrusting the Labor party, they wished a minimum of state control. In foreign policy they wished to withdraw from continental commitments, to give the League of Nations only limited support, and to stabilize Europe in order to increase trade. Naturally, they were deeply suspicious of Russia and hostile to communism.

The left, on the other hand, drew its strength from the great mass of workers, from trade unions and socialistic societies, and from dissatisfied Liberals, who now joined the Labor party. The left was composed of men of various shades of socialism. In 1918 the Labor party drew up a new constitution which committed its members to socialistic objectives, though in moderate form. Its aims were

> to secure for the producers by hand and by brain the full fruits of their industry, and the most equitable distribution thereof that may be possible, upon the basis of the common ownership of the means of production and the best obtainable system of popular administration and control of each industry and service.[2]

The left thus registered its opposition to capitalism. It wished to nationalize key industries, it opposed the gold standard, and it advocated an ambitious housing program and an extension of old-age pensions and national insurance. In foreign affairs the left supported the League of Nations and the concept of collective security; it also stood for disarmament. Toward Russia its tone was friendly though cautious. Hostile to imperialism, it sympathized with India's national aspirations. This moderate socialism should not be regarded as revolutionary, for the vast majority of the members of the Labor party assumed that their objectives would be attained through the normal process of parliamentary legislation. There was an element that favored direct action in the form of a general strike, but the party as a whole was moderate; it rejected affiliation with the small group of British Communists.

Nonetheless, to many workers the time seemed ripe for an advance toward socialistic goals. The war had given workingmen a new confidence in themselves and in their unions. Labor leaders had gained political experience both as members of the

---

[2]Quoted in Charles Loch Mowatt, *Britain between the Wars 1918–1940* (Chicago: University of Chicago Press, 1955), p. 18.

War Cabinet and as spokesmen for the opposition. After the war the Trades Union Congress, which met only once a year, established a general council to direct policy between the annual meetings; the party's new constitution, drawn up in 1918, made it a national party that might in time attract middle-class support. Though Labor leaders might already regard the Russians with some skepticism, the Russian Revolution was still an inspiration to the rank and file. The war, moreover, had seen a vast extension of government controls. New ministries had been established; the civil service had greatly expanded; and a Ministry of Reconstruction, created in 1917, had made voluminous reports. Thus the machinery of the state was fully adequate for an extension of a socialistic or collectivist program.

Lloyd George and Labor

Lloyd George, however, though he had once been a radical, was now surrounded by Conservative colleagues who opposed an extension of the activities of the state or any move toward nationalization. On the contrary, they wanted decontrol, and Lloyd George yielded to this demand. Wartime restrictions were permitted to lapse, factories and surplus commodities were sold, and rationing was ended. The production of electric power was placed under the loose supervision of a government board. The railways were returned to private companies. In dealing with labor unrest Lloyd George appeared to be playing for time. In February 1919 he summoned a National Industrial Conference attended by employers and trade-union representatives. Lloyd George sent a message saying that he would listen sympathetically to labor's grievances, and there was high hope that the conference would open a new chapter in the relations of labor and management. But once the conference ended, nothing more was accomplished.

Lloyd George's greatest difficulty was with the coal miners, who expected that after the war the coal industry would be nationalized and that their working conditions would be improved. When the government took no action, they threatened to strike in 1919. Thereupon Lloyd George persuaded the labor leaders to postpone the strike while a royal commission—the Sankey Commission—investigated the industry. The commission recommended nationalization, but the government, rejecting this solution, kept the industry under temporary control and appeased the miners by wage increases. Trouble was merely postponed until 1921, when the situation had altered completely. A short business boom following the war had ended during 1920, after which date the continental market for British coal collapsed and the industry was in a serious depression. With heavy losses imminent, the Cabinet hurried coal mining back to private operators, who could not make ends meet without a reduction in wages. In their strike in 1921 the miners called on their allies, the railway and transport unions, to support them by a sympathy strike, but these unions refused. The miners, thus left alone, went down to bitter defeat and were forced to accept lower wages.

Lloyd George's government extended the social services in two directions. The first was housing. There had been very little building during the war, and it was estimated that 800,000 new houses were required. An act of 1919 provided subsidies through which some 200,000 houses were built in the next four years, and the principle was established that housing was a concern of the state. An Unemployment Insurance Act of 1920 extended benefits to some 12 million workers, whereas the former law had covered only about 4 million. Small contributions, as before, were made by the worker, the employer, and the government; benefits covered fifteen weeks of continuous unemployment in any one year.

Losses in Foreign Trade

After the collapse of the boom in 1920, a long depression settled on Britain. Even before the war, as we have seen, her share of world trade had been diminishing; the war accelerated this tendency. While Britain was intent on war production, foreign competitors, especially the neutral nations, pressed into her old markets. Underdeveloped countries, unable to buy goods from Britain as they had formerly done, began to develop their own manufacturers. In the years after the war, Britain found that she was selling much less to Russia than before 1914 and that the important German market had all but collapsed because of Germany's poverty. Italy, developing her hydroelectric potential, ceased to import large quantities of British coal. The newly created countries of Europe eagerly expanded their industries; the United States not only competed with Britain but raised tariffs against her. Moreover, the staple British exports—coal, textiles, iron, and steel—were losing their former position in international trade. British exports of coal declined from eighty-two million tons in 1907 to seventy million in 1930; her exports of cotton cloth from an annual value of £105 million to £86 million. Her foreign trade in the 1920s was no more than eighty percent of its former value.

The result was widespread unemployment. It was worst in the shipbuilding industry along the Clyde, in the area of Newcastle, in Lancashire, and in the coal fields of South Wales. During the decade before the war, unemployment had averaged 4.5 percent of the labor force; in 1921, when 2 million persons were unemployed, the figure reached 22.4 percent; for the next ten years it averaged 10 to 12 percent.

The sudden slump in 1920 caused a great outcry for economy in the expenditures of the government and for a reduction of taxation. To answer these demands the Cabinet in 1921 appointed a committee of business leaders to suggest economies; but the committee, headed by Sir Eric Geddes, recommended such drastic reductions that the government itself was aghast. The "Geddes ax" would have crippled the normal functioning of the state. Its suggested economies were only partially carried out, though even so there were sharp reductions in expenditures. At the same time the government raised interest rates. The result was a deflation which discouraged business and depressed the entire economy. Nor did a few cautious moves toward a protective tariff or a slight reduction of taxation make matters better.

Indeed, Britain would have faced an impossible situation if certain things had not helped her. She enjoyed so-called favorable terms of trade. This meant that agricultural products and other raw materials were cheap in the years following the war, while manufactured articles were expensive, so that British exports of manufactured goods brought a high price in relation to the cost of imported raw materials. Britain also possessed certain invisible exports. She retained about three-fourths of her prewar investments overseas, and although she was unable to increase them, they brought her handsome dividends. London continued to be a world center of insurance, shipping, and international exchange. The city could still perform many services for foreign customers. It was to retain these customers that Britain clung to the gold standard, although these measures kept her exports high in price and low in volume.

The Fall of Lloyd George

The fall of Lloyd George in 1922 was partly the result of a revolt against him by the rank and file of Conservative members and partly the result of the Chanak crisis. Lloyd George was a man who was either admired or detested. His extraordinary cleverness, his promptness in decision and action, his occasional ruthlessness, and his lack of loyalty to his colleagues inspired some men and alienated others. He was supported by the leaders of the coalition—by Austen Chamberlain, Arthur Balfour, Lord Birkenhead, Winston Churchill, and, for a long time, Bonar Law. On the other hand, most of the Conservatives disliked him intensely. He was so clever that he was not trusted. He was accused of minor corruption in bestowing honors on wealthy men who contributed to his Liberal party chest. His solution of the Irish question irritated Conservatives, who had fought home rule all their lives. They wanted a protective tariff, which Lloyd George opposed for fear of losing Liberal support.

The Chanak crisis in 1922, which might have led to a war with Turkey, further alienated Conservatives. Although a portion of Turkish Anatolia had been awarded to the Greeks after the war, the Turks, under their national leader, Mustapha Kemal, turned on the Greeks and drove them out. In this affair the Conservatives were pro-Turkish; Lloyd George, pro-Greek. It was said that Lloyd George would destroy the Conservative party as he had destroyed the Liberals. This fear turned Bonar Law against him. At a famous meeting of the Conservative parliamentary party at the Carlton Club in October 1922—despite the pleadings of Austen Chamberlain and Arthur Balfour—the Conservatives voted to withdraw from the coalition; Lloyd George resigned that afternoon. After his interview with George V the king remarked, "He will be prime minister again." But he never was. He remained in the Commons for many years, admired but out of office. The men who succeeded him as prime minister were less likely to inspire hostility.

THE CONSERVATIVES IN POWER, 1922–1924

The fall of the coalition restored the pattern of three political parties functioning independently. But divisions and anomalies remained, and it was several years before any one strong and united party held a long tenure of office. Bonar Law formed a Conservative Cabinet, but some of the ministers of the late coalition—Lord Birkenhead, Austen Chamberlain, and Arthur Balfour—angry at the way in which the coalition had been dissolved, refused to join the new government. Thus Conservative leadership was divided; and a number of younger men, such as Stanley Baldwin, secured high office and established themselves so firmly in the party hierarchy that they never were dislodged. Bonar Law held an election in November 1922. The Conservatives won 347 seats in the Commons, the Asquith Liberals 60, the Lloyd George Liberals 57, Labor 142. The Liberals remained divided, while Labor, increasing its strength from 59 to 142 members, became the second largest party in the Commons.

Bonar Law's Cabinet, with Lord Curzon as foreign secretary, was more concerned with foreign than with domestic problems. At a conference at Lausanne, Curzon secured a new treaty with the Turks following the Chanak crisis. He also had to deal with Germany and France during the French occupation of the Ruhr—the desperate effort of the French to secure payment of reparations after the Germans defaulted. The French occupation of the Ruhr revealed a sharp division of policy: France was determined to obtain reparations; Britain wanted to restore the German economy in the hope of creating a better market for her exports. Curzon's attempted mediation led in time to a new approach to the problem of reparations, a new plan of payment (the Dawes Plan), and an American loan to Germany. Reparations were closely linked with war debts. In 1923 Baldwin, then chancellor of the Exchequer, and Montagu Norman, the governor of the Bank of England, visited the United States to negotiate a settlement of Britain's enormous debt. The best they could obtain was an arrangement for payment over a period of sixty-one years at interest of three percent for the first ten years and 3.5 percent thereafter. The attitude of the United States was neither generous nor wise.

In May 1923 Bonar Law resigned because of ill health. He died in October. A man of integrity and with a high sense of duty, he was narrow, uninterested in ideas, and unable to inspire devotion. His opponents thought that he worshipped nothing but success. The selection of the next prime minister lay between Stanley Baldwin and Lord Curzon. Baldwin, a wealthy industrialist and country gentleman, was a newcomer to high office whose character was as yet obscure, though he was obviously conciliatory, friendly, and moderate. Curzon, on the other hand, was a brilliant man who had had a brilliant career. He had been viceroy of India, he had been a member of the War Cabinet, he was now foreign secretary, deputy prime minister, and Conservative leader in the House of Lords. He had every reason to assume that he would be Bonar Law's successor. However, he was a peer. Leading Conservatives advised the king that the prime minister must be in the Commons; hence the king sent for Baldwin and not for Curzon. Curzon was stunned. He praised Baldwin in public, saying that he possessed many merits, among them the "supreme and indispensable qualification of not being a peer."

Baldwin remained in office only from May 1923 to January 1924. His principal aim was to unite the Conservative party. To appease Austen Chamberlain he appointed Austen's younger brother, Neville Chamberlain, as chancellor of the Exchequer. When Baldwin announced his conversion to a protective tariff the country was taken by surprise. The Conservatives united and rallied behind their leader, but Liberal and Labor members joined in strong opposition. Controversy became so heated that Baldwin held an election in December 1923. The Conservatives came back with 258 seats in the Commons (as opposed to 346 before the election); the two wings of Liberals, with 158; and Labor, with a great advance to 191. Though Baldwin's strategy was to be triumphant in the end, it began with an electoral defeat.

THE FIRST LABOR GOVERNMENT, JANUARY TO NOVEMBER 1924

It was not at first clear what kind of government would follow the election of 1923. The Conservatives were the largest single party in the Commons. But the country had rejected protection; Labor was the strongest antiprotection party and with Liberal support could outvote the Conservatives. Hence the possibility arose of the formation of a Labor cabinet. Some politicians wished to exclude Labor at all costs. The city of London professed great alarm at the prospect of a socialist government. Wild predictions were made of the dire results of Labor rule; it was suggested that Labor might break down the bonds of marriage and give official sanction to immorality. Despite the furor, however, it was clear that Labor could never assume office under safer conditions than those which then existed. Labor would be helpless without Liberal support. It would be too weak to do much harm, as Neville Chamberlain remarked, but not too weak to be discredited. Asquith decided that the Liberals would support a Labor government and thus give it a temporary majority. The Labor leaders, for their part, felt that to refuse office would be to acknowledge incompetence. Hence, when Baldwin was defeated by a combination of Labor and Liberal votes, he resigned, and the king called upon Ramsay MacDonald to form a Cabinet. The king noted in his diary: "Today 23 years ago dear Grandmama died. I wonder what she would have thought of a Labor government."

As an experiment in politics, Labor's first tenure of power was highly interesting. MacDonald had some difficulty in forming his Cabinet. His initial choice of J. H. Thomas, a former locomotive engineer, genial, easygoing, and somewhat given to profanity, as foreign secretary was killed by the ridicule of the press. MacDonald became his own foreign secretary; Thomas accepted the Colonial Office. Philip Snowden, a weaver's son, a keen debater with a very sharp tongue, was made chancellor of the Exchequer. Other ministers included Arthur Henderson, the son of a Glasgow cotton spinner; J. R. Clynes, who once worked in a cotton mill; and the radicals John Wheatley and F. W. Jowett. MacDonald brought in two men from outside the party, Lord Haldane as lord chancellor, and Lord Chelmsford, once viceroy of India, as first lord of the Admiralty. On the whole, it was a moderate Cabinet, which reassured the country.

A Labor member remarked, "At any rate we have the handsomest of all prime ministers." MacDonald's fine face, brilliant eye, and noble presence gave him an aristocratic appearance. His pride and courage confirmed the impression. He was master of an emotional, poetic eloquence. But his weaknesses were obvious.

Ramsay
MacDonald.
(National Portrait
Gallery, London)

"Gentleman Mac" was never popular with trade union leaders, toward whom he was rather distant. Far too sensitive to criticism, jealous, given to intrigue, under heavy pressure he was prone to make sudden decisions that were too drastic and were often irrevocable. Very much the moderate, he was determined to tame the wild men of his party and to make the party respectable. MacDonald believed that socialism could come only through evolution and only with the consent of the majority of the people.

The atmosphere of the House of Commons quickly tamed the wild members. The first visit of the ministers to Buckingham Palace to receive their seals of office was a unique occasion. The king was genial and friendly and put the ministers at their ease. Some Labor members were astonished that "Wheatly—the revolutionary—went down on both knees and actually kissed the king's hand," but the majority of workingmen took pride in seeing their own people moving in such exalted circles. Despite some snobbery, many members of the Commons were friendly and conciliatory toward the new ministers, who were invited to social functions. The "aristocratic embrace," the willingness of politicians to accept the Labor Cabinet, was much in evidence, and the Labor members liked it.

The achievements of the first Labor government were necessarily limited. Most of the new ministers were without experience in office and had much to learn. It was obvious they dared not offend the Liberals. An unexpected bar to socialistic experiment was the rigid orthodoxy of Philip Snowden's budget, which provided no surplus funds to spend on public works in an effort to relieve unemployment. Labor, like the Conservatives before them, failed to solve the problem posed by the unemployed. But the Cabinet improved the social services, liberalized unemployment insurance, and passed an excellent housing bill which provided houses that were within the means of the working classes.

The government was also successful in foreign policy. MacDonald helped to initiate the Dawes Plan for the payment of German reparations, improved Franco-German relations, and arranged for the French withdrawal from the Ruhr. At the League of Nations, Labor ministers supported the Geneva Protocol, which provided

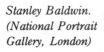

Stanley Baldwin. (National Portrait Gallery, London)

for the compulsory arbitration of international disputes. Wishing to draw closer to Russia, the Cabinet recognized the Soviet Union, concluded a commercial treaty with Russia, and provided the Russians with a British loan. These actions were bitterly opposed by the Conservatives, who raised a furor over the case of a British Communist, J. R. Campbell, the author of an article that appeared to incite mutiny in the army. The Conservatives, accusing the government of leniency toward communism, called for a vote of censure. Rather surprisingly, MacDonald announced that he would regard the vote as a vote of confidence. He demanded all or nothing but was defeated, and thereupon dissolved Parliament in October 1924. A few days before the election the *Times* published a letter supposedly from a Russian leader, Zinoviev, to the British Communist party outlining a plan for revolution. This letter counted heavily against Labor in the election. The conservatives returned with an enormous majority, winning 414 seats, whereas Labor won only 151 and the Liberals only 42. For the first time since the war a political party came into power with the overwhelming support of the people. The defeat of Labor was temporary, but the Liberals were shattered beyond repair.

BALDWIN'S SECOND MINISTRY, 1924–1929

Baldwin's second ministry lasted from 1924 to 1929, the full five years permitted by law without an election. During these years his prestige was high. He created an image of himself as a plain, sensible man who expressed simple ideas in simple words that everyone could understand, an honest country gentleman who loved rural life and enjoyed nothing better than gazing fondly at his pigs. This image was a pose, for Baldwin was an able politician who healed the divisions in his party, handled crises well, won the confidence of the nation, and showed that on occasion he could fight. He had no policy beyond moderation and good will. He wished to soften the clash of capital and labor and to maintain a balanced and harmonious society; he sought stability and respose. To his discredit, however, Baldwin was a lazy man who disliked business, who hated to make decisions, who could fight in a crisis but sought to delay fighting as long as possible.

Baldwin's Cabinet included Austen Chamberlain, Lord Birkenhead, and later Arthur Balfour. Their presence in the Cabinet healed the breach in Conservative ranks and strengthened the party. Baldwin also invited Winston Churchill to become chancellor of the Exchequer.

In foreign affairs, with Austen Chamberlain as foreign secretary, the Conservatives undid much of the work of the Labor government. The treaties with Russia were abandoned; in 1927 diplomatic relations with Russia were broken off. The Geneva Protocol was rejected, though Chamberlain pursued an alternate policy of bringing Germany into the orbit of nations without disturbing the French insistence on security. Chamberlain secured the Locarno Pact of 1925 which guaranteed the Franco-German frontier. The Rhineland was demilitarized; Germany and France agreed not to make war on each other but to settle their differences through arbitration; and Germany was admitted to the League of Nations. A better spirit prevailed for a time in international affairs.

In 1925 Britain returned to the gold standard at prewar parity, which meant that the pound was raised to its old value of $4.86.[3] This action represented the climax of Britain's attempt to return to conditions existing before the war. The hope was to enhance the position of London as a financial and commercial center and to increase its business with foreign customers, but the result was disappointing: the price of British exports was pitched too high for the world market. As a result of the world depression, Britain abandoned gold in 1931.

The General Strike

The most dramatic event of these years was the general strike in 1926. This strike, though often described as the climax of labor unrest following the war, in reality took place after the crisis was over. By 1926 labor was moving away from the militant socialism of the first postwar years. The leaders of the labor movement— MacDonald, Henderson, J. H. Thomas, and Ernest Bevin—were moderate men who wished to quell the zeal of left-wing elements. These elements, however, remained among the rank and file. For a moment in 1926 they gained the upper hand and precipitated the general strike. Once the strike was over, the labor movement as a whole returned to a moderate course. The strike was really a sympathy strike in support of the coal miners, though it was organized on so extensive a scale as to be called a general strike.

The coal-mining industry, as we have seen, had been depressed since the end of the war. It fell into new difficulties when the French evacuated the Ruhr, thus increasing the continental output of coal, and when Britain returned to the prewar gold standard. The operators declared that a slight increase in wages since 1921 would have to be abandoned. The miners threatened to strike and were strongly supported by the powerful general council of the Trades Union Congress. A widespread strike, involving many workers besides the miners, seemed likely. In order to gain time, as Lloyd George had done, Baldwin appointed a new commission, headed by Sir Herbert Samuel, to investigate the coal industry. Reporting in March 1926, this commission accepted a number of reforms suggested by the miners but rejected a policy of government subsidies to keep the industry afloat. This meant that either wages would have to be temporarily reduced or else the working day made longer. The miners stood firm: "Not a penny off the pay, not a minute on the day." The strike began on 4 May 1926. Some three million workers—miners; railway workers; transport workers; dockers; printers; workmen in steel, chemical, and power plants; and men in the building industries—went on strike.

Very few had revolution in mind, but the government assumed they did. Police and soldiers were used to protect volunteer workers, to convoy food, and to keep essential services in operation. Baldwin declared that the strike was unconstitutional. He was supported by Sir John Simon, a distinguished lawyer who asserted in the

---

[3]An act of 1920, which had prohibited the export of gold, was now allowed to lapse.

Commons that the strike was illegal and that its leaders were liable for damages. These statements frightened the general council of the Trades Union Congress. The council, already nervous lest the strike get out of control, began to seek an excuse for bringing it to an end. When Sir Herbert Samuel suggested that reduction of miner's wages be postponed until the recommendations of his commission had been put into effect, the council grasped at the proposal and ended the strike after nine days, though no agreement with the Cabinet had been reached. In a word, the council surrendered. Many workers felt they had been betrayed. The coal strike ended in total defeat, with lowered wages and much unemployment.

The collapse of the strike was a personal triumph for Baldwin, but in the years that followed he did very little either to relieve the miners, many of whom fell into a wretched state, or to attack the broader problem of unemployment. The Trades Dispute Act passed in 1927 outlawed the general strike as well as sympathy strikes. Workers would no longer be required to contribute to the Labor Party through their unions without the workers' specific consent. Baldwin had not sought this statute but did acquiesce in its passage.

There was some advance in the social services during this period, thanks to Neville Chamberlain, minister of health, and to Winston Churchill, chancellor of the Exchequer. An act in 1925 provided allowances for widows and orphaned children and enabled a worker who made contributions to obtain a pension at sixty-five instead of at seventy. In 1927 a new act for insurance against unemployment lowered both contributions and benefits in an effort to extend the length of time during which benefits could be paid. The act was a move away from insurance to a policy of assistance based on need, for widespread and continuous unemployment was undermining the principle of true insurance. A Local Government Act in 1929 abolished the system of local guardians of the poor and transferred their powers to the county councils.

The Election of 1929

Baldwin held an election in 1929. His prestige was now somewhat tarnished because of his failure to improve the economy, though he seemed to believe that the Conservatives were assured of victory. Both the Liberals and the Labor party made strenuous preparations for the electoral campaign. Lloyd George, with the aid of an able economist, J. M. Keynes, set forth a broad program of public works and economic planning to relieve unemployment and to make better use of surplus captial. The Labor party proposed to increase unemployment benefits, extend other social services, nationalize a number of industries, and lessen British imperial commitments. In the election that followed, Labor won 289 seats, the Conservatives 260, and the Liberals only 58. Labor, for the first time, was the strongest party in the Commons. The Conservatives suffered a severe though not a crushing defeat. On the other hand, the slight gain made by the Liberals was in reality a reverse in view of the efforts Lloyd George had been making: his attempt to revive the Liberal party had failed.

THE GREAT DEPRESSION

Ramsay MacDonald, now prime minister for the second time, formed a Cabinet which remained in office from June 1929 to August 1931. Of the nineteen ministers who had served in his first government, twelve reappeared in his second, with most of the radicals excluded. Snowden returned as chancellor of the Exchequer, Arthur Henderson became foreign secretary, J. H. Thomas was assigned the task of dealing with unemployment. Among the newcomers was Miss Margaret Bondfield, minister of labor, the first woman to be a member of a British Cabinet.

The government announced a broad and attractive program of legislation to relieve unemployment and to improve other aspects of the economy. Unhappily, Britain was shortly engulfed in a world depression touched off by a crash on the New York Stock Exchange in the autumn of 1929. Trouble spread quickly from the United States to the Continent and then to Britain. Foreign trade declined and unemployment mounted. The figures of unemployment, which had stood at 1,200,000 when Mac-Donald assumed office, rose to 1,600,000 in March 1930 and to the staggering figure of 2,500,000 by December of that year. The Cabinet appeared to be paralyzed by this disaster. It took no decisive action, nor did it carry through the program it had announced when it came into power. MacDonald, whose enthusiasm for socialism had long since waned, made his weak position in the Commons an excuse for doing nothing. Snowden's finance remained rigidly orthodox, avoiding all heroic measures. J. H. Thomas failed miserably in dealing with unemployment. Meanwhile, the funds available for the relief of unemployment were exhausted, so that the Cabinet was faced with a large deficit.

A crisis arose in August 1931. As the financial position of the government steadily worsened, Snowden had appointed a committee in March under Sir George May, a businessman prominent in insurance, to suggest economies. His report, issued on 31 July, called for drastic reductions in expenditures, including smaller benefits for the unemployed. This report precipitated a run on sterling by Britain's foreign creditors. To meet the emergency, Britain would have to borrow heavily in New York and Paris. Foreign bankers, however, hesitated to lend money until they were assured that the recommendations of May's committee would be carried out. Their hesitation caused a crisis in the Cabinet. A number of ministers refused to sanction cuts in unemployment benefits, and MacDonald warned the king that unless the Cabinet could agree he would have to resign.

Faced with the possibility of MacDonald's resignation, the king consulted with the leaders of other parties: with Baldwin for the Conservatives, and with Sir Herbert Samuel, who spoke for the Liberals during an illness of Lloyd George. They made various suggestions, but both agreed to serve in a coalition or National Cabinet under MacDonald. The king then summoned MacDonald, Baldwin, and Samuel; the resolution was taken to form such a government. Returning to an awkward interview with the Labor ministers, MacDonald informed them that the Labor Cabinet was at an end, that they were no longer in office, but that he was to remain as the head of a National government. He asked them whether they would follow him into a coalition with Conservatives and Liberals. Only three agreed to do so. The Labor party, astounded as these events, repudiated MacDonald and went into opposition.

Much controversy has raged around this crisis. Labor members have regarded it as a plot to drive them from power. This belief appears to be unfounded. Yet MacDonald should have consulted his Labor colleagues before consenting to form a new Cabinet; certainly he did not treat them with frankness. The question has also been raised as to whether King George, impelled by a sense of urgency, was more active than a constitutional monarch should have been in promoting the formation of a national government. One should add that these events were infinitely more complex than any brief sketch can indicate. One can only speculate as to the secret motives of public figures acting under great pressure.

Credits were obtained in New York and Paris, and the financial crisis passed, but Britain was forced to abandon the gold standard in September. The pound sank to a dollar value of about $3.40.

SOCIETY IN THE 1920s

Social conditions in the 1920s were naturally very different from those before the war. Indeed, the danger is that one may see nothing but change and may miss the evidence of continuity from an earlier period and the stability of an older social order. Many of the changes in the 1920s were in manners and fashions and in the uses of a new technology rather than in the basic structure of English society.

The population of Great Britain increased slowly from 40,831,000 in 1911 to 44,795,000 in 1931. The greatest growth was in London and in the counties of southeastern England. Since many of the newer industries were located in this area, it attracted population from other parts of the country, from the northern and eastern counties, from the Midlands, and from Wales. This was a process that has continued to the present day and will probably continue in the future. Britain was more urban than ever. In 1931 only about one-fifth of the people lived in the country. The number of women in the population was greater than that of men, though the ratio was closer than it had been at the end of the war. Due to a declining birth rate, the proportion of persons over sixty-five years of age had increased. The sufferings and the awful wastage of war were keenly felt in the years following the peace. Men who had been maimed or crippled, widows left to rear fatherless children, young women who had lost their fiancées, shortages, rationing, and restraints, industrial unrest—all underlined the price that had been paid for victory.

The upper and middle classes, of course, continued to dominate politics and to fill the higher positions in the civil service, in business, and in the professions. Although fashionable society was not as glittering as before the war, its gatherings in London and at sporting events began to be chronicled by the press once more. The nobility, which numbered 708 persons in 1923, had been augmented by 176 creations since 1910. It was true that after the war a good many country houses were sold and large estates broken up; taxes and death duties redistributed wealth and property.

Nonetheless, the aristocracy remained a wealthy class, and a new plutocracy, often enriched by the war, was seeking admission to society. A similar story can be told of the middle classes. Prices had risen much faster than salaries and inflation had sharply diminished the value of prewar savings. Some members of the middle classes called themselves the new poor. But this was an exaggeration. The middle classes continued to send their children to expensive private schools. There was no great change in the percentage of the national income that went to various classes of society.

Class distinction and inequality of opportunity were perpetuated by the educational system. The upper and middle classes sent their children to the public schools; these were boarding schools and were in fact very private, exclusive, and costly. Attendance at a public school, followed by a university education, was the first and essential step in a career of importance. The education of the working classes in the publicly supported elementary and secondary schools was quite another matter. In the early 1920s, despite hope from an education act of 1918, only some twelve percent of the children leaving the elementary schools continued full time in secondary education, and only a few more than four in every one thousand attended a university. Attendance in school was compulsory until the age of fourteen. An important step was taken, as the result of the Hadow Report, in 1926. Children were sorted out according to their skills and abilities at the age of eleven and were placed in one of three types of secondary schools: grammar schools that prepared them for university work; technical schools; or so-called modern schools that gave a rounded education combining features of the other two. But the government provided so few university scholarships that the number of ex-elementary school children who obtained a university education was microscopic. By 1931 some thirty thousand students were attending British universities.

A generation gap existed in the 1920s. The older generation, still very much in control, was followed by an appalling gap among the men who had done the fighting. The next generation, which came of age after 1918, was inclined to go its own way and to set its own standards of thought and conduct. Typical of this set was the emanicipated young woman—the "flapper"—who supported herself in London as a secretary or a salesgirl and who attended lively parties, smoked cigarettes and drank cocktails, and talked about sex with some freedom. Dancing to jazz music from America was popular. These uninhibited young people gave an impression of reckless gaiety that did not represent society as a whole.

The flapper was a step in the emancipation of women. The movement for woman suffrage before the war had grown so militant that the public had turned against it. But the response of women to the call of duty during the war years had been so magnificent that in 1918 they were given the vote almost as a matter of course. The act enfranchised all men over twenty-one and all women over thirty who qualified, or whose husbands qualified, for the franchise in local government. The act redrew the boundaries of constituencies with the aim of creating single member units each representing seventy thousand people. Plural voting was restricted, though not abolished, all elections were to be held on one day, a candidate must post a bond of £150 which was forfeited if he or she did not obtain one eighth of the votes cast.

By this act two million men and 6 million women were added to the franchise. In 1928 women were given the vote on the same terms as men; this act increased the number of women voters by another six million. In 1920 Oxford University admitted women both as students and as candidates for degrees, though Cambridge did not follow for another quarter of a century. The emancipation of women and doubtless the excess of women over men led to fashions in dress which minimized femininity and gave women a curveless schoolboy shape, though before the end of the decade short skirts and curves began to reveal the female figure more gracefully. Men's clothes tended toward informality, comfort, and brighter colors.

Wages, which had risen during the war, remained at a level about eleven percent higher than before 1914. Thus a worker's position was improved unless he or she was swept up in the dreadful wave of unemployment. Even if unemployed, workers benefited from extended social services including unemployment insurance. A good deal of new housing was built for the working classes. In the inner cities, after a slum area had been cleared, there was not much to be done except to construct apartments which the poor could afford to rent. However, municipalities also built housing estates on the outskirts of the city. These consisted of enormous numbers of two story semidetached houses built in units of two or four dwellings on curving streets with a yard for each family. The housing estates gave the working classes better quarters than they had ever had before. Unfortunately, as things turned out, they were too expensive for most of the workers; only the upper crust of artisans, who merged with the lower middle classes, could afford them. They were often a long journey from the place of employment. And while they were bright and fresh, they were sometimes bleak, lacking trees and amenities such as churches and town halls.

Like all suburbs, they were dependent upon transportation to the city. In London some of the underground lines were extended on the surface into the country and the railways provided suburban service, which was gradually electrified. But the great development was the bus. The number of buses increased enormously, not only in the city and its suburbs but also in rural areas. Motor trucks or lorries carried all kinds of goods. Long-distance motor coaches competed successfully with the railways, for they could pick up passengers in out of the way places. As for the railways, they improved in speed and safety without startling innovations; they were slipping in their ability to produce good profits. The commercial use of the airplane did not develop as rapidly as had been anticipated. The first companies, offering flights to the Continent, were failures. Imperial Airways, however, founded in 1924 with a government subsidy, consolidated earlier lines and opened service to distant parts of the empire. The number of privately owned automobiles increased threefold, reaching the million mark in 1930.

The changes of the era naturally were reflected in literature and art. Some of the older writers—G. B. Shaw, W. B. Yeats, and John Galsworthy—retained their popularity. Galsworthy's *Forsyte Saga*, a picture of Victorian life, was widely read. On the whole, however, literature was dominated by a younger generation who turned against what it regarded as ornate and artificial writing. Ready to experiment and strongly influenced by Sigmund Freud, the younger writers were interested in the psychology of sex, in the impact of a changing world upon the individual, in

Thomas Sterns Eliot. (A.P. Wide World Photos, Inc.)

scenes and thoughts of violence. D. H. Lawrence glorified sexual love; Evelyn Waugh satirized the smart young set in London. A more versatile writer was the younger Aldous Huxley, whose *Point Counter Point* was much admired. A new type of poetry—learned, symbolic, highly intellectual—appeared in the writings of T. S. Eliot. *The Waste Land,* expressing the dreariness of a great modern city, appealed to those who regarded the era as one of disintegration. Writers who employed a stream-of-consciousness technique were Virginia Wolf and, in a different way, James Joyce. In painting a struggle arose between traditional artists and more radical painters who preferred works of abstraction. The Royal Academy sponsored exhibits of traditional art, while an exhibit arranged by Osbert and Sacheverell Sitwell in 1919 stirred interest in modern art in France. The Tate Gallery, aided by a generous gift, purchased excellent examples of modern abstraction; gradually the public was won over to this kind of painting. In sculpture the work of Jacob Epstein, which was very modernistic, aroused the wrath of conventional people. Epstein was an American Jew who had settled in England before the war. His *Risen Christ* sculpture evoked the following response from a Jesuit priest:

Rising Christ, *by Jacob Epstein. (City University of New York, Graduate Center)*

> I felt ready to cry out with indignation that in this Christian England there should be exhibited the figure of a Christ which suggested to me some degraded Chaldean or African, which wore the appearance of an Asiatic-American or Hun-Jew, which reminded me of some emaciated Hindu, or a badly grown Egyptian swathed in the cerements of the grave . . .

Architecture, on the other hand, remained largely traditional, condemned by moderns as lacking in originality and imagination. In the 1930s it grew more adventurous. The love of good music rapidly increased. It was stimulated by excellent orchestral conductors such as Sir Thomas Beecham and Sir Henry Wood, by broadcasting, by phonograph records, and by the establishment in 1930 of the orchestra of the British Broadcasting Corporation.

Many new forms of amusement—in which the lower classes largely joined—came into existence after the war. One was the motion picture or cinema. The production of motion pictures had been begun in England before the war but had faded away in the war years. The American industry, on the other hand, had grown enormously; it dominated the British market in the postwar period. By 1930, however, four important British corporations produced films and operated chains of theaters where the films were shown. Talking pictures, which appeared in the United States in 1926, were not at first taken seriously in England.

Broadcasting began in England on an experimental basis in 1922. A good many companies, seeing the broadcasting boom in the United States, wished to broadcast programs in the hope of selling receiving sets. But the Post Office, which controlled wireless under an act of 1904, eventually decided in favor of a monopoly; the British Broadcasting Corporation, therefore, came into existence in 1926 as a monopoly controlled by the government. Its policy was influenced strongly by its director, J. C. W. Reith, a Scot who insisted that broadcasting should be used for instruction as well as entertainment and that it should preserve a high moral tone as a matter of paramount importance. Thus the character of the BBC was set in its infancy. Its news bulletins may have weakened the power of the press but they did not diminish

Recumbent Figure, *by Henry Moore. (Tate Gallery, London)*

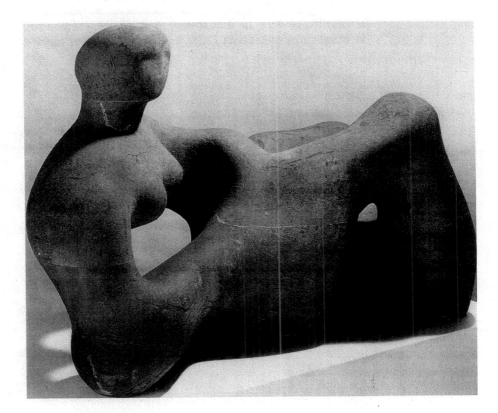

the enormous circulation of the cheaper daily papers, whose ownership became concentrated in a few large combinations.

Great sporting events, at which huge crowds watched contests between professional teams, became extremely popular. Cricket matches, soccer, and rugby football games, as well as horse racing and racing by greyhounds after a mechanical hare were attended by millions of people. Betting, of course, added zest to these sports. It increased at such an enormous pace that it may be called a national vice, though close supervison kept it from becoming corrupt. These sports had their drawbacks, but at least they provided rivals to the pub; convictions for drunkeness steadily decreased.

The years following the war were difficult ones for the British farmer. Due to the decline of agriculture in the last quarter of the nineteenth century, Britain was growing only about one-fifth of the wheat it consumed when the war broke out in 1914. The war brought about a determined effort to increase production: three million acres of pastures were ploughed and planted; farmers were guaranteed against loss on wheat and oats; a minimum wage was established for agricultural laborers. But after the war there came a slump: the world market was glutted with agricultural produce and prices fell sharply. Faced with large payments to honor its pledges, the government abandoned the farmer and the farm laborer. Hence wages fell and agriculture began to decline once more. In 1931 the acreage under wheat was smaller than before the war, though the yield per acre was larger. The food produced in Britain was only about forty percent of what was needed.

C H R O N O L O G Y

Politics and Depression

1916	Easter Rising, Dublin
1918	Lloyd George Coalition won re-election
1918–27	*Forsyte Saga* by John Galsworthy
1919	Paris Peace Conference—Treaty of Versailles; League of Nations; Irish Republic proclaimed
1920	Unemployment Insurance Act; *Risen Christ* by Jacob Epstein
1921	Miners' strike defeated; "Geddes Ax"

(continued on next page)

Chronology, continued

1922	Washington Naval Conference; Irish Free State recognized; Lloyd George resigned; Bonar Law prime minister; *The Waste Land* by T. S. Eliot
1923	Dawes Plan; Bonar Law resigned; Baldwin prime minister; election without a winner
1924	First Labor government; Ramsay MacDonald prime minister; Zinoviev Letter; Conservative landslide; Baldwin again prime minister
1925	Locarno Pact; Gold Standard restored
1926	General Strike; Hadow Report; BBC founded
1927	Trades Dispute Act
1928	D. H. Lawrence's *Lady Chatterley's Lover;* Aldous Huxley's *Point Counter Point*
1929	Conservatives defeated; MacDonald forms minority Labor government; Depression began
1931	Labor cabinet resigned; MacDonald leader of national government

34 The Struggle for Peace and the Second World War, 1931–1945

THE NATIONAL GOVERNMENT, 1931–1940

As a result of the events described in the previous chapter, Ramsay MacDonald formed a National Cabinet which came into office late in August 1931. It was supported by the Conservatives, who were strong in the Commons; by the Liberals, who were weak; and by a handful of Labor members who adhered to MacDonald. The bulk of the Labor party, still the largest single party in the Commons, was in angry opposition. Soon there was talk of an election. It was urged by the Conservatives, who saw an opportunity to appeal to the country on patriotic grounds for support of the National government (in which they would predominate), and at the same time to denounce the Labor party as the source of the nation's ills and to push for a protective tariff. The Labor and the Liberal members of the Cabinet opposed an election but yielded to Conservative pressure. They refused to support a tariff; hence it was decided that the ministers should agree to disagree. MacDonald should ask the electors for a vote of confidence without committing himself on tariff policy; other ministers could advocate what they pleased—they could at least agree in attacking Labor. The result was a confusing, vindictive, and rather fraudulent election in which ministers contradicted each other and in which the Labor party was denounced in violent terms. The National government won by a landslide. Its supporters consisted of 472 Conservatives, 68 Liberals, and 13 National Labor members. The Labor party in opposition won only 46 seats.

The results of this election were highly important. For the next nine years the Conservatives enjoyed an overwhelming supremacy in the Commons. Behind the facade of a National government they yielded a power they could not have obtained through their own electoral strength. MacDonald might be prime minister, but the key men in the Cabinet were Baldwin and Neville Chamberlain. There was no need to pay attention to the wishes of the opposition nor to bring in new blood. Neither Lloyd George nor Winston Churchill was a member of the coalition. "It was no 'national' government," wrote a contemporary. "It was simply a get-together on the part of the Boys of the Old Brigade, who climbed on the Bandwagon and sat there, rain or shine, until they brought the British Empire to the verge of destruction."

MacDonald's captivity was soon evident, for Neville Chamberlain, chancellor of the Exchequer, pressed for tariff reform. He was strong enough to have his way, though Labor and Liberal ministers protested and some of them later resigned. A tariff, established early in 1932, imposed general duties of 10 percent on imports (with certain exceptions); and an advisory board was empowered to fix additional duties up to 33½ percent. Shortly after the tariff became law, an imperial economic conference was held in Ottawa for the purpose of concluding preferential agreements with the Dominions. The result was disappointing. Britain had no intention of sacrificing her farmers, and the Dominions were determined to protect their growing industries. British trade with the Dominions increased to some extent. But it was the Dominions, not Britain, that profited, for increased imperial trade disturbed old links with other markets; British exports made only a slight recovery after 1932.

Ministers and Kings

MacDonald remained prime minister until June 1935. He became a rather tragic figure. He was of great use to the Conservatives, for he enabled them to maintain the fiction of a national government. However, his effectiveness declined, his speeches were evasive and confused, and there was less and less reason for his remaining in office. In 1935 he and Stanley Baldwin, who was lord president of the Council, exchanged places; in 1937 MacDonald retired and died shortly thereafter. Although he had done much to build the Labor movement, Labor never forgave him for his desertion of the party in 1931.

Baldwin held office as prime minister for two years. It was his misfortune that these were years of crisis in foreign affairs about which he cared very little. Meanwhile a domestic problem of a most unusual character arose. King Edward VIII, who had succeeded to the throne in January 1936, had little sympathy with the symbolic duties of a British monarch. Moreover, he became interested in an American divorcée, Mrs. Wallis Warfield Simpson, and was constantly in her company. When it was indicated to him that Mrs. Simpson should leave the country, he angrily told the prime minister, "I mean to marry her and I am prepared to go." The country, at least the country outside London, was solidly against the marriage. Baldwin confronted Edward with the alternative of either renouncing Mrs. Simpson or abdicating the throne. Baldwin's speech of explanation in the House of Commons was plausible. An abdication bill was passed. Edward went into exile with the title of duke of Windsor, and his brother, the duke of York, became George VI. Many people felt that Edward had been hustled along rather brusquely. Shortly after this crisis Baldwin retired. It is evident that behind his pose of being a simple country gentleman there was more cleverness and less frankness than appeared on the surface. It would be at least a generation before Baldwin's role was appreciated.

Society in the 1930s

The problems facing the nation in the 1930s were very difficult indeed: continued depression; appalling unemployment; the rise of Hitler and Mussolini; and the Spanish Civil War which sharply divided British sympathies. The prevailing mood in this period was serious and somber, without the buoyancy of the 1920s. The sad plight of the depressed areas and the glaring inequalities between rich and poor led to introspection and self-criticism; the nation was more inclined to look inward at its domestic problems than outward toward the rest of the world. Much thought was given to social and economic questions. The era was one of awakened social conscience, of surveys, and of apprehension about the nation's future.

The hard core of unemployment centered in the areas that depended upon the staple industries of the nineteenth century—coal, textiles, shipbuilding, iron and steel. These areas included most of northern England, almost all of industrial Scotland, all of South Wales, and parts of North Wales. At the beginning of 1933 the unemployed reached the dreadful figure of three million persons. The distress in Wales and Lancashire was acute; half of Glasgow was unemployed and in the shipbuilding town of Jarrow on the Tyne two-thirds of the workers were without jobs. A number of books, such as J. B. Priestley's *English Journey* (1934), described the derelict towns. They were all much alike—the shops closed, the houses in need of repairs, the men standing idly at the street corners with their hands in their pockets. The unemployed fell into three categories. The first contained those who were temporarily out of work or were working part time. Then came the young men who had never had employment. Finally there were the long-term unemployed who had not had jobs for years. They included the older men who would probably never find employment. The evils of unemployment were obvious: the hopelessness of continual idleness, the loss of self-respect, the frustrations of chilling poverty. For many families a major problem was to keep warm; the easiest solution was to go to bed early and get up late. Little luxuries—the cinema and small bets—offered some diversion. Moreover, a great many agencies sprang up to keep the men occupied and physically fit. The government sponsored training centers of various kinds. Much more, however, was done by voluntary bodies who helped workmen form clubs for amusement, training, education, and for work on farms or in workshops or in the operation of abandoned coal mines. The government did not offer employment on public works; indeed, it cut the amount of relief payments in 1931. It did, however, attempt to relieve distress. The machinery for the administration of relief was improved, although an attempt to gauge the means of each family as a whole (the "means" test) was resented. It penalized thrift, invaded privacy, and led to petty gossip.

Although the unemployed were kept from starvation, there was great hardship and distress. It became clear, moreover, that inadequate housing, malnutrition, infant and maternal mortality, insufficient medical attention, and the incidence of tuberculosis were much more prevalent in the depressed areas than in more prosperous ones. This situation formed the background of the welfare state.

These sad conditions in unemployed Britain were only dimly understood by the

more prosperous areas in the south. As a matter of fact, a significant economic revival occurred in Britain during the second half of the 1930s. It was due very largely to the cheapness of imported raw materials, which kept down the cost of living and provided some money for increased investment at home. Manufacturers gave greater attention to production for the home market. Profits were less than those in foreign trade, but real wages were increasing and with them the purchasing power of the middle and lower classes. Neville Chamberlain encouraged business by forcing down the rates of interest. A notable increase occurred in the building of houses. Some recovery took place in steel, china, and railways; and the new industries, such as chemicals, rayon, electrical goods, motor cars, packaged and prepared foods, expanded. These new industries centered in the southeast of England, especially in the London area, and to some extent in the western midlands around Birmingham. It was natural that young men and women from the depressed areas in the north migrated to localities that offered greater hope of employment. Population, which had shifted northward more than a century earlier, began to turn south again. In southeastern England large numbers of modest families enjoyed higher standards of living than they had known before.

Many persons outside of politics were giving serious thought to social and economic problems. The quest for new solutions was evident in the work of the economist J. M. Keynes. His important book, *General Theory of Employment, Interest, and Money* (1936), developed the doctrine that governments should combat, and might prevent, depressions by adjustments of credit and investment, by reducing interest rates, by deficit spending for public works to relieve unemployment and to increase the purchasing power of the people. Within a decade this book revolutionized government policy toward economic questions. A belief in the value of economic planning by the state steadily grew. It was noticed that Russia had escaped the impact of the world depression; hence much of the economic thinking and writing of the time contained admiration for Russian communism. When the civil war in Spain developed into a struggle between communist and fascist Europe, the Communist Party in Britain sent volunteers as well as munitions and medical supplies. Young people, especially students, regarding the Labor Party as out of date, were prepared to join communists and other elements in a popular front against fascism. A *Left Book Club,* managed by Victor Gollancz, issued books in rather uncritical support of Russia. Poetry with a socialist or communist slant was published by a *Left Review.*

Behind this furor, social changes begun in the previous decade continued to develop. Road transport of all kinds grew steadily; the city dweller enjoyed rides in the country in his car. There was a great increase in hiking, fostered by youth hostels and by campaigns to keep physically fit. Facilities developed for indoor ice skating, for lawn tennis in the public parks, for swimming and sun bathing, which led to abbreviated swim suits. The cinema was popular. Newspapers, partly because of their keen competition, held contests for readers.

The public also desired matter for serious reading; this accounts for the popularity of the Penguin paperbacks, some of them selling for as little as 6*d.*, of the *Listener,* a magazine issued by the BBC, and of popular accounts of mathematics, science, and philosophy. Good taste in music continued to improve. The other arts, unfortunately, became rather highbrow and experimental. Painters and sculptors produced abstractions that were difficult to understand. Architecture grew more imaginative but did not win popular approval.

Britain and the Dictators

The softness and appeasement of British policy toward Hitler and Mussolini during the 1930s are invariably associated with Neville Chamberlain, who became prime minister in 1937. But this policy began under MacDonald and Baldwin; Chamberlain merely carried it forward. In 1931, when the depression was at its worst, Japan made war on China in Manchuria and then created the satellite state of Manchukuo. In 1932 the weakness of the Weimar Republic in Germany enabled Hitler to rise to power. Becoming chancellor in January 1933, he withdrew Germany from the League of Nations and began to rearm. In 1935 he announced the existence of the German air force; in violation of the Treaty of Versailles he introduced conscription for his army. In the same year Mussolini attacked Ethiopia in eastern Africa. It is easy to see, as we look back, that Britain should have taken an early stand against these violations of international law, but it is also easy to understand why she did not.

Churchill and Lloyd George, 1934. (A.P. Wide World Photos, Inc.)

Britain had suffered terribly from the First World War. The filthy war in the trenches, the frightful casualties, and the sufferings of the bereaved made many people in Britain regard another war as unthinkable. No international problem, it was held, could justify another carnage. Every crisis brought the longing that it would pass without a war or at least without a war involving Britain. Great faith was placed in the League of Nations as a means of achieving collective security. Opposition to rearmament was widespread. Such thinking was confused, for if Britain did not arm and if other nations followed her example, the League would not be strong enough to resist aggressors.

Constant clashes with France in the 1920s made British sentiment rather pro-German. Germany, it was felt, had been poorly treated at Versailles. The danger to Europe lay in communism, not in fascism, and so the Nazis could be regarded as a bulwark against Russia. With such ideas current in Britain, statesmen faced the duty of educating the public to the need for rearmament and for a tougher policy toward the dictators. But MacDonald and Baldwin were not energetic, Chamberlain believed in appeasement, and Labor opposed rearmament; moreover, ministers were carefully attuned to the wishes of the voters. Hence it was easy to believe that when Hitler spoke of peace he could be trusted and that when he threatened war he could be contained by negotiation. In 1935 the Cabinet announced its intention to rearm and to

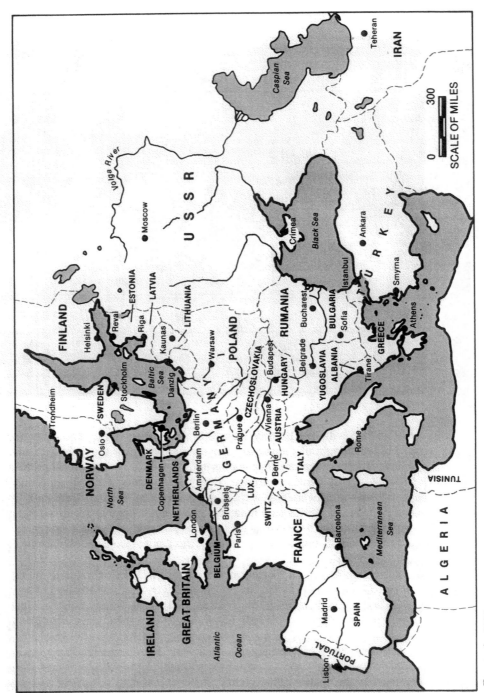

Europe in 1930.

strengthen the Royal Air Force, but little was done. In an election in the same year (won by the national government) Baldwin told the people what they wanted to hear: that Britain would make the League of Nations the keystone of her policy and would take her stand on collective security.

Unfortunately the League was showing that it could not stop aggression. When Mussolini attacked Ethiopia in 1935 the British public assumed that the League would assert its authority and would apply sanctions against Italy, but Baldwin's policy was to stay out of the Italian-Ethiopian crisis. An agreement was made with the French by which Mussolini would be allowed to seize about half of Ethiopia. In this instance British statesmen were softer than was the British public. A storm of protest arose over the action of the government, but in the meantime Mussolini had completed his conquest.

In the same year Baldwin concluded a treaty with Germany permitting Hitler to increase his naval strength to thirty-five percent of that of Britain. British policy was to play off one dictator against the other so that she would not be quarreling with both of them at the same time. But Hitler was insatiable. In 1936 he sent his troops into the Rhineland even though the Rhineland had been demilitarized by treaty. Baldwin accepted this coup without demur and caught at German proposals to secure the future peace of Europe. The people as a whole agreed. Hugh Dalton, a Labor member, remarked in the Commons: "It is only right to say bluntly and flatly that public opinion in this country would not support and certainly the Labor party would not support the taking of military sanctions or even economic sanctions against Germany at this time in order to put German troops out of the German Rhineland." One of the few voices of protest was that of Winston Churchill, who attacked the Cabinet's slowness in rearmament. The government, he declared, "simply cannot make up their minds, or they cannot get the prime minister to make up his mind. So they go on in strange paradox, decided only to be undecided, resolved to be irresolute, adamant for drift, solid for fluidity, all-powerful to be impotent."

The Spanish Civil War

The Spanish Civil War, which broke out in July 1936, influenced Britain profoundly and proved to be the first step in awakening the people to the dangers of appeasement. A Republican government, supported by liberals and by various left-wing parties, had been established in Spain in 1931. In 1936, however, a revolt against this government was begun by the fascist General Francisco Franco. Franco at once received aid from Hitler and Mussolini, who saw in the revolt a pattern of fascist intervention and a dress rehearsal for a larger war to come. The Republican government was aided by volunteers from many lands and by tanks and planes from Russia. The British government announced its neutrality. At first this policy won general support, and the Cabinet accepted a French proposal that the major powers not intervene in Spain. Hitler and Mussolini, under thin disguises, continued to send aid to Franco. In practice, nonintervention was a farce that played into Franco's hands. It denied assistance to the Republicans, undermined the doctrine of collective security, bypassed the League, exalted the dictators, and increased the bitterness of liberals everywhere at the brutality of Franco's campaign.

There were sharp attacks on the government in England. The Labor party, forgetting its pacifism, denounced nonintervention. Opposition arose from such totally different persons as Winston Churchill and Clement Attlee, the leader of the Labor party. Churchill attacked the Cabinet for its neglect of imperial interests, for a victory by Franco would endanger Gibraltar. Attlee charged that the Cabinet was motivated by upper-class sympathy for Franco, by concern for business, and by a fondness for the dictators. To the average Englishman the war symbolized the clash of communism and fascism, and there was general sympathy with the former. But the more the people protested, the more tenaciously the Cabinet clung to the fiction of nonintervention, ignored its infringement by the dictators, and seemed determined on peace at any price. Meanwhile, Franco won the war.

Neville Chamberlain and Appeasement

In May 1937 Baldwin was followed as prime minister by Neville Chamberlain. Honest, industrious, patient, and methodical, he was essentially the efficient civil servant who handled administrative problems with careful skill, but he was also narrow, cold, and overconfident. He was scornful of the Labor members, one of whom remarked that he must have been "weaned on a pickle." Toward Conservatives he was a disciplinarian. He was inclined to follow his own ideas without seeking proper advice and resented criticism even from his friends.

Although his training and experience lay in domestic affairs, he made foreign relations the principal sphere of his activity. He expected the Foreign Office and the foreign secretary (Anthony Eden) to follow the lead he gave them; yet he did not hesitate to bypass them and to deal directly with Hitler and Mussolini. He believed that the League of Nations had failed, that collective security had failed with it, that no reliance could be placed on the United States, and that direct negotiations with dictators could lead to compromise. He let Hitler know that Britain would not oppose changes in central Europe provided those changes came about through peaceful agreement. This policy was interpreted in Germany as meaning that Britain would offer no serious objection to Hitler's plans. The Germans saw that the pretense of negotiations must be maintained. Ribbentrop, the German Ambassador in London, wrote to his master, "We must continue to foster England's belief that a settlement and an understanding between Germany and England are still possible." But in the meantime German plans for aggression must not be interrupted. And thus, while Chamberlain strove to remove tensions through negotiation, the Nazis were preparing for military conquest. Chamberlain hoped to strengthened his hand against Hitler by agreements with Mussolini. His softness toward Italy caused the resignation of Anthony Eden in February 1938. Unfortunately, Eden had just been criticized by Hitler, so that his resignation looked like another humiliation for the democratic powers. In the following month Hitler sent his troops into Austria and absorbed that country into the Reich. Britain protested but made no other move.

Neville Chamberlain. (National Portrait Gallery, London)

Attention turned quickly to the more vital question of Czechoslovakia, an important country with an army of thirty divisions, with strong defensive fortifications, and with the Skoda munition works. She was the ally of France and she might well have received assistance from Russia. But after Austria's incorporation into the Reich, Czechoslovakia was ringed by German territory. Moreover, there were some 3,500,000 Germans in an area called the Sudetenland. Hitler determined upon Czechoslovakia's destruction. He protested violently against the supposed ill treatment of the Sudeten Germans, and events moved swiftly to a crisis.

Chamberlain hoped that the Sudeten question could be settled without undermining the independence of Czechoslovakia. Rejecting French and Russian moves to organize resistance, he assumed full control of British policy and engaged in direct talks with Hitler to prevent German military action against the Czechs. He talked with Hitler twice in September 1938. In the first interview he agreed that the Sudetenland should be surrendered to Germany after a plebiscite. In the second

Anthony Eden,
Foreign Secretary.
(A.P. Wide World
Photos, Inc.)

Hitler demanded immediate occupation before the plebiscite was held. This Chamberlain refused. War now appeared inevitable, and Britain made hasty preparations for the safety of the people.

Then suddenly Hitler asked for a conference at Munich to which he invited Chamberlain, Mussolini, and Premier Daladier of France. Here it was agreed to permit Hitler to occupy the Sudetenland on his own terms without a plebiscite. Hitler guaranteed the integrity of what remained of Czechoslovakia and signed an innocuous agreement suggested by Chamberlain promising to negotiate any new difference that might arise between England and Germany. The immediate reaction in England was one of profound relief. Chamberlain was hailed with enthusiasm as he proclaimed, "I believe it is peace in our time." However, he met sharp attacks in the House of Commons. Churchill called Munich "a total and unmitigated defeat." It was soon clear that Hitler had every intention of taking the rest of Czechoslovakia. The blow fell in

March 1939, when Hitler sent troops into Bohemia and Moravia. Czechoslovakia disappeared.

The reaction in Britain was violent. Even Chamberlain was convinced at last that he had been wrong and that appeasement had failed. A revolution took place in British policy. The production of military aircraft was stepped up. The navy was empowered to build its strength to a level equal to that of the German and Japanese navies combined. Conscription was introduced to raise an army quickly. Moreover, Chamberlain pledged British support to various nations—Poland, Rumania, Greece, and Turkey. An attempt was made, though rather feebly, to reach an agreement with Russia.

Events now rushed to a climax. Hitler determined to attack Poland. He also made secret approaches to Russia; a sure indication of impending war was the announcement on 23 August of a German-Russian nonaggression pact. As everyone suspected, it contained secret clauses for the partition of eastern Europe between the two powers. Russia had found she had more to gain from Germany than from England; and Hitler, facing war in the west, wished to protect his eastern frontier. On 1 September German troops invaded Poland. Britain honored her pledges, and war began on 3 September.

It would be unfair to place all the blame for the humiliating era of appeasement upon Chamberlain's shoulders. The policy began before he became prime minister, and to the end he received strong support from many quarters in Britain. The Labor party long opposed rearmament in a blind and doctrinaire way. Men in public life felt the shame and humiliation of Munich but secretly hoped that Hitler could be bought off by acquiesence in his villainies toward smaller nations. The people as a whole during this era were listless, frightened, and confused. One cannot blame them for dreading war, but they could have been heartened by a bolder government. Criticism must fall on the leaders—Baldwin, Simon, Hoare, and Halifax, as well as Chamberlain—who permitted their country to drift into such weak and disastrous policies.

THE SECOND WORLD WAR

The Twilight War

The Second World War began with Hitler's smashing assault on Poland, which broke that country in seventeen days. England and France could not aid the Poles. France, it is true, might have attacked Germany along the Rhine, but the French were dominated by a strategic concept of static defense. They occupied their magnificent fortifications known as the Maginot Line and felt secure, though the Maginot Line faced eastward and did not extend along the frontier between France and Belgium. A British army under Lord Gort was sent to northwestern France but it was not in contact with the enemy. Land operations, therefore, were at a standstill in western Europe during the winter of 1939–1940, and there ensued the strange

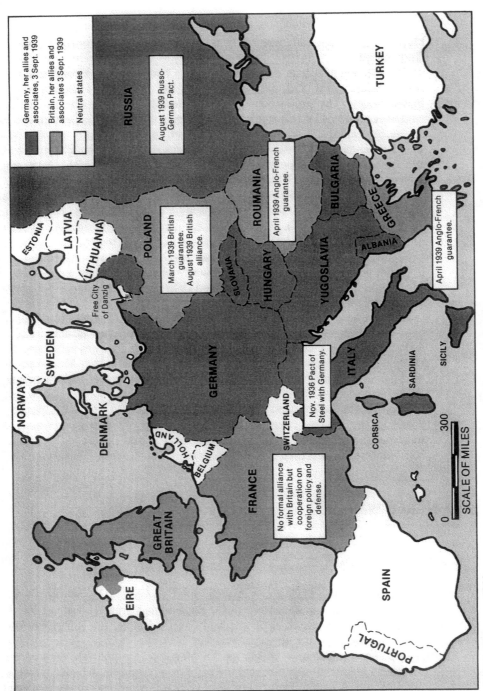

Germany, her allies and associates, 3 Sept. 1939

Britain, her allies and associates 3 Sept. 1939

Neutral states

August 1939 Russo-German Pact.

RUSSIA

ROUMANIA

April 1939 Anglo-French guarantee.

BULGARIA

POLAND

March 1939 British guarantee.
August 1939 British alliance.

ESTONIA

LATVIA

LITHUANIA

Free City of Danzig

GREECE

ALBANIA

April 1939 Anglo-French guarantee.

SLOVAKIA

HUNGARY

YUGOSLAVIA

TURKEY

NORWAY

SWEDEN

DENMARK

GERMANY

HOLLAND

BELGIUM

SWITZERLAND

Nov. 1936 Pact of Steel with Germany.

ITALY

SARDINIA

SICILY

CORSICA

FRANCE

No formal alliance with Britain but cooperation on foreign policy and defense.

GREAT BRITAIN

EIRE

SPAIN

PORTUGAL

300

SCALE OF MILES

0

British diplomacy 1939.

period that Churchill dubbed the twilight war (Americans called it the phony war) in which very little happened.

There was some activity at sea. A German submarine sank the British aircraft carrier *Courageous;* a second submarine daringly penetrated the defenses of the British naval base at Scapa Flow in the Orkneys and sank the battleship *Royal Oak.* These were serious losses. On the other hand, the German pocket battleship *Admiral Graf von Spee,* which had been raiding British commerce, was cornered by British cruisers off Montevideo in Uruguay and scuttled by her crew. The British began a naval blockade they believed was having some effect. An element of unreality about the war persisted during the first winter, and there was a natural decline in the morale of the people. Air-raid precautions, rationing, and evacuation from large cities began to be considered annoyances; many evacuated persons drifted back to their homes. The sense of unreality was intensified when Hitler declared that he would welcome peace. Having crushed the Poles and divided their country with Russia, he asked blandly, "Why should the war in the west be fought?" Although Chamberlain insisted in public that the German proposals were worthless, he hoped in secret that war might be avoided in western Europe.

Such dreams were rudely shattered by events in Scandinavia. In November 1939 the Russians had attacked Finland in order to secure a stronger western frontier, and this led to a British decision to assist the Finns. A British force was to have driven across northern Norway, but Hitler acted first. In a lightning attack on 9 April 1940 he overwhelmed Denmark in a few hours and Norway in a few days, though not without serious naval losses from Norwegian and British resistance. The British landed troops near Trondheim on the Atlantic coast of Norway and later at Narvik farther to the north. But the Trondheim campaign was abandoned because of fear of German air power; and by the time the Germans were pushed out of Narvik their invasion of France had reduced the operations in Norway to small importance.

The campaign in Scandinavia ended Chamberlain's government. At the beginning of the war he sought to broaden his ministry by bringing in a number of new men, including Churchill at his old post at the Admiralty and Anthony Eden as Secretary for the Dominions. But neither the Labor nor the Liberal party would form a coalition with Chamberlain. When he announced the withdrawal of British forces from the area of Trondheim, the demand arose that he resign. He fought to retain his leadership but could not do so. He resigned in favor of Winston Churchill on 10 May 1940.

Arms and the Man[1]

On the very day that Churchill became prime minister of Britain, Hitler's forces invaded Holland and Belgium on their way to attack the French. Churchill's supreme opportunity had come. He had been one of the few who denounced appeasement during Chamberlain's ministry and he had had no part in that policy. Now, at a moment of grave national peril, he came into office with great power and prestige. By daily contact with the chiefs of staff he directed the entire war effort. He evoked a

[1]This is the title of a chapter in D. C. Somervell, *British Politics Since 1900* (London: Dakers, 1950).

Churchill views damage at the House of Commons, May 1941. (A.P. Wide World Photos, Inc.)

new spirit in the British people. He never minimized difficulties and hardships; yet he called forth courage, determination, unity, and sacrifice. In his first speech in the House of Commons as prime minister he declared that he could offer nothing but

> blood, toil, tears, and sweat . . . You ask, what is our policy? I will say: It is to wage war, by sea, land, and air with all our might and with all the strength that God can give us . . . What is our aim: . . . Victory—victory at all costs, victory in spite of all terror; victory, however long and hard the road may be.

A deep and emotional patriotism transformed the nation as it prepared for the battle for survival. Pacificism vanished. Leaders of all parties accepted places in Churchill's War Cabinet or in ministries outside it. Within a month the number of airplanes produced by British factories greatly increased. An astonishing piece of legislation placed all persons and all property at the disposal of the government to be employed in the best interests of the nation.

This steadfast, determined, and unified spirit was indeed necessary in the days that followed. On May 13–14 the Germans broke through the French lines at Sedan in the Ardennes sector west and north of the Maginot Line. Within ten days they had swept westward to the Channel, dividing the British and some French units from the main French armies. The British Expeditionary Force was in great danger of annihilation, but a corridor was kept open to Dunkirk, German naval units were held at bay, the Royal Air Force gave adequate protection, and some 338,000 troops (about two thirds of them British) were evacuated from the beaches at Dunkirk to England, most of them by the navy but many in small boats of all kinds that crossed and recrossed the Channel. Dunkirk was a triumph of British valor and determination, but the equipment of the troops was lost and a front on the Continent became impossible. On June 21 the new French premier, General Pétain, signed an armistice with Germany. Its terms gave Hitler possession of the northern half of France, including Paris, and the entire French Atlantic coast. An inland, unoccupied zone was left to the Pétain government with a capital at Vichy.

The Battle of Britain

The fall of France left Britain exposed to immediate invasion, and the summer and autumn of 1940 formed the most dangerous period of the war. There was scarcely enough equipment in Britain to arm two divisions, but Churchill's fighting spirit never wavered. "We shall defend our Island," he declared, "whatever the cost may be, we shall fight on the beaches, we shall fight on the landing grounds, we shall fight in the fields and in the streets, we shall fight in the hills; we shall never surrender." Home defenses were hastily prepared, the coastal areas strengthened, obstructions set up to prevent the landing of enemy planes. The Local Defense Volunteers, later known as the Home Guard, swelled to a force of half a million.

It was assumed that Hitler had a master plan for invasion but he did not. In fact, he had hardly looked beyond the defeat of France; he had assumed that once France was knocked out of the war the British would recognize the folly of further resistance. It was apparently not until May that he contemplated invasion and not until the middle of July that he began determined preparations for a landing in Britain. Such an operation required both naval power and command of the air. After long debate with his advisers, Churchill came to the "hateful decision" that the French fleet could not be allowed to fall into German hands. Superiority at sea was the one advantage left in British hands and it could not be threatened. British warships thereupon bombarded and put out of action French naval units at Oran in Algeria and at Dakar in French West Africa.

Meanwhile the German air raids against Britain increased in intensity. On August 1 Hitler issued instructions for an all-out campaign to destroy the Royal Air Force and the British aircraft industry. For three weeks in late August and early September an average of a thousand German planes was over Britain daily, attacking airfields, factories, radar stations, and the docks of East London. The Blitz was on. Fire fighting in London and elsewhere became a major concern of the government. Many Londoners slept in the stations of the Underground, or in "Andersons"—small shelters accommodating four or six people and protecting them from flying glass and splinters though not from direct hits—or trickled into the countryside at night. But in defiant London there was a high degree of discipline and order, and essential services continued. During the last week of August and the first week of September the issue of the battle in the air was doubtful. Thereafter the Royal Air Force grew in strength and effectiveness; by the middle of September it was downing two German planes for every British one lost. The German effort to gain control of the air over Britain was a failure. Hitler postponed and then canceled the invasion, the shipping assembled for the descent on Britain was dispersed, and by the end of September the British knew there would be no invasion in 1940. But heavy air raids on Britain continued at night when darkness made defense more difficult. Hitler then began a systematic attempt to destroy British centers of industry. Throughout the winter of 1940–1941 there were constant raids on London. On the night of December 8–9, four hundred German bombers swept over the city, inflicting heavy damage. Other cities— Coventry, Birmingham, Plymouth, and Liverpool—were also under heavy attack. It was not until June 1941, when Hitler turned on Russia, that the pressure on Britain from the air diminished.

North Africa and the Mediterranean

Very heavy fightng also developed in the Mediterranean. Mussolini, who entered the war as France was falling, had visions of conquering Greece as well as securing Egypt as a connecting link between Libya and the Italian possessions in East Africa. Both efforts met with failure. In September 1940 the Italians invaded Egypt from Cyrenaica, but soon came to a halt because of lack of transport and were pushed back into their own territories by a British counterattack from Egypt. Another British force drove from Kenya into Italian Somaliland and Ethiopia, forcing the Italians from those areas. A pro-German regime in Iraq quickly was smashed; British and Free French forces occupied Syria and Lebanon. Mussolini also failed in his war against Greece; and in two fierce assaults the British defeated the Italian navy at its base in Taranto in southern Italy and in a battle at sea off Cape Matapan in Greece.

The situation altered early in 1941, when the Germans decided to intervene. Hitler sent General Rommel to stiffen the Italians in North Africa; a powerful German offensive was launched in the Balkans against Yugoslavia and Greece. To meet this danger, some fifty-eight thousand British troops were brought to Greece from Egypt. When the Greeks did not cooperate, however, Yugoslavia was quickly overrun by the Germans. It soon became necessary to evacuate the British forces, first to Crete, and then, after a brilliant assault on Crete by German airborne troops, from Crete back to Egypt. The whole campaign in Greece and Crete was a sharp reverse for Britain. Rommel, opposed by weaker British forces, made alarming progress in North Africa.

Aid from the United States

Meanwhile the United States was moving closer to all-out aid to Britain. At the beginning of the war, when American sentiment was overwhelmingly against involvement, Congress would do no more than permit the sale of war materials to Britain on a cash-and-carry basis. This meant that goods must be picked up by British ships in American ports and must be paid for at once. But the fall of France drove home the fact that Britain might be overwhelmed and that all of Europe might soon be under the domination of the Nazis. Keenly aware of this threat, President Roosevelt pledged in June 1940 that the United States would supply material assistance to "the opponents of force." Late in the summer he transferred to Britain fifty overage American destroyers in exchange for air and naval bases in British America, chiefly in the West Indies. Then in December he announced his policy of lend-lease, an

Churchill addresses joint session of Congress, December 1941. (A.P. Wide World Photos, Inc.)

arrangement by which the United States might sell, exchange, lend, or lease materials of war to any nation whose defense was deemed essential to American security. Becoming law in March 1941, the lend-lease measure made vast quantities of war materials available to Britain, though it would be some time before their impact was felt on the battle fronts.

Too large an amount of these supplies was being lost at sea. German submarines could operate from any port along the western seaboard of the Continent north of Spain, while Irish neutrality denied to Britain the use of ports in southwestern Ireland which would have been of great value. In April 1941—when Hitler intensified the submarine war—Britain lost 195 ships, totaling some 700,000 tons. So great was the pressure on the British navy that, whereas in the First World War a convoy had often been protected by eight or ten destroyers, it was now escorted by two or three or sometimes by only one. Roosevelt did what he could. He began an American patrol in the western North Atlantic which broadcast the whereabouts of German ships and aircraft. He occupied Greenland and assisted in the defense of Iceland. More decisive steps were taken in the autumn in 1941, when American naval units began to escort British convoys in the North Atlantic and armed American merchantmen carried goods directly to Britain. A vast program of shipbuilding was begun in the United States. Yet the Battle of the Atlantic was far from won.

Attacks on Russia and on the United States

Hitler's massive invasion of Russia along a broad front in June 1941 and the Japanese air attack on the American fleet at Pearl Harbor in December drew these countries into the war and altered the entire complexion of the conflict. Hitler apparently believed that the Russian army, which had been purged in 1937, could be conquered in a single campaign and that the wheat of the Ukraine and the oil of the Caucasus could be won before the coming of winter. The Germans met with initial success, especially in the south. But in the north neither Leningrad nor Moscow was captured, and with the arrival of winter and with a Russian counteroffensive in December the Germans suffered great hardships and heavy losses.

Relations between Japan and the United States had become very strained as the Japanese had extended their power in China and in Southeast Asia while Europe was engulfed in war. In 1940 Japan had concluded a military alliance with Germany and Italy directed primarily against the United States. Hence the attack on Pearl Harbor brought America into the war not only against Japan but also against Germany and Italy.

Britain was no longer alone. Russia and the United States proved to be far more formidable military powers than Hitler had imagined. Yet their entry into the war was followed by a long series of disasters. For the first year, as Churchill remarked, Russia was a major obstacle to Allied success, for she was sent large quantities of supplies badly needed elsewhere. Stalin made insistent and embarrassing demands for a second front in western Europe, though an Allied invasion of the Continent would be impossible for a long time to come. In June 1942 the Germans began a new and dangerous offensive in southern Russia. Sebastopol and Rostov fell in rapid succession; a series of great battles was fought in the vicinity of Stalingrad for the control of the Volga Basin.

The attack on Pearl Harbor also was followed by shattering losses in the Far East. The Japanese, knowing that success depended on speed, began a series of lightning strikes against American, British, and Dutch possessions. Hong Kong fell on Christmas Day, 1941. The Japanese pushed south along the Malay Peninsula, destroyed by air attack two British warships, the *Repulse* and the *Prince of Wales,* and captured Singapore along with 100,000 prisoners. The Americans were driven from the Philippines in April 1942; by May the Dutch East Indies were in Japanese hands and Burma was overrun. The Japanese were in a position to harass British and Indian commerce in the Bay of Bengal, to cut off Allied aid to China over the Burma Road, and to invade both India and Australia. In North Africa Rommel began a new offensive in June 1942. Defeating British tanks, he captured Tobruk, which had withstood his earlier attacks, and pushed on to El Alamein in Egypt, only seventy-five miles from Alexandria. Meanwhile the Battle of the Atlantic seemed to be going in favor of the Germans. German submarines began to operate off the eastern coast of the United States, and for a time the American navy, lacking small craft for patrol, was unable to cope with this danger. Submarines and airplanes also took a heavy toll of British convoys sailing north of Scandinavia to Russia or fighting their way through the Mediterranean to bring supplies to Malta.

The Turning of the Tide

It was in the last months of 1942 and in the first half of 1943 that the tide of victory began to turn in favor of the Allies. In Russia the Germans were stopped at Stalingrad on the Volga. As the winter of 1942–1943 approached, they should have retreated, but Hitler ordered them to hold their ground. Thenceforth the Russians were able to take the offensive and to push the Germans back. As Churchill acknowledged later, it was the Russians who did "the main work of tearing the guts out of the German army."

In the Pacific the United States reacted quickly despite the disaster at Pearl Harbor. In two remarkable naval engagements, fought almost entirely by airplanes from rival carriers, the Japanese navy was severely damaged. The first, the Battle of the Coral Sea in May 1942, stopped a sea-borne attempt to invade Australia. The second, the Battle of Midway in June, was a decisive victory over the Japanese fleet. The Japanese were moving south through New Guinea and were attempting to cut the supply line from the United States to Australia by attacks on the Solomon Islands. In the severe fighting that took place in both areas the Japanese were turned back and the foundations were laid for American counterattacks from New Guinea toward the Philippines and across the Pacific from Hawaii toward Japan. It was some time before the British could do more than defend India against the Japanese in Burma.

Another crucial factor in "turning the tide" was the Ultra, the British system for decoding German messages which had been coded by the enigma machine.

The cracking of the enigma codes was a military secret even more closely guarded than that of the atomic bomb. Whereas the Germans at least suspected that a bomb was being developed, they never imagined that the enigma had been violated. At times the need to keep the Ultra's secret was more important than using the information it revealed. It was a secret whose very existence was kept for a generation after the conclusion of the war. The success of the Ultra does not, however, imply that the war was less hazardous or that the ultimate victory was less deserved.

In North Africa, as the flow of Allied supplies around the Cape of Good Hope became established and as new generals, Sir Harold Alexander and Sir Bernard Montgomery, assumed command, the British inflicted an important defeat on Rommel. In a tremendous battle lasting twelve days in October 1942 Rommel's defenses at El Alamein were broken and he was driven westward. He continued to retreat for more than a thousand miles. Meanwhile in November a powerful Anglo-American army landed in Algeria and in Morocco and began to move eastward toward Rommel in a vast pincers movement. The German game in Africa appeared to be over. But Hitler, who hated above all things to relinquish ground that he had conquered, sent strong reinforcements to Tunisia and ordered Rommel to turn on his pursuers. The fighting in North Africa thus was prolonged for six months. In May 1943, however, the Allies closed in on Tunisia, capturing more than a quarter of a million Germans and Italians. This ended the fighting in North Africa. It was the best the Allies could do at the time to satisfy Stalin's constant demand for a second front in Europe.

The battle against the submarine became much more successful during 1943. During the second half of the year the rate of destruction of submarines greatly increased while that of transport and merchant vessels greatly declined. The U-boat all but disappeared from the Mediterranean, and convoys sailing north of Scandinavia slowly were freed from attack by German warships. The strategic bombing of Germany was only beginning to gather strength during this year.

The Invasion of Europe

Ever since the American entry into the war there had been frequent meetings between Churchill and Roosevelt and their chiefs of staff. Hopeful communiqués were issued after each of these conferences, but a good deal of disagreement existed below the surface. Where should the war effort be concentrated and how should vital supplies be apportioned among the various fronts? Some American officers thought that the United States should put its main strength in the war against Japan, but Roosevelt supported Churchill in believing that the European theater must take precedence over the Far East. Americans wished an offensive in northern Burma to reopen the Burma Road to China, but the British wished to concentrate on the defense of India. Above all, the Americans urged an invasion of France at the earliest possible moment. The prolonged fighting in North Africa, however, made such a plan impossible for 1943; in any case, Churchill preferred an offensive in the Mediterranean, perhaps in the Balkans, to strike "at the soft underbelly of the Axis." A strong believer in strategic bombing, he hoped to secure bases in the Mediterranean from which to destroy the German war machine.

Amid these conflicting proposals a compromise was found in an invasion of Sicily and Italy from North Africa. In July 1943 the Allies moved into Sicily and shortly cleared the Germans from that island. At this point Mussolini fell from power and a new Italian government was formed by Marshal Badoglio, who concluded an armistice with the Allies. But the Germans quickly seized control of Italian affairs, so that when the Allies pushed into Italy in September they found themselves opposed by strong German forces who took advantage of the mountainous terrain and fought with skill and determination. Progress was therefore very slow, the Allies were halted south of Rome during the winter of 1943–1944, and it was not until June 1944 that Rome was occupied. Thereafter the Italian front became less important because of the invasion of France, although the fighting in Italy pinned down large numbers of German troops to the very end of the war.

The great assault on the fortress of Europe was now in the making. It required elaborate planning and a gigantic build-up of American forces in Britain. It was preceded by massive air attacks on Germany which, although they did not cripple German industry, went far toward destroying the German air force. The invasion

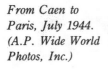

From Caen to Paris, July 1944. (A.P. Wide World Photos, Inc.)

began on June 6, 1944, when a vast fleet assembled south of the Isle of Wight. From that position, wrote Churchill,

> in an endless stream, led by the mine-sweepers on a wide front and protected on all sides by the might of the Allied navies and air forces, the greatest armada that ever left our shores set out for the coast of France.

The British General Montgomery was in charge of field operations, though the supreme commander was the American General Eisenhower. The plan was to seize the coast of Normandy, the British on the left flank holding back the Germans while the Americans on the right broke through to the south and then turned east.

This plan succeeded, though there were initial setbacks. It was not until late in July that the American General Patton broke out into Brittany at St.-Lô. The Germans held for some time at Caen, but in August they retreated and large numbers of them were captured after complicated flanking movements by the Allies at Falaise. Meanwhile another Allied invasion from the French Mediterranean coast pushed up the valley of the Rhone. The Germans were now in full flight from France. By September

British troops occupy Lisieux, August 1944. (A.P. Wide World Photos, Inc.)

the Allies held a very large area, their lines extending from Antwerp southward to Namur and Metz and then west to Orléans and Nantes. The end of the war appeared to be in sight. But Germany did not collapse. On the contrary, Hitler launched a counteroffensive in December which drove a large salient into American lines north of Luxembourg and threatened Liège and Namur. These attacks in the Battle of the Bulge were contained, but the hope of ending the war in 1944 disappeared.

Meanwhile, new problems arose concerning the future of eastern Europe and the Balkans as the Russian armies pushed westward. It had been partly to preserve some British influence in these areas that Churchill had advocated an Allied front in the Balkans. In October he flew to Moscow in the hope of striking a bargain with Stalin, and some arrangements were made, though the Russians disregarded them later. In February 1945, Churchill, Roosevelt, and Stalin met for a conference at Yalta in the Crimea. Here, with considerable misgivings, Churchill and Roosevelt made concessions to Russia both in the Far East and in eastern Europe in order to maintain the alliance, to bring Russia into the war against Japan, and to induce Stalin to cooperate in forming the United Nations. These concessions opened the way for Russian predominance throughout eastern Europe. But there was not much that the British and the Americans could do. "What would have happened," Churchill asked later, "if we had quarrelled with Russia while the Germans still had three or four hundred divisions on the fighting front?"

It was February 1945 that the final thrusts at Germany began. They were accompanied by massive air raids on German industry, oil refineries, and railway connections. British and American armies pushed to the Rhine and then across it. By the end of April the Russians had surrounded Berlin. Early in May the Germans surrendered, first in Italy and then to Montgomery in Germany; to Montgomery's commander, Eisenhower; and to the Russians in Berlin.

The war against Japan was not yet won, but the Allies were closing in from various directions. Lord Louis Mountbatten, the head of the British Southeast Asia command, was instructed to begin an invasion of Burma early in 1945, a tremendous undertaking. A number of armies commanded by General Slim converged from India on Mandalay in Upper Burma and captured that city, along with many Japanese prisoners. Slim then raced south to Rangoon, which he also captured, taking it just before the coming of the monsoon rains. Thus Burma was cleared of the Japanese.

Two other movements were converging on them. One was lead by General MacArthur, who moved north from New Guinea to the Philippines, where there was severe fighting for six months. Meanwhile the United States navy was pushing westward from Hawaii toward Japan. The Mariana Islands were taken in 1944, Iwo Jima in March 1945, and Okinawa in May. The Americans were now close to the Japanese home islands. Elaborate plans were evolved for an invasion of Japan which, it was feared, would be very costly in human lives. But with the dropping of the first atomic bombs on Hiroshima (6 August) and on Nagasaki (9 August) and with a Russian declaration of war against Japan, the Japanese had had enough. They surrendered unconditionally on 14 August; the formal document was signed on 2 September. This ended the Second World War.

THE HOME FRONT DURING THE WAR

As the danger from Hitler unfolded in May 1940, Churchill was able to form a truly national government. He established a War Cabinet of five men. He himself took the post of minister of defense; Lord Halifax, a veteran Conservative politician, remained as foreign secretary; and Chamberlain agreed to serve as lord president of the Council. His loyalty to Churchill in the Cabinet preserved the unity of the Conservative party and rendered a service to the country. Clement Attlee, the leader of the Labor party, became lord privy seal and deputy leader of the Commons; Arthur Greenwood, another Labor member, served at first without portfolio and later was placed in charge of postwar reconstruction. Members of all three parties served as ministers outside the Cabinet. Two of the most important were Ernest Bevin, the secretary of the Transport and General Workers Union, who became minister of Labor and National Service, and Lord Beaverbrook, a newspaper magnate of drive and energy, who was appointed minister of Aircraft Production. They were shortly brought into the Cabinet. Sir John Anderson, an eminent civil servant, was added in 1941, and Anthony Eden replaced Halifax. Beaverbrook later was replaced by Oliver Lyttelton, a Conservative; and Greenwood first by Sir Stafford Cripps and then by Herbert Morrison, both Labor members. These men conducted the war for several years. The Cabinet concentrated on major decisions, leaving details to powerful committees.

Most ministers had had experience in administration during the First World War and had also had time during Chamberlain's regime to consider what should be done in another conflict. Hence they were able to avoid earlier mistakes and to establish at once the full control that had come only in the later stages of the First World War. The country was governed during the Second World War with admirable firmness and judgment. Its entire resources of human and material power were channeled into the war effort with completeness and success.

The process began in September 1939 while Chamberlain was still prime minister. The Cabinet assumed wide powers. New ministries were created for Economic Warfare, Information, Food, and Shipping. A national registration was carried through and identity cards were issued to everyone. Much more drastic measures were taken after Churchill assumed office. As mentioned earlier, an unprecedented law passed in June 1940 placed all persons and all property at the disposal of the government. An Essential Work Order of March 1941 enabled the Cabinet to place workers in occupations in which their skills would be most beneficial to the war effort. By the summer of 1941 about eight million men and women were in the armed forces, in home defense, or in factories producing war materials. It was estimated then that about two million more would be required by the summer of 1942 and that the army would have to be enlarged, although a high percentage of skilled labor would have to be retained in war factories, especially in plants producing aircraft. These objectives were achieved only by the strictest budgeting of human resources and by the use of women and of men over military age in all sorts of employment. Nonessential industry was curtailed, utility standards were introduced for consumer goods, rationing was intensified, all persons between the ages of eighteen and fifty were made eligible for national service. A number of young men—the Bevin Boys, as they were called—were detailed to work in the mines. Of every nine men in Britain's labor force in 1944, two were in the armed services and three were in war production.

There was comparatively little unrest in the factories because labor strongly supported the war and because labor leaders, such as Bevin and Morrison, were given authority to deal with labor problems. Bevin pleased labor by forcing employers to provide social services, such as nursery schools for the children of women workers. Even the Communists were willing to cooperate after Russia entered the war. Taxation was very high. The income tax was imposed on incomes that had not been taxed before the war and was made to increase more rapidly on incomes in the higher brackets. At the same time the government held down the cost of living by price controls and by subsidies to farmers.

Plans for Reconstruction

Thus the life of the nation was carefully planned during the war and the economy was closely controlled. The war inspired ideals of social and economic equality. Despite the austerity of wartime conditions, many laboring people were economically better off than ever before, whereas the middle and upper classes found their standard of life reduced by scarcities and by heavy taxation. Some of the officials in the Treasury, such as the economist J. M. Keynes, were quite willing to use the budget to redistribute wealth and to encourage planning. A pamphlet by the historian R. H. Tawney, *Why Britain Fights,* set forth ideals of social justice and of opportunity for all to enjoy the fruits of civilization.

Churchill was not greatly interested in planning: his mind was on the war. He disliked anything that might detract from the war effort and he feared that plans for reconstruction might become so ambitious as to be unattainable and thus an ultimate disappointment. But he could not ignore the national urge to look toward the future. He asked Arthur Greenwood to study the problems of reconstruction. A number of committees of investigation were appointed. One such committee, headed by Sir Montague Barlow, dealt with the relocation of industries and of factory workers in areas away from congested urban districts. Its aim was to spread employment more evenly thoughout the country. A Location of Industries Act was passed in 1945. The Scott Committee, concerned with the utilization of land, stressed the need to foster agriculture, to preserve places of natural beauty, and to induce industry to use old sites in decaying towns in order to restore their prosperity, The Uthwatt Report recommended that the state purchase land both in towns and in the country so as to control the course of future building. Some of these recommendations were contained in the Town and Country Planning Act of 1944.

The most ambitious and controversial of these reports was that of Sir William Beveridge, which dealt with social insurance and which proposed that social insurance be made a part of a larger plan of social security. All the social services, Beveridge believed, should be united under the control of a new ministry. He advocated compulsory insurance for everyone under a uniform system of payments and benefits. A minimum income at the subsistence level should be guaranteed to all, and there should be special benefits to cover the expenses of marriage, childbirth, and death. His report, said Beveridge, was a statement of the uses to which the nation could apply its victory when victory had been achieved.

The Beveridge Report was received with enthusiasm by the Labor party and by the public as a whole, but the government, intent on the war, did not wish to commit itself to such far-reaching proposals, and only tentative steps were taken to implement the report. Churchill appointed as the minister of reconstruction, Lord Woolton, who issued a number of white papers on social insurance, national health, and full employment. One of these papers contained a pledge that the government would use its financial power to ensure full employment after the war. Thus the social legislation of the postwar era, which will be examined in the next chapter, was clearly foreshadowed during the war period.

C H R O N O L O G Y

Peace and War

1931	National Government won landslide election; relief payments cut; the "means test" begins
1932	Tariff Reform adopted; Imperial Economic Conference
1933	Hitler became chancellor of Germany
1935	Baldwin again prime minister; Mussolini attacked Ethiopia; Anglo-German Naval Agreement
1936	Death of George V; accession of Edward VIII; Abdication; George VI king; J. M. Keynes's *General Theory of Employment, Interest, and Money;* Spanish Civil War; German occupation of Rhineland
1937	Neville Chamberlain prime minister
1938	Anthony Eden resigns as foreign secretary; German occupation of Austria; Munich Agreement
1939	German occupation of Czechoslovakia; British rearmament accelerated; guarantee to Poland; World War II
1940	Churchill prime minister; Coalition Government; Dunkirk; Battle of Britain; Anglo-U.S. destroyers for bases agreement

(continued on next page)

Chronology, continued

1941	Lend-Lease Act passed in U.S.; German invasion of Russia; Pearl Harbor
1942	Anglo-American landings in North Africa; Battle of El Alamein; Beveridge Report
1943	Germans driven from Africa; landings in Sicily and Italy
1944	Fall of Rome; D-Day landings in Normandy; Town and Country Planning Act; Education Act
1945	Yalta Conference; victory in Europe; Labor landslide; Attlee prime minister; atom bombs dropped on Japan; Japan surrendered

35

Post-War Britain: 1945–1970

After the Second World War, as after the first one, Britain faced many problems of readjustment. Fundamentally these problems were much the same, but the intensity of Britain's difficulties in 1945 and the emergence of the United States and Russia as the two world giants forced Britain to recognize, as she had not done in 1918, that her old predominance as a great power had ended. She was left with a certain moral grandeur but had sacrificed much of her economic strength to obtain the victory.

THE ELECTION OF 1945

In the spring of 1945, when Allied success over the Axis Powers was assured, there was talk in Britain of an early election. Churchill, who assumed that his great prestige as the architect of victory would bring the Conservatives success at the polls, set 5 July as the day of the election. Actually, the Labor party was much better prepared to fight an election than were the Conservatives. Determined to end the political truce after the war was won, Labor had kept its views before the public through a series of pamphlets dealing with such matters as housing, full employment, public health, and the nationalization of industry. Labor's electoral manifesto, *Let Us Face the Future,* set forth in clear and temperate language a program of expanded social services, limited nationalization, and continued controls to ease the transition to a peacetime economy.

The Conservatives, with no such clear-cut program, declared that after the peace they would examine each industry in turn, and would do what seemed best in individual cases. Churchill clearly favored an abandonment of government controls and the encouragement of private enterprise. He launched an attack on socialism, comparing it with the totalitarian regimes of the fascists. The reaction of the people was one of amused skepticism. A Labor leader remarked that "Winston was having a night out." Unafraid of economic planning, the people were thinking of housing, employment, and social security; their mood for the moment was rather radical. They did not regard the winning of the war as the achievement of any one party. Many voters recalled the Conservative policy of appeasement during the 1930s and were determined to throw out the "men of Munich." Hence the Labor party won by a landslide in the election of 1945. The new House of Commons contained 393 Labor members and only 189 Conservatives. The nation was rather astonished at what it had done. So was Churchill. He wrote later that he had exercised power during more than five years of war, "at the end of which time, all our enemies having surrendered unconditionally or being about to do so, I was immediately dismissed by the British electorate from all further conduct of their affairs."

LABOR AND THE WELFARE STATE

The Labor Cabinet of 1945

Clement Attlee, the Labor prime minister, was a moderate man, cool in temperament, and persuasive in maintaining harmony within his Cabinet. An able debater, with long experience in the Commons, he was industrious, honest, and loyal. But he lacked Churchill's glamour and oratorical power. As he drove to Buckingham Palace in his small family car to kiss the royal hand as prime minister, he was a symbol of postwar Britain—sensible, practical, and patient, but a little drab. His most important colleague in the new Cabinet was Ernest Bevin, the foreign secretary. Other Cabinet ministers included Hugh Dalton, the sharp-tongued chancellor of the Exchequer; Herbert Morrison, leader of the House of Commons; Sir Stafford Cripps, president of the Board of Trade; and Aneurin Bevan, the radical and controversial minister of Health.

For the first time in history the Labor party commanded a large majority in the Commons. It could claim a mandate to move ahead with a program of expanded social services and nationalization. About half the Labor members were in the Commons for the first time. Like the Liberals in 1906, they were inexperienced yet zealous. They pushed their program with rapidity, but they were harassed and hampered by the desperate economic plight in which Britain found herself.

The Economic Problem

Although the loss of life in the British armed forces during the Second World War was much less than during the earlier war, the material damage at home was much greater. Sections of London and of other cities had been leveled to the ground, some five million houses had been destroyed or rendered unsafe for habitation, and eighteen million tons of shipping had been lost. British railways, factories, and power

plants had been subjected to constant and grueling use in war production without normal maintenance and modernization. The cost of rebuilding and replacement was greater than Britain could afford, for she had liquidated about a third of her foreign securities and had lost many of her invisible exports.

It was essential for Britain to restore her factories, regain some portion of her foreign trade, and expand her shrunken exports until they balanced the cost of imported goods and raw materials. It was hoped that American assistance in the form of lend-lease would be continued after the war, but the United States brought lend-lease to a rather abrupt termination in September 1945, following the surrender of Japan. To meet this crisis Britain obtained from the United States a loan of $3750 million, which was to carry interest of two percent and was to be repaid in fifty annual installments beginning in 1951. A loan of $1250 million was secured from Canada on somewhat more generous terms. These credits, it was hoped, would carry Britain over the first years of reconstruction. Unfortunately, the cost of raw materials was high in 1945 and the money was spent more quickly than had been anticipated.

The Labor government, in handling economic problems, relied on strict controls. This seemed the natural thing to do: controls had been successful during the war, and economic planning was in fashion. Wartime restrictions were therefore continued into the peace. Through an elaborate system of licenses and allocations the government regulated the importation of raw materials and their distribution to British manufacturers, favoring those industries which fed the export trades. Steel, machine tools, and other necessities also were allotted carefully among industrialists. To conserve the supply of machines and raw materials required by industry, the government established a system of licenses for exports as well as imports. Expansion by industry was regulated, prices were fixed, and foreign exchange was carefully controlled. The government, though retaining ample powers of coercion, preferred to employ persuasion and consultation in dealing with labor and management; many of these controls were exercised by industrial magnates who worked closely with the Board of Trade and with other ministries. At the same time domestic consumption and private building were curtailed through rationing, price controls, taxation, and building permits.

The price of food was held at a low level. The Ministry of Food bought agricultural products from British farmers and sold them to the public at substantially lower prices; imported food often was bought in bulk in order to obtain it at a cheap rate. The result was that even persons with very low incomes could obtain a nutritious diet, though there were many complaints about its monotony.

The effect of this control of industry was disappointing. Strict regulation, which had achieved its purpose during the war, failed to produce the desired results in time of peace. One difficulty was that the workers no longer felt the stimulus of war conditions; many years of tension and struggle now were followed by a natural decline in morale. Although the demand for labor was high and employment had risen, productivity did not increase correspondingly. There were stoppages and evidence of slackness. Diminished incentive affected manufacturers, for excessive controls hampered private enterprise. Rising wages and cheap interest rates increased purchasing power, but rationing and restrictions severely limited what people were permitted to buy. Manufacturers saw no reason to produce articles the public was not allowed to purchase.

The economy improved very slowly. It was stronger in 1946 than it had been in 1945, but a severe slump occurred in 1947, a year that began badly with an unusually severe winter, during which snow and ice blocked roads and railways. As reserves of coal shrank, factories closed for lack of fuel, and some two million workers were temporarily idle. British exports declined during the first half of 1947, just as the American and Canadian credits were running out. A new austerity program was announced by the government, and a new drive for greater productivity was begun.

It was fortunate for Britain that late in 1947 the American government decided to give economic aid to Europe under the Marshall Plan. The Americans feared that if Europe did not develop economically the way would lie open for an advance of communism. Hence the Organization for European Economic Cooperation was established early in 1948 to place large American credits at the disposal of European countries and to induce them to cooperate in removing tariff barriers. Marshall

Plan aid helped to improve the British economy in 1948. There were other reasons for the advance: several of the controls over British industry were now relaxed, industry throve under less rigid supervision, and both labor and management made a greater effort to increase productivity. The year 1949 was rather disappointing. A slight depression in the United States caused a decline in American imports from Britain, and so precarious was the basis of the British economy, that this moderate drop forced a devaluation of the pound from $4.03 to $2.80 in September. Conditions improved once more in 1950.

Nationalization

A time of such uncertain economic conditions as the period following a war might well appear inappropriate for socialistic experiment. Yet the Labor party, from the moment it came into office, followed a policy of partial nationalization of industry. A nationalized industry was one whose total assets had been purchased by the state. Private owners received a fair price for their property, all nationalization being based on acts of Parliament. The industries thus acquired were operated by public corporations responsible to various ministries for general policy but not for the details of management. In some cases the business executives who had managed industries before nationalization were employed to continue their direction. The position of labor was unaffected. Without participating in the guidance of nationalized industry, labor continued to deal with management through collective bargaining and through the right to strike.

The Cabinet began by nationalizing the Bank of England in 1946. Stockholders received government stock in place of their old certificates; the directors of the bank were to be appointed by the Cabinet. The relations of the bank and the Treasury, however, had been so close before nationalization that they were changed very little. A member of Parliament dubbed the entire proceeding "an elaborate game of make-believe." The government acted partly because it regarded nationalization as a kind of retribution for the role the bank was supposed to have played in overthrowing the Labor Cabinet in 1931.

A Coal Industry Nationalization Act also was passed in 1946. Although the Conservatives criticized the details of this measure, its principles were accepted by both parties. There was an obvious need to bring the independent mining companies—some eight hundred in all—under central regulation; the state of the industry was most unsatisfactory, with low productivity, low morale among the miners, bad blood between labor and management, and poor living conditions in mining areas. The act established a national coal board to control the industry under the general supervision of the minister of Fuel and Power. Nationalization also was applied to civil aviation, to cables and wireless, and to electricity and gas. A drastic, complicated, and far-reaching measure dealt with inland transport—railways, canals, docks and harbors, buses, and road haulage.

Controversy arose over Labor's desire to nationalize iron and steel, an industry which could claim that it was efficient and productive and that it had established effective controls over itself, with machinery for fixing prices and for allocating production quotas. On the other hand, the Cabinet asserted that the industry was semimonopolistic and that, intent upon profits, it did not attempt to meet the nation's demand for steel or the laborer's need for full employment. The nationalization of iron and steel became a symbol of the success or failure of Labor's program. The Conservatives feared that, if this industry was nationalized, the way would be opened for the nationalization of many others. Labor believed that failure in this case might jeopardize all its efforts. A division arose over this measure between the doctrinaire socialists and the more practical politicians in the Labor party. Further, it became obvious that because of opposition in the House of Lords the legislation on iron and steel would be a lengthy business. In 1949 Labor passed an act which limited to one year instead of two the power of the Lords to delay legislation. The iron and steel bill passed through Parliament in 1949, but it was not to become effective until 1951, before which date there would be a general election.

Labor pressed forward with its program of nationalization in a spirit of idealism and crusading zeal, but the results were disappointing. Socialists had hoped that workers in nationalized industries would develop a sense of indirect ownership, would take pride in their participation in public enterprises, and would acquire some influence through consultation with management. Few of these expectations were fulfilled. Public ownership failed to stir the imagination of workingmen. In their view, conditions remained as they had always been, and the boss was still the boss. Socialists had also hoped that public ownership would result in lowered salaries for business managers and would thus advance equalization of income. Nationalized industries, however, had to compete with private enterprise for able executives and had to pay them roughly comparable salaries. Nor was public ownership a cure for the ills of industry, though it is true that conditions were sometimes improved. The coal-mining industry, for example, was in a more satisfactory state following nationalization. Yet the production of coal was less than the goals that were set, and the morale of the men was low despite high wages and fringe benefits. Having paid a fair price for the industries it acquired, the state expected them to show a profit. But profits did not necessarily follow. The railways, now feeling the full competition of airplanes and motor cars, had been operated at enormous loss. The nationalization of iron and steel became a political liability. Public ownership was neither a cure for economic ills nor a factor in reshaping society.

The Extension of the Social Services

Another portion of Labor's program dealt with the extension of the social services. Several acts, closely following the recommendations of the Beveridge Report, were passed between 1946 and 1948. The most comprehensive was the National Insurance Act, by which older legislation dealing with old-age pensions and with insurance against illness and unemployment was consolidated into one vast insurance plan for the entire population. Almost every adult now paid small weekly sums to the government, and employers made similar payments for each employee. These contributions amounted to about thirty percent of the cost of the insurance plan; the remainder was met by general taxation. Benefits included weekly payments during periods of illness and unemployment, old-age pensions, and supplementary sums to meet special cases and emergencies, such as pregnancy, childbirth, widowhood, and death.

Industrial injuries also were placed on an insurance basis. Each workman paid a few pennies a week (matched by his employer) into a central fund from which benefits were drawn. A Family Allowances Act, passed by Churchill's government in 1945, provided small sums to every family for each child (except the first) until that child reached fifteen. A National Assistance Act abolished the old poor laws, offered the minimum cost of food and shelter to every applicant, and provided for half a million persons who because of age or infirmity required special care.

The most popular item in the extension of the social services was the National Health Service Act of 1946. This act had a longer history than is often supposed: for many years the medical profession, the public, and various governments had considered plans for the improvement of medical services, but a white paper issued by the Cabinet in 1944 alarmed the doctors. They were afraid that a national service would undermine the freedom of their profession and that bureaucrats at the local level would mismanage hospitals. Aneurin Bevan, the minister of Health, who piloted the bill through Parliament, was roundly abused. The bill had a stormy passage but once it became law it was received gratefully by the people. It provided free medical and dental service, free glasses, dentures, and prescriptions for medicine, and free hospitalization for the entire population. It called for clinics and health centers, though these were too costly to be introduced at once. The plan retained as much flexibility as possible. Physicians could continue in private practice if they wished; patients could select their doctors. There can be little doubt that the health service improved the health of the nation. Persons who had gone to doctors only in emergencies, or who could not afford specialists, now received adequate attention. Used far more than had been anticipated, the health service became very costly. Yet so great was its popularity, that the Conservatives campaigning in 1950 promised to continue the plan if they were returned to power.

A number of other measures should be mentioned, including two important housing acts. The first, in 1946, curtailed private building and aimed at the construction of low-priced houses the state could rent for as little as 10s. a week. Rising costs soon made this figure unrealistic, but rents were kept very low. A second act, passed in 1949, encouraged local authorities to improve large city houses, which had degenerated, through subdivision into apartments and cheap lodgings. The housing program, supervised by Aneurin Bevan, was subjected to severe criticism because of the acute shortage, the high cost, the arbitrary fixing of rents, and some unavoidable waste. Nonetheless, within five years Bevan built 806,000 permanent houses and apartments and 157,000 temporary houses; he also created 333,000 new units through the conversion of older dwellings.

The government hoped to implement an ambitious Education Act passed in 1944, but was badly hampered by a shortage of trained teachers and of school buildings. Some progress was made, especially in training teachers. The school-leaving age was raised to fifteen and the state began to give greatly increased assistance to universities and to university students. A New Towns Act in 1946 empowered the government to build new industrial and residential towns on the outskirts of large cities, thus drawing industry and population away from congested urban centers. An Atomic Energy Act authorized experiments in the uses of atomic energy for peaceful purposes. Two measures dealt with the constitution. The first abolished the last vestiges of plural voting. The universities lost their representation in the Commons; businessmen who had voted both in the constituencies in which they resided and also in those in which they worked were now allowed to vote only in the first. In 1949, as we have seen, the power of the House of Lords to delay legislation was reduced from two years to one.

Relations with Russia

In conducting foreign affairs the Labor government experienced the dissillusionment of worsening relations with Russia. The radicals of the party believed that if her policy were truly socialistic Britain should be able to get on with the Russians. But it was quickly evident that Russian aims were incompatible with British interests. British influence disappeared in most of eastern Europe as the countries of that area were reduced to Russian satellites. The Russian *coup d'état* in Czechoslovakia in 1948 was as ruthless as Hitler's nine years before. Russian efforts to obtain one of the former Italian colonies in North Africa, as well as Russian intrigues in Greece, threatened the British position in the eastern Mediterranean. Moreover, Russia refused to participate in the Marshall Plan and prevented her satellites from doing so. Finally, in Germany, where lay the central problem, Russia's attitude was distinctly hostile. In 1948 she attempted to block the access of the Western Powers to their sectors of Berlin, a move adroitly countered by a massive airlift to Berlin from the West. Meanwhile there was constant vilification of the West by Russian propaganda.

Ernest Bevin, foreign secretary in the Labor Cabinet, a trade-union man rather than a doctrinaire socialist, followed tradition by defending British interests as best he could. He thought in terms of a defensive alliance of western European nations to fill the power vacuum created by Germany's defeat. In 1947 he concluded such an alliance with France; in the next year he brought in Holland, Belgium, and Luxembourg. The culmination of this policy was the North Atlantic Treaty Organization (NATO) established in 1949. This organization included the powers along the western seaboard of Europe (except for Spain and Ireland), together with the United States, Canada, Iceland, and Italy. Greece and Turkey entered NATO in 1951, West Germany in 1955, and Spain in 1982. It was a military alliance aimed at keeping the Russians at bay.

Evaluation of Labor's Tenure of Power

What had the Labor government accomplished during its five years of power? Britain's position in international affairs, after the establishment of NATO, was more secure and influential than it had been at the end of the war. Labor's principal achievement at home was not nationalization, of which the benefits were doubtful, but, rather, the establishment of the welfare state. By 1950 the social services were expanded greatly, unemployment scarcely existed, income sufficient to meet the minimal cost of food and shelter was guaranteed to all, and a free medical service was available. The housing problem was being attacked with vigor, and educational policy, though not achieving all that had been hoped, was set on a more democratic course. There were fair shares for all. This advance had come, not as the result of a sudden revolution in thought or action, but through an evolutionary trend toward greater concern for the welfare of the population as a whole. An all-important question remained: could the welfare state become an affluent state with a rising standard of living for all classes, or must the wealth of the country remain static and the condition of the poor improved solely by taxing away the resources of the well-to-do? This was the question posed through the 1950s.

THE TRANSITION TO CONSERVATIVE GOVERNMENT

The Labor party, after its strenuous five years of advanced legislation, could hardly hope for another great victory at the polls. The bulk of its proposed reforms had been enacted; it could offer the public only a continuation of the same bill of fare. Its time in office had been marked by high taxation and by irksome shortages and controls. The economic crisis of 1947 had brought great discomfort and unwelcome austerity. Labor, moreover, was threatened by a revolt of its radical wing in opposition to Bevin's foreign policy. The party program in 1950, therefore, was moderate. Ministers proposed to extend the welfare state but would act with caution. They affirmed their faith in nationalization, but they had little to say about economic planning and they recognized the role of private enterprise in industry. As Mr. Attlee toured the country in his small automobile with his wife at the wheel, he presented an image of sensible economy and disarming moderation.

The Conservatives, despite a good deal of frustration, had been growing in strength, had improved their party organization, and had acquired an adequate party chest. Their problem was whether to accept the welfare state. Although there were many things about it they did not like, they knew that it had the backing of the majority of voters and hence they wisely regarded it as something permanent. They claimed they could improve its administration and reduce its cost. They opposed nationalization. But, with the exceptions of iron and steel and road haulage, they agreed not to disturb those industries already nationalized. The two parties were closer together in 1950 than might be supposed.

The election in February 1950 proved to be a stalemate. Labor lost its large majority, though with 315 seats it remained the strongest party in the Commons. The Conservatives, with 298, were not far behind; Labor's majority over all other parties combined was only 6. Attlee remained as prime minister. Unable to press contentious measures, he offered only a limited program of legislation in the speech from the throne which opened the new Parliament. The fear of defeat in a snap vote forced Labor members to be diligent in their attendance in the Commons.

Although the Labor party remained in office for about a year and a half, it was beset with many difficulties, barely escaping defeat when it gave effect to the act of 1949 nationalizing iron and steel. The act had provided that nationalization should take place in 1951, but the Conservatives, pointing to Labor losses in the recent election, now pressed for further delay, which the government refused. Other problems arose from the conflict in Korea. This broke out in June 1950 when the United States, acting under a resolution of the Security Council of the United Nations, defended South Korea against Communist attack from the north. The Cabinet approved this action and sent naval units to Korea. But Britain did not wish to lose her trade with China; moreover, she feared that the United States would broaden the war into a general conflict, and she felt the necessity of increasing her armaments. Rearmament, which caused new division between the moderate and radical wings of the Labor party, was denounced by Aneurin Bevan, who declared that its cost would take money away from the social services. In April 1951 he resigned from the Cabinet. Other resignations, coming at a time when several key ministers were ill, reduced the drive and momentum of the government. The national economy, having done very well in 1950, sagged in 1951, so that a new balance-of-payments crisis was in the making. Under these circumstances Attlee held an election in October 1951.

The trend away from Labor continued in this election, though the Commons remained very evenly divided between the two major parties. The Conservatives won 321 seats whereas Labor won 295. Over all other parties combined the Conservative majority was only 17. Yet this shift in strength, though small, was sufficient to bring in the Conservatives and to end Labor's term of office. The election was more decisive than was imagined at the time, for the Conservatives were to remain in power for the next thirteen years.

THE CONSERVATIVES IN POWER

Churchill's Cabinet, 1951–1955

Winston Churchill, still surprisingly vigorous at seventy-seven, immediately formed a Conservative government. He assumed his old post of minister of Defense and brought into the Cabinet several elder statesmen with whom he had worked during the war. One was Lord Woolton, who became a coordinating minister for Food and Agriculture. Another was Lord Cherwell, a physicist who was placed in

HOUSE OF WINDSOR (MOUNTBATTEN)

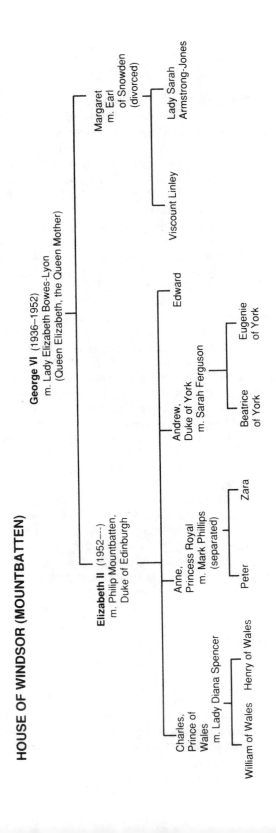

George VI (1936–1952)
m. Lady Elizabeth Bowes-Lyon
(Queen Elizabeth, the Queen Mother)

Elizabeth II (1952——)
m. Philip Mountbatten,
Duke of Edinburgh

Margaret
m. Earl
of Snowden
(divorced)

Anne,
Princess Royal
m. Mark Phillips
(separated)

Andrew,
Duke of York
m. Sarah Ferguson

Edward

Viscount Linley

Lady Sarah
Armstrong-Jones

Charles,
Prince of
Wales
m. Lady Diana Spencer

Peter

Zara

Beatrice
of York

Eugenie
of York

William of Wales   Henry of Wales

control of atomic energy and research. Younger ministers included Sir Anthony Eden as foreign secretary, R. A. Butler as chancellor of the Exchequer, and Harold Macmillan as minister of Housing.

A few months after Churchill resumed office, his friend King George VI died of cancer while only in his fifties. His daughter Elizabeth became queen at age twenty-six and immediately inspired talk of a new Elizabethan Age. Her marriage to Philip, duke of Edinburgh, in 1947 had been the first grand occasion for the nation to celebrate since before the war. Churchill gave an inspiring send-off to the new era when he spoke fondly of his long service to the Crown and of a return to the days of Queen Victoria. On the eve of the queen's coronation in June 1953 Mount Everest was climbed for the first time, and by a British team. A new Elizabethan Age indeed!

Churchill's majority was so small that he acted cautiously. He dropped his idea of restoring to the universities their former seats in the Commons. He left the nationalized industries as they were, with two exceptions. One was iron and steel, which was returned to private ownership, though an iron and steel board supervised the industry, determined prices, and directed capital investment. The nationalized transport industry also was altered so as to permit haulage by road in privately owned trucks. Again, the supervision of the government by no means disappeared. Churchill faced a balance-of-payments crisis. Rearmament, the high cost of raw materials, and the constant tendency to increase imports had caused a heavy drain on the pound and on dollar reserves. Churchill curtailed imports, raised the bank rate, discouraged capital investment, and retarded the accumulation of inventories. Fortunately the balance of payments soon improved. Between 1952 and 1954 manufactured articles rose in price in the world market while the cost of raw materials declined. These favorable trends were accompanied by an increase in British productivity. It was possible to end the rationing of food in 1954, and Butler reduced taxation slightly, though this advantage was offset by his discontinuance of food subsidies. Hence the price of food rose somewhat. Macmillan won praise by building over 300,000 new houses a year.

In April 1955 Sir Winston Churchill at eighty stepped down from his office of prime minister. With his lion's heart, his magnificent confidence in himself and in his country, his ability to inspire others, his capacity for prompt decision, and his power over words, he was one of England's greatest warrior-statesmen. His life was an epitome of British history for almost sixty years. He was succeeded as prime minister by his foreign secretary, Sir Anthony Eden, who at once dissolved Parliament.

The Election of 1955

The election of 1955, coming in the middle of the decade, illustrates a number of trends and developments. There was, in the first place, a continued swing to the right. Having increased their strength in the elections of 1950 and 1951, the Conservatives now further improved their position by winning a comfortable majority of fifty-eight seats over all other parties combined. This was an unusual occurrence.

It is normal for a party, once in power, to enact its program and then decline in popularity until it grows weak and tired. The Conservatives, reversing this pattern, were making the 1950s a Conservative decade.

Their success was due in large measure to the improved condition of the economy. They had been fortunate in coming to power at a time when world economic conditions were moving forward; they had made the most of their opportunity. The working classes, with full employment and good wages, were tasting an increased prosperity. With many of the old controls now lifted, industry was thriving and was pushing new techniques and new products. The great success story was that of the automobile. The production of motor cars was four times as large in 1955 as it had been in 1946. Everybody wanted a car. Automobiles became an important article of export. There was, of course, a price to be paid, for Britain is a small and crowded island whose country lanes, blind corners, and crooked city streets are ill adapted to motor traffic. Nonetheless, the manufacture of automobiles was giving an important stimulus to the economy. Other industries, such as the production of aircraft, radios, chemicals, electrical goods, and new machines of all kinds, were doing well— appealing to the home market and competing successfully in world trade. There was also a great amount of building.

The election of 1955 indicated a certain apathy toward politics. The number of persons who voted was less in 1955 than in 1951, a decline more harmful to the Labor party than to the Conservatives. Apathy was due perhaps in part to a feeling that the destiny of the world was no longer controlled by Britain, but rather by the Soviet Union and the United States. It was due in part to greater contentment with conditions as they were and to a belief that policy would be much the same no matter which party was in power.

In December 1955, when Clement Attlee resigned as leader of the Labor party, Bevan was passed over, and the leadership went to Hugh Gaitskell, an economist of high integrity and of moderate socialistic views. Bevan became more temperate. There were differences between the moderate and radical wings of the party. The radicals urged a further nationalization of industry, the disestablishment of the Church of England, withdrawal of Britain from imperial commitments, reduction in the size of the army, and abandonment of close relations with capitalistic America. They opposed nuclear defense because they held that Britain, whether prepared or not, would be destroyed in the course of a war involving nuclear weapons.

Sir Anthony Eden, 1955–1957

Sir Anthony Eden, an attractive gentleman in manners and appearance, remained as prime minister only from April 1955 to January 1957. As foreign secretary under Neville Chamberlain he had resisted the policy of appeasement toward Hitler and Mussolini. He had long enjoyed the confidence of Churchill, who thought of him as his successor both during the war and during Churchill's last premiership. As prime minister, however, Eden was a disappointment. It was a great disadvantage to him—or to anyone—to follow such an outstanding figure as Churchill. Eden did not arouse enthusiasm among the rank and file of the party, nor did he appear to give the full commitment to his office that was necessary for success. He had to deal with a serious crisis in 1956 when Britain and France intervened in a war between Egypt and Israel, sent troops into the Suez Canal zone, and then, under strong pressure both from to U.S.S.R. and the United States, agreed to withdraw their forces. This episode greatly weakened Eden's government. He resigned as prime minister in January 1957, though his party remained in power.

Harold Macmillan, 1957–1963

It was thought that Eden's successor as Conservative prime minister would be R. A. Butler, who had been chancellor of the Exchequer in Churchill's last Cabinet. Butler, however, was passed over, perhaps because he had privately expressed his opposition to the venture in Suez; the premiership went to Harold Macmillan. A member of the Commons for many years, Macmillan had first held office in 1951 as Churchill's minister of Housing, when he had been a brilliant success and had served as foreign minister and later as chancellor of the Exchequer under Eden. His position as prime minister was at first precarious: his party was divided by the Suez crisis, and the public was critical of it. Had Labor been stronger and more united it might have overthrown the Conservatives and formed a Labor government.

But Macmillan quickly proved his ability. He established his leadership among the Conservatives. His economic policy was successful. The Suez crisis, which had been very costly, forced Britain to purchase oil from the United States at a time when the balance of payments was already unfavorable. To meet this crisis, Macmillan resorted to the usual methods of checking capital expenditures and curtailing imports. His principal weapon was an extremely high bank rate of seven percent, which held borrowing to a minimum. The balance of payments righted itself, foreign trade increased, and soon the economy again was permitted to expand. The year 1959 was an excellent one and the government was able to reduce taxes. It is not surprising, therefore, that when the Conservatives held an election in October they won a handsome victory, increasing their majority in the Commons to 100.

In the early 1960s, however, the Conservatives found themselves in difficulties of various kinds. Weaknesses appeared in the economy. Hoping to expand trade with the Continent, Macmillan applied in 1961 for admission to the European Economic Community, known as the Common Market, an economic association of six countries (France, West Germany, Italy, the Netherlands, Belgium, and Luxembourg) among whom tariff barriers had been substantially reduced. The economies of these countries were developing at a faster rate than was that of Britain. Membership in the Common Market would expand British exports and would assist her in maintaining sterling as an international currency as well as in developing backward areas in the Commonwealth. Negotiations continued for more than a year. But in January 1963 the French president, Charles de Gaulle, who did not wish to admit a rival to French leadership in the Common Market, managed to close the door against British participation. He contended that British membership and the changes Britain pro-

Harold
Macmillan.
(Carlton Club,
London)

posed would alter the nature of the Common Market. His action was a rebuff to Macmillan, who had been basing his economic and political policy on the assumption that Britain would be admitted.

Macmillan was further embarrassed by decisions in the United States which showed that Britain was depending on America for missiles to carry her nuclear weapons. The winter of 1962–1963 was a severe one, with a power shortage and with a greater amount of unemployment than had existed since before the war. Then came the Profumo scandal, in which the secretary for War was involved with a woman who might have been a security risk. In October 1963 Macmillan resigned as prime minister. After a rather bitter intraparty contest, he was succeeded by the earl of Home who, renouncing his peerage, took his seat in the Commons as Sir Alec Douglas-Home.[1]

---

[1]A Peerage Act of July 1963 gave all existing peers the right to renounce their peerages within the next six months. Persons succeeding to peerages subsequent to the act were allowed a year in which they might do the same. Another change in the law of the peerage had been made in 1958 when life peerages were created.

An aristocrat of charm and intelligence, Sir Alec had a quiet manner which was effective over television and in the House of Commons. He had done well as foreign secretary under Macmillan. On the other hand, some people considered him too old at age sixty and too conservative; they doubted whether he would prove a dynamic leader. He came to power at a time when an election was approaching and when the Conservatives were thought to be heading for a severe defeat. During the year of Sir Alec's ministry, however, their chances improved. Forecasts indicated that the country was again very evenly divided between the two major parties; the election, held on 15 October 1964, resulted in a narrow victory for Labor with 317 seats, as against 304 for the Conservatives and 9 for the Liberal party. If Conservatives and Liberals voted together, Labor's majority would be only 4.

LABOR IN POWER

After the election of October 1964 the Labor party came into office for the first time in thirteen years. Its *Party Manifesto* issued before the election was a vigorous document promising new ministries for economic affairs and for technology, greater scope and expansion for the nationalized industries, and the nationalization of iron and steel. Harold Wilson, the Labor prime minister, who had become leader of the party in 1963 at the death of Hugh Gaitskell, was regarded, if not as a radical, at least as a man around whom radicals gathered. A politician of vigor, perserverance, and skill, he echoed the tone of the *Party Manifesto*, declaring that despite his small majority he intended to govern with decisiveness.

During his five and a half years in office, however, he was not in a position to push controversial legislation. His majority, as we have seen, was very small, sometimes shrinking to the vanishing point, until in March 1966, sensing a favorable moment, he called unexpected election and won a handsome majority of ninety-seven seats. A far greater cause for moderation was the fact that throughout his premiership he was faced with serious economic problems: inflation, demands for higher wages, and crises in the balance of payments. Unfortunately in Britain, when the economy is booming and wages and profits are high, as was the case under Macmillan, inflationary pressures begin to mount. The demand for goods and services increases, imports multiply, foreign holders of sterling sell short in hope of devaluation, and a balance-of-payments crisis is shortly at hand. This was the situation when Wilson took office, and similar problems plagued him year after year.

To maintain the parity of the pound and to reverse the unfavorable balance of payments, Wilson employed the same tactics that the Conservatives had used in the past: surtaxes on many imports, tax relief to exporters, emergency budgets increasing general taxation, tight money, discouragement of economic expansion, an attempt to find "an incomes policy," that is, to regulate wage increases (even by legislation) and to retain a correlation between them and increased productivity. Britain reduced her military budget, curtailed her imperial commitments, and

increased the payments by employers and employees to support the social services. Even so, Wilson was forced to devaluate the pound from about $2.80 to about $2.40 in November 1967. He also turned toward the Conservative policy of seeking English membership in the European Economic Community or Common Market.

Thus Wilson's radicalism disappeared. He defended his moderate policies by saying that the two parties were moving toward a consensus; in the election of 1966 he referred to his government as a national government. But many of his followers were unhappy with his measures. He felt great pressure from trade unions demanding wage increases. Indeed, the whole field of labor relations was in ferment, with many work stoppages and with orderly bargaining disturbed by wildcat strikes. Wilson also was under attack from Labor members who wanted lower interest rates and greater economic expansion and disliked British support of the United States in Vietnam.

The economic situation improved in 1969. In June 1970, again believing that the moment was opportune, Wilson dissolved Parliament and held an election. To the consternation of the Labor party, the Conservatives won by some thirty seats, Wilson resigned, and Edward Heath, who had succeeded Sir Alec Douglas-Home as Conservative leader, formed a Cabinet.

THE EMPIRE SINCE 1918

Changes of a fundamental nature have taken place in the British Empire since the end of the First World War. The maturing of the older Dominions into sovereign states, the insistent nationalism among the peoples of Asia and Africa, the grant of independence to many of these peoples, and the evolution of what is sometimes called the Second Commonwealth have transformed the empire into something very different from what it once was. The crucial points, as we shall see, were the granting of independence to India and to Pakistan in 1947 and their desire to become republics, though within the Commonwealth. It was fortunate that the Labor party, with its liberal approach to colonial questions, was the party in power at that time. The truth was that Britain lacked the resources to continue her former imperial commitments and could not hope to check the tide of nationalism nor to defend and develop the empire as she had done in the past. It was possible for Labor to give independence to India, Pakistan, Burma, and Ceylon quickly and easily. The Conservatives, on the other hand, when in power during the 1950s reverted for a moment to older concepts in dealing with Egypt and the Suez Canal. This policy proved a failure. Thereafter, the Conservatives accepted the new order, which called for liberation of the colonies at a very rapid pace.

India

Nationalism in India increased greatly in intensity during the years following the First World War. A new constitution granted to India in 1919 was regarded as disappointing, for it did little more than make Indian ministers responsible for the less important parts of local government. Public opinion, already irritable, was alienated by two other events. One was a series of statutes enlarging the powers of the government to suppress plots and conspiracies. These statutes were regarded as oppressive. The other was the Amritsar incident, a most unfortunate episode in which a British commander opened fire on an unarmed crowd that had assumed a threatening tone.

These were the circumstances which brought Mohandas K. Gandhi to the fore as the leader of the nationalist movement. Gandhi was a strange combination of saint and revolutionary, of holy man and cunning politician, modest yet dictatorial, gentle yet wholly unreasonable. He soon produced great changes, turning the nationalist movement, largely confined to the educated classes, into a movement of the people. He transformed the Congress party into a revolutionary body, pledged to overthrow the existing government by all peaceful means. The Congress became a kind of rival government to that of the British. Gandhi refused self-government by installments;

he demanded it immediately and completely. In 1919 Gandhi began the first of his campaigns for passive disobedience.

Ramsay MacDonald, with Baldwin's support, obtained the passage of a new India Act in 1935. This act entrusted the whole field of local government to Indian ministers responsible to the provincial legislatures. It also envisaged a federal framework at the center, with a legislature and a Cabinet responsible to it, though the viceroy still retained control of defense, foreign affairs, and religious policy. The portion of the act concerning provincial government went into effect in 1937 and made a fair beginning. The formation of the federal framework at the center was deferred, pending negotiations with the native princes, and was still in abeyance at the beginning of the Second World War.

Meanwhile, the Congress party was becoming more and more autocratic. It claimed to represent all India, to be the one true party of Indian nationalism, the sole heir of British power. No other party and no other leadership were to count in the India of the future. When the Congress party won elections to the provincial legislatures it refused to share power with any other party, and Congress members conducted themselves as the future rulers of India. This attitude greatly alarmed the Muslims. If the Congress was to dominate the government after independence was won, the Muslim position would be hopeless. Hence the Muslims drew together and improved the strength of their organization, the Muslim League. They found an able leader in the fiery and impressive Mr. Mohammed Ali Jinnah. Forming the Muslim League into a compact fighting party, Jinnah declared that the Muslims would accept no constitution of either Hindu or British manufacture but would achieve their own destiny in their own way. The Muslims, he asserted, were not an Indian minority but a separate nation. Those parts of the population with a clear Muslim majority should be formed into a separate state, cut off from the rest of the country. Thus the policy of partition, which resulted later in the creation of Pakistan, came into existence.

During the Second World War the Congress party, refusing to fight for Britain until India was free, demanded immediate independence. The Muslim League, taking a middle course, did not tell its members to stay out of the war effort but refused to cooperate officially unless its policy of partition was accepted. The British made many efforts to win over the major parties. At one point Sir Stafford Cripps flew to India and offered complete independence after the war, with a settlement to be devised by the Indians, if only they would cooperate in the war effort. His offer was rejected. In 1942 Gandhi prepared for a new passive disobedience campaign, though the Japanese army was now on India's eastern frontier. He was arrested, and the British remained in full control of the country. Many thousands of Indians, it should be added, played their part in the war as soldiers and civilians.

The Labor party, which came to power at the end of the war, was prepared to grant India its independence. By a strange paradox, the problem now was to bring Hindus and Muslims together in some sort of government which both would accept. Negotiations continued with no end in sight. In February 1947, in the midst of Britain's coal shortage, Mr. Attlee declared that Britain would withdraw from India, whatever the situation might be in that country, at a date no later than June 1948. Even so, Hindus and Muslims could not agree. To Lord Mountbatten, the last British viceroy, partition appeared the only possible solution. It was, moreover, a solution that must come quickly in order to prevent a civil war. With great skill Mountbatten won both the Hindu Congress and the Muslim League to accept his proposals. On 15 August 1947, India was divided into the two independent states of India and Pakistan. They agreed to remain within the Commonwealth with Dominion status. India became a republic in 1950; Pakistan, in 1956. East Pakistan broke away and became Bangladesh in 1971. When Bangladesh joined the Commonwealth, Pakistan resigned but rejoined in 1989.

Egypt

Although Britain recognized with promptness and decision that independence for India was inevitable, she was slower to see the necessity for a comparable change of policy toward the Middle East. Britain was, of course, intensely aware of the importance of the Suez Canal; having controlled the Arab world during the war and having defended Egypt against Mussolini and Hitler, she was inclined to think of the Middle East in the old imperial terms. In the Suez crisis of October-November 1956 she acted as she might have done in the late nineteenth century. The result was a sharp reminder that times had changed.

In 1922 Britain took the unusual course of declaring unilaterally that Egypt was an independent country, though with certain reservations; Britain insisted that the passage of shipping through the canal must be secure; she reserved the right to defend Egypt against aggression, thus warning other powers to keep away; and the administration of the Anglo-Egyptian Sudan was to remain in her hands. Egypt refused these terms. But in 1936, alarmed at Mussolini's attack on Ethiopia, the Egyptians concluded a treaty with Britain.

This alliance was in operation during the Second World War. But once the war was ended, a new wave of nationalism arose in Egypt. The Labor government, hoping to preserve the military alliance, agreed to withdraw British troops from Cairo and from the Nile Delta, though not from the canal zone. But the Egyptians became more and more hostile and harassed the British troops remaining along the canal. After a number of military *coup d'états* in Egypt, the dominant power in 1954 was the premier, Lieutenant Colonel Nasser, a fiery army officer and ardent nationalist. Britain now agreed, very reluctantly, to withdraw her troops within the next two years. By June of 1956 British soldiers had evacuated the canal zone, leaving one of the world's largest military bases in the hands of civilian caretakers.

Palestine

Events in Palestine also formed part of the background of the Suez crisis. Unfortunately for the British, their mandate in Palestine, begun in 1920, was an impossible one that contained a basic contradiction. Britain undertook to build a Jewish national state in Palestine and at the same time to foster the free development of the Arabs, who hated the Jewish immigrants. Hostility between the two peoples became uncontrollable after the Second World War. Various plans for a binational state, for partition, and for cooperation with the United States in finding a solution came to nothing, and in 1948 Britain brought her mandate to an inglorious end by withdrawing her forces and leaving Jews and Arabs to fight out the issue among themselves. A number of Arab countries, including Egypt, made war on the Jews. But the Jews proved to be surprisingly tough; they repulsed the Arabs and established the independent state of Israel. The Arabs smarted under this defeat, and Nasser, when he came to power, made the destruction of Israel one of his prime objectives. In 1955, by a sudden deal with Russia, he obtained a large quantity of armaments from Czechoslovakia; he then stepped up Egyptian raids into Israeli territory. A new war seemed inevitable.

The Suez Crisis

The United States and Britain, alarmed at Nassar's action in obtaining Russian arms, agreed to help Egypt build a dam at Aswan on the Nile. When the United States suddenly withdrew her offer, Nasser reacted with furious violence. On 26 July 1956, only a few weeks after British forces had evacuated the canal zone, Nasser proclaimed that Egypt would nationalize the Suez Canal, that it would be operated by Egypt, and that the tolls would be used to build the Aswan Dam. There was great alarm in London and Paris and great pressure to intervene. Suddenly Israel determined to attack the Egyptians before they learned to use their Russian arms. On 29 October, Israeli troops pushed toward the canal, easily routing the Egyptians.

The next day England and France issued an ultimatum to both parties demanding that they cease hostilities and withdraw ten miles from each side of the canal. Egypt was asked to allow Anglo-French forces to protect the canal by occupying key points in the canal zone. Israel agreed to these demands but Egypt rejected them. Britain and France then bombarded Egyptian airfields and sent troops into the canal zone on 5 November. World opinion was hostile, Russia threatened to intervene, and the United States, angry because she had not been consulted, denounced the action of her allies. British opinion was divided. Under enormous pressure, Eden decided on 6 November to withdraw British forces if troops were sent by the United Nations to protect the peace in Egypt. To this all parties eventually agreed, and the crisis subsided. The episode was most unfortunate for Britain. It damaged her prestige among the Arabs, it exalted Nasser as an Arab hero when his weakness might well have been exposed by Israel, it left bitterness between England and America, and it showed beyond question that imperialism of the old kind was not only out of date but dangerous.

FROM EMPIRE TO COMMONWEALTH

Changes of a fundamental character have taken place in the structure of the British empire during the twentieth century. The major units of the old empire, both the dominions and many former dependencies, have become sovereign states, loosely associated together as a Commonwealth of Nations. Since 1947 the term "dominion" has fallen into disuse. All sovereign states are known as "Members of the Commonwealth" and include many Asiatic and African peoples as well as those of European stock. There are, of course, a small number of British dependencies, but these are rapidly achieving their independence. The word "Commonwealth" is now used as a comprehensive term to include all British territories, whatever their status.

Development of the Dominions

Before the First World War the empire was divided sharply into two parts. The first consisted of the Dominions of Canada, Newfoundland, Australia, New Zealand, and South Africa. Except for Newfoundland, where there were few inhabitants,[2] the dominions contained large permanent populations predominantly of British origin, though there were many French Canadians and the Boers in South Africa outnumbered the British. The dominions were self-governing in their domestic affairs. The other portion of the empire was composed of a large number of dependencies inhabited by non-European peoples. In general, the dependencies were not considered as candidates for self-government. India was perhaps an exception for the British talked as if India might one day become self-governing, though the British timetable, if left to itself, would have been a slow one.

Though the dominions had achieved self-government in their internal affairs, they had not done so in their foreign policy. Diplomatically the empire functioned as a unit, with policy formulated in London. The dominions, for example, were automatically at war in 1914 when Great Britain declared war on Germany. This conflict, in which they played so notable a part, increased their sense of independence and nationhood; the time had come when they must either be allowed to cooperate in constructing a common foreign policy or be permitted to develop foreign policies of their own. The second alternative took place. The dominions secured separate representation at the Peace Conference at Paris, they were entrusted with the administration of mandated territories, and they became members of the League of Nations. Ireland, a dominion since 1922, wished to become a republic. During the 1920s Canada developed her own diplomatic service and sent an ambassador to Washington in 1927. When the dominions obtained control of their foreign policy, they became sovereign states. Their position was clearly phrased in a famous resolution drafted by Lord Balfour at the Imperial Conference in 1926. The dominions, this statement read,

> are autonomous communities within the British Empire, equal in status, in no way subordinate one to another in any aspect of their domestic or external affairs, though united by a common allegiance to the Crown, and freely associated as members of the British Commonwealth of Nations.

The Statute of Westminster in 1931 gave parliamentary sanction to this statement and spelled out some of its implications by repealing certain laws infringing on the

---

[2]Newfoundland ceased to be a dominion in 1934 and reverted to the status of a Crown colony. In 1949 it became a Canadian province.

sovereignty of the Dominions. No British statute was applicable to a dominion without its consent, any alteration in the succession to the Crown must be approved by the dominions, a dominion might withdraw from the Commonwealth if it so desired. The new diversity in foreign policy was clearly evident when war again broke out in 1939. Australia and New Zealand considered themselves automatically at war with Germany after the British ultimatum to Hitler. But the decision to enter the war was taken in Canada and in South Africa only after a vote in their parliaments; and in South Africa, where the prime minister was opposed to war, he resigned and was succeeded by one in favor of it. Ireland remained neutral, and in 1949 left the Commonwealth and became a republic.

The Commonwealth of Nations

The grant of independence to India and Pakistan in 1947 proved to be a new departure in the history of the Commonwealth. In the first place, the decision was taken to offer these countries the status of dominions, which they decided to accept. This meant that Britain would treat them as she treated the older dominions; thus a pattern was set for dealing with other non-European nations within the empire as they received their independence from it. Secondly, India expressed her desire to become a republic and yet remain within the Commonwealth. Such an arrangement was possible only by abandoning the common allegiance to the Crown which had previously been regarded as essential to membership in the Commonwealth. A meeting of Commonwealth prime ministers in 1949, recognizing that India was to become a sovereign, independent republic, noted:

> The government of India have declared and affirmed India's desire to continue her full membership of the Commonwealth of Nations and her acceptance of the king as the symbol of the free association of its independent member nations and as such the Head of the Commonwealth.[3]

Thus the king became a symbol of the free association of member nations; he held the title of head of the Commonwealth, the title assumed by Queen Elizabeth II when she succeeded to the throne in 1952. In that year it was decided that each nation might use a form of title suitable to its own circumstances.

Following the Indian pattern, other portions of the empire, as they became independent, sovereign states, could, if they so desired, remain within the Commonwealth whether they were monarchies or republics. Some have declined membership—Burma in 1948, Ireland in 1949, the Sudan in 1956—but most of them have not done so. Their numbers have been very large. Sri Lanka (Ceylon) became independent and a member of the Commonwealth in 1948. Then, after a lapse of some years, others followed in rapid succession (see Appendix II).

The Commonwealth displays both strength and weakness. The ties of kindly sentiment toward Britain among overseas populations of British origin are a potent force. The voluntary nature of the Commonwealth promotes good will.

---

[3]Quoted in Arthur C. Turner, "The Commonwealth: Evolution or Dissolution?" *Current History*, XLVI (May 1964), p. 260.

Britain in Africa 1947–1968.

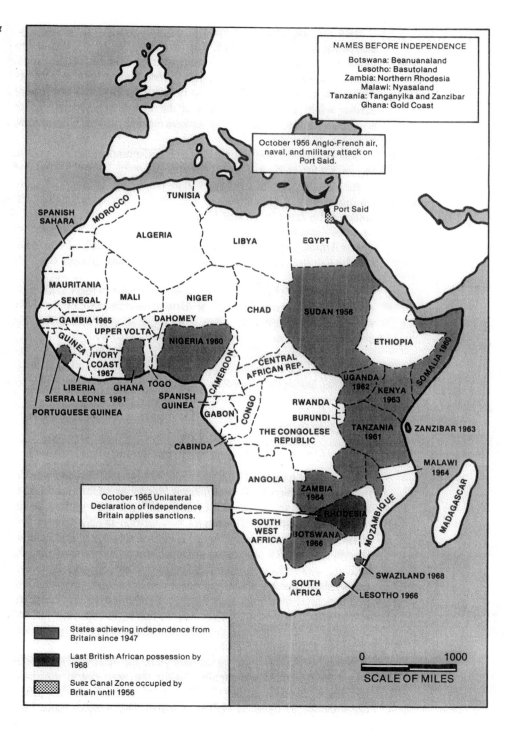

NAMES BEFORE INDEPENDENCE

Botswana: Beanuanaland
Lesotho: Basutoland
Zambia: Northern Rhodesia
Malawi: Nyasaland
Tanzania: Tanganyika and Zanzibar
Ghana: Gold Coast

October 1956 Anglo-French air, naval, and military attack on Port Said.

SPANISH SAHARA

MOROCCO

TUNISIA

Port Said

ALGERIA   LIBYA   EGYPT

MAURITANIA

SENEGAL   MALI   NIGER   CHAD

GAMBIA 1965   SUDAN 1956

GUINEA   DAHOMEY   ETHIOPIA

UPPER VOLTA

IVORY COAST 1967   NIGERIA 1960   CENTRAL AFRICAN REP.   SOMALIA 1960

LIBERIA   GHANA   TOGO   CAMEROON   UGANDA 1962   KENYA 1963

SIERRA LEONE 1961   SPANISH GUINEA   RWANDA

PORTUGUESE GUINEA   GABON   CONGO   BURUNDI   TANZANIA 1961   ZANZIBAR 1963

CABINDA   THE CONGOLESE REPUBLIC

MALAWI 1964

ANGOLA   ZAMBIA 1984   MADAGASCAR

October 1965 Unilateral Declaration of Independence Britain applies sanctions.

RHODESIA

SOUTH WEST AFRICA   BOTSWANA 1966   MOZAMBIQUE

SWAZILAND 1968

SOUTH AFRICA   LESOTHO 1966

States achieving independence from Britain since 1947

Last British African possession by 1968

Suez Canal Zone occupied by Britain until 1956

0   1000
SCALE OF MILES

With the final demise of the white-dominated colony of Southern Rhodesia and its independence as Zimbabwe, the gravest threat to the cohesion of the Commonwealth had been, at least temporarily, ended. Britain joined with the rest of Africa in working for a free Namibia (South West Africa) and for liberalization in South Africa itself. Britain put its stress on working with and encouraging change in South Africa, while all other members of the Commonwealth stressed the need for economic sanctions. This led to serious strains in the Commonwealth and the near isolation of Britain.

Political ties among the nations of the Commonwealth have been strengthened by the desire for union in a world dominated by the United States and Russia. But in the event of a third world war, Britain could not defend the Commonwealth in any adequate way, the success of the Falklands campaign not withstanding. Indeed, some of the most important Commonwealth countries—Canada, Australia, and New Zealand—are linked to some extent with the United States for purposes of defense. South Africa, where the whites are following a policy of domination over the blacks, left the Commonwealth in 1961—or, rather, was virtually expelled from it—over this issue.

The former British colonies, especially those in the Caribbean and in West Africa, showed great sympathy for the British re-conquest of the Falkland Islands in the spring of 1982, refusing to see it as a question of colonialism, but rather as one of self-determination.

The Commonwealth of Nations is a unique experiment in combining liberty with voluntary cooperation among peoples of very different kinds. It is based on noble and generous instincts as well as on necessity and the hope of profit.

SOCIETY IN POST-WAR BRITAIN

For almost a decade after the end of the war in 1945 life was dull and depressing to many Englishmen. The demobilized soldier or sailor came home to austerity, to an acute housing shortage, and to more meager rations than he had had in the armed forces. Although the government was forever urging greater productivity, the more attractive articles produced were reserved for export and could not be bought by the British public. So severe was the shortage in housing that for a time almost all building was forbidden except the construction of schools, factories, and houses for the working classes. Local authorities, attempting to provide these houses, built ugly prefabricated dwellings that were not intended to last more than ten years. Permanent houses met higher standards, but style and embellishments were sacrificed to utility. It is small wonder that such austerity, after the strain of a great war, dampened the spirits of the people.

Nonetheless the working classes were far better off than before the war. Wages, which had been rising rapidly during the war years, continued to improve after the peace. Moreover, unskilled laborers were now better paid, so that their wages drew closer to those of skilled artisans. The welfare state brought many benefits,

Elizabeth II, by Pietro Annigoni. (National Portrait Gallery, London)

especially in medical attention. Yet by far the most important cause of growing prosperity among the lower classes was full employment. At the end of World War II a tremendous amount of building was essential, city planning was in the air, manufacturers were urged to produce exportable goods at top speed, the demand for coal was enormous, and both political parties—following Keynesian economics—were committed to full employment as a policy of state. Nor were labor-saving devices widely available. Thus the working classes—backed by strong trade unions—stood to gain greatly in the postwar period.

Fashionable society did not emerge as quickly as it had done in the 1920s, partly because the royal family discouraged ostentation and partly because social functions could hardly be held at hotels while the price of a dinner was restricted to 5s. The aristocracy, as well as the working classes, faced a housing problem. Country houses, some of them enormous, were taxed heavily, required an army of servants, and produced little or no income. The only way that many owners could maintain them was to open them to the public and charge a small admission fee. Or they could be sold to schools or nursing homes or given to the nation, in which case they were administered by the National Trust, a public body that cares for ancient monuments. Many upper-class families were now content with handsome London apartments.

Foreign travel, stimulated by the automobile and improved roads on the Continent, became popular as soon as it was permitted; vacationers favored France, Italy, Spain, and Yugoslavia. British films were superior to those before the war. The annual Edinburgh Festival of Music and Drama, which drew talent from all over the world, began in 1947. Two public celebrations, the Festival of Britain, a world's fair held in 1951, and the coronation of Queen Elizabeth II in 1953, may be taken to mark the transition from postwar austerity to a happier and more affluent period.

The population of Great Britain in 1971 was 53,979,000, a figure indicating only moderate growth but laying to rest the fear of a sharp decline, which had often been predicted in the 1930s. At that time the birth rate was decreasing; but it shot forward in the years after the war, though it was leveling off by 1960. A notable feature of the postwar period was the influx into Britain of immigrants from the British West Indies, West Africa, India, and Pakistan. The highly controversial question arose of whether to bar a further increase in their number. With the passage of a series of acts, each more restrictive than those preceeding, the rate of immigration was reduced enormously. The Immigration Act of 1971 limited immigration to those who could demonstrate British ancestry through at least one parent. All preference for those from the Commonwealth was at an end. Former Conservative cabinet minister Enoch Powell's warnings about "rivers of blood" flowing if "colored" immigration was not stopped had had its effect.

Development of Urban Areas

A striking feature of post-war Britain was the development of the conurbation, which is the urban area formed when a number of neighboring towns expand toward each other until they become one continuous city. The term conurbation is used for seven areas: Greater London, West Midlands (Birmingham), Southeast Lancashire (Manchester), Merseyside (Liverpool), West Yorkshire (Leeds), Tyneside (Newcastle), and Clydeside (Glasgow). Greater London, containing over eight million persons in 1961, is, of course, unique. New office buildings of streamlined glass and modern design made their appearance, as have also skyscrapers such as the Shell Building, the Hilton Hotel, and Vickers House. A telecommunications tower 580 feet in height was erected by the General Post Office. The parks had not been disturbed; Kew Gardens and the Royal Park at Windsor were enlarged.

City planning became an absolute necessity. It was essential in bombed-out cities such as Coventry and Plymouth and even more essential in London. The first plan for Greater London, prepared by Patrick Abercrombie in 1944, was conceived in terms of four concentric circles. The first was inner London, from which some factories and many factory workers were to be removed; the second a ring of old suburbs, to be left much as it was; the third a green belt ring of small towns and villages in rural settings; the fourth an outer circle of existing towns and of new towns to be built under an act of 1946. This plan was only partially fulfilled. A million factory workers were removed from the inner ring, but for the most part they settled in the outer rings and their places were quickly taken by people working in offices.

In the new towns an effort was made not only to build houses, schools, and shopping centers, but also to locate factories. They were attractive communities, fresh, neat, and well planned; the factories were built in good modern designs; there was a picturesque blending of old and new—one may find an Anglo-Saxon church around the corner from an electronics factory. Another aspect of city planning was an attack on the problems of modern traffic. There was also regional planning for large areas. This led to the wholesale restructuring of the counties of England and Wales in the early 1970s. The boundary lines were redrawn and, in many cases, names were changed. (In Wales Welsh names were introduced.) The new counties and metropolitan areas created a new tier of local government, resulting in the increased cost of local government and in a decline in individual identification with the local authority. This was Heath's attempt to make Britain more efficient. Even though the restructuring other than in London has not been undone, it is not popular.

C H R O N O L O G Y

Post-War Britain

1944	Education Act
1945	Labor landslide; Attlee prime minister
1946	U.S. and Canadian loan; Bank of England nationalized; coal nationalized; National Health Service; National Insurance Act
1947	Marshall Plan; railways nationalized; India and Pakistan granted independence; Edinburgh Festival began
1948	Electricity production and distribution nationalized
1949	Devaluation of pound; Parliament Act reduced power of Lords; iron and steel scheduled to be nationalized; NATO formed; Republic of Ireland recognized
1950	Labor won slender majority; Korean War
1951	Conservatives won narrow victory; Churchill prime minister; Festival of Britain
1952	George VI died; Elizabeth II
1954	Rationing and most controls ended

(continued on next page)

Chronology, continued

1955	Churchill retired; Eden prime minister; Conservative election victory; Gaitskill succeeded Attlee as Labor leader
1956	Suez Crisis
1957	Eden resigned; Macmillan prime minister
1959	Conservative landslide
1963	Profumo scandal; Macmillan resigned; Douglas-Home prime minister
1964	Labor victorious; Wilson prime minister
1966	Labor landslide
1967	Pound devalued
1970	Labor defeated; Heath prime minister

36

Britain Enters Europe

Harold Wilson had come to office in 1964 promising "the white heat of the technological revolution." By 1970 it had become clear that no such revolution had taken place or was about to take place. There were grave doubts as to whether or not the decline of Britain could ever be arrested. The sixties ended in a certain malaise. The newly triumphant Conservatives were committed to creating a more efficient economy run on market, or capitalist, lines. A meeting of Conservative leaders at Selsden Park had agreed on such a program and the press conjured up the image of the new Briton as "Selsden Man." In fact, Edward Heath was to move forward on lines already anticipated by Harold Wilson in the closing phase of his administration.

THE DECLINE OF CONSENSUS POLITICS

Edward Heath and the Miners

In spite of a temporary revival in Labor support preceding the 1970 election, Harold Wilson had presided over a deeply divided Labor party. His proposals to curb the powers of the trade unions and to limit wage increases did not succeed but, in the eyes of the left wing in his party, he had deserted the cause of socialism. He also had to drop his plans to reform the House of Lords. His support of British entry into the Common Market also antagonized many of his colleagues. The defeat in 1970 precipitated the split between right and left within the Labor party. Edward Heath's administration was to contribute to an increasing polarization within the nation itself.

Heath inherited an increasingly shaky economic situation. Wilson's devaluation of the pound in 1967 had contributed to inflation, increasing demands for wage in-

Edward Heath.
(A.P. Wide World
Photos, Inc.)

creases to offset inflation, and an adverse balance of payments. Heath's initial response was to curb the unions by legislation and to hold down wages by controlling the money supply. He saw Britain's ultimate salvation, however, in membership of the Common Market. British entry into the Common Market found the British economy stagnating, which induced Heath and his chancellor of the Exchequer Anthony Barber to begin a rapid economic expansion. Previously, economic expansions had been halted at the onset of inflation and trade imbalances. This time, Heath and Barber decided to let expansion have a free rein. This set the stage for a rapid increase in the rate of inflation which would come to challenge the Western economies from the mid-seventies until the mid-eighties.

The original Common Market, or European Economic Community, consisted of France, Italy, West Germany, the Netherlands, Belgium, and Luxemburg. After refusing to join in 1958, Harold Macmillan brought the Conservatives around to supporting entry. Harold Wilson supported entry while he himself was in office and opposed it when out of office. Heath came to see entry as the cornerstone of his and Britain's destiny. Parliament ratified the treaty of accession in 1972 and entry took place on 1 January 1973. Ireland and Denmark also joined. (Greece eventually did also, followed by Spain and Portugal.)

Membership in the Common Market has been part of a radical change in Britain's position in Europe and the world. For supporters of entry it was to bring economic salvation. For its opponents it was the end of national independence. In truth it was neither. It did, however, create deep divisions in the Labor party and gradually saw Britain's trade being Europeanized. In addition, Europe was to replace the Commonwealth as the principal external forum for British economic and political activities.

Heath's success in entering the Common Market was followed within a year by struggles with the miners which led to the most severe strike-induced crisis since the General Strike of 1926. Oil had been discovered in the North Sea in 1970 but production was minimal at the time of the Arab-Israeli war in October 1973. The resulting fourfold increase in oil prices made coal and the men who mined it more valuable. After one wage concession to the miners, Heath decided to draw the line at further demands. The resulting coal miners' strike in February 1974 was taken by Heath as a direct challenge to the government. He called for a general election. The miners' slow-down beginning in the previous November had led to such a shortage of fuel that industry was already on a three-day week. The nation was cold, dark, and depressed. The voters were asked to decide "who should govern," the miners or an elected government. Their answer was not a clear one. The Labor party won the largest number of seats, but without having a majority. Wilson formed a minority government on 4 March. The next election was on 10 October.

Two Elections in One Year

Campaigning for the October 1974 election began the moment the votes were counted in February. The results then were: Labor 301, Conservatives 296, and Liberals 14. The Liberals had been encouraged by the polls to expect a substantially greater number of seats. With 19.3 percent of the votes and only 14 seats, the Liberals were now determined to push for proportional representation. If Heath had agreed to this demand, he might have put together a Conservative-Liberal coalition. Neither of the large parties wanted proportional representation, however.

Wilson's new minority government quickly settled the miners strike by agreeing to their demands for a 31 percent wage increase. The three-day week drew to a close. One harbinger of future trouble was the fact that industrial production during the period of the three-day weeks was about as high as during a normal week. This seemed to prove the Conservative argument that British industry was overmanned, thus contributing to low productivity and high prices in world trade.

In the inevitable October election Labor was credited with putting the nation back to work and was rewarded with a tiny overall majority: 319 seats for Labor, 276 Conservatives, and 13 for the Liberals. The Scottish Nationalists rose from 7 to 11

*European
Community 1987.*

Common Market Members
(with dates of admission)

and the Welsh Nationalists (Plaid Cymru) rose from 2 to 3. The new forces of
Scottish and Welsh nationalism were to add to the burdens of a Labor party
committed to the principle of a strong central government. The Nationalists were
determined to secure "devolution" or the establishment of regional governments
somewhat like that found in Northern Ireland before 1973.

The great issue in the October election was the Common Market. Labor had pledged withdrawal if it won, but this was only to take place after the electorate had expressed itself in an advisory referendum. The use of a referendum was in itself a controversial innovation. As the referendum campaign wore on, it was clear that Wilson, again in office, continued to support membership in the Common Market. The Conservatives largely supported membership, as did the Liberals. The result was a 2 to 1 victory for continued membership. The 2 to 1 margin was reached in England, Scotland, and Wales. In Northern Ireland the margin was 52 to 48.

Once the issue of membership in the Common Market was settled, Labor did not reunite its factions. The underlying weakness of the economy proved to be too much. The three main elements in the party were becoming increasingly estranged from each other. On one hand, there were the Labor members of Parliament, the greatest number of whom backed Wilson and his deputy James Callaghan in attempting to hold down inflation and maintain employment by means of an incomes policy labeled the "Social Contract." Continued high government spending and borrowing would provide workers with a "social" wage so that "employment" wages could be restrained. This "social contract" required the cooperation of the trade union leaders.

The union leadership had traditionally been in the center or on the right of the Labor Party. This position now was changing. The Wilson government had repealed Heath's union regulations and the British trade unions were now totally free to conduct their affairs without any restrictions. Many union leaders saw the "social contract" as the first step toward the creation of a union-dominated government; a Labor government that would be answerable to the unions, not to the electorate.

A third group within the party were the local constituency associations. A dwindling number of members on the constituency level had resulted in an increasingly militant left-wing force. The leader of the faction was Anthony Wedgwood Benn (Tony Benn) who had years before renounced his inherited peerage and become the leading parliamentary spokesman for greater party democracy. That would mean a greater voice for the constituencies and the unions at the expense of members of Parliament and the parliamentary leadership.

The loss of two elections in one year led to the fall of Edward Heath as Conservative leader. In 1965 the Conservatives had replaced a secretive system by which leaders "evolved" with a complex procedure for electing the leader. Heath had been the first beneficiary of the new system. He was also to be its first victim. When Heath sought a vote of confidence from his party, Mrs. Margaret Thatcher joined others in running against him. On the second ballot she secured her majority. The Tories thus became the first major British party to be led by a woman. She was even given membership in the hitherto all male Carlton Club. Margaret Thatcher would bring several significant changes to the government, in addition to breaking ground for future female leaders.

James Callaghan and the Nationalists

With no warning the sixty-year-old Harold Wilson retired from the premiership in March 1976. The party election went to the foreign secretary, James Callaghan, Wilson's choice. Being an avuncular Welshman who had mastered the party bureau-

cracy and had befriended the trade unions, it was thought that Callaghan would consolidate the Labor party after the divisive years under Wilson. This was not to be.

The economy suffered from increased inflation and the "social contract" began to unravel. Increased revenues from North Sea oil merely held down the rise in the budget deficits. A string of by-election defeats stripped Labor of its majority. The narrower the majority the more Callaghan depended upon the support of the Liberals and the Nationalists. Finally Labor became a minority government allied with the Liberals and supported by Scottish and Welsh Nationalists and the Ulster Unionists. Callaghan in turn had to allow for bills which would create devolved government in Scotland and Wales if each of the respective electorates voted "yes" in a referendum, and if the "yes" vote constituted at least 40 percent of the eligible voters. The referendum of 1 March 1979 lost in Wales. It got a favorable majority in Scotland, but the total "yes" vote did not meet the 40 percent requirement. Labor had failed to deliver "devolution." The Nationalists did not need Labor any longer.

The winter of 1978–1979 had been plagued with strikes by public employees resistant to Labor's attempt to hold down public expenditures and to set an example of wage restraint. The breakdown in the smooth delivery of public services came to be called the "winter of discontent." The government's failure to carry "devolution" was the last straw. In a no-confidence vote on 28 March, the Callaghan government became the first government in half a century to be defeated on a confidence vote. It was accomplished by a margin of one vote.

Parliament was dissolved and the election took place on 3 May. The result was a solid Conservative majority of thirty seats over all others. Mrs. Thatcher became the first woman prime minister. The Liberals and Nationalists lost support along with Labor.

MRS. THATCHER AND THE TURN TO THE RIGHT

As leader of the opposition, Mrs. Thatcher had already earned the sobriquet of "iron lady." She was an outspoken critic of big government, high taxes, deficit-financing, and of many aspects of the welfare-state. She favored smaller govern-

Margaret Thatcher, "the Chemist–Candidate." Oxford student and Parliamentary candidate, 1958. (A.P. Wide World Photos, Inc.)

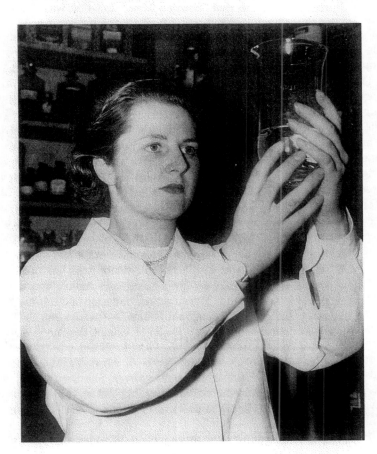

ment, lower taxes, a balanced budget, a stronger national defense, and a more forceful foreign policy. She appeared to be the most consistently conservative leader since Bonar Law in the early 1920s. The defeat of Labor was in its turn to lead to a rush of left-wing ideas and groups. The nation was abandoning the center for the edges. Thatcher said that the policies of the center since World War II had reduced Britain to the status of a second-class power with one of the weakest economies in the developed world. She was determined to arrest the decline and set the stage for recovery.

The first three years of the new government saw inflation climb up to the 20 percent figure and unemployment slowly climbed as well. A modest tax cut failed to satisfy Conservatives and enraged Labor. An economic policy called "monetarism" by its critics created high interest rates, rapidly rising unemployment, a cutback in social services, and continued budget deficits. Inflation, however, did decline, reaching 5 percent by the fall of 1982.

Ten years earlier, Edward Heath had reversed his policies in the face of a declining economy and had begun the "Barber boom." Mrs. Thatcher was "not for turning," and proved to be the real "Selsden Man." Inflation was to be fought as a menace greater than unemployment, in a reversal of all post-war economic and social policy. Ever since 1945, the political consensus agreed that unemployment as seen in the 1920s and 1930s must never return. It was Thatcher's view that this war against unemployment had been the root cause of inflation, inefficiency, low productivity, high taxes, increasing national indebtedness, and an increasing role for the public sector at the expense of the private. Whether or not she would be given time to see through this reversal was not yet certain.

The strengthening of the national defenses proved to be costly and less was done than had been promised. The decision to purchase the Trident missle and to remain a nuclear power was largely taken at the expense of the traditional naval forces. Except for the solution of the colonial problem in Africa by the creation of an independent Zimbabwe out of the old Southern Rhodesia, Thatcher's foreign policy was one of strong and vocal anti-Communism. She made a strong effort to ensure that membership in the Common Market did not prove to be too costly.

Until the Argentine occupation of the Falkland Islands in March 1982, Mrs. Thatcher was the most divisive and unpopular prime minister since the use of opinion polls. However, the war in the South Atlantic was her turning point. The British government had for years sought a solution in conjunction with Argentina, yet the Islanders always objected. The Argentine invasion of the Islands resulted in a popular explosion of indignation throughout Britain. All parties and all classes were caught up in a public demand for action. Thatcher caught the mood almost immediately and launched a counterattack. The speed and efficiency with which the British forces responded and the forceful response of Mrs. Thatcher herself won her great popularity. Her standing in the polls soared. She became for a time the focus of a newly patriotic and self-confident Britain. Victory for Britain over Argentina was quick, if not sure. Victory in the next election for Mrs. Thatcher began to look more and more likely.

With unemployment over three million, all expected Labor to be far ahead in the

Mrs. Thatcher shown as a pirate on the cover of the Argentine review El Porteno. *(Sipa Press/Art Resource)*

polls and eventually victorious. Yet the Labor party entered the mid-80s more deeply divided than at any time since 1933. As Thatcher moved the center of politics to the right, the left was becoming more powerful in the Labor party.

James Callaghan had resigned as leader of the Labor party, and in a complex and divisive party election Michael Foot was chosen to replace him, with Dennis Healey as his deputy. The new electoral machinery reflected the party spirits. The leaders were now elected by a mechanism giving the members of the House of Commons and the delegates from the constituencies each 30 percent of the vote, with the trade unions controlling 40 percent of the vote. Foot had the support of all three. Healey was vigorously opposed by the left and by the constituency associations led by Tony Benn, the "reluctant peer." The disordered party expected defeat, but rallied round their "beloved Michael," hoping for a calming influence in the face of a Tory whirlwind. A few dozen former members formed a new Social Democratic party led by former chancellor of the Exchequer and Home Secretary Roy Jenkins. The Social Democrats joined forces with the Liberals under David Steel to capture the center which the Conservatives and Labor had abandoned, at least temporarily. The alliance's chief demand was for proportional representation. Conservatives and Labor could at least unite in opposition to that. However, the appearance of unity among Conservatives may have been put on for electoral purposes. Mrs. Thatcher's determination to reverse the course of British life had deeply divided her Cabinet, her party, and the country. She called her opponents "wet" and treated them with cold disdain. Some had already left her Cabinet before the election; others were to be removed later.

NORTHERN IRELAND

The act by which Britain recognized the Irish Republic maintained the status of Northern Ireland as part of the United Kingdom. However, it was stated that if ever a majority of the North wanted unity with the Republic of Ireland, they would have it. The fact was, however, that a million protestants and a half million Catholics in the North shared different political allegiances. The Protestant "loyalists" had dominated the government in Belfast (Stormont) since its inception. Catholics were second-class citizens at best. Even in Catholic communities the elections were won by Protestants. The North is the poorest province in the United Kingdom and the Catholics suffered the brunt of that.

In 1969 a civil rights movement began. After pressure from London the Protestants made concessions, however the legalizing of civil rights did not end the violence. The Provisional wing of the I.R.A. demanded that the "Brits" get out and that Ireland be united. The Protestants retaliated with violence on their part. A large British army was installed in the province to separate the two sides. At first the Catholics welcomed the army. Soon the army became part of the problem. "The troubles" have led to over two thousand deaths and untold destruction of property. "Bloody Sunday," 30 January 1972, was the worst single incident, when British troops fired on illegally parading Catholics. This soon led to the abolition of the Northern Ireland government and the imposition of direct rule from London.

The governments of Britain and Ireland have publicly called for the end of violence and for "power sharing" in the North. An Anglo-Irish agreement on power sharing was reached at Sunningdale in 1973. Direct rule was temporarily ended. However, the Sunningdale Agreement was destroyed by a Protestant general strike in the spring of 1974, when the Wilson government stood by while the Unionists walked out of the Assembly. Direct rule from London was resumed. The Irish and the British both had hoped that "power sharing" would lead to peace and to Irish unity. In the North, Catholics believed that the British would prevent unity, while the Protestants feared the British would "betray" them. The two sides in the North were more polarized in the mid-80s than ever before. The death of ten Catholics during the hunger strike at the Maze prison in the spring of 1981 resulted in an upsurge of support for the Sinn Fein, the political wing of the I.R.A. It also enhanced the strength of the Protestant extremists led by the Rev. Ian Paisley.

In the summer of 1984 the British and Irish governments began to negotiate a new form of power sharing. The result was the Anglo-Irish Agreement of 15 November 1985. The Irish Republic was given the right to advise on Northern Ireland policy by means of an Anglo-Irish Conference of ministers authorized to discuss political, legal, and security matters on an ongoing basis. The Unionist leaders of the North denounced this British "treachery." The Irish in the Republic were wary of being saddled with the responsibility for the North without any real power. The Republic was also divided within itself as to what goal it sought in the North: was it the withdrawal of the British and a union with the Republic? Or did it seek true equality for Catholics in the North, while the North remained within the United Kingdom? While the latter was probably the real goal, it could never be admitted publicly. Catholic support for the Agreement was also questioned because of the provision calling for the arrest and trial of terrorists in either part of the island, regardless of the scene of the violence.

The Agreement has seen the decline of I.R.A. violence directed at civilians but an increase in that directed at British military forces, their families, and employees. The attacks have spread to the British mainland and to areas occupied by British forces on the Continent. Dublin and London and their electorates grow weary, as militants on both sides in the North show no signs of abating.

Thatcher Wins Again and Again

The Tory "whirlwind" came indeed, and with such force that the election itself was an anticlimax. The results in 1983 were Conservatives 397, Labor 209, the Liberal-SDP Alliance 23. The overall Conservative majority was 144 seats, second only to the Labor landslide of 1945 in the post-war era.

Mrs. Thatcher's second term saw the economic hardships of the first term begin to pay off. The economy began to grow, unemployment stopped rising after going above three million, and a showdown with the coal miners seemingly transformed the relationship between the government and the labor movement. Nationalized industries began to be sold off to the general public ("privatization") and taxes would be cut before the next election. The prime minister never seemed to waver in her determination to transform the national psyche and to win the next election, and perhaps the one after that as well. The "Iron Lady" had spoken for a defiant nation during the Falklands campaign. She was able to build upon that foundation a structure of change and confrontation that seemed to carry all before it. The "green and pleasant" land was once again to be the "workshop of the world."

The Labor party quickly said goodbye to their "beloved Michael" and elected Neil Kinnock as leader. A young Welshman with no experience as a cabinet minister, Kinnock came from the "soft" left wing of the party and was in that respect a new Harold Wilson. He was hailed as a man of the people, with an attractive and energetic wife campaigning at his side. As a skilled speaker before an audience of his own supporters, Kinnock was expected to keep the numerous "militant tendency" in place while guiding Labor in reaching out to the liberal-minded middle-class supporters of Attlee and Wilson. Arthur Scargill and the miners were a test for Kinnock and the Labor party, as they were for the Conservative government and the country itself.

In the spring of 1984 the coal miners struck in opposition to government proposals for voluntary retirement with cash subsidies for thousands of miners. Scargill knew that oil and nuclear energy were long-run threats to the coal industry. A reduced industry meant a smaller work force and a smaller miners' union. He suspected that Thatcher was seeking revenge upon the miners for the strike in the winter of 1974, which had led to the fall of the Conservative government. Scargill was determined to stop the retirement of thousands of miners, even when those affected were willing to accept the cash and stop work. The ten-month strike involved many incidents of violence by frustrated miners and clashes with police brought in to enforce the newly adopted Conservative restrictions on "flying" pickets and secondary pickets. Though Kinnock felt compelled to support the miners once more, Thatcher clearly had a better sense of public opinion against Scargill and the violence committed by his more militant followers. To have repudiated the miners would have destroyed the unity of the Labor party. The miners lost, Thatcher won, and Kinnock and Labor emerged divided and unsure of themselves and their purposes. As with the Falklands, Thatcher knew when and where to draw the line and make a stand.

The triumph over the miners was not to eliminate opposition within the Conservative party, however. The Thatcher program and her personal style were still resented by large segments of the party and the nation. Much of her personal power was based upon a divided opposition rather than positive support. This was as true within the party as within the nation itself. Her opponents within the party bided their time until their opportunity came in late December 1985. Westland Helicopters, the last British-owned firm in the helicopter business, was nearly bankrupt. Michael Heseltine, the defense minister, sought a financial rescue from continental European sources while the company itself sought a deal with an American company. Thatcher opposed Heseltine and allowed her staff, including civil servants, to conduct a campaign on behalf of the company and its American friends. Correspondence to Heseltine was leaked to the press, embarrassing him and resulting in a backlash of anger against the "unscrupulous woman." She consistently denied any wrongdoing and let it be known that Leon Brittan, the secretary for Trade and Industry, had authorized the leak. Brittan shortly resigned and for a time it seemed that Thatcher's tenure as prime minister would also be brief. She weathered the storm, but her reputation suffered. Many doubted that she had no role in authorizing a leak of private correspondence. Many in the Labor party believed that she had lied about the events leading to the sinking of the Argentinian cruiser *Belgrano* during the Falklands campaign. (Lying to the House of Commons is one of the most serious offenses a member can commit.) Thatcher's personal standing has never fully recovered from either of these episodes. Heseltine has declared his ambition to be prime minister, and would eventually challenge her directly.

The last two years of the second Thatcher government found the leaders of both major parties seriously wounded. The Conservatives, however, did benefit from a rapidly growing economy, a low level of inflation, and declining unemployment. Chancellor of the Exchequer Nigel Lawson had adopted the Thatcherite goal of an overall balanced budget in order to reduce income taxes. The Thatcher government had in fact stopped the increase in public expenditure as a percentage of the gross domestic product. Overall tax receipts were still rising and the result was a balanced budget, with surpluses just around the corner. Lawson, in fact, began to pay off the national debt. Whereas Lawson wanted to cut taxes, Labor and many Conservatives wanted to use the surpluses to increase public spending, especially in the social and health areas. A compromise was reached and increases were allowed for health, job training, and some social benefits.

The Labor party faced the coming election still deeply divided on defense issues. Kinnock was personally committed to unilateral nuclear disarmament and to the removal of all NATO nuclear forces from British soil. All opinion polls showed that this was not acceptable to a large majority of the electorate. Since the Labor party had already been wounded by the coal strike, the defense issue made a Labor victory nearly impossible.

During the fourth year of her second administration, Thatcher sensed victory and was determined to face the electorate armed with an agenda for action in the third term. There was to be no resting on laurels. The Lawson tax cuts quickly led to an economic boom and the election was called for June 1987, before the boom resulted

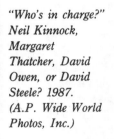

"Who's in charge?"
Neil Kinnock,
Margaret
Thatcher, David
Owen, or David
Steele? 1987.
(A.P. Wide World
Photos, Inc.)

in renewed inflation. Even though parliaments are allowed to run for five years, Thatcher called for elections after just four years in both 1983 and 1987, expecting victory each time. The results, though not so spectacular as in 1983, were still decisive. The Conservatives won 375 seats, Labor 229, and the Alliance 22. The overall majority was 101.

The election was a defeat for the Labor party but a personal triumph for Neil Kinnock. He had mastered the use of television and the press conference. This personal triumph made him determined to restructure the party and make it a winner in the elections of the 1990s. The Labor party has used the years since the 1987 election to reshape its policies and to renew its personnel. In the process Kinnock has modified, if not abandoned, traditional Labor commitments to unilateral nuclear disarmament and to nationalization of industry. Labor is becoming more accepting of market forces in the economy and of Britain's role in the European community. The newly adopted policies passed their first test in the European Parliament elections in 1989, with Labor winning an absolute majority of the United Kingdom seats for the first time.

The Conservative party was shaken by this unexpected defeat, but Thatcher insisted upon continuing the program she had begun in her third term. Her agenda included the rapid privatization of nationalized industries. British Telecom (telephone) had already been sold to an eager public, instantly creating a vast number of new capitalists. Combined with the tremendous success of the sale of council houses to their tenants, Britain was on the way to becoming the property-owning Conservative-voting democracy that Conservative politicians had dreamed of since the times of Eden, Neville Chamberlain, and Disraeli. These successes were to be followed by less popular sales of the local water companies and of the electricity production and distribution industries. The Conservatives hoped that these sales of public utilities would create capitalists by the millions, reduce the size of government, bring in large revenues in the short run, and provide the cash to justify lower taxes and a reduced percentage of the economy in the public domain. It was also hoped, especially in the case of water, that environmental regulations could be more easily enforced upon private industries and their customers than upon government agencies answerable to voters and taxpayers. The most radical of the many items on the Thatcher agenda was the abolition of real estate taxes (rates) for homeowners and their replacement by a community charge or "poll tax" payable by all adults. Thatcher had called for the abolition of rates in the mid-1970s when she was still leader of the opposition. Local governments, many in Labor party hands, were not easily restricted in their spending or in their willingness to raise rates on nonvoting businesses or nonresident homeowners. The new laws would provide for a standard rate of tax for all businesses nationwide. The community charge or poll tax would be set by each local authority. It was Thatcher's hope that high-spending and high-taxing local authorities who were dominated by Labor would be punished by the voters. Since approximately 25 percent of local spending will be financed by the community charge, the adoption of a tax not tied to income is a major turn from the principle of progressive taxation that all modern industrial democracies have adopted in the twentieth century. This truly revolutionary tax was first introduced in Scotland, where hundreds of thousands have refused to pay. Its enforcement in England is expected to be equally difficult and politically divisive.

As the 1980s drew to a close, the greatest issues facing the nation, as seen by Thatcher, were the overriding need to control inflation, to guide European unity in the direction of an expanded free trade rather than toward a united states of Europe, and to educate the nations of the world about environmental dangers, especially in the area of global warming. As a trained chemical engineer, Thatcher could speak with authority on these environmental issues.

Whereas the 1980s had been a decade of unbroken electoral triumph for the Conservatives and Margaret Thatcher, the prospects for the 1990s suggest that a revitalized Labor party with more electorally relevant policies and leaders adept at using the newly televised House of Commons will provide a challenge to the Conservatives not seen since the 1960s. Thatcher and the Conservatives, however, do not seem to be as worn out from their duties as was the case in 1963 and 1964. Thatcher is determined to go on, and moreover, her Cabinet are equally determined to go on, with or without her. The new decade will be dominated by two parties generating new ideas, led by people anxious to win and to set the agenda. The prospects for the Alliance and its heirs are indeed dim: Britain will once again be a two-party political arena.

Opportunity and the Quality of Life

The standard of living of the British people has risen spectacularly since World War II in absolute terms. In comparison with other advanced industrial nations, Britain's performance has not been so spectacular. In fact, she now ranks above only Italy, Spain, Portugal, and Ireland in Western Europe. Inflation and slow economic growth carried average wages from £500 per year to over £7,000 in the early 1980s. The major cause of higher living standards, however, was that more and more women joined the work force. The two and even three-earner family meant new expectations and new realities. Wages generally kept ahead of inflation and unemployment benefits have been sufficiently high to maintain a decent standard for the unemployed.

Few features of modern society in Britain have contributed more to the general welfare than has the National Health Service, hailed as a notable achievement. Although it was denounced at first by the medical profession, official inquiries into its functioning and costs have concluded that it has not been widely abused and, considering its accomplishments, has not been unreasonably expensive. The income of the doctors who work in it has been a serious difficulty. Speaking very broadly, doctors have not been well paid in England, but under the Health Service many have felt that they were more poorly paid than ever. The problem has been investigated a good deal and has been the subject of many negotiations between the government and the British Medical Association. But although the income of physicians has increased, the problem is far from solution. Nurses and other hospital workers also feel badly treated. Nearly 15 percent of all medicine is now private, largely financed through insurance. By the close of the 1980s the Health Service was once again a great political issue. Labor had called for the total abolition of private medicine. Thatcher has proposed a major restructuring of the National Health Service designed to make it more cost effective and more responsive to patients and taxpayers. The proposals have met with great opposition from doctors and have aroused fears among the general population that Thatcher is not really a friend of the NHS.

The changes in English education have been tremendous, though this has not been true of elementary education, where the problems were largely those of coping with a growing number of children. Issues in secondary education have been more controversial. The system in operation before the war sorted out the children at the age of eleven and placed them according to their abilities and interests in grammar schools, or technical schools, or so-called modern schools which combined character-istics of the other two. This system was criticized on the ground that a child's capabilities could not be judged accurately when the child was only eleven years of age. An answer has been found in the establishment of comprehensive schools which offer all types of education and permit children to pass from one type to another as their abilities appear to warrant. The school-leaving age had been raised to fifteen by an act of 1944; a further rise to sixteen, recommended in 1959, is now in effect. The examination of all students at eleven (plus) years of age was dropped as being socially divisive. The strict separation of grammar schools and secondary modern (vocation-al) schools was also gradually replaced by what is now an almost universal system of comprehensive secondary schools in the public sector. Many middle-class parents are not convinced that the new schools and the new certificates they award are of the same standard as the old grammar schools. The conflict between the twin goals of a meritocracy and a socially egalitarian society is still clearly seen in the field of education. The influx of large numbers of immigrant children from Asia, Africa, and the Caribbean has added to the potential conflict.

It is at the university level, however, that an educational explosion has taken place. In 1961 more than 100,000 students were registered in British universities, twice the number of those before the war. Moreover, four-fifths of these postwar students were receiving aid from the government; indeed the government was paying more than half the cost of all university education. The percentage of the population in post-secondary education has leveled off since the sixties and is among the lowest in the industrial world. A system of thirty polytechnics has been es-tablished since the 1960s and enrolls seventy percent of all first-year students in higher education. A large number of new universities have been founded since the war, including those at Keele, Southampton, Hull, Exeter, Leicester, Brighton, York, Norwich, Lancaster, Colchester, Canterbury, and Coventry. These often take their name from the county in which they are located. Together with Oxford and Cambridge and with a number of universities founded in the nineteenth and early twentieth centuries, they provide Great Britain with a superior system of higher education. Moreover, the children of working-class parents now have an opportunity for university training equal to that of children from wealthy and influential homes. However, the enrollments in universities are still overwhelmingly middle class. The polytechnics have a stronger working class mix, but Britain continues to lag behind in providing higher education for the bulk of its people. Such fundamental and far-reaching changes leave the future of the public schools in some doubt. In 1964 the Labor party daringly proposed to absorb them into the national system, and in 1982 the party was prepared to call for their eventual abolition.

Leisure and Entertainment

The growing affluence of Britain has created a greater amount of leisure for all classes and also new ways in which that leisure can be used. In the suburban areas around the large towns one finds a lively set of well-to-do business people who live in fine houses with extensive grounds; they form what has been called the cocktail belt. Social life, as with the same set in America, centers in golf and country clubs; weekend guests devote their time to golf, tennis, picnics, and parties. Some of the wealthier suburbanites belong to fox hunts; there is much riding with ponies for the children. Thus country life persists, though it is less sedate than of old. Hunting is constantly under attack by animal lovers.

Middle- and lower-class families must live more frugally than this, but here also old forms of entertainment are givng way to new. The interest in cricket matches and football (soccer) games has somewhat abated, and attendance at the cinema has declined. The reason for this change is the television, which was introduced in the 1950s and has become so popular that nearly all families possess a set. Until 1955 broadcasting of this type was a monopoly of the BBC. In that year, after violent debate, the decision was taken to permit commercial television, though the programs were to be carefully supervised by an Independent Televison Authority. Many British TV programs are popular in America. Competition for both audiences and revenues is increasingly intense. In order to ensure sufficient revenues, the BBC compulsory fees have become so high as to become politically controversial. Some have suggested that the BBC be partially financed by advertising. The introduction of cable TV, linked to worldwide satellites and to continental European producers, has greatly increased competition and the quantity of programs available. Quality remains a matter of debate.

Older forms of amusement have other rivals. Automobile racing, both by professionals and by amateurs who do such things as race up high hills, is popular. These meets are not the fastidious gatherings that attend horse races at Ascot or Goodwood. The crowd is noisy, the air foul with gasoline fumes, and the audience is composed of young people. Another sport is bowling, which can be made a family affair and offers a hilarious evening at low cost. Gambling laws have been modified to permit bingo, a game that supplies a small thrill without danger of great loss. Sailing has also grown popular. There are numerous yacht clubs; a growing problem is reminiscent of the automobile—where does one park one's yacht? A major problem of violence among soccer fans has arisen during the 1980s. Because of close geographical proximity, fans follow their teams when playing away from home. The visitors standing on the terraces have frequently become so violent that exhorbitant

The Beatles in
rehearsal for a
royal show, 1963.
(A.P. Wide World
Photos, INc.)

The Rolling Stones
in Philadelphia,
1989. (A.P. Wide
World Photos,
Inc.)

damages and personal injuries or even deaths are not infrequent. These violent rampages have also broken out on visits to the Continent, threatening Britain's future participation in European soccer.

Foreign travel has grown enormously, for rich and poor alike. An American staying in a London hotel may hear the chambermaid announce that she is about to take a holiday to Spain. To rent a foreign villa for a few weeks is quite the vogue. Travels in southern Europe have produced an interest in wine, sidewalk cafes, foreign restaurants, and foreign clothes such as Italian shoes and Paris fashions. In fact, London has become a center for designers of women's clothes, which are far more stylish than they used to be. Dancing is very popular, and, like other amusements, lends itself to the formation of clubs.

As in other countries, the young people show tastes that their elders find difficult to understand. The craving for "socially unacceptable" popular music and outrageous fashion trends attest to the determination of youth to go its own way. The British have become the great exporters of popular culture as well as the more traditional

Mary Quant wears a mini-skirted dress as she displays her Order of the British Empire, 1966. (A.P. Wide World Photos, Inc.)

elite culture. The dress, hair styles, music, and dance of the British working class youth are spreading throughout the world. Until the 1960s the culture and style of the upper classes were exported and emulated abroad, while the lower classes imported American styles and fashions. That changed with the Beatles and Carnaby Street. The variety of culture and styles exported by Britain today is truly stagger-ing. The new immigrants from Africa and the Caribbean have had a great influence upon the young. The televison series "East Enders" typifies the newer dress, music, and morals of many of the young, especially among the working class. The immi-grants have had an impact upon Britain. Britain, in turn, through her cultural exports, continues to have an impact on the world.

Intellectual entertainment is also available. The London theaters present good

The Barbican Centre, 1982. (A.P. Wide World Photos, Inc.)

drama and are well attended. Of special note are the National Theatre Company, the Royal Shakespeare Company, and the Sadler's Wells Ballet, incorporated in the Royal Ballet in 1957, and the Barbican Centre. London has become a great musical center. Orchestral concerts, recitals by outstanding artists, and a full season of opera attract large crowds. The University of London, by far the largest university in Britain, adds to the intellectual climate of the city, as do famous libraries, museums, and art galleries. Although much of the press is sensational, many newspapers, as well as weeklies and quarterlies, contain material for the serious reader.

The Great Depression, World War II, and the new Britain which the Attlee government tried to create in the 1940s had led to a literature of anger in the 1950s. John Osborne's *Look Back in Anger* had captured the imagination at home and seemed to typify the new Britain for foreign audiences. It appeared in 1956, the same year as the Suez Crisis. The anger was of dual origins: the nation was in decline with respect to the wider world and the old class system was surprisingly persistent at home.

John Osborne, August 1957. (A.P. Wide World Photos, Inc.)

The 1960s and 1970s ushered in a new morality. Sexual restraints were removed, homosexuality was legalized, divorce and abortion were made easier, capital punishment was abolished, and the reduction in the voting age to eighteen made youth fashionable, if not supreme. Drama, dance, music, and the ballet flourished. The novel, poetry, and serious reading in general declined as leisure-time activities. The plays of Harold Pinter and Samuel Beckett were classless, but also depicted a separation from society, and a stress upon the inner feelings and urges of the isolated individual. The place of the individual in the community was missing.

Who can deny that Great Britain has met with marked success in solving the tremendous problems of the twentieth century and in creating a more humane, enlightened, and equalitarian society than it could boast a century ago? England also is producing a new type of Englishman, less conventional and less inhibited than of

Samuel Beckett, 1966. (A.P. Wide World Photos, Inc.)

Mrs. Thatcher was the first Western leader to recognize Mikhail Gorbachev as a revolutionary world leader, 1987. (A.P. Wide World Photos, Inc.)

old, but also more isolated. Mrs. Thatcher has said that "there is no such thing as society."

However, the seeming abandonment of a policy of full employment and a turn away from a search for greater equality in the name of preserving greater individual liberty may see the return of a more conservative and class-stratified society. The prosperity of the 1950s and 1960s brought many changes in the British life style. A less socially cohesive 1980s have placed the future of many of these things in doubt.

The competition from Europe will only increase as the single market approaches in 1992. Britain's ability to compete successfully is not taken for granted. Many Scots see the new Europe as an opportunity for greater Scottish automomy. The Labor party looks forward to seeing some aspects of the Continental labor management relations introduced in Britain. The banking, insurance, and stockbroking industries feel confident. Manufacturing industry and its workforces are fearful. Some see a future for a greater Britain in Europe. Others see a need to remain merely English. The Channel Tunnel will open a new decade and a new world for all.

Mrs. Thatcher and presidential hopeful Vice President George Bush. London, 1987. (A.P. Wide World Photos, Inc.)

THE NINETIES' MONARCHY

As Britain prepares for the new world of the 1990s, it is well to take a look at the ultimate symbol of her national life—the monarchy. The sovereignty of Queen-in-Parliament has been and will be continually reduced by legislation and decrees from the European Community. In spite of this, or perhaps because of this, the bonds between the mass of British people and the royal family have never been closer. All public opinion polls consistently show the queen herself to be held in the highest respect. Queen Elizabeth, the Queen Mother, continues to be everyone's favorite grandmother or great aunt. The Princess of Wales has captivated the world and outshines the greatest movie stars. Princess Anne has emerged as a hardworking leader of the worldwide Save the Children Fund and is increasingly treated with respect and sympathy. The Prince of Wales has found a role as the spokesman for the "man in the street" on questions of architecture and the environment. He has

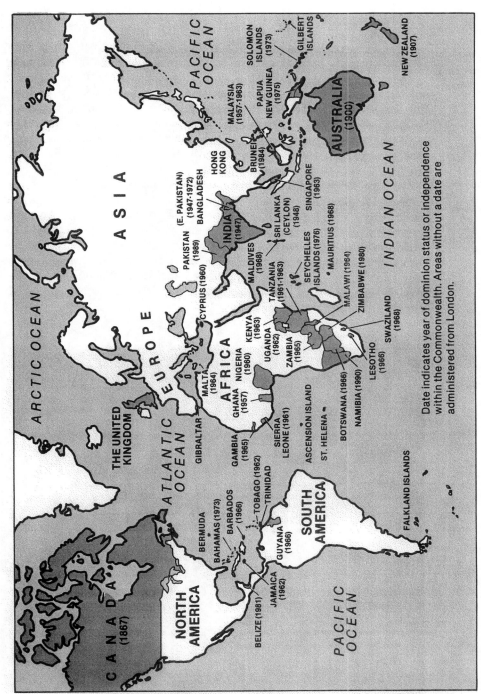

The Commonwealth 1987.

ARCTIC OCEAN

PACIFIC OCEAN

ASIA

EUROPE

AFRICA

ATLANTIC OCEAN

INDIAN OCEAN

PACIFIC OCEAN

NORTH AMERICA

SOUTH AMERICA

CANADA (1867)

THE UNITED KINGDOM

AUSTRALIA (1900)

NEW ZEALAND (1907)

GILBERT ISLANDS

SOLOMON ISLANDS (1973)

PAPUA NEW GUINEA (1975)

MALAYSIA (1957-1963)

BRUNEI (1984)

SINGAPORE (1963)

HONG KONG

BANGLADESH (E. PAKISTAN) (1947-1972)

INDIA (1947)

PAKISTAN (1989)

CYPRUS (1960)

MALDIVES (1968)

SRI LANKA (CEYLON) (1948)

SEYCHELLES ISLANDS (1976)

MAURITIUS (1968)

TANZANIA (1961-1963)

KENYA (1963)

UGANDA (1962)

MALAWI (1964)

ZIMBABWE (1980)

SWAZILAND (1968)

LESOTHO (1966)

ZAMBIA (1965)

BOTSWANA (1966)

NAMIBIA (1990)

MALTA (1964)

GIBRALTAR

GHANA (1957)

NIGERIA (1960)

GAMBIA (1965)

SIERRA LEONE (1961)

ASCENSION ISLAND

ST. HELENA

BERMUDA

BAHAMAS (1973)

BARBADOS (1966)

TOBAGO (1962)

TRINIDAD

JAMAICA (1962)

BELIZE (1981)

GUYANA (1966)

FALKLAND ISLANDS

Date indicates year of dominion status or independence within the Commonwealth. Areas without a date are administered from London.

825

become a source of anguish for the architectural profession and has raised some eyebrows because of the fine line he walks between the political and the nonpolitical.

Prince Philip, duke of Edinburgh remains one step behind when the cameras are on, but he does a great deal of hard work inspiring and directing the duke of Edinburgh's Award Scheme in Britain and fifty other countries around the world. The Scheme assists young people from average backgrounds in developing their talents and aspirations in order to improve themselves individually and to be of service to their communities. He would like all young people to be in the mold of those who attended Gordonstoun School, as did he and his sons.

The royal family and their marriages have been TV spectaculars. The divorce of Princess Margaret and the Earl of Snowden and the separation of Princess Anne and Mark Phillips have led to public acceptance and public sympathy. Prince Andrew's marriage outside the traditional circle of royalty and nobility was fully accepted also. While the Duchess of York's boisterous behavior has led to much criticism of her personally, her husband and the wider family remain largely unscathed. Britain's role and status in Europe and the world have changed and will continue to do so. The royal family adjusts to these modulations and carries on, themselves seemingly unmoved. Their future at least, is secure.

Family group—the Prince and Princess of Wales with Prince William and Prince Henry, 1984. (A.P. Wide World Photos, Inc.)

C H R O N O L O G Y

Britain in Europe

1969	Civil Rights Movement in Northern Ireland
1970	Conservative victory; Edward Heath prime minister
1972	"Bloody Sunday" in Londonderry
1973	Britain enters European Common Market; Sunningdale Agreement; "three-day week"
1974	Heath defeated in February election; Labor victorious in February and October; Wilson again prime minister; direct rule in Northern Ireland
1975	Common Market supported in referendum; Margaret Thatcher Conservative leader; Labor adopts "Social Contract"
1976	Wilson resigned; James Callaghan prime minister
1979	"Winter of discontent"; devolution referenda defeated in Scotland and Wales; Conservatives won election; Margaret Thatcher prime minister
1980	Michael Foot Labor leader
1981	Maze prison hunger strikes; Social Democratic party founded; marriage of Prince of Wales and Lady Diana Spencer
1982	Falklands War
1983	Conservative landslide; Neil Kinnock Labor leader
1984	Coal strike began
1985	Coal strike ended; Anglo-Irish Agreement; Westland Helicopter crisis
1987	Thatcher won again

Suggestions for Further Reading

BIBLIOGRAPHIES

Bonser, Wilfred, *An Anglo-Saxon and Celtic Bibliography* (450–1087), 2 vols., 1957.

Brown, L. M. and I. R. Christie, *Bibliography of British History, 1789–1851,* 1977.

Davies, Godfrey, *Bibliography of British History: Stuart Period, 1603–1714,* rev. Mary Keeler, 1970.

Gross, Charles, *The Sources and Literature of English History,* 1915.

Hanham, H. J., *Bibliography of British History, 1815–1914,* 1976.

Pargellis, Stanley and D. J. Medley, *Bibliography of British History: The Eighteenth Century, 1714–1789,* 1951.

Read, Conyers, *Bibliography of British History: Tudor Period, 1485–1603,* 2d ed., 1959.

Smith, Robert A., *Late Georgian and Regency England, 1760–1837,* 1984.

The North American Conference on British Studies has sponsored the following bibliographical handbooks:

Altschul, M., *Anglo-Norman England, 1066–1154,* 1969.

Wilkinson, Bertie, *The High Middle Ages in England, 1154–1377,* 1978

Guth, D. J., *Late-Medieval England, 1377–1485,* 1976.

Levine, Mortimer, *Tudor England, 1485–1603,* 1968.

Sachse, William L., *Restoration England, 1660–1689,* 1971.

Altholz, J. L., *Victorian England, 1837–1901,* 1970.

Havighurst, A. F., *Modern England: 1901–1970,* 1976.

REFERENCE WORKS

Cockayne, George E., *The Complete Peerage of England, Scotland, Ireland, Great Britain, and the United Kingdom,* ed. Vicary Gibbs, et al., 13 vols., 1910–1959.

Drabble, Margaret, ed., *The Oxford Companion to English Literature,* 5th ed., 1985.

Fryde, E. B., D. E. Greenway, S. Porter, and I. Roy, eds., *Handbook of British Chronology,* 3d ed., Royal Historical Society, 1986.

Gilbert, Martin, *British History Atlas,* 1968.

Haigh, Christopher, *The Cambridge Historical Encyclopedia of Great Britain and Ireland,* 1985.

Langer, William L., ed., *An Encyclopedia of World History: Ancient, Medieval, and Modern, Chronologically Arranged,* 5th ed., 1973.

McEvedy, Colin and Richard Jones, *Atlas of World Population History,* 1978.

Rogers, Pat, *The Oxford Illustrated History of English Literature,* 1987.

Stephen, Leslie and Sidney B. Lee, eds., *The Dictionary of National Biography from the Earliest Times to 1900,* 1921–1922.

JOURNALS

Albion
American Historical Review
Bulletin of the Institute of Historical Research
Economic History Review
English Historical Review
Historical Journal
History
History Today
Journal of British Studies
Journal of Modern History
Past and Present
Times Literary Supplement (London)

THE STUARTS (1603–1714)

The causes of the English (Puritan) Revolution continue to be of interest, and regional studies have become very important. How things actually worked is of more concern than are the great clashes of ideologies. Scholars of the Revolution are examining local governmental, economic, and social institutions and their impact upon the national scene. The rise of modern science and its political and broader intellectual influences is a subject of increasing importance. Scholars are also seeking the origins of the modern family and modern gender roles in the Tudor and, especially, the Stuart years.

Church and State

Aylmer, G. E., *The King's Servants*, 1961.

———, *Rebellion or Revolution? England, 1640–1660*, 1986.

Baxter, Stephen, *William III*, 1966.

Bottigheimer, Karl, *English Money and Irish Land*, 1971.

Bowen, Catherine Drinker, *The Lion and the Throne: The Life and Times of Sir Edward Coke*, 1956.

Brailsford, H. N., *The Levellers and the English Revolution*, 1961.

Bridenbaugh, Carl, *Vexed and Troubled Englishmen, 1590–1642*, 1968.

Brunton, D. and D. H. Penninton, *Members of the Long Parliament*, 1954.

Canny, Nicholas, *Kingdom and Colony: Ireland in the Atlantic World, 1560–1800*, 1988.

Churchill, Sir Winston S., *Marlborough, His Life and Times*, 6 vols., 1933–1939.

Clarendon, Earl of, *History of the Great Rebellion*, 1888.

Clark, Sir George, *The Later Stuarts, 1660–1714*, 1934.

Davies, Godfrey, *The Early Stuarts, 1603–1660*, 1959.

———, *The Restoration of Charles II*, 1955.

De Krey, Gary Stuart, *A Fractured Society: The Politics of London in the First Age of Party, 1688–1715*, 1985.

Feiling, Keith, *A History of the Tory Party*, 1924.

Fink, Zera, *The Classical Republicans*, 1962.

Firth, C. H., *The Last Years of the Protectorate*, 1909.

———, *Oliver Cromwell and the Rule of the Puritans in England*, 1900.

Fletcher, Anthony, *The Outbreak of the English Civil War*, 1981.

———, *Reform in the Provinces: The Government of Stuart England*, 1986.

Foster, Elizabeth Read, *The House of Lords, 1603–1649: Structure, Procedure, and the Nature of its Business*, 1983.

Gardiner, S. R., *History of England, 1603–1656*, 18 vols., 1894–1904.

Green, David, *Queen Anne*, 1971.

Gregg, Pauline, *Free Born John: A Biography of John Lilburne*, 1961.

Haley, K. H., *First Earl of Shaftesbury*, 1968.

Haller, William, *Liberty and Reformation in the Puritan Revolution*, 1955.

———, *The Rise of Puritanism, 1570–1643*, 1938.

Havran, Martin J., *Catholics in Caroline England*, 1962.

Hexter, J. H., *The Reign of King Pym*, 1941.

Hill, Christopher, *Puritanism and Revolution*, 1958.

Holmes, Geoffrey, *Britain after the Glorious Revolution*, 1969.

———, *British Politics in the Age of Ann*, 1968.

Horewitz, Henry, *Parliament, Policy and Politics in the Reign of William III*, 1977.

Hulme, Harold, *The Life of Sir John Eliot*, 1957.

Hutton, Ronald, *The Restoration: A Political and Religious Victory of England and Wales, 1658–1667,* 1985.

Jones, Colin, Malwyn Newitt and Stephen Roberts, eds., *Politics and People in Revolutionary England,* 1986.

Jones, J. R., *Charles II: Royal Politician,* 1987.

———, *The First Whigs: The Politics of the Exclusion Crisis, 1673–83,* 1961.

———, *The Revolution of 1688 in England,* 1972.

Judson, Margaret, *The Crisis of the Constitution,* 1949.

Keeler, Mary F., *The Long Parliament, 1640–41,* 1954.

Kenyon, J.P., *Robert Spencer, Earl of Sunderland, 1641–1702,* 1958.

———, *The Stuart Constitution, 1603–1688,* 1966.

Kishlansky, Mark, *The Rise of the New Model Army,* 1979.

Macaulay, T. B., *History of England,* 6 vols., 1849–1861.

MacCormack, J., *Revolutionary Politics in the Long Parliament,* 1974.

Moir, Thomas L., *The Addled Parliament of 1614,* 1958.

Morrill, J. S., *The Revolt of the Provinces,* 1976.

Ogg, David, *England in the Reign of Charles II,* 2 vols., 1956.

———, *England in the Reign of James II and William III,* 1953.

Ogilvie, Charles, *The King's Government and the Common Law, 1471–1641,* 1958.

Pawlisch, Hans P., *Sir John Davies and the Conquest of Ireland: A Study of Legal Imperialism,* 1985.

Pearl, Valerie, *London and the Outbreak of the Puritan Revolution, 1625–1642,* 1961.

Plumb, Sir John H., *The Growth of Political Stability in England, 1675–1725,* 1967.

Prall, S. E., *The Agitation for Law Reform during the Puritan Revolution, 1640–1660,* 1966.

———, *The Bloodless Revolution: England, 1688,* 1972.

———, *The Puritan Revolution: A Documentary History,* 1968.

Richardson, R. C., *The Debate on the English Revolution,* 1989.

Roberts, Clayton, *The Growth of Responsible Government in England,* 1966.

Roots, Ivan, *The Great Rebellion, 1642–1660,* 1966.

Russell, Conrad, *The Origins of the English Civil War,* 1973.

———, *Parliaments and English Politics, 1621–1629,* 1979.

Schwoerer, Lois, *The Declaration of Rights, 1689,* 1981.

———, *"No Standing Armies": The Antiarmy Ideology in Seventeenth-Century England,* 1974.

Snow, Vernon, *Essex the Rebel: The Life of Robert Devereux, the Third Earl of Essex, 1591–1646,* 1970.

Solt, Leo, *Saints in Arms,* 1959.

Speck, W. A., *Reluctant Revolutionaries: Englishmen and the Revolution of 1688,* 1989.

Stone, Lawrence, *The Causes of the English Revolution, 1529–1642,* 1972.

Trevelyan, G. M., *England Under Queen Anne,* 3 vols., 1930–34.

———, *The English Revolution, 1688–1689,* 1938.

Trevor-Roper, H. R., *Archbishop Laud,* 1940.

———, *Catholics, Anglicans and Puritans: Seventeenth-Century Essays,* 1988.

Tyacke, Nicholas, *Anti-Calvinists: The Rise of English Arminianism, c. 1590–1640,* 1987.

Underdown, David, *Pride's Purge: Politics in the Puritan Revolution,* 1971.

Van der Zee, H. and B., *William and Mary*, 1973.

Wedgwood, Dame Veronica, *The King's Peace*, 1955.

———, *The King's War*, 1958.

———, *The Trial of Charles I*, 1964.

Western, J. R., *Monarchy and Revolution: The English State in the 1680s*, 1972.

Willson, David Harris, *King James VI and I*, 1956.

———, *The Privy Councillors in the House of Commons, 1604–1629*, 1940.

Worden, Blair, *The Rump Parliament, 1648–1653*, 1974.

Zaller, Robert, *The Parliament of 1621*, 1971.

Economic, Social and Intellectual

Astor, Margaret, *England's Iconoclasts*, Vol. I, *Laws against Images*, 1988.

Brooks, C. W., *Pettyfoggers and Vipers of the Commonwealth: The 'Lower Branch' of the Legal Profession in Early Modern England*, 1986.

Chambers, J. D., *Population, Economy, and Society in Pre-Industrial England*, 1972.

Clarkson, L. A., *The Pre-Industrial Economy in England, 1500–1750*, 1971.

Cliffe, J. T., *Puritans in Conflict*, 1988.

Collinson, Patrick, *Godly People: Essays on English Protestantism and Puritanism*, 1983.

Earle, Peter, *The Making of the English Middle Class: Business, Society and Family Life in London, 1660–1730*, 1988.

Gooch, G. P., *English Democratic Ideas in the Seventeenth Century*, 1959.

Harris, Tim, *London Crowds in the Reign of Charles II: Propaganda and Politics from the Restoration until the Exclusion Crisis*, 1987.

Hill, Christopher, *The Economic Problems of the Church, from Whitgift to the Long Parliament*, 1956.

———, *Society and Puritanism in Pre-Revolutionary England*, 1964.

———, *A Tinker and a Poor Man: John Bunyan and His Church*, 1988.

———, *The World Turned Upside Down*, 1972.

Jacob, James R., *Henry Stubbe, Radical Protestantism and the Early Enlightenment*, 1983.

Jacob, Margaret, *The Newtonians and the English Revolution*, 1974.

Katz, David, *Sabbath and Sectarianism in Seventeenth-Century England*, 1988.

Laslett, Peter, *The World We Have Lost: England Before the Industrial Age*, 1965.

Manning, Brian, *The English People and the English Revolution*, 1976.

Notestein, Wallace, *The English People on the Eve of Colonization*, 1954.

Phillips, John, *The Reformation of Images: Destruction of Art in England, 1535–1600*, 1973.

Pocock, J. A., *The Ancient Constitution and the Feudal Law*, 1957.

Prest, W. R., *The Rise of the Barristers: A Social History of the English Bar, 1590–1640*, 1986.

Sharpe, Kevin, *Criticism and Compliment: The Politics of Literature in the England of Charles I*, 1987.

Stone, Lawrence, *Family, Sex, and Marriage in England, 1500–1800*, 1977.

Supple, B. E., *Commercial Crisis and Change in England 1600–1642*, 1959.

Tawney, R. H., *Business and Politics Under James I*, 1959.

———, "The Rise of the Gentry, 1558–1640," *Economic History Review*, XI (1941), 1–38.

Thomas, Keith, *Religion and the Decline of Magic: Studies in Popular Beliefs in Sixteenth and Seventeenth Century England*, 1971.

Thompson, Roger, *Women in Stuart England and America*, 1974.

Trevor-Roper, H. R., "The Gentry, 1540–1640," *Economic History Review*, Supplement I, 1953.

Turner, F. C., *James II*, 1948.

Underdown, David, *Revel, Riot and Rebellion: Popular Politics and Culture in England, 1603–1660*, 1987.

Walzer, Michael, *The Revolution of the Saints*, 1965.

Westfall, R. S., *Science and Religion in Seventeenth-Century England*, 1958.

Zagorin, Perez, *The Court and the Country: The Beginning of the English Revolution*, 1969.

———, *A History of Political Thought in the English Revolution*, 1954.

THE HANOVERIANS (1714–1837)

The continuing influence of the Jacobites is receiving great attention. The older views of Namier and the Whig oligarchy are being re-examined. Ideas from lower as well as upper classes are seen to be more important than was previously thought. The years of George II and George III are increasingly being studied as a society in the throes of economic and social change with great political ramifications. Change, rather than stability, is now the object of interest. The wars with France, culminating in the victory at Waterloo, are of significance to scholars studying the broader themes of the rise and fall of nations and empires. The economic and social foundations upon which wars and empires are built are also of concern. Besides these grand themes, there is an increasing interest in the emergence of women as writers, thinkers, and proponents of feminist ideas accompanying the creation of a working class, all as part of the Industrial Revolution.

Church and State

Ayling, Stanley, *The Elder Pitt*, 1976.

———, *George the Third*, 1972.

Bartlett, J. C., *Castlereagh*, 1967.

Baugh, Daniel, ed., *Aristocratic Government and Society in Eighteenth-Century England: The Foundations of Stability*, 1975.

Beattie, John M., *The English Court in the Reign of George I*, 1967.

Black, Jeremy, *British Foreign Policy in the Age of Walpole*, 1985.

Brewer, John, *The Sinews of Power: War, Money and the English State, 1688–1783*, 1989.

Brock, W. R., *Lord Liverpool and Liberal Toryism, 1820–1827*, 2d ed., 1967.

Brooke, John, *King George III*, 1972.

Colley, Linda, *The Defiance of Oligarchy: The Tory Party, 1714–1760*, 1982.

Cone, Carl B., *The English Jacobins*, 1968.

Corbett, Julian S., *England in the Seven Years' War: A Study in Combined Strategy*, 2 vols., 2d ed., 1918.

Derry, John W., *Charles James Fox*, 1972.

Ehrman, John, *The British Government and Commercial Negotiations with Europe, 1789–1793*, 1962.

————, *The Younger Pitt, The Years of Acclaim*, 1969.

Feiling, Keith, *The Second Tory Party, 1714–1832*, 1938.

Foord, Archibald, *His Majesty's Opposition, 1714–1830*, 1964.

Gipson, Lawrence, *The British Empire Before the American Revolution*, 15 vols., 1958–70.

Glover, Michael, *Wellington as Military Commander*, 1968.

Hatton, Ragnhild, *George I, Elector and King*, 1978.

Hill, B. W., *British Parliamentary Parties, 1742–1832: From the Fall of Walpole to the First Reform Act*, 1985.

Keir, David L., *The Constitutional History of Modern Britain, 1485–1950*, 1953.

Kissinger, Henry, A., *A World Restored: Metternich, Castlereagh and the Problems of Peace, 1812–22*, 1957.

Kronenberger, Louis, *The Extraordinary Mr. Wilkes*, 1974.

Landau, Norma, *The Justices of the Peace, 1679–1760*, 1984.

Longford, Elizabeth, *Wellington: Pillar of State*, 1973.

————, *Wellington: The Years of the Sword*, 1969.

Mackesy, Piers, *The War for America, 1775–1783*, 1964.

Marcus, G. J., *The Age of Nelson: The Royal Navy, 1793–1815*, 1971.

Marshall, P. J., *The Impeachment of Warren Hastings*, 1965.

Mitchell, Austin, *The Whigs in Opposition, 1815–30*, 1967.

Namier, Sir Lewis, *England in the Age of the American Revolution*, 1933.

————, *The Structure of Politics at the Accession of George III*, 2 vols., 2d ed., 1957.

Pares, Richard, *George III and the Politicians*, 1953.

Plumb, Sir John H., *Sir Robert Walpole: The King's Minister*, 1960.

————, *Sir Robert Walpole: The Making of a Statesman*, 1956.

Porritt, E. and A., *The Unreformed House of Commons*, 2 vols., 1903.

Priestley, J. B., *The Prince of Pleasure and His Regency*, 1969.

Richardson, Joanna, *George IV: A Portrait*, 1970.

Smith, Robert A., *Eighteenth-Century English Politics, Patrons and Place-Hunters*, 1972.

Speck, W. A., *Stability and Strife, England, 1714–1760*, 1977.

Temperley, Harold, *The Foreign Policy of Canning, 1822–1827*, 1925.

Thomas, P. D. G., *The House of Commons in the Eighteenth Century*, 1971.

————, *Lord North*, 1976.

————, *The Townshend Duties Crisis: The Second Phase of the American Revolution, 1767–1773*, 1987.

Thomis, Malcolm I. and Peter Holt, *Threats of Revolution in Britain, 1789–1848*, 1977.

Watson, J. Steven, *The Reign of George III, 1760–1815*, 1960.

Webster, Charles K., *The Foreign Policy of Castlereagh*, 2 vols., 1925–1931.

Western, J. R., *The English Militia in the Eighteenth Century: The Story of a Political Issue, 1660–1802*, 1965.

Wickwire, Franklin and Mary, *Cornwallis: The American Adventure*, 1970.

Willcox, William B., *Portrait of a General: Sir Henry Clinton in the War of Independence*, 1964.

Williams, Basil, *The Whig Supremacy, 1714–1760*, 2d ed., 1962.

Williams, E. Nevell, *The Eighteenth Century Constitution, 1688–1815: Documents and Commentary*, 1960.

Ziegler, Philip, *King William IV*, 1973.

Economic, Social, and Intellectual

Ashton. Thomas S., *An Economic History of England: The Eighteenth Century*, 1955.

———, *The Industrial Revolution, 1760–1830*, rev. ed., 1964.

Bersay, Peter, *The English Urban Renaissance: Culture and Society in the Provincial Town, 1660–1770*, 1989.

Butterfield, Herbert, *George III and the Historians*, 1957.

Christie, Ian R., *Wilkes, Wyvill and Reform*, 1962.

Clarke, J. C. D., *English Society, 1688–1832*, 1986.

Cone, Carl B., *Burke and the Nature of Politics*, 2 vols., 1957–64.

Crafts, N. F. R., *British Economic Growth During the Industrial Revolution*, 1985.

Deane, Phyllis, *The First Industrial Revolution*, 1965.

Deane, Phyllis and W. A. Cole, *British Economic Growth, 1688–1959: Trends and Structure*, 2d ed., 1967.

Donaldson, William, *The Jacobite Song: Political Myth and National Identity*, 1988.

Flinn, M. W., *British Population Growth, 1700–1850*, 1970.

———, *Origins of the Industrial Revolution*, 1966.

Gay, Peter, *The Enlightenment: An Interpretation*, 2 vols., 1967–70.

Goodwin, Albert, *The Friends of Liberty: The English Democratic Movement in the Age of the French Revolution*, 1979.

Harris, R. W., *Reason and Nature in the Eighteenth Century, 1714–1780*, 1969.

———, *Romanticism and the Social Order, 1780–1830*, 1969.

Hartwell, R. M., *The Industrial Revolution and Economic Growth*, 1971.

Hobsbawm, E. J., *Industry and Empire*, 1968.

Malcomson, R. W., *Popular Recreation in English Society, 1700–1850*, 1973.

Marshall, Dorothy, *Dr. Johnson's London*, 1968.

———, *Eighteenth-Century England, 1714–1783*, 1962.

———, *English People in the Eighteenth Century*, 1965.

———, *John Wesley*, 1965.

Marshall, J. D., *The Old Poor Law, 1795–1834*, 1968.

Mathias, Peter, *The First Industrial Nation*, 1969.

Mingay, G. E., *English Landed Society in the Eighteenth Century*, 1963.

Musson, A. E. and Eric Robinson, *Science and Technology in the Industrial Revolution*, 1969.

Olson, Donald J., *Town Planning in London: The Eighteenth and Nineteenth Centuries*, 1964.

Perkin, Harold, *The Origins of Modern Society, 1789–1880*, 1969.

Plumb, Sir John H., *England in the Eighteenth Century*, 1963.

———, *Man and Society in Eighteenth-Century Britain*, 1968.

Poynter, J. R., *Society and Pauperism: English Ideas on Poor Relief, 1795–1834*, 1969.

Price, Jacob M., *Capital and Credit in British Overseas Trade: The View from the Chesapeake, 1770–1776*, 1980.

Quennell, Peter, *Romantic England: Writing and Painting, 1717–1851*, 1970.

Rostow, W. W., *The Stages of Economic Growth*, 1960.

Rude, George W., *Hanoverian London: 1714–1808*, 1971.

———, *Wilkes and Liberty*, 1962.

Semmel, Bernard, *The Methodist Revolution*, 1974.

———, *The Rise of Free Trade Imperialism*, 1970.

Stone, Lawrence and Jeanne Stone, *An Open Elite? England, 1540–1880*, 1984.

Sutherland, Lucy S., *The East India Company in Eighteenth-Century Politics*, 1952.

Thompson, Edward P., *The Making of the English Working Class*, 1963.

———, *Whigs and Hunters: The Origin of the Black Act*, 1975.

Vann, Richard, *Social Development of English Quakerism, 1655–1755*, 1969.

Webb, Robert K., *The British Working-Class Reader, 1790–1848*, 1955.

VICTORIAN ENGLAND

Scholars are increasingly looking to the Victorian era as one of instability and of anticipation of twentieth-century problems. The rise of the trade unions is of greater interest than the rise of the Labor Party. The conflict between the Liberal and Conservative parties is more often related to the wider economic and social problems of a deeply divided nation. The role of Ireland and the Irish in British politics and the impact on Gladstone and Gladstonian liberalism is of great significance. Studies of women for their own sakes, not just as participants in a wider society, are increasingly prevalent. The roles of workers, women, and the Irish are more interesting than the older interest in Church, State, and Empire.

Church and State

Arnstein, Walter L., *The Bradlaugh Case: Atheism, Sex, and Politics among the Late Victorians*, 1984.

Bagehot, Walter, *The English Constitution*, 1867.

Beales, Derek, *From Castlereagh to Gladstone, 1815–1885*, 1969.

Blake, Lord, *The Conservative Party from Pitt to Churchill*, 1970.

———, *Disraeli*, 1966.

Briggs, Asa, *The Age of Improvement, 1783–1867*, 1959.

Bulmer-Thomas, Ivor, *The Growth of the British Party System*, 2 vols., 1965.

Chadwick, Owen, *The Victorian Church*, 2 vols., 1966–1970.

Clive, John, *Macaulay: The Shaping of the Historian*, 1973.

Conacher, J. B., *The Peelites and the Party System, 1846–1852*, 1972.

Cooke, A. B. and John Vincent, *The Governing Passion: Cabinet Government and Party Politics in Britain, 1885–1886*, 1974.

Cowling, Maurice, *1867: Disraeli, Gladstone, and Revolution,* 1967.

Curtis, L. P., *Coercion and Conciliation in Ireland, 1880–1892,* 1963.

Davis, Lance, E. and Robert A. Huttenback, *Mammon and the Pursuit of Empire: The Political Economy of British Imperialism, 1860–1912,* 1986.

Emy, H. V., *Liberals and Social Politics, 1892–1914,* 1973.

Ensor, R. C. K., *England, 1870–1914,* 1936.

Gash, Norman, *Politics in the Age of Peel,* 1953.

——, *Reaction and Reconstruction in English Politics, 1832–1852,* 1965.

——, *Sir Robert Peel,* 2 vols., 1961–1972.

Hamer, D. A., *Liberal Politics in the Age of Gladstone and Rosebery,* 1972.

Hanham, H. J., *Elections and Party Management: Politics in the Time of Disraeli and Gladstone,* 1959.

——, *The Nineteenth Century Constitution, 1815–1914,* 1969.

Hardie, Frank, *The Political Influence of the British Monarchy, 1868–1952,* 1970.

Harrison, J. F. C., *The Early Victorians, 1832–1851,* 1971.

Hoppen, K. Theodore, *Elections, Politics, and Society in Ireland, 1832–1885,* 1984.

Hovell, Mark, *The Chartist Movement,* 1918.

Judd, Denis, *Radical Joe, A Life of Joseph Chamberlain,* 1977.

Longford, Elizabeth, *Queen Victoria: Born to Succeed,* 1965.

Lowe, C. J., *The Reluctant Imperialists, 1870–1902,* 1968.

McCaffrey, Lawrence J., *The Irish Question, 1800–1922,* 1968.

Maehl, William H., Jr., *The Reform Bill of 1832,* 1967.

Magnus, Philip, *Gladstone,* 1954.

Mansergh, Nicholas, *The Irish Question, 1840–1921,* 3d ed., 1975.

Meacham, Standish, *Lord Bishop: The Life of Samuel Wilberforce,* 1970.

Monypenny, W. F. and G. E. Buckle, *Life of Disraeli,* 6 vols., 1910–1920.

Morley, John, *Life of Gladstone,* 3 vols., 1903.

Parris, Henry, *Constitutional Bureaucracy: The Development of British Central Administration Since the Eighteenth Century,* 1969.

Pelling, Henry, *The Origins of the Labour Party, 1880–1900,* 1954.

——, *Popular Politics and Society in Late Victorian Britain,* 1968.

Poirier, Philip, *The Advent of the British Labour Party,* 1958.

Radzinovicz, Leon, *A History of English Criminal Law and Its Administration from 1750,* 4 vols., 1948–1969.

Ridley, Jaspar, *Lord Palmerston,* 1970.

Seton-Watson, R. W., *Britain in Europe, 1789–1914,* 1937.

Shannon, Richard, *The Crisis of Imperialism,* 1974.

Smellie, K., *A History of Local Government,* 4th ed., 1968.

Smith, Francis Barrymore, *The Making of the Second Reform Bill,* 1966.

Smith, Paul, *Disraelian Conservatism and Social Reform,* 1967.

Stansky, Peter, *Gladstone: A Progress in Politics,* 1979.

Taylor, A. J. P., *The Struggle for Mastery in Europe, 1848–1918,* 1954.

Thornton, A. P., *The Imperial Idea and Its Enemies: A Study in British Power,* 1959.

Vincent, John, *The Formation of the Liberal Party,* 1967.

Ward, J. T., *Chartism*, 1973.

Woodward, E. L., *The Age of Reform, 1815–1870*, 2d ed., 1962.

Economic, Social, and Intellectual

Altick, Richard D., *Victorian People and Ideas*, 1973.

Ashworth, William, *The Economic History of England, 1870–1939*, 1960.

Ausubel, Herman, *In Hard Times: Reformers Among the Late Victorians*, 1961.

Best, Geoffrey, *Mid-Victorian Britain, 1851–1875*, 1971.

Blodgett, Harriet, *Centuries of Female Days: Englishwoman's Private Diaries*, 1988.

Bridenthal, Renate, C. Koonz, and S. Stuard, *Becoming Visible: Women in European History*, 1987.

Briggs, Asa, *Victorian Cities*, 1963.

Cannadine, David, *Lords and Landlords: The Aristocracy and the Towns, 1774–1967*, 1980.

Clark, G. Kitson, *An Expanding Society: Britain, 1830–1900*, 1967.

————, *The Making of Victorian England*, 1962.

Crow, Duncan, *The Victorian Woman*, 1972.

Davis, L. and R. Huttenback, *Manor and the Pursuit of Empire: The Political Economy of British Imperialism, 1860–1912*, 1987.

Fieldhouse, C. M., *Economics and Empire, 1880–1914*, 1972.

Fox, Alan, *History and Heritage: The Social Origins of the British Industrial Relations System*, 1985.

Gartner, Lloyd, *The Jewish Immigrant in England, 1870–1914*, 1960.

Halevy, Elie, *History of the English People in the Nineteenth Century*, 6 vols., 1949–52.

Himmelfarb, Gertrude, *Victorian Minds*, 1972.

Holcombe, Lee, *Victorian Ladies at Work*, 1973.

Kadish, Alon, *Historians, Economists, and Economic History*, 1989.

Lees, Lynn, *Exiles of Erin: Irish Migrants in Victorian London*, 1979.

Marsh, Peter, *The Conscience of the Victorian State*, 1979.

Olsen, Donald J., *The Growth of Victorian London*, 1976.

Owen, David, *English Philanthropy, 1660–1960*, 1964.

Pelling, Henry, *A History of Trade Unionism*, 1963.

Phillipps, K. C., *Language and Class in Victorian England*, 1984.

Reader, W. J., *Professional Men: The Rise of the Professional Classes in Nineteenth-Century England*, 1966.

Roberts, David, *Victorian Origins of the British Welfare State*, 1960.

Rose, Michael E., *The English Poor Law, 1880–1930*, 1971.

Rostow, W. W., *British Economy in the Nineteenth Century*, 1948.

Semmel, Bernard, *Imperialism and Social Reform*, 1960.

Soffer, Reba, *Ethics and Society in England: The Revolution in the Social Sciences, 1870–1914*, 1978.

Thompson, F. M. L., *English Landed Society in the Nineteenth Century*, 1963.

Vicinus, Martha, *Suffer and be Still: Women in the Victorian Age*, 1972.

Wiener, Joel, *Radicalism and Freethought in Nineteenth-Century Britain,* 1983.
Wohl, Anthony, *Victorian Family,* 1978.
Young, G. M., *Victorian England: Portrait of an Age,* 1936.

THE TWENTIETH CENTURY

The biographical approach is becoming dominant in the scholarship of the twentieth century. The Edwardian era, World Wars I and II, the Great Depression, and the welfare state are all central issues studied through the writings and lives of individual leaders. There is also a great interest in social issues and the economy. A declining Britain on the world stage is juxtaposed with a domestic Britain, with increasing parity for all its citizens. Future world relationships will undoubtedly be formed to further the emergence of a European Britain, rather than to maintain the image of a "septered isle" in its "splendid isolation."

Church and State

Attlee, Clement, *As It Happened,* 1956.
Beer, Samuel H., *British Politics in the Collectivist Age,* 1965.
Beloff, Max, *Imperial Sunset,* 1969.
Blake, Lord, *The Unknown Prime Minister: The Life and Times of Andrew Bonar Law,* 1954.
———, *The Decline of Power, 1915–1964,* 1985.
Bowman, John, *De Valera and the Ulster Question, 1917–1973,* 1982.
Boyce, D. G., *Englishmen and Irish Troubles: British Public Opinion and the Making of Irish Policy, 1918–22,* 1972.
Churchill, Randolph and Martin Gilbert, *Life of Winston Churchill,* 8 vols (to 1965), 1966–88.
Churchill, Winston S., *History of the Second World War,* 6 vols., 1948–1954.
———, *The World Crisis,* 4 vols., 1923–1929.
Cole, G. D. H., *History of the Labour Party Since 1914,* 1948.
Cross, Colin, *The Liberals in Power, 1905–1914,* 1963.
Eden, Anthony, *Memoirs,* 3 vols., 1960–1965.
Feis, Herbert, *Roosevelt, Churchill, Stalin,* 1957.
Fisk, Albert, *In Time of War: Ireland, Ulster and the Price of Neutrality, 1939–45,* 1983.
Foot, Michael, *Aneurin Bevan,* 2 vols., 1962–1973.
Gilbert, Bentley B., *David Lloyd George: a Political Life: The Architect of Change, 1863–1912,* 1987.
Gilbert, Martin, *The Roots of Appeasement,* 1967.
Graubard, Stephen R., *British Labor and the Russian Revolution, 1917–1924,* 1956.
Grigg, John, *Lloyd George: The People's Champion: 1902–1911,* 1978.
Havighurst, Alfred, *Twentieth-Century Britain,* rev. ed., 1966.
James, Robert Rhodes, *Ambitions and Realities: British Politics, 1964–70,* 1972.

Jenkins, Roy, *Asquith*, 1964.

———, *Mr. Balfour's Poodle*, 1954.

Koss, Stephen E., *Asquith*, 1976.

———, *Lord Haldane: Scapegoat for Liberalism*, 1969.

———, *Nonconformity in Modern British Politics*, 1975.

Lloyd, T. O., *Empire to Welfare State: English History, 1906–1967*, 1970.

Macleod, Ian, *Neville Chamberlain*, 1960.

Macmillan, Harold, *Memoirs*, 6 vols., 1966–1973.

Magnus, Philip, *King Edward VII*, 1964.

Mansergh, Nicholas, *The Commonwealth Experience*, 1969.

Marder, Arthur, *From the Dreadnought to Scapa Flow: The Royal Navy in the Fisher Era, 1904–1919*, 5 vols., 1961–1970.

Marquand, David, *Ramsay MacDonald*, 1977.

Marwick, Arthur, *Britain in the Century of Total War, 1900–1967*, 1968.

Medlicott, W. N., *British Foreign Policy Since Versailles, 1919–1963*, 2d ed., 1968.

———, *Contemporary England, 1914–1964*, 1967.

Middlemass, Keith and John Barnes, *Baldwin*, 1969.

Morgan, Kenneth O., *Labor People: Leaders and Lieutenants, Hardie to Kinnock*, 1987.

Nicolson, Harold, *King George V*, 1951.

Pelling, Henry, *A Short History of the Labour Party*, 1961.

Sked, Alan and Chris Cook, *Post-War Britain: A Political History*, 1979.

Skidelsky, Robert, *Politicians and the Slump: The Government of 1929–1931*, 1967.

Stevenson, Frances, *Lloyd George: A Diary*, 1971.

Taylor, A. J. P., *English History, 1914–1945*, 1965.

———, *the Origins of the Second World War*, 1961.

Thomas, Hugh, *The Suez Affair*, 1967.

Wheeler-Bennett, J. W., *King George VI: His Life and Work*, 1958.

———, *Munich: Prologue to Tragedy*, 1948.

Wilson, Harold, *Final Term: The Labour Government, 1974–1976*, 1979.

———, *A Personal Record: The Labour Government, 1964–1970*, 1971.

Wilson, John, *CB: A Life of Henry Campbell-Bannerman*, 1973.

Young, Kenneth, *Sir Alec Douglas-Home*, 1972.

Zebel, Sydney H., *Balfour: Political Biography*, 1973.

Economic, Social, and Intellectual

Bruce, Maurice, *The Coming of the Welfare State*, 1961.

Cairncross, Alec, *Years of Recovery: British Economic Policy, 1945–51*, 1985.

Clegg, H. A., *A History of British Trade Unions Since 1889, Vol. 1, 1889–1910; Vol. 2, 1915–1933*, 1964 and 1987.

Cole, Margaret, *The Story of Fabian Socialism*, 1961.

Dangerfield, George, *The Strange Death of Liberal England*, 1935.

Gilbert, Bentley B., *Britain Since Nineteen Eighteen*, 2d ed., 1980.

———, *British Social Policy, 1914–1939*, 1970.

Graves, Robert and Alan Hodge, *The Long Week-End: A Social History of Great Britain, 1918–1939,* 1940.

Gregg, Pauline, *The Welfare State: An Economic and Social History of Great Britain from 1945 to the Present Day,* 1969.

Halsey, A. H., *Change in British Society,* 3d ed., 1986.

———, *Trends in British Society Since 1900: A Guide to the Social Structure of Britain,* 1972.

Lekachman, Robert, *The Age of Keynes,* 1966.

Mowat, Charles L., *Britain Between the Wars, 1918–1940,* 1955.

Pollard, Sidney, *The Development of the British Economy, 1914–1980,* 3d ed., 1983.

Sampson, Anthony, *The New Anatomy of Britain,* 1973.

Sissons, Michael and Philip French, *The Age of Austerity, 1945–1951,* 1963.

Stansky, Peter and William Abrahams, *Orwell: The Transformation,* 1980.

Webster, Charles, *The Health Services Since the War,* Vol. 1: *Problems of Wealth Care; The Material Wealth Services before 1957,* 1988.

Wiener, Martin, *English Culture and the Decline of the Industrial Spirit, 1850–1980,* 1982.

Appendix I

Heads of Cabinets and Prime Ministers (with dates of taking office)

April 1721	(Sir) Robert Walpole (later Earl of Orford)	Whig
	Earl of Wilmington	
February 1742	John Lord Carteret (Earl Granville)	Whig
August 1743	Hon. Henry Pelham	Whig
February 1746	Earl of Bath	Whig
February 1746	Hon. Henry Pelham	Whig
March 1754	Duke of Newcastle	Whig
(Resigned November 1756)	Duke of Devonshire	Whig
November 1756	Duke of Newcastle	
June 1757	William Pitt	Whig
March 1761	Duke of Newcastle	
	Earl of Bute	Whig
May 1762	Earl of Bute	Whig
April 1763	George Grenville	Whig
July 1765	Marquis of Rockingham	Whig
July 1766	William Pitt, Earl of Chatham	
August 1766	Duke of Grafton	Whig
November 1768	Duke of Grafton	Whig
February 1770	Lord North	Whig
March 1782	Marquis of Rockingham	
	Earl of Shelburne	Whig
July 1782	Earl of Shelburne	Whig
April 1783	Duke of Portland	
	Lord North	Whig
	Charles James Fox	

December 1783	William Pitt, the Younger	Whig
March 1801	Henry Addington	Whig
May 1804	William Pitt, the Younger	Whig
January 1806	Lord Grenville	
	Charles James Fox	
	Henry Addington, Lord Sidmouth	Coalition
	(The Ministry of All the Talents)	
March 1807	Duke of Portland	Tory
September 1809	Spencer Perceval	Tory
June 1812	Earl of Liverpool	Tory
April 1827	George Canning	Tory
September 1827	Viscount Goderich	Tory
January 1828	Duke of Wellington	Tory
November 1830	Earl Grey	Whig
July 1834	Viscount Melbourne	Whig
December 1834	Sir Robert Peel	Conservative
April 1835	Viscount Melbourne	Whig
September 1841	Sir Robert Peel	Conservative
July 1846	Lord John Russell (Earl Russell, 1861)	Whig
February 1852	Earl of Derby	Conservative
December 1852	Earl of Aberdeen	Coalition
February 1855	Viscount Palmerston	Whig
February 1858	Earl of Derby	Conservative
June 1859	Viscount Palmerston	Whig
October 1865	Earl Russell	Whig
June 1866	Earl of Derby	Conservative
February 1868	Benjaming Disraeli (Earl of Beaconsfield, 1876)	Conservative
December 1868	W. E. Gladstone	Liberal
February 1874	Benjamin Disraeli (Earl of Beaconsfield, 1876)	Conservative
April 1880	W. E. Gladstone	Liberal
June 1885	Marquess of Salisbury	Conservative
February 1886	W. E. Gladstone	Liberal
August 1886	Marquess of Salisbury	Conservative
August 1892	W. E. Gladstone	Liberal
March 1894	Earl of Rosebery	Liberal
June 1895	Marquess of Salisbury	Conservative
July 1902	A. J. Balfour (Earl of Balfour, 1922)	Conservative
December 1905	Sir Henry Campbell-Bannerman	Liberal
April 1908	H. H. Asquith (Earl of Oxford and Asquith, 1925)	Liberal
May 1915	H. H. Asquith (Earl of Oxford and Asquith, 1925)	Coalition
December 1916	David Lloyd George (Earl Lloyd George of Dwyfor, 1945)	Coalition
October 1922	A. Bonar Law	Conservative
May 1923	Stanley Baldwin (Earl Baldwin of Bewdley, 1937)	Conservative
January 1924	J. Ramsay MacDonald	Labor

November 1924	Stanley Baldwin	Conservative
June 1929	J. Ramsay MacDonald	Labor
August 1931	J. Ramsay MacDonald	National
June 1935	Stanley Baldwin	National
May 1937	Neville Chamberlain	National
May 1940	Winston S. Churchill	Coalition
May 1945	Winston s. Churchill	Conservative
July 1945	Clement R. Attlee (Earl Attlee, 1955)	Labor
October 1951	Winston S. Churchill	Conservative
April 1955	Sir Anthony Eden (Earl of Avon, 1961)	Conservative
January 1957	Harold Macmillan (Earl of Stockton, 1984)	Conservative
October 1963	Sir Alec Douglas-Home (previously Earl of Home, later Lord Home of the Hirsel, 1974)	Conservative
October 1964	Harold Wilson (Wilson of Rievaulx, 1983)	Labor
June 1970	Edward Heath	Conservative
February 1974	Harold Wilson	Labor
March 1976	James Callaghan (Lord Callaghan of Cardiff, 1987)	Labor
May 1979	Margaret Thatcher	Conservative
November 1990	John Major	Conservative

Chancellors of the Exchequer

February 1559	Sir Walter Mildmay
June 1589	John Fortescue
May 1603	Sir George Home (Earl of Dunbar, 1605)
April 1606	Sir Julius Caesar
October 1614	Sir Fulke Greville (Lord Brooke, 1621)
January 1621	Sir Richard Weston (Lord Weston, 1628; Earl of Portland, 1633)
July 1628	Edward Barrett (Lord Barrett of Newburgh-Scotland)
March 1629	Francis Cottington (Lord Cottington, 1631)
January 1642	Sir John Culpepper (Lord Culpepper, 1644)
March 1643	Sir Edward Hyde (Earl of Clarendon, 1661)
1654–1659	(Treasury Commissioners during Protectorate)
May 1661	Anthony Ashley Cooper (Earl of Shaftesbury, 1672)
November 1672	Sir John Duncombe
April 1676	Sir John Ernle
April 1689	Henry Booth, Lord Delamer (Earl of Warrington, 1690)
March 1690	Richard Hampden
April 1694	Charles Montagu (Lord Halifax, 1700)
May 1699	John Smith
March 1701	Henry Boyle
February 1708	John Smith
August 1710	Robert Harley (Earl of Oxford and Mortimer, 1711)
June 1711	Robert Benson (Lord Bingley, 1713)
November 1713	Sir William Wyndham
October 1714	Sir Richard Onslow (Lord Onslow, 1716)

October 1715	Robert Walpole (Earl of Orford, 1742)
April 1717	James Stanhope (Viscount Stanhope, 1717; Earl Stanhope, 1718)
March 1718	John Aislabie
February 1721	Sir John Pratt
April 1721	Robert Walpole (Earl of Orford, 1742)
February 1742	Samuel Sandys (Lord Sandys of Ombersley, 1743)
December 1743	Henry Pelham
March 1754	Sir William Lee
April 1754	Henry Bilson Legge
November 1755	Sir George Lyttelton (Lord Lyttelton, 1756)
November 1756	Henry Bilson Legge
April 1757	William Murray (Lord Mansfield, 1756; Earl of Mansfield, 1776)
July 1757	Henry Bilson Legge
March 1761	William Wildman Barrington-Shute (Viscount Barrington-Ireland)
May 1762	Sir Francis Dashwood (Lord le Despenser, 1763)
April 1763	George Grenville
July 1765	William Dowdeswell
August 1766	Charles Townshend
September 1767	Lord Mansfield
October 1767	Frederick North, Lord North (Earl of Guildford, 1790)
April 1782	Lord John Cavendish
July 1782	William Pitt
April 1783	Lord John Cavendish
December 1783	William Pitt
March 1801	Henry Addington (Viscount Sidmouth, 1805)
May 1804	William Pitt
February 1806	Lord Henry Petty (Marquess of Lansdowne, 1809)
March 1807	Spencer Perceval
June 1812	Nicholas Vansittart (Lord Bexley, 1823)
January 1823	Frederick John Robinson (Viscount Goderich, 1827; Earl of Ripon, 1833)
April 1827	George Canning
September 1827	John Charles Herries
January 1828	Henry Goulburn
November 1830	John Charles Spencer, Viscount Althorp (Earl Spencer, 1834)
December 1834	Sir Robert Peel
April 1835	Thomas Spring Rice (Lord Monteagle of Brandon, 1839)
August 1839	Sir Francis Thornhill Baring (Lord Northbrook, 1866)
September 1841	Henry Goulburn
July 1846	Sir Charles Wood (Viscount Halifax, 1866)
February 1852	Benjamin Disraeli (Earl of Beaconsfield, 1876)
December 1852	William Ewart Gladstone
February 1855	Sir George Cornewall Lewis
February 1858	Benjamin Disraeli (Earl of Beaconsfield, 1876)
June 1859	William Ewart Gladstone

July 1866	Benjamin Disraeli (Earl of Beaconsfield, 1876)
February 1868	George Ward Hunt
December 1868	Robert Lowe (Viscount Sherbrooke, 1880)
August 1873	William Ewart Gladstone
February 1874	Sir Stafford Henry Northcote (Earl of Iddesleigh, 1885)
April 1880	William Ewart Gladstone
December 1882	Hugh Culling Eardley Childers
June 1885	Sir Michael Edward Hicks Beach (Earl St. Aldwyn, 1915)
February 1886	Sir William George Granville Venables Vernon Harcourt
August 1886	Lord Randolph Henry Spencer Churchill
January 1887	George Joachim Goschen (Viscount Goschen, 1900)
August 1892	Sir William Harcourt
June 1895	Sir Michael Hicks Beach (Earl St. Aldwyn, 1915)
July 1902	Charles Thomson Ritchie (Lord Ritchie, 1905)
October 1903	Joseph Austen Chamberlain
December 1905	Herbert Henry Asquith (Earl of Oxford and Asquith, 1925)
April 1908	David Lloyd George (Earl Lloyd George of Dwyfor, 1945)
May 1915	Reginald McKenna
December 1916	Andrew Bonar Law
January 1919	Joseph Austen Chamberlain
April 1921	Sir Robert Stevenson Horne (Viscount Horne, 1937)
October 1922	Stanley Baldwin (Earl Baldwin of Bewdley, 1937)
October 1923	Arthur Neville Chamberlain
January 1924	Philip Snowden (Viscount Snowden, 1931)
November 1924	Winston Leonard Spencer Churchill
June 1929	Philip Snowden (Viscount Snowden, 1931)
November 1931	Arthur Neville Chamberlain
May 1937	Sir John Allsebrook Simon (Viscount Simon, 1940)
May 1940	Sir Howard Kingsley Wood
September 1943	Sir John Anderson (Viscount Waverley, 1952)
July 1945	Hugh John Neale Dalton
November 1947	Sir Richard Stafford Cripps
October 1950	Hugh Todd Naylor Gaitskell
October 1951	Richard Austen Butler (Lord Butler of Saffron Walden, 1965)
December 1955	Maurice Harold Macmillan (Earl of Stockton, 1984)
January 1957	George Edward Peter Thorneycroft (Lord Thorneycroft, 1967)
January 1958	Derick Heathcoat Amory (Viscount Amory, 1960)
July 1960	John Selwyn Brooke Lloyd (Lord Selwyn-Lloyd, 1976)
July 1962	Reginald Maudling
October 1964	Leonard James Callaghan (Lord Callaghan of Cardiff, 1987)
November 1967	Roy Harris Jenkins (Lord Jenkins of Hillhead, 1987)
June 1970	Iain Norman Macleod
July 1970	Anthony Perrinott Lysberg Barber (Lord Barber, 1974)
March 1974	Denis Winston Healey
May 1979	Sir Richard Edward Geoffrey Howe

June 1983	Nigel Lawson
October 1989	John Major
November 1990	Norman Lamont

Secretaries of State for Foreign Affairs

March 1782	Charles James Fox
July 1782	Thomas Robinson, Lord Grantham
April 1783	Charles James Fox
December 1783	George Nugent-Temple-Grenville, Earl Temple (Marquess of Buckingham, 1784)
December 1783	Francis Godolphin Osborne (Duke of Leeds, 1789)
June 1791	William Wyndham Grenville, Lord Grenville
February 1801	Robert Banks Jenkinson (Earl of Liverpool, 1808)
May 1804	Dudley Ryder, Lord Harrowby (Earl of Harrowby, 1809)
January 1805	Henry Phipps, Lord Mulgrave (Earl of Mulgrave, 1812)
February 1806	Charles James Fox
September 1806	Charles Grey (Earl Grey, 1807)
March 1807	George Canning
October 1809	Henry Bathurst, Earl Bathurst
December 1809	Richard Wellesley, Lord Wellesley, Marquess Wellesley-Ireland
March 1812	Robert Stewart, Viscount Castlereagh (Marquess of Londonderry, 1822)
September 1822	George Canning
April 1827	John William Ward, Viscount Dudley and Ward (Earl of Dudley, 1827)
June 1828	George Hamilton-Gordon, Earl of Aberdeen-Scotland, Viscount Gordon
November 1830	Henry John Temple, Viscount Palmerston-Ireland
November 1834	Arthur Wellesley, Duke of Wellington
April 1835	Viscount Palmerston
September 1841	Earl of Aberdeen
July 1846	Viscount Palmerston
December 1851	Granville George Leveson-Gower, Earl Granville
February 1852	James Howard Harris, Earl of Malmesbury
December 1852	Lord John Russell (Earl Russell, 1861)
February 1853	George William Frederick Villiers, Earl of Clarendon
February 1858	Earl of Malmesbury
June 1859	Lord John Russell (Earl Russell, 1861)
November 1865	Earl of Clarendon
July 1866	Edward Henry Stanley, Lord Stanley (Earl of Derby, 1869)
December 1868	Earl of Clarendon
July 1870	Earl Granville
February 1874	Earl of Derby
April 1878	Robert Arthur Talbot Gascoyne-Cecil, Marquess of Salisbury
April 1880	Earl Granville

June 1885	Marquess of Salisbury
February 1886	Archibald Philip Primrose, Earl of Rosebery-Scotland, Lord Rosebery (Earl of Midlothian, 1911)
August 1886	Stafford Henry Northcote, Earl of Iddesleigh
January 1887	Marquess of Salisbury
August 1892	Earl of Rosebery
March 1894	John Wodehouse, Earl of Kimberley
June 1895	Marquess of Salisbury
November 1900	Henry Charles Keith Petty-Fitzmaurice, Marquess of Lansdowne
December 1905	Sir Edward Grey (Viscount Grey of Fallodon, 1916)
December 1916	Arthur James Balfour (Earl of Balfour, 1922)
October 1919	George Nathaniel Curzon, Earl Curzon (Marquess Curzon of Keddleston, 1921)
January 1924	James Ramsay MacDonald
November 1924	Sir Joseph Austen Chamberlain
June 1929	Arthur Henderson
August 1931	Rufus Isaacs, Marquess of Reading
November 1931	Sir John Allsebrook Simon (Viscount Simon, 1940)
June 1935	Sir Samuel John Gurney Hoare (Viscount Templewood, 1944)
December 1935	Robert Anthony Eden (Earl of Avon, 1961)
March 1938	Edward Frederick Lindley Wood, Viscount Halifax (Earl of Halifax, 1944)
December 1940	Anthony Eden (Earl of Avon, 1961)
July 1945	Ernest Bevin
March 1951	Herbert Stanley Morrison (Lord Morrison of Lambeth, 1959)
October 1951	Anthony Eden (Earl of Avon, 1961)
April 1955	Maurice Harold Macmillan (Earl of Stockton, 1984)
December 1955	John Selwyn Lloyd (Lord Selwyn-Lloyd, 1976)
July 1960	Alexander Frederick Douglas-Home, Earl of Home (later, 1963, Sir Alec Douglas-Home; later still, Lord Home of the Hirsel, 1974)
October 1963	Richard Austen Butler (Lord Butler of Saffron Walden, 1965)
October 1964	Patrick Chrestien Gordon-Walker (Lord Gordon-Walker, 1974)
January 1965	Robert Maitland Michael Stewart (Lord Stewart of Fulham, 1979)
August 1966	George Alfred Brown (Lord George-Brown, 1970)
March 1968	Robert Maitland Michael Stewart (Lord Stewart of Fulham, 1979)
June 1970	Sir Alexander Frederick Douglas-Home (formerly Earl of Home; later Lord Home of the Hirsel, 1974)
March 1974	Leonard James Callaghan (Lord Callaghan of Cardiff, 1987)
April 1976	Charles Anthony Raven Crosland
February 1977	David Anthony Llewellyn Owen
May 1979	Peter Alexander Rupert Carington, Lord Carrington
April 1982	Francis Leslie Pym (Lord Pym, 1987)
June 1983	Sir Richard Edward Geoffrey Howe
July 1989	John Major
October 1989	Douglas Hurd

Archbishops of Canterbury

597–604	Augustine		1191	Reginald FitzJocelin
604–619	Laurence		1193–1205	Hubert Walter
619–624	Mellitus		1205–1206	Reginald and John de Grey
624–627	Justus		1206–1228	Stephen Langton
627–653	Honorius		1228–1229	Walter de Eynesham
653–664	Deusdedit		1229–1231	Richard Grant Wethershed
666–668	Wigheard		1231	Ralph Nevill
668–690	Theodore		1232	John of Sittingbourne
692–731	Berhtwald		1232–1233	John Blund
731–734	Tatwine		1233–1240	Edumund of Abingdon
735–739	Nothhelm		1241–1270	Boniface of Savoy
740–760	Cuthbert		1270–1272	Adam of Chillenden
761–764	Bregowine		1272–1278	Robert Kilwardby
765–792	Jaenberht		1278–1279	Robert Burnell
792–805	Aethelheard		1279–1292	John Pecham
805–832	Wulfred		1293–1313	Robert Winchelsey
832	Feologild		1313	Thomas Cobham
833–870	Ceolnoth		1313–1327	Walter Reynolds
870–888	Aethelred		1327–1333	Simon Meopham
890–923	Plegmund		1333–1348	John Stratford
923–926	Aethelhelm		1348–1349	John Offord
926–941	Wulfhelm		1349	Thomas Bradwardine
941–958	Oda		1349–1366	Simon Islip
958–959	Aelfsige		1366–1368	Simon Langham
959	Byrhthelm		1368–1374	William Whittlesey
959–988	Dunstan		1375–1381	Simon Sudbury
988–990	Aethelgar		1381–1396	William Courtenay
990–994	Sigeric		1396–1397	Thomas Arundel
995–1005	Aelfric		1397–1399	Roger Walden
1006–1012	Aelfheah		1399–1414	Thomas Arundell
1013–1020	Lyfing (Aelfstan)		1414–1443	Henry Chichele
1020–1038	Aethelnoth		1443–1452	John Stafford
1038–1050	Eadsige		1452–1454	John Kempe
1051–1052	Robert of Jumièges		1454–1486	Thomas Bourgchier
1052–1070	Stigand		1486–1500	John Morton
1070–1089	Lanfranc		1501	Thomas Langton
1093–1109	Anselm		1501–1503	Henry Deane
1114–1122	Ralph d'Escures		1503–1532	William Warham
1123–1136	William of Corbeil		1532–1553	Thomas Cranmer
1138–1161	Theobald of Bec		1555–1558	Reginald Pole
1162–1170	Thomas Becket		1559–1575	Matthew Parker
1173–1184	Richard of Dover			
1184–1190	Baldwin			

1575–1583	Edmund Grindal	1828–1848	William Howley
1583–1604	John Whitgift	1848–1862	John Bird Sumner
1604–1610	Richard Bancroft	1862–1868	Charles Thomas Longley
1611–1633	George Abbot	1868–1882	Archibald Campbell Tait
1633–1645	William Laud	1883–1896	Edward White Benson
1645–1660	Church of England abolished	1896–1902	Frederick Temple
		1903–1928	Randall Thomas Davidson
1660–1663	William Juxon	1928–1942	Cosmo Gordon Lang (Lord Lang of Lambeth, 1942)
1663–1677	Gilbert Sheldon		
1677–1690	William Sancroft		
1691–1694	John Tillotson	1942–1944	William Temple
1694–1715	Thomas Tenison	1945–1961	Geoffrey Francis Fisher (Lord Fisher of Lambeth, 1961)
1715–1737	William Wake		
1737–1747	John Potter		
1747–1757	Thomas Herring	1961–1974	Arthur Michael Ramsey (Lord Ramsey of Canterbury, 1974)
1757–1758	Matthew Hutton		
1758–1768	Thomas Secker		
1768–1783	Frederick Cornwallis	1974–1980	Frederick Donald Coggan (Lord Coggan, 1980)
1783–1805	John Moore		
1805–1828	Charles Manners Sutton	1980–1991	Robert Alexander Kennedy Runcie
		1991–	George Carey

Appendix II

The Commonwealth of Nations (with dates of independence)

Queen Elizabeth II is head of state of:
United Kingdom of Great Britain and Northern Ireland
Antigua and Barbuda (1981)
Australia (1901)
Bahamas (1973)
Barbados (1966)
Belize (1981)
Canada (1867)
Grenada (1974)
Jamaica (1962)
Mauritius (1968)
New Zealand (1907)
Papua New Guinea (1975)
St. Christopher and Nevis (1983)
Saint Lucia (1979)
Saint Vincent and the Grenadines (1979)
Solomon Islands (1978)
Tuvalu (1978)

Republics and Others

Bangladesh (1971)
Botswana (1966)

Brunei (1984)
Cyprus (1960)
Dominica (1978)
The Gambia (1965)
Ghana (1957)
Guyana (1966)
India (1947)
Kenya (1963)
Kiribati (1979)
Lesotho (1966)
Malawi (1964)
Malaysia (1957)
The Maldives (1982)
Malta (1964)
Namibia (1990)
Nauru (1968)
Nigeria (1960)
Pakistan (1947–1971; 1989)
Seychelles (1976)
Sierra Leone (1961)
Singapore (1963)
Sri Lanka (1948)
Swaziland (1968)
Tanzania (1961)
Tonga (1970)
Trinidad and Tobago (1962)
Uganda (1962)
Vanuatu (1980)
Western Samoa (1962)
Zambia (1964)
Zimbabwe (1980)

Index

Page numbers in italics refer to illustrations. Page numbers followed by "n" refer to footnotes.